THE LIFE OF CHRIST

THE NEWMAN PRESS · WESTMINSTER, MARYLAND

1959

THE LIFE
OF CHRIST

by Andrés Fernández, S.J.

Former Professor and Rector
The Pontifical Biblical Institute

Translated by PAUL BARRETT, O.F.M.CAP.

Illustration on title page: NAZARETH: *Panorama. In the center are the Convent and Basilica of the Annunciation.*

Second Printing January, 1959

This is a translation of the second edition of *Vida de Nuestro Señor Jesucristo* published by Biblioteca de Autores Cristianos, Madrid, 1954

Nihil obstat:
   FR. HILARIUS A CARLOW GRAIG,
   O.F.M.Cap.
   Censor theol. deput.

Imprimatur:
   FR. JACOBUS A MITCHELSTOWN,
   O.F.M.Cap.
   Min. Prov. Hib.

die 21 Januarii, 1958

Nihil obstat:
   EDWARDUS A. CERNY, S.S.,
   D.D.
   Censor Librorum

Imprimatur:
   FRANCISCUS P. KEOUGH, D.D.
   Archiepiscopus Baltimorensis

die 5 Augusti, 1958

Translator's Foreword

THE AUTHOR NEEDS NO INTRODUCTION AS AN authority in his field: he has been a professor of Sacred Scripture for more than forty years, twenty of which he spent in Rome and twenty more in Jerusalem. While in Rome he was Rector of the Biblical Institute for seven years. During his long sojourn in Palestine he made an intensive study of the country, and, convinced that familiarity with the Holy Land is a tremendous aid to a deeper knowledge of Him who was born there, he resolved to put the fruits of his years of research at the disposal of the public. Hence this book. Yet his dedication to geographical and topographical detail is but one aspect of his work, for he also discusses disputed texts of Scripture openly and fearlessly, and sheds new light on the Gospel narrative. With a skill born of love and long acquaintance he describes the physical features of the Holy Land; but he also recreates for us the prevailing atmosphere, the spirit of the people at the time of Christ. Not only does he enable us to walk with our Lord across the pleasant rolling plains and climb with Him up the tortuous mountain trails; he also gives us a deep insight into the mind and heart of Him who came to seek and save that which was lost.

I am very grateful to Father Fernández for allowing me to translate his inspiring book, for being so co-operative in the course of the work, and for supplying the gracious Preface to my effort. I should also like to express my gratitude to Very Rev. Father Hilary, O.F.M.Cap., for reading the manuscript and making many helpful suggestions; to Rev. Father John Baptist Weldon, O.F.M.Cap., for reproducing the maps; and to Mrs. Marian F. Gough for typing the manuscript and assisting me in the necessary research work.

Many of the New Testament quotations in this book are taken from the Confraternity Edition by permission of the copyright owners, the Confraternity of Christian Doctrine. I have followed the author's own version in the following texts: Matthew 5:4, 32; 8:28; 9:15; 11:12; 19:9; 20:30; 23:32; 26:69–75; Mark 1:2, 4, 13, 14, 24; 5:41; 8:26; 14:66–72; Luke 1:35, 46–55; 3:3; 4:1–2; 5:17, 39; 6:26; 8:26; 12:1; 22:56–62; 24:22; John 1:9, 15–16, 20, 22, 25, 42, 47; 2:4; 4:9; 5:10; 10:29; 18:16–18, 25–27; 19:14, 27, 31; 20:17; Acts 1:16–19; I Corinthians 5:1.

PAUL BARRETT, O.F.M.CAP.

La Canada, California
July 16, 1957

Author's Preface

IT IS NOT WITHOUT A CERTAIN SATISFACTION THAT I undertake the writing of this short Preface to the English translation of my study of the life of Christ. I suppose that it is the dream of every author to see his work made available to as many people as possible; and although it is not within my realm to praise my own book, I think that I can certainly say a few words of commendation of Father Barrett's translation of it. My contacts with this assiduous worker have been restricted to correspondence, in the course of which Father has shown himself to be not merely a good translator but also a genuine scholar. His knowledge of Sacred Scripture, his familiarity with the Spanish language, and his past experience as a translator have enabled him to produce a charming narrative which is deserving of my full approval.

It should be noted that this English translation undergoes certain changes from the Spanish second edition. A few details of little interest to the general reader have been omitted. This is especially true of the sections which treat of our Lord's parables and the indissolubility of marriage, where the discussion seemed slightly cumbersome. On the other hand, further study has prompted a few additions to the original text. The sections on the

Holy Women, diabolical possession, and the reality of the Ascension are entirely new, while other sections have been amplified. The net result has been to make the present volume more readable and more up-to-date.

Finally, I would like to say a word of thanks to Father Barrett for his wholehearted dedication to the work of translating this book, to the Newman Press for making it available to the English-speaking world, and last but not least, to Rev. John Dewing S.J. for his inexhaustible generosity and invaluable help in going through the manuscript. It is my hope that many will find this effort a source of truth and inspiration.

ANDRÉS FERNÁNDEZ, S.J.

San Cugat del Vallés
July 9, 1957

Acknowledgments

THE TRANSLATOR, REV. PAUL BARRETT, O.F.M. Cap., and The Newman Press wish to thank the following publishers for their kind permission to reproduce quotations from the copyrighted publications listed below:

The Bruce Publishing Company, Milwaukee, for *Jesus Christ: His Life, His Teaching, and His Work,* by Ferdinand Prat, S.J., translated by John J. Heenan, S.J.

Burns, Oates & Washbourne, Ltd., London, for *A Two Year Public Ministry,* by Edmund Sutcliffe, S.J.

Harper & Brothers, New York, for *Light From the Ancient East,* by Adolf Deissman, translated by L. Strachan.

The Harvard University Press, Cambridge, Massachusetts, for *Select Papyri* by A. S. Hunt and C. C. Edgar, published in the Loeb Classical Library.

B. Herder Book Company, St. Louis, for *The Life of Christ,* by Louis C. Fillion, S.S., translated by Newton Thompson.

The Macmillan Company, New York, for *Jesus of Nazareth,* by Joseph Klausner.

The Oxford University Press, Inc., New York, for *The Mishnah,* translated by Herbert Danby.

Charles Scribner's Sons, New York, for *A Critical and Exegetical Commentary on the Gospel According to St. Luke,* by Alfred Plummer.

Contents

Introduction

The Infancy of Christ

The Public Life

List of Illustrations

List of Abbreviations

Ant.	Flavius Josephus, *Antiquities of the Jews*
Baldi, *Enchiridion*	D. Baldi, *Enchiridion Locorum Sanctorum: Documenta Sti. Evangelii loca respicientia* (Jerusalem, 1935)
Bibl. Zeit.	*Biblische Zeitschrift* (Freiburg im Breisgau, 1903–1927; Paderborn, 1931 *et seqq.*)
Braun, *S. Jean*	*La Sainte Bible,* Tome X (Paris, 1950)
Buzy, *S. Matt.*	*La Sainte Bible,* Tome IX (Paris, 1950)
Cornelius a Lapide	*Commentarium in quatuor Evangelia: Opera* (Paris: Ed. L. Vivès, 1881), Vols. 15–16
Dict. Apolog.	A. D'Alès, *Dictionnaire Apologétique de la Foi Catholique* (Paris, 1909–1930)
Dict. d'Arch. Chrét.	*Dictionnaire d'Archéologie Chrétienne et de Liturgie* (Paris, 1907 *et seqq.*)
Dict. de la Bible	F. Vigouroux, *Dictionnaire de la Bible* (Paris: 1891–1912); F. Vigouroux et L. Pirot, Suppléments I–III (Paris, 1926 *et seqq.*)
Dict. de Théol. Cath.	A. Vacant, E. Mangénot, E. Amann, *Dictionnaire de Théologie Catholique* (Paris, 1899 *et seqq.*)
Est. Bibl.	*Estudios Bíblicos* (Madrid, 1929–1936, 1942 *et seqq.*)
Est. Ecles.	*Estudios Eclesiásticos* (Madrid, 1922 *et seqq.*)
Geyer, *Itinera*	*Itinera Hierosolymitana saeculi IV–VIII* (Vindobonae, 1898)
JPOS	*Journal of the Palestine Oriental Society* (Jerusalem, 1921 *et seqq.*)

Knabenbauer, *In Matt.,*   J. Knabenbauer, *Commentarius in quatuor*
  In Marc., In Luc.,   *Sancta Evangelia,* Cursus Scripturae Sacrae (5
  In Ioan.   vols.) : I (2 vols.), *In Matt.* (ed. 3ª, 1922) ; II,
    In Marc. (ed. 2ª, 1907) ; III, *In Luc.* (ed. 2ª,
    1905) ; IV, *In Ioan.* (ed. 2ª, 1906).

Marchal, *S. Luc*   *La Sainte Bible,* Tome X (Paris, 1950)

Mishnah   *The Mishnah,* translated from the Hebrew by
    H. Danby (New York : Oxford University Press,
    1933)

n.   note

Nouv. Rev. Théol.   *Nouvelle Revue Théologique* (Tournai, 1869 *et*
    seqq.)

PG   J. P. Migne, *Patrologiae Cursus Completus,*
    Series graeca (Paris, 1857–1865)

PJB   *Palästinajahrbuch* (Berlin, 1905 *et seqq.*)

PL   J. P. Migne, *Patrologiae Cursus Completus,*
    Series latina (217 Vols., Paris, 1844–1855 [Vols.
    1–30, altera ed., 1865 *et seqq.*])

Pirot, *S. Marc*   *La Sainte Bible,* Tome IX (Paris, 1950)

RB   *Revue Biblique* (Paris, 1892 *et seqq.*)

Rech. de Sc. Rel.   *Recherches de Science Religieuse* (Paris : 1910
    et seqq.)

Rev. Sc. Phil. et Théol.   *Revue des Sciences Philosophiques et Théologi-*
    ques (Paris, 1907 *et seqq.*)

Rev. Sc. Rel.   *Revue des Sciences Religieuses* (Strassbourg,
    1921 *et seqq.*)

Schürer   E. Schürer, *Geschichte des jüdischen Volkes im*
    Zeitalter Jesu Christi (Leipzig, 1901)

Str.-Bill.   H. L. Strack und Paul Billerbeck, *Kommentar*
    zum Neuen Testament aus Talmud und Mid-
    rasch (München, 1922-1928)

Verb. Dom.   *Verbum Domini* (Romae, 1921-1943)

Wars   Flavius Josephus, *The Wars of the Jews*

ZDPV   *Zeitschrift des deutschen Palästina-vereins*
    (Leipzig)

Zeit. f. kath. Theol.   *Zeitschrift für katholische Theologie* (Inns-
    bruck, 1877 *et seqq.*)

Introduction

1. The Geography

of Palestine

The Name

Who would ever have imagined that the land occupied by the people of Israel would come to be generally known by the name of their bitterest enemies? For the word "Palestine" is derived from *Philistia*, "the country of the Philistines," that uncircumcised people which established itself in the southwest of Canaan. However, in Sacred Scripture the usual name for Palestine is *Erets Israel* or *Admat Israel*, that is, "the Land of Israel" (1 Kings 13:19; Ezech. 7:2), a title which has been revived in abbreviated form by the establishment of the new Jewish state, Israel. The country was also called "the land of the Hebrews" (Gen. 40:15), and "the land of promise" or "the promised land" (Heb. 11:9) because it had been promised by God to the Patriarchs (cf. Gen. 13: 14 *ff.*).

Topography

It has been said, and with good reason, that Palestine is the land of contrasts, a statement which is immediately borne out by the great disparity between its physical insignificance and its moral greatness.

From the foot of Mount Hermon in the north, to the Negeb in the south, or, according to the ancient formula, from "Dan to Bersabee" (1 Kings 3:20), Palestine measures only about 149 miles. The area west of the Jordan is a little more than 6,000 square miles, while the region east of the Jordan is 3,660 miles, so that the whole country contains only about 9,700 square miles; that is to say, it is considerably smaller than Belgium (11,755 square miles), slightly smaller than Sicily (9,860 square miles), and practically the same in area as the state of Vermont (9,609 square miles).

Insignificant though it is in physical size, Palestine towers above the other nations of the world in moral grandeur, for it was this unpretentious strip of land that God selected as the home of His Chosen People, and it was here that He willed the Word Incarnate to be born, to live and to die. Here, then, were fulfilled the sacred mysteries of our Redemption, and from this small country the divine light shone out over the world to dispel the darkness that enshrouded mankind. This is the country of Jesus and therefore, by antonomasia, the Holy Land.

There are great contrasts to be found also in the very geographical configuration of Palestine, for from east to west it is divided into four very dissimilar zones, namely, the 'Arabah, the mountain region, the Sephela, and the seacoast (cf. Deut. 1:7; Jos. 9:1). The 'Arabah is the great depression that separates the region west of the Jordan from the territory east of the Jordan, and it extends north from the Gulf of 'Aqaba to the Dead Sea (cf. Deut. 2:8), and from there to the Lake of Gennesareth (cf. Deut. 4:49). The mountain region is the middle section, the spine of the country, as it were, running from north to south, and known by various names, such as "the mountain of Juda" (Jos. 20:7; 21:11), "mount Ephraim," and "mount Nephtali" (Jos. 20:7). The Sephela is the western zone, covered with low hills and sloping in folds of ground from the high mountains down to the seacoast. This division of Palestine into four regions applies particularly to the southern half of the country.

If we take in the whole country at a glance we shall see that three totally dissimilar zones run parallel to each other from majestic Mount Hermon in the north to the low hills that lose themselves in the Negeb to the south, each zone varying in width but retaining its distinctive character.

The eastern belt, at the extreme north of which the springs of the Jordan rise, begins by broadening out into a beautiful oval-shaped plain on whose eastern side sleep the quiet waters of the small Lake of el-Huleh, also known erroneously as "the waters of Merom." About 9½ miles farther south, the floor of the valley dips down to form the Lake of Gennesareth, the surface of which is 682 feet below sea level, and on whose western shore lies the plain of Gennesareth, nowadays known as el-Ghuwer, which is 3 miles long and about 2½ miles wide at its broadest point. South of the lake is the district known as el-Ghor. The latter is, in fact, the valley of the Jordan, which at this point measures only about 3 miles across and which, widening and narrowing gently as it runs south, reaches a width of about 12½ miles at Jericho. The Jordan river bed drops 610 feet between the Lake of Gennesareth and the Dead Sea, a distance of 65 miles as the crow flies, but due to its meandering the actual course of the river measures 186 miles between the two points mentioned. The Dead Sea, also known as "the most salt sea" (Jos. 18:19), is about 47 miles long and almost 10 miles across at its widest point. It is divided into two very unequal sections by the small peninsula of el-Lisan, a tongue of land which projects into the water west of Kerak; the northern section reaches a depth of about 1,310 feet, while the southern is only 20 to 30 feet deep. The surface of this sea is 1,290 feet below sea level. At the extreme south of the sea is Jebel Usdum, in which popular fancy still professes to see Lot's wife turned into a pillar of salt, while to the north, on the eastern coast, stand the ruins of Machaerus, where John the Baptist was beheaded by order of Herod Antipas (cf. Matt. 14:3 ff.; Josephus *Ant.* xviii. 5. 2). Quite a few authors are of the opinion that the wicked cities of Sodom and Gomorrha (Gen. 19) lie buried beneath the waters of this sea, whose wild and deserted surroundings seem to be accursed by God.

The central zone is the series of mountains that runs from north to south in a twisting chain, broken at intervals, sometimes only partially, by *wadis* and plains. The principal plain in this region is the great one of Esdrelon, which is 96 square miles in area and which, stretching from the plain of Accho in the northwest to that of Jezrael in the east, forms the valley that separates the mountains of Galilee from those of Samaria. Smaller in size but very fertile and beautiful is the Sahel el-Askar, which lies to the east of Sichem and upon which Jesus gazed as he said to His disciples: "Behold that the fields are already white for the harvest" (John 4:35). The mountains of this region most noted for their height or their historical significance are: Jebel Jermaq (3,936 feet), the highest in all Palestine, situated on the border between upper and lower Galilee; Mount Thabor (1,844 feet); el-Muchraqa, or Mount of Sacrifice (1,811 feet) in the Carmel range; Jebel Fuqqu'a, or Mountains of Gelboe (1,700 feet); Jebel Eslamiyeh, or Mount Ebal (3,077 feet), and Jebel et-Tor, or Mount Garizim (2,848 feet), on either side of Sichem; el-'Asur, or Baal Hasor (3,316 feet), a little to the north of et-Taiyibeh or Ephrem; Nebi Samwil (2,936 feet), northwest of Jerusalem; the Mount of Olives (2,664 feet); and Sirat el-Bella (3,369 feet), north of Hebron.

The western zone, which includes the Mediterranean coast line, stretches from Ras en-Naqura, or Scala Tyriorum, to Egypt, and is divided into four sections, of which the great plain of Accho is the first, measuring about 22 miles to the promontory of Carmel and reaching at some points a width of 8 miles, with the great bay, nearly 9½ miles wide, guarded at its extremities by the two cities of Accho or Saint-Jean d'Acre, and Haifa. Then comes the plain of Saron, at first compressed between the Carmel range and the sea, but gradually broadening out until at Caesarea it reaches a width of nearly 10 miles; it continues to widen as it runs south. The ruins of the fortress of Athlit, or Castellum Peregrinorum, the last bulwark of the Crusades, are imposing even today; and in Qaisariyeh, or Caesarea, there are still traces of the magnificent city which Herod built in honor of Augustus and which was later the seat of the Roman procurator and the place where St. Paul was imprisoned (cf. Acts 23:33). South of the plain of Saron, between the mountains of Judea and the seacoast, stretches the Sephela with its cities of Lydda, Emmaus, and Beit Jibrin, or Eleutheropolis, a region which was, at least in part, the country of the Philistines. Finally comes the Negeb, an arid desert extending as far as "the torrent of Egypt," or the Wadi el-'Arish, and containing the famed city of Gerara near which Abraham lived (cf. Gen. 20:1 ff.).

We shall supply more geographical details in the course of this work.

Division of Palestine at the Time of Christ

When Herod the Great died, he left his kingdom divided between his three sons: to Archelaus went Idumea, Judea and Samaria, with the title of king, a title which Rome did not confirm but replaced by that of ethnarch only; to Philip went Batanea with Gaulonitis, Trachonitis and Auranitis, and the title of tetrarch; while Herod Antipas received Galilee and Perea, also with the title of tetrarch.[1]

JUDEA, SAMARIA, AND GALILEE

The border between Judea and Samaria was variable: in Josephus' day it passed through Korea, or Kerawa, in the valley of the Jordan, near the ford of ed-Damiyeh;[2] then it went up through Anuat-Borkeos, or 'Ain Berqit, some 10 miles south of Nablus,[3] and turned south, probably not far from Antipatris. The border between Samaria and Galilee must have crossed the plain of Esdrelon, since Josephus assigns to Galilee Kesalot, or Iksal, which is on the north edge of this plain,[4] while he includes in Samaria Ginea, or Jenin, in the extreme south of the plain.[5] In this last passage he explicitly says that Samaria "begins in Ginea [Jenin] and ends in the toparchy of Acrabathane."

Galilee was divided into two sections, upper and lower Galilee; the dividing line probably ran from east to west from the Wadi el-'Amud, a little to the south of Safed, through Kefr 'Anan, the great valley of esh-Shaghur, to Accho. This division is indicated by the very conformation of the terrain.

PEREA

Perea, as is indicated by its very name coined by Josephus,[6] was the region situated on the other side of the Jordan. Its boundaries were, according to the same historian,[7] Machaerus on the south, Pella on the north, Philadelphia ('Amman) on the east, and the Jordan on the west. Its capital was Gadara,[8] which stood on the site now occupied by modern es-Salt. Consequently, es-Salt is not ancient Ramoth Galaad, as some have thought, but rather ancient Gador. The other city named Gadara, situated near the River Yarmuk, in the Decapolis, is the modern Umm Keis.

THE DECAPOLIS

The Decapolis mentioned in the New Testament (cf. Matt. 4:25; Mark 5:20; 7:31), was a group of Hellenistic cities, some distance

---

[1] *Ant.* xvii. 8. 1.
[2] *Wars* i. 6. 5.
[3] *Ibid.* iii. 3. 5.
[4] *Ibid.* iii. 3. 1.
[5] *Ibid.* iii. 3. 4.
[6] *Ibid* iii. 3. 3.
[7] *Ibid.*
[8] *Ibid.* iv. 7. 3.

from each other, which were directly under Roman authority. Some of these cities had been brought under Jewish dominion by Alexander Janneus,[9] but had been liberated in 64 B.C. by Pompey.[10] We do not know for certain if there was a political bond between these cities, that is, if they formed a real confederation. At first they were ten in number, hence the name, the Decapolis, but others were soon added until the total reached fourteen, and some authors believe that there were even more. With the exception of Scythopolis, all were in the Trans-jordan, and they were named as follows: Damascus; Hippos, the ruins of Qal 'at el-Hosn, across the lake from Tiberias; Gadara, modern Umm Keis, overlooking the River Yarmuk; Pella (Khirbet Fahil), farther to the south, on the northern border of Perea; [11] Gerasa, the present-day imposing ruins of Jerash; Philadelphia, ancient Rabbath Ammon, today called 'Amman, capital of Jordan; Raphana (er-Rafeh), near Karnaim; Canatha (Kanawat), not far from er-Rafeh; Capitolias, present-day Beit er-Ras, a little to the north of Irbid; Abila (Tell Abil), about 5 miles north of Beit er-Ras and 11 miles east of Gadara; Adra, modern Der'a, one of the capitals of the kingdom of Og; Dion, the position of which is not known with certainty but which has been variously located at Eidun in the district of 'Ajlun, at el-Hosn, and at Tell el-Ash'ari; and Samulis, about which we know nothing except the name. Scythopolis, the only city of the Decapolis situated west of the Jordan, is the modern Beisan, which lies across the Jordan from Pella.

The Fertility of the Land

On a certain occasion I was travelling with a group of pilgrims down through the desert of Juda towards the Dead Sea, when one of the party, a young lady, turned to me and asked with an air of ingenuous skepticism: "Father, is *this* the land described as flowing with milk and honey?"

No doubt this is the reaction, expressed or silent, of all who cross not only the desert of Juda, whose very name proclaims it a wild and barren land, but also the mountains of Judea, arid and rocky, without trees or vegetation, and baked by the sun's rays. How could God have said to Moses: ". . . I am come down to deliver them out of the

---

[9] *Ant.* xviii. 13. 3.   [11] *Wars* iii. 3. 3.
[10] *Ibid.* xiv. 4. 4.

hands of the Egyptians: and to bring them out of that land into a good and spacious land, into a land that floweth with milk and honey"? (Exod. 3:8.)

Some authors think that the explanation is that the Promised Land seemed fertile to the Hebrews in comparison with the desert through which they had wandered with so much hardship for forty years.

Undoubtedly that was the case, but we know that even before the Jews began their weary pilgrimage, God had told Moses that Canaan was a good and fertile land. And Moses had promised his people that their future home would be better than Egypt: "For the land, which thou goest to possess, is not like the land of Egypt, from whence thou camest out: where, when the seed is sown, waters are brought in to water it after the manner of gardens. But it is a land of hills and plains expecting rain from heaven" (Deut. 11:10–11). And he also told them: "The Lord thy God will bring thee into a good land, of brooks and of waters, and of fountains: in the plains of which and the hills deep rivers break out. A land of wheat, and barley, and vineyards, wherein fig trees and pomegranates, and olive yards grow: a land of oil and honey. Where without any want thou shalt eat thy bread, and enjoy abundance of all things . . ." (Deut. 8:7–9).

It may well be that these descriptions were somewhat exaggerated, but they must have corresponded in some way to the reality. How, then, are we to reconcile them with the Palestine of today?

The solution is that the present state of the country is not a faithful reflection of the conditions that obtained in ancient times. Since it is not possible to review every section of the land, we shall have to limit ourselves to a few regions.

Many years ago, when for the first time I crossed the plain of Gennesareth, near the lake, I found it covered with thorn-patches, inhabited by a handful of Bedouins, and having every appearance of being poor and unproductive. Yet this is the very plain that Josephus described [12] as a veritable paradise where every type of tree flourished and a great variety of fruits was produced. And even granting that a Jewish historian such as he may have exaggerated, there is undoubtedly much truth in his description.

If we follow the valley of the Jordan to the south, we see that the whole region from Kerawa to the vicinity of Jericho is nowadays a real

[12] *Wars* iii. 10. 8.

desert. But we know that, at the time of Christ, in the then flourishing cities of Phasaelis and Archelais (Khirbet Fusail and Khirbet el-'Audja et-tachta respectively), there were groves of palm trees producing dates that were highly praised by Pliny in his writings. And on the eastern side of the Jordan, towards the south, instead of the depressing, arid desert that one sees today, there stood Livias, Abila and other cities which also boasted palm groves yielding delicious fruit.[13] We need make only brief mention of Jericho, at the mouth of the Wadi el-Qelt, which Herod made into a true garden of delights. In the fourteenth century A.D., sugar cane was grown in the eastern valley of the Jordan, as we know from the testimony of travellers and the mute evidence of the millstones that have been found between Tell Kefrein and Tell er-Rameh. And the same held good for the region to the north at the mouth of the Jabbok (the Wadi ez-Zerqa), while centuries ago the beautiful oval plain of el-Huleh, at the foot of Mount Hermon, was covered with extensive plantations of rice.

But what of the mountain region? It is certain that many if not all of the mountains that are now completely bare were once clothed with woods, olive-groves and vineyards. According to tradition, the hill of Tell el-Ful (ancient Gabaa, home of Saul and first capital of the kingdom of Israel), which lies 3 miles north of Jerusalem, was once covered by a grove. Recent excavations here have borne out the tradition by uncovering the remains of trees. A little farther to the north, the hills of the village of Mikmas, now almost totally denuded, were once clothed with olive and fig trees; and a short distance to the east, between Mikmas and Khirbet ed-Dwer, one can still see, hollowed out in the ground, an ancient press that must have been used to extract the olive oil. A little more than half-way from Bethlehem to Herodium, in a region that has all the appearances of a desert and which is now inhabited by poverty-stricken Bedouins, we saw a cave which contained a great millstone that was used, no doubt, for pressing the olives that once grew in that district, now entirely devoid of trees.

About 10 miles west of Jerusalem and very near Abughosh (ancient Qiryathiarim, or Qiryat el-'enab, significant names which show that this was once a city of woods and a city of grapes), a few years ago we saw only bare, rocky mountains that apparently would never produce anything. Yet today the traveller will find there a broad

---

[13] Cf. *Wars* iv. 7. 6; *Ant.* iv. 8. 1.

expanse of groves and fruit trees of various types that make the region an excellent summer resort.

We shall end our survey by saying a few words about the Negeb. This is the name given to the southern part of Palestine whose northern boundary probably passed through the village of ed-Dahariyeh, about half-way between Hebron and Bersabee, and extended to the desert of the Sinaitic peninsula. The soil here is arable and yields good harvests when it gets sufficient rain, but since rain is often lacking, there are many years when the crops are meager. At present the Negeb is sparsely populated, the few inhabitants being Bedouins; however, several Jewish colonies have been established here in the past few years. In ancient times it was much more densely populated. In fact, when David took refuge in Geth under the protection of King Achish, he made sallies into the Negeb of Juda, the Negeb of the Jerameelites, and that of the Quenites (cf. 1 Kings 27:10), while the Amalecites, the Calebites and other tribes also lived there (cf. 1 Kings 15:2 *ff.*; 30:14). Centuries later, in the Byzantine epoch, this region attained a degree of prosperity surprising to us, considering its present state. One can still see the ruins of several ancient basilicas, and no doubt there were others which have since disappeared completely. For example, in Sbeitha alone, some 25 miles south of Bersabee, there are preserved the apses and part of the naves of three churches which must have been magnificent buildings, if we are to judge by the ruins that remain. And in el-'Audjeh, not far to the west of Sbeitha and about 31 miles southwest of Bersabee, two churches of considerable size have been discovered. Naturally, all this architecture presupposes a population that was rather numerous and enjoyed a certain amount of prosperity. The wealth of these people was derived in part from commerce. As regards agriculture, they assured themselves of an adequate supply of water by building large cisterns and sinking numerous wells, many of which are now blocked up due to negligence and lack of proper care.

From what we have said—and much more could be written on the subject—it is plain that the present deplorable state of Palestine must be attributed principally, if not wholly, to the way the land has been allowed to run down, due to the indolent character of the inhabitants and the bad administration of the Turkish government. The progress that has resulted from the efforts of new colonists is a clear indication of how the fertility of Palestine's soil can be increased by persevering labor.

Population

It is very difficult to calculate the density of population in Palestine at the time of Christ. Josephus tells us [14] that in Galilee alone there were 204 towns and cities, the smallest of which had more than 15,000 inhabitants.[15] Even if we grant that each of these centers had only 15,000 people, the total population would then be more than 3½ million, a figure that would have to be increased to more than 5 million if we took into consideration the fact that there were many large cities (*"urbes frequentes"*). Josephus supplies additional, although indirect, data [16] when he tells us that in A.D. 66, at the request of Cestius Gallus, the priests counted the sacrifices that were offered in the celebration of the Passover and found that they numbered 256,500. He then goes on to note that since the number partaking of each Paschal lamb might not be less than ten and sometimes went as high as twenty, the total number of participants was about 2,700,000, that is, 3 million in round numbers. Obviously these figures are exaggerated, yet we have no other data from which to make a true estimate. Therefore we shall content ourselves with quoting the words of Father Szczepanski: [17] "It is not possible to fix the number of inhabitants in the whole province of Judea at the time of Christ. Various calculations and certain indications may perhaps lead us to the following figures: total population 1,500,000, of which about 600,000 were in Judea and Idumea, 400,-000 in Samaria, 300,000 in Galilee, and 200,000 in Perea." The same author calculates that of the whole population about 300,000 were non-Jewish.

According to the latest figures available (1957), the population of Israel is 1,885,000 (1,670,000 Jews and 215,000 non-Jews). It seems that exaggerated figures of displaced Arabs have been quoted, and that the actual number does not exceed 700,000.

As regards Jerusalem in particular, we read in the Second Book of Machabees (5:14) that 80,000 inhabitants of the city fell victims to the fury of Antiochus, 40,000 being killed and the remainder sold as slaves. Yet it is certain that some of the citizens escaped death or slavery. Hecateus of Abdera, whom Josephus quotes,[18] writes that in

[14] *Life* 45.
[15] *Wars* iii. 3. 2.
[16] *Ibid.* vi. 9. 3.
[17] *Geographia historica Palaestinae anti-* quae (Romae: Scripta Pont. Inst. Bibl., 1928), pp. 214 *f.*
[18] *Against Apion* i. 22.

his day, 312 B.C., the city of Jerusalem counted 120,000 inhabitants. But apart from Josephus' accounts, which we have just mentioned, we possess no literary data about the time of Christ, and there is great diversity of opinion among modern authors. C. Schick made a very detailed study of this problem [19] and, basing his arguments on the area of the city, the amount of space ordinarily required for each inhabitant (on this point he quotes examples from European and Eastern cities),[20] and the way families are crowded together in a small space in the Jerusalem of our day,[21] he concludes that the population of ancient Jerusalem must have varied from time to time between 200,000 and 250,000 inhabitants.[22]

However, Professor Joachim Jeremias arrives at a very different conclusion.[23] He, too, starts with the territorial extent of the city, and by calculating the space needed for each inhabitant, he deduces that the population of Jerusalem at the time of Christ was probably from 25,000 to 30,000 inhabitants.

If we had to express our opinion, we should say that Jeremias' figure seems rather low and Schick's excessively high, but we should hesitate to suggest a definite number ourselves. We shall probably never know the answer, whatever it may be. In a short study published in 1923,[24] the same Professor Jeremias gives the figure as 55,000, on the supposition that Agrippa's wall coincided with the present one; however, if it followed the longer circuit, then a much higher figure seems indicated, say 95,000. No doubt the author has since modified his opinion.

---

[19] *ZDPV*, IV (1881), 211–228.
[20] *Idem.*, p. 216.
[21] Cf. *Idem.*, p. 217.
[22] *Idem.*, p. 216.

[23] *ZDPV*, LXVI (1943), 24–31.
[24] *Jerusalem zur Zeit Jesu* (Leipzig, 1923), p. 96. We have only this first edition at hand.

2. Historical

Background

From Hyrcanus II to Herod the Great (63–37 B.C.)

Caesar conquered Pompey at Pharsalus on August 9th, 48 B.C., and when in the summer of the same year he passed through Palestine, he showed himself very generous and favorable to the high priest Hyrcanus II and to his minister, Antipater the Idumean, the father of Herod the Great.

He restored to Hyrcanus, with the title of ethnarch, the political power which Gabinius had taken from him; and the high priest and his sons were officially declared friends and allies of the Romans. Caesar made Antipater and his sons Roman citizens and confirmed Antipater as procurator (ἐπίτροπος) of Judea, an office which in fact he had been exercising already.[1]

On his return from Syria whither he had accompanied Caesar, Antipater took advantage of the strong position in which his patron's great favors had placed him, and appointed one of his sons, Phasael, governor of Jerusalem and its district, and made another, Herod, governor of Galilee, although he was only twenty-five years old. In their new posts, both Phasael and Herod gave clear proofs of their energy and intelligence. Herod particularly distinguished himself, so much so that Cassius Longinus, the proconsul of Syria, entrusted him with the government of Celesyria. As regards Phasael, Josephus testifies that he governed Jerusalem with such

[1] *Ant.* xiv. 8. 1; 5. 1; 6. 4.

14

prudence and moderation that he won the people over; and the same historian says that because of the benefits they received from Antipater "the whole nation respected him as if he were a king and honored him as if he were the absolute lord of the country." [2] However, despite all this, it is certain that, deep down, the Jews hated Antipater and his sons, mainly because they were Idumeans, traditional enemies of the Jewish nation, and because they represented a foreign power, Rome. The day was to come when this hatred would explode violently.

On March 15th, 44 B.C., Caesar fell beneath the daggers of his assassins at the foot of Pompey's statue. Cassius Longinus, one of the conspirators, fleeing from Marc Antony who wished to avenge Caesar's death, went to Syria where he had been proconsul from 53 to 51 B.C. The Roman garrisons rallied to his aid, and since he needed money for the campaign he had in mind, he demanded a heavy tax of 700 talents from Judea. Antipater, eager to curry favor with the new proconsul, hastened to comply with the demand, and charged his sons with the task of collecting the tribute. Among those who had a hand in this work was a certain Malichos who had ambitions of supplanting Antipater. But seeing that he could not overthrow the procurator by force, this Malichos bribed the cup-bearer of Hyrcanus to administer poison to Antipater when both he and Antipater were guests at the high priest's table. Herod, however, quickly avenged his father's death by having Malichos killed near Tyre.[3]

In 42 B.C. Cassius left Syria, and in the great confusion that reigned there, Antigonus, the ever-conquered but still undaunted son of Aristobulus, supported by some of the leaders of Cassius' party, such as Ptolemy of Chalcis, Fabius of Damascus, and Marion of Tyre, believed that the opportune moment had come to make another attempt at regaining power. He advanced with his army towards Judea, but Herod went out to meet him and forced him to retire.

Naturally Hyrcanus was grateful to Herod for thus averting a grave danger to the nation. And Herod, although he was already married to Doris, the mother of his eldest son, Antipater, wished to strengthen the bonds between himself and the high priest. Therefore he became betrothed to Mariamne, daughter of Alexander, Antigonus' brother, and of Alexandra, Hyrcanus' only daughter, and hence the high priest's granddaughter.[4]

[2] *Ant.* xiv. 9. 2.
[3] *Ibid.* xiv. 11. 3, 6.
[4] *Ibid.* xiv. 12. 1.

A complete change in the political scene was produced in the autumn of 42 B.C. by the battle of Philippi, at which Marc Antony and Octavian defeated Brutus and Cassius, both of whom committed suicide. This victory made Marc Antony lord of all Asia and rendered very critical the position of Hyrcanus, Phasael and Herod, who had hitherto shown themselves favorable to Cassius. A delegation of discontented Jews took advantage of the situation to approach the conqueror, who was still in Bithynia, with the accusation that Phasael and Herod had usurped power and that Hyrcanus was incapable of governing properly. But Herod the opportunist was not unduly perturbed: he simply changed sides and embraced the cause of Antony. He took precautions to neutralize the effect of the Jewish delegation by hastening in person to present Antony with regal gifts and to remind him of his former friendship with Antipater. So successful was Herod that the delegation was not even given a hearing, and another Jewish group who were later sent to Antioch fared no better. A third deputation of a thousand Jews met a much worse fate, however, for they were treated barbarously, some of them being killed. The triumph of the Idumeans was complete when Antony appointed Phasael and Herod tetrarchs, that is, rulers of Judea.

But this triumph was not to endure for long. An invasion of the Parthians became a daily-increasing threat; yet Marc Antony, whose task it was to resist them, had thoughts for nothing but feasting and enjoyment. In fact he abandoned his Syrian legions and spent the winter of 41 to 40 B.C. with Cleopatra in a mad round of pleasure. In addition he burdened his subject peoples, those of Judea included, with heavy taxation to pay for his amusements and his preparations for war. The gathering storm broke at the beginning of 40 B.C. when the Parthians attacked. Some, led by a Roman, Quintus Labinius, headed for Asia Minor, and others, under their king Pacorus and the satrap Barzophernes, descending on Syria and Palestine. In Judea they were welcomed as liberators, for with their help the Jews hoped to shake off the yoke of the hated Idumeans and to free themselves from the crushing Roman taxes.

Happiest of all at the turn of events was Antigonus, the ill-starred and obstinate pretender, for he looked upon the invaders as allies who would aid him to mount the coveted throne of Judea and rid himself of his rivals. He made the Parthians a promise—one which he never fulfilled [5]—that he would give them 1,000 talents and 500 women (a new and shameful price) if they would give him the kingdom and put Herod to death.[6] The Parthians accepted the offer; Antigonus advanced on Jerusalem with an army of Jews who had joined him, and took possession of the Temple. Phasael and Herod entrenched themselves in the royal palace and harassed Antigonus. The citizens were divided and civil war broke out. Then Antigonus called in a Parthian general as arbitrator under the pretense of arranging for a peaceful settlement. At the invitation of the Parthian, Phasael and Hyrcanus presented themselves to Barzophernes, who had his headquarters in Galilee, to explain their reasons for resistance. But, once there, they were imprisoned and later handed over to Antigonus, who with his own teeth, as Josephus affirms, bit off Hyrcanus' ears, thus rendering him forever ineligible for the office of high priest.[7] Phasael, to escape being put to shame, killed himself by dashing his head against the wall. Herod, however, suspecting the trap that was being laid for him, escaped by night with his family to the fortress of Masada and from there set out for Petra.

Thus, through the support and favor of the Parthians, Antigonus was finally able to enjoy the long-coveted dignities of king and high priest, and to give himself the satisfaction of issuing coins bearing the Greek words "Of King Antigonus" and the Hebrew inscription "Mathathias, high priest," Mathathias being his Jewish name.

But the struggle had not yet reached its end. Rome had lost Palestine, and Antigonus, who had triumphed on the field of battle, was about to be defeated on the field of diplomacy.

While on his way to Petra, Herod found out that Malchus, the king of the Nabateans, had no desire to give him shelter for fear of becoming embroiled with the Parthians. He was left, therefore, without anyone to whom he could turn for aid. In these terrible straits he made a desperate decision and, proceeding to Alexandria, he embarked for Rome in the autumn of 40 B.C., apparently with the intention of getting help to wrest the crown from Antigonus and to pass it on to his future brother-in-law, the young Aristobulus, Mariamne's brother, at whose court he would then be an all-powerful minister.

The outcome of his maneuver exceeded all his hopes, for he was favorably received by both Marc Antony and Octavian, and had no

---

[5] *Wars* i. 13. 2.
[6] *Ant.* xiv. 13. 2.

[7] *Wars* i. 13. 9.

difficulty in obtaining a decree from the Senate which made him, and not Aristobulus, king of Judea. This was more than he had even dreamed of, and his joy was equalled only by his surprise. No doubt the Romans believed that the son of Antipater would prove a more useful and trustworthy ally than the Hasmonean Aristobulus.

Herod, then, was king by the consent of Rome the omnipotent and assuredly against the wishes of the immense majority of the Jews. But he had still to win his kingdom with the sword.

He set out for Palestine in 39 B.C., landing at Ptolemais and capturing the city. With the recruits that he was able to gather, and assisted by the Romans, he went south to Joppa, seized it and went on to Masada to free the members of his household who were besieged there. In the following year, 38 B.C., there was a new invasion of Parthians, and Herod was fighting in Galilee when Antigonus in the south defeated and killed his brother Joseph. Seeing that he could not possibly conquer his rival with Jewish troops alone, Herod obtained two legions from Marc Antony and with them, after several battles, he laid siege to Jerusalem in the spring of 37 B.C. Then, leaving the Romans encamped about the city, he went to Samaria to marry his betrothed, Mariamne.[8]

After this, Sossius, proconsul of Syria, arrived with a large army sent by Marc Antony to help Herod seize Jerusalem. Josephus records [9] that the besiegers had eleven legions and 6,000 horses, as well as other auxiliary troops from Syria. After forty days, the first wall was taken; fifteen days later they took the second; and then the defenders retreated to the Temple. Thus the city had held out for almost three months, that is, through the summer of 37 B.C. The slaughter was terrible, old and young, men and women, being put to the sword. Antigonus came down from the citadel and threw himself at the feet of Sossius, who mocked him, calling him a woman. He was taken as a prisoner to Antioch and there, some time later, Marc Antony, persuaded by Herod's insistent pleas and perhaps even more by his gold, ordered the prisoner to be put to death.[10]

Herod's dream had finally come true; in 37 B.C., he, an Idumean, was seated on the throne of the illustrious family of the Hasmoneans. Certainly he never suspected that the royal couch would prove to be for him a bed of sharp thorns. But such, in fact, it turned out to be.

[8] *Ant.* xiv. 15. 14.
[9] *Ibid.* xiv. 16. 1.
[10] *Ibid.* xiv. 16. 2–4; xv. 1. 2.

Herod the Great

Historians usually divide the life of Herod into three periods: [11] first, consolidation of his authority (37–25 B.C.); second, period of greatest prosperity (25–13 B.C.); and third, dissensions and domestic strife (13–4 B.C.), although these latter were not lacking during the first period.

First period (37–25 B.C.). Throughout these years he had to contend with many enemies—the people, the aristocracy, and the Hasmoneans—and he had to defend himself against Cleopatra as well.

The people did not want Herod, for they considered him a usurper who was occupying the throne that belonged by right to the national dynasty of the Hasmoneans. Furthermore, he was only half-Jewish since he was an Idumean by race, and there was a long-standing enmity between the two peoples. Such a traditional hatred could not be completely hidden, and Herod was well aware of the Jews' real feelings towards him. But being both daring and astute, he ruled the rebellious with an iron hand and courted the pacifists with lavish generosity.

Although Antigonus had been defeated and now lay in a faraway prison in Antioch, he still had many supporters among the aristocrats of Jerusalem. The unscrupulous new king therefore took care to rid himself of these dangerous men by having no less than 45 of the principals killed and their property handed over to him.

The Hasmoneans naturally found it difficult to accept Herod, and Alexandra, Mariamne's mother, treated her son-in-law with disdain. No wonder then that there was ill-feeling and domestic strife, which Herod's jealous and meddling sister Salome, always her brother's evil genius, inflamed still further by her calumnies. All the Hasmoneans who gave the suspicious tyrant the slightest grounds for distrust were disappearing one after the other. In Jericho, the young high priest Aristobulus, Mariamne's brother, was strangled by order of his brother-in-law.[12] Next, Herod had his uncle, Joseph, killed; then the aged Hyrcanus,[13] and in 29 B.C. even his own wife, Mariamne.[14] Finally, a year after her daughter's murder, Alexandra fell victim to her son-in-law's hatred, and with her death disappeared the last of the Hasmoneans who could threaten the throne of the cruel and ambitious monarch.

[11] Cf. Schürer, I, 377.
[12] *Ant.* xv. 3. 3–4.
[13] *Ibid.* xv. 6. 2.
[14] *Ibid.* xv. 7. 3–6.

With all his wiles, however, Herod could not prevent Marc Antony from giving Cleopatra several parts of his kingdom, including the extremely rich and fertile region of Jericho.[15]

Second period (25–13 B.C.). Concerning this stage of Herod's career Josephus, not without a certain tinge of bitterness, writes that, "Since no one remained of the family of Hyrcanus and since he [Herod] had established his authority so firmly that none could oppose him even if he worked against the Law, he departed from the national customs, and with new and foreign institutions he corrupted the old state of things which ought always to have remained inviolate." [16]

This is the period of Herod's great building projects, of his prodigality in raising monuments and in constructing or embellishing whole cities. We shall limit ourselves to a brief survey of these activities, which earned him the title "Herod the Great."

First he built in Jerusalem a theatre about which nothing is known for certain, but which is believed to have been near the present south wall, half-way between the Gate of David and the Cedron; he also built an amphitheatre which some identify, apparently not without good reason, with a kind of semicircle cut into the north side of the hill called er-Ras, a little to the south of the city. He restored and embellished the Baris of the Machabees, renaming it Antonia in honor of his patron, Marc Antony, and it was here that he lived until he built, to the northwest of the city, the magnificent palace, one of whose three towers is still preserved. He reconstructed the city of Samaria, which he called Sebaste, in honor of Augustus, where a beautiful colonnade can still be seen. He rebuilt Anthedon, a short distance to the north of Gaza, renaming it Agrippeion. On the western plain, not far north of Jaffa, he constructed Antipatris, as he did Phasaelis in the valley of the Jordan. On the Mediterranean coast he transformed the Tower of Straton into the splendid city of Caesarea. He built the palace-fortress at Herodium, a little to the south of Bethlehem, and restored the fortresses of Hyrcania, Machaerus and Masada. He raised no less than three temples in honor of Augustus, one in Caesarea, one in Sebaste (which is still partly preserved), and one in Paneion, or Baniyas, as it is called today. But all these projects were surpassed by the magnificent Temple in Jerusalem, which he built or enlarged and beautified to ingratiate himself with the Jewish people.

[15] *Ant.* xv. 4. 1–2.　　　　[16] *Ibid.* xv. 7. 10; 8. 1.

We shall not linger to describe the many costly constructions which he completed outside Palestine.[17]

Obviously Herod needed immense quantities of gold and silver for these vast building schemes, and he got the money by extorting it from his subjects. No wonder then that the people were discontented; yet so great was the fear he inspired that no one dared defy him. But although he kept the populace in subjection, he could not control the members of his own family.

Third period (13–4 B.C.) The last ten years of Herod's life were filled with untold domestic dissension, suspicion, hatred and bitterness. Peace seemed about to be restored to the royal palace when Herod was reconciled in Rome with Alexander and Aristobulus, his two sons by the Hasmonean Mariamne. But the scheming Salome was there to continue her spiteful poisoning of her brother's mind, and all the hatred which her evil heart had nursed against Mariamne was now directed against the unfortunate queen's sons. No doubt the sons had not been able to forget their mother's murder, and it is not to be wondered at if they were sometimes imprudent in their speech. For the rest, since they were both very handsome and belonged to the great Hasmonean family on their mother's side, the people spontaneously showed them marks of affection which awakened jealousy in Herod's suspicious heart. In addition, Glaphyra, Alexander's wife, and Berenice, the wife of Aristobulus, did not help to promote peace, for the former boasted continually about her royal blood, since she was the daughter of Archelaus, king of Cappadocia, while Berenice always ran to tell her mother, Salome, everything she heard from her husband.

But perhaps all this would not have caused trouble between father and sons if Salome's viperish tongue had not succeeded in poisoning the king's mind with exaggerations and calumnies. In order to humiliate and curb the two brothers, Herod brought to the palace his own brother, Pheroras, and Antipater, his son by his first wife Doris. The two newcomers joined with Salome against the young brothers, and gave Herod to understand that the young princes were plotting to avenge their mother's death and seize the throne. Finally, these three calumniators were so successful that the unhappy, angry king decided to condemn his two sons to death, and, after a trial held in Beirut, he

---

[17] For an account of these consult Josephus, *Ibid.* xv-xvi; *Wars* i. 21. 1–13. For particular reference to the Temple see *Ant.* xv. 11. 1–7.

had them sent as prisoners to Sebaste and there at his orders they were strangled.

But even this did not bring Herod peace, for his son Antipater continued to plot against him, and he had him recalled from Rome and thrown into prison.

The king now fell ill of a very painful disease and had himself carried to the baths at Callirrhoe, but did not obtain relief. From here he was brought to Jericho and there, five days before his death and with the permission of Augustus, he ordered the execution of Antipater. His last act of cruelty was to bring the principal men of the kingdom to Jericho, and to order Salome and her husband to have them all killed as soon as he breathed his last. However, in this case Salome was less cruel than her brother, for she let them go free after his death.

Herod died a short time before the Passover in 4 or perhaps 5 B.C., at the age of seventy.[18] His body, which was being eaten by worms even while he was still alive, was carried with great pomp to Herodium and interred in the palace-fortress which he had built to commemorate a signal victory.[19]

Without doubt Herod was a man of great ability; he was intelligent, courageous and enterprising, but these qualities were overshadowed by his insatiable ambition, to which he sacrificed justice and morality and for which he crushed all who opposed his designs. He won his title "the Great" for his magnificent buildings, certainly not for the unhappiness of his private life and his despicable maneuvering to gain and keep his throne. He began his reign by shedding the blood of his people and brought it to a close with the slaying of his sons, while the blood of the Holy Innocents will always be a blot upon his name.

Josephus sums up Herod's career in two phrases by saying that he was outwardly great and glorious but unhappy and miserable in his domestic relations.[20]

Dynasty of Herod the Great

Herod made three wills, in the last of which he left Judea, Samaria and Idumea to Archelaus with the title of king; Galilee and Perea to

---

[18] Cf. *Ant.* xvi-xvii; *Wars* i.
[19] Cf. *Ant.* xvii. 8. 3–4.
[20] *Ibid.* xvii. 8. 1; cf. *Ibid.* xvi. 5. 4, where he gives a longer and more judicious verdict.

Dynasty of Herod the Great

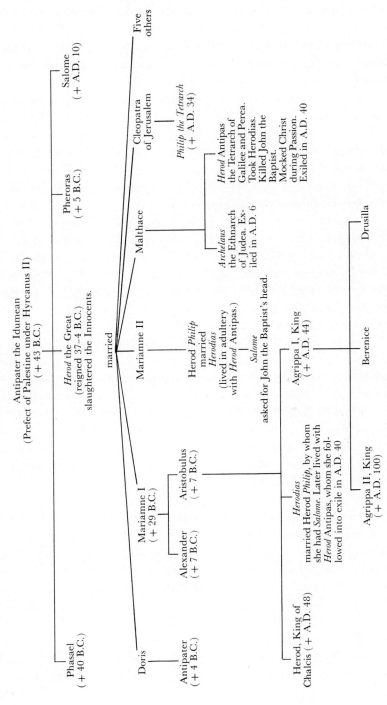

Antipater the Idumean
(Prefect of Palestine under Hyrcanus II)
(+ 43 B.C.)

Phasael
(+ 40 B.C.)

Doris

Antipater
(+ 4 B.C.)

Herod the Great
(reigned 37–4 B.C.)
slaughtered the Innocents.

married

Mariamne I
(+ 29 B.C.)

Alexander
(+ 7 B.C.)

Aristobulus
(+ 7 B.C.)

Herodias
married Herod Philip, by whom
she had Salome. Later lived with
Herod Antipas, whom she followed into exile in A.D. 40

Herod, King of
Chalcis (+ A.D. 48)

Mariamne II

Herod Philip
married
Herodias
(lived in adultery
with Herod Antipas.)

Salome
asked for John the Baptist's head.

Agrippa I, King
(+ A.D. 44)

Agrippa II, King
(+ A.D. 100)

Berenice

Drusilla

Pheroras
(+ 5 B.C.)

Malthace

Archelaus
the Ethnarch
of Judea. Ex-
iled in A.D. 6

Herod Antipas
the Tetrarch of
Galilee and Perea.
Took Herodias.
Killed John the
Baptist.
Mocked Christ
during Passion.
Exiled in A.D. 40

Cleopatra
of Jerusalem

Philip the Tetrarch
(+ A.D. 34)

Salome
(+ A.D. 10)

Five
others

Names italicized are mentioned in the Gospels.

Herod Antipas with the title of tetrarch; and to Philip, also with the title of tetrarch, five districts to the northeast and east of the Lake of Gennesareth, two of which are mentioned by St. Luke (3:1), namely, Iturea and Trachonitis. To his sister Salome, he left the cities of Jamnia, Azotus and Phasaelis. Augustus ratified this will in all particulars except the title of king for Archelaus, to whom he conceded only that of ethnarch.

After nine years of rule by Archelaus, a commission of Jews and Samaritans went to Rome to complain of his cruelty, with the result that he was deposed by Augustus in the following year, A.D. 6, and exiled to Vienne in Gaul. His territory was placed under the authority of a Roman procurator, dependent on the great province of Syria.

Philip the Tetrarch seems to have been a man of good character and temperate habits. He married Salome, daughter of Herodias, and lived peacefully in his dominions. He restored Paneion, near the source of the Jordan, and called it Caesarea (the Gospel "Caesarea Philippi"); and near ancient Bethsaida he founded the so-called Bethsaida Julias which is probably identifiable with present-day et-Tell. He died in A.D. 34 and his territory was annexed to the Roman province of Syria.

In A.D. 37 Tiberius died and was succeeded by Caligula, who from his youth had been a friend of Agrippa, the son of Aristobulus and brother of Herodias. On ascending the throne he wished to give his friend proof of his affection and so he ceded to Agrippa all the territory formerly held by Philip the Tetrarch, and bestowed on him the title of king.

Antipas established himself in Sephoris (Diocaesarea), embellished Livias in the valley of the Jordan, and later, towards A.D. 20, built near the Lake of Gennesareth a city which he named Tiberias in honor of Tiberius, and in which he took up residence. We all know of his adulterous union with Herodias, whom he stole from his half-brother Herod Philip, her lawful husband; and we know, too, that he murdered John the Baptist and played a part in the trial of Christ. Antipas was satisfied with his title of tetrarch, but when his adulterous consort Herodias saw her brother Agrippa receiving the title of king, she became so envious that, in spite of Antipas' reluctance, she gave him no rest until she had persuaded him to go to Rome to obtain the same honor from the Emperor.

But things turned out badly for him. Agrippa learned of his proposed journey to Rome and sent his own freedman, Fortunatus, to the

Emperor with a document in which he accused Antipas of being wanting in fidelity to Rome. Caligula believed the accusation and deprived
Antipas of his tetrarchy, which he then gave to Agrippa along with
the personal property of Herodias, who followed her lover into exile
at Lyons in Gaul in A.D. 40.[21]

Agrippa I had taken possession of his kingdom in A.D. 38. When
Caligula was assassinated on January 24th in the year 41, Agrippa was
in Rome and helped Claudius to mount the imperial throne. As a mark
of gratitude the new Emperor gave Agrippa Judea, Samaria and
Idumea, so that he then ruled the whole kingdom of his grandfather,
Herod the Great. As was to be expected, he took up residence in
Jerusalem, and desiring to enlarge the city, he began to build a wall
around the northern hill called Bezetha, but did not finish it because
the Emperor Claudius ordered the work to be stopped. To ingratiate
himself with the Jews he began to persecute the Christians, having St.
James the Greater killed and St. Peter imprisoned with the idea of
murdering him also after the Passover. But, as we know, an angel freed
Peter before the king could carry out his plan (cf. Acts 12:1 ff.).
Agrippa's reign was a short one, for in the year 44 he went to Caesarea
to attend the games being held in honor of the Emperor, and there he
died a wretched death (cf. Acts 12:19–23; *Ant.* xix. 8. 2) at the age
of fifty-four, after a reign of seven years. During his reign he had conformed to the customs and religion of the Jews and had been generous
and liberal to them, so that the people had really loved him and were
sincerely sorry at his death.

His son Agrippa II was in Rome when the father died. Because he
was only seventeen years old, it was not deemed prudent to give him
his father's kingdom, and so it passed to the Roman administration
under the authority of a procurator. But in 48 or 49 when his uncle,
Herod, king of Chalcis, died, Claudius gave him Chalcis, which he
relinquished later, in 53, to take over the former tetrarchy of Philip.
In the following year, 54, he was given the cities of Tiberias and
Tarichea in Galilee, and that of Julias (also called Livias) in Perea,
along with several of the surrounding small towns. In honor of Nero
he gave the name Neronias to the capital of his tetrarchy, a name
which, however, soon fell into disuse. The Emperor also committed to
him the inspection of the Temple, a task which took him often to
Jerusalem, where he resided at the palace of the Hasmoneans, from

---

[21] Cf. *Ant.* xviii. 7. 1–2.

which he used to watch the Temple priests. He made several improvements in the edifice, and had the city streets paved with slabs of white marble. On one occasion, when he went to Caesarea with his sister, Berenice, he met St. Paul and showed him some signs of sympathy (cf. Acts 25:13–26, 32). He does not seem to have been hostile to the Christians. He was always a faithful ally of the Romans, both before and after, as well as during, the war of 70. It appears that he died in 93 or 94, although some hold that it was not until 100.[22]

Roman Procurators

In the tenth year of his rule (i.e., in A.D. 6), Archelaus was deposed by Augustus, who placed his territory under the authority of procurators residing in Caesarea. These officials were: Coponius (6–9), Marcus Ambivius (9–12), Annius Rufus (12–15), Valerius Gratus (15–26), Pontius Pilate (26–36), Marcellus (36–37), and Marullus (37–41).

From 41 to 44 the whole kingdom of Herod the Great was ruled by his grandson Agrippa I, at whose death it once more came under the authority of Roman procurators, who were: Cuspius Fadus 44–?), Tiberius Alexander (48–?), Ventidius Cumanus (48–52), Antonius Felix (52–60), Porcius Festus (60–62), Luceius Albinus (62–64), and Gessius Florus (64–66).

Social and Religious Background

The social and religious conditions that obtained among the Jews at the time of Christ are best seen in the various sects then flourishing in Palestine. Flavius Josephus has left us a mass of interesting detail about three of these sects—the Pharisees, the Sadducees and the Essenes.[23] We cannot do better than summarize, if not transcribe, what the Jewish historian has to say.

THE PHARISEES

The Pharisees live frugally, they do not give themselves over to a life of pleasure and comfort, and in their actions they follow the dictates of right reason. They show great respect for the ancients and do not permit themselves to act contrary to the traditions they have received from them.

[22] E.g., Schürer, I, 599. On Agrippa I and Agrippa II, see *Ant.* xviii-xx; *Wars* ii.
[23] First in *Wars* ii. 8. 2–14, and later in *Ant.* xviii. 1. 2–5.

They hold that all things are directed by Providence, yet they acknowledge that man is free in his actions. They believe in the immortality of the soul and hold that in the next world there will be a reward for the good and punishment for the bad. They are very united among themselves and preserve peace and harmony for the common good. They enjoy great authority with the people, so much so that the public follows their advice in whatever touches upon religion, and particularly in the matter of prayers and sacrifices.

Thus, according to Josephus, the Pharisees' distinctive characteristics were austerity, and love of peace and harmony; in religious matters they believed in Providence, free will, the immortality of the soul, and reward or punishment in the next life. Furthermore, they accepted not only the written word, that is, the Sacred Scriptures, but tradition as well.

Josephus' description is rather flattering: we can believe that such were indeed the principles which the Pharisees professed, but their very austerity and respect for the traditions of the ancients carried them to deplorable excesses. Hence the difference between the picture which Josephus paints and the impression we get of the Pharisees from the Gospels.

In their scrupulous and, we could almost say, morbid preoccupation with the perfect observance of the Law, they descended to minute details and lost themselves in endless discussions on secondary and completely unimportant points, particularly with regard to legal purity. And this very scrupulosity led them to pay less attention to interior purity, wherein lay the essence of the Law, for they stopped at the externals and neglected to extract the marrow. Therefore when Christ insisted on purity of heart and on the practice of virtue, and placed less importance in outward trifles, these worshippers of the purely external opposed him openly or in secret. And when they saw the people following the new Teacher whose "word was with authority" and realized that they were losing the crowds, they were consumed with envy and tried by every means in their power to destroy the influence of the young Prophet of Nazareth.

These brief considerations enable us to see in true perspective the generally hostile relations that existed between Jesus and the Pharisees, and to reconcile perfectly the Jewish historian's account with the Gospel narrative. However, there is solid foundation for believing that not all the Pharisees went to the extremes which the Saviour condemned so severely, and that there were some who paid more attention to the practice of virtue than to legal hairsplitting. Thus we have the example of Nicodemus, who came to Jesus in search of enlightenment with good faith and humility (cf. John 3:1 *ff.*); of Gamaliel, who came to the defense of St. Paul (cf. Acts 5:34 *ff.*); while verse five in the fifteenth chapter of the Acts speaks in general of Pharisees who embraced the Christian Faith.

THE SADDUCEES

The Sadducees deny the immortality of the soul, and hence all notion of reward for the good or punishment for the bad in the next world. They reject every kind of tradition and accept the written Law alone. They have no respect for the teachers, but rather consider it a virtue to contradict them. Not many belong to this sect but the few who do are members of the upper classes. They take little part in public affairs and when they are forced against their will to do so they act in conformity with the doctrine of the Pharisees since otherwise the people would not tolerate them.

As we can see, the Sadducees were generally aristocrats who rejected tradition and denied the soul's immortality. The latter point is confirmed by Christ's reply in Matthew 22:29–33 regarding the resurrection of the body. The attitude of the Sadducees as portrayed in the Gospels corresponds closely to the description left us by Josephus. Finally, it is interesting to note that most of the priests were members of this sect.

THE ESSENES

The Essenes do not live in one city alone but in several,[24] forming a community in which there is no private property, all goods being held in common. They observe celibacy, believe in the immortality of the soul and give themselves over with great zeal to the practice of the virtues. They do not go to the Temple to offer sacrifice but send their gifts there. They apply themselves to agriculture; everyone works and no one is allowed to keep a servant. In all things they lead the common life. Those who wish to embrace this kind of life are put on trial for a whole year; and after that there is a second trial lasting not less than two years; only then, and provided that he has acquitted himself well and is judged worthy, is the

---

[24] Many of them lived outside cities altogether. They were very numerous to the west of the Dead Sea, and the fountain of Engaddi seems to have been their principal center.

applicant admitted to full membership in the community. Next, he has to take several oaths—that he will always worship God; that he will practice justice to man; that he will never do harm to anyone; that he will always hold the wicked in horror and always go to the aid of the good; that he will always keep faith with all and most especially with those who rule, and that if one day he is called to govern, he will be modest in his bearing, not wishing to be different from his subjects in anything, even in clothing; that he will always be a lover of truth; that he will keep himself far from all stealing and even from all gain; that he will not keep anything secret from the members of the community but that he will do so rigorously as regards outsiders; and that, finally, he will never change in any particular the doctrine which he has received.

Josephus puts their number at more than 4,000.[25]

Their *horarium*, as we would call it, was interesting. They kept perfect silence until sunrise, then after saying some prayers they began their work, which lasted until the fifth hour, i.e., 11:00 A.M. They engaged in agriculture principally, but they also raised cattle, kept bees, and did all types of domestic tasks. At eleven they went to the pool to bathe, an act which they regarded as a religious rite. Then, dressed in white tunics, they came together in the refectory, into which no stranger was ever admitted. Some prayers were said, all seated themselves in the prescribed order, and before each was placed a dish of food and some bread, which were eaten in silence. When the frugal meal was finished, they put on their ordinary garments once more and went back to work until evening fell. Then came supper, at which the procedure was the same as at the morning meal.

The Essenes are not mentioned in the Gospel, but some authors claim that they can discover traces of Essenism in John the Baptist, who, they continue, probably took his baptism of penance from these sectaries. Some even say that John may have been an Essene himself for a time. For our part, we do not think that he had any such connections with the sect; see below, pages 185 *ff.,* where we speak of the baptism of John.

There are others who go still further and claim that Christ Himself had direct dealings with the Essenes, and that from them He derived certain points of doctrine found in the Gospel, for example, fraternal charity, celibacy, the spurning of worldly things, etc.

[25] *Ant.* xviii. 2. 5.

Certainly there is a resemblance between the practices of the Essenes and the Gospel teaching, but such a resemblance does not by any means prove that the Gospel was derived from the sect.

At all events, information about these sectaries is interesting because it shows us a current of thought and a system of social and religious practices that otherwise we would never have expected to find in the Jewish world of the time.

New light has been shed on the Essenes by the now-famous manuscripts of Qumran.[26] Of particular interest is the manuscript which the editors have entitled *Manual of Discipline* and which has points of similarity to the Sadokite document of Damascus [27] and reveals the existence of a socio-religious organization that is reminiscent of the community of the Essenes. Since the Essenes lived in the very place where the manuscripts were found, and since the contents of the manuscripts appear to reflect their doctrine, the obvious conclusion is that the owners and compilers of these singular and, to us, very precious documents, were none other than the Essenes themselves. But because there are certain differences between the practices of the Essenes and the *Manual of Discipline,*[28] we may suspect that these documents do not deal with the Essenes directly but only with a similar older community whose spirit, however, continued to live in the Essenes.

This well-founded probability suggested by the documentary evidence has been confirmed by archaeological findings. The excavations made at Khirbet Qumran at the end of 1951 and the beginning of

[26] Also known as the Dead Sea Scrolls or the Documents of 'Ain Feshka. Regarding these manuscripts and the topographical position of Qumran, see below pp. 31 *f.*

Several interpretations of the name "Qumran" have been suggested. The one proposed by Michaud (*Revue d'Histoire et Philosophie Religieuses* [1955], pp. 71 *f.*) is interesting. According to this author the name comes from the Arabic word *qamira*, "to be white," or "to keep vigil by moonlight." Thus Khirbet Qumran would mean "the ruin belonging to those who dress in a white tunic or who keep vigil by moonlight." We know from Josephus (*Wars* ii. 8. 5) that the Essenes, who were very similar to, if not identical with, the ascetics of Qumran, wore white tunics on certain occasions, and it is not unlikely that, at least sometimes, they performed their spiritual exercises by the light of the moon.

[27] This document was discovered in Cairo and published in 1910. For further information concerning it see J. B. Frey, *Dict. de la Bible,* Suppl. I, cols. 396–403; Lagrange, *RB* (1912), pp. 213–240, 321–360. Recently much has been written on the relationship between this document and the manuscripts of Qumran; see below, n. 28.

[28] For these see *Est. Bibl.* (1952), pp. 394 *f.* In *The Biblical Archaeologist,* 13 (1950), 50–72, a very detailed comparison is made between the Qumran (Dead Sea) documents and the Sadokite document of Damascus, and between the Essenes and the Therapeutae on the one hand, and John the Baptist and his disciples on the other.

1952 brought to light a rectangular building of considerable size (about 92 by 118 feet) with several rooms, in one of which there was a stone bench running along the wall.[29] Everything points to the supposition that it was a meeting place for the scattered inhabitants of that desert region.[30]

Near the site of the excavations there is a cemetery with a thousand graves; [31] and since there is no proportion between the size of the ruin and the number of burials, we are forced to conclude that the dead of the surrounding district were brought to Qumran for interment in the common graveyard.

The first documents discovered at Qumran were as follows:

> Isaias (complete).
>
> Commentary on Habacuc.
>
> Manual of Discipline.
>
> Apocalypse of Lamech.[32]
>
> Isaias (incomplete).
>
> War of the Sons of Light.
>
> Hymns or psalms of thanksgiving.
>
> A very small portion of the Book of Jubilees.[33]

[29] See Père de Vaux's articles in *RB* (1953), pp. 83–106, 245–267, 541–561; (1954), pp. 207–236; (1956), pp. 533–577.

[30] Later excavations revealed the remains of much older buildings which seem to date back as far as the eighth and seventh centuries B.C. (see *RB* [1956], pp. 535 *ff.*); and there are grounds for suspecting that this was the site of the *'Ir ham-Meah* ("the city of salt") mentioned in Josue 15:62 (see *RB* [1956], pp. 537 *ff.*). Perhaps this building had some connection with the constructions of Josaphat and Ozias (2 Par. 17:12; 26:10).

To judge by the data available at present, the building belonging to the ascetics of Qumran was probably constructed in the time of Hyrcanus I (134–104 B.C.), extended under Alexander Janneus (103–76 B.C.), destroyed by an earthquake in 31 B.C., restored at the beginning of the Christian era, and destroyed once more in A.D. 68. A short while afterwards, it was taken over by a garrison of soldiers and it remained a military post until the end of the century. During the second war, which ended in A.D. 135, the ruin was used by the followers of Bar Kokeba, and then it was abandoned for good (*RB* [1956], p. 569).

[31] The first excavations at the site uncovered the skeletons of several women (*RB* [1953], p. 103). At first sight it seemed that there had existed communities of women whose corpses had been carried to the common cemetery for burial. But later, the skeletons of four children between six and ten years of age as well as the remains of more women were discovered (*RB* [1956], pp. 570 *f.*). The most plausible explanation is that the women and children were the wives and families of those Essenes who, according to Josephus (*Wars* ii. 8. 13), did marry.

It should be noted that several other cemeteries have been discovered within short distances of the one just mentioned.

[32] The latest opinion is that this is an "apocalyptic Genesis."

[33] Other documents have been found, but not all of them have a bearing upon the

The documents were found by chance in the spring of 1947 by a Bedouin of the tribe of the Taamireh who was searching for a lost sheep. They were in a cave called Ma'aret Qumran, which is in the desert of Juda, a little less than three-quarters of a mile west of the Dead Sea, about half a mile north of Khirbet Qumran, two and a half miles north of 'Ain el-Feshkha, and seven and one-half miles south of Jericho. They were in the form of several rolls of leather preserved in jars and containing biblical, liturgical and religious writings in Hebrew. It was not until April, 1948, that the news of the discovery of the manuscripts was published in the United States. On January 28th, 1949, the cave was relocated by a search party, and from mid-February to March 5th of the same year, Mr. Harding and Père de Vaux explored it and gathered more than 600 small fragments of leather and about forty pieces of papyrus. It seems that in November, 1948, the Bedouins had searched the cave again, and had dug up the floor in search of more relics.

Later, in 1952, in another cave not far from the one just mentioned, two copper rolls were found which at first could not be unfolded. It was not until 1956 that experts at the University of Manchester succeeded in reading the writing engraved on the copper scrolls, which were found to contain a list of some seventy places between Hebron and Mount Garizim (many of them near Jerusalem) where numerous objects of great value, some being made of gold and silver, had been buried for safekeeping.[34]

In December, 1951, and January, 1952, more work was done at Khirbet Qumran, and the above-mentioned building and cemetery were discovered.

Excavations were next made at the Wadi el-Murabba'at, eleven miles south of Khirbet Qumran, eight and one-half miles north of 'Ain Jidi, a little less than three-quarters of a mile north of the Wadi ed-Deradjeh, and about fifteen and one-half miles southeast of Jerusalem. An examination was made of four caves in the northern side of the *wadi,* about six miles from the Dead Sea. The digging went on for a full six weeks: two of the caves yielded nothing of interest, but in the other two the excavators found an abundance of earthenware frag-

community at Qumran. They are listed in some of the books and articles given below on p. 34, n. 36.
[34] Cf. *Biblica*, 37 (1956), 387 *f.*; *Chemical and Engineering News* (Sept. 3, 1956); Rand McNally *Bible Atlas* (New York, 1956), p. 18.

ments, coins of the era of the procurators of Palestine, of Agrippa I, Hadrian, and the second Jewish war (133–135), as well as *ostraka* in Hebrew, many fragments of leather and papyrus in Greek, Hebrew and Aramaic, some of them biblical, from Genesis, Exodus, and Deuteronomy, and seemingly more recent than those found at Qumran. Also discovered there was a matrimonial contract in Greek dating from the seventh year of Hadrian (A.D. 124). But most surprising of all were two letters signed by one Simon Bar Koseba and addressed to a certain Jesus (Yeshua') Ben Galgola. One of these letters dealt with administrative affairs only, but the other spoke of the political activity of the Gentiles (*goyim,* the Romans) against whom war was being waged. This seems to indicate that the signature on the letter was that of the well-known Bar Kokeba ("son of the star," a name given him by his followers) whose real name was Bar Koseba (from his native town; his enemies used to mispronounce it Bar Kozeba, "son of a lie," or "liar"), the leader of the second insurrection against Roman domination.[35]

At the close of 1952, in a cave above Ma'aret Qumran and more difficult of access, the Bedouins found more fragments of manuscripts in Hebrew, Aramaic and Greek, apparently dating back to A.D. 40. Among these various documents, the one that holds most interest for us is the *Manual of Discipline,* from which we shall quote some passages indicative of the spirit that animated the community which lived by it.

> All who enter the rule of the Community shall cleave to the Covenant in the presence of God, obliging themselves to act in conformity with all He commanded (col. I, 16).
> This is the rule for those who have offered themselves to form part of the Community, that they withdraw from all evil and persevere in all good, and turn aside from the assembly of perverse men . . . acting according to the disposition of the sons of Sadoq, priests, custodians of the Covenant. . . . (col. V, 1–2).

Therefore there was an association which professed a certain common rule of which the official custodians were the priests, sons of Sadoq.

> In this manner shall they act in their habitations. Wherever there are

---

[35] Cf. *RB* (1953), pp. 276–294: "Une lettre de Simon Bar Kokheba."

two together, let the younger obey the elder. . . . . Let all eat in common, and in the same manner let them give the blessing and make their deliberations. Wherever there are ten let there be not lacking a priest among them, and in his presence let each one sit in his proper place and let them seek counsel in due order. . . . At the meal, let the priest bless the bread and the wine. . . . Wherever there are ten let there be not lacking among them one who applies himself day and night to the study of the Law for the common good. All shall pass a third part of the night in reading the Book, in the study of justice and in the common blessing (col. VI, 2–14).

In his dealings with his brothers let each one practice truth, justice, uprightness, benevolent charity, and modesty in speech (col. VIII, 2).

Let the prudent man fulfill the will of God in everything; . . . and let him take pleasure in nothing outside the will of God (col. IX, 23 *f.*).

These short quotations give us fresh insight into the religious atmosphere at the time of our Lord. The principal virtues recommended in this community—contempt for riches, isolation from the world, love of neighbor, continence, humility—were those which the Essenes practiced, a fact which confirms to a certain extent the hypothesis that the two sects or associations were identical, a point upon which authors are not agreed.

Lively discussions have arisen as to the date of these manuscripts, especially of those found at Qumran; and these discussions still continue, although with less intensity, since there is a wide diversity of opinions. Some authorities hold that the manuscripts date back to the first half of the second century before Christ, to the time of the Machabees, while others put them as late as the Middle Ages, truly an exaggerated view. It should be held as solidly probable that they belong to the pre-Christian era, and it is by all means certain that they are anterior to A.D. 70.[36]

---

[36] Countless articles have been written about these documents; we shall cite but a few: A. Bea, *Biblica*, 29 (1948), 44, 446–448; 30 (1949), 128 *f.*, 293–295, 474 *f.*, 446–448; 31 (1950), 242–245. *Civiltà Cattolica*, I (1950), 480–494, 612–624; IV (1952), 128–142. Tournay, *RB* (1949), pp. 204–238; de Vaux, *ibid.*, pp. 530–549; (1952), pp. 187–218; (1953), pp. 83–106, 245–275. Pérez Castro, *Sefarad*, II (1951), 115–153 (with copious bibliography on 151–153); XII (1952), 167–197. L. Arnaldich, *Est. Bíbl.*, 11 (1952), 359–398. Raymond E. Brown, "The Qumran Scrolls and the Johannine Gospel and Epistles," *Catholic Biblical Quarterly*, 17 (1955), 403–419, 559–574. Roland E. Murphy, "Insights into the New Testament from the Dead Sea Scrolls," *American Ecclesiastical Review*, 135 (1956), 9–22. J. Schmitt, "Les écrits du Nouveau Testament et les textes de Qumran," *Revue des Sciences Religieuses*, 29 (1955),

THE NAME AND ORIGIN OF THE PHARISEES, SADDUCEES AND ESSENES

The Hebrew word *perushim,* Pharisees (from the verb *parash,* to separate), means "the separated ones," a name given them, probably somewhat con'emptuously, because of their excessive and scrupulous preoccupation with keeping themselves apart from persons and things liable to endanger in the slightest their legal purity.

Their origin is uncertain. Some think that they go back to the time of Esdras and Nehemias, at whose command the Jews promised under oath to keep from association with other races and in particular to send away the foreign women whom they had married (cf. 1 Esdras 10; 2 Esdras 10:28 *ff.*). But this was a single episode concerning the people as a whole, and there is no indication that it resulted in the formation of a group of men with the characteristics of the Pharisees. The first mention which Josephus makes of the sect [37] is in reference to the time of Jonathan (161–143 B.C.), that is, towards the middle of the second century before Christ.

On the other hand, we can say, if not with absolute certainty at least with great probability, that the Pharisees are the successors or rather the spiritual heirs of the Assideans (Hebrew *chasidim,* "the pious ones") whom we find mentioned in the Books of the Machabees (1 Mach. 2:42; 7:12; 2 Mach. 14:6). These Assideans joined the Machabees' movement and had already been in existence for some time before.

According to some, the name *Sadducee* comes from the Hebrew word *tsaddiq,* "just," an adjective which consorted ill with their character, since they apparently possessed little justice or piety. More likely the name comes from that of the priest Sadoq (Tsadoq), who was raised to the high priesthood by Solomon (cf. 3 Kings 2:35); hence they probably were the Sadokite priests, or sons of Sadoq. They formed as it were the Jewish aristocracy. And since, as we have already mentioned, the majority of the priests were Sadducees, the members of the sect were sometimes called "Boethusians," a name taken from Boethus,

381–401; 30 (1956), 55–74, 261–282. Albert Vincent's *Les manuscrits hébreux du Désert de Judà* (Paris, 1955), Geoffrey Graystone's *The Dead Sea Scrolls and the Originality of Christ* (New York, 1956), Roland E. Murphy's *The Dead Sea Scrolls and the Bible* (Westminster, Md., 1956), Géza Vermès' *Discovery in the Judean Desert* (New York, 1957), and Antonio G. Lamadrid's *Los descubrimientos de Qumran* (Madrid, 1956), are thorough studies of the documents from every angle.
[37] *Ant.* xiii. 5. 9.

the head of one of the principal priestly families.[38] The Sadducees played an important part during the whole reign of the Hasmoneans, in contrast with the Pharisees, whose influence waxed and waned. Josephus also mentions the Sadducees in connection with the time of Jonathan.[39]

The name and origin of the Essenes are extremely obscure. Depending on the word from which one derives the name Essene (in Josephus, from *essenoi;* in Philo, *esaioi*), it signifies "holy ones," "silent ones," "physicians," "prophets," etc. Absolutely nothing is known about the time of founding of this society. As in the case of the Pharisees and Sadducees, the first mention which Josephus makes of the Essenes is in connection with the era of Jonathan.[40]

THE HERODIANS

The Herodians appear twice in the Gospels, once when, after Jesus had cured the man's withered hand, they conspired with the Pharisees to destroy Him (Mark 3:6), and again when, along with the disciples of the Pharisees, they approached our Saviour, asking Him guilefully whether or not it was lawful to pay tribute to Caesar (Matt. 22:16; Mark 12:13).

Some authors (e.g. Lagrange, Holzmeister) think that these Herodians were soldiers of the tetrarch Antipas, or else members of his court, that is, courtiers (*aulici*). We, however, believe that they were a true party.

When Josephus speaks of the war which Herod the Great fought against Antigonus before ascending the throne, he mentions the Herodians in two passages, referring to them as "Herodians" [41] and "those that were on the side of Herod." [42] It is obvious that Josephus considered them as partisans of Herod, for he places them over against the "Antigoneans" [43] who were, as is evident, the partisans of Antigonus. This party of the Herodians continued to exist after the war with Antigonus and even after Herod's death. It was composed of Jews devoted to the Herodian dynasty, who no doubt hoped that the Roman procurators would cease to govern the land and that the whole territory would be restored to the line of Herod.

---

[38] Cf. Schürer, II, 478; *Mishnah, Menahoth* 10:3, where the name *Boethusians* is found.

[39] *Ant.* xiii. 5. 9.

[40] *Ibid.*

[41] *Wars* i. 16. 6.

[42] *Ant.* xv. 15. 10.

[43] *Wars* i. 16. 6.

It was a purely political party, but its members must have felt little affection for the Prophet of Nazareth, for they undoubtedly knew of Jesus' connections with John the Baptist, whose attitude towards Antipas was no secret. Then, too, they may well have heard about the name with which, one day in Pella, Jesus stigmatized the tetrarch— "That fox!" (Luke 13:32). Hence they formed these temporary alliances with the Pharisees against Jesus, although they, as a party, had nothing to do with religious matters, and even though the Pharisees' mode of life was far removed from their own worldly, careless conduct.

THE SCRIBES

The Scribes (γραμματεῖς) appear frequently in the Gospel story, especially in the Synoptics (they appear only once in St. John, in the episode of the adulterous woman, John 8:3). They were men skilled in the Law, or, as we would call them, jurists or lawyers. They were not necessarily priests although they could be, nor did they necessarily belong to a particular sect, such as that of the Sadducees and Pharisees, though there were Scribes who were Pharisees (cf. Mark 2:16); however, they had close connections with the latter sect. Thus we often find the Scribes and Pharisees linked together in the Gospels (e.g. Mark 7:1; Luke 5:30), and the censures which our Saviour launched at the latter were also directed against the Scribes, for they, by their subtlety in interpreting the Law, had emptied it of its spirit, leaving behind only the dead letter; and in this they were like the Pharisees. No wonder then that their attitude towards Jesus was generally hostile, although there were some of them who were sympathetic to Him, such as the one to whom He said: "Thou are not far from the kingdom of God" (Mark 12:34). They enjoyed great authority and were honored with the title *rabbi*, "master."

The Book of Ecclesiasticus, written about 180 B.C., speaks highly of the Scribes (chapters 38 and 39). But they were in existence long before that, and the origin of these men "skilled in the Law" probably dates back to the time of the Babylonian captivity. In fact this is what Esdras is called in the book which bears his name (1 Esdras 7:6). The Hebrew title was *sofer*, plural *soferim*.

There were two parts or elements in the interpretation of the Law, the *haggadah* ("narration," from the verb *nagad*, "to manifest" or "to relate") and the *halakah* ("way" or "road," from the verb *halak* "to march"). The first was narrative; the second, doctrinal and moral.

Naturally, whoever wished to become a scribe or a lawyer had to apply himself to the study of the Law under the direction of a teacher. St. Paul tells us that he sat at the feet of Gamaliel and was intructed by him in all the rigor of the Law (cf. Acts 22:3). One who studied thus was called *talmîd tôrah,* "a disciple of the Law." In the Talmudic era, that is, several centuries after Christ, full authority to teach was not given before the candidate had completed his fortieth year, and it was conferred by a kind of imposition of hands.

Although the Scribes fell into grave abuses in their manner of interpretation and did not give an example of humility but rather of refined pride, we must agree that they did not cease to do good service by contributing to the strict observance of the Law.

HELLENISM

Hellenism was another element that influenced the lives and thoughts of the Jewish people. It was Alexander the Great's ambition not only to conquer but also to Hellenize: he wished to dominate nations physically, but desired even more to conquer them spiritually. He proposed to teach the subject nations Greek culture in all its aspects, in religion, art, customs, and all the manifestations of national life. Hence his conquering troops were followed by another army, one of colonizers whose function was to spread peacefully the spirit of Greece among the peoples whom he had subdued by the sword. The Macedonian hero's undertaking was eventually crowned with success, since those who divided the spoils of his empire followed in his footsteps and fostered the triumph of Greek culture.

As was bound to happen, this culture spread to Palestine, especially to the cities on the seacoast. Josephus calls Gaza "Greek," [44] and Anthedon, a little farther to the north, was a Greek foundation. Some of the cities along the coast, although they had not been founded by the Greeks themselves, were intensively Hellenized; such were Ascalon, Jaffa, Apollonia, Dora (Tantura), Ptolemais (ancient Accho, which has reassumed its former name). There were also Hellenized cities in the interior of the country—Scythopolis (Beisan); Paneion (the Caesarea Philippi of the Gospel, which has returned to its ancient

[44] *Wars* ii. 6. 3.

name, Baniyas)·; Philotheria, which some locate at Khirbet Kerat at the southwestern end of the Lake of Gennesareth. And in the Transjordan, Josephus applies the adjective "Greek" to Hippos (Qal'at el-Hosn, southeast of the lake) and Gadara (Umm Keis), a little farther to the south; also Hellenized were Pella and Dion, Gerasa and Philadelphia (the ancient capital of the Ammonites and now capital of Jordan with the old name, 'Amman).

It is obvious that the Jews, surrounded by these cities with which they had of necessity to maintain more or less close connections, could not withdraw completely from their influence. In fact, at the beginning of the second century before Christ, many of the Jews, without any physical coercion, abandoned their national traditions and adopted the Greek mode of life. Thus the author of the First Book of the Machabees is forced to admit that: "In those days there went out of Israel wicked men and they persuaded many, saying: Let us go and make a covenant with the heathens that are round about us, for since we departed from them many evils have befallen us. And the word seemed good in their eyes. And some of the people determined to do this and went to the king: and he gave them license to do after the ordinances of the heathens" (1 Mach. 1:12–14).

And so eager were they to ape foreign ways that they hastened to build in Jerusalem a gymnasium in the pagan style, as was to be found in Hellenized cities. They introduced the games and the boxing so popular in those centers, and since they were ashamed of having been circumcised they had the foreskin restored artificially. In short, a strong Hellenistic trend had begun which was not confined to the gymnasium and the games but influenced minds and hearts as well.

The Second Book of the Machabees (4:7 ff.) is even more explicit than the first. Jason, who had thus Hellenized his real name, Jesus,[45] dissolved the legal, truly Jewish institutions and introduced foreign customs. He erected a gymnasium under the very Citadel of David, where he fitted up an *ephebeum* in which youths from the most distinguished families practiced for the games. In fact, enthusiasm for Hellenism reached such a peak that even the priests, instead of devoting themselves to the service of the altar, flocked to the *palestra* to take part in the exercises.[46]

Hellenism, therefore, had succeeded in insinuating itself among the

[45] *Ant.* xii. 5. 1.   [46] *Ibid.*

Jewish people. But it was to meet there a resistance which it had not encountered in other nations, for monotheism, the worship of one God alone, was deeply rooted in the Jewish heart, and the Mosaic Law was held in profound veneration and influenced the whole life of the nation. Thus it was that Hellenization reached only the upper class of society and not even all of that: it did not affect the mass of the people; furthermore, it was quickly opposed, first by the Assideans, that is to say, the "just ones," those who kept up zeal for the observance of the Law (cf. 1 Mach. 2:42; 7:12; 2 Mach. 14:6), and then by their successors, the Pharisees, whose example the general public followed.

On top of all this came the insane persecution of Antiochus IV Epiphanes, the badly-advised king who thought that by using violence he would be able to overcome the resistance of the great mass of the Jews. But his cruelty produced the opposite effect: instead of wiping out the Jewish religion, he succeeded only in increasing the Jews' religious fervor and in stemming, or at least lessening, the current of Hellenism that had already caught up part of the upper classes. The cry of Mathathias in Modin: "Every one that hath zeal for the law and maintaineth the testament, let him follow me" (1 Mach. 2:27), electrified souls and began that titanic struggle in which the great hero's five sons finally gained a glorious victory after immense sacrifices and stirring exploits. This obviously does not mean to say that Hellenism was wiped out, for it certainly existed in the time of Christ, as we have said. It does mean, however, that its wings were clipped and its influence greatly lessened.

LANGUAGE

Did the infiltration of Hellenism into Palestine implant the Greek language there? What tongue did the Jews speak at the time of Christ? The common language was certainly Aramaic, which had supplanted Hebrew. We need only recall the words of our Lord on the Cross: "*Eloi, Eloi, lama sabacthani?*" (Mark 15:34); the numerous names beginning with *bar,* such as Bartholomew, Bartimeus, Barnabas, Barabbas, etc.; the words *abba* (Mark 14:36), *haceldama* (Acts 1:19), *gabbatha* (John 19:13), *golgotha* (Matt. 27:33) etc.; and Peter's name, *Cephas.* An unequivocal proof that the people no longer even understood Hebrew is found in the fact that, since the Sacred Scriptures were read in Hebrew in the synagogues, they had to be translated into Aramaic for the benefit of the congregation. It is interesting to read in the *Mishnah* the provisions made in this respect: "He that reads in the Law [of Moses] . . . may not read to the interpreter more than one verse [in order that the interpreter may easily recall and translate it] or, in [a reading from] the Prophets, three verses . . ." "He that is blind may receive the *Shema' with its Bene-* dictions and *interpret.*" "The story of Reuben [Gen. 35:22] is read out but not *interpreted;* the story of Tamar [Gen. 38:13 *ff.*] is read out and *interpreted.*" [47] In *Sotah* 7, verse 2, we read: "These [pas-sages] must be said in the Holy Language," [48] that is, in Hebrew, and then they are quoted one by one. It is clear, then, that since the mass of the people did not understand Hebrew, much less were they able to speak it; and it is no less evident that Aramaic was the language used by our Lord. We know that the people as a whole neither spoke nor understood Greek. Josephus records that during the war when Titus wished to persuade the besieged to cease all resistance, he used an "interpreter," [49] and that on other occasions Josephus himself was the one charged with speaking to his compatriots in their own tongue,[50] an indication that they did not understand Greek. Later still, in the third and fourth centuries, Aramaic was spoken and there were many who did not know Greek. Schürer cites two significant cases in point.[51] The rabbi Yochanan, who taught in Sephoris and Tiberias in the third cen-tury, allowed young women to learn Greek, a concession which caused some surprise; so that evidently Greek was far from being in general use. And in the time of Diocletian, in the Christian community in Scythopolis, there was a man whose duty it was to translate into Aramaic the portions of the religious functions that were read in Greek.

It is interesting and instructive to read what the pilgrim Etheria wrote for her nuns in Galicia at the end of the fourth century:

In that province [Palestine] one section of the people knows Greek and Aramaic [Etheria writes *"siriste"*], another section Greek alone and a third Aramaic only; and so, since the bishop, although he knows Aramaic, always speaks in Greek and never in Aramaic, there is always a priest

[47] *Mishnah, Megillah* 4:4, 6, 10.
[48] *Ibid.*
[49] *Wars* vi. 6. 2.
[50] *Ibid.* v. 9. 2–4; vi. 2. 4–5.
[51] II, 85.

present who translates into Aramaic what the bishop says in Greek, so that all may understand. The lessons are read in Greek but there is always one who translates them into Aramaic in order that all the people may understand them.

Etheria then adds a detail concerning the Latin tongue:

There are also Latins, that is, those who know neither Aramaic nor Greek; and so that they may not feel slighted ["*ne contristentur*"] explanation is made for them too, for there are other Graeco-Latin brothers and sisters ["*fratres et sorores*"] who explain to them in Latin.[52]

However, although the Greek language did not spread among the mass of the people, it was certainly known and spoken in the cities on the coast and in the Hellenized cities of the interior; and there is no doubt that in Jerusalem it was known by educated people as well as by many of the aristocrats and the priestly caste. Nor is it improbable that a certain number of the common people also understood it, and perhaps even spoke it more or less perfectly.[53]

In conclusion we can say that, despite the undoubted infiltration of Hellenism into Palestine, our Lord lived in a specifically Jewish atmosphere; and this is also the impression one receives from reading the Gospels. His lessons to the people, His discussions with the Pharisees, and His dialogues with the authorities of Jerusalem, all belong to the purely Jewish world of ideas and interests, without any trace of Hellenic influence.

LITERATURE

Numerous writings of the last two centuries before Christ have come down to us. We shall not try to review them all, but shall confine ourselves to a few, enough, however, to enable us to get a sufficiently clear conception of the principal ideas that were dominant in the last years of Judaism and the beginning of the Christian era.

The two principal ideas were *Messianism* and *Wisdom,* i.e., practical wisdom. One can say that the others revolved about these two. Messianism appears clearly in the so-called *Psalms of Solomon,* written

---

[52] Geyer, *Itinera Hierosolymitana saeculi IV–VIII* (Vindobonae, 1898), p. 99.
[53] Gustaf Dalman, *Jesus-Jeshua,* trans. by P. Levertoff (New York: The Macmillan Co., 1929), pp. 1–37.

towards the middle of the first century before Christ, perhaps a short time after the taking of Jerusalem by Pompey in 63 B.C. The idea of *Wisdom* appears in the deuterocanonical book, Ecclesiasticus, which dates back to the beginning of the second century before Christ, as well as in the section of the *Mishnah* called *Aboth,* a collection of the sayings of the wise men of Israel who lived between the first century before Christ and the end of the first century A.D.

MESSIANISM

Some authors claim that, with the disappearance of the Prophets after the exile, the idea of a Messias also disappeared, or at least faded into the background, and they also claim that at the time when Christ came on earth the Messianic idea was almost forgotten. Nothing could be further from the truth, as the Gospels suffice to prove. The delegation of Jews who approached John the Baptist and the dialogue that took place between him and them (John 1:19 *ff.*), are clear indications that the Messianic idea was still current, as is also evident from the words of the Samaritan woman: "I know that Messias is coming (who is called Christ). . . ." (John 4:25), and the confession of St. Peter: "Thou art the Christ" (Matt. 16:16). Moreover, the book of the prophet Daniel was well-known, a book which our Lord quoted before Caiphas (Matt. 26:24), and one which was wholly impregnated with Messianism: "I beheld therefore in the vision of the night, and lo, one like the son of man came with the clouds of heaven. And he came even to the Ancient of days: and they presented him before him. And he gave him power and glory and a kingdom: and all peoples, tribes and tongues shall serve him. His power is an everlasting power that shall not be taken away: and his kingdom that shall not be destroyed" (Dan. 7:13–14). One could not speak in clearer terms of the Messianic kingdom; and so the Jews understood the passage.

In the aforementioned *Psalms of Solomon,* eighteen in number, written by a Pharisee or at any rate penetrated with the spirit of the Pharisees, the writer speaks of a future glorious kingdom in which a good and just king will reign; he predicts that the nation's enemies will be wiped out and that victorious Israel will enjoy peace and happiness. Without any doubt, the author is here concerned with the kingdom which the ancient prophets of Israel depicted in such glowing colors.

WISDOM

The Jews had the highest esteem for wisdom, practical wisdom, that is, a norm of life and a rule for upright action. It is thus that it appears in Ecclesiasticus, or as it is also called, "The Wisdom of Jesus, son of Sirach," which was written orginally in Hebrew, although until 1896 it was known only in the Greek translation made by a grandson of the author. It is very similar to the Proverbs of Solomon since for the most part it is composed of moral sayings or maxims such as these taken from the fifth chapter:

"Follow not in thy strength the desires of thy heart" (v. 2).

"Be not anxious for goods unjustly gotten: for they shall not profit thee in the day of calamity and revenge" (v. 10).

"Honor and glory is in the word of the wise: but the tongue of the fool is his ruin" (v. 15).

And the same author says that wisdom is in the fear of the Lord: "The fear of the Lord is the beginning of wisdom. . . ." "The fear of the Lord is a crown of wisdom. . . ." "The root of wisdom is to fear the Lord. . . ." "For the fear of the Lord is wisdom and discipline. . ." (chap. 1, vv. 16, 22, 25, 34).

The Book of Wisdom, or the "Book of the Wisdom of Solomon," as it is sometimes called, although written by a Jew, is permeated with Greek philosophy; the author was an Alexandrian Jew who wrote in Greek and lived in an atmosphere other than that of the Jewish world of Palestine.

It will be sufficient to quote a few maxims from the *Pirke Aboth* (i.e., "Maxims of the Fathers") : [54] ". . . the men of the Great Synagogue . . . said three things: 'Be deliberate in judgment, raise up many disciples, and make a fence around the Law.' " "Simon the Just was of the remnants of the Great Synagogue. He used to say: 'By three things is the world sustained: by the Law, by the [Temple-]service, and by deeds of loving-kindness.' " "Nittai the Arbelite said: 'Keep thee far from an evil neighbor and consort not with the wicked and lose not belief in retribution.' " These maxims are taken from chapter one (vv. 1, 2, 7) ; the rest of them are of the same type.

It is clear that besides Messianism and wisdom, eschatology played a large part in Jewish thought during the last two centuries before Christ. In this regard the apocryphal *Book of Henoch (Ethiopic)* and

[54] *Mishnah, Aboth* 1:1, 2, 7.

the *Sibylline Oracles* are of singular importance, but actually eschatological dissertations were usually coupled with the Messianic ideas.

Although the subject is very interesting, we do not think that this is the place to write at length on the interpretation of Jewish literature.[55]

[55] See Schürer, III, for abundant material on the subject.

3. The Gospels:

Chronology

We have not judged it opportune to treat here of the authenticity and historical validity of the Gospels, a subject which is dealt with specifically and at due length in numerous other works. But we shall give a brief outline of the four documents which form the basis of the life of Christ, and shall endeavor to bring out the special nature and the distinctive characteristics of each Gospel.

The Gospel of St. Matthew

In a quick reading of the first Gospel, two characteristics leap to the eye: its markedly apologetic purpose and the systematic marshalling of the material. The evangelist, writing for his fellow-Jews who were well versed in the Sacred Scriptures, wishes to prove to them that Jesus of Nazareth is the Messias foretold by the prophets (cf. 1:22 f.; 2:5 f., 15, 17 f., 23, etc.). He does not, of course, in any way exclude the Divinity of Christ, which appears in numerous passages (His baptism, 3:17; His Transfiguration, 17:5; His speaking to the Father, 11:25–27, etc.); but the most striking thing about this Gospel, and the object which the evangelist has most in mind, is the messianic character of Christ.

Another characteristic to Christ's Gospel is the proportion of space devoted to Christ's teachings. Naturally, the miracles are not passed over in silence (cf. chaps. 8–9), nor does the evangelist fail to relate numerous episodes, but there is no doubt that, in comparison with the three other Gospels, the first shows that St. Matthew sets out to give a certain preponderance to the doctrinal element over what we may call the narrative element.

Unlike Mark and Luke, who had not lived close to Christ, St. Matthew had at his disposal two sources of material—his own experiences as an eyewitness of almost everything he wrote about, and the body of oral tradition that very soon began to form. However, in arranging his narrative he does not seem to have adhered strictly to either the one or the other. His Gospel was rather like a thesis, a didactic work, and he molded his material with that aim in view, setting down both the doctrinal and the narrative elements in order of importance. He grouped many teachings around the Beatitudes (chapters 5–7), and set down many more where he tells of Christ's sending forth the Apostles (chapter 10); in chapters 8 and 9 he collected a great number of miracles, while in chapter 13 he gathered together a considerable proportion of the parables. It is easy to see that with this desire for systematization the author was not greatly concerned about chronological order. The exact time or place of an event mattered little to him; what interested him was the event itself, its apologetic force or its dogmatic implications. But he does not always depart from the chronological order: for example, chapters 14 to 18 contain a series of episodes (the first multiplication, journey to Tyre and Sidon, the second multiplication, St. Peter's confession, the Transfiguration, several incidents in Capharnaum) which certainly followed each other in the order related. Nevertheless, this sequence, which is very real and objective, is, as it were, only incidental to the evangelist's main purpose.

Therefore when we wish to ascertain the chronological order of our Lord's life, we shall not use the first Gospel as our guide; however, when St. Matthew's account does coincide in time with the others we can take it as opportune and valuable confirmation.

The Gospel of St. Mark

In the second Gospel we find a different atmosphere, for St. Mark's narrative is like a limpid stream which runs freely and swiftly, not pausing to spread out into quiet pools, but ever moving onward as if it were eager to reach the end of its journey. Delightfully it flows along, now rapidly and turbulently, now muted and calm, but always advancing, always reaching out towards its goal.

What plan had Mark in mind when he was writing his Gospel, so spontaneous, so different from the others? We are of the opinion that he had no special, personal object in mind. He merely wished to put down in writing the "good tidings," which he found stereotyped, as it were, in the teaching of Peter. On this point we have the explicit testimony of Papias,[1] who calls him "Mark, the interpreter [ἑρμηνευτής] of Peter," meaning that Mark wrote what he had heard from Peter and retained in his memory. Consequently, if his Gospel did follow a plan, it was not Mark's plan but Peter's. But had Peter himself a fixed mode of procedure? Papias supplies the answer: Peter "gave his teachings with a view to the profit [of the listeners], and not as one composes a history properly so-called [σύνταξιν] of the words [λογίων: words and deeds] of the Lord."

This description of Peter's method excludes all intention on his part of following a strict sequence, whether logical or chronological, and of giving a complete history of Christ. His only norm was the benefit of his audience; and Mark confined himself to putting down in writing these oral instructions of Peter. Unlike the other Synoptic writers, he did not revise his material, shaping it to conform to a personal plan, and this is precisely what gives his narrative its charming freedom, vivacity and spontaneity.

We are now in a better position to estimate the true value of Papias' observation that Mark did not write with order (οὐ μέντοι τάξει). There has been, and still is, much discussion as to whether Papias meant logical or chronological order. For our part, we suspect that Papias' phrase is given a precision which he did not intend it to have. Remembering Matthew with his logical order, Luke with his chronological order and both with their historical completeness—for they took in the *whole* life of Christ—Papias found that Mark lacked the order that was so evident in the other Synoptics. Hence when he used the word "order," he wished to express both logical and chronological order, as well as completeness of material, since a perfectly-arranged history must not appear incomplete and, in a certain sense, mutilated. Papias undoubtedly valued the three elements, logical and chronological order,[2] and completeness of material, and it was no wonder

[1] Eusebius *Hist. eccles.* iii. 39; *PG* 20, 300.
[2] We think that Prat exaggerates when he says: "Chronological order, for Papias, as for most of his contemporaries, was a kind of disorder." (*Jesus Christ*, trans. by John J. Heenan, S.J. [Milwaukee: Bruce Publishing Co., 1950], I, 18.)

that, finding all three lacking in Mark, he referred to them all when he spoke of "order."

We do not believe, then, that Mark was concerned with the exact sequence of events. However, he does generally follow the chronological order of things, not because he set out expressly to write down his narrative in due sequence, but simply because the events were presented to him in this form.

Mark seems to have had a lively interest in realistic touches that throw a personality into sharp relief, make us almost see an action being performed or show us the inner feelings of his characters; with a few swift strokes he can sketch a scene that comes alive before our eyes and draws us in to take part in it. What the other evangelists express vaguely and impersonally, he pins down and makes vivid by the use of telling details and direct speech. Rather than accumulate long quotations, we shall content ourselves with a few brief examples of his style: "The whole town had gathered together at the door" (1:33); "There was no longer room, not even around the door" (2:2); ". . . a paralytic, carried by four" (2:3); "And he himself was in the stern of the boat, on the cushion, asleep" (4:38; Matt.: "but he was asleep"; Luke: "he fell asleep"); "And looking round upon them with anger, and being grieved at the blindness of their hearts. . . ." (3:5; Luke: "And having looked around upon them all"); ". . . they could not do so much as take their food" (3:20); "And they . . . said to him, 'They are all seeking thee'" (1:37; Luke: "And the crowds were seeking after him, and came to him").

It would be easy to multiply passages which show this love of the concrete, this keen psychological observation, and this preference for direct quotation which give the second Gospel a special character and an additional charm and interest. Was Peter's preaching like this, or were these characteristics the product of the evangelist's own genius? It would be difficult to say, since we have no means of judging.

The Gospel of St. Luke

Unlike the other Synoptic writers, Luke tells us clearly and explicitly from the very start the aim he had in writing his Gospel and the plan he followed (cf. 1:1–4). He was familiar with the Gospels of

Mark and Matthew,[3] and other writings as well, and although he esteemed and respected the first two Gospels, they did not satisfy him, one because it was too concise and fragmentary, containing little of Christ's teachings and nothing about the Infancy, the other because he found that it lacked order in the narration of the events. With the object of avoiding these two defects and after having inquired carefully into all things from their very beginnings,[4] he decided to set them down in order so that deeds and words are unfolded in the narrative just as they occurred in reality [5]—all for the purpose of confirming his "most excellent Theophilus" more and more in the Faith.

Consequently, we know that Luke, and Luke alone, specifically proposed to hand down to us the Gospel story in the same sequence in which it developed. His general intention is by no means rendered ineffectual by the fact that his placing of events may not always follow the strict chronological order or that sometimes he may have purposely inverted that order. It is not strange to find that, no matter how carefully he endeavored to ascertain the exact sequence of the Gospel episodes, he did not always succeed in doing so; nor should we wonder if he departs from the chronological order when good pedagogy or greater clarity requires him to do so. We shall speak in due course (pp. 70 ff., 459 ff., 503 f.) of what is known as the "Lucan section" (Luke 9:51 to 19:14).

[3] Authors discuss whether or not the two other Synoptic Gospels should be numbered among the various works to which Luke refers. We believe that he had the first two Gospels particularly in mind, for they suffered from the two very defects which he set out to avoid writing with a certain *completeness* (a reference to Mark) and by following the *objective succession* of events (an allusion to Matthew).

[4] This is how we should interpret ἄνωθεν, which refers to the following word πᾶσιν. Luke wished to be complete, and therefore he informed himself not only about the public life of Christ but also about His very beginnings. There is nothing here that can be called tautology. Our interpretation—common among authors—is much more probable than the other one, "for a long time," which some prefer.

[5] Καθεξῆς should be understood in this chronological sense. St. Luke uses it again in 8:1; Acts 3:24, 11:4, 18:23; and in all these passages the word has a temporal tinge and even a sense of succession: it is a rule of good exegesis that we should give it the same force in Luke 1:3. We should do so all the more because this meaning harmonizes much better with the context than the other sense of *logical* order. If Luke wished to signify only that he proposed to write with order and not confusedly so that there would be coherence between the various parts of his narrative, his observation would be pointless and out of place since, as Knabenbauer (*In Luc.*, p. 33) rightly observes, what good writer would think of giving notice to his readers that he proposes to write without confusion or that he will not fail to follow a certain order in his narrative?

The Gospel of St. John

Although the fourth Gospel is very appropriately called the *spiritual* Gospel, it is actually the one which best places events in their proper chronological setting and which paints scenes with a most vivid and picturesque realism. In it, discourses on abstract and profound doctrines alternate with concrete descriptions, firmly and vividly drawn. St. John is the only evangelist who mentions the three Passovers; he alone provides chronological details on the ministry of John the Baptist and the beginning of the public life of Christ—"The next day . . ." (1:29, 35, 43); the precise time when the visit of the two disciples took place—"It was about the tenth hour" (1:39); the date of the wedding-feast at Cana—"And on the third day a marriage took place . . ." (2:1); the time of our Lord's conversation with the Samaritan woman—"It was about the sixth hour" (4:5), etc. Therefore it is to the *spiritual* Gospel, to the Gospel that offers us the most elevated, abstract doctrine, that we turn in search of concrete and exact data to fix the chronology of the Gospels.

The fourth Gospel contains delightful scenes and dialogues—Andrew and his companion following Jesus and remaining with Him (1:37–39); the conversation with Nathanael (1:47–51), with the Samaritan woman (4:7–26), and above all, that literary gem, the account of the man born blind (9:1–41). In short, this Gospel is a combination of idealism and realism in the best sense of the word; it is like the eagle, which now soars above the mountain peaks, and now sweeps down to skim the plain; here Heaven bends to earth in a holy kiss, sanctifying it and losing nothing by the contact.

If we were asked to characterize each evangelist in one word, we should say that Matthew is the *Apologist,* Mark the *Catechist,* Luke the *Historian,* and John the *Theologian.* In Matthew the ruling thought is "Jesus is the promised Messias"; in Mark, "Jesus Christ, the Son of God, came to proclaim the Gospel of the Kingdom"; in Luke, "Jesus came to bring peace and salvation to the world" (in reference to the angels' hymn and the Benedictus); in John, "Jesus of Nazareth is the Word who lived from all eternity in the bosom of the Father."

In Matthew events are set down in logical order; in Luke they follow the order of time, while Mark did not work according to any plan properly so-called, either logical or chronological. John did not propose, as Luke did, to give us a chronologically accurate account of the life of Christ, since his object was to develop and expound clearly the basic idea of his Prologue; but his analytical cast of mind and his love for the concrete caused him to scatter throughout his Gospel numerous details of time and place which are of inestimable value to us in fitting our Lord's life into its correct chronological setting.

Problems Presented by the Gospels

From what we have said it is easy to conjecture that the authors' diversity of purpose and personal character must be clearly reflected in their works, that the order of events must differ from one to the other, and that the mode of presentation will not always be the same. And the reality bears out the conjecture. It would be needless labor to accumulate quotations, since they are known to anyone who has so much as skimmed lightly over the four Gospels. These accounts of our Lord's life are like four musical instruments, each with its own special sound, which blend together in beautiful harmony. They are four differently-colored rays of light which, when they come together, form a many-hued picture. This is the Gospel harmony, this is the *concordia evangeliorum.*

But in order to perceive and appreciate this harmony we need a criterion that is at once wide and discerning: wide, to allow us to recognize the same reality under different appearances; discerning, so that we may not mistake a new fact for an old one in different guise. The history of exegesis in our own times and the extremes to which some authors have gone are sufficient proof that it is dangerous to make one's criterion either too wide or too narrow. We must admit, however, that it is not always easy to strike the golden mean. There are, of course, obvious cases which present no difficulty, such as those in which the evangelists give the same episodes a different chronological sequence, using such vague formulas as "then," "afterwards," "at that time," etc. Here, by their very lack of precision, they show clearly enough that they do not intend to pin the event down to a definite moment. But we must proceed with greater caution when the evangelist uses a concrete and well-defined expression, such as "The next day . . ." (John 1:29, 35, 43); "And on the third day . . ." (John 2:1); "after six days . . ." (Matt. 17:1; cf. Luke 9:28, "about eight days after . . ."), etc. In these cases it is difficult to avoid the impression that the writer knew the date and fully intended to indicate it. As regards the evangelists' mode of expressing themselves, there is no doubt that they had a perfect right to use different phrasing to pass down to us the same idea. It was not necessary, nor, for that matter, was it possible without very special assistance, for them to agree so closely with each other that they would repeat the very words pronounced by their Master.

There is another problem which must be treated with caution and prudence, and that is, did the evangelist at any time take the liberty of putting words in our Lord's mouth which He actually never said but which reflect His thought and are in harmony with His teaching, as for example when in Mark 10:12 He says: ". . . and if the wife puts away her husband, and marries another, she commits adultery"? There are some authors, Prat [6] for example, who favor the affirmative answer to this question. While not claiming to reject flatly this opinion, we should, however, be more reserved, and in this particular case we should choose the negative answer. In the Roman world it was an accepted thing for a woman to seek a divorce, and very possibly this custom had infiltrated into the higher classes of Jewish society. Consequently, we cannot say that the words in question would have sounded strange on the lips of Christ.

A special and certainly a much-discussed problem is presented by certain of the parables, for example, the parables of the talents and the gold pieces [7] (Matt. 25:14–30; Luke 19:11–27). The fundamental teaching is the same in both parables, but the circumstances of time and place, the modes of expression, and the numbers involved are not the same; in fact, the whole literary atmosphere is different. Are they really two parables or are they only one? The problem is of ancient date and will probably never be solved satisfactorily. Possibly each evangelist, concentrating on the doctrinal basis of the parable, intended to limit his historical guarantee to that alone without including the details, which he may have known only vaguely and whose concrete form had no bearing on the doctrine he wished to hand down. Whether or not that was what happened here, the evangelist's thought must be studied attentively and minutely in each particular case.

Even more complex and delicate, if that were possible, is the

[6] *Op. cit.,* I, 34–35.

[7] In Luke 19:11–27, the Challoner-Rheims Version has "pounds" and the Confraternity Edition has "gold pieces": a gold piece, also called a *mina,* was worth about $35.00, or one-sixtieth of a talent ($2,100.00). See below, p. 617, n. 20. (Translator's note.)

problem posed by St. John. Did our Lord actually pronounce those discourses which form a considerable part of the fourth Gospel? How could the evangelist have retained them entire in his memory and have reproduced them faithfully in writing? It would be easy and convenient to give a short, definite answer in the affirmative or the negative, but such a reply would hardly satisfy the reader, nor would it, in our opinion, correspond to the objective reality.

It is immediately apparent that in its narrative portions the well-named spiritual Gospel is a faithful reflection of reality. Its author was the beloved disciple who was always close to the Master. His love lent keenness to his eyes and made his memory especially retentive; even the minutest details did not escape him, and during the course of his long life he kept turning over in his mind the loving memories of his Lord. We can easily understand this tenacity in keeping fresh the recollection of concrete and intensely vivid facts. But can we say the same of long discourses, often on abstract subjects and always on the sublimest doctrine?

First we must accept as firmly established the fundamental principle that the Apostle never put on Christ's lips a discourse which He had in no way pronounced. We know that it was then a generally-admitted practice for an historian to attribute pronouncements to his subjects corresponding to their state of mind and in harmony with the circumstances of time and place. Whatever the legitimacy of such a procedure, we are convinced that St. John never used it, for his respect and veneration for his Master would not have allowed him to do so. However, we are not going to claim that he reproduced Christ's discourses word for word. Neither divine inspiration nor historical veracity requires that, nor was it the evangelist's avowed intention. The ideas were important, not the words, although it would be a great consolation for us to possess not only the ideas but even the very terms in which they were clothed. Yet fortunately in not a few cases we have the moral certainty that our Lord's very words have been recorded for us.

The Apostle had carefully gathered the teachings of Christ; he had lived them, meditated lovingly upon them and had made them, as it were, part of himself. And these teachings of the Divine Master have been transmitted to us through the ardent soul and crystal-clear mind of him who was the beloved disciple. It may well be, and it is even natural to expect, that they have come down to us colored by the spirit of John; yet this coloring, this shading, is not a distortion; it is a quality that harmonizes faithfully with the spirit of Christ Himself.

Did the evangelist allow himself the liberty of filling out the Master's ideas with his own personal observations? If it is a question of interpolating some words or phrases to make our Lord's thought stand out more clearly and render it more accessible, then the answer is in the affirmative, in conformity with St. Augustine's teaching.[8] But if it is a question of a more or less lengthy commentary which the disciple presents as a continuation of the Master's discourse, the answer must be in the negative. It is inconceivable that St. John would think, even for a moment, of putting his own commentary on the same plane as the words of Christ in such a way that his addition would form a unity with our Lord's utterances and would give the impression that the whole discourse had come from Christ's own lips. It is possible, and it may actually have happened in one case or another—for example, in the dialogue with Nicodemus (John 3)[9]— that we are unable to draw a clear and definite line between the words of the Master and those of the disciple, due to the fact that writers in those days used neither quotation marks nor parentheses and also because John succeeded in assimilating Christ's doctrine so perfectly that even when he speaks for himself, his words vibrate with a divine resonance.

Must we hold that the discourses reproduced by the fourth evangelist are not only Christ's own words but also that they were pronounced in the circumstances of time and place indicated by the Apostle? Could St. John have put a discourse in the wrong place, or even have combined pronouncements made at different times and in different places and presented them as one continuous whole? Several authors observe that it is unjust to deny St. John a liberty which is conceded to St. Matthew,[10] and they are perfectly right. For, since Matthew's literary procedure is compatible with divine inspiration and preserves historical truth, it is allowable also to John. Hence the possibility of such a method is not automatically ruled out, and the Apostle could have linked together discourses pronounced at different times

[8] ". . . sive ad illuminandam declarandamque sententiam, nihil quidem rerum, verborum tamen aliquid addat" (*De cons. Ev.; PL* 34, 1091).

[9] Cf. pp. 256 *ff.* below.

[10] "Quod Matthaeo licitum erat, Ioanni denegandum non est a priori." H. Höpfl and B. Gut, *Introductio specialis in Novum Testamentum* (Romae, 1938), no. 262.

and in different places and presented them as one uninterrupted speech. But did he actually do so?

We believe that if we look into the minds of the evangelists and try to find out what was their attitude or general intention regarding the point in question, we shall find a very noticeable difference between the Synoptics and the fourth Gospel, and we must take strict account of this difference when dealing with particular cases. In St. Matthew and St. Luke, Christ's discourses ordinarily appear against a vague, imprecise chronological background. Thus in several of His pronouncements (e.g., Luke 17:1-10) we can discover no connection with the immediate or the proximate context, and throughout the whole "Lucan section" (Luke 9:51—18:14) it is difficult to ascertain the time and place of many of Christ's discourses.[11] Just the opposite happens in St. John. He tells us that Christ conversed with Nicodemus in Jerusalem, during the Passover and at night (2:23; 3:2); that He spoke to the Samaritan woman at noon beside Jacob's well when He was returning from Judea (4:1-7); that the dialogue which he mentions in chapter 5 took place between Christ and the Pharisees in Jerusalem soon after the curing of the paralytic at the pool of Bethesda; that the discourse on the Bread of Life occurred in the synagogue at Capharnaum after the first multiplication of the loaves; that the considerations on the good shepherd were uttered in Jerusalem in connection with the miracle worked on the man born blind (10:1-18), etc. All these discourses are fitted into a well-defined framework of time, place and persons involved. Here we do not have to rely on such vague indications as "then," "at that time," "in a certain place," which leave us in such a fog as regards date and location that we do not know exactly when or where the action occurred or the words were said. On the contrary, St. John gives us concrete data and draws his pictures with firm strokes and clean outlines. Of course, sometimes the Synoptic writers, too, provide facts of time and place, but not as markedly, as precisely and as frequently as the fourth Gospel, and it is this striking difference that gives a special, personal character to St. John's narrative, and distinguishes it sharply from that of the other evangelists. Therefore we cannot but conclude that the author remembered the exact circumstances in which Christ pronounced His

11 "Now after this. . . . And he said to them. . . ." (10:1); "And it came to pass as he was praying in a certain place. . . . " (11:1); "Now when immense crowds had gathered together . . ." (12:1); "And it came to pass, when he entered the house of one of the rulers of the Pharisees . . ." (14:1), etc.

discourses and that he wished to frame our Lord's words in the very setting of time and place in which they were spoken.[12] There remains only one hypothesis, namely, literary artifice: is it possible that, in order to give Christ's words an added sense of reality, the Apostle may have set them down against a concrete and tangible background which served as a kind of counterpoise to the subtlety and abstract quality of the thought expressed? In our opinion, it would have been psychologically impossible for John to have used such an artifice. We are not going to prove this statement; the best proof is to be found in an attentive, repeated reading of the fourth Gospel. And we would almost go so far as to say that anyone who fails to perceive the impossibility of this theory after such a perusal, is ill-equipped to pass judgment on St. John's work.

Naturally, our general conclusion does not dispense us from diligently examining particular cases, some of which we shall discuss in due course.

It will not be out of place here to say something about St. John's "symbolism." As we have already remarked, the fourth Gospel has been justly called the "spiritual Gospel." Its recurrent references to *light, life, truth* and *love* give it a special character of its own. Its very prologue (1:1-13) is impregnated, as it were, with light, truth and life, for St. John contemplated the Incarnate Word, whom he was about to make known to men, as the principle and source of light, truth and life: "I am the way, the truth and the life" (14:6); "I came that they may have life, and have it more abundantly" (10:10).

In addition, certain material elements, such as water, wine, bread and life appear again and again in the narrative. Now, in view of the markedly spiritual character of the fourth Gospel, the question spontaneously arises as to whether these material elements have a higher, spiritual significance in addition to their primary meaning. For example, are the wine and water mentioned at the marriage feast at Cana symbols of light and love, of faith and charity respectively? Is the conversion of Israel prefigured in our Lord's colloquy with Nicodemus, and the conversion of the Gentiles in the episode of the Samaritan woman? It is noteworthy that in both these incidents, there is

---

[12] This does not mean to say that, in reproducing one of Christ's discourses, the Apostle might not have interpolated some sentences which he remembered having heard the Master speak in other circumstances of time and place. We cannot point to a definite concrete instance of this, but such a procedure is not excluded by what we have said.

mention of water. Is the multiplication of the loaves a symbol of the
Eucharist, the Bread of Life? Does the episode at the pool of Siloe, the
healing of the man born blind, symbolize the light which the Word,
the Envoy of the Father, came to shed upon the world? Is the raising
of Lazarus meant to be a symbol of the highest manifestation of life? [13]

There is no denying that there are points of contact between such
material elements as water, wine, bread and life, and the most exalted
concepts of light and love or heavenly bread and supernatural life.
And, obviously, the former can readily serve as symbols of the latter.
But did St. John intend them so to serve? In describing the wedding
feast at Cana, did he mean to use the water as a symbol of supernatural life and the wine as a figure of love? The terms used in the
narrative itself and the circumstances of the episode give no indication
that such was the evangelist's intention; and there is no need to give
the water and wine a second, deeper meaning in order to appreciate
the full force of the miracle. Nor does it seem that St. John meant to
refer to the conversion of the Jews when he wrote of our Lord's telling
Nicodemus the conditions necessary for entering the kingdom of
heaven. And it is just as unlikely that he wished to speak symbolically
of the conversion of the Gentiles in his description of the meeting between Jesus and the Samaritan woman.

At first glance, the healing of the man born blind seems the most
markedly symbolical miracle of all. Nevertheless our Lord's use of
water as the instrument of healing is easily explained by the circumstance that the pool of Siloe was close at hand. He had just before left
the Temple and was probably in the district of Ophel, at the southern
end of which the pool lay, when He met the blind man. The fact that
St. John gave the translation of the Hebrew word "Siloe" (i.e.,
"sent") does not mean that he was referring to Him whom the Father
had *sent* into the world. In 19:13, he gives the Hebrew translation of
Lithostrotos (Gabbatha), and surely no one will try to see some
symbolism in his supplying that information.

But there is one episode the possible symbolical meaning of which
must be treated with greater reserve than that of the others mentioned
above, and that is the multiplication of the loaves. The fact that our
Lord took bread as the matter of the Blessed Sacrament and the
further fact that in St. John's narrative there is a close connection be-

[13] See Fr. Allo's "Symbolisme de Saint Jean," in *L'Évangile spirituel de Saint
Jean* (Paris, 1944), pp. 67–94, particularly pp. 73–75.

tween the miracle worked in the neighborhood of Bethsaida and the great discourse in the synagogue at Capharnaum, invite us to see a true symbolical meaning in the multiplication of the loaves: the earthly bread which nourishes the body is a symbol of the heavenly bread that nourishes the soul.

The fourth Gospel certainly deserves the title "the spiritual Gospel." But "spiritual" does not mean "symbolical." St. John's Gospel is eminently spiritual because it is intimately and consciously penetrated with the highest spiritual concepts, which give it a character all its own and mark it off clearly from the Synoptic narratives. The beloved disciple shows our Lord as the Eternal Word who, possessing the fullness of life, came into the world to make men sharers in that life: "I came that they may have life, and have it more abundantly" (John 10:10). That is the central idea about which the whole Gospel revolves, for this divine life is light and truth and love: "I am the light of the world. . . . I am the truth. . . . A new commandment I give you . . . that as I have loved you, you also love one another." All this beauty stands out in high relief and needs no abstruse and, in reality, very problematic symbolical meanings to reveal or enhance it.

As we have already pointed out, we are not here attempting to prove the authenticity and historical value of the Gospels. However, since we have menioned oral tradition or, if you will, *catechesis,* as being, at least partially, the basis and fount of the Gospel narrative, perhaps someone may ask, "Is this basis solid enough and is this fount pure enough to allow us to vindicate the truly historical character of the Gospels?"

In the last few decades there has arisen a new school called the *Formgeschichte* ("Form Criticism") school, which studies the development of the literary-religious activity of the Christian community or communities and seeks to ascertain what part these communities played in the elaboration of the Gospels as we have them today. Praiseworthy indeed is the desire to discover in minutest detail the way in which that collection of deeds and words which make up our Gospels was formed in the first Christian generation. But the *Formgeschichte* school is vitiated by two grave faults in method. First, it gives such prominence to the community, and attributes to it such a preponderance in the elaboration of the Gospels that the personality of the evangelist almost disappears; and when there is question of analyzing what can be called the community movement, this school, instead

of citing objective historical facts to support its thesis, describes with
great aplomb and much pseudo-scientific display the curve which the
movement *must have* followed. Obviously, such a procedure is bound
to be highly subjective. The second fault, no less grave than the first,
is in the criterion used to draw a distinction between the primitive
historical nucleus and the parasitic elements which came from the
community. It is set down as a principle that each of the statements
attributed to Christ must be reduced to its simplest form, so that if it
contains two parts, one of which is limited in reference while the other
is universal, then the latter is to be considered as an addition—the
community's comment, as it were, on the original primitive nucleus of
the statement. The members of this school go further and maintain
that everything that goes beyond the purely natural order is also to be
considered an addition.

A few examples will make clear the method employed by these
critics. In Mark 11:15-18, we read about the expulsion of the vendors
from the Temple. According to the *Formgeschichte* school, this account of the act itself can belong to the original nucleus but the sentence in verse 17, "My house shall be called a house of prayer for all
the nations" is a foreign element added to the primitive idea, which can
stand without it, and so this addition should be eliminated. In the
anointing at Bethany (Mark 14:3-9), this school says, the sole primitive statement of Christ is: "She has done me a good turn. For the
poor you have always with you . . ." while what follows is the commentary made by the community and inspired by the thought of
Christ's passion.

We do not claim that oral tradition put all the actions in their due
geographical and chronological positions, nor that it reproduced the
very words spoken by our Lord and the other personalities in the
Gospels; the variety found in all sections of the Synoptics is evidence to
the contrary. But we do say that it would be wrong to suppose that an
evangelist, when recording this tradition, would have dared to present
as an historical element of our Lord's life an action which he himself
had invented, or that he would have put on Christ's lips a statement
that he well knew our Lord never uttered. The respect which the
evangelists had for Christ, for the *Kyrios*, did not allow them to take
such liberties. Perhaps someone will say that either the catechist or the
community could have added to the Master's authentic words by way
of amplification or commentary, and that this new element then came

to form an integral part of the Gospels. We acknowledge willingly that such a possibility cannot be excluded, but we also hold that it would be shallow and unscientific to concede without solid arguments the existence of such additions or amplifications.[14]

Chronology

THE BIRTH OF CHRIST

The death of Herod is the most definite point of departure for fixing, though it be only approximately, the date of Christ's birth. Herod died in the year 750 after the foundation of Rome, four years before the beginning of the Christian era (which, as is well known, the Scythian monk, Dionysius Exiguus, mistakenly made to coincide with the Roman year 754), thirty-seven years from the time the Romans had given him the title of king, after thirty-four years of actual rule,[15] a short while before the Passover, either at the beginning or at the end of March,[16] and at the age of almost seventy years.[17] This date for the death of Herod is well-established and should be regarded as certain from every point of view.

According to Josephus,[18] the battle of Actium, from which Octavian emerged victorious over Antony, and which was fought in September of the Roman year 723 (that is, 31 B.C.), occurred in the seventh year of Herod's reign. Since this reign lasted thirty-four years, if we add twenty-seven to 723 we shall get the Roman year 750 as the end of Herod's rule and the year of his death. Josephus also tells us [19] that between the capture of Jerusalem by Pompey (63 B.C. or Roman year 690–691) and the taking of the same city by Herod (in the war against Antigonus), there elapsed twenty-seven years (or possibly only twenty-six depending on whether or not the historian includes the year already begun): [20] from which it follows that the second conquest of

---

[14] Publications on the *Formgeschichte* method are almost countless, but since we touch upon it only in passing we refrain from giving a bibliography. A comprehensive account of it can be found in the learned and judicious article by E. Florit, "La 'storia delle forme' nei Vangeli in rapporto alla dottrina cattolica," *Biblica* 14 (1933), 212–248.

[15] *Ant.* xvii. 8. 1; *Wars* i. 33. 8.

[16] *Ant.* xvii. 9. 3; *Wars* ii. 1. 3.

[17] *Ant.* xvii. 6. 1; *Wars* i. 33. 1.

[18] *Ant.* xv. 5. 2; *Wars* i. 19. 3.

[19] *Ant.* xiv. 16. 4.

[20] Cf. Schürer, I, 415.

Jerusalem took place in the Roman year 716–717; and therefore Herod's reign, lasting as it did for thirty-four years, came to an end in the Roman year 750, four years before the Christian era.[21]

Other arguments in support of this date can be derived from an eclipse of the moon on the night of March 12th or 13th, 4 B.C.,[22] and from the chronologies of Archelaus [23] and of Antipas, but there is no need to go into these arguments here: suffice it to say that they point towards the same year 750.[24]

Therefore Herod's death occurred in the Roman year 750, four years before the Christian era, and hence it is certain that our Lord was born before 750. But the question is, how long before? The visit of the Magi may perhaps shed some light on the point. Basing his calculations on the time at which the Magi had seen the star, Herod ordered the slaughter of all male children two years of age and under, since he took it for granted that the appearance of the star had co-incided with the birth of the new King. The suspicious monarch evidently wished to make completely sure that he would achieve his purpose; thus we can reasonably infer that Christ must have been born a year and a half, or at least a year, before Herod's terrible decree.

But this does not solve the problem, for we must now ascertain how much time elapsed between the coming of the Magi and Herod's death. We know that Herod had himself carried to the thermal springs at Callirrhoe in a vain search for relief from his illness, and everything seems to indicate that this journey occurred a short time before his death at Jericho.[25] But we do not know how much time intervened between his visit to Callirrhoe and the coming of the Magi and we have no positive means of ascertaining it. The common opinion is that the interval was rather a short one.

Another chronological fact, and one which, to all appearances, is very exact, is provided by St. Luke (2:1–2): "Now it came to pass in those days, that there went forth a decree from Caesar Augustus that

[21] Cf. Joseph Felten, *Neutestamentliche Geschichte, oder Judentum und Heiden-tum zur Zeit Christi und der Apostel* (zweite und dritte Auflage) (Regensburg, 1925), I, 178.

[22] *Ant.* xvii. 6. 4.

[23] Notice that in *Wars* ii. 7. 3, the *ninth* year of Archelaus' reign is given as the date of his exile, while *Ant.* xvii. 13. 2, gives the *tenth* year. This second date should be taken as the true one. Cf. Schürer, I, 415.

[24] See Schürer, I, 416 where the arguments are given briefly and clearly.

[25] *Ant.* xvii. 6. 5; 8. 1; *Wars* i. 35. 5, 8.

a census of the whole world should be taken. This first census took place while Cyrinus was governor of Syria." Since this census was precisely the reason for Mary's journey to Bethlehem, it provides us with a definite point of reference for fixing the date of our Lord's birth. But we prefer to lay this argument to one side because it bristles with difficulties. The reader will see what we mean if he turns to pp. 112 *ff.*, where we discuss the way to harmonize it with the Gospel narrative.

From what we have said the reader can deduce that it is not possible to fix with complete exactitude the date of Christ's birth and that we must be content with an approximation. In practice we can safely conclude that our Lord was born about two years before Herod's death, and therefore about six years before the beginning of the Christian era as we reckon it.

PUBLIC LIFE

In regard to the beginning of the public life we have several pieces of evidence which allow us to fix it in a reasonably satisfactory manner. When our Lord was speaking with the Jews during the first Passover which He celebrated in Jerusalem, they said to Him: "Forty-six years has this temple been in building, and wilt thou raise it up in three days?" (John 2:20). From Josephus [26] we know that Herod began his magnificent construction in the eighteenth year of his reign, which corresponds with the Roman year 734–735, granting that he began to rule in 717. When he died in 750, the building had been going on for fifteen years; and since it lasted for forty-six years all told, it continued for thirty-one years after his death in the Roman year 750. And seeing that the present era began, not in 750, but in 754, the thirty-first year after the death of Herod corresponds to A.D. 27–28. Hence we can say that Christ celebrated the first Passover of His public life in the year A.D. 28.

We obtain a similar result from the text of Luke (3:1–2): "Now in the fifteenth year of the reign of Tiberius Caesar . . . the word of God came to John . . . in the desert." Augustus died on August 19th of the Roman year 767 (A.D. 14); hence the fifteenth year of Tiberius corresponds with the Roman year 782 or A.D. 29. It must be noted, however, that in 765, two years before his death, Augustus made Tiberius a *collega imperii*, that is, his associate in the imperial rule.

[26] *Ant.* xv. 11. 1.

Therefore if St. Luke took this latter date as his point of departure, we get the year 27 and not 29 as the beginning of Christ's ministry.

We must remember one circumstance which may cause a slight variation in estimating this date; according to all appearances, the period of time between the death of a sovereign and the beginning of the next year was considered as the first year of his successor's reign, even though this interval covered only a few months or less. We do not know whether or not the evangelist followed this method of reckoning.

In the passage we quoted, Luke is primarily concerned with John the Baptist's ministry, but we know that our Lord's public life began very soon after that of His Precursor.

Luke provides us with another valuable piece of evidence when he says: "And Jesus himself, when he began his work, was about [ὡσεί] thirty years of age. . ." (3:23). If the evangelist meant to give a categorical and precise indication, then this would be the clearest and most decisive of all the chronological data. However, the particle of approximation with which he qualifies his statement leaves the way open for a variation of several years either way.[27] Thus a double hypothesis is possible, that at the time mentioned, Christ was thirty-two or thirty-three, or, on the contrary, only twenty-eight or twenty-nine years of age. Hence this text does not narrow down the dates we have already estimated, but it does, in a way, corroborate and confirm them.

DURATION OF THE PUBLIC LIFE

First of all we must exclude the hypothesis that the public life of our Lord lasted only one year, even prescinding from the question of whether or not it is possible to fit the whole Gospel account into such narrow limits.

Actually, St. John definitely mentions three Passovers: "Now the Passover of the Jews was at hand, and Jesus went up to Jerusalem" (2:13; cf. v. 23); "Now the Passover, the feast of the Jews, was near" (6:4); "Before the feast of the Passover . . ." (13:1). This mention of three Passovers implies a period of at least two years and some months. This conclusion cannot be avoided except by eliminat-

---

[27] This is the well-founded opinion of U. Holzmeister, S.J., *Chronologia Vitae Christi* (Romae, 1933), pp. 96–98; in *Verb. Dom.*, 7 (1927), 369, Funk holds the same view. A somewhat different way of interpreting the text can be seen in *Razón y Fe*, 43 (1915), 181 f.

ing one of the Passovers, which is exactly what some authors do, claiming that the word "Passover" in John 6:4 is not authentic.[28]

Such a procedure must be termed purely arbitrary, for the word in question appears in all the manuscripts and in all the versions. But even if we allow the unjustified removal of the word, the very text itself protests that the "feast of the Jews" mentioned here is and can be none other than the Passover. In referring to the same episode which St. John here relates, the multiplication of the loaves, St. Mark says (6:39) that Jesus ordered the people to sit down on the *"green* grass," an indication that it was spring (March-April). Hence the feast of the Tabernacles is excluded, since it was celebrated in the month of Tishri (mid-September-mid-October), and it is inconceivable that at that time of year the desert or semi-desert scene of the miracle (cf. Luke 9:10) would have been covered with green grass.

Discarding, then, the hypothesis of only one year of public life, we are left with two theories worthy of consideration, both of them with many supporters—namely, that the public life lasted three *complete* years, or that it lasted three *incomplete* years. In the first case *four* Passovers were celebrated during our Lord's public life; in the second, only *three*.

Let us begin by acknowledging that this problem is not susceptible of a wholly satisfactory solution, and that we are dealing solely with probabilities. The elements of the discussion are provided almost exclusively by St. John, for, as we have remarked before, it is the *spiritual* Gospel that supplies the most numerous and most concrete chronological data. We can say, although with some exaggeration, that the whole controversy revolves around the interpretation of two passages from this Gospel, John 5:1, and 4:45.

[28] J. Belser in *Bibl. Zeit.*, 1 (1903), 55–63, 160–174, refutes the arguments which are brought against the hypothesis of only one year. He concludes that the only effective argument against this hypothesis is the mention of the Passover in John 6:4; this mention is probably unauthentic, he says, since distinguished Fathers of the first centuries do not refer to it, and since such a Passover alters the whole plan of the fourth Gospel. Once this Passover is suppressed, he continues, the whole public life of Christ in St. John's Gospel extends from the Passover of the Roman year 782 to 783, with which the Synoptic Gospels are in perfect agreement (p. 174). In *Bibl. Zeit.*, 2 (1904), 373–376, E. Nagle makes some interesting observations on Belser's articles; and he is rather skeptical about the omission of the word "Passover" in John 6:4. With erudition and great ingenuity, H. J. Cladder (*Unsere Evangelien* [Freiburg im Breisgau], 1919, pp. 205–221) endeavors to prove that the "Passover" of John 6:4 is not authentic, and he concludes: "Without trying to impugn other viewpoints, I am of the opinion that the hypothesis of only one year finds solid support in the Gospel of St. John" (p. 221).

In John 5:1, we read: "After this there was a feast of the Jews. . . ." What feast is he referring to—the Passover? Here, textual criticism must come into play. The Greek text offers a double reading: ἑορτή without the article (*a* feast), and ἡ ἑορτή with the article (*the* feast). Neither of the two readings can be regarded as certain, but the first seems to be critically the more probable.[29] In this case we can conclude that St. John is not speaking here of the Passover, for if he were he would certainly have used the article. But even if he had used the article, we should still not be sure that he meant the Passover, for why then did he not identify it by its proper name as he does in 2:10; 6:4; 13:1?[30] On the other hand, the article was always employed if there was question of any one of the three feasts which the Israelites had to celebrate in Jerusalem (cf. Deut. 16:16). Pentecost was one of these, and, in our opinion, it is this feast that is referred to in the passage under discussion.[31]

In John 4:35, our Lord says to His disciples: "Do you not say, 'There are yet four months, and then comes the harvest'? Well, I say to you, lift up your eyes and behold that the fields are already white for the harvest." These are two difficult sentences which appear to be incompatible and mutually contradictory. The first seems to indicate that the time is winter and the second that it is summer. There are two possible interpretations and both have been advanced, but neither can be regarded as definitive.

If we understand the first sentence in its real sense, that is, that there were actually four months to go before the harvest, then the time would be the month of January, since in that region of Sichem the crops were gathered during the first half of June. In this case the second sentence has a symbolic meaning, i.e., the fields which were already white were the Samaritans who were then ripe for conversion.

[29] The new papyrus of St. John (P 66, or Bodner Papyrus II), which dates back to the end of the second century, does not have the article. This papyrus, containing no less than fourteen chapters of the fourth Gospel, was found in 1952 and published in 1956 by Victor Martin under the title *Papyrus Bodner II, Évangile de S. Jean, Chap. 1–14* (Bibliotheca Bodneriana, Cologny-Genève, 1956). Cf. *Ephemerides Theologicae Lovanienses,* 32 (1956), pp. 547 f., and, for a fuller treatment, *Orientirung* (Zurich, 5 Januar, 1957).

[30] It is true that the "feast" of John 4:45 is the Passover, but we must note that this "feast" is the Passover referred to in John 2:23, which had been celebrated a short time before.

[31] Braun (*S. Jean,* p. 351), who reverses the order of chapters 5 and 6 of St. John, believes that "the feast of the Jews" in 5:1, is the Passover of 6:4. Even prescinding from the difficulties raised by the reversal of order (cf. pp. 296 ff.), this identification seems to us in no way probable.

In the second interpretation the process is reversed. The first sentence was a proverb which was current among the people and which had no real relationship to the actual state of the crops. But in the second, Jesus wished to point out that the waving wheat upon the plain was about to be gathered in, and that it was a symbol of the good disposition of the Samaritans, who were ready for conversion. Our Lord recalled the proverb on account of the contrast which it offered with the actual state of the fields, for they did not need four more months of growth, but had already attained complete maturity.

We regard this second interpretation as the more probable one, for although we have no positive evidence to prove that the first sentence contains a proverb, the very manner in which our Lord introduces it ("Do you not say . . .") seems to hint that it was a current saying.[32]

The enthusiastic reception which the Galileans gave our Lord (cf. John 4:45) seems to have followed very soon (one or two months) after the feast of the Passover, during which they had seen the marvels wrought by their Fellow-Countryman (cf. John 2:23). It was these wonders that caused them to be so well disposed towards Christ, and thus it is not likely that eight or nine months had passed since the feast and the miracles. Again, if the interval had been a long one, most likely spent by our Lord in the ministry in Judea, it is not easy to understand why the Synoptic writers say nothing about it and why St. John records only a few brief episodes from it.

Hence we conclude that the fourth Gospel mentions only three Passovers[33] and that, consequently, our Lord's public life did not last three complete years but only two years and some months, or about two years and a half—in other words, three incomplete years.

In conformity with what we have said, we arrange the chronology of Christ's life thus:

The Nativity should be placed approximately two years before Herod's death, about the Roman year 748, and hence some six years before the Christian era as it is commonly reckoned; His baptism in

---

[32] Thus it is understood by Lagrange, Prat, Murillo and many others. As Murillo puts it: "In His words in v. 35, Christ undoubtedly alludes to a popular proverb which went like this: 'From now to the harvest there are still four months,' and which the Hebrews employed to indicate that there was still a long time to go before some event was due to occur." (*El Cuarto Evangelio* [Barcelona, 1908], p. 231.)

[33] It may be objected that St. John does not mention all the Passovers. However, in view of the particular interest which the evangelist shows in the feasts celebrated in Jerusalem, even the less important ones like the Dedication, it is highly improbable that he would fail to mention one of the Passovers.

the year 27 (probably in the final months) ; the years 28 and 29 spent in the full ministry; His death in the year 30. In this year 30, the 14th of Nisan fell on Friday, April 7th; [34] and on this day, sunrise was at 5:44 and sunset at 6:23.

It is difficult to fix the duration of the public life of Christ, but it is harder still to coordinate chronologically the events of His ministry, for the evangelists, particularly the three Synoptics, reflect oral tradition, in which our Lord's life was not set forth in its fullness or in its strict time sequence. Rather, those events were selected which seemed most interesting, or perhaps most cogent from an apologetic point of view, or which had remained most deeply engraved on the disciples' minds. Of course, in the latter case the judgment and particular tastes of the catechist would have played a very important part. Thus several series of narratives were formed, which through being repeated day after day, gradually hardened into a set, stereotyped form. This explains, on the one hand, the common background of our evangelists, the Synoptics, and on the other, the differences between their accounts, without excluding, of course, the fact that each evangelist, due to his character and the particular aim he had in view or his relationship to the Apostles, left on his own Gospel the more or less well-marked impression of his personality.

As we have already indicated, the public ministry of Christ includes three Passovers: the first (John 2:13, 23) in the year 28, for the celebration of which He went up to Jerusalem; the second (John 6:4) in 29, during which He remained in Galilee; and the third (John 13:1) in 30, which was that of the Passion. Hence the public life of our Saviour extended over two complete years, 28 and 29, part (about three months) of 27, and about the same number of months in 30.

In order to arrange the various episodes of these years as far as possible in chronological order, the best procedure seems to be to take each of the Passovers as a center and point of reference, and group about it the events that fall within its orbit. This method fixes the general outlines and allows us with greater facility and assuredness to complete the picture by tracing in the secondary lines and the minor details. Naturally, however we may arrange it, the time sequence of the numerous episodes will in many points be only probable to a greater or lesser degree: but in any case, despite the uncertainty and the great number of different combinations possible, it will always be of marked

[34] Cf. *Biblica*, 9 (1928), 55.

advantage to have singled out a certain proportion of events which are grouped around the feasts of the Jews, the dates of which are definitely known.

(1) Before and a little after the *first Passover* (John 2:23): baptism, temptations, first disciples, return to Galilee, the wedding feast at Cana, short visit to Capharnaum; *going up to Jerusalem for the Passover,* conversation with Nicodemus; ministry in Judea, imprisonment of John the Baptist; departure for Galilee, conversation with the Samaritan woman; arrival in Galilee and second miracle at Cana (healing the son of the official).

There is no reasonable doubt about the sequence of these events. At this point, however, we come across a problem upon whose solution depends the order of the subsequent episodes. This problem is the burning question concerning the inversion of chapters 5 and 6 of St. John. If the inversion is accepted, the episode at the pool of Bethesda (John 5:1-9) must be put forward until after the sermon on the Bread of Life (John 6:32 *ff.*), which followed shortly after the first multiplication, and which consequently fell within the year 29. But since we prefer to keep the present order of chapters [35] and to regard the feast mentioned in John 5:1 as the feast of Pentecost, we date the aforementioned Bethesda episode fifty days after the first Passover. Therefore it was shortly after the second miracle at Cana that our Lord once more went up to Jerusalem for the feast of Pentecost, during which He healed the paralytic at Bethesda.

(2) *The second Passover* (John 6:4): the first multiplication ("Now the Passover, the feast of the Jews, was near," John 6:4), the sermon on the Bread of Life, journey to the region of Tyre and Sidon, second multiplication, return to Capharnaum, curing the blind man of Bethsaida, Caesarea Philippi, Transfiguration, return to Capharnaum.

(3) The fourth Gospel provides some precious points of reference for *the last six months:*

a. in the month of Tishri (September-October) Jesus went from Capharnaum to Jerusalem for the feast of Tabernacles (John 7:2 *ff.*).

b. in Kislev (November-December) Jesus went from Perea to Jerusalem for the feast of the Encoenia or Dedication (John 10:22), and from Jerusalem He returned to Perea (John 10:40).

c. at some point not long before the Passion, Jesus went to Bethany, where He raised Lazarus (John 11:1 *ff.*).

[35] See below, pp. 296 *ff.*

The so-called "Lucan section," (Luke 9:51—18:14),[36] of great
importance in the ordering of the events of the last six months, covers
the period from the feast of Tabernacles in the third year (September-
October, 29) until the journey from Jericho to Jerusalem for the last
Passover and the Passion (March-April, 30). These ten chapters are
rich in doctrine and contain many beautiful lessons:

> They provide Christian piety with incomparable treasures. In them
> we read those moving stories and parables which the other evangelists
> have not preserved for us—the good Samaritan, Martha and Mary, the
> cry of the woman who called the Mother of Jesus blessed and our Lord's
> reply, the prodigal son, the rich man and Lazarus, the Pharisee and the
> Publican. . . . Never was the evangelical light softer and, at the same
> time, more penetrating; never did it make us see so deeply into the
> divine and human mercy of our Saviour.[37]

But in contrast to their rich fund of doctrine, these chapters provide
few points of chronological reference.

Luke mentions a journey to Jerusalem no less than three times
(9:51; 13:22; 17:11). If these journeys could be identified with those
of the fourth Gospel, some headway would be made. Some writers
have tried so to identify them; thus Wieseler, for example, sets up the
following scheme of relationship: 9:51, Christ's journey to Jerusalem
for the feast of Tabernacles (John 7:2 ff.); 13:22, from Perea to
Bethany where He raised Lazarus (John 11); 17:11 from Ephrem to
Jerusalem for the last Passover.[38] But we think that the various passages in Luke refer to one and the same great journey which included
several others of lesser importance and which was directed towards the
ultimate end announced in 9:51—the supreme immolation in Jerusalem.

How are we to fit Luke's narrative into the framework of our
Lord's life? Here we meet with two difficulties: we do not know if the

---

[36] Innumerable theories have been advanced concerning the character of this section and the chronological order of the events related therein; to list them here
would take us too long and would be superfluous. Suffice it to say that none of
these theories can claim more than a greater or lesser degree of probability. For
further information see the succinct and very pertinent observations of Lagrange
on this "Lucan section" (Évangile selon S. Luc. [Paris, 1927], pp. 38–41).
Much longer but less skillful is Louis Gerard's treatment of the problem
(L'Évangile des voyages de Jésus [Paris, 1951], pp. 130 ff.).

[37] Lebreton, Études, 193 (1929), 136.

[38] Ibid., p. 137.

narrative unfolds in strictly chronological order, and we cannot exclude the possibility that the evangelist may have included in chapters 8:51 to 18:14 lessons or events that belong to another time and place. The three callings to follow Christ, found one after the other in Luke 9:57–62, arouse the not unfounded suspicion that we have here an artificial linking of events, and cause us to wonder if this is the only example of such a device in the "Lucan section." We must, therefore, proceed with the greatest caution. But since, on the other hand, there seems to be no positive evidence against the chronological order, we cannot deem it unscientific to accept this order as being probably true to life in its general outlines and insofar as the contrary is not proved. Upon the basis of this hypothesis, then, we shall try to coordinate the "Lucan section" with the data supplied by St. John.

Between the feast of Tabernacles (John 7:2—John 8) and the feast of Dedication (John 10:22), should come Luke 9:51—10:42 (the three callings, and the sending of the seventy-two disciples, both while our Lord was still in Galilee; and then, in Perea, "I praise thee, Father . . . ," the good Samaritan, Martha and Mary). Between the feast of Dedication (John 10:40) and the raising of Lazarus, or more precisely our Lord's withdrawal to the town of Ephrem (John 11:54), comes Luke 11–17:10. This section opens with the teaching of the "Our Father," contains the doctrine of Providence and the "parables of mercy," and closes with the various lessons on scandal, the forgiveness of injuries, faith and humility. Between the raising of Lazarus and the last journey before the final Passover we should probably have to place Luke 17:11—18:14 (the healing of the ten lepers, the words on the sudden appearance of the kingdom of God, the parables of the unjust judge and the Pharisee and the publican). From 18:15 onwards, Luke's account has its parallels in the other two Synoptics.

In conformity with these indications we arrange the events of the last six months in this fashion:—

(1) Jesus went up from Capharnaum to Jerusalem for the feast of Tabernacles (Tishri—roughly, mid-September to mid-October of the year 29; John 7:2; Luke 9:51).

(2) A little later our Lord paid a quick visit to Galilee during which He launched the terrible "Woes" against Capharnaum, Corozain and Bethsaida (Luke 10:13–15).

(3) He left Galilee for the last time to go to Perea: ". . . He departed from Galilee and came to the district of Judea beyond the

Jordan" (Matt. 19:1); "And leaving that place, he came to the district of Judea beyond the Jordan . . ." (Mark 10:1). The district referred to is the low-lying region which stretches to the east of the Jordan and which, properly speaking, was part of Perea and under the rule of Herod Antipas. But since this section of Perea bordered upon Judea and, topographically speaking, seemed to be more of a piece with it than with the mountainous region which constituted the principal part of Perea, both evangelists called it "Judea beyond the Jordan," or simply, transjordanic Judea.[39]

(4) Our Lord, coming from Perea, went up through the desert of Juda where he related the parable of the good Samaritan, then was a guest at the house of Martha and Mary (Luke 10:30–42), and entered Jerusalem for the feast of Dedication (John 10:22. Kislev= November-December of the year 29). When the feast was over He returned to Perea to the place where John had been baptizing (John 10:40).

(5) Not long before the Passover, our Lord was called to Bethany, where He raised Lazarus (John 11:1 ff.). From Bethany He retired to Ephrem on account of the hostility of the Jews (John 11:54).

(6) From Ephrem He made His third journey to Perea, passing through Jenin (Luke 17:11).

(7) He passed through Jericho on His last journey to Jerusalem, where He made His triumphal entry (Matt. 20:17–29; Mark 10:32– 46; Luke 18:31–35; John 12).

Hence our Lord was certainly twice in Perea, and from there He went up once to Jerusalem and once to Bethany. Did He make a third journey to Perea? That would depend on the road He took on leaving Ephrem (cf. John 11:54). Some think that He followed the road that led directly to Jericho. We believe it more probable that He went north, passed along the border between Samaria and Galilee (cf. Luke 17:11), and returned to Perea.

There still remains to be filled the period of nine or ten months between the first Pentecost (May of 28) and the first multiplication, a little before the second Passover (March-April of 29). This is the Galilean ministry, a period of intense activity—the calling of the Apostles, miracles, parables, the Sermon on the Mount, the enthusiasm of the crowds, the sending forth of the Apostles, and the single episodes of the paralytic, the widow of Naim, the daughter of Jairus, the peni-

[39] Cf. Buzy, *S. Matt.*, p. 247.

tent woman, the beheading of John the Baptist, etc. It is not possible to fix adequately either the chronological sequence or even the location of all the events in this period. However, the episodes are so vivid and so full of atmosphere that they give us a concrete and striking idea of our Lord's apostolic activity during this lengthy interval. The chronological succession of events which we consider most probable will appear in the course of our narrative.

If we now glance over the whole public life of our Lord, we shall see that He labored, in a permanent way, exclusively in Galilee and Perea: in Galilee from the first Pentecost until the feast of Tabernacles in the following year, a period of about fifteen months, a long space of time which is divided into two very different periods by His leaving Capharnaum and His consequent journey to the region of Phoenicia; in Perea, He labored from soon after the feast of Tabernacles until the third and last Passover. He exercised His ministry in Jerusalem, we might say, only as a visitor, on the occasion of the great feasts—the first Passover and Pentecost of 28, and the feasts of Tabernacles and Dedication of 29. So far as we know, our Lord did not go up to Jerusalem apart from those feasts; nor did He remain in any way permanently in Judea, but only from shortly after His conversation with Nicodemus to the end of that more or less long period—in our opinion more short than long—during which His disciples were baptizing at the same time as John the Baptist (cf. John 3:22 *ff.*).

The Infancy of Christ

4. The Annunciation

and Visitation

The Heavenly Message [1]
(Luke 1:26–38)

Nestling humbly almost at the bottom of a valley, completely shut in by low hills, Nazareth appeared to be hiding itself from the eyes of men.[2] It was a poor village, off the great commercial routes and with no outlet to the plain of Esdrelon except through a narrow pass. So unknown and forgotten was it that its name does not appear even once in the whole of the Old Testament. This hamlet, though

[1] On the heavenly message, or, in other words, the mystery of the Annunciation, see the two interesting monographs: Otto Bardenhewer, *Maria Verkündigung* in *Biblische Studien*, X, Fasc. 5 (1905), and A. Médebielle, "Annonciation in *Dict. de la Bible,* Suppl. I, cols. 262–297.

[2] As regards the exact site of the old town, there are some authors, such as Dr. Clemens Kopp, who draw a distinction between primitive, Jewish, and Byzantine Nazareth. They hold that the galleries which run beneath the church known as the Workshop of St. Joseph are probably relics of the primitive town, and that Jewish Nazareth was built near Mary's Well, a short distance east of the present town, which stands on the site occupied by Byzantine Nazareth.

Because water is necessary for life, we know that towns naturally grew up around adequate water sources, such as an abundant spring. But we must also remember that the primitive settlers at Nazareth may have chosen an elevated site near the spring in preference to the floor of the valley. Then, too, no traces of ancient dwellings have been found around the spring itself. Therefore we believe it more probable that Jewish Nazareth was situated on the lower slope of the hill, where part of the present town stands. G. Dalman (*Sacred Sites and Ways,* trans. by Paul Levertoff [New York, The Macmillan Co., 1935], pp. 61 *ff.*) is of the same opinion.

Matson Photo

NAZARETH: *In the background, the Basilica of the Annunciation and the Franciscan Monastery.*

despised, was nevertheless the "flower of Galilee," [3] and in it grew another flower whose singular beauty attracted the gaze of the Most Blessed Trinity. This flower was the daughter of Joachim and Anne; her name was Mary, which means "exalted" or "lady," [4] and she was betrothed to a young artisan named Joseph.

This view has recently been confirmed by the excavations directed by Fr. Bagatti when the small Church of the Annunciation was being replaced by a magnificent basilica. See *Noticias cristianas de Israel,* Vol. VI, nos. 3 and 4 (Dic., 1955), 28–31.

[3] "Ibimus ad Nazareth et juxta interpretationem nominis ejus florem videbimus Galileae": St. Jerome, *PL* 22, 491. For the probable justification for this title see p. 149 below.

[4] Many meanings of the name Mary have been proposed—"lady," "beloved of God," "star of the sea," "enlightener," "beautiful." Bardenhewer, who has written a very complete monograph on the subject, prefers the last meaning, "beautiful" (see *Der Name Maria, Biblische Studien,* I, Fasc. 1 [1895], 1). Zorell believes that the name was of Egyptian origin and made up of *Meri* or *Mari* (beloved) and *Yam* (Yahweh), i.e., *Meri-Yam*—"beloved of Yahweh" (*Verb. Dom.,* 6 [1926], 257). This explanation has many elements of probability and is very tempting; however, we prefer the one advanced by Vogt—"exalted" or "lady" (*Verb. Dom.,* 26 [1948], 163–168). In the texts of Ras Shamra we find the word *mrym* (maryam[u] or miraym[u]) which means "high," "exalted" (*ibid.,* 165). In his article "El nombre de la Virgen María" in *Lumen,* 2 (1953), 24–37, Fr. Leal seems inclined to favor this opinion.

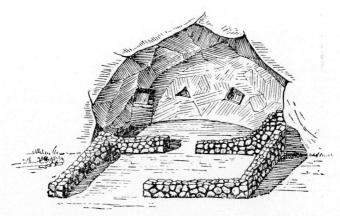

This drawing gives some idea of the manner in which many of the houses in Nazareth were constructed. The inner room was formed by building a wall across the mouth of a natural cave, and a second compartment was made by adding two projecting walls and a front.

The maiden, Mary, lived in a modest little house which, like the other dwellings in Nazareth, was composed of two parts, a natural cave, perhaps somewhat improved upon by the occupants, and a kind of second room formed by walls built in front of and enclosing the cave-mouth. This cave has been providentially preserved to the present day for the loving veneration of the faithful, and it may still be seen, haloed with a tradition of sixteen centuries. Like a precious jewel it was set in a basilica built probably in the fourth century by the converted Jew, Count Joseph of Tiberias, and replaced by the magnificent temple of the Crusaders which even today in the midst of its ruins shows its three great apses.

The neighbors had no idea of, and could not even have suspected, the inestimable riches of grace within the soul of the young village girl; but they did see and admire her angelic modesty as she passed on her way to draw water from the hamlet's only well, and they knew her exquisite charm of manner and her dignified, humble and recollected deportment.

Now the fullness of time foretold by the prophets of Israel had come. The Eternal Father, about to send His only-begotten Son on earth, contemplated the orb of the world and His gaze came to rest lovingly on the humble virgin of Nazareth.

Mary was in her home, perhaps meditating on the approaching advent of the promised Messias, when suddenly there appeared to her

NAZARETH: *Mary's Well.*

an angelic spirit, the Archangel Gabriel, who greeted her with this
singular salutation:

> "Hail, full of grace,
> the Lord is with thee.
> Blessed art thou among women."

Truly a unique form of greeting, for its three parts express a triple
greatness: such abundance of grace that she is called *"full* of grace";
the loving presence of God whose delight is in her; and her privileged
position of eminence above all other women.[5]

These magnificent words are preceded by a salutation which in the
text takes a Greek form ($\chi a\hat{\iota}\rho\epsilon$), but which, when addressed to a young
Hebrew maiden in Aramaic, the common language of the day, would
actually be "Peace be with thee," the salutation used by Christ after
His Resurrection (Luke 24:36; John 20:19, 26; *Pax vobis;* cf. Luke
10:5) and which is still used by the Jews (*shalôm,* "peace") and the
Arabs (*salam 'alek,* "peace be with thee").[6]

Considered in itself, the second phrase, "the Lord is with thee,"

[5] This last sentence, "Blessed art thou among women," is missing in a good number
of codices and is not admitted by quite a few authors, e.g., Lagrange, Marchal.
But be that as it may, we find it again on St. Elizabeth's lips (Luke 1:42).
[6] In *Biblica,* 20 (1939), 131–141, Lyonnet regards the expression not as a saluta-

could also be taken as a salutation in the same way as that used by Booz to his reapers: "The Lord be with you" (Ruth 2:4), to which they gave the beautiful response: "The Lord bless thee." But in the archangel's message to Mary it is a question of a good already present, as in Judges 6:12, where the angel says to Gedeon: "The Lord *is* with thee," assuring him of God's presence and protection.

On hearing the angel's words, Mary was troubled, not so much because she was being addressed by a heavenly messenger, as because in her profound humility she could not understand the import and motive of the high praise with which she was greeted.

Then the angel communicated to her the divine message: "Do not be afraid, Mary, for thou hast found grace with God. And behold, thou shalt conceive in thy womb and shalt bring forth a son; and thou shalt call his name Jesus. He shall be great, and shall be called the Son of the Most High; and the Lord God will give him the throne of David his father,[7] and he shall be king over the house of Jacob forever; and of his kingdom there shall be no end."

tion, but as an invitation to exult and rejoice, and he believes that the Greek verb is equivalent to the Hebrew *ronni or gîli,* as in Sophonias 3:14; Joel 2:21; Zacharias 9:9, passages in which the idea of rejoicing and happiness is expressed. This interpretation fits easily into the context; nevertheless we are more inclined to think that the archangel used the expression as a salutation.

[7] According to the prophecies, the Messias was to be born of David, and the angel actually says that He has David for His father. The two genealogies, St. Matthew's (1:1–17) and St. Luke's (3:23–28), are agreed on this point, for in both of them David is counted among our Saviour's ancestors. But otherwise they differ notably from each other: in the whole series of names from David to Joseph there are only two corresponding names, Salathiel and Zorobabel. How explain such divergence? Two hypotheses have been proposed. According to the first, which dates back in origin to Julius Africanus (cf. *PG* 10, 52 *ff.;* 20, 89 *ff.*), both evangelists give the genealogy of *St. Joseph,* St. Matthew writing the natural, and St. Luke the legal genealogy. That is to say, Heli died without male issue and, according to the decree of the Levirate Law (cf. Deut. 25:5–10), his brother Jacob married his widow and from her begot St. Joseph, who, consequently, was the natural son of Jacob and the legal son of Heli (some authors reverse the terms, i.e., legal son of Jacob and natural son of Heli). According to the second hypothesis, St. Matthew gives the genealogy of *St. Joseph,* who was descended from David through Solomon, while St. Luke gives that of *Mary,* who was also descended from David but through his other son, Nathan.

Both theories are acceptable; neither is certain. We are more inclined to favor the first, although we acknowledge the force of the arguments for the second. A brief, clear treatment of the problem can be found in Prat (*Jesus Christ,* I, 478–482) who prefers the first, and in Simón-Dorado (*Praelectiones Biblicae: Novum Testamentum I* [Taurini, Marietti, 1951], 265–274) who believes that the second is the more probable. The question is treated at much greater length by Vogt in *Der Stammbaum Christi bei den heiligen Evangelisten Matthäus und Lukas* (*Bib-*

NAZARETH: *The Grotto of the Annunciation.*

What greatness is enshrined in these brief sentences! Mary will be the mother of a king who will sit on the throne of David, the mother of a king whose kingdom shall not pass away like so many others, but shall last through all eternity. Even more, she will be the Mother of the Son of the Most High, the Mother of God made man, of the promised Messias. What was the reaction of the humble maiden when she was confronted with this glorious perspective? Did she feel joy, complacency, satisfaction?

"How shall this happen, since I do not know man?"

This was her answer, an answer which reveals to us her deepest concern and the most intimate recesses of her heart. The whole of Christian tradition has taken these words to mean that Mary had resolved to remain a virgin. And there is good reason for this inference, for otherwise her answer to the angel would be altogether meaningless. She was already betrothed, in the ordinary course of events the marriage would soon be consummated, and then the angel's prediction would be fulfilled. But since the virgin objected that she did not know man, it is a clear indication that she was not going to consummate the marriage, that she had resolved to preserve her virginity. Her use of the present tense, "I do not know man," does not invalidate the argument, for, as we are all aware, in everyday speech we often use the present tense when referring to the future. For example we say: "I'm not doing it!" when we mean "I'm not doing it now and I shall not do it: I don't want to do it."

Some authors have thought that Mary took the message to mean that the conception had already occurred, since the Aramaic participle ("Behold, *conceiving* . . .) could refer to the *past* as well as to the *future*.[8] Thus her reply would then mean: "It is not possible that I

---

lische Studien XII, Fasc. 3 [Herder 1907]) and by J. M. Heer in *Die Stammbäume Jesu nach Matthäus und Lukas* (*Biblische Studien* XV, Fasc. 2–3 [1910]). Both uphold the natural genealogy of St. Joseph in Matthew and the natural genealogy of Mary in Luke. They discuss at length all the problems raised by the two Gospel passages.

[8] S. Landersdorfer puts forward this explanation in *Bibl. Zeit.*, 7 (1909), 30–48. His main, not to say his only, argument is that Mary was "a child of her times" ("ein kind ihrer Zeit war") and that therefore she shared the ideas of her contemporaries, unless God had taught her otherwise by means of a revelation. He goes on to say that we know nothing of any such revelation and if there had been one the evangelist should have told us of it (p. 37). Certainly Mary was a child of her times in her dress, her food, her ordinary occupations, and her social conduct; but within, in the sanctuary of her soul, she was a world apart, a unique world. She did not need a special revelation, as we shall show later on (pp. 85 f.); and we are in no position to sit in judgment on the evangelist and declare

have conceived since up to the present I have never known man." But such an opinion is untenable. It would indeed be very strange if the virgin destined to be the Mother of God had been the victim of so great an error at such a solemn moment and in regard to a divine message brought by an angel and expressed in a form that clearly looked to the future. Moreover, the heavenly visitor's reply plainly indicates that Mary had not been mistaken, but had understood perfectly the import of the message he had brought her.

Nor is it reasonable to conclude that the Virgin thought there was question of an immediate conception and that, consequently, she objected that she could not then see how it could be realized, since hitherto she had only been betrothed and the ceremonies of the matrimony had not yet been performed.[9] We must note that the angel's announcement was couched in general terms only, and that his words did not contain the least indication that the conception was to take place immediately. To read that meaning into the text would be to falsify it, and to claim that Mary understood the message in that sense would be to attribute to her a strange lack of judgment. If she had so misunderstood him, the angel could have said to her: "Why propose an imaginary difficulty? Wait a few months and everything that I have foretold will come to pass."

Some Protestant and rationalistic authors, finding the path of exegesis thus effectively barred against them, have recourse to the *deus ex machina* and declare that the passage is spurious. This is a completely arbitrary assertion, totally at variance with the unanimous testimony of the codices, the versions and tradition.

what he should or should not have written. Cf. Médebielle, *loc. cit.*, cols. 287 *f.;* Bardenhewer, *loc. cit.*, pp. 121 *f.*

Recently both Fr. Paul Gächter in *Maria im Erdenleben* (2nd ed., Innsbruck, 1953), pp. 92–98, and Fr. J.-P. Audet in "L'annonce à Marie" in *RB* (1956), pp. 346–374, have maintained that Mary's question did not imply that she had resolved to remain a virgin. We have examined closely the arguments of these authors but we can see no reason for altering in the slightest our opinion on the matter. We regard as highly improbable Fr. Audet's interpretation of verse 34 (*loc. cit.*, p. 370): "Comment celà se fera-t-il, puisque (dans ce cas), je ne dois point connaître d'homme?"

[9] This is the interpretation given by Donatus Haugg, *Das erste biblische Marienwort* (Stuttgart, 1938). Few have followed Haugg in this, while many have refuted him, e.g., Holzmeister, "Quomodo fiet istud quoniam virum non cognosco?" in *Verb. Dom.*, 19 (1939), 70–77, and J. Collins, "Our Lady's Vow of Virginity," in *Catholic Biblical Quarterly*, 5 (1943), 371–380, where the arguments brought forward by Haugg are examined and refuted one by one, and where the reader will find an abundant bibliography. See likewise the brief but effective refutation by K. Prümm in *Zeit. f. kath. Theol.*, 63 (1939), 128 *f.*

But if Mary had resolved to remain a virgin, *why did she contract marriage?* We must not forget that here we are in a sphere that is more divine than human, that in the unfolding of these events, unknown to the world but great in God's eyes, Divine Providence plays a principal and exceptional part, and that God's thoughts are beyond the reach of man. For the rest, it was fitting and even morally necessary that she who was to be the Mother of God should have a husband at her side, for how else could her honor have been safeguarded? The marriage was necessary so that under its protection the great mystery of the Incarnation could fittingly come to pass. And even apart from this reason, celibacy was frowned upon rather than esteemed in the society of the time, and it is very likely that the young maid of Nazareth had to resign herself, very much against her will, to contracting marriage, making sure, of course, that her husband was prepared to respect her virginity. To outline the general attitude of the epoch towards marriage, we shall recall briefly the doctrine then current among the Jews. For a man, marriage was a strict obligation, but the rabbis were not agreed that it was so for a woman, some asserting while others denied that it was. "The Rabbi Yochanan ben Beroqa [about the year 110] used to say: For both [man and woman] the Scripture says: 'And God blessed them, saying: Increase and multiply. . . .' (Gen. 1:28); hence marriage is obligatory for woman, too." [10] At any rate, even though there might not be a true obligation, a young Hebrew maiden would be morally compelled to marry, and all the more so since at the usual age, between twelve and thirteen years, she was completely subject in this matter to her father's wishes, a dependence which, in practice if not in theory, no doubt continued even longer.[11] But it is exactly this traditional attitude towards marriage which gives rise to what some authors do not hesitate to call a grave problem: namely, if the whole atmosphere in which Mary lived was so unfavorable, and even hostile, to celibacy, *how can we explain why she decided to remain a virgin?*

We must acknowledge that this question would be difficult to answer satisfactorily if we were dealing with an ordinary, commonplace Hebrew girl. We should certainly need to have some very real reason for thinking that such a girl would have withdrawn from the

[10] Hermann L. Strack and Paul Billerbeck, *Kommentar zum Neuen Testament aus Talmud und Midrasch* (München, 1922–28), II, 372 *f.*
[11] *Ibid.,* p. 375.

culture in which she lived and would have set herself apart from the women of her time. But who would be so bold as even to suspect, let alone assert, that Mary's spiritual horizon was confined to the same limits as that of her companions at Nazareth, that her thoughts and aspirations were restricted to the same orbit as those of the poor peasant girls of Galilee? It is irreverent, and not only irreverent but unscientific, to place the Blessed Virgin on the same level as ordinary women. She did not need a revelation properly so-called before making a resolve or taking a vow to remain a virgin; the supernatural light which the Holy Spirit shed on her mind was sufficient, for the rays of this light were powerful enough to dissipate the fog of contemporary prejudice and to reveal the hidden excellence of virginity.

Yet we must not think that the value of virginity was so hidden as to be wholly unknown. As we have seen, at this very period of history there flourished the sect of the Essenes, a body of men who renounced the pleasures of the world and who lived in perfect continence, considering celibacy as a sacrifice pleasing in the eyes of God.[12] In the Old Testament, too, the excellence of virginity was not completely unknown, since the prophet Jeremias practiced it, and did so at the express command of God (Jer. 16:1-2).

Mary's reply to the angel confronts us with a rather more difficult problem. If she knew that the Messias was to be born of a virgin she had no reason to be perturbed at the announcement of a conception which, by divine decree, was bound up with virginity; thus her words "I do not know man" are meaningless. We are therefore faced with a dilemma: either Mary did not understand that the angel was speaking of the Messias, or she was ignorant of the virginal conception of the promised Redeemer.

The first part of the dilemma must be regarded as wholly improbable, for the glowing words of the angel left no room for doubt; the characteristics of the Child who was to be conceived could belong to no one but the Messias foretold by the prophets of Israel. As Médebielle observes: "The angel described the Messias, the object of universal expectation, as having the characteristics foretold in the best-known and most expressive prophecies, and he described Him in such a way that any Jew, no matter how unfamiliar he was with the Scrip-

---

[12] See pp. 28 *ff.* above. The discovery of the Qumran documents has fully confirmed this point of Essenian discipline.

tures and the national expectations, would have understood immediately that it was the Messias who was being announced." [13]

Yet we are spontaneously inclined to believe that Mary could not have been ignorant of the prophecy in Isaias 7:41 concerning the Virgin-Mother, which St. Matthew quotes (1:23), and that, therefore, she knew of the virginal conception of Him whose coming was being announced to her. If we remember, however, that it is very doubtful that the Jews interpreted the passage from Isaias in this sense,[14] perhaps we shall be less surprised to find that Mary did not even then know of the great mystery of the virginal conception.

We could avoid these difficulties by maintaining that Mary asked the question, not because she believed that maternity and virginity were incompatible, but because she wished to inquire about some other circumstance of the mystery. Perhaps this interpretation would be possible if she had merely asked: "How shall this happen?"; but it seems to be completely ruled out by the second part of her question, "since I do not know man," a phrase which clearly expresses the reason for her inquiry and reveals her innermost thoughts. The same conclusion is to be drawn from the very answer of the angel: "The Holy Spirit shall come upon thee, and the power of the Most High shall overshadow thee; and, for this reason, that which shall be born, holy, shall be called Son of God." [15] And then he added, as if in confirmation of the

[13] *Loc. cit.* col. 290.

[14] We cannot find any Jewish doctor in favor of this interpretation. It is true that the Septuagint translated the *almah* of Isaias by παρθένος, which certainly means *virgin*, but Lagrange observes that "l'oracle d'Isaïe est resté isolé dans le judaïsme" (*Évangile selon S. Matthieu*, Paris, 1927); and Prat (*op. cit.* I, 48, n. 10) says: ". . . There is nothing to indicate that they [the Septuagint translators] understood 'the virgin shall give birth' *in sensu composito*," i.e., that she would be a mother while remaining a virgin.

[15] Διὸ καὶ τὸ γεννώμενον ἅγιον κληθήσεται Υἱὸς Θεοῦ. Of the several accepted ways of construing this sentence (not less than four or five), the one we have given in the text seems to us to be by far the most probable. First of all, the particle διὸ is causal (cf. Matt. 27:8), not simply inferential, and it is reinforced by the particle καί, which should not be translated by *etiam*. Then ἅγιον is in apposition to τὸ γεννώμενον and should not be rendered *"shall be* holy" but simply "holy"; and the force of the causal διὸ falls principally and directly, not on the word "holy," but on the expression "Son of God." This title does not here imply the hypostatic union, but is given to the Child because He is to be born of God in the sense that He will be conceived by the direct intervention of God and not by man. Understood in this way, the phrase is in perfect harmony with the preceding one in which the Holy Spirit and the power of the Most High are mentioned, for it is this power which is going to be exercised in the conception of the Child who is announced. The dominant idea is not that the Child will be holy, but rather that He will not be the son of a man, that He will owe the formation of His human nature directly and exclusively to the power of

stupendous miracle which was about to be worked: "And behold, Elizabeth thy kinswoman also has conceived a son in her old age, and she who was called barren is now in her sixth month; for nothing shall be impossible with God."

Mary's virginity was assured; humbly, generously, she pronounced the *fiat* which the Eternal Father seemed to be awaiting in order to bring to pass the great mystery: "Behold the handmaid of the Lord; be it done to me according to thy word." From that moment on, Mary was the Mother of God and Co-redemptress of the human race.[16]

The womb of a humble virgin enclosed the Almighty; the Most Holy Trinity rejoiced, the angels adored; the world had received its Saviour. In the grotto at Nazareth, beneath the table of the altar, the devout pilgrim can read this inscription carved in a medallion of white marble:

HIC VERBUM CARO FACTUM EST

Here the Word was made flesh

Such is the august majesty of this place that the soul feels itself suddenly seized by a holy fear, for here was accomplished the mystery of mysteries, the ineffable union of the divine nature with human nature in the Person of the Word. Here, at the *fiat* of the handmaid of the Lord, a new heaven and a new earth were created and a new era

God. In the second phrase, the Child is presented to us as being both *holy* and *Son of God*, but the latter title is expressed more directly and with greater emphasis. The whole sentence, as is easy to see, is in the same psychological atmosphere as the entire passage and, like it, is directed towards removing the Virgin's concern.

This is Maldonatus' interpretation: "Neque enim de Christi natura, sed de modo generationis angelus agebat."

Nevertheless, if we take the message as a whole, we also find in it the title "Son of the Most High," and so we can say that it contains, if not the explicit and categorical assertion of the hypostatic union, at least a very pronounced allusion thereto.

The reader will find in the commentaries other interpretations, among them the one which reads "that which shall be born shall be called holy, Son of God," and which understands the latter title in the sense of the hypostatic union. See, in particular, Bover, *Biblica,* 1 (1920), 92–94; *Est. Ecles.,* 8 (1929), 381–392; Médebielle, *Dict. de la Bible,* Suppl. I, cols. 276 *ff.*

[16] Mary's words "fiat mihi secundum verbum tuum" can and should be regarded as being *soteriological.* We can truly say that with these words she began or inaugurated, as it were, the office of Co-redemptress. See the magnificent treatise by Bover, *Deiparae Virginis consensus corredemptionis ac mediationis fundamentum* (Matriti, 1942), where the author proves this thesis by rigorous theological reasoning and especially by an abundance of testimony from the Fathers and ecclesiastical writers.

begun for the world, the era of that kingdom which the archangel announced as the Kingdom of the Son of the Most High, which shall never end.

The Word
(John 1:1–18)

This Word which became flesh in time and among men, is revealed to us by the Eagle of Patmos as living in the bosom of God and exercising His power from all eternity.

1	In the beginning was the Word,
	and the Word was with God;
	and the Word was God.
2	He was in the beginning with God.
3	All things were made through him,
	and without him was made
	nothing that has been made.[17]
4	In him was life,
	and the life was the light of men.
5	And the light shines in the darkness,
	and the darkness grasped it not.
6	There was a man,
	one sent from God,
	whose name was John.
7	This man came as a witness,
	to bear witness concerning the light,
	that all might believe through him.
8	He was not himself the light,
	but was to bear witness to the light.
9	It was the true light
	that enlightens every man,
	coming [18] into this world.

[17] Vv. 3–4. There are two ways to construe these sentences:
   1. "Factum est nihil quod factum est. In ipso vita erat."
   2. "Factum est nihil. Quod factum est, in ipso vita erat." We prefer the first, and it is this version which we have used in the text.
[18] Here also there are two ways of construing the sentence:
   1. "Erat lux vera, quae illuminat omnem hominem *venientem* in hunc mundum."
   2. "Erat lux vera, quae illuminat omnem hominem *veniens* in hunc mundum."

10   He was in the world,
    and the world was made through him,
    and the world knew him not.

11   He came unto his own,
    and his own received him not.

12   But to as many as received him,
    he gave the power of becoming sons of God;
    to those who believe in his name:

13   Who were born [19] not of blood,
    nor of the will of the flesh,
    nor of the will of man,
    but of God.

14   And the word was made flesh,
    and dwelt among us.
    And we saw his glory—
    glory as of the only-begotten of the Father,
    full of grace and of truth.

15   John bears witness concerning him,
    and cries, "This was he of whom I said,
    'He who comes after me
    is placed before me,
    because he was before me.' "

16   And of his fullness
    we have all received,
    and grace upon grace.[20]

In this second construction, which we regard as the more probable one, it is the *light* which comes into the world.

[19] Several codices and some Fathers give the singular "was born" instead of the plural. The few authors, including Loisy and Zahn, who prefer this reading, make it refer to Christ and see in this text an allusion to His virginal conception. One of their reasons for this preference is that, in this passage, St. John "fait trop de part [of the spiritual generation of the sons of God] dans ce prologue où tout converge vers l'Incarnation du Verbe." But Lagrange, in *Évangile selon S. Jean* [Paris, 1927], rightly observes that "ce n'est pas notre jugement qui doit prévaloir; c'est le sien [St. John's]." This idea of the spiritual generation of the sons of God appears repeatedly in the First Epistle of St. John—2:29; 3:9; 4:7; 5:4,18. In actual fact, it seems to harmonize better with the remainder of the passage. For the rest, the literary foundation for the reading referred to is very shaky. Fr. D. Mollat also favors the singular, "was born." He calls it an "allusion à la génération éternelle du Verbe, mais sans doute aussi, vu l'insistance sur l'exclusion du sang et de la chair, à la naissance virginale de Jésus" (*La Bible de Jérusalem* [Paris, 1950]).

[20] V. 16: *et gratiam pro gratia:* καὶ χάριν ἀντὶ χάριτος. This phrase has been, and still is, much discussed, and many different interpretations of it have been given. The version in the text seems to us the most probable one, although it is not

17   For the law was given through Moses;
             grace and truth came through Jesus Christ.

18   No one has at any time seen God.
          The only-begotten Son,[21]
          who is in the bosom of the Father,
          he has revealed him.

Such is the Prologue of St. John, a worthy introduction to what the Fathers call the spiritual Gospel,[22] a preface in which the Apostle summarizes his whole Gospel.

In a literary work, the higher and more sublime the thought, the more obscure and untraceable the orbit it describes; hence the great variety of opinions on the proper disposition of the various parts and the development of the ideas in the Prologue to St. John's Gospel. Quite a few authors believe that the same thought underlies each of the three passages into which the Prologue is generally divided (vv. 1–5, 6–13, 14–18), and that this one thought takes different forms and is developed in concentric circles. Thus the basic idea remains fundamentally the same in each passage, although in each it is clothed in different words, or rather, set forth with increasing clarity.[23]

For our part, however, we view the matter in a somewhat different light, and we think that not only the form but also the idea itself progresses, unfolding in three stages which are not concentric but march forward in a straight line, each being distinct from the others:

wholly satisfactory. The evangelist does not appear to have had in mind a *concrete* and *specific* grace, the replacing of the Law by the Gospel, nor was he thinking of a *state* of grace, but rather of an *abundance* of graces in general. The plenitude of the Word made flesh is such that from it, as from an inexhaustible spring, there flow graces which we receive one after the other and which, in a certain sense, replace one another, without the divine current ever ceasing to run, provided, of course, that we do not place any obstacle in its path. Cf. Bover, *Biblica,* 6 (1925), 454–460; Médebielle, *Verb. Dom.,* 2 (1922), 141; and in particular the learned and concise article by D. Frangipane, "Et gratiam pro gratia," in *Verb. Dom.,* 26 (1948), 3–17.

21 Although many recent authors (e.g., Lagrange, Braun, etc.) prefer the reading μονογενὴς Θεὸς (One God, Only Son), we favor the other version ὁ μονογενὴς υἱὸς (the Only-begotten Son). Cf. Calmes, *RB* (1899), p. 243, who also prefers this second reading and gives, in our opinion, very sound reasons for his choice.

22 Or as Fr. Spicq says, without any recourse to metaphor: "The Prologue of St. John . . . constitutes a solemn preface, perfectly adapted to the main body of the work." ("Le Siracide et la structure littéraire du Prologue de Saint Jean," in *Mémorial Lagrange* [Paris, 1940], p. 183.)

23 Cf. U. Holzmeister in *Verb. Dom.,* 11 (1931), 65–70: "*Activitas salutifera Verbi divini ter depingitur ita, ut sermo de generalissimis principibus descendat ad describenda ea, quae adhuc generaliora sunt, et tunc ad specialia*" (p. 66).

the Word in God; the Word in the world, creating and enlightening it; and then the Word made flesh and dwelling among men.

St. John tells us that the Word was in the bosom of God, that He was God, equal to the Father and the Holy Spirit (vv. 1–2). Then he describes the activity of the Word unfolding itself in creation, bringing out of nothingness and giving being to everything that is, so that nothing exists without the Word's creative power (v. 3). But the world, called into existence, was sunk in darkness, and the Word, in His infinite goodness, willed to enlighten men, making them partakers in His life, which is light. And although the darkness did not accept the light but rather tried to smother it, yet the light continued to shine in some fashion through the darkness (vv. 4–5).

But since the light was weak and flickering, men had difficulty in finding the path which they were to follow. Then the Word, moved by compassion, willed to come and dwell among men. The ancient prophets had foretold His coming, yet it was fitting that He should be immediately preceded by a herald who would warn men of the approaching arrival of the great King. This herald was the son of Zachary and Elizabeth, he who had been pointed out centuries before by the prophet Malachias (3:1). Therefore the evangelist very fittingly presents John to us as giving testimony of the light for which all men were hoping and which had not yet appeared (vv. 6–8). Then, after stating that although John the Baptist had come "to bear witness concerning the light . . . he was not himself the light" (vv. 6–8), the evangelist goes on to declare that the true light was already in the world, enlightening all men without exception, that light which is the Word, by whom the world was created (vv. 9–10). Developing the last phrase of verse 10, "and the world knew him not," St. John widens the horizons of his perspective and describes the Word now Incarnate in the midst of His public life, rejected by some but accepted by others to whom He "gave the power of becoming sons of God," who were born not of flesh or blood, but of God Himself (vv. 11–13).

And after this brief digression, as it were, the Apostle shows us plainly and in clear, concise terms that Word "made flesh and [dwelling] among us" (vv. 14 ff.).

What is the central theme of the Prologue—what thought was uppermost in St. John's mind when he wrote it? We do not think that it is the mystery of the Trinity, or the Divine Sonship, or even the Incarnation strictly so-called. In our opinion the central theme is

Christ Jesus, the God-Man, and His infinite greatness. In his Prologue St. John wished to say to us: "This Jesus whom I am going to present to the world as living in time among men, is the *Logos* who lived in the bosom of God from all eternity."

Recently a new conception of the Prologue has been proposed, namely, that it is a *liturgical hymn to Christ, the God-Man*, which was used by the first Christian communities and which St. John incorporated into his Gospel.[24] Thus the *Logos* in the first verse is not the Word before the Incarnation but rather the Word Incarnate, the Man-God. And because the verses referring to John the Baptist (vv. 6–8) are evidently foreign to the hymn as a whole, the proponents of the hymn theory hold that they were inserted when the Prologue was made part of the Gospel.

We shall not pause here to discuss this very interesting problem but shall simply make some brief observations on the matter.

We find no difficulty in admitting that St. John could have used an existing document in his Prologue if it formed a suitable opening for his Gospel. Such a procedure would not be opposed to inspiration. But we do not think that the arguments for this hypothesis are strong enough to make it solidly probable.

We must acknowledge that the use of *liturgical hymns* in the first Christian communities has been sufficiently proved. In fact, even if their use had not been positively established, we could have presupposed it: indeed, to a certain extent we would have had to presuppose it. But are the Pauline passages, cited in this regard,[25] liturgical hymns which the Apostle incorporated into his Epistles? We do not believe that the available historical and literary evidence is strong enough to warrant an affirmative answer to this question.

The whole structure of St. John's Prologue, the succession of ideas, and the piling of clause upon clause, give the impression that the author wished to expound the *doctrine* of the *Logos* and not merely to write a hymn in praise of the God-Man. Then, too, if the Prologue was a liturgical hymn, already consecrated by use, the introduction of a foreign element like the passage referring to John the Baptist's ac-

---

[24] This interpretation is expounded and defended at length in *Bibl. Zeit.* (Neue Folge), 1 (1957), 69–109, in an article entitled, "Logos-Hymnus und johanneischer Prolog," by R. Schackenburg, and in *Est. Bibl.*, 15 (1956), 223–277, 381–427, "¿ Es un himno a Cristo el prólogo de San Juan?" by Fr. Serafín de Ausejo.

[25] Phil. 2:6–11; Col. 1:15–20; 1 Tim. 3:16; Heb. 1:2–4.

tivity would have destroyed its unity. On the other hand, however, the passage in question fits very well into the Prologue when the latter is viewed purely as a vehicle of doctrine.

An account of the Prologue of St. John, however short, would be incomplete without some observations on the Word, the *Logos*.[26] The word *logos* is proper to St. John in the particular sense in which he uses it in his Prologue (four times, vv. 1 and 14), and elsewhere (twice only, in 1 John 1:1, and Apoc. 19:13). The fact that the word does not appear anywhere else in the fourth Gospel raises a problem, namely, the relationship between the Prologue and the Gospel itself. Some have thought that they are foreign to each other and that when St. John had written his Gospel, he went back and wrote a preface which had nothing to do with the main body of the work. In reality, however, the Prologue is very closely connected with the rest of the Gospel. John's purpose in writing his account of Christ's life was to present Jesus the Messias as the source of light and life,[27] and the Prologue is full of references to light and life. Throughout the whole work John says to the reader: "This Jesus whom you see radiating life and light is precisely that *Logos* which you have contemplated in the bosom of God and which communicates light and life to men." It matters little whether the evangelist began his Gospel with the Prologue or added it afterwards (the first opinion seems to us the more probable one); the important thing is that in conceiving the Gospel with its special character and particular purpose, St. John also conceived the Prologue.[28]

But there remains a twofold question to be answered: why did St. John use the word *logos* in the Prologue, and refrain from using it in the rest of the Gospel? Although it is not possible to give a definite and sure answer to these questions, we can at least advance an acceptable explanation of the evangelist's procedure. In the Prologue he was writing freely without having to follow the course of our Lord's earthly life and, as we shall see later, he wished to accommodate his mode of ex-

---

[26] On the Logos see the lengthy and profound treatise by Lebreton in *Histoire du dogme de la Trinité* (Paris, 1927), I, 56–251. For a briefer treatment of the subject, see L. de Grandmaison, *Jesus Christ*, trans. by B. Whelan (New York: The Macmillan Company, 1930), I, 164–171; Vosté, *Studia Joannea* (Romae, 1930), pp. 79–100.

[27] The passages are too well known to need quoting.

[28] On this point Vosté very aptly observes: "Prologus ergo est clavis totius Evangelii. . . . Prologus est tamquam divinus sol, ac vere coelestis illuminans ex alto—ex Deo et aeternitate—totum Evangelium." (*Op. cit.* p. 77.)

pressing his thoughts to an intellectual atmosphere which we can call Hellenic and within which the concept of the *Logos* was known and even disseminated. But when he began his account of our Lord's deeds and teaching, he left aside the word because he had never heard Christ using it.

In accordance with its very etymology (λέγειν), *logos* basically means "word" (*verbum*), and since a word is an echo or reflection of thought or *verbum mentis, logos* also means a concept and, by extension, the source of the concept, i.e., the intellectual faculty or reason.

The common opinion is that the theory of the *logos* first appeared in the few and variously-interpreted fragments of Heraclitus (about 600 B.C.), and that the Stoics (e.g., Zeno, about 200 B.C.) developed and amplified it. These Stoics believed that the world was animated by a spirit which they called *logos,* and which informed each individual being, giving each its particular essence. Therefore every individual had its *logos* which, however, was not independent and self-subsistent, but was part of the universal *logos* which was called *logos spermatikos* (σπερματικός), since it penetrated all beings as the sperm in the animal. The human *logos* was considered in its internal aspect (reason, intellect), when it was called ἐνδιάθετος, or in its external aspect (word), when it was named λόγος προφορικός. As is evident, the *logos* of the Stoics was not transcendent and distinct from the world, but was immanent in and an essential part of it; hence the absolute monism of the Stoics.

Very different was the conception of the Neo-Platonists, who admitted a dualism between God and the world, regarding the one as being distinct from the other. But since they conceived God as being so far removed from the world that any direct communication between Him and it would be beneath Him, they had to imagine an intermediate being which they called *logos* and which was at once the efficient and the exemplary cause of the world.

Philo, a Jew faithful to his national religion but born and educated in Alexandria, wished to harmonize the ideas of the Stoics and the Neo-Platonists with the Sacred Scriptures. He was always a monotheist, but since he regarded God as being so transcendent that He could not communicate directly with the world, he evolved the idea of a series of intermediate beings which served as links between God and man, and the most exalted of these beings was the *logos.* Thus we can see that even though the word *logos* is common to the Jewish philosopher and the evangelist, the underlying reality of the term is essentially different. With Philo the *logos* is inferior to God, a kind of demiurge, a vague personification, while the *Logos* of St. John *is* God, identical in nature with the Father, a definite individual Being, the historical Christ Himself, whose deeds the evangelist narrates.

We must also take into account the Old Testament and rabbinical literature, both of which speak of personifications worthy of note; in the Old Testament we find *Hokmah* and *Sophia,* and in the writings of the rabbis we read of *Memra* and *Shekinah,* ideas which could be said to prepare, more or less indirectly, for St. John's doctrine of the *Logos*. The pertinent passages in the Old Testament are: Job 28:12–28; Proverbs 8; Ecclesiasticus 24:1–30; Wisdom 8–10. Here *Wisdom* figures so prominently and is described as possessing such characteristics that it is difficult not to see in it more than a mere poetic personification.[29] However, the same cannot be said of the *Memra* (word) and the *Shekinah* (dwelling or abode) of the Targums and the Talmud, for they are very different in character from the *Hokmah* and *Sophia* of the sapiential books, and are really only substitutes for the sacred name of God.[30]

Finally, in the New Testament St. Paul presents Christ as the image of the Father and as Co-creator and Sustainer of the world (1 Cor. 8:6; 2 Cor. 4:4; Col. 1:13–20), and in the Epistle to the Hebrews (1:1–5) he sets down the attributes of the *Logos,* although he does not use the actual word itself here or in the passages just mentioned.

Considering all these antecedents, it is not difficult to account for the doctrine contained in St. John's Prologue and for his use of the word *Logos*.

The various teachings on the *logos* as efficient cause, exemplary cause, soul of the world, the bond of union between the parts of the universe, etc., were current among educated people, and it is not altogether unlikely that they had also reached beyond the circle of the philosophers and had, to a certain extent, spread among the less learned classes. St. Paul must have known these doctrines, and he surely was familiar with the concept of *Sophia* and *Hokmah* found

---

[29] Cf. Vaccari, "Il concetto della Sapienza nell'A.T." in *Gregorianum,* 1 (1920), 218–251.

[30] On the real nature of *Memra* cf. Str.-Bill. II, 302–333 (Ersatz für "Gott," p. 308; für "Jahve," p. 311); and Grandmaison's brief remarks, *op. cit.,* I, 165, n. 1.

Murphy Photo

The path leading from Nazareth down to the plain of Esdrelon.

in the sapiential books of the Old Testament. Therefore he understood that the reality which philosophy was striving to reach in a thousand ways and amid a thousand errors and which was found only in outline in the Old Testament, was none other than Jesus, the Son of God, who verified and united in Himself in a sublime and harmonious synthesis the attributes which the philosophers credited to their absurd *logos*. And like St. Paul, St. John knew this too. Both Apostles took their teaching on the *Logos* from the sources of revelation. As regards the use of the word itself, it is probable that St. John was indebted in some way, not precisely to one or the other of the philosophers, be he Philo, Plutarch or anyone else, but to the intellectual atmosphere in which he lived, which may have occasioned his use of the word *logos* and perhaps also the concrete and particular form in which he expressed the attributes of the *Logos,* the Son of God.

Mary and Elizabeth

(Luke 1:39–56; cf. Map I)

When Mary heard from the angel that Elizabeth was six months pregnant, her tender heart would not allow her to remain at home when her presence could be useful to her cousin, now advanced in years. Thus, motivated by charity which "is patient, is kind; . . . is

'Ain Karim: *The white tower at the far right*

not self-seeking . . ." (1 Cor. 13:4, 5), she set out for the mountain region of Juda. Since she was so young herself, she undoubtedly had some good woman, a relative or neighbor, as a companion. If we were to credit the artists we would believe that her betrothed accompanied her, for in several paintings Joseph is seen at a respectful distance from Zachary's house. But Joseph's presence there is not in harmony with the Gospel account of his anguish when he found that Mary was with child.

The journey was a long and arduous one of about ninety-four miles, but charity "bears with all things, . . . endures all things" (1 Cor. 13:7). Following the rocky path that winds around the foot of Jebel el-Qafseh, Mary and her companion came out onto the broad plain of Esdrelon, and leaving on the left Mount Thabor, which no doubt reminded her of Debbora, a prophetess of Israel (cf. Judges 4–5), she continued on towards the orchards of Engannim, present-day Jenin, and it was perhaps in this town that she spent the first night of her journey. From Engannim she went south through Qubatiyeh and Sanur (perhaps ancient Bethulia, reminiscent of the prowess of the courageous Judith), then on through Geba (Jeba') and past the city of Samaria, leaving it to the right; then through the valley that runs between Mount Ebal and Mount Garizim, to Sichem, a place

belongs to the Church of the Visitation.

sanctified by the patriarchs Abraham and Jacob. From Sichem her path continued south, passing near Lubban where there still exists a *khan* which is possibly the successor to the ancient inn where pilgrims were wont to spend the night. Then perhaps after passing through the city of Silo, the repository of the Ark of the Covenant, and on by Bethel where she no doubt saw again in spirit the ladder of Jacob (cf. Gen. 28:12), Mary arrived at the house of Elizabeth after a journey of not less than four days.

Where was this blessed house that was sanctified by the presence of the Mother of God? As many as ten different sites have been proposed, among them Hebron, Bethlehem, Jerusalem, Yutta and 'Ain Karim. The first three can be discarded without further discussion. As regards Yutta, a town situated some six miles south of Hebron (cf. Jos. 15:55; 21:16), there is no foundation for reading its name in place of "Juda" in the Gospel text, as some wish to do, nor is any importance to be attached to the existence there of a church dating back to the sixth or seventh century. Actually, 'Ain Karim is the only site that has solid, although not completely convincing, arguments in its favor. It is true that the first clear testimony on its behalf dates back only as far as the beginning of the twelfth century (the Russian *hegumenos,* Daniel); but since there are several more or less explicit references dating from the sixth century (Theodosius, *c.* A.D. 530), and since in the Byzantine epoch (fifth or sixth century) there was a church at the place of the Visitation and at that of the Baptist's birth, we have some basis for concluding that, even from the first centuries, tradition probably acknowledged the small town of 'Ain Karim as the birthplace of John the Baptist.[31]

The town itself is situated about four and one-half miles southwest of Jerusalem. Its name means "noble fountain," and is taken from the free-flowing spring that rises in a fold of the mountains and forms a nest of verdure where the terrain slopes gracefully in beautiful, well-cultivated terraces.

"And [Mary] entered the house of Zachary and saluted Elizabeth. And it came to pass, when Elizabeth heard the greeting of Mary, that the babe in her womb leapt. And Elizabeth was filled with the Holy Spirit, and cried out with a loud voice, saying, 'Blessed art thou among women and blessed is the fruit of thy womb! And how have I deserved that the mother of my Lord should come to me? For behold, the moment that the sound of thy greeting came to my ears, the babe in my womb leapt for joy. And blessed is she who has believed, because the things promised her by the Lord shall be accomplished.' "

And Mary answered Elizabeth by pouring out her soul in the sublime canticle of the Magnificat, which was really more the humble, spontaneous reaction of her heart to her cousin's praise than a response to her greeting. She recognized the gifts that Heaven had showered upon her, but she attributed to God, and to God alone, all the glory that resulted from them. Hence her first words were a glorification of God:

> "My soul glorifies the Lord,
>   and my spirit rejoices in God my Saviour;"

It was in God she rejoiced; in Him she placed her joy and her hope. Elizabeth had called her "blessed among women." Mary did not deny but rather confirmed this title, but she protested that it was due solely to the goodness and mercy of God, and not to her own merits. All her greatness stemmed from God's having deigned to look upon her lowli-

---

[31] Buzy, *Saint Jean-Baptiste* (Paris, 1922), deals at length with this question (pp. 47–60). Recently, Fr. Saller, O.F.M. made some very interesting excavations in the Sanctuary of John the Baptist's birthplace and uncovered some beautiful mosaics belonging to the ancient church.

ness, and it was precisely through this glance that He wrought such great things in her, His handmaid:

> "Because he has regarded the lowliness
>   of his handmaid,
>   for, behold, henceforth all generations
>   shall call me blessed;
> Because he who is mighty has done
>   great things for me,
>   and holy is his name."

But God was ready to turn this glance of mercy on all men, provided that they disposed themselves to correspond with it:

> "And for generation upon generation is
>   his mercy to those who fear him."

Then, developing this thought and raising her mind from the particular and personal to the general, Mary showed us how God lays low the proud, exalts the humble, and how He gave proofs of His fidelity in fulfilling His promises to Israel:

> "He has shown might with his arm,
>   he has scattered the proud in the
>   conceit of their heart.
> He has put down the mighty from their thrones,
>   and has exalted the humble. . . .
> He has given help to Israel, his
>   servant, mindful of his mercy—
> Even as he spoke to our fathers—
>   to Abraham and to his posterity
>   forever."

As the years have slipped by, as the centuries have passed, over all the earth, amid the clamor of great cities, in the silence of the deserts, in the depths of wild forests, and soaring high above the vicissitudes of human life, there has resounded the sweet and consoling canticle in which all generations have acclaimed Mary as the *Blessed* Virgin.

What a beautiful tableau, enacted in a delightful setting, was this meeting between the two holy cousins—the affectionate concern on the lovely face of the young maid of Nazareth, the look of joyful surprise mingled with humble confusion in the bearing of the older woman, the

'AIN KARIM: *Church of the Visitation. In the foreground one can see the convent of the Russian Orthodox nuns, who live in little huts set apart from each other and built around their church.*

spouse of Zachary. Elizabeth humbled herself, Mary gave glory to God; and the Son of the Virgin caused the son of the once-barren woman to leap with joy in his mother's now fertile womb.[32]

Though it may seem strange, there are some authors who hold that Elizabeth and not Mary uttered the Magnificat. The only critical basis for this claim is found in three Latin codices which have the words "et ait Elisabeth" in verse 46. Certainly a very flimsy foundation, for how

[32] At this moment the angel's promise to Zachary was fulfilled (Luke 1:15): "Spiritu Sancto replebitur adhuc ex utero matris suae." Although, strictly speaking, the expression ἐκ κοιλίας μητρὸς αὐτοῦ, "from his mother's womb," could mean "from his *birth*" (cf. Isai. 48:8), it is clear from the context that there is question here of the time in which John was still (ἔτι) in his mother's womb. In fact, according to v. 44, the child's joyful leap was the cause of his mother's enlightenment and of her being filled with the Holy Spirit ("et repleta est Spiritu Sancto Elisabeth." v. 40); consequently, and with greater reason, the son, too, was filled with the Holy Spirit.

In itself the phrase "to be filled with the Holy Spirit" can indicate the bestowal of the gift of *prophecy* as, for example, in the case of Zachary (Luke 1:67); but since, in the circumstances, such a gift would have been fruitless, the phrase should rather be understood as indicating *sanctification* properly so-called: "Intelligi autem veram sanctificationem, ablato peccato originali et gratia sanctificante infusa, ei esse collatam sententia est omnino communis et certa" (Knabenbauer, *in loc.*). Cf. Buzy, *Saint Jean-Baptiste*, pp. 64–96.

can one allow these few pieces of evidence to outweigh the immense testimony of the rest of the codices and of all the versions? The incongruity of such a procedure is immediately obvious. Nor can it be held that the primitive text read simply "and said," that is to say, that the subject was omitted originally but was afterwards supplied, some inserting the word "Mary," and others "Elizabeth." Such a supposition is purely arbitrary, and not one codex or even one version has preserved this alleged original reading. Moreover, in the immediately preceding context it is Elizabeth who is speaking, and therefore, in the absence of a subject in verse 46 it would be natural to suppose that it was she who continued to speak, so that if a subject was to be supplied, surely it would be "Elizabeth" and not "Mary." Yet, as we have said, almost all the codices have "Mary" in this place.

For the rest, the very content of the Magnificat requires Mary as the author, and not her cousin. After all, how could Elizabeth have dared to say that all generations would call her blessed? Very different were the emotions felt by the wife of Zachary as she stood in the presence of the Mother of God.

Mary's improvisation of the canticle need not prove a difficulty, for she had read the Sacred Scriptures and the memory of her reading enabled her to express aptly and fluently the feelings of her heart. Some may object that the sentiments she expressed are more in keeping with the great mystery of the Incarnation than with the object of her visit, and that consequently the Magnificat was composed at the Annunciation rather than at the Visitation. But the contrary is the case, for the canticle was inspired by Elizabeth's words: "And how have I deserved that the mother of my Lord should come to me?" The great grace which Mary had received through the power of the Holy Spirit caused her heart to overflow in words of thanksgiving, praise and humility. Thus the whole tenor of the canticle is in perfect accord with the historical setting and with Mary's state of mind. Finally this has always been, and still remains, the common opinion of the Fathers and ecclesiastical writers.[33]

[33] All these reasons are pointed out in the decree of the Biblical Commission of June 26th, 1912: "Utrum rarissima illa et prorsus singularia documenta, in quibus Canticum *Magnificat* non beatae Virgini Mariae, sed Elisabeth tribuitur, ullo modo praevalere possint ac debeant contra testimonium concors omnium fere codicum tum graeci textus originalis, tum versionum, necnon contra interpretationem, quam plane exigunt non minus contextus, quam ipsius Virginis animus et constans Ecclesiae traditio? *Resp.*: Negative." (Denzinger, *Enchiridion symbolorum,* no. 2158). Cf. Durand, "L'origine du 'Magnificat,' " in *RB* (1898),

Mary remained with her cousin, attending to her needs and serving her with delicate and solicitous charity, and when three months had passed, "Elizabeth's time was fulfilled that she should be delivered, and she brought forth a son," the son of the promise which God had made to Zachary, the child's father, a priest of the class of Abia. We must note here that the priests of the Old Law were divided into twenty-four groups, each of which took its turn at performing the Temple services for a week. These services included, among other things, the placing of incense on the altar in the Holy Place, the second part of the Sanctuary properly so called, between the *pronaos* or vestibule and the Holy of Holies. The Holy Place contained the gold-covered altar of incense, which stood in front of the Holy of Holies; to the left of the altar, on the north side, stood the table of the loaves of proposition, and to the right, on the south side, stood the seven-branched gold candlestick.

To avoid possible jealousy and to ensure order, the various duties were assigned by lot. But each priest could offer the incense only once in his lifetime, apart from the very rare case when all the priests present had already performed this duty. The one chosen to offer the incense was accompanied by two assistants whose duty it was to help him in the sacred function, which, in a certain sense, formed part of the perpetually-repeated sacrifice offered twice a day, morning and evening, from whence came the titles "morning sacrifice" and "evening sacrifice."

Zachary belonged to the eighth of the twenty-four groups of priests, and in time it fell to his lot to perform the noble and exalted service; it is believed that he did so in the morning rather than in the evening, although there is no cogent reason for saying so. Having sacrificed the lamb and recited the liturgical prayers, and accompanied by two assistants whom he himself had chosen, Zachary prepared to offer the incense. One of the assistants took a gold censer on a silver plate and filled it with incense, while the other placed in a golden vessel glowing coals taken from the altar of the holocausts. Then the three priests ascended the twelve steps leading to the Sanctuary. As they entered

pp. 74–77; Bardenhewer, *Ist Elisabeth die Sängerin des "Magnificat,"* in *Biblische Studien*, VI, Fasc. 1–2 (1901), 189–200. In *Verb. Dom.*, 2 (1922), 194–198, Zorell divides the canticle into strophes and supplies brief, clear, exegetical notes. Knabenbauer, *In Lucam*, pp. 92 f. points out those Old Testament passages that are in any way parallel to the various ideas expressed in the Magnificat, particularly the Canticle of Anna in 1 Kings 2:1–10.

the vestibule an instrument called *magrephah* was struck, and at the sound all the priests and Levites hastened to take their assigned places and prepare themselves to pray, as did all the faithful who were present. Once inside the Holy Place, one of the assistants scattered the burning coals on the altar of incense while the other placed the censer in the celebrant's hands. Both assistants then left the Holy Place and Zachary was alone. When the sound of the liturgical words "He is offering the incense!" reached him from without, he scattered the incense on the coals. At this solemn moment, the culminating point of the whole sacred ceremony, the priests, Levites, and people prayed in a profound religious silence as the cloud of fragrant smoke ascended to the Lord. This was the earthly counterpart of the vision later beheld by the Seer of Patmos: "And I saw the seven angels who stand before God, and there were given to them seven trumpets. And another angel came and stood before the altar, having a golden censer; and there was given to him much incense, that he might offer it with the prayers of all the saints upon the golden altar which is before the throne. And with the prayers of the saints there went up before God from the angel's hand the smoke of the incense" (Apoc. 8:1–4).

When the incense had been sprinkled on the fire, the officiating priest was supposed to make a profound prostration, withdraw from the Holy Place and stand at the top of the stairway where, surrounded by his ministers and by all the priests, who took their places on the steps below him, he recited the liturgical prayer. Thus the people waited for Zachary to appear after completing the sacred rite, but as the moments passed and he did not come, the onlookers' wonder grew. At last, however, he came forth, and the Temple resounded with the great affirmation of faith:

"Truly art Thou, O Yahweh, our God and the God of our fathers;

Our King and the King of our fathers;

Our Saviour and the Saviour of our fathers;

Our Creator and the Rock of our salvation;

Our Help and our Redeemer.

Thy Name is eternal, and there is no other god besides Thee."

The ceremony was supposed to close with the blessing of the people prescribed in Numbers 6:24–26, given by the officiating priest and repeated by the other priests:

"The Lord bless thee, and keep thee.

The Lord show his face to thee, and have mercy on thee.

The Lord turn his countenance to thee, and give thee peace." [34]

But when Zachary did not give the blessing, the priests and people realized that he was unable to speak and concluded that he had had a vision. Their surmise was correct, for there had appeared to him an angel standing at the right of the altar near the candlestick, at the south side of the Holy Place. At the sight of the apparition, Zachary "was troubled, and fear fell upon him," but the angel, who was none other than the Archangel Gabriel, reassured him, saying: "Do not be afraid, Zachary, for thy petition has been heard. . . ."—no doubt referring to the petition which he had made on behalf of the people while he was offering the incense. Then the angel continued: ". . . and thy wife Elizabeth shall bear thee a son and thou shalt call his name John [i.e., "Yahweh is propitious"]. . . . He shall be great before the Lord . . . and shall be filled with the Holy Spirit even from his mother's womb. . . ." But Zachary could not bring himself to believe this promise, since he and his wife were advanced in years. The angel therefore said to him: "Behold, thou shalt be dumb and unable to speak until the day when these things come to pass, because thou hast not believed my words, which will be fulfilled in their proper time."

As we have seen, the promise was fulfilled and the child was born; the friends and neighbors of the family rejoiced and congratulated the mother. On the eighth day after the birth, preparations were made to circumcise the child; and it was decided that, as was the custom, he should be called Zachary after his father. But Elizabeth said: " 'Not so, but he shall be called John.' And they said to her: 'There is none of thy kindred that is called by this name.' " Turning to Zachary, they asked him what name he wished to give his son, and he, taking a writing tablet, wrote: "John is his name." Immediately his tongue was loosed, and, filled with the Holy Spirit, he intoned that magnificent canticle, the Benedictus:

"Blessed be the Lord, the God of Israel,
because he has visited and wrought

[34] For a fuller account of the ceremonies we have just described, see the treatise *Tamid* in the *Mishnah,* in particular 3:6–9; 5:4–6; 6:1–3; as well as Str.-Bill., II, 71–73, and Alfred Edersheim, *The Temple—Its Ministry and Services as They Were in the Time of Jesus Christ* (Grand Rapids, Mich.: Wm. Eerdmans Publishing Co., 1950).

redemption for his people. . . .
And thou, child, shalt be called the
prophet of the Most High,
for thou shalt go before the face of
the Lord to prepare his ways. . . .''

Mary was there, and with what love she took the child in her arms, that child whose conception the angel had announced to her, and who, she knew, was the fruit of the merciful power of God! It is true that the order in which the evangelist narrates the events would seem to indicate that the Blessed Virgin had already left for Nazareth when the Precursor was born. In fact, in 1:56, St. Luke says: "And Mary remained with her [Elizabeth] about three months and returned to her own house." And then in the next line (v. 57), he tells of the child's birth: "Now Elizabeth's time was fulfilled that she should be delivered, and she brought forth a son." But, as we have said, the order of narration in the Gospels does not always correspond to the chronological order of the events, and in this particular case the reason for the divergence is easy to guess, for before passing on to the account of John's birth, St. Luke wanted to finish what he had to say about Mary, just as in 3:20-21, where, wishing to complete one subject before starting another, he first tells of John's imprisonment and only then of Christ's baptism, although the latter obviously preceded the former.

By saying in verse 36 that Elizabeth was in her sixth month with child and then in verse 56 that Mary stayed with her about three months, the evangelist seems to hint that the Blessed Virgin was still with her cousin when the baby was born. As Plummer rightly observes, it would be strange if Mary had left just before the birth, particularly when it was to be such a singular and blessed one which was bound to bring great rejoicing to the whole district. Some authors think that it would have been indecorous for a virgin to have been present at the birth; but as Cornelius a Lapide has sensibly pointed out, Mary could have retired to another room and prayed there for mother and child, leaving the midwives to assist at the actual delivery. And surely no one will think of denying that Zachary's house had some place suitable for recollection and prayer. Other critics have said that Mary's love for solitude was so great that she would have left to escape the great gathering of people who undoubtedly would arrive to celebrate the birth. Again Cornelius a Lapide supplies the answer by saying that if a large crowd had come, it would have given Mary an opportuinty to enlighten and edify a greater number of people.[35]

Return to Nazareth
(Matt. 1:18–25)

No doubt Joseph awaited with loving impatience the return of his betrothed, but his joy soon turned to deep pain. Mary had been away more than three months, and after her return Joseph realized that she was going to be a mother. Yet although sorrow and bewilderment filled his soul, not the slightest reproach escaped his lips. He knew the spotless virtue of his betrothed, but the fact that she was with child was clear and evident. What was he to do? Receive her into his house? Impossible! Denounce her? But he could not bring himself to believe that she was guilty. Day and night these harrowing doubts gnawed at him, while Mary suffered too: each was in pain on the other's account and neither was responsible for the anguish caused. Their suffering was a Providential mystery of love and pain, one which provided a shining example for future generations—in Mary, an example of modesty, reserve, humility and abandonment to Providence; in Joseph, of prudence, delicacy and charity.

After long consideration, Joseph came to the reluctant conclusion that he would have to repudiate Mary. But how? St. Matthew tells us: "But Joseph her husband, being a just man, and not wishing to expose her to reproach, was minded to put her away privately" (1:19). He was a just man, a faithful observer of the Law of God (the word δίκαιος should not be translated as "kind," "merciful," as some think), and therefore his honor and his conscience would not allow him to receive into his house and definitively take as his wife a girl who was going to be the mother of a child which he knew was not his. On the other hand, however, he was convinced of Mary's great virtue, and he did not wish to defame her by denouncing her to the tribunal, as was his right. Therefore he decided on the middle course; he would give her a private bill of divorce which would free him from the embarrassing situation and yet avoid a public denunciation of Mary.[36]

But before he could act, an angel came and lifted the veil from

---

[35] "Turba affluentium parva fuit; et si magna fuisset, maiorem fecisset Virgo fructum, pluribus annuntiando praecursorem Christi iam esse natum, aliisque suis piis sermonibus." (In loc.)

[36] There are authors, e.g., Lagrange and others, who give Joseph's being a just

the mystery: "Do not be afraid, Joseph, son of David, to take to thee Mary thy wife, for that which is begotten in her is of the Holy Spirit. And she shall bring forth a son, and thou shalt call his name Jesus; for he shall save his people from their sins" (Matt. 1:20–21).

Joseph did as the angel of the Lord commanded: freed now from anxiety and sorrow, and filled with a holy joy, he received Mary, his wife, into his house. And the evangelist adds: "And he did not know her till she had brought forth (her first-born) son: *Et non cognoscebat eam donec peperit filium (suum primogenitum)*" (v. 25).[37]

man as a reason for his not wanting to defame Mary. We believe it more probable that his resolve to give her a secret bill of divorce was the result of *two* factors: of his being a just man and of his wishing to avoid anything that would bring dishonor on Mary. There is no solid basis for the opinion that Joseph knew of the mystery of the Incarnation and was too humble to dare receive Mary into his house; nor is there any foundation for the theory that the holy patriarch had a positive suspicion that his betrothed was guilty of infidelity.

[37] Many Protestants claim that this sentence excludes Mary's perpetual virginity; to quote only one among the moderns, W. C. Allen writes: "The imperfect ἐγίνωσκεν is against the tradition of perpetual virginity" (*A Critical and Exegetical Commentary on the Gospel According to S. Matthew* [New York, Scribner, 1913], p. 10); while others take their stand especially on the particle *donec*, "till," as if the limit of Joseph's "not know(ing)" Mary were her "(bringing) forth her first-born son."

While the words used both in Greek (ἕως οὖ) and in Hebrew ('ad ki) excludes action in the past, it does not presuppose action in the future as does the English "till" or "until"; a few examples of its use in the Scriptures will suffice to prove our point: e.g., in Genesis 8:7 we are told that the raven did not return "till the waters were dried up upon the earth," and in 2 Kings 6:23 we read that Michol had no child *usque in diem mortis suae,* whereas actually the raven did not return after the waters had dried up, and Michol obviously had no children after her death. The phrase in question can very well be translated as Joüon and Buzy render it: "without his having known her, she brought forth a son."

This interpretation is wholly satisfactory. In recent years, M. Peinador, C.M.F., has proposed a rather unusual version of this passage (*Est. Bibl.* [1949], p. 390). He understands the verb *cognoscere* in the sense of "intellectual cognition" and translates the sentence: "And Joseph took Mary as his wife, although he did not understand [what the angel had revealed to him] until she brought forth her son." We do not think that many will accept this explanation.

The expression *suum primogenitum*, which we have put in parenthesis, should be eliminated from the text; it seems to be a gloss taken from Luke 2:7. Certain authors have concluded from these words (cf. Frey, *Biblica* 11 (1930), 383 *f.*) that the Blessed Virgin had other children; obviously they did not stop to reflect that the *first-born* "est non tantum *post quem alii* sed etiam *ante quem nullus*" (St. Jerome, *Contra Helvidium,* 10; *PL* 23, 202). Frey (*loc. cit.,* pp. 373 *ff.*) deals very fully with this point and discusses a Jewish epitaph (pp. 385–390) of the very time of Augustus, in which Arsinoe, the dead woman, is depicted as saying: "In the birth-pangs of my first-born son(πρωτοτόκου τέκνου), fate brought me to the end of my life." Obviously she had no other children after the first since she died in childbirth, and yet she called the child her first-born. There could be no more convincing proof. Cf. also Van Kasteren, *RB* (1894), pp. 56 *f.*

Did the Annunciation and the painful misunderstanding just described take place while Mary was still living with her parents and as yet only betrothed, or was she already formally married to, and living with, Joseph? Some favor the second viewpoint, among them Fr. Frangipane, who supports this thesis with great erudition.[38] However, the great majority of authors prefer the first opinion, and, we believe, with very good reason.

Among the Hebrews a clear distinction was made between the espousals (*erusin-sponsatio,* or *qiddushin-segregatio*) and the marriage (*nissu'in-ablatio*), which took place when the bride was brought and introduced into the groom's house. Both of these stages are clearly referred to in Deuteronomy 20:7: "What man is there, that hath espoused a wife, and not taken her [i.e., taken her into his house]?" We must remember that the espousals were not just a promise of future marriage but that, in a certain sense, they constituted the marriage, for, as Philo says: "The espousals have the force of marriage." [39] In fact, if the man died, his fiancée was considered a widow, and therefore the high priest could not take such a woman as his wife, for the *Mishnah* [40] laid down that: "A High Priest may not marry a widow whether she had become a widow after *betrothal* or after wedlock." If an espoused woman had carnal intercourse with another man she was looked upon as an adulteress and was punished by stoning. Dissolution of the espousals had to be done by a bill of divorce (*libellum repudii*). Strictly speaking, the espousals gave the right to marital intercourse, although ordinarily this did not take place until after the bride had been introduced into the groom's house. As Strack-Billerbeck say: "By the espousals the union of a man and a woman in matrimony among the Jews was perfect in every respect: (*rechtlich in jeder Hinsicht perfekt*)." [41]

From the two expressions which St. Matthew uses, we can clearly deduce that Mary had not yet been introduced into Joseph's house at the time of his mental anguish. The first of the two phrases employed by the evangelist is: "before they *came together*" (1:18); this is to be understood as referring to *local* cohabitation and not to marital intercourse, for although in itself it can mean the latter, it is never used in this sense in the New Testament. The passage from St. Paul which

[38] In *Verb. Dom.,* 25 (1947), 99–111.
[39] *De legibus specialibus* iii. 12.
[40] *Mishnah, Yebamoth* 6:4.
[41] *Op. cit.,* II, 393; see *ibid.,* 394 *ff.* for the proof of what we have just said.

some propose as a parallel (1 Cor. 7:5: καὶ πάλιν ἐπὶ τὸ αὐτὸ συνέρχησθε; *et iterum revertimini in idipsum;* "and return together again") is not completely parallel, since the verb is not used alone but is accompanied by a complement.

The second phrase used by the evangelist is found where the angel says to Joseph: "Do not be afraid, Joseph . . . *to take to thee* Mary thy wife: noli timere *accipere* [παραλαβεῖν] Mariam" (1:20); and in verse 24 we read "and [he] took unto him his wife: et *accepit* [παρέλαβεν] coniugem suam." This refers to the second part of the marriage, the introduction of Mary into Joseph's house. But how could he be said to have taken her into his house if she was already there? If she had been living under his roof at the time, the word "retained" or "kept" would be the one to use; but παραλαμβάνω has not this meaning.

How was Mary's reputation to be saved if she had not yet entered Joseph's house as his wife? As we have pointed out, espousal was, in a certain sense, equivalent to full marriage, and the conjugal act between the espoused couple was regarded as lawful. It is true that, according to the rabbinical writings, there was a certain irregularity in such an act, but we do not know with certainty how it was regarded at the time of which we speak. We are sure of one thing, however; we know that the Blessed Virgin's good name did not suffer the least blemish.[42]

---

[42] This point is treated at greater length by Holzmeister, *De sancto Joseph quaestiones biblicae* (Romae, 1945), pp. 68–79; *Verb. Dom.,* 24 (1944), 202–212; 25 (1947), 145–149.

See Fr. Paul Gächter, *op. cit.,* pp. 111–116, where the author gives very good reasons why the inhabitants of Nazareth did not know, or at least might not have known, about Mary's condition when she returned from her visit to Elizabeth.

5. The Birth of Christ:

Flight into Egypt

Bethlehem
(Luke 2:1–7; cf. Map I)

Several months had passed since Joseph had received the angel's message, months which he and his young wife Mary had spent in sweet and holy companionship beneath the same roof. The clouds of sorrow had been lifted and the radiant Sun which Mary carried beneath her heart shed rays of peace, joy and serene contentment throughout the modest dwelling. Tranquilly, gently, the days slipped by in that home sanctified by the presence of Jesus and perfumed by the sweet odor of the virtues of the angelic spouses. Mary's heart and mind were concentrated upon the Child within her, while Joseph was filled with reverent awe at the presence of her who was the living tabernacle containing his God.

While the days passed thus silently and peacefully in the hidden and unknown village of Nazareth, preparations were being made in imperial Rome, the capital of the world, for an event which would harshly disrupt the calm tenor of the Holy Family's daily life. As St. Luke tells us: "Now it came to pass in those days, that there went forth a decree from Caesar Augustus that a census of the whole world should be taken. This first census took place while Cyrinus [Quirinius] was governor of Syria. And all were going, each to his own town, to register."

There was nothing extraordinary about such a decree nor about the fact that everyone had to go to his family's place of origin. We know that Augustus ordered several censuses [1] and that he arranged to have one taken in Egypt every fourteen years for which everyone had to go to his city of origin to register.[2] But the mention of Quirinius presents some difficulty, for we know from the official list of the legates of Syria that in 8 B.C. the legate was C. Sentius Saturninus, who was succeeded by P. Quintilius Varus, the latter being still in office at the death of Herod the Great. Herod died in 4 B.C., some three years after the birth of Christ, which therefore occurred about 6 or 7 B.C. But in 6 or 7 B.C., the legate of Syria was not Quirinius but C. Sentius Saturninus. Hence the problem which from early Christian times has taxed the ingenuity of critics and exegetes.

Many solutions have been proposed, but we shall mention only a few:

(1) We know that Quirinius was the legate of Syria at the time of Archelaus' death in A.D. 6 and that he then took a census in Syria and Judea.[3] It has also been ascertained that he had held the office in former years,[4] and that this term as legate must have been between 12

---

[1] Some of them were listed in the inscriptions at the entrance to the temple which was erected in his honor at Ancyra (Ankara) in Galatia. Cf. Schürer, I, 110.

[2] This is seen from the text of an edict of Vibus Maximus (A.D. 104): "Proclamation of Gaius Vibius Maximus, praefect of Egypt. The house-to-house census having started, it is essential that all persons who for any reason whatsoever are absent from their homes be summoned to return to their own hearths, in order that they may perform the customary business of registration and apply themselves to the cultivation which concerns them." (A. S. Hunt and C. C. Edgar, *Select Papyri* ["The Loeb Classical Library"; Cambridge, Mass.: The Harvard University Press, 1934], II, 108 *f.* Cf. *Verb. Dom.*, 1 (1921), 208, regarding the various types of census in Egypt.

[3] *Ant.* xvii. 13. 5; xviii. 1. 1; 2. 1. Gamaliel refers to this census in Acts 5:37: "in the days of the census"; "in diebus *professionis*"; τῆς ἀπογραφῆς. This census is also fully confirmed by an inscription found in Venice, the full text of which can be seen in *Dict. Apolog.*, I, col. 1426.

[4] The fact that Quirinius had already been the legate of Syria is deduced from the Tibur inscription, so called because it was found near Tivoli in 1764; it is now preserved in the Lateran Museum. The text as reconstructed by Mommsen can be seen in *Dict. de la Bible*, II, cols. 1187 *f.*, and in Schürer, I, 325. The most interesting part of the inscription is the last line, which reads: ". . . DIVI AVGVSTI (I)TERVM SYRIAM ET PH(OENICEN OPTINVIT)." As can be seen, it certainly refers to a second legation in Syria, but unfortunately the part containing the name of the person in question has been lost. Mommsen and the great majority of authors hold that the inscription refers to Quirinius, but some deny that it does (cf. Schürer, I, 324). An inscription from Antioch of Pisidia, transcribed by Ramsay in 1912, corroborates the opinion held by Mommsen, for it mentions Sulpicius Quirinius as a *duumvir* of the Antiochean colony (P. SVLPICI QVIRINI DVVMVIRI), from which it is evident that

B.C. and 8 B.C., since in 12 he was consul in Rome and in 8, C. Sentius Saturninus was the legate of Syria. The census mentioned by St. Luke took place duing this first legation.[5]

(2) The second solution to the problem is as follows: about the year 9 B.C. Quirinius *began* the census and it was completed, perhaps in 7 B.C., by his successor Saturninus, who, as we saw, was legate from 8 to 6 B.C.[6]

(3) We know that there were sometimes two imperial legates in the same region at once. Thus, for example, in Africa in A.D. 75 one legate was at the head of the troops while another was put in charge of taking the census. We can, therefore, suppose that Quirinius' first legation coincided, in the years 8–6 B.C., with the legation of Saturninus.[7]

(4) Finally, there is a fourth solution, which is based on philology. The sentence in St. Luke is translated to read: "This census was *previous to that which* took place while Quirinius was governor of Syria." Obviously, this version removes every difficulty, and it is possible, philologically speaking.[8] The proponents of this solution argue further that the evangelist was probably referring to the census taken during the legation of Quirinius because this census was well known to all; and that actually Gamaliel does refer to it in Acts 5:37.[9]

he was in the East during the years 10–7 B.C., the date of the inscription. Cf. *Verb. Dom.*, 1 (1921), 207, and *RB* (1913), p. 617, for the text of this inscription; see also Deissmann, *Light from the Ancient East*, pp. 5 f. Finally, according to Tacitus (*Annales* iii. 48), Quirinius, a short time after his consulate (12 B.C.), subjugated the Homonadenses, whose territory was in the province of Syria. Thus Schürer, I, 325 f.; E. Ruffini, *Chronologia Veteris et Novi Testamenti* (Romae, 1924), who also gives the text of Tacitus.

[5] Thus O'Rourke, Ruffini and others.

[6] Tertullian (*Adv. Marcion.* iv. 19; *PL* 2, 434) attributes it to Sentius Saturninus, and seems to indicate that it was he who *finished* it.

[7] Prat, *Jesus Christ*, I, 484 f.; L. Fillion, *The Life of Christ*, trans. by N. Thompson (St. Louis: B. Herder Book Co., 1946), I, 588 f.

[8] Passages can be found in which πρῶτος is equivalent to πρότερος, e.g., in 2 Kings 19:44 (LXX v. 43) we read: Ὁ λόγος μου πρῶτός μου τοῦ Ἰούδα, which Lagrange and Prat (*op. cit.*, I, 484) translate as "My cause prevails over (that of) Juda," and in which, as can be seen, the second term of the comparison is understood; see also John 1:15, 30. Schürer (I, 535) admits that the suggested translation is grammatically correct but, for other reasons, he does not accept it in the text in question.

[9] This was the solution proposed by Hervart in 1612 (cf. Prat, *op. cit.*, I, 484) and adopted by a good number of Protestants (cf. Schürer I, 535) and Catholics, including Calmet and Lagrange. In a learned opusculum entitled *S. Luca e il censo di Quirinio* (Gerusalemme, 1934), Canon D. Filippo Talvacchia gives the word πρώτη the meaning of "beginning" and translates Luke 2:2 as: "This census *began* when Quirinius was governor of Syria" (p. 27).

The first solution seems improbable since it requires that the date of Christ's birth be put back too far, but any one of the other three must be regarded as plausible, the fourth being the one which removes the difficulty at its very source. At any rate, it has been well established that St. Luke's statement can, and indeed must, be accepted as truly historical.[10]

In obedience to the imperial decree, Mary and Joseph gathered together a few necessities for the journey and set out for Bethlehem. Women were not obliged to present themselves at the census-taking, but it is most likely that Mary did not wish Joseph to go alone, and he no doubt was reluctant to leave her side when her time was so near. At all events, Divine Providence arranged that Mary, too, should make the journey in order that the prophecy of Micheas (5:1; Vulgate 5:2), which said that the Messias was to be born in Bethlehem, might be fulfilled. The whole march of events is a clear example of how God can make use of men—in this case, of the Emperor Augustus—to bring about His secret designs gently and effectively.

Most probably, the travellers followed the same road which Mary had traversed on her way to visit St. Elizabeth [11]—down the steep and narrow path by Jebel el-Qafseh to the Plain of Esdrelon, across the plain to Engannim (Jenin), then on to Sichem, Silo, Bethel, and finally to the hill which Josephus calls Mount Scopus, from which they had their first clear view of the Holy City. From Jerusalem to Bethlehem was a distance of only about five miles, and no doubt they followed the road which began at the northwest corner of Jerusalem, where Herod's palace stood near the Gennath Gate. It is very likely that this road did not descend to the bottom of the valley of Ben-Hinnom as does the present highway which passes through Birket es-Sultan, but rather crossed the northern part (the Wadi el-Meis) of the valley, and then, climbing the hill now known as Nikefurieh, passed through a little hamlet called "the House of the Terebinth," mentioned

[10] On the points treated here, there is an erudite discussion, from a frankly negative point of view, in August Pauly, *Realenzyclopädie,* Vol. IV A1 (Stuttgart, 1931), cols. 828–843, where a copious bibliography is given. Schürer (I, 508 *f.*) also gives a long, but now somewhat dated, bibliography. Cf. the short article by M. Barquero in *Reseña Ecclesiástica* (1913), pp. 577–588; of interest also is the article by E. W. Seraphin, "The Edict of Caesar Augustus (Luke 2:1–5)," in *Catholic Biblical Quarterly,* 7 (1945), 91–96. Simón-Dorado, *op. cit.,* pp. 316–332, is very learned on the subject.

[11] See above, pp. 98 *f.*

Sira Photo

BETHLEHEM AND THE SURROUNDING COUNTRYSIDE: *1. The Franciscans' "Casa Nova," behind which stands the great basilica; 2. Beit Sahur, called "the town of the shepherds"; 3. The Field of Booz, where the ruins and crypt of an*

by Josephus,[12] and, according to him, situated very near the tomb of Herod's family, opposite the site now occupied by the Pontifical Biblical Institute. From there the road runs to the southwest, approaching the present Greek colony, where the ancient road can still be seen.[13] This old road crosses the Beqa'a (=the ancient valley of Raphaim, cf. 2 Kings 5:18–22), parallel to the main highway, with which it merges a short distance from Mar Elias.[14]

[12] Cf. *Wars* v. 12. 2.

[13] It is possible and even probable that there was a crossroads a short distance outside Jerusalem, and therefore travellers coming from the north direct to Bethlehem would not have had to go up to the capital but could have by-passed it, leaving it a little to the left.

[14] As a result of the recent Jewish-Arab war this highway was cut in half, the northern section being held by the Jews and the southern by the Arabs. The upshot was that it could not, and still cannot, be used for travel between Jerusalem and Bethlehem. Since the latter town fell within their zone, the Arabs, almost at the very start of the war, opened a new road which made a long detour through Deir Dosi, a total distance of about fifteen miles. Because this road was so roundabout and also because of the difficult terrain through which it passed, another shorter and easier road seven miles long was built towards the close of

ancient church are preserved; 4. "The Field of the Shepherds," under the care of the Franciscans; 5. The location of the ancient monasteries of Deir Dosi and Mar Saba; 6. The Mountains of Moab; 7. The Dead Sea.

The well, or rather, the cistern which can still be seen there by the side of the road, is called Bir-Kadismu (later called also "the Well of the Magi"), in reference to the stone upon which the Blessed Virgin probably sat to rest (κάθισμα = seat). On this spot a church and monastery were built towards the middle of the fifth century in memory of the Holy Family's brief pause there, and it was this monastery, perhaps, which owned the old cistern that is still preserved a short distance from the present highway. A few minutes' travelling brings one to the crest of the hill which divides the northern region from the southern, and upon which the ancient Greek monastery of Mar Elias stands like a watchtower. Looking north from there one can see, against an arid, depressing background, the city of sorrow, the city in which our Saviour died, and in which the sorrowing Mother wept bitter

1952. This route branches off from the Jericho highway near Jebel Baten el-Hawa or the "Mount of Scandal," as it is called, down the eastern side of which it descends to the Cedron or the Wadi en-Nor; then it rises to Ras el-Mukabber, and then, passing through the little town of Sur-Bahir, it continues on to merge with the Bethlehem highway between Mar Elias and Tantur. This second route was used for the great feast of the Nativity of 1952.

BETHLEHEM: *A typical street.*

tears. To the south lies the smiling town of Bethlehem,[15] girt about with

[15] Called in Hebrew *Beit Lehem,* which is commonly interpreted as "house of bread." There are some (e.g., Abel, Ricciotti) who give it the meaning of "house of the god, Lahamu," i.e., the second element is the name of a pagan deity. It is true that a god named Lahamu was known in Babylon: cf. Deimel, *Pantheon Babylonicum* (Romae 1914), p. 161; Juan Rovira, *Enuma Elish,* or *Poema babilónico de la creación* (Barcelona, 1922), p. 22, ("towards Lahmu

verdant almond, fig, and olive trees; the town where Jesus was born, where the Virgin Mother's heart beat with ineffable joy as she first embraced her Divine Son. To the east lies a wide and fertile plain, delighting the eye with its natural beauty and the mind with the memory of the angels' song that rang across it on the first Christmas night; beyond the plain rise the mountains of Judea, and beyond them again lie the leaden-hued waters of the Dead Sea dominated by the steep Mountains of Moab.

When the Saviour of the world came on earth, Bethlehem was an insignificant little town with scarcely more than a thousand inhabitants, but even then it could boast of a glorious past and point with pride to the names of Booz, Ruth and David, which sealed its claim to a noble and ancient inheritance.

A short while before they arrived at the town itself, the Holy Family undoubtedly passed near the tomb of Rachel, who was buried where she died, near Bethlehem Ephrata (cf. Gen. 35:19–20; 48:7) on her way back from Mesopotamia. The tomb was still extant at the time of St. Jerome and he acknowledged its authenticity.[16]

At length, after a weary journey lasting at least four days, Mary and Joseph arrived at the city of David, the abode of their ancestors, and Joseph immediately began to seek a lodging for the few days they expected to spend in the town. Did he have relatives living there to

and Lahamu, the gods, their fathers"); see also pp. 15, 23, 34. But there is nothing to prove that this god was venerated or even known in Palestine; Jirku's observations in *Altorientalischer Kommentar zum alten Testament* (Leipzig, 1923), pp. 71 *f.*, are far from being convincing. Certainly there are names in which the second element is the name of a god, but there are also many others in which it is a common noun, e.g., Beit emir, Beit ej-jemal, Beit el-Khalil, Beit Meis, Beit el-milh, etc.

16 Since 1 Kings 10:2 speaks of the tomb of Rachel as being within the limits of Benjamin, quite a few authors believe that Jacob's wife was buried in the territory of the tribe mentioned. Therefore they deny the authenticity of the sepulchre that pilgrims visit today near Bethlehem, and they eliminate as a gloss the phrase in Genesis 35:19; 48:7 which identifies Ephrata with Bethlehem. But even if the phrase is a gloss, it is a most ancient one and reflects a very noteworthy Jewish tradition. It is possible, as Schulz correctly observes (*Die Bücher Samuel*, 10:2 [Münster, 1919]), that there was a twofold tradition. The reasons advanced by Dhorme (*Les Livres de Samuel*, 10:2 [Paris, 1910]) are not sufficient to deny solid probability to the opinion that regards as authentic the sepulchre of Joseph's and Benjamin's mother near Bethlehem. See the excellent article by Bover in *Est. Ecles.* 7 (1928), 226–237, in which, after examining and weighing the reasons for and against each of these two theories, the author decides in favor of the sepulchre near Bethlehem. It may be that in the territory of the tribe of Benjamin there was a monument which was taken to be the tomb of Rachel, the mother of Benjamin.

whom he could appeal for hospitality? We do not know, for the Gospel is completely silent on the matter. At all events, even if he did have kinsfolk in Bethlehem, either his delicate reserve prevented him from asking them for shelter, or all the houses were already taxed to capacity by the extraordinary influx of visitors. We do know, from the evangelist's explicit mention of the fact, that the holy Patriarch endeavored to find lodging at the inn. This inn was not what the present-day Arabs call *el-medafeh,* a kind of hostelry found in every town, great and small, in which the inhabitants gather daily and where travellers put up for the night. Instead it was what we today would call a hostel, night-shelter or caravanserai, known in the East as a *khan.* These *khans* were usually rectangular in shape with a large courtyard in the center for the pack-animals and a kind of covered porch running around the inside of the four walls for the travellers, with perhaps a few alcoves set apart for important visitors. Even today there are some *khans* to be seen in Palestine; there is one, for example, just outside Nazareth and another in Lubban, not far from ancient Silo, standing probably on the same location as the *khan* which Mary and Joseph came upon as they journeyed south and in which they very likely spent the night. It is difficult to say exactly where the *khan* at Bethlehem was situated; [17] no doubt it was either inside or close to the town, which, as we have seen, was then very small.

Today Bethlehem covers a much larger area than it did at the time of Christ's birth. In all probability, the town was then limited to the little group of houses which now faces the basilica.[18] On this level space there may have been in ancient times a *bamah* (a kind of altar) upon which Samuel offered sacrifice (cf. 1 Kings 16:1–5); it is certain, however, that in 347 St. Cyril of Jerusalem said that "ten years before there was a small grove there," [19] and that, according to St. Jerome,[20] this grove was standing in the time of Hadrian and that

[17] The text of Jeremias 41:17 cannot be used to prove that the inn was situated *near* the city (Prat, *op. cit.,* I, 82). First of all, it is very problematic whether or not this text speaks of an *inn,* since the meaning of the word *gerût* is uncertain. Furthermore, people travelling to Egypt—and it is to these that the text refers—undoubtedly took the Hebron road and would not have had to turn aside towards Bethlehem. Then, too, it is not improbable that, instead of *gerût,* we should read *gidrôt* ("sheepfolds"), as some good commentators do.

[18] Cf. Dalman, *Sacred Sites and Ways,* pp. 29 f.

[19] *PG* 33, 752.

[20] See below, p. 122.

A KHAN *or inn.*

Tammuz-Adonis was venerated in the sacred grotto where Christ had been born.

St. Joseph failed to find room at the inn, either because there actually was none or because the innkeeper was reserving the alcoves for more prosperous-looking guests. This is certainly the meaning of St. Luke's observation: ". . . there was no room for them in the inn," the implication being that Mary and Joseph had asked for shelter there and had been refused. What may well have happened is that, in view of Mary's condition, Joseph did not wish to take lodgings in the open porches of the *khan* where privacy was impossible, but wanted to find a more retired place which, for one reason or another, was denied him. Hence he was forced to seek shelter in one of the caves which can still be seen near the town. Thus St. John's sad pronouncement was verified at the very beginning of Christ's earthly life: "He came unto his own, and his own received him not" (1:11). The designs of the Eternal Father for His Son were being manifested even before His birth.

By speaking of the "manger" in which Mary laid her Son, St. Luke indicates indirectly that the cave was one where animals were kept, although he does not say so explicitly. It is merely unfounded conjecture to say that this cave formed part, the cellar or basement, as it

BETHLEHEM: *Grotto of the Nativity. The Star set in the floor under the altar in the background marks the place which tradition regards as the very spot upon which our Lord was born.*

were, of the inn. A tradition dating back to the second century and handed down in the *Protoevangelium of James* (chap. 18) and by St. Justin in his *Dialogue with Trypho*,[21] testifies to the fact that the Gospel narrative is to be understood as referring to an actual cave; and in Origen's day (third century) this was the generally accepted interpretation.[22] There is no positive reason to doubt the authenticity of this traditionally accepted cave, which today is preserved beneath St. Helena's basilica at Bethlehem. In fact, according to St. Jerome's testimony, from the time of the Emperor Hadrian, A.D. 136, "Venus' lover [i.e., Tammuz-Adonis] was lamented in the cave where the Christ-Child once cried." [23] This pagan cult was introduced here with

[21] Cap. 28: *PG* 6, 657: "Since he had nowhere to go in the village, Joseph took refuge in a *cave* near the village."

[22] *Contra Celsum* 1. 51: *PG* 11, 756: "There the *cave* where He was born is shown, and in the cave, the *manger*."

[23] "Bethleem nunc nostram, et augustissimum orbis locum, de quo Psalmista canit: Veritas de terra orta est, lucus inumbrabat Thamuz, id est, Adonidis; et in

BETHLEHEM: *Basilica of the Nativity.*

the object of wiping out the memory of Christ, but it really achieved the contrary purpose, since it served to assure more than ever the authenticity of the site. Thus the spot was easily identified when St. Helena wished to build the great basilica.

It was here, then, that the Virgin Mary "brought forth her first-born son, and wrapped him in swaddling clothes, and laid him in a manger," that Son of whom Isaias prophesied: "For a child is born to us, and a son is given to us and the government is upon his shoulder: and his name shall be called, Wonderful, Counsellor, God the Mighty, the Father of the world to come, the Prince of Peace" (9:6).

It was midnight, but brighter than noon; midnight, when all things cease from toil and are wrapt in silence and peace. When the Blessed Virgin finished her prayer, the heavens began to drop down honey and sweetness, and she, without pain, without distress, without suffering the loss of, or the least stain upon, her virginal purity, saw before her the fruit of her womb. He who came for the benefit and salvation of the world lay before her, brighter and more resplendent than the sun itself, but

specu, ubi quondam Christus parvulus vagiit, Veneris amasius plangebatur." (Ep. 58 *ad Paulinum: PL* 22, 581.)

BETHLEHEM: *Basilica of the Nativity, Interior.*

shivering with cold and, with His tears, already beginning His task as Redeemer. Words cannot tell nor human mind conceive the joy which the most pure Virgin felt at that moment, or the awe and wonder which were hers at seeing Him whom she knew to be true God, so lowly and so humble; and prostrating herself before Him with deepest reverence, she said, as we are told: *"Bene veneris, Deus meus, Domine meus et Filius meus:* Welcome, my God, my Lord, and my Son." And thus she adored Him, kissing His feet, for He was her God; His hand, for He was her Lord; and His face, for He was Her Son.[24]

Glory in Heaven: Peace on Earth
(Luke 2:8–20)

From the high ground at Bethlehem the land slopes gently to the east until, a little beyond Beit-Sahur, known as "the town of the shepherds," it opens out into a spacious and somewhat rolling plain already famous in the Old Testament as the scene of the meeting between Booz and Ruth (cf. Ruth, chap. 2), an incident which is commemorated in the name, "the Field of Booz," given to a strip of land which lies in the center of the extensive valley, and near which are preserved the ruins of a Byzantine church. But luster greater than that imparted to this region by the ancestors of Christ was given to it by the angels who

[24] Luis de Granada, "Sermón de la Fiesta del Nascimiento de Nuestro Redemptor" in *Obras de Fr. Luis de Granada* (Madrid, Ed. Cuervo, 1906), XIII, 477.

descended upon it to proclaim His birth, and by the fortunate shepherds who received there the joyful announcement. These shepherds
were "living in the fields and keeping watch over their flock by night,"
that is to say, they guarded the flock, each taking his turn at watching.

Seeing that tradition has fixed the birth of Christ in the winter
months, it may at first seem surprising that the shepherds were passing
the night in the open country at that season of the year. We must remember, however, that the Jews had two types of livestock which they
called "of the house" and "of the desert" respectively. The first type
was driven out to pasture in the morning and brought back to the
stable at night; the second remained in the fields from the Passover to
November, according to some rabbis, or the whole year round, according to others.[25] The flock of the shepherds at Bethlehem was probably
of this last type. Actually the winter in Palestine is not severe, and
snow never falls on the "Field of the Shepherds," although Bethlehem
itself is sometimes covered with it. And there are years when, even on
the high land, the temperature is very moderate and almost spring-
like, not only by day but also at night, as the writer has experienced
more than once.

As regards the exact spot where the shepherds were when the
angel "stood by them," a tradition dating from the fourth century
points to a little knoll, about a mile and a quarter east and somewhat
to the north of Bethlehem. This site bears the significant name of Siyar
el-Ghanem ("the sheepfold"); it was excavated in 1859 by Guarmani,
and is nowadays administered by the Franciscans.[26] There is a tower
here, as well as a spacious cave 63 by 50 feet; north of the tower, the
foundations of a three-naved church, some 86 by 79 feet, still can
be seen; and finally, there are three tombs dug out of the rock within a
burial cave. All these details correspond exactly with the description
written by Arculf in 670: "In the church, I visited the three tombs of
those three shepherds who are buried near the tower of Gader, these
tombs being about a thousand paces east of Bethlehem. In this very
place, near the tower of the flock, an angelic light had shone round
about these shepherds at the Lord's birth, and on this spot was built
the aforesaid church which now contains the shepherds' tombs." [27] The

---

[25] Cf. Str.-Bill., II, 114 *f*.
[26] On February 15, 1951, excavations were begun at Siyar el-Ghanem under the
direction of Fr. Virgilio Corbo, O.F.M.; cf. *La Terra Santa* (1951), pp. 95 and
326, and especially Fr. Corbo's recent book, *Gli scavi di Kh. Siyar el-Ghanem
(campo dei Pastori) e i Monasteri dei dintorni* (Roma, 1955).
[27] Geyer, *Itinera*, p. 258.

A Palestinian shepherd.

shelter provided by the cave and the elevation of the place above the plain made it a very convenient camp site from which the shepherds could watch their flocks.

About fifteen minutes' walk to the southwest of this site there is another one owned by the Greeks and called Deir er-Ra'wat ("monastery of the shepherds") or Keniset er-Ra'wat ("church of the shepherds"), where the ruins and crypt of an ancient church are preserved. Dalman [28] prefers this site to that of the Franciscans; but we think that the latter has better guarantees of probability and we know that it is the one which Arculf visited. Meistermann [29] intimates that the Greek site, in the center of the plain, was first called Deir er-Raut ("monastery of Ruth") and was dedicated to Ruth the Moabitess, and that later this name was changed to Deir er-*Ra'wat* ("monastery of the *shepherds*"), a statement which Dalman rejects.

The Eternal Father willed that these rough, unlettered shepherds should be the first men to adore His Son. He did not choose the proud leaders of the Jews, the haughty Sadducees or the hypocritical Pharisees, for high birth and worldly glory count for nothing with God, who looks with love and favor upon the simple of soul and the humble of heart.

The shepherds were terrified when the sky was suddenly filled with

[28] *Op. cit.,* pp. 45 *f.*   [29] *Ibid.,* p. 51, n. 2.

light and an angel appeared to them. But the angel calmed their fear
with the words: "Do not be afraid, for behold, I bring you good news
of great joy which shall be to all the people; for today in the town of
David a Saviour has been born to you, who is Christ the Lord. . . ."
And in order that they might recognize Him, the angel gave them a
sign: ". . . you will find an infant wrapped in swaddling clothes and
lying in a manger."

Then a multitude of celestial spirits joined the heavenly messenger
and made the sky resound with their joyous hymn:

> "Glory to God in the heights,
>   and peace on earth to men of good will,"—

a beautiful canticle which could more fittingly be divided into three
distinct strophes referring respectively to the glory of God in the
heavens, happiness on earth, and God's benevolence towards all men.
Such a division harmonizes admirably with the proof of His infinite
love which God gave to men in the birth of His Divine Son.

The shepherds set out in haste to search for the Child, "and they
found Mary and Joseph, and the babe lying in the manger." Enlightened as they were by the Holy Spirit, with what simple faith and
burning love they must have adored the Babe! No doubt they brought
Him such gifts as they could offer—some cheese, a few handfuls of
dried figs and raisins, a small jar of milk, and perhaps a lamb. Then
they returned to their flocks "glorifying and praising God for all that
they had heard and seen. . . ." As for Mary, when she saw her sweet
Jesus already being adored and acknowledged as the Messias, she "kept
in mind all these things, pondering them in her heart."

"Peace to men of good will": this angelic song—"*praeconium
vocis angelicae*," as St. Augustine calls it [30]—at first glance seems very
simple, yet, as Maldonatus has pointed out, although it is quite short,
it contains many difficulties, which in turn give rise to several different
interpretations. Since this hymn of the angels is of special importance,
and since the Church has incorporated it into her liturgy, we shall
pause a moment to consider how it should be interpreted.

First of all, the word *eudokía* (εὐδοκία), which is translated as "good
will," can of itself be understood in two ways, each of which has many
supporters. Thus, for example, Knabenbauer, Plummer, Fillion,
Dausch, Lebreton, Simón-Dorado and Gomá interpret it as meaning

[30] *PL* 38, 998.

BETHLEHEM

Albina Photo

"*God's* good will," while others, such as Lagrange, Valensin, Marchal and Joüon prefer *"man's* good will." Let us discuss briefly which of the two opinions is the more acceptable one.[31]

[31] See Van Kasteren on this specific subject in *RB* (1894), pp. 58–61.

In the New Testament, *eudokía* means:

(1) *God's good pleasure:* Matthew 11:26; Luke 10:21; Ephesians 1:5, 9; Philippians 2:13.

(2) *Man's good will:* in Romans 10:1 it means "desire" or "wish"; in 2 Thessalonians 1:11 "good pleasure," and in Philippians 1:15 "good will." In none of these passages does it signify that the will is good in the sense of being *upright* or *just,* i.e., in the *moral* sense. Cremer says that not even once is it taken in this sense.[32]

In the Old Testament, the meaning of *eudokía* is usually the same as that of the Hebrew *ratson,* which occurs 56 times, 40 in reference to *God* and only 16 in reference to *man.* In the Septuagint it is translated by many different words. Apart from Ecclesiasticus, the word *eudokía* appears only ten times in the Old Testament, eight of which correspond to *ratson* and all of which refer to God. Thus it is obvious that in the Old Testament the use of the word in connection with God is much more frequent than its reference to man. In addition we must note that when it has this latter sense, it does not properly refer to a *just* or *upright* will but rather to *complaisance,* or a *benevolent inclination.* This is the way the Greek fathers, from the fourth century on, have understood it, and hence the first sense ("God's good pleasure") is the preferred one.

But who are these "men of God's good pleasure," the objects of the divine benevolence? Some believe that they are the Jews, the Chosen People, to whom God had given so many proofs of predilection; others think that it is rather a question of the people of God in general or of those men with whom God is pleased. In any event, all authorities agree that the phrase indicates a certain particularization, since peace is not announced for *all* men but is limited to a special group, to those in whom a definite condition is fulfilled. It excludes therefore what we may call "universalism."

However, the angel's hymn does have this universal application if we admit the reading given in the *textus receptus,* where we find the nominative *eudokía* and not the genitive *eudokías,* so that the phrase becomes "to men, the good pleasure of God." That is to say, in the birth of our Saviour, God showed His benevolence, His good will, to *all* men without exception, a meaning which seems to us to be more in conformity with the context. In fact, there is nothing extraordinary in

---

[32] Cf. *Biblisch-theologisches Wörterbuch der Neutestamentlichen Gräcität,* p. 102, for the exact meaning of the passages mentioned.

an announcement of peace for these men who merit divine benevolence.[33] That is the normal thing, and it was always thus. But the angels
certainly announced something extraordinary and unusual produced at
the birth of Christ. Why proclaim as exceptional, and with such
solemnity, a state of affairs that had existed from the beginning?
Lagrange has no difficulty in proving from Luke 1:17, 51 *ff.*, 76 *f.*,
and Isaias 57:19 *ff.* that "salvation for men is a conversion and presupposes certain moral dispositions," and that "there is no peace for
the ungodly." All this is true, but it has no application here. The passages he cites speak about what is normal, whereas our passage deals
with something extraordinary, i.e., the effect of the great event which
the angels announced.

Therefore it seems that we must give the preference to *eudokía* in
the nominative, provided that it does not lack a solid critical foundation. And it does have very solid backing, for it is the reading of the
textus receptus, as we have already pointed out, and is found in many
manuscripts, both uncial and minuscule, in all the Syriac versions as
well as the Coptic, the Armenian, and the Ethiopic, in the redactors
of *Codex Vaticanus* and *Codex Sinaiticus,* and in the Greek fathers in
general; and it is the reading preferred by such exegetes as Cremer,
Crampon, Zorell and others.[34] By reading *eudokía* in the nominative
the hymn can be divided into three harmonious strophes. The universal
character of the first strophe ("Glory to God in the heights [of
heaven])" is repeated in the second ("and on earth peace") and the
third ("good will to men").

> *Glory to God* in the heights of [heaven],
> and on earth *peace,*
> [*divine*] *good will* to men.

There is also perfect harmony between the various elements: *Glory to
God, peace, (divine) good will; in the heights, on earth, to men.* And
in each strophe there are two elements, since "Glory to God" is but one
element in itself.

But some object to this division which, at first glance at least, seems
well founded; they say that the third strophe is superfluous since it is
already contained in the second, for the "earth" certainly includes

---

[33] Fillion, *op. cit.,* I, 307–308.   [34] See *Bibl. Zeit.,* 5 (1907), 382.

"men." As we see it, however, the difficulty is only apparent. The second strophe embraces the whole world in general and includes inanimate nature, which in the descriptions of the prophets partakes of the universal joy at the coming of the Messias. Now the word "peace" in the angels' hymn means precisely this joy, and not simply the tranquillity of a good conscience. Therefore, it is not surprising to find that, among such a host of benefits, particular mention is made of one which affects men alone,[35] and which is much greater than the rest, namely, divine good will. Who would dare to say that such a reference is mere tautology? And be it noted that this divine benevolence is not restricted to upright men, to those who are on the path of salvation; instead, it extends to all men, Jews and Gentiles, just men and sinners, for, at His only-begotten Son's coming into the world, the Father is manifesting His good will towards all, without exception. How wide then are the horizons opened up by this magnificent canticle! Here there are no limits, no exceptions, but only a heart-lifting and truly divine universality.[36]

We trust that the reader will pardon us if we have dwelt too long on this passage. We have gone into such detail with the sole purpose of giving a clear idea of the interesting and difficult problem it presents, one which is of very ancient date and which is still being discussed by exegetes.

The Circumcision
(Luke 2:21)

God enjoined circumcision upon Abraham as the distinctive mark of the male members of the Chosen People and as a seal on the covenant made between Him and the holy patriarch: "This is my covenant which you shall observe, between me and you, and thy seed after thee: All the male kind of you shall be circumcised. And you shall circum-

---

[35] On this point there is a very apt observation in *Verb. Dom.*, 12 (1932), 362: "Si vero legitur εὐδοκία in nominativo, habentur tria membra quae ita coordinantur: Gloria in excelsis Deo; pax in terra; benevolentia hominibus. Simile quid habetur in cantico trium puerorum (Dan. 3:52–90), ubi post elogium generale (vv. 52–56) primo invitantur ad Dei laudem creaturae caelestes (57–73), dein terra (73–81), denique homines (82–90); item in psalmo 148; caelum (1–6), terra (7–10a), homines (10b–14)."

[36] The reader will find a very complete dissertation on the meaning of the word *eudokía*, both in the Old and New Testaments, in Gerhard Kittel *et al., Theologisches Wörterbuch zum Neuen Testament* (Stuttgart, 1935), II, 740–748.

cise the flesh of your foreskin: that it may be for a sign of the covenant between me and you. An infant of eight days old shall be circumcised among you, every man child in your generations. He that is born in the house, as well as the bought servant shall be circumcised, and whosoever is not of your stock" (Gen. 17:10–12). It is well known that various peoples, the Arabs, for example, have practiced, and still do practice, circumcision, and that the ceremony is an occasion for a family feast. Much has been written about the character and motive of the rite, some authors regarding it simply as an hygienic measure, while others think that it was a sign of the child's incorporation into his people or tribe. But in Israel, as is plain from God's words to Abraham, the ceremony had, and continues to have, a purely religious character. As a faithful observer of the Law, our Lord willed to submit Himself humbly to this rite and, at the very outset of His earthly life, to offer to His Eternal Father some drops of that Precious Blood which He was later to pour out in such abundance.[37]

As we have just said, the Jews still practice circumcision, and, according to the Talmud, there are certain prayers to be recited during the ceremony. The circumciser says: "Praised be He who sanctified us by His commandments and enjoined circumcision upon us." The child's father says: "Praised be He who sanctified us by His commandments and commanded us to introduce him [i.e., the child] into the covenant of our father Abraham." Those present say: "Just as he entered into the covenant, so also he can enter into the Law." Thus the very words used clearly show the completely religious and national character of the rite.[38]

As was customary on the occasion, the new-born Child was given a name, which was none other than that revealed by the angel: Jesus ("Saviour"), a most holy name, the only one through which men can attain salvation (cf. Acts 4:12), a name that is above every other name, most sweet and yet most terrible, since "at the name of Jesus every knee should bend of those in heaven, on earth and under the earth; and every tongue should confess that the Lord Jesus Christ . . . [triumphs] in the glory of God the Father" (Phil. 2:9–11).

[37] Where did the Circumcision take place? In Bethlehem, no doubt; but was it in the cave or in a house to which the Holy Family had moved? It is difficult to say. St. Epiphanius thinks that our Lord was circumcised in the cave itself.
[38] Cf. Str.-Bill., IV, 30.

Purification and Presentation
(Luke 2:22–38; cf. Map VII)

The Law of Moses prescribed that a woman who had given birth to a son should present herself for purification at the Temple forty days after the birth. She had to offer to the priest a yearling lamb for a holocaust, as a symbol of union with God, and a young pigeon or turtledove as a sacrifice for sin to blot out her legal impurity. If the family was poor, she could offer two young pigeons or two turtledoves, one for the holocaust and one as the sacrifice for sin (cf. Lev. 12:1–8). If the son was her first-born, she had to consecrate him to the Lord (cf. Exod. 13:11–16), for God demanded the first things of the flock and the first fruits of the fields, and, in like manner, He claimed for Himself the first-born son of each family, and the parents had to redeem the child by paying five shekels (about $7.00 in our money) to the Temple (cf. Num. 18:15 f.).

Our Lady, who had conceived by the power of the Holy Spirit, was not subject to the law of purification; and Jesus, being King and Lord of Heaven and earth, did not need to be ransomed. Yet both the Son and the Mother wished to fulfill the Law, giving thereby a lofty example of deep humility and perfect obedience. Then, too, since the virginal birth was not generally known, they wished to avoid every possible occasion of scandal by conforming to the custom.

And so, forty days after our Saviour's birth, Mary, carrying Jesus in her arms and accompanied by Joseph, set out for the Holy City. Since they came from Bethlehem they would naturally enter the Temple precincts through one of the gates on the south side, probably the Huldah Gate, which perhaps can be located where one sees today the Triple Gate, now walled up. When the Temple was being rebuilt after the Babylonian captivity, the ancients of the people, who had beheld the magnificence of Solomon's Temple, wept to see the poverty of the structure that Zorobabel was raising (cf. 1 Esd. 3:12); but the prophet Aggeus, seeing in spirit the entrance of the Messias into the new Temple, exclaimed: "The Desired of all nations shall come: and I will fill this house with glory. . . . Great shall be the glory of this last house more than of the first. . . : and in this place I will give peace, saith the Lord of hosts" (Agg. 2:8 ff.). But little or nothing of that glory was visible to those present at our Lord's entry into the Temple, or to those other mothers who, along with Mary, had come thither to undergo the rite of purification.

When Mary had entered the Temple proper, perhaps through the Gate of the First Born, on the south side, she ascended from the Court of the Women by the staircase of fifteen semicircular steps on which, according to the *Mishnah,* the Levites used to sing the fifteen gradual Psalms (Ps. 119–133) on the feast of Tabernacles. Then she prostrated herself in humble recollection on the eastern side of the Court of Israel. It was here that the ceremony of purification took place: the priests, in Mary's name, offered the twofold sacrifice commanded by the Law by immolating the two doves which she had brought. Then the Child was presented to the priest, who, in accordance with the rite, took Him in his arms, blessed Him and returned Him to His Mother, receiving in exchange the sum of five shekels. At that moment Jesus no doubt repeated in His heart the oblation He had made on entering the world: "Behold, I come . . . to do thy will, O God" (Heb. 10:7).

He who humbles himself shall be exalted: Jesus willed to humble Himself, and the Eternal Father at that moment exalted Him through the mouth of the venerable Simeon. This just and God-fearing man had besought the Holy Spirit not to let him die without having seen the Anointed of God, and his wish was granted to him. Inspired by the Holy Spirit, he came to the Temple, and beholding the humble Child in Mary's arms, recognized in Him the Messias whom he had so ardently desired to see. His yearning fulfilled, he took the Infant in his arms and exclaimed:

> Now thou dost dismiss thy servant, O Lord,
>   according to thy word, in peace;
> Because my eyes have seen thy salvation,
>   which thou hast prepared before the
>   face of all peoples:
> A light of revelation to the Gentiles,
>   and a glory for thy people Israel.

This beautiful canticle was, as it were, the venerable Simeon's swan song; with his own eyes he had beheld the Messias, and now nothing remained for him to see.

Joseph and Mary, wondering at the unusual occurrence, were overjoyed to hear Simeon's great praise of the Child. But the holy old man had not finished speaking yet. He had torn aside the veil of the future and had revealed the light that shone there; but all was not light in his vision, for he had also perceived the dark and menacing shadows of death. Turning to Mary, he transfixed her heart with this fearful prophecy: "Behold, this child is destined for the fall and for the rise of many in Israel, and for a sign that shall be contradicted. And thy own soul a sword shall pierce, that the thoughts of many hearts may be revealed."

Simeon's prophecy was as harsh and tragic as his *Nunc dimittis* was gentle and full of joy. The tender Infant was light and glory, but He would also be the occasion of the fall of many. His mission would be opposed by the hardness of heart of His compatriots in Israel, many of whom would be scandalized by the humble circumstances of His appearance, His family and His words. Yet, through faith in Him, many others would be raised from abasement and spiritual death to true and blissful life.

Jesus was, as it were, the visible sign of this conflict of spirits, of this war between two opposing camps. In fact, the Gospel narrative is the story of the Jews' enmity to the Person of Jesus, an enmity which culminated in Calvary, but which has not died down with the centuries and which will not cease until the end of time. Just as Christ is a perennial source of grace and sanctification, of benediction and love for those who live according to His will, so He is an occasion of reprobation, despair and hatred for those who find that His doctrine, example and disciples are obstacles to their pride and concupiscence. Twenty centuries of history have fully confirmed Simeon's predictions.

Anna the prophetess, a woman at least eighty-four years old, now joined her praise to that of Simeon. Appearing on the scene just at that moment, and also enlightened from above, she began to speak of the wonders of God to all who were awaiting the redemption of Israel.

Having fulfilled the prescriptions of the Law, the Holy Family returned to Bethlehem. Immediately after telling about the purification, St. Luke adds: "And when they had fulfilled all things prescribed in the Law of the Lord, they returned to Galilee, into their own town of Nazareth" (2:39). It is possible that the Holy Family left for Nazareth at this time and returned shortly afterwards to Bethlehem, since it was there that the Magi found them, and from there that they fled to Egypt. The object of such a flying visit to their home would have been to settle some business matters, to collect a few household utensils and perhaps to say goodbye to relatives and friends, because Joseph had decided to leave the little Galilean village and establish himself in Bethlehem. This is the way several authors (e.g., Vilariño) interpret the passage. But the evangelist's observation can be given another and, we believe, a much more probable interpretation, one which many exegetes, such as Knabenbauer, Prat, Lagrange and others, prefer: namely, that since Luke has said nothing about the adoration of the Magi or the flight into Egypt, he simply passes over these two episodes in silence, and speaks here of the Holy Family's definitive return to Nazareth after the flight into Egypt; hence this would be the same incident to which St. Matthew refers in 2:23.

The Adoration of the Magi
(Matt. 2:1–12)

The shepherds who came to adore the Child were the representatives of the Jewish people; the Magi who came from afar were the representatives of the Gentiles, and in showing Himself to them, Christ, as it were, revealed Himself to all the nations of the world. The Church, therefore, calls this mystery the Epiphany, the "manifestation."

The palace of Herod the Great was one of the scenes in this drama of revelation, and the present citadel, called the Tower of David and situated at the northwest corner of Jerusalem near the Jaffa Gate, can surely be regarded as a true Christian sanctuary, since Herod received the illustrious strangers in one of its sumptuous halls, and since it was in this building, too, that the Jews gave public testimony that the Messias was to be born in Bethlehem.

The Magi came "from the East," in itself a very vague designation. Job counted himself among the "people of the East" (Job 1:3), and, according to one tradition, the holy patriarch's homeland was to the east of the Lake of Gennesareth in the region of Jolan, where, in a town called Sheikh Sa'ad, a stone is still pointed out as "the Stone of Job." [39] "From the East" could also mean from Persia, Media, Arabia or Mesopotamia. Since this last-named region was part of the ancient Babylonian empire, where astronomy was especially studied, it seems

[39] Cf. A. Fernández, *Problemas de topografía palestinense* (Barcelona, 1936), p. 93.

JERUSALEM: *The Citadel, occupying part of the site of Herod's palace.*

to fit in well with the Gospel narrative, in which the star plays such an important role. Yet, on the other hand, because the first known *magi* were Medes, the region of Media-Persia perhaps merits our preference.

According to its etymology, the word *magi* seems to mean "followers of Mazdeism." Herodotus says that these *magi* were one of the six tribes of Media and that they wielded great influence at the court, where they were consulted on all matters of importance. This author goes on to say that they also acted as priests for the Persians, and he calls them astrologers, soothsayers, philosophers, etc.[40] It cannot be maintained that they were kings, despite their popular title, "the Three Kings," but they certainly were important personages who devoted themselves to the study of the sciences in general and perhaps of astronomy in particular. There has not always been unanimity as regards their number, and the tradition has varied over the centuries, some authors maintaining that there were as many as twelve, while the frescoes in the catacombs generally depict three, but sometimes also two or four. In the end, however, the number three prevailed, due

[40] Cf. G. Messina, *Der Ursprung der Magier und die Zarathustriche Religion* (Roma, 1930).

perhaps to the fact that they brought *three* gifts, gold, frankincense and myrrh.

Their names have taken many, and often very strange, forms. Syriac tradition has preserved no less than twelve names, the first three of which are, for example, *Zarvandad,* son of Artaban; *Hormizd,* son of Sitruq; and *Gushnasaph,* son of Gunaphar. But the most generally accepted names, the first mention of which apparently dates back to the eighth or ninth century, are Gaspar, Melchior and Balthasar.[41]

Various theories about the star have been proposed. Some say that it was the conjunction of Saturn, Jupiter and Mars which occurred in the Roman year 747 or 7 B.C. in our reckoning; this was Kepler's theory, and it won many supporters. Others, including Origen, say that the star was a comet; according to some it was Halley's comet, which appeared twelve years before our era and was seen again in 1910. A third hypothesis is that the star was a special one that did not follow the laws of nature.

The first opinion is not in accord with the word used by St. Matthew, ἀστήρ, which, unlike ἄστρον, never refers to a constellation or any group of stars, but always to a single isolated star. Nor does Halley's comet suit the circumstances, since it appeared too long before the birth of Christ. This last objection cannot be applied to the appearance of an unidentified comet, but if the star was a comet, how explain the fact that it appeared anew to the Magi on the road to Bethlehem, a difficulty that applies to the first theory as well? Hence precisely because of this second appearance of the same star, its movement from Jerusalem to Bethlehem, and its standing still over the house where Jesus was, we prefer to accept the third hypothesis, for it is the only one which accounts satisfactorily for all the circumstances. Thus the star that was seen in the East was a most unusual one, whose appearance cannot be regarded as an ordinary phenomenon, and therefore every purely naturalistic explanation is excluded.

The Magi well understood that the star portended something far above the natural order. It is possible that the mere sight of it led them to suspect that it was an indication of the birth of the Messias-

[41] As a matter of curiosity, it is interesting to read what Zacharias Chrysopolitanus wrote in the twelfth century on this matter: "Nomina trium magorum, graece: Apellius, Amerus, Damascus. Apellius interpretatur *fidelis,* Amerus *humilis,* Damascus *misericors.* Hebraica lingua vocati sunt Magalath, Galgalath, Saracin. Magalath interpretatur *nuntius,* Galgalath *devotus,* Saracin *gratia*" (*PL* 186, 83).

King, a possibility heightened by the fact that at the time, particularly in Persia, the hope of a new era for humanity was in the air, the conviction that a mysterious personage was going to come and bring about a great renewal in the world. But be that as it may, only an internal supernatural enlightenment could have assured those who beheld the star that it was a sign of the coming of the Messias. Perhaps God gave this supernatural insight to others besides the Magi, but the hardships of a long and difficult journey, their unwillingness to leave their homeland, and perhaps also their doubt as to the success of the quest caused them to turn a deaf ear to the divine invitation to partake in such a glorious adventure. Only the Magi answered the heavenly summons, and so they can very fittingly be held up as models of fidelity in following the call of God.

From the Magi's own words, *"We have seen his star in the East,"* we know that the star did not accompany them to Jerusalem, and we can gather as much also from the great joy they felt when they saw it again on their way to Bethlehem. Its guidance was not necessary, however, because they must have been well aware that the King of the Jews would be born in His native land, the capital of which was Jerusalem, a city of note lying on a well-marked route.

The route which the Magi followed towards Palestine depended, of course, on their point of departure. If they had come from Mesopotamia, they would have taken the great caravan trail which followed the Euphrates and crossed it at Karkemish. Then going down through Aleppo, they would probably have advanced towards Damascus, from which point they would have followed the ancient *Via Maris* into Israel. Then they would have taken the road that ran through the country from north to south, passing through Sichem and, therefore, reaching the capital from the north. In a word, they would have followed practically the same route as did the patriarch Abraham. If, on the contrary, they had come from Arabia, there were two roads open to them: the first was the southern one which crossed the 'Arabah, the ancient kingdom of Edom, and which perhaps went up through Bersabee and Hebron. But they do not seem to have come this way, since everything indicates that they did not pass through Bethlehem on the journey to Jerusalem. Hence they would have come by the other path, more to the north, through the ancient land of Moab, passing through Jericho down to the Jordan valley and across the river; then they would have come up through the Wadi el-Qelt and arrived at Jerusalem from the eastern side. On their return home it is extremely likely that they took the southern road, because it was the more direct.

By whatever route they came, it was a long and hazardous journey, but finally they arrived at Jerusalem on their richly-caparisoned camels and accompanied by a large retinue of servants. As they made their way into the city, their exotic appearance attracted attention and a crowd quickly gathered around them. Little suspecting the disturbance that their innocent question was to cause in the city, they asked the on-lookers eagerly: "Where is he that is born king of the Jews? For we have seen his star in the East and have come to worship him." With one stroke of the pen the evangelist describes the effect of their inquiry: "But when King Herod heard this he was troubled, and so was all Jerusalem with him."

And why would not the hated Idumean tyrant have been disturbed, for was he not always suspicious, always imagining intrigues on every side and living in continual fear of losing the throne he had usurped? The wily old king's astute hypocrisy was matched only by his cruelty, and he set about using the one vice to achieve the aims of the other. He resolved to rid himself of the menace of the new king, but he knew he would have to proceed cautiously. First of all he had to find out where the rival monarch had been born, and so he called together the chief priests and the scribes, who were well versed in the Sacred Scriptures, and asked them where the Messias was to be born. The doctors of Israel knew the prophecy of Micheas (5:2) and they answered without hesitation: "In Bethlehem of Juda."

Now that he knew the place of the birth, Herod had to ascertain the time. Accordingly he summoned the Magi, but secretly, in order not to show his courtiers his deep trepidation, and from the visitors found out the time of the star's appearance. He presupposed, and not without foundation, that the appearance of the star coincided with the new king's birth. Then as he said farewell to the Magi, he requested, with sacrilegious hypocrisy: "Go and make careful inquiry concerning the child, and when you have found him, bring me word, that I too may go and worship him."

The plot was skillfully contrived, and for the moment Herod was satisfied and at ease, assured that his scheme could not fail. Meanwhile, little suspecting the king's criminal designs, the Magi remounted their

Albina Photo

BIR KADISMU: *or "The Well of Resting," also called "The Well of the Magi," halfway between Jerusalem and Bethlehem.*

camels and took the road to Bethlehem. Great was their joy when, on leaving the city, they once more beheld the star that they had seen in the East but which, as we have indicated, had not accompanied them on their journey towards Jerusalem.

The Holy Family was no longer living in the lowly cave, for it is most likely that when the crowds who had come to register had left Bethlehem, St. Joseph had sought better quarters and had been able to obtain a small house which, though unpretentious and simple, was much more comfortable and habitable than the miserable stable. This supposition is upheld by the expression which St. Matthew uses: "εἰς τὴν οἰκίαν: and entering *the house*" (Matt. 2:11); absolutely speaking, this could mean simply a dwelling, but it should be taken here in the common and obvious sense of a house properly so-called. And it was over this holy house that the star came to rest.

How surprised the illustrious visitors must have been when they saw the "palace" of the new King, to whom they had come so far to render homage! Certainly they had reason enough to think that they had been mistaken and that the whole affair had been an illusion. But the light from on high, which had enabled them to see the significance of the star, now revealed to them the true nature of the new King, and humbly prostrating themselves they respectfully and devoutly offered Him their gifts—gold, as to a king; incense, as to God; and myrrh, as to a mortal man.[42]

Flight Into Egypt and Massacre of the Innocents
(Matt. 2:13–18)

After paying their respects to the new King, the Magi no doubt prepared to return to Jerusalem to fulfill the promise they had made to Herod, believing as they did that his request was sincere and devout. But God, who had led them to Bethlehem with such loving providence, intervened to save them from the tyrant's trap and to warn them not to return to him. And so, obedient to the divine command, they took the desert road and, crossing the Jordan valley, returned directly to their own country.

Herod, meanwhile, was anxiously awaiting their arrival. Uneasy and perhaps a little alarmed at the delay, he undoubtedly sent out his spies, who returned with the news that the Magi had already departed over the desert route. And, most disquieting of all, they added that the visitors had found a child to whom they had rendered homage and presented royal gifts.

---

[42] See the interesting opuscule by Fr. (now Canon) Pedro A. Mattheu in the series *Florilegio Biblico,* No. 14, in which the author deals more fully with all these points concerning the Magi.

When the trembling spies reported their findings to him, Herod's rage knew no bounds. Anger, suspicion, and alarm surged through his heart. Enraged and humiliated by the failure of his hypocritical scheme and now completely obsessed by the fear that the new king would despoil him of his crown, he resolved to have his revenge. His cunning had availed him nothing; therefore he would resort to violence. The Magi had told him the date of the star's appearance, and now, using this meager information to gain his ends, he ordered the death of all male children of two years and under in Bethlehem and the surrounding district. Surely, he thought, the pretender would not escape this time; his death would be secured.

On that terrible day the streets of the peaceful, smiling city of David ran red with the blood of the Innocents and resounded with the wails of their heartbroken mothers. Seven centuries before, the prophet Jeremias had described the bloody holocaust:

> A voice was heard in Rama,[43]
> > weeping and loud lamentation;
> Rachel weeping for her children,
> > and she would not be comforted,
> > > because they are no more.
>
> > > > (Matt. 2:18; cf. Jer. 31:15.)

Much fantasy has been woven about the number of children slain in this massacre. Some authors (St. Paschasius and the Ethiopic liturgy), taking Apocalypse 14:1 as a basis, make the number as large as 144,000. One tradition interprets the word ὁρίοις in the sense of *villages* and includes in this term even the birthplace of John the Baptist, 'Ain Karim, which is almost four and one-half miles from Bethlehem, as the crow flies; this interpretation would, of course, considerably increase the number of children killed. In 1940 Bethlehem had a population of about 7,000, and the children of two years and under, i.e., those born between April 1, 1938, and April 1, 1940, numbered 561, of whom 262 were male and 299 female. Taking these figures as a term of reference and reckoning the population of Bethlehem at the time as about 1,000, we find that the number of male children would then

---

[43] Rama is the present er-Ram, about five miles north of Jerusalem, in the center of the former territory of the tribe of Benjamin. When Jerusalem was destroyed, Nabuchodonosor ordered all the unfortunate Jews who were destined for exile to be assembled at this town. Jeremias imagines Rachel bewailing the sad fate of the Benjamites, because she was Benjamin's mother (cf. Gen. 35:18).

have been approximately thirty-seven. Therefore we can fairly safely estimate that Herod slew between thirty and forty children.

But what man, however powerful, can thwart God's plans? The Lord has His own designs and, when necessary, He sweeps aside the most complicated schemes of men. And so the one Child that Herod sought was no longer in Bethlehem, for an angel had appeared to Joseph in a dream and had commanded him to flee to Egypt with the Child and His Mother: "Arise, and take the child and his mother, and flee into Egypt, and remain there until I tell thee. For Herod will seek the child to destroy him."

The command was a hard one to obey; it was humiliating, too, since it meant that the Creator was fleeing from His creatures, and there was the added hardship of having to set out hurriedly and at such an hour. But Mary and Joseph obeyed the divine command without question and without delay, giving us thereby a sublime example of the obedience, peace and serenity which we should practice in the trying circumstances of life. If God was with them, who could harm them?

The journey was a lengthy and fatiguing one. In order to go to Egypt they had first to go to Hebron, and there were two possible routes thither. The principal one was the continuation of the road which from very ancient times ran from north to south through the whole land of Canaan; but this passed some distance to the west of Bethlehem, leaving the town on the left and following practically the same route as the present highway. The other and much less frequented road started from the town itself, and it was most probably the one that still leaves Bethlehem from the southeast side not far from the basilica, descends towards the valley and follows it for some distance. Then, after crossing the Wadi Artas, the road ascends towards the west and goes on to pass above the sanctuary of the *Hortus Conclusus*. This is probably the way the Holy Family went.

About two miles outside of Hebron they turned to the right and, passing through Beit Jibrin, went on towards Gaza where they came out on the *Via Maris,* which was the usual route for caravans and armies and which they could easily follow to the Egyptian border. Or they might have continued on into Hebron itself and from thence to Bersabee, and soon they would have reached the open desert. It is difficult, even impossible, to say which of the two routes they followed.

The second was somewhat more direct, but the first was easier and safer and St. Joseph would probably have selected it for that reason.

If we were to believe the apocryphal gospels, the Holy Family's path through the desert was an uninterrupted series of miracles—palm trees which bent down to give them shade, fountains that sprang up to quench their thirst, and wild beasts which suddenly became tame. In reality, the travellers had to suffer the hardships always entailed in a long journey across arid and inhospitable terrain, hardships that were here the first trials in the life of Him who was one day to be for our sakes the Man of Sorrows.

We have no completely trustworthy evidence as to where the Holy Family settled in Egypt. One tradition, apparently dating from the fifth century, says that they went up the Nile valley as far as the city of Hermopolis in upper Egypt, about 212 miles from the Egyptian frontier. It is, however, most unlikely that they would have undertaken so long a journey when there was no real necessity for it. Furthermore, although they did not know when they would be told to return home, they could have presupposed that their exile would be a relatively short one. It is much more probable and almost certain that St. Joseph chose some place in the Nile delta as a temporary home, but it is not possible to ascertain the exact location. In the old city of Cairo, the Coptic church of Abu-sarga is pointed out as the site on which the Holy Family's house stood. According to a tradition which, however, does not appear to go back further than the thirteenth century, the holy pilgrims halted at Matarieh, about four and one-half miles north of Cairo. If we wish to choose a site, which has more probabilities in its favor than the others, we can perhaps give the preference to Leontopolis, the present Tell Yehudiyeh, about sixteen miles north of ancient Heliopolis and about twenty miles from Cairo. There was a flourishing colony of Jews in this city, and they even had a temple there, erected in 170 B.C. by the priest Onias.[44] It is most likely that St. Joseph would have elected to live in a place where he would be among his compatriots who could help to ease the burden of exile and render life less difficult for his spouse and her Child.

[44] Cf. *Ant.* xiii. 3. 1–3, where Josephus writes that Onias, wishing to build in Egypt a temple to the true God, sent a petition to King Ptolemy and Queen Cleopatra, in which he said that "having . . . come with the Jews to Leontopolis," he was requesting permission to build there a temple to Almighty God after the pattern of that in Jerusalem, wherein the Jews who lived in Egypt could come together. And the monarchs graciously gave him the permission he asked.

We can easily imagine how hard life must have been for them, especially at the beginning. They were exiles, strangers in a foreign land, compelled to earn their bread in the sweat of their brow, and perhaps being treated with indifference or even contempt because of their poverty. It was thus that the Eternal Father treated His Son and those nearest Him; unsearchable indeed are the mysteries of Divine Providence!

Return From Egypt
(Matt. 2:19–23)

Since the flight into Egypt had been a consequence of Herod's cruelty, it was natural that the Holy Family's exile should end with the tyrant's death. Herod died in the spring of 4 B.C. (750 from the foundation of Rome), and probably between March 27 and April 11,[45] five days after having had his son Antipater killed. He was seventy years of age and had reigned for thirty-seven years. Towards the end he had perpetrated new acts of cruelty, and his painful, ignominious death was commonly regarded as a just punishment for his sins. Josephus has left us a very detailed and frightening account of Herod's last days: [46]

Herod's illness grew worse every day in punishment for his sins. He felt that he was being consumed by a fire which glowed within his entrails. His intestines were ulcerated and certain parts of his body were rotting away, crawling with worms and giving off an unbearable stench. On the advice of his doctors he had himself brought to the warm baths at Callirrhoe [near the Dead Sea and almost at the foot of Machaerus, where later John the Baptist was beheaded]; but getting no relief from the baths, he had himself carried again to Jericho. When he saw that death was near he ordered the principal men of the kingdom to come to Jericho, and he commanded his sister Salome to kill them all as soon as he died so that, since the people would not mourn him, there would at least be great wailing and lamentation throughout the land when he departed from life. In these last days, Herod discovered that his son Antipater, believing his father already dead, had begun to act as if he were king, and the dying monarch immediately ordered him to be slain. When Herod finally died, and before the news of his death was divulged, Salome freed

[45] Cf. Schürer, I, 415, n. 167.
[46] Cf. *Ant.* xvii. 6–8. We give here a condensation and free translation of Josephus' description.

Sénès Photo

HERODIUM: *near Bethlehem.*

the great men of the kingdom, who had been shut up in the hippodrome where they were to have been slain; thus she left unfulfilled the tyrant's cruel command.

Archelaus gave his father a funeral worthy of a king and had the rotting corpse brought with great pomp and ceremony from Jericho to the palace-fortress of Herodium, where it was interred.

When Herod was dead, the angel appeared once more to Joseph and said to him: "Arise, and take the child and his mother, and go into the land of Israel, for those who sought the child's life are dead." The command was a general one, and did not specify where in Israel Joseph was to take up his abode. He seems to have had the intention of returning to Bethlehem and perhaps settling there, for what place could be more suitable for them than the town where Jesus had been born? Then, too, Bethlehem was Joseph's own town of origin and he undoubtedly had relatives there; and although his first contact with the town had not been pleasant, the inhabitants would now welcome him and his family back as old friends. In addition, they would once more be close to the holy cave where they had received the greatest Gift God ever gave to men.

However, when they entered their native land they discovered, perhaps at Gaza, that Archelaus had succeeded Herod in Judea. The dead king had first named his son Antipas as his heir, but he later changed his will and left Judea, Samaria and Idumea to Archelaus. The people acclaimed Archelaus as king on his father's death, but he did not possess this title, for although he had gone to Rome to beg for it, he had been refused, and Augustus had conceded him only the dignity of ethnarch.[47] Archelaus was considered to be a true son of his father in every kind of vice, but particularly in cruelty.[48] Thus, scarcely had he come into power when, to put down an uprising, he slaughtered no fewer than three thousand men.[49]

Naturally St. Joseph feared that if he settled within reach of the new tyrant, the Child's life would again be in danger, and so, when his fears were confirmed by a warning from heaven, instead of turning northeast along the Beit-Jibrin road which led to Bethlehem, he continued north along the *Via Maris,* crossed the plain of Saron and rounded the northern end of Mount Carmel; or perhaps upon reaching the present-day Tell Assawir, a short distance south of Caesarea, he headed east, entered the Wadi 'Ara, and reached the great plain of Esdrelon through Megiddo. From there the Holy Family would have seen the mountains of Nazareth, and after a short journey they would have joyfully entered the humble village amid the affectionate greetings of the inhabitants.

There is the greatest difference of opinion as to the duration of the exile in Egypt, some authors believing that it was as long as ten years, and others reducing it to a few months or even a few weeks. Obviously, it corresponded roughly with the period of time that elapsed between the visit of the Magi and the death of Herod. As we said above, Herod died at the end of March or the beginning of April in the Roman year 750; and the Magi apparently visited Bethlehem at least a year after our Saviour's birth, which, as we have seen, took place about the Roman year 748 or 6 B.C. in our reckoning. Hence it follows that barely two years intervened between Christ's birth and Herod's death, and since the adoration of the Magi cannot have taken place before the beginning of the second of these two years, it also follows that the exile in Egypt did not extend over more than a year, and perhaps lasted only a few months.[50]

---

[47] *Ant.* xvii. 11. 4; cf. 9. 3, 7.

[48] Cf. Schürer, I, 451, and *Ant.* xvii. 13. 2, where we read that "the Jews and Samaritans, no longer able to bear his cruelty and tyranny," denounced him to the Emperor, who condemned him to exile.

[49] *Ant.* xvii. 9. 3.

[50] Lagrange says "one month," Vilariño "a few months," Gomá "about three

St. Matthew closes his brief description of the return to Nazareth with the words: ". . . that there might be fulfilled what was spoken through the prophets, 'He shall be called a Nazarene' " (Matt. 2:23).

The word Ναζωραῖος is found in various forms, but the differences are slight and unimportant, and of much less interest than the real meaning of the term. It is evident that the word is closely connected with the name of the village, which in Greek is written Ναζαρέτ, a form that presupposes the letter *zain* in the original Hebrew, which would therefore come from the root *nzr* (=to make a vow). But it seems that the Hebrew name of the village was not written with the letter *zain* but with *tsade* [51] from the root *natsar* meaning "to guard or protect," or from *netser*, "a shoot or young plant." Hence Nazareth means *guardian* or *protector,* or else *young plant, branch* or *flower.* St. Jerome translates *netser* in this second sense in Isaias 11:1: "*Et flos* [netser] *de radice eius ascendet.*" But how can Ναζωραῖος be derived from *natsara* if the Greek *zeta* corresponds, not to the Hebrew *tsade,* but to *zain?* This is certainly a difficulty, but there are cases in which the Hebrew *tsade* is transcribed by the Greek *zeta,* as, for example, in Genesis 13:10 where the Hebrew *tso'ar* is transliterated into Greek as Ζόγορ.

What we have just said explains how Christ's being a Nazarene, i.e., from the city of Nazareth, is the fulfillment of the prophecy of Isaias 11:1.[52]

---

months"; Fillion thinks it was longer, "at least two or three years." (*Op. cit.,* I, 360.)

[51] We know this from the Syriac versions of the Gospel, which transcribe the name as *nosrath,* and from the name *hannosrî* which the Jews gave the Christians, and also from the present name for the village, *en Nasira.*

[52] Besides the usual commentaries, see Holzmeister, *Verb. Dom.,* 17 (1937), 21–26; Lyonnet, *Biblica,* 25 (1944), 196–206; Dalman, *op. cit.,* pp. 57 *ff.;* Albright, *Journal of Biblical Literature,* 65 (1946), 397–401, where other explanations of the word are given.

6. Hidden Life

at Nazareth

Thirty years spent in the obscurity of a workshop in a little village hidden in the hills of Galilee! Here is yet another unfathomable mystery of Divine Providence. Truly, as God said through Isaias: "My thoughts are not your thoughts: nor your ways my ways. . ." (55:8).

Men love noise, self-advertisement and glory, but the Son of God delighted in silence and retirement, and wished to be unknown not only by the world, but even by his closest neighbors. During the years which He spent in Nazareth, the world was in a turmoil; the gates of the temple of Janus in Rome were opened and the Roman eagles once more flew to the borders of the Empire to hold back the wave of invading barbarians, while in the capital itself the noble senatorial families paraded their wealth in magnificent displays, poets sang to the music of their lyres, great orators gloried in their own eloquence, and battle-scarred warriors dreamed of new conquests. In Judea, Archelaus, the son of the tyrant Herod, was outdoing his father in cruelty and all kinds of vice to such an extent that he was denounced by his subjects, exiled by Augustus, and his territory put under the direct rule of a Roman governor.[1]

But among all these vicissitudes, amid this continuous ebb and flow of events, the life of Christ passed

[1] *Ant.* xvii. 13.

quietly and peacefully behind a veil of silence and obscurity. Apart from the finding in the Temple, the evangelists have left us only a few short sentences concerning this long period of time: "And the child grew and became strong. He was full of wisdom and the grace of God was upon him" (Luke 2:40); "And Jesus advanced in wisdom and age and grace before God and men" (Luke 2:52); ". . . and [he] was subject to them" (Luke 2:51).

Yet in these years of the hidden life, devout souls find abundant food for contemplation; the very obscurity is a light to guide their steps, while the silence is a voice that instructs, consoles and animates them. And the little house at Nazareth is a school for Christian families; there fathers can learn how to rule gently and to provide for their family's necessities by their labor; mothers have there a perfect model of loving submission and of untiring attention to household tasks; and children can behold and copy the Son of God's modesty, industry, and perfect obedience to His earthly parents. In that poor and humble dwelling all can breathe in the sweet perfume that strengthens the soul and gives it the power to bear the trials of life with resignation and even with joy.

The Finding in the Temple
(Luke 2:41–50; cf. Map I)

Every male Israelite was obliged to go up to the Temple three times a year, as prescribed by the Law: "Three times in a year shall all thy males appear before the Lord thy God in the place which he shall choose: in the feast of unleavened bread [=the Passover], in the feast of weeks [=Pentecost], and in the feast of tabernacles" (Deut. 16:16; cf. Exod. 23:14–17; 34:23). But those living at a considerable distance from Jerusalem were permitted to reduce their visits to one a year, or they might even be exempted altogether. As is evident from the text, women were not bound by this obligation, but they frequently went to Jerusalem for these feasts out of devotion. The Law laid down no rule for children, but, as might be expected, the rabbis drew up a very full code of rules for them. A boy was bound to observe the whole Law when he reached puberty, which, in the opinion of the doctors of Israel, was at the age of thirteen years complete,[2] when he was given

---

[2] It was not enough for him to have *begun* his thirteenth year. In the *Mishnah*, *Niddah* 5:6, we read: "A boy twelve years old and one day—his vows must be

the name *bar misvah,* son of the precept or of the Law. However, he was bound by certain laws even before that age; how long before depended on the nature of the precept in question. According to the school of Hillel, the male children of Jerusalem were bound to present themselves before Yahweh on the three feasts mentioned above from the moment they were able to go up to the Temple holding their father's hand. A great rabbi used to say: "At five years old [one is fit] for the Scripture, at ten years for the *Mishnah,* at thirteen for [the fulfilling of] the commandments. . . ." [3] But even before the children reached the required age, the parents were to accustom them to the practice of the Law, so that its observance would be easier when they were obliged to keep it. [4]

Thus it can be seen that our Lord's visit to the Temple at the age of twelve was not obligatory, and that He would not be considered a "son of the Law" until a year later. However, as was the common practice, His parents brought Him with them to accustom Him little by little to the fulfillment of the precepts. Therefore we can say that, contrary to the opinion of Knabenbauer, Plummer, Prat and others, this visit was probably not His first since His infancy. St. Luke mentions the age of twelve, not because that was the first time the Child made the pilgrimage, but rather because he wished to record that our Lord remained in the Temple and spoke with the doctors precisely in that year and at that age. The very tone of the text shows that this was the evangelist's intention, for he does not say that "when he was twelve years old *they brought him,*" or *"he went up,"* but "when he was twelve years old they went up to Jerusalem . . . and . . . [he] *remained"*; from which it is clear that the mention of His age refers to what He did on that occasion and that the pilgrimage to the Temple is spoken about only incidentally. [5] Jesus, then, set out with Mary and

examined; if he is thirteen years old and one day, his vows are valid. . . ." The reason was that only at that age did he reach puberty, which was deemed to indicate the possession of full responsibility. We do not know what basis Marchal (*S. Luc,* p. 51) had for citing the authority of Lagrange and affirming that "the young Israelite began to be a *son of the precept,* not at twelve, but at fifteen years of age." He would have done well to have given some definite quotation. Actually, according to the *Mishnah,* a Jewish boy became subject to the whole Law, not at twelve or fifteen but at the end of his thirteenth year.

[3] *Mishnah, Aboth* 5:21.

[4] On these points cf. Str.-Bill., II, 144–147.

[5] The Vulgate preserves the relationship between the various grammatical parts of the sentence: "Et cum factus esset annorum duodecim, ascendentibus illis Jerosolymam secundum consuetudinem diei festi, consummatisque diebus, cum redirent, remansit puer Jesus in Jerusalem, et non cognoverunt parentes ejus."

Joseph in the caravan which was leaving Nazareth and which, after crossing the great plain of Esdrelon, would pass through present-day Jenin, Qubatiyeh, Sichem, Lubban, Bethel, and el-Bireh,[6] taking four or five days to cover the distance between Nazareth and Jerusalem (about eighty-seven miles by the present road). On reaching Mount Scopus they would see and greet with psalms the Holy City.

We do not know where the Holy Family stayed in Jerusalem; perhaps it was in the house of some relative or friend, or maybe in one of the many tents which were pitched on the Mount of Olives, since the city could not provide accommodation for the great multitude of pilgrims. From there they would descend every morning to attend the ceremonies in the Temple. With what reverence and love must Christ have entered His Father's house! What an example of modesty, recollection and deep devotion the Holy Family must have been to all who saw them!

At sunset on the first day of the Azymes, i.e., the 14th of Nisan, the lamb was sacrificed and eaten (Deut. 16:6; Ex. 12:6). The pilgrims had to spend that night in Jerusalem, but on the following morning, in conformity with Deuteronomy 16:7, they could return home.[7] However, the Holy Family, out of devotion, remained for all the feasts of the Passover and set out for Nazareth only after the eighth and most solemn day (Deut. 16:8).

At this point, Divine Providence had a heavy trial in store for Mary and Joseph. Amid the confusion of the crowds, it was easy for a child to leave his parents' side without their noticing it. This Jesus did, and when Mary and Joseph found that He was missing they were not immediately alarmed, for it was very likely that He had joined some relatives or neighbors and that they would find Him at the first halt on the journey home, at the place where they were going to spend the night. Or perhaps Mary and Joseph became separated from each other in the confusion of starting the return trip, and each thought that Jesus was with the other.

All unsuspecting, then, they went a day's journey or, as the text says, "a day's road" ($\dot{\eta}\mu\acute{\epsilon}\rho as\ \dot{o}\delta\acute{o}\nu$), an expression that is found in other passages, e.g., 3 Kings 19:4. According to Josephus,[8] a day's journey would be about twenty miles for a good walker, for he says that such a

---

[6] For a more detailed description of the route, see pp. 98 f. above.
[7] Cf. Str.-Bill., II, 147 f.
[8] *Life* 52.

person could cover the distance from Galilee to Jerusalem (about sixty-two miles as the crow flies) in three days. But for a travelling party which included women, old people and children, a day's journey would be much less than twenty miles, especially on the first day when they would start late in order to allow everyone to do last-minute errands. Taking all this into account, we can place some faith in the tradition, unfortunately not very ancient, which points to the present-day town of el-Bireh, ten miles from Jerusalem, as the first stage of the journey. Here one can still see the ruins of a church of the time of the Crusades, which may have been built to commemorate the Gospel incident.[9]

We can imagine how solicitously Mary and Joseph went searching for Jesus among their relatives and friends when the caravan halted for the night. As they went from group to group without result, their anxiety grew, and when they found that no one had seen the Child during the whole journey, they became thoroughly alarmed. Only the heart of a mother, the heart of the Mother of God, could fully appreciate Mary's grief, pain and anxiety as she and Joseph set out to retrace their steps to Jerusalem. As they went, they questioned everyone they met, particularly the stragglers from their own caravan who were slowly making their way to the stopping place. But no one knew anything of the Child. They spent the whole of the next day combing the city, searching streets and squares, and asking about Jesus at the houses of relatives and friends. They traversed the city from end to end, but all in vain. Finally, on the third day,[10] they went up to the Temple, and to their great joy found Him there, "sitting in the midst of the teachers, both listening to them and asking them questions."

It is not possible to ascertain in which part of the Temple they found Him, since the word "Temple" should be taken here in the wide sense as designating the whole building, including the porches. The Gospel is not here referring to the lessons which the rabbis used to give to the public during the feasts, for during these classes the listeners were not allowed to pose questions, although discussion was permitted and was common in the schools which were usually attached to

---

[9] See D. Baldi, *Enchiridion Locorum Sanctorum: Documenta Sancti Evangelii loca respicientia* (Jerusalem, 1935), pp. 208 *ff.*: "Item Albiera [el-Bireh] castrum, ubi est ecclesia S. Mariae Virginis in qua recognovit perdidisse filium puerum Yhesum" (fourteenth-century text).

[10] We are of the opinion that they reached Jesusalem on the evening of the same day on which they had set out, and therefore this day would be counted as the first of their search.

the synagogues and in which the teachers not only allowed but encouraged the pupils to ask questions and propose difficulties.[11] But St. Luke was not speaking of a school, for there were many teachers and not, as usually happened, only one. The gathering was probably one of those meetings which the rabbis were accustomed to hold in one of the outer parts of the Temple or perhaps in one of the courtyards, during which points of the Law or the Holy Scriptures in general were discussed. The public was permitted to attend these gatherings and allowed to ask questions, while the teachers in their turn might interrogate the listeners. The teachers usually sat on stools, and the listeners on mats upon the ground, as St. Paul did when he sat "at the feet of Gamaliel" (Acts 22:3). Hence Jesus was not seated on a chair in the center of and overlooking the assembly, as if He were teaching a class, although that is the way many painters have mistakenly depicted Him. Instead, He had humbly taken His place among the listeners and was asking questions and answering the teachers in the same way as the others. But his searching inquiries and skillful replies had won the admiration of these men who had grown old in the study of the Sacred Books. As they listened to Him, no doubt they were thinking that He would in time become a great doctor; and perhaps they followed the example of the Rabbi Gamaliel who, having received a wise reply from the young Chananya ben Chananya, tenderly kissed the boy and predicted that in due time he would be an oracle in Israel.[12] Would that these questions and answers of the Son of God had been preserved for us! Would that we, like the doctors in the Temple, were allowed to admire the wisdom and discretion displayed by the young Christ! Did the discussion turn upon the coming of the Messias and the wonders that He was to work? We do not know, and must content ourselves with adoring wordlessly what God has willed to keep hidden under the veil of silence.

Inexpressible indeed must have been the joy of Mary and Joseph at the sight of Christ! Though Mary was the holiest among the daughters of men, she still had all a mother's natural feelings. Therefore, without waiting for the grave assembly to disperse, she must have spontaneously embraced her Son, and uttered the loving reproof: "Son,

---

[11] Rabbi Pinechas used to say: "In Jerusalem there were 480 synagogues, and each one had a primary school for the teaching of the Bible and a secondary school for the teaching of the *Mishnah*" (Str.-Bill., II, 150). The number of the synagogues is obviously exaggerated; but there were certainly many of them.

[12] Str.-Bill., II, 151.

why hast thou done so to us? Behold, thy father and I have been seeking thee sorrowing." Our Lord's reply was somewhat surprising. It was very natural that His mother and foster father should have gone in search of Him, yet He said to them: "How is it that you sought me? Did you not know that I must be about my Father's business?" [13] It is difficult not to feel a certain harshness in these words of our Lord's, a harshness which some authors, like Lagrange and Prat, try to soften by assuming, more or less gratuitously, that Christ smiled as He spoke them. The Word Incarnate undoubtedly practiced the humble obedience of a son, yet He also showed His sovereign independence as God. This was not to be the last time the Man-God showed His transcendence above all the laws of flesh and blood, and precisely in regard to His mother.

Mary and Joseph did not understand the meaning of Jesus' reply. They knew that their Son had to be about His Father's business, but they could not understand why the service of His Father had led Him to separate Himself from them without warning and to cause them so much sorrow and pain. Nor was it given to them to foresee the other great sufferings which His perfect obedience to His heavenly Father

---

[13] As Joüon rightly remarks (*L'Évangile de N.S. Jésus-Christ* [Paris, 1930], the phrase ἐν τοῖς τοῦ πατρός μου can have a twofold meaning: (1) "in the *house* of my Father"; "near my Father," e.g., as in Esther 7:9, ἐν τοῖς 'Αμάν; in Job 18:19, ἐν τοῖς αὐτοῦ, and in the classics; or (2) "in the *things*, in the *service* of my Father," e.g., as in Matthew 16:23 and Mark 8:33; τὰ τοῦ Θεοῦ; τὰ τῶν ἀνθρώπων; in Matthew 20:15, ἐν τοῖς ἐμοῖς; and in 1 Corinthians 7:32, 34, τὰ τοῦ κυρίου; τὰ τοῦ κόσμου. From the philological point of view, both versions are perfectly justified. The Peschitto version and a good number of Fathers give the first; the Vulgate and many commentators give the second. Among modern authors, Zahn, Lagrange, Prat, Plummer and others prefer the first, while Joüon, Dalman (*Jesus-Jeshua*, p. 36), Fillion and others choose the second. Zahn explains at length the sense of our Lord's reply in conformity with the first interpretation: Jesus wonders that they went looking in the houses of the city instead of going immediately to the Temple, since they should have known that the house of His Father was more important to Him than all else. But according to this reasoning, our Lord was replying only to the second part of our Lady's statement: "Thy father and I have been seeking thee sorrowing," and not to the first: "Son, why hast thou done so to us?", which was obviously the principal part and which conveyed a loving reproof. It would have been strange if Jesus had disregarded this question completely in replying. However, if we accept the second interpretation ("in the *things*, or the *service* of my Father"), His reply is a full one, as if to say: "There was no reason for so much anxiety and affliction in seeking me, for you should have known where I would be. As regards my having left you, I did it for higher motives, to attend to the things of my Father." On this point see the booklet by Juan José Gómez, O.F.M., *Jesús en el templo* (Murcia, 1930), pp. 43–59; also Patrick J. Temple's article " 'House' or 'Business' in Luke 2, 49?" in *The Catholic Biblical Quarterly*, 1 (1939), 342–352, which upholds the interpretation that we prefer.

would occasion.[14] Carefully His Mother kept in her heart these, and no doubt many other things that He said down through the years.

Wisdom and Grace

"And the child grew and became strong. He was full of wisdom and the grace of God was upon him" (Luke 2:40). "And Jesus advanced in wisdom and age and grace before God and man" (Luke 2:52).

The Word made flesh was true man and wished to be like other men in everything, sin excepted. Therefore the Child Jesus passed through the same stages of development as other children. He grew in wisdom, that is to say, His mind developed, His judgment matured, His powers of observation increased and He was continually adding to His knowledge. While His mind was being formed, His body also developed—that is the meaning of the word ἡλικία [15]—His limbs growing stronger and His height increasing. And God was pleased [16] with this twofold growth, His pleasure becoming greater, as it were, in proportion to His Son's development because the Child's acts became increasingly perfect, according as His mind and body matured. Men, too, were pleased at His progress, for it gave them a certain joy to see Him grow up healthy and robust, increasing day by day in intelligence and good judgment.

His physical development was a real growth and followed exactly the normal human lines. But we cannot say the same of His mental development, and the problem which it presents is a delicate one, requiring several distinctions. In Christ as man we must distinguish between three types of knowledge—*beatific* knowledge or knowledge of *vision, infused* knowledge, and *experimental* or *acquired* knowledge. There could be no development of the first or the second since He possessed

---

[14] René Thibault (*Le sens des paroles du Christ* [Bruxelles, 1940], pp. 17 *f.*) supposes that Jesus had warned His parents that He would remain in the Temple, but that they had not understood Him or had forgotten. We do not think that this is the true interpretation; the evangelist's words contain something more profound and hidden than that.

[15] This word can mean either "age" or "stature." The second meaning is evident in Luke 19:3, where it is said that Zacchaeus, being τῇ ἡλικίᾳ μικρός ("small in stature"), was not able to see Jesus because of the crowd. This meaning of "stature" is more in harmony with the context here.

[16] In this passage χάρις should not be taken to mean sanctifying grace but rather the favor of God or of man, as, for example, in Acts 2:47.

them in all their fullness from the first instant of the hypostatic union. But the third could increase since it depended on the sensible objects around Him.[17]

Experimental knowledge is that which man acquires by the use of his senses and by the elaboration of the ideas which the intellective faculty derives from the elements supplied to it by the senses. As the Apostle says (Heb. 5:8), Jesus grew in this knowledge as other men do, in the sense that He widened His human horizons. He learned His trade from Joseph, and from Mary and Joseph He learned the lessons of daily life. From the human point of view, His cast of mind and His mode of expressing Himself were shaped by the prevailing intellectual atmosphere, by His race, His nation and His city.[18]

He could not, of course, grow in sanctity as such, but only as considered in its effects; in other words, His actions became increasingly perfect as actions but they did not, indeed they could not, increase grace in Him, for He already possessed the fullness thereof.[19]

Obedience and Toil

"And he . . . was subject to them" (Luke 2:51).

"Is not this the carpenter's son?" (Matt. 13:55).

"Is not this the carpenter [ὁ τέκτων], the son of Mary?" (Mark 6:3).

Men fell under the power of the devil through the disobedience of

---

[17] On this point St. Thomas has written the following beautiful words: "Tam scientia infusa animae Christi quam scientia beata fuit effectus agentis infinitae virtutis, qui potest simul totum operari; et ita in neutra scientia Christus profecit, sed a principio eam perfectam habuit. Sed scientia acquisita causatur ab intellectu agente, qui non simul totum operatur, sed successive; et ideo secundum hanc scientiam Christus non a principio scivit omnia, sed paulatim et post aliquod tempus, scilicet in perfecta aetate" (*Summa Theologica*, III, q. 12, a. 1, ad 1).

[18] I. Gomá, *El Evangelio explicado,* 4 vols. (Barcelona, 1940), *in. loc.*

[19] As St. Thomas says: "Cum in Christo fuerit omnis gratiae plenitudo, et fuerit simul comprehensor ac viator, impossibile fuit aliquo modo in illo gratiam augeri." And more explicitly: "In sapientia et gratia aliquis potest proficere dupliciter. Uno modo secundum ipsos habitus sapientiae et gratiae augmentatos; et sic Christus in eis non proficiebat. Alio modo secundum effectus, inquantum scilicet aliquis sapientiora et virtuosiora opera facit; et sic Christus proficiebat sapientia et gratia, sicut et aetate; quia secundum processum aetatis perfectiora opera faciebat, ut se verum hominem demonstraret, et in his quae sunt ad Deum, et in his quae sunt ad homines" (*Summa Theologica*, III, q. 7, ad 3).

the first Adam, and God willed to save them through the obedience of the second Adam. From His first entry into the world, Jesus exclaimed: "Behold, I come—(in the head of the book it is written of me)—to do thy will, O God" (Heb. 10:7). He began His life with an act of obedience, He continued it in obedience and He ended it with obedience, "becoming obedient to death, even to death on a cross" (Phil. 2:8). The little house at Nazareth was indeed a house of obedience, for in it God obeyed man, the Creator the creature, and He who was All obeyed two human beings who, of themselves, were nothing. The three members of the Holy Family played roles very different from the ones which worldly wisdom would have assigned them. Jesus, the Lord of Heaven and earth, who could command the angelic hierarchy, who with a single word created the entire universe from nothing, obeyed Mary and Joseph, and gave commands to none. Mary, though full of grace and the holiest soul that came from the hands of God, was still a mere creature; but she gave commands to her Creator and, in her turn, obeyed Joseph. And Joseph, a great saint but far below his spouse in sanctity, gave commands to Jesus and to Mary, and was not subject to either of them. " 'He was subject. . . .' Who? To whom? God was subject to man, not only to Mary but also to Joseph. . . . What a stupendous miracle! That God should obey a woman, what unparalleled humility! That a woman should give commands to God, what unheard-of sublimity!" [20]

The house at Nazareth was also a house of toil. Joseph had to support the family with the work of his hands and the sweat of his brow. Mary had to prepare the meals, grind the wheat in the little hand mill and bake the bread; she had to spin, sew and wash the clothes; in a word, she spent the day engaged in the household tasks proper to a mother of a poor family. And when Jesus was a child He would help His Mother to sweep the house, light the fire, grind the wheat, and carry home her purchases from the market; and when she went to the fountain He would accompany her, carrying His own small pitcher to fill. This fountain was no doubt the same one that is still there today at the eastern end of the town, for it is the only fountain in Nazareth, apart from another towards the northwest near the Maronite church, which gives only a meager and intermittent supply of water. In ancient times the spring from which our Lady drew water

[20] St. Bernard, *Sermo I super "Missus est."*

rose more to the north, from which point it was later channeled to the present site.

Since our Lord wished to be like us in all things except sin, He studied with the other boys of His own age, going to the synagogue, listening to the teacher, learning and reciting His lessons as the rest of the pupils did. And when He grew older He set to work to help support the family. In those days there were certainly public schools for the children, and although there was not one in every village, Nazareth probably had its own. Classes were generally held in a room adjoining the synagogue, but sometimes there was a separate school building. Tradition attributes to Josue ben Gamla (A.D. 63–65?) an ordinance which made school attendance obligatory for boys of six and over.[21]

Even today in Palestine one can still see little hand mills being used for grinding grain. The peasants, however, rarely use them but the Bedouins frequently do, for in their nomadic life a portable mill is always useful and often indispensable. This utensil was common among the Jews, and our Lord mentions its use in Luke 17:35: "Two women will be grinding together; one will be taken, and the other will be left." And the Book of Judges (9:53) records that a woman broke Abimelech's skull by throwing a piece of a millstone down on him. As regards the baking of bread, two of the methods used are worthy of note. The present writer saw the simplest and most rudimentary one being used in the valley of the Jordan. The dough was merely placed on the ground and covered with glowing embers (*panis subcinericius:* bread baked under the embers); after a few minutes it was retrieved and, though not fully baked, it was nevertheless edible. Perhaps the bread which the angel gave Elias (3 Kings 19:6) was of this type, although the Hebrew expression strictly means bread baked on hot stones. The second method required the use of the *tannur* which, one could say, is no longer employed in Palestine and which we saw only in upper Galilee, while in Jerusalem and the surrounding district we found only one, and that was in a Syrian household. The *tannur* is a circular cavity about three feet deep and two feet in diameter. It is first heated to a high temperature by burning branches in it and then the cook rapidly and skillfully spreads thin cakes of dough all around the smooth, concave sides of the open oven. At present in Palestine baking is most commonly done with the *tabun* and the *sadj*. The *tabun* is a kind of clay oven built on the ground and shaped like a beehive

21 Cf. Str.-Bill., III, 664: see 155, n. 11.

with a hole in the top. The dough is inserted through this hole and the oven is then covered with embers. The *sadj* is an iron basin that is placed bottom-up on the fire. When the metal is heated the dough is spread thinly on top and requires only a few minutes to bake. This utensil has the advantage of being easily portable, and we have seen families break their journey for a few moments to bake their bread on the *sadj* and then continue on their way.

St. Joseph worked as a carpenter (Matt. 13:55) and, as was natural, Jesus learned the trade from His foster father (Mark 6:3). The Word Incarnate, who was to be our Model in everything, wished to give us the good example of manual labor. His work was humble but by no means despised, for persons of good position did not disdain to teach their sons a trade. As Rabbi Gamaliel used to say: "To what can we compare a man who works at a trade? To a vineyard surrounded by a wall, and a garden protected by a hedge." [22]

It is not surprising to find that the Fathers are not fully agreed on the nature of St. Joseph's trade, since the word τέκτων means simply a craftsman, a man who works one type of material, be it iron, wood or stone. The Hebrew counterpart is *horesh*, which is made more specific by adding the name of the material worked, e.g., "artificers in *wood* and *stone*" (2 Kings 5:11), which the Septuagint translated as τεκτόνας ξύλων καὶ τεκτόνας λίθων; see also "an artificer in *brass*" (3 Kings 7:14). Several Fathers, St. Hilary included, interpreted the word in the sense of an *ironworker*.[23] But from a very early date popular opinion has leaned towards carpentry as Joseph's trade: St. Justin wrote that Jesus was regarded as a tradesman, "one who did manual work making plows and yokes." [24] This view, favored in pictures and paintings, is the one that has prevailed and that is now generally accepted.[25]

---

[22] Str.-Bill., II, 10. A short distance north of the Basilica of the Annunciation, and adjoining the Franciscan monastery, there is a church called the Workshop of Joseph, or the Church of the Nutrition, under which there are several interesting chambers. A little to the west of the basilica, in the ground beneath the church and convent of the Dames de Nazareth, extensive ruins have been found which have awakened great interest, for some authorities believe that the Holy Family lived here and that this was the site of the Church of the Nutrition mentioned by many pilgrims, and particularly by Arculf (seventh century). Others (e.g., Dr. Kopp) identify the old Church of the Nutrition with the present Greek Orthodox church of St. Gabriel, near the fountain.

[23] "Sed plane hic erat fabri filius, *ferrum igne vincentis*," PL 9, 996.

[24] *Dial. cum Tryph.* 88: PG 6, 687.

[25] See Höpfl's article, "Nonne hic est fabri filius?" in *Biblica*, 4 (1923), 41–55, and Sutcliffe's article, "S. Joseph Faber Lignarius" in *Verb. Dom.*, 5 (1925),

Christ's Appearance

When we set out to consider what our Lord looked like, we spontaneously recall the psalmist's words: ". . . beautiful above the sons of men" (Ps. 44:3), for we cannot think of the Son of the Virgin as other than handsome and graceful, displaying in His face and bearing a charming and attractive dignity. But others have not felt that way, and, strange as it may seem to us, some of the Fathers not only believed that Christ was not particularly handsome but that He was uncomely or even positively ugly. For example, St. Justin says that it was prophesied of Christ that He would be of lowly aspect and without beauty,[26] and Clement of Alexandria, Tertullian, St. Basil and others were of the same opinion. This strange conclusion was based, on the one hand, on Isaias' description (chapters 52–53), and, on the other, on the contrast between the humility and lowliness of His first coming and the glory and splendor of His second.[27] So ill-founded an opinion could not be generally accepted or entertained for long. The whole Gospel represents Christ as being so attractive and so charming that it is impossible to picture Him as ugly and repulsive in appearance. And so, from the very earliest times, the great majority of the Fathers and ecclesiastical writers have pictured Him as possessing physical beauty, a dignified and manly attractiveness which was the reflection, as it were, of the incomparable beauty of His soul.

The fact that the most ancient representations of our Saviour differ greatly from one another makes it abundantly clear that no authentic outline of His features has been handed down to us.[28] From the combination of these primitive representations in the Byzantine period there evolved the portrait which is nowadays regarded as classical and which corresponds at least in its main outlines to the description left us by St. John Damascene and to the detailed word-picture which was supposedly written by one Publius Lentulus, who claimed that he was

74–79. In a searching and very learned article entitled "Charpentier ou maçon?" in *Revue de Théologie et de Philosophie* (1948), pp. 161–192, Émile Lombard concludes in favor of carpentry.

[26] *Dial. cum Tryph.* 14: *PG* 6, 506.

[27] "Ex his et aliis eiusmodi prophetarum dictis, o Trypho, aiebam, alia in primum Christi adventum dicta sunt, in quo ingloriam et informem et mortalem speciem habiturus praedicatur; alia in alterum eius adventum, cum in gloria ex nubibus aderit." (St. Justin, *loc. cit.*)

[28] A number of ancient portraits of Christ are reproduced in *Dict. d'Arch. Chrét.* (Paris, 1927), VII, 2399–2462.

the predecessor of Pontius Pilate, but which really dates back no further than the twelfth century:

He [Jesus] is tall in stature, distinguished in appearance, commanding respect and inspiring both love and reverence. His hair, chestnut brown and reaching to his shoulders . . . is parted in the middle after the manner of the Nazarenes. His forehead is smooth and serene, His face is handsome, slightly ruddy in complexion and without wrinkle or blemish. . . . His beard is full . . . and forked at the chin. His eyes are clear and bluish in color. When He reproves He is terrible to behold; when He admonishes He is kind and gentle. His whole bearing is joyful, yet grave. He has been seen to cry but never to laugh. . . . He speaks little, and then modestly. . . . He is the most beautiful of the sons of men.[29]

The Gospel of the Infancy

Before we go on to the public life of our Lord, we shall say a few words about the "Gospel of the Infancy," as it has been called. St. Mark passes over the Infancy in silence and begins his Gospel with the Precursor, while St. John opens his with Christ's eternal generation. Thus only St. Matthew and St. Luke write about the mysteries of the Infancy.

St. Matthew's Gospel (1:18–2, 23) contains the following episodes: the miraculous conception of Christ and the marriage of Mary and Joseph; the visit of the Magi, and references to the birth of Christ; the flight into Egypt and the slaughter of the Innocents; the return from Egypt to Nazareth. St. Luke records the following events: the foretelling of the Precursor's birth, the Annunciation to Mary; Mary's visit to Elizabeth and the birth of the Precursor; Birth of Christ; adoration of the shepherds; Circumcision; Presentation and Purification; return to Nazareth; the Child's growing up; His being lost, and the finding in the Temple. St. Matthew gives Christ's genealogy at the beginning of his Gospel (1:1–17), while Luke gives it when referring to His baptism by John (3:23–38).

Thus, of the two accounts, St. Luke's is the more complete, and it is he who has preserved for us the three canticles, the Magnificat, Benedictus and Nunc dimittis, which St. Matthew does not even mention. The two narratives are very different in character, but do not

[29] Cf. F. Vigouroux, "Lentulus," in *Dict. de la Bible,* IV, cols. 168–172.

contradict each other in the smallest detail; rather, they harmonize perfectly and are mutually complementary. Even a superficial examination of the two Gospels shows that St. Matthew's narrative revolves around Joseph, and St. Luke's around Mary: in the latter account alone do we find the angel's message to Mary, i.e., the Annunciation, her visit to Elizabeth, and her Purification in the Temple. Hence it is with good reason that the two first chapters of St. Luke are called "the Gospel of Mary." But where did the evangelist get his information about events which were witnessed only by the Blessed Virgin and about which only she could know—for example, her conversation with the archangel at the Annunciation? St. Luke himself seems to hint at the answer when, after relating the adoration of the shepherds, he writes: "Mary kept in mind all these things, pondering them in her heart" (2:19; cf. 2:51). He must, therefore, have received these precious confidences either directly or indirectly from Mary, and was thus able to record them for our instruction and consolation. If he knew our Lady personally, and though not probable it is still not impossible that he did, he could have heard them from her own lips. And if he never met her, he could have gleaned reliable information from those who had known her.

The authenticity and even the historical reliability of the "Gospel of the Infancy," and of St. Luke's account in particular, have been and still are impugned. Hostile critics maintain that St. Luke's first two chapters are written in a style that is markedly Hebrew and very different from that employed in the rest of the Gospel, and that therefore both sections cannot have been written by the same author. Furthermore, these critics say, the first two chapters form a complete unit by themselves and could very well be regarded as a small Gospel distinct from the rest, which, since it is wholly concerned with the public life of our Lord, would lose nothing by the separation. And if the first two chapters were removed, the account of John the Baptist's ministry would then serve as a very fitting prologue to the remainder. The critics then conclude that St. Luke's Gospel originally opened with John the Baptist's preaching, and that the account of our Lord's Infancy was added later.

We unhesitatingly grant that St. Luke's first two chapters are different in style from the rest and that the Gospel could well begin without them, but we deny the conclusion which the critics draw from these premises. The opening chapters are written in a distinctively

Hebrew style, but it is not difficult to explain why. It is quite possible and even probable that when St. Luke was composing his Gospel there were in circulation several accounts of Christ's Infancy written in Aramaic. There is nothing strange about that, since there was considerable literary activity at the time. And what would be more natural than that the evangelist should have translated these documents into Greek and used them as source material? Thus his first chapters, drawn as they were from such sources, would have a decidedly Hebrew tinge which would not carry over into the rest of the Gospel.

It is also true that St. Luke's Gospel could fittingly begin with the third chapter, the preaching of John the Baptist, and that the first two chapters would not be missed, as they would in the case of St. Mark. But this is no compelling argument against the authenticity of these chapters. By its very nature, the account of the Infancy is completely different from the story of the public life. What wonder, then, that each forms a complete unit in itself, perfectly comprehensible even when standing alone? And yet, despite the mutual independence of the two sections, the account of the Infancy provides a very suitable prelude to, and complement of, the public life.

There is another objection of a general nature which is raised against the historical validity of the whole Gospel of the Infancy. In the case of great men, the objectors say, attention is first fixed on their public life, on their achievements and glorious deeds, and it is not until later, and sometimes only after an extended period, that public curiosity is aroused concerning the childhood of these men who, in their mature years, accomplished such great things. Then fancy is given free rein and childhood legends are concocted to suit the adult attainments of each hero. However, no matter how persuasive the concrete examples of this tendency may be, we know that the Gospel of the Infancy is not just a popular fable. For one thing, a notable lapse of time is required for building up such a legend, but the first two chapters of St. Luke were part of his Gospel from the beginning, and there is not the slightest evidence that the public life of Christ was recorded first and the account of His Infancy not composed until much later. Furthermore, our Lord possessed characteristics which were totally lacking in those heroes whose biographies are cited as examples of the addition of childhood legends. For centuries the Jews had been awaiting the coming of the Messias, and among many other prophecies there was one which specified the place of His birth. It was, therefore, very natural that the faithful should have been interested in His birthplace and in everything that referred to His first years on earth; and this all the more so since they not only marvelled at His wondrous works, but also felt an ardent and tender personal love for Him, a love which wished to know and treasure even the smallest details about the Beloved. Hence it is neither reasonable nor scientific to apply to our Lord the norms which do hold good or can hold good for other men, no matter how important these men may seem.

The "Gospel of the Infancy" has also been attacked because of the miraculous nature of many of its episodes, such as the prophecies, the angelic apparitions, etc. Obviously anyone who rejects the supernatural must refuse to believe that these things could have happened; for such a one supernatural events, by the mere fact of their being supernatural, are not, and cannot be, historical. But here we are no longer in the field of exegesis and history but rather in that of apologetics, which is outside the scope of this work. A person who admits the Incarnation will not be surprised to find events of a supernatural nature in the account of the Infancy; rather he will regard them as connatural and in perfect harmony with the great mystery of God's becoming man.[30]

---

[30] A very full treatment of our Lord's Infancy will be found in Patrick J. Temple's *Pattern Divine: Our Lord's Hidden Life* (St. Louis: B. Herder Book Co., 1950).

The Public Life

7. Beginning of the Public Life (Late A. D. 27)

The Precursor

Near the east bank of the Jordan, opposite Jericho and close to the Monastery of St. John, the ruins of an ancient church can still be seen. This venerable monument has stood here for fifteen hundred years, yet, about A.D. 27, five hundred years before it was built, these now-deserted banks of the Jordan were swarming with crowds who had come from Perea, Judea and from far-off Galilee, as well as from the neighboring cities of Bethannabris, Abila, Livias and Bezemoth (Bethsimoth), from Jericho and even from Jerusalem itself. For something unusual was happening and the stirrings of a new spirit were being felt throughout Israel.

The angel whose coming had been foretold five hundred years before by the prophet Malachias, had finally appeared:

"Behold I send my angel,

and he shall prepare the way before my face" (3:1). The voice which Isaias had heard in his prophetic ecstasy was now ringing through Israel:

"The voice of him who cries:

Prepare ye in the desert the way for the Lord:

Make straight in the wilderness a path for our God" (40:3). After four centuries of silence the voice of a prophet was once more raised in the land. The longed-for

Messias was about to appear, and John was His Precursor: the great King was coming, and John was His herald.

VOCATION OF JOHN THE BAPTIST

St. Luke begins his narrative of John's public ministry with an unusually solemn formula: "Now in the fifteenth year of the reign of Tiberius Caesar, when Pontius Pilate was Procurator of Judea, and Herod tetrarch of Galilee, and Philip his brother tetrarch of the district of Iturea and Trachonitis, and Lysanias tetrarch of Abilene, during the high priesthood of Annas and Caiphas, *the word of God came to John,* the son of Zachary, in the desert" (3:1–2). This is the formula which is used in the Old Testament to announce the supernatural vocation whereby God sent a prophet to fulfill some mission (cf. Jer. 1:1; Isai. 38:4 *f*.). St. Luke also indicates that John had been preparing himself for the call, for he tells us that the Baptist had been living in the deserts from his youth until the day of his manifestation to Israel (1:80). Upon hearing the voice of God, the Precursor abandoned his life of retirement and began his ministry. The Lord was sending him; he had nothing to fear. Another prophet, Jeremias, had said to God: "Ah, ah, ah, Lord God, behold, I cannot speak, for I am a child." And the Lord had replied: "Say not: I am a child: for thou shalt go to all that I shall send thee, and whatsoever I shall command thee, thou shalt speak. Be not afraid at their presence. . . ." And the supreme reason why Jeremias was not to be afraid was: "I am with thee to deliver thee, saith the Lord" (Jer. 16–8). John, too, had the same assurance.

BACKGROUND
(Matt. 3:1; Mark 1:4; Luke 3:3; cf. Map IV)

"Now in those days," writes St. Matthew (3:1), "John the Baptist came, preaching in the desert of Juda . . ." And St. Mark says: "John the Baptist was in the desert, preaching a baptism of penance (1:4)." [1] We can readily understand John's going into the desert to live a life of solitude and prepare himself for his ministry. But it is

---

[1] This reading, adopted by Knabenbauer, Lagrange and others, is to be preferred to that of the Latin version: "Fuit Joannes in deserto baptizans [or, rather, baptizans in deserto] et praedicans baptismum . . ."; which is also that of the *textus receptus.*

Sira Photo

The Desert of Juda.

rather strange that he should also have chosen the desert as the scene of his preaching. There is no doubt that the place in question is the region which is still called the desert of Juda, the arid and sparsely cultivated territory that extends east from the crest of the mountains of Judea, or in other words, from a line running from Jerusalem towards Bethlehem, Thecua and still farther south—certainly not a place well suited for gathering crowds.

St. Luke gives us the explanation of this apparent enigma when he says: "And he went into all the region about the Jordan, preaching a baptism of penance." By collating this text with the ones quoted above, we gather that the valley of the Jordan was considered to be part of the desert region. Josephus tells us that the valley was known as "the great plain" (τὸ μέγα πεδίον); [2] but he also calls it "the desert region, through which the Jordan flows." [3] In the Old Testament there is a distinction made between the *'Arabah* (valley of the Jordan, cf. Jos. 8:14; 11:2) and the *midbar yehudah* ("desert of Juda"), a term found only in Judges 1:16 and Psalm 62:1. St. Mark seems to maintain this distinction when he says: '. . . the Spirit drove him [Jesus] forth into the desert" (1:12), i.e., the Spirit drove our Lord from the *Jordan,* where He had been baptized (v. 9), into the desert.

From these facts we gather that the valley of the Jordan was

[2] *Wars* iv. 8. 2. [3] *Ibid.* iii. 10. 7.

known by its own special name, and that it was distinct from the desert of Juda, but that in general it, too, was a desert region. The evangelists, who were not concerned with distinguishing rigidly between the various regions, regarded as a unit the whole territory between Mount Olivet and the River Jordan; and they were all the more likely to do so since the country south of Jericho is very dry and can reasonably be looked upon as an extension of the desert of Juda. However, we must remember that the valley of the Jordan did not then present the same aspect as it does now. The Jericho of Herod was much larger than the wretched town of today,[4] and there was much more land under cultivation, with groves of palm and balsam trees.[5] In the north, almost at the foot of the Alexandreion (=Qarn Sartabeh), flourished the city of Phasaelis, also founded by Herod. On the other side of the Jordan, at the foot of the mountains of Moab, lay Bethannabris, at the entrance to the Wadi Nimrin; and more to the south were Abila and Livias, formerly called Betharamphtha, where Herod had a palace; [6] and almost on the shores of the Dead Sea stood Bezemoth.[7] Although these cities were only oases in the desert, they made the Jordan valley a very different place from the barren expanse it is today. All that remains of Phasaelis is a few ruins; the very site of Bethannabris is scarcely discernible; Tell-Kefrein (=Abila) and es-Sweimeh (=Bezemoth) are inhabited by a handful of Bedouins, while er-Rameh has been replaced by a sleepy hamlet built a short distance from the ancient Tell. When we consider this bygone glory we can readily understand how a large crowd could easily have come from the region about the Jordan to hear the preaching of John.

St. Matthew and St. Mark speak only of John's public ministry, while, as we have already seen, St. Luke also mentions his life of preparation: "[John] was in the deserts until the day of his manifestation to Israel" (1:80). Should we regard these "deserts" as being identical with the desert of Juda where, as the other Synoptic writers tell us, John preached? The great majority of commentators, including Knabenbauer, Lagrange and B. Weiss, reply in the affirmative. We must note that in Luke 5:16 and 8:29, the same expression is used (ἐν ταῖς ἐρήμοις), and that it indicates simply the isolated and sparsely

---

[4] For the exact site of Jericho, see pp. 555 f. below.
[5] Cf. *Wars* iv. 8. 3; Schürer, I, 380.
[6] Cf. *Wars* ii. 4. 2; Schürer, I, 214.
[7] *Wars* iv. 7. 4. 6.

cultivated regions in the neighborhoods of Capharnaum and Gerasa. Therefore, in Luke 1:80, the phrase could be understood to indicate isolated places which were little frequented because they were not intensively cultivated.[8] Nevertheless, we, too, believe that the region in question is most probably the desert of Juda. There John, in silence, retirement and penance, prepared himself for the great mission which was in store for him.

At the time of which we speak, the solitary life was certainly not commonly followed, yet neither was it wholly unusual. We know from Josephus that the Essenes lived in the desert and that, in order to find out more about the sect, he himself went to live with one of them, a man named Banus whose only clothing was leaves and who ate only herbs. The historian seems to have lived with this Banus from his sixteenth to his nineteenth year.[9] Since there is a certain similarity between the life of the Essenes and that of John, the question of a possible relationship between the two naturally arises. It is very probable that John knew the sect but there are no grounds for saying that he was influenced in any way by them; in fact, the Gospel narrative seems rather to indicate the contrary. Hence the great majority of authors find grounds for denying that the Precursor was an Essene.[10]

[8] Today the name, the Desert of St. John, is given to a delightful spot, about four miles southwest of 'Ain Karim, where there is a free-flowing spring—'Ain el-Habis—and a cave, both well suited to provide a hermit with water and shelter. Perhaps this very suitability for the solitary life gave rise to the tradition which dates back, at the most, to the twelfth century and probably only to the thirteenth. (Cf. Baldi, *Enchiridion.* . . . , pp. 56, 76.) Dr. Clemens Kopp's article, "Le désert de saint Jean près d'Hébron" in *RB* (1946), pp. 547–558, is well worth reading. With a wealth of data, the author argues in favor of a site near the present town of Taffuh, five miles west of Hebron, where there is a spring called 'Ain Ma'mudiyeh, a name which is reminiscent of baptism, and where one can still see the ruins of a church and some other monuments which, according to Fr. Esteve (*loc. cit.,* pp. 559–575), date back to the last period of the Byzantine epoch.

[9] *Life* 2: Josephus speaks at greater length about the Essenes in *Wars* ii. 8. 2. 13, where he describes their ideas and manner of life. For further material on the Essenes see Schürer, II, 651–680; Buzy, *Saint Jean-Baptiste* (1922), pp. 182–185; also pp. 30–34, 36 above.

[10] Even Goguel denies it: see *Jean-Baptiste* (Paris, 1928), pp. 108 *ff.*; *Vie de Jésus* (Paris, 1952), pp. 250 *f.* See also Marchal, "Esséniens," in *Dict. de la Bible,* Suppl. II, Col. 1128. However, the documents of Qumran (cf. above pp. 30–34) impose upon us a degree of reserve in dealing with the subject. These documents clearly prove that the solitary, and, in a certain sense, monastic life, was more intense and widespread in that era than we had been led to believe by the sparse data upon which we had to rely before. There is no positive evidence that John belonged to one of these communities, but the mere fact of their existence, and precisely in the desert of Juda, as shown by the newly-discovered

Solitude, fasting and penance are the best preparation for doing God's work. Silence is the strength of great souls, who concentrate and conserve their energy therein. And it is in silence, too, that God communicates Himself: "I . . . will lead her into the wilderness: and I will speak to her heart" (Osee 2:14). The soul grows strong by taming the appetites of the flesh and bringing them into subjection to the will. Moses and Elias had thus prepared themselves for their missions, and our Lord Himself was later to go into the desert to fast and to pray before beginning His public life.

JOHN'S APPEARANCE
(Matt. 3:4; Mark 1:6)

John the Baptist had come to preach penance, and his austere mode of life was in conformity with his preaching: "But John himself had a garment of camel's hair and a leathern girdle about his loins, and his food was locusts and wild honey" (Matt. 3:4); "And John was clothed in camel's hair, with a leathern girdle about his loins, and he ate locusts and wild honey" (Mark 1:6). Thus his very clothing, coarse and rough as it was, reminded the crowds of the ancient prophets (cf. 4 Kings 1:8); and his food, the plainest and rudest fare, was in perfect harmony with his harsh vesture.

Our Lord also came to preach penance (cf. Matt. 4:17), yet how different were His appearance and manner of life from those of John! But He did not for that reason reprove His chosen Precursor; instead, He praised him, drawing attention to his rough clothing and pointing out that those who clothe themselves in soft fabrics dwell in the palaces of kings (Luke 7:25). There is a diversity of spirits, each good and laudable, and none worthy of condemnation; yet there are people whose evil disposition turns everything to poison. As our Lord Himself said: "John the Baptist came neither eating bread nor drinking wine, and you say, 'He has a devil.' The Son of Man came eating and drinking, and you say, 'Behold a man who is a glutton, and a wine-drinker, a friend of publicans and sinners!' " (Luke 7:33.) Nothing satisfied these murmurers, and they always found something to condemn.

manuscripts, demand that we proceed very cautiously in forming opinions on the matter. Some authors have also tried to prove a relationship between John and Mandeism; but the point is not worth dwelling upon. For a very complete treatment of the subject see L. Tondelli's monograph, *Il Mandeismo e le origini cristiane* (*Orientalia*, no. 33, 1928), especially pp. 70 ff.; *Biblica*, 9 (1928), 206–228.

Both the Latin word *vestimentum* and the Greek ἔνδυμα are general terms and can mean both "tunic" (χιτών) and "cloak" (ἱμάτιον), two completely distinct garments which together formed the ordinary clothing of the ancient Hebrews (cf. Matt. 5:40; Acts 9:39). In the case of John the Baptist, it seems that the evangelists, as if wishing to stress the Precursor's austerity and poverty, referred rather to the tunic, since this garment was absolutely indispensable and was worn by even the poorest people, whereas the cloak could be done without and was actually laid aside at work. The ζώνη was the leather girdle or belt which bound the tunic about the waist, or as Zorell aptly defines it: "cingulum zona quam veteres vestibus circumdabant, ne diffluerent," [11] (as do the natives of Palestine at the present day). He cites Acts 21:11; Apocalypse 1:13; 15:6, where the word is used in this identical sense. Many Old Testament passages could also be quoted in favor of this definition, Leviticus 16:4 in particular, where there is not the slightest doubt that the ζώνη was used to gird the tunic about the priest's waist. In view of all this, the interpretation of the word which Lagrange gives in his commentary on St. Mark [12] is rather strange; he says that the girdle (the ζώνη) took the place of a tunic, and that it was not a leather strap but rather a kind of leather loincloth ("une sorte de pagne") which was wrapped about the loins. This meaning does not seem admissible for there is only one text in the whole Bible that can be used to support it, namely, Genesis 3:7; and even there the Greek translation does not use ζώνη but περιζώματα, while verse 27 of the same chapter says that "God made for Adam and his wife *garments of skins*" which, as is clear from the context, covered not only their loins but also their whole bodies. According to Lagrange's interpretation, then, John the Baptist was clothed in a cloak of camel's hair and a leather loincloth.[13]

We know that the ancient Hebrews ate locusts, since they are mentioned in Leviticus 11:22 as being clean animals and therefore not forbidden food under the Law. The *Mishnah* provides evidence that they were also eaten in later times, for it distinguishes between clean and unclean locusts,[14] and says that "no flesh may be cooked in milk ex-

---

[11] *Novi Testamenti Lexicon Graecum, Cursus Scripturae Sacrae* (Paris, 1931).

[12] *Évangile selon S. Marc* (Paris, 1929).

[13] Cf. *Rech. de Sc. Rel.*, 23 (1933), 589–598, where Buzy refutes this interpretation of the text in a note entitled "Pagne ou ceinture?"

[14] "Among locusts [these are clean]: all that have four legs, four wings, and jointed legs, and whose wings cover the greater part of their bodies," *Hullin* 3:7. See Str.-Bill., I, 98–100.

cepting the flesh of fish and locusts." [15] Locusts were also pickled in brine.[16] Even in modern times "the Arabs eat locusts, first removing the head, wings and hind parts; they mix them with dates . . . or toast them and eat them as one would a piece of meat." [17]

More than once Sacred Scripture mentions the honey which was found in holes in the rocks and in cavities in tree trunks, and which, since it was made by non-domesticated bees, was called wild honey (cf. Deut. 32:13; Judges 14:8; 1 Kings 14:25 *ff.*). The juice of certain plants was also called honey; e.g., Josephus [18] says that when pressure was applied to palm trees of a certain type found in Jericho, they gave "an excellent kind of honey not very inferior in sweetness to the other honey." Some authors (e.g., Lagrange) believe that the honey which John ate was of this vegetable type, obtained perhaps from the tamarinds of the Jordan valley: but it is more probable that he ate honey properly so-called as Durand, Pirot and commentators in general believe.

JOHN THE BAPTIST'S MISSION

In the Greek Orthodox Monastery of St. John (Qasr el-Yehud), near the Jordan, a visitor's eye was caught by what seemed to be a statue of John the Baptist, but he was not sure about its identity because it had two wings like an angel's. He asked the monk who was acting as guide, and found that the image was indeed that of John; and when he objected that the statue had wings, the monk replied: "*Malek:* he is an *angel.*" St. Mark (1:2) actually does apply to John the words of Malachias (3:1): "Behold, I send *my angel* before thee, who shall prepare thy way," [19] and our Lord also applies these words

---

[15] *Hullin* 8:1.

[16] Cf. *Terumoth* 10:9.

[17] Jaussen, *Coutumes des arabes du Pays de Moab* (Paris, 1903), p. 250. See also Musil, *Arabia Petraea,* III (Wien, 1908), 151. The present writer can testify that, during two plagues of locusts which occurred in Palestine in recent times, many of the natives took advantage of the invasion to gather the insects for food.

[18] *Wars* iv. 8. 3.

[19] In the same verse, Malachias speaks of "the angel of the testament," words which have been interpreted in very different ways (cf. W. Nowack, "Die kleinen Propheten," *Handkom. z. Alt. Test.,* III, 4 [Göttingen, 1903]). The most probable interpretation seems to be the one which identifies this angel with the Lord (*ha'adon*) and which says that he is distinct from the angel mentioned in the first part of the verse (thus Knabenbauer).

The quotation in Mark 1:2 creates a difficulty. The evangelist attributes the words to Isaias, whereas in reality they are found in Malachias 3:1. Several

to John in Matthew 11:10. Therefore John was an *angel*, that is, a messenger, sent by God on a special mission, namely, to be the Precursor of the Messias, to go before Him and prepare the way for Him: "who *shall prepare* thy way" (Mark 1:2; Matt. 3:3; Luke 3:4–6). The three Synoptic writers quote the same passage from Isaias (40:3), and Luke adds verses 4–5. It is true that Isaias was really referring to Israel's return from exile, which involved the crossing of the desert between Babylon and Palestine; yet we must remember that the whole second part of Isaias is also Messianic. The image which he uses is a reference to the messengers whom oriental princes used to send before them to prepare the roads along which they were to pass. St. Luke undoubtedly understood the prophet's words in a moral sense: the valleys that are to be filled represent the poor and humble who are to be exalted; the mountains which are to be brought low are the mighty and proud who will be humbled; the crooked paths that are to be straightened signify the unjust and the dishonest who will be converted. St. John also speaks of the Baptist in his Gospel, crediting him with the same mission, but in different words and using a different image. In the fourth Gospel, John the Baptist is the man sent by God to point out the light to men; he himself is not the light, but he will be the path which will lead men to the light (John 1:6–8). This mode of expression suits perfectly "the evangelist of the light."

John the Baptist himself said (John 1:19–23) that he was not the Messias, or Elias, or a prophet, or, rather, *the* prophet (ὁ προφήτης), i.e., the great prophet of Deuteronomy 18:15, promised by Moses and expected by the Jews. He said he was "the voice of one crying in the desert," applying to himself the words of Isaias 40:3. In speaking of this passage, the Fathers, with perfect justice, praise the profound humility of John in regarding himself as something so unsubstantial and so passing as a voice. But it was none other than our Lord who uttered the most glowing praise of John; John is a firm and immovable pillar, not a reed shaken in the wind; he is more than a prophet, he is the angel sent by God to prepare the paths of the Messias; he is Elias;

MSS have "the prophets" instead of "Isaias," but this is probably an intentional change: the authentic reading is "Isaias" (Knabenbauer, Lagrange). Some commentators hold that the quotation from Malachias is a later gloss on the original text, but there is not sufficient reason for their assertion. The obvious and most probable solution is that St. Mark combined two prophecies, one from Malachias and the other (v. 3) from Isaias (40:3) and used the latter's name since his words were more to the point. This is Knabenbauer's solution.

he is the greatest of the sons of women (Matt. 11:7–19); "he [is] the lamp, burning and shining" (John 5:35).

Several of these expressions seem to be in opposition to others found in the Gospels; and some are so pregnant with meaning that they need to be explained. Thus our Lord says that John is Elias (Matt. 11:14; 17:12 *f.*), but the Baptist himself had denied that he was (John 1:21). We find the explanation of the apparent contradiction in the words which the angel addressed to Zachary (Luke 1:17): ". . . he [John] shall himself go before him [the Lord=the Messias] in the spirit and power of Elias." The Precursor was not Elias in person but he was to be animated with his spirit, his fortitude, and his ardent zeal; and in his external appearance, austerity, dress and mode of life in the desert, he was to display a striking similarity to the great prophet of the divine retribution.

Our Lord also says of John that "among those born of woman there has not risen a greater than John the Baptist" (Matt. 11:11). Is John, then, holier than all other men? This is not the meaning of our Lord's words, for "greater" does not refer to John's personal sanctity but to his office, as is clearly indicated by the rest of the sentence: "yet the least in the kingdom of heaven is greater than he." [20] And in fact, the

---

[20] Our Lord's words: "the least in the kingdom of heaven is greater than he," give us to understand that John the Baptist did not belong to the kingdom of heaven, that he was not included in the new spiritual economy which the Messias had come to establish. But, on the other hand, in Luke 17:21, our Lord also said: "Behold, the kingdom of God is within you." These two passages present a problem whose solution is not easily seen at first glance.

The kingdom of heaven is the new order of things foretold by the prophets; it is the New Law as opposed to the Old; it is the substitution of the Gospel for the Mosaic Law. But when did the Old Law cease and the New begin? When was the Mosaic Law abrogated and when did the Gospel of Christ come into force?

St. Paul says (Gal. 3:24 *f.*) that just as the tutor withdraws and relinquishes his office when his pupil reaches his majority, so also the Old Law ceased at the coming of Christ, for which it had prepared mankind. But the Apostle does not specify whether the cessation of the Law coincided with our Lord's actual coming on earth, or with the beginning of His public life, or with His death. What he does say (Heb. 9:11 *ff.*) is that just as the old covenant was sealed with the blood of animals, in like manner the New Covenant was sealed with the blood of the immaculate Lamb. And since this New Covenant is nothing other than the Gospel and the kingdom of heaven which Jesus Himself came to preach, we must conclude that it was precisely at the moment of Christ's death that the New Covenant was sealed, the law of grace began, the kingdom of heaven was inaugurated, and the Mosaic Law was abrogated to make way for the Gospel. Therefore we can regard the death of Christ as the dividing line between the old economy and the new. It is not without reason that the Fathers say that the Church sprang forth from the heart of Christ. At the moment of His death, the history of the world was divided into two great eras, the era of

least in dignity in the kingdom of heaven, i.e., in the New Covenant, is greater than the greatest in the old, since the old covenant is far inferior to the new. Within the old covenant, John is the greatest because he not only announced the Messias but also was His immediate Precursor; he saw Him with his own eyes and baptized Him with his own hands. Note, too, that Luke (7:28) says: "among those born of women there is not a greater *prophet* than John the Baptist," which clearly shows the aspect under which John possesses this supremacy over others. Therefore, as Toledo correctly observes, there is question here of John's office as a *prophet*. And it is also clear that our Lord was not speaking here of greater or lesser sanctity, but of the dignity and excellence of John's mission.[21] Finally, making Christ's words refer to personal sanctity would lead to the absurd conclusion that any member of the New Covenant is holier than John.

Our explanation of these passages would seem to presuppose that John belonged to the Old Testament and not to the New. St. Thomas holds that the Precursor belonged to the New,[22] but he explains this statement in the sense that John was the end of the Old Law and the beginning of the Gospel.[23] It can be said that John was the extrinsic beginning of the New Law, as the dawn is said to be the beginning of the day and the end of the night. Strictly speaking, he was not a member of the Church instituted by Christ, since he died before our Lord had definitively founded the Church. Yet he can truly be regarded as belonging in a certain sense to the New Testament because he announced Christ already present and not merely to come, as the ancient prophets did.

In one of the passages to which we have just referred (Matt. 11: 12), our Lord goes on to say: "And from the days of John the Baptist until now, the kingdom of heaven *suffereth violence* [$\beta\iota\acute{a}\zeta\epsilon\tau\alpha\iota$], and *the*

---

slavery and that of freedom, the freedom of the sons of God; the era of death conquered by Christ on the cross, and the era of life. From that moment, by virtue of the blood of Christ, all humanity was introduced into the new economy of the kingdom of heaven.

Our Lord's words, "the kingdom of God is within you" (Luke 17:21), do not negate what we have just said. In fact, when He made this declaration, He was announcing the kingdom, and implying that He Himself was its King. For the rest, if anyone objects that the verb is in the present, "is within you," we can point to those other words of Christ (Matt. 1:17): "Repent, for the kingdom of heaven is *at hand*."

[21] Cf. Knabenbauer, *in loc.*
[22] *Summa Theologica*, IIa-IIae, q. 174, a. 4, ad 3.
[23] "Terminus legis et initium evangelii." *Ibid.*, IIIa, q. 38, a. 1, ad 2.

violent bear it away." These words are very difficult to interpret and no one can claim to have found a completely satisfactory solution to the problem. The sentence can be translated in two ways:

(1) "The kingdom of heaven is violated ("suffereth violence": *vim patitur*), and the violent bear it away." But this version, in which βιάζεται is regarded as passive, can be understood in two totally different senses—(a) "the kingdom . . . is violated," i.e., is taken by main force; men hurl themselves forward violently in order to enter it (hence their attitude towards the kingdom is *favorable* and not hostile); "and the violent," i.e., those who strive mightily, who do not shrink before the difficulty of their task, "bear it away" for themselves, i.e., they attain to it, they succeed in entering it. This is the interpretation given by many of the Fathers and it is the most common one in Catholic exegesis.[24] (b) "The kingdom . . . is violated," i.e., it is oppressed, it is opposed; men resist it and fight against it (their attitude, then, is *hostile*); "and the violent," i.e., those who make war on it, "bear it away" from the others, i.e., they hinder others from entering it.[25]

(2) "The kingdom of heaven presents itself violently; it makes its appearance with strength (βιάζεται taken as the middle voice, in an intransitive sense); [26] and the violent bear it away." Again, the second part of the sentence can be understood in two senses, *favorable* or *hostile*.

In endeavoring to solve the problem we must take account of the parallel passage in Luke 16:16: "The Law and the Prophets were until John; from that time the kingdom of God is preached: and every one uses violence towards it [βιάζεται εἰς αὐτήν]," i.e., the Law and the Prophets ended in John, and from then on the good news of the kingdom of God has been announced and everyone endeavors to enter that kingdom. The first part of this passage presents no difficulty: the Law and the Prophets endured until John came but since then (ἀπὸ τότε), i.e., with John, a new era has begun; the kingdom of God, which in

---

[24] Among recent exegetes, Lagrange, Buzy, Valensin-Huby, Bover, and others.

[25] This is the interpretation favored by Knabenbauer, Merx (*Die vier kanonischen Evangelien: Das Evangelium Matthaeus* [Berlin, 1902], *in loc.*) and others.

[26] Dausch, *Die drei älteren Evangelien* (Bonn, 8th ed.), pp. 187 *f.* Knabenbauer, Merx, and Cremer (*Bibl.-theol. Wörterbuch der Neut. Gräcität* [9th ed.], pp. 231 *f.*) refute this interpretation. The important thing is to find out whether βιάζομαι in the intransitive sense can be used absolutely and without any complement. The examples adduced (cf. Zorell, *N.T. Lex. Graec.*) have a complement, but this does not seem sufficient proof that the word cannot be used without one.

former times had only been prophesied, has begun to be announced as already present. The word βιάζεται in the second part of the sentence is certainly in the middle voice, i.e., everyone *struggles, makes great efforts;* but the other expression, εἰς αὐτήν, is not as clear, since it can be taken to mean *towards it,* i.e., everyone exerts himself to enter the kingdom, to take it by main force; or it could mean *against it,* i.e., everyone exerts himself to resist the kingdom, maintaining, therefore, a hostile attitude towards it.

Comparing the two passages, we believe that the βιάζεται of Matthew should be taken in the middle, intransitive sense and as a parallel of Luke's εὐαγγελίζεται (*evangelizatur:* "is preached").[27] And, actually, the preaching of the Gospel was its appearance; except that βιάζεται expresses the somewhat violent manner in which it appeared. This shows clearly the meaning of the words "from the days of John the Baptist" (Matt. 11:12), which undoubtedly refer to verse 13: "For all the Prophets and the Law have prophesied until John." The relationship between the two parts of the sentence appears more clearly in Luke.

But in what sense should we understand the second part of Matthew's sentence (11:12): "and the violent bear it away"? (Luke has: "every one useth violence towards it.") Since the phrase in itself can have two meanings, we should seek the answer in the context and the historical circumstances in which it was uttered. In Matthew, just after saying these words (vv. 16 *ff.*), our Lord reproached John's contemporaries for not having heeded the Baptist's preaching. He recalled the grave injury they had done him by saying that he was possessed by the devil (v. 18), and the calumnies they were now spreading about the Son of Man Himself, calling Him "a glutton and a wine-drinker, a friend of publicans and sinners" (v. 19). Then He immediately raised His voice against Corozain, Capharnaum and Bethsaida because they did not wish to do penance, i.e., because they were resisting the kingdom of Heaven. And in Luke 16:14–15 He reproved the Pharisees, saying that their consciences were an abomination in the eyes of God. Now it is not likely that, in such circumstances, our Lord would have affirmed that everyone was hastening to enter the new kingdom and to seize it by main force. Instead, He repeatedly stated that obstacles were being placed in the way of those who wished to enter the kingdom:

---

[27] Lagrange (*Év. selon S. Matt.,* [3e éd.], p. 221) seems to take the βιάζεται of Matthew as being parallel to that of Luke.

"Woe to you, Scribes and Pharisees, hypocrites! because you shut the kingdom of heaven against men. For you yourselves do not go in, *nor do you allow those going in to enter*" (Matt. 23:13); "Woe to you lawyers! because you have taken away the key of knowledge; you have not entered yourselves and *those who were entering you have hindered*" (Luke 11:52). Consequently, we hold that the second interpretation given above (p. 180, No. 1 b) is the more probable one.[28]

However, in spite of our favoring the second interpretation, we believe that preachers may freely use the first one, the commonest among Catholic commentators, for it also is probably correct, and even more so than the one we favor if we are to judge by the number who uphold it. Our Lord's words, understood in this second sense, find an echo in the *Imitation of Christ:* "The greater violence thou offerest to thyself, the greater progress wilt thou make." [29]

THE PEOPLE'S OPINION OF JOHN THE BAPTIST

The three Synoptic Gospels depict the crowds gathering around the Precursor to listen to his words and to receive the baptism of penance (Matt. 3:5 f.; Mark 1:5; Luke 3:10–14). St. Luke enumerates various classes of people, including publicans and soldiers, who came to John asking what they should do and receiving from him a clear-cut answer. Some had not been content to follow him sporadically only, but had formed themselves into a group of disciples who seem to have accompanied him everywhere (cf. John 1:35). And so greatly was he esteemed that people began to ask themselves if he were not the Messias (cf. Luke 3:15; Matt. 11–2; 14:12). Even Herod Antipas had a high opinion of him, for when he later heard of the wonders which our Lord was performing, he thought that the Miracle-worker was none other than John the Baptist risen from the dead (Matt. 14:1 f.); and we are also told that while he had John in prison, the monarch followed his advice on many occasions (Mark 6:20).

However, amid this chorus of praise there were discordant voices raised against John. Our Lord Himself said that there were some who, when they saw the austere life the Baptist lived, "neither eating nor drinking," and were unwilling to imitate him, claimed that he was possessed by the devil. But no doubt these detractors were Scribes and

---

[28] Cf. Simón-Dorado, *op. cit.,* pp. 565 f. for a lucid account of the various interpretations.
[29] Bk. I, Chap. 25, 11.

Pharisees, who, as we know, did not believe in the baptism of John (Matt. 21:26; Mark 11:31; Luke 20:5), whereas the people regarded it as coming from heaven, for they venerated the Baptist as a true prophet (Matt. 21:26; Mark 11:32; Luke 20:6). We find an echo of this veneration in Flavius Josephus: "Among the Jews there were those who believed that Herod's defeat was a punishment for what he had done to John, called the Baptist. . . . The latter was a good man who taught the Jews the practice of virtue"; and the Jewish historian goes on to speak with high praise of the Baptist.[30]

THE PREACHING OF JOHN THE BAPTIST
(Matt. 3:1–12; Mark 1:4–8; Luke 3:3–18)

St. Matthew (3:2) sums up John's preaching in two phrases: "Repent, for the kingdom of heaven is at hand," the latter phrase being the principal one, although at first glance it may seem only secondary. The sense of the whole is: the kingdom of heaven is near; therefore, you must prepare to receive it by doing penance. It was with almost identical words that Christ later began His own preaching: "The kingdom of God is at hand. Repent and believe in the gospel" (Mark 1:15).

John was the herald of Christ; he was the apostle of penance. His speech was harsh and even violent: "Brood of vipers! who has shown you how to flee from the wrath to come?" (Matt. 3:7) i.e., from the punishment which the Messias in His capacity as Supreme Judge will bring upon the unjust and the sinners (cf. Rom. 2:5; 1 Thess. 1:10). We should note that although in Luke 3:7 these words seem to be addressed to the people in general,[31] they were actually launched by John against the Pharisees and Sadducees, as St. Matthew explicitly declares: "But when he saw many of the Pharisees and Sadducees coming to his baptism, he said to them. . . ." He knew them well, for this undoubtedly was not the first time he had had to deal with them. Probably more than once they had smiled disdainfully at the burning zeal of the unpolished speaker. They were the just ones, the masters of Israel; what need had they of penance? Furthermore, were not they sons of Abraham, a title which in itself assured their salvation? Cer-

---

[30] *Ant.* xviii. 5. 2.

[31] Luke's manner of speech is justified, for since the Pharisees and Sadducees were part of a crowd of listeners, John appeared to be speaking to everyone present; but his invective was directed only against the members of the two parties.

tainly it must have been these hypocrites who spread the calumny that John was possessed by the devil (Matt. 11:18). Against this background the Precursor's violent outburst is not surprising, for he had to unmask his detractors and show them up for what they were; and he could do so freely because he knew that the crowd was with him, and that the Pharisees and Sadducees did not dare oppose popular opinion (cf. Luke 20:6). Vehemently he attacked the proud hypocrites for their smug self-complacency: "Bring forth therefore fruit [32] worthy of penance," (Matt. 3:8), i.e., do not be satisfied with your merely external practices; an inner change (μετάνοια) of heart is necessary for you, a change which must show itself outwardly in your deeds just as the tree shows its true nature in its fruit (Matt. 7:20); in other words, your deeds should correspond with inner dispositions of penance and should be a sign thereof (cf. Acts 26:20). "Rend your hearts and not your garments" (Joel 2:13); "By their fruits you will know them" (Matt. 7:20); "Not everyone who says . . . 'Lord, Lord,' shall enter the kingdom of heaven" (Matt. 7:21).

It was certainly a privilege to be a descendant of Abraham, as St. Paul freely admitted,[33] but the Jews exaggerated the privilege and had reached the point where they imagined that the mere fact of being corporally descended from Abraham was a sure guarantee of salvation. As proof of this we need only recall the reply which their pride of race inspired them to give to Christ: "We are the children of Abraham, and we have never yet been slaves to anyone" (John 8:33). Hence John, answering their unspoken thoughts, said to them: "Do not think to say within yourselves, 'We have Abraham for our father. . . .'" (Matt. 3:8–9). Then, exploring the full meaning which these words had for the Pharisees and Sadducees, namely, that the promise had been made to the sons of Abraham and to no others, and that therefore this promise was to be fulfilled in them and in no one else, John added: "I say to you that God is able out of these stones to raise up children to Abraham" (v. 9), thereby implying that God did not need them in order to fulfill His promise. The true sons of Abraham are those who do as he did; thus to those who proudly proclaimed: "Abraham is our father," our Lord said: "If you are the children of Abraham, do the works of Abraham" (John 8:39).

[32] The singular here should be maintained against the plural of the *textus receptus.*
[33] ". . . qui sunt Israelitae, quorum adoptio est filiorum, et gloria, et testamentum, et legislatio, et obsequium, et promissa. . . ." (Rom. 9:4).

John insisted that penance should not be deferred, for the kingdom of Heaven was near: "For even now the axe is laid at the root of the trees; every tree, therefore, that is not bringing forth good fruit is to be cut down and thrown into the fire" (Luke 3:9; cf. Luke 13:6 *ff.*). This is the same doctrine which St. Paul was to preach later: "Behold, now is the acceptable time; behold, now is the day of salvation!" (2 Cor. 6:2); "Therefore while we have time, let us do good to all men" (Gal. 6:10).

The impression which John made on the people, and their resultant desire to change their lives, can be seen in their inquiries as to what they should do to reform. St. Luke alone has preserved this interesting detail of the Baptist's preaching (3:10–14). To each one who asked him, John gave an appropriate answer; to the crowd in general he recommended the practice of mercy in almsdeeds (vv. 10 *f.*); to the publicans charged with collecting taxes, that they should not exact more than was due (vv. 12 *f.*); to the soldiers, that they maltreat no one, accuse no one falsely, and refrain from taking money from anyone by fraud or violence, but rather be content with their pay. These soldiers could well have been a kind of Jewish bailiff like the publicans, whom they assisted in their taxgathering. It is also possible that they were Gentiles hired by Herod Antipas,[34] or, less probably, by the Roman procurator. At all events, it is not necessary to hold that they were Jews.[35]

THE BAPTISM OF PENANCE

St. Mark (1:4) and St. Luke (3:3) say that John preached "the baptism of penance for the remission of sins," i.e., a baptism that was received as an indication of interior penance, of a change of heart by which one turned from sin to embrace virtue, a penance that brought with it the forgiveness of sins. As St. Thomas observes,[36] the evangelists' words could give the impression that John's baptism conferred grace of itself and by its own power, especially since Mark (1:5) goes on to

---

[34] Josephus (*Ant.* xvii. 8. 3; *Wars* i. 33. 9) speaks of Thracians, Galatians and Germans as being hired by Herod the Great.

[35] Dausch believes that he can discover in the text itself an indication that they were not Jews but pagans; so does Zahn, who, following the best codices, reads: Τί ποιήσομεν καὶ ἡμεῖς, and sees a special emphasis in this placing of καὶ ἡμεῖς, as if they had said: "What shall *we* do, we who are not Jews but Gentiles?"

[36] "Videtur quod in baptismo Ioannis gratia daretur. Dicitur enim . . . praedicans baptismum poenitentiae in remissionem peccatorum. Sed poenitentia et remissio peccatorum est per gratiam" (*op. cit.,* IIIa, q. 38, ad 3).

say that the baptism was accompanied by the confession of sins. But John himself took care to remove any false impression there might be by declaring: "I indeed baptize you with *water*. . . . But he who is coming after me . . . will baptize you with *the Holy Spirit and with fire*" (Matt. 3:11; Luke 3:16). Concerning these words, Suárez remarks that they clearly establish a difference between the two baptisms, and since both were in water, John's "with water" should be understood as meaning his baptism was conferred "in water alone," but that Christ's baptism would contain both elements, "namely, water and the spirit." [37] The word "fire" does not indicate a separate element in Christ's baptism, but is included only to show with what strength and purifying power the Holy Spirit operates therein.[38] St. Thomas says that John's baptism did not confer grace but only prepared its recipients for grace, and did so in three ways (*tripliciter*).[39] Hence Suárez rightly observes that "John's baptism was instituted solely for the purpose of ministering to Christ's manifestation and appearance, and of preparing the way for His baptism." [40] John himself was explicit on this point: "That he may be known to Israel, for this reason have I come baptizing with water" (John 1:31).

John's baptism was different also from *circumcision*, the *ablutions* of the Jews, and the so-called *baptism of the proselytes*. *Circumcision*, as St. Thomas remarks, "was instituted as a remedy for original sin," [41] but it was not properly speaking a cause of grace, as is Christian baptism.[42] Suárez, quoting St. Gregory Nazianzen, notes that John's baptism was not wholly similar to the *ablutions* of the Jews, since it was performed with a view to penance while the ablutions were not.[43]

In our day, some have wished to see in John's baptism a copy, as

[37] *Opera*, ed. L. Vives (Parisiis, 1860), XIX, *In III Part., disp.* 25, *sect.* 2, *no.* 2.

[38] See the article "Baptême par le feu" in *Mélanges de Science religieuse,* 8 (1915), 285 *ff*.

[39] "Per doctrinam Ioannis inducentem homines ad fidem Christi; assuefaciendo homines ad ritum baptismi Christi; per poenitentiam praeparando homines ad suscipiendum effectum baptismi Christi." (*Loc. cit.*)

[40] *Loc. cit., no.* 3.

[41] *Loc. cit.*

[42] "In circumcisione conferebatur gratia . . . , aliter tamen quam in baptismo. Nam in baptismo confertur gratia ex virtute ipsius baptismi; quam habet in quantum est instrumentum passionis Christi iam perfectae. In circumcisione autem conferebatur gratia non ex virtute circumcisionis, sed ex virtute fidei passionis Christi, cuius signum erat circumcisio." Before circumcision was instituted, faith in Christ, who was to come, was sufficient for justification. (IIIa, q. 70, a. 4.)

[43] *Loc. cit.*

it were, of the so-called *baptism of proselytes*. The Talmud lays down
three conditions for the admission of a Gentile to the Jewish community—circumcision, a baptism (*tebilah*) or a cleansing by immersion, and a sacrifice. Authors are not agreed as to whether or not
this was the practice at the time of Christ. We find this baptism first
mentioned in the Talmud on the occasion of a dispute between the
schools of Shammai and Hillel.[44] But both Schürer and Strack-
Billerbeck conclude that it existed long before this time, since it seemed
to be traditional and was admitted without discussion by the various
schools, an opinion towards which Lagrange also leans. But Bernard
Weiss, on the contrary, holds that this baptism does not go back farther
than A.D. 70, and he bases his argument principally on the fact that
neither Philo nor Josephus makes the slightest mention of it.[45]

The facts which we have briefly covered scarcely justify an un-
qualified conclusion. For our part, we think it at least very probable
that the baptism of proselytes did exist in the time of our Lord, and
that it came into special prominence only in the first century of our
era. For the rest, it was a spontaneous result of the ruling ideas and
practices that had been current among the Jews from time im-
memorial. We know that to rid themselves of legal impurity, the
Chosen People had to perform numerous ablutions which sometimes
extended to the whole body, e.g., in the case of a leper who had been
cured of his disease (Lev. 14:8 *f.*). Therefore, since the Gentiles were
considered unclean (cf. John 18:28; Acts 10:28), it was only to be
expected that they should be obliged to purify themselves by bathing
the entire body before being incorporated into the Jewish people, the
people of God, the holy people. Did John take this baptism of proselytes
as a model for the external rite of his baptism? Did he draw any inspiration from the Jewish ceremony? It is possible that he did, for
dogma offers no opposition to such a procedure; yet, on the other
hand, there is no positive evidence in favor of this hypothesis. The historical and especially the prophetical books of the Old Testament were
more than enough to give John the idea of a baptism by water; and
Strack-Billerbeck acknowledge that he "lived and moved in the atmos-

---

[44] Str.-Bill., I, 102.
[45] *Das Matthäusevang.* (Göttingen, 1898–1902), p. 93, note. Schürer (1, 184) tries
to weaken this argument by saying that no one can point out a passage in
Philo or Josephus in which these authors would have been bound to speak of
such a baptism.

phere of the Old Testament and that his baptism was certainly inspired by the prophecies contained therein." [46]

But whatever the form, we know that John's baptism, in its basic significance, had nothing to do with the baptism of proselytes, which was concerned with Levitical, legal purification, while John's ceremony, on the contrary, was centered on morality, which penetrates into the soul. His baptism was one of *penance* for the *remission of sins,* an expression which is never found in connection with the baptism of proselytes.[47] Furthermore, the latter was the rite whereby one entered and became a member of a new community, namely, the Jewish people, whereas there was nothing like this in John's baptism, the object of which was to prepare the way for the coming of the Messianic kingdom by a change of heart.[48]

The confession of sins which accompanied John's baptism ("confessing their sins," Matthew 3:6; Mark 1:5) was, as it were, a spontaneous unburdening of the heart oppressed by the weight of sin. It would be fruitless to discuss whether only a general accusation of sin was made or whether the penitents mentioned their individual sins. Doubtless that was left to each one's judgment and depended on the character and fervor of each. In Acts 19:18, James 5:16 and several times in the Old Testament, e.g., in 1 Esdras 9:6, we read of a confession of sins, apparently a general confession. It is interesting to read the confession of a rabbi of the third century A.D.: "Lord, I have sinned and done evil; I have persevered in evil and have walked in wrong paths. No longer do I wish to act as I have done until now. Pardon me, O Yahweh, my God, all my faults and sins!" [49] Perhaps the penitents on the banks of the Jordan accused themselves in similar terms.

[46] I, 112.

[47] Str.-Bill., I, 110, describes the way in which the baptism of proselytes was administered. Cf. also B. Ugolinus, *Thesaurus antiquitatum sacrarum* (Venetiis, 1744–1769), XXII, 922 *ff.*

[48] Both Str.-Bill. (I, 112) and Schürer (I, 185, n. 90) freely admit this essential difference. However, *The Jewish Encyclopedia* (New York: Funk & Wagnalls, II, 499 *f.*) tries to place both baptisms on the same level by saying that the object of the baptism of proselytes was moral, and not simply, Levitical purity, and even insinuates that Jewish baptism did not differ essentially from the Christian rite since, in a certain manner, it too conferred the Holy Spirit.

No one will deny that the Jews knew about purification of the heart, for it is mentioned on every page of the prophets as well as in the historical books of the Old Testament, while there are also references to it in rabbinical literature. But this has no bearing on the particular point concerning the relationship between John's baptism and that of the proselytes.

[49] Str.-Bill., I, 113.

JOHN'S FIRST TESTIMONY

The Precursor had come to point out the Messias to men (John 1:8: "He . . . was to bear witness to the light"), and he did so clearly and humbly. No doubt he spoke often of the Messias, but the Gospels have recorded only four of his proclamations, one in the three Synoptics and three which St. John alone has preserved.

The first proclamation of the Messias (Matt. 3:11–12; Luke 3: 15–17; Mark 1:7–8) took place before Christ's baptism, although all three Gospels mention the baptism first (Matt. 3:13; Luke 3:21; Mark 1:9).[50] Here John the Baptist confessed that the Messias ("he who is coming [ὁ ἐρχόμενος] after me [in time]") was mightier than he. This frank admission fits in best with the context in St. Luke, where it appears to have been motivated by the crowd's surmise—no doubt expressed in words—that perhaps John was the Christ (3:15). Therefore, wishing to remove any such misapprehension, he spoke out plainly, using as his main argument the fact that the baptism which the Messias would institute would be "with *the Holy Spirit* and with *fire*," whereas his was only "with *water*" (v. 16). And in order to show Christ's immense superiority, he added with profound humility: "His sandals I am not worthy to bear" (Matt. 3:11). In Mark (v. 7) and Luke (v. 16) we find: "the strap of whose sandals I am not worthy to stoop down and loose." [51] If one were not worthy to carry or to loose another's shoes, then one was not worthy to be his servant, his slave. The Talmud said that one of a slave's duties was to put on and to untie his master's shoes; and this service was regarded as being so lowly that a certain rabbi, when declaring that a disciple ought to act as his teacher's slave, expressly excluded the untying of the teacher's shoes.[52] Among the Greeks and Romans also this task was proper to slaves.[53]

---

[50] B. Weiss (*Das Johannes evangelium* [Göttingen, 1902], p. 68), without reason, identifies this proclamation with that of John 1:26 *f*. It is true that, in this passage in John, we find the expression used by the Synoptics: "non sum dignus . . ."; but there would be nothing extraordinary in the Precursor's using such words more than once.

[51] Cf. St. Augustine's well-known discussion of this apparent contradiction (*De consensu evang.* 2. 12: *PL* 34, 1090 *f*.) ; also, A. Fernández, *De Interpretatione Sacrae Scripturae*, in *Institutiones Biblicae*, ed. 4 (Romae: Pont. Instit. Bibl., 1933), I, 440–442.

[52] "Rabbi Josue, son of Levi, used to say: 'A disciple ought to do for his teacher all the things that a slave has to do for his master, with the exception of loosing his shoes.' " (Str.-Bill., I, 121.)

[53] Plautus (*Trinummus* 252) mentions the *sandaligerae*, the slave-girls who followed their mistresses about, carrying their sandals (Pauly, *Realenzyclopädie*,

In order to throw into greater relief the power and greatness of the Messias, John went on to represent Him as the Supreme Judge. To impress his meaning more deeply on the minds of his listeners he used a metaphor drawn from the current method of winnowing wheat, with which they were thoroughly familiar (Matt. 3:12). Christ, with His irrevocable verdict, would separate the good from the evil as the farmer separates the straw from the wheat with his winnowing-fork. He would gather the good into His granaries in Heaven and would cast the evil into the fire that never dies.

The Baptism of Jesus
(Matt. 3:13–17; Mark 1:9–11; Luke 3:21–23; cf. Map IV)

The glory of the Herald culminated in the baptism of the great King whom he had come to announce. While still in His Mother's womb, the Son of Mary had sanctified the son of Elizabeth; and now the roles were reversed, as it were, and Christ came to receive the baptism of penance from His Precursor.

The fame of the austere prophet who was calling the people to do penance filtered through to the obscure and isolated village of Nazareth, where it provided a subject for conversation among the people of the district, and no doubt some of those who felt a yearning for spiritual renewal decided to join the crowds on the banks of the Jordan. Others from Galilee and places farther away than Nazareth had already done so: thus two fishermen from Bethsaida, John and Andrew, had not only gone to see the great penitent but had become his disciples. Therefore a small group of people from Nazareth set out on a pilgrimage of penance to the Jordan where John was baptizing, and among them was the young tradesman, the Son of Mary the modest housewife who had been left a widow by the death of her husband, Joseph the carpenter.

This journey to the south was a solemn event, for this was the hour which, from all eternity, the Heavenly Father had appointed for His Son to show Himself to the world, after some thirty years of

Vol. IA 2 [*Sandalia*], col 2.261). Merx says that the Arabs have a proverb: "Perhaps I ought to carry your shoes?" meaning, "I am not your slave." (*Die vier kanonischen Evangelien*, Vol. I, *Das Evangelium Matthaeus* [Berlin, 1902], p. 43.) However, we have questioned several Arabs and none of them could vouch for the existence of such a proverb. It is possible that it is used in some localities only and not in others.

The River Jordan.

hidden life, and to preach the "good tidings" which, down through the centuries, the prophets had come to announce.

The parting of Son and Mother must have been heartbreaking. Mary was aware that this departure of her Son was no ordinary leave-taking; she knew that it was definitive and for good. She knew, too, whither her Son was bound, and the prophetic words of the aged Simeon: "And thy own soul a sword shall pierce" came back to her mind and heart, more distinct and more threatening than ever. But the Father's will had to be accomplished, and Mary made the sacrifice demanded, generously, humbly and lovingly.

The small caravan from Nazareth probably took the eastern route rather than the mountain road that went through Samaria. Descending to the plain of Esdrelon the travellers passed near Mount Thabor, leaving it on the left, breasted the hill not far from Endor in order to enter the valley of Beisan and then, turning south, crossed the region which the fourth Gospel calls Aennon (3:23) and which abounds in springs. Then, continuing south, they reached the Jordan, approximately opposite Jericho.

From St. Luke's account (3:21) we know that when they reached the river there was a crowd of people there who wished to be baptized, and we can well suppose that our Lord joined the crowd and awaited His turn. What an example of humility, observe the Fathers, that the Innocent One should mingle with sinners, the Just with the unjust, as if He, like them, had need of being purified!

John did not know Jesus by sight, as he himself was to tell us later: "And I did not know him. But he who sent me to baptize with water said to me, 'He upon whom thou wilt see the Spirit descending, and abiding upon him, he it is who baptizes with the Holy Spirit' " (John 1:33). There is nothing strange in the fact that Jesus and John had never met, for John had retired to the desert while still young, and Nazareth lay almost ninety miles to the north. But the Precursor knew that the Messias would one day come to the place where he was baptizing, and with what yearning he must have awaited Him! When Jesus did present Himself to be baptized, His bearing, His humble recollection, His angelic modesty, and, above all, an inspiration from on high, showed John who it was that had come to ask him for baptism.[54] Then there occurred that loving contest in humility:

"It is I who ought to be baptized by thee, and dost thou come to me?" (Matt. 3:14)—a very natural reaction of the herald as he stood before his King, of the servant in the presence of His Lord.

But Christ, pleased with the humility of His Precursor, answered: "Let it be so now, for so it becomes us to fulfill all justice."

This justice was not legal justice, as if our Lord had to be cleansed from impurity, nor was it the fulfillment of an obligation to receive baptism from John, since the reception thereof was completely voluntary. It was simply a question of our Lord's following out His Father's plan and submitting to His will. The Father had willed the Messias to be baptized by John and both had to bow before this ordinance, the One by being baptized, the other by performing the rite.

The baptism was by immersion; the person being baptized waded into the river and remained there while he confessed his sins. It is probable that John pronounced some formula during the ceremony, but neither the evangelists nor tradition has preserved it for us. Then the newly-baptized person left the water and returned to the river-bank. Most likely this was the rite employed by John when baptizing

---

[54] As Fr. Murillo says: "The sign of the dove's descent was not given to John for his own enlightenment but for a public testimonial to the people. Thus there is no contradiction between John's words and the private knowledge of Christ which he could have had and actually did have before the descent of the dove." (*Evangelio de San Juan* [Barcelona, 1908], p. 168.)

our Lord. In the divine plan, Christ's baptism was to be accompanied by the Father's solemn declaration, and His profound humility was to be followed by His sublime glorification: "The heavens were opened to him, and he saw the Spirit of God descending as a dove and coming upon him. And behold, a voice from the heavens said, 'This is my beloved Son, in whom I am well pleased' " (Matt. 3:16 *f.*).

The three Synoptic evangelists say that it was the Holy Spirit (Luke), the Spirit of God (Matt.), the Spirit (Mark), that descended, and that He descended in the form of a dove.[55] And the words the Gospels used to describe the event [56] indicate that the dove either came to rest on our Lord's very head, or at least came down low enough to show clearly for whom it had appeared.

Why did the Holy Spirit appear precisely in the form of a *dove?* The Fathers give various reasons: (1) the dove is the symbol of peace; after the Flood it brought back an olive branch, the sign of peace; and at the birth of the Messias, the angels had sung: "And *peace* on earth . . ."; (2) it was the symbol of simplicity; "Be . . . wise as serpents, and *guileless as doves*" (Matt. 10:16); (3) in the Canticle of Canticles (2:10; 5:2), the Holy Spirit calls the spouse "my *dove*,"; (4) St. Thomas adds a fourth reason, namely, to signify the seven gifts of the Holy Spirit, which have a certain similarity with the properties of the dove.[57] The same holy Doctor quotes St. Augustine [58] to the effect that the Holy Spirit manifested Himself visibly in two ways: by the *dove* and by *fire*. By the dove God wished to make it known that those who are sanctified by the Spirit should not retain any duplicity but should rather be animated by simplicity; and in order to show that this simplicity should not remain cold or inactive, the Lord willed to manifest Himself by fire. In rabbinical literature, the dove is considered the symbol of the people of Israel. Perhaps it was also regarded as a symbol of the Spirit of God, although this significance does not appear clearly.[59]

The words that were heard coming from Heaven are identical in the three evangelists except that St. Matthew uses the third person

---

[55] Some believe that it was a real dove, and it has even been said that the bird was expressly created by God for the purpose. Suárez thinks it more probable that it was only the *figure* of a dove (*Disp.* 27, *sect.* 2 [ed. L. Vives], XIX, 406). This appears to be the most reasonable assumption, since the formation of such a figure in the air was sufficient for God's purpose.

[56] καταβαῖνον εἰς αὐτόν; ἐρχόμενον ἐπ᾽ αὐτόν .

[57] IIIa, q. 39, a. 6, ad 4.

[58] *In Ioan.* tr. 6. 3: *PL* 35. 142.

[59] Cf. Str.-Bill., I, 123–125.

("*This is* my beloved Son. . . ."),[60] while the others use the second
person ("*Thou art* my beloved Son. . . .").[61] This testimony is very
similar to that which the Father was to give later at the Transfiguration, the sole difference being that in the latter mystery there is greater
variety in the formula as preserved for us by the three Synoptic authors.
The solemn words heard at the baptism of Christ are like an echo of
Psalm 2:7 and Isaias 47:1.

Exactly when did these supernatural phenomena take place, during
the baptism itself or after it? If we were to judge by the way painters
usually portray the scene, we should have to say that the opening of
the heavens and the descent of the dove coincided with the actual administration of the baptism. But this is not the impression given by the
evangelists' descriptions. Matthew says that "when Jesus *had been
baptized,* he immediately came up from the water. And behold, the
heavens *were opened* . . ."; Mark writes that *"immediately on coming up* from the water he saw the heavens opened . . ."; while Luke
adds an interesting detail: "Jesus also having been baptized *and being
in prayer* . . . heaven was opened. . . ." Thus when our Lord had
been baptized, He returned to the riverbank and began to pray; and
it was at this moment that the heavens opened, the dove appeared, and
the Father's voice was heard.

Luke explicitly says that our Lord saw these miracles (v. 22), and
John the Baptist later said that he, too, had seen them (John 1:32–
34). Authors are not agreed as to whether or not the people also saw
them. Buzy holds that "Jesus and John were the only witnesses of the
theophany," but the proofs he puts forward seem to us insufficient.[62] If
our Lord presented Himself for baptism in order that His real identity
might be announced (John 1:31), it was natural that the signs which
pointed Him out should have been seen by those to whom He was
going to reveal Himself, namely, the people; for the manifestation of
Christ was not done for His own benefit, and John the Baptist's words
seem to imply that it was not meant for him alone. This is the opinion
held by the majority of commentators, e.g., Knabenbauer, Lagrange,
Gomá, and others.[63]

---

[60] We believe that this was the form used by the Father; however, the meaning
is the same.

[61] ὁ υἱός μου ὁ ἀγαπητός, ἐν σοὶ (Matt. ἐν ᾧ) εὐδόκησα.

[62] *S. Matt.,* p. 35.

[63] As Suárez says: "Verisimilius est ita descendisse, ut ab omnibus qui aderant con-
specta sit" (*Disp.* 27, *sect.* 2, XIX, 404).

St. Augustine sees the mystery of the Holy Trinity depicted in the scene at the baptism: "The Trinity manifests Itself very plainly: the Father in the voice, the Son as man, the Spirit as the dove." [64]

The place where the baptism occurred was certainly the Jordan, for St. Matthew says: "Then Jesus came from Galilee to *John* at the *Jordan*, to be baptized by him" (3:13; cf. Mark 1:9). But was it the eastern or the western bank? The fourth Gospel explicitly says that John was baptizing beyond the Jordan,[65] but this obviously does not rule out every other possibility, and there is no reason to presuppose that John remained all the time on the same side of the river; he could have crossed and recrossed it. However, since he was "beyond the Jordan" when he received the delegation from Jerusalem (John 1:19–28) and since our Lord's baptism had most likely taken place a short time before the arrival of the delegates (1:32), we may conclude, with some probability at least, that Christ was baptized beyond the Jordan, and all the more so since the phrase which the fourth evangelist uses, "when John was baptizing," seems to imply a certain continuity. Neither the Synoptic Gospels nor tradition contains anything against this conclusion. The first three evangelists give only extremely vague data (cf. Matt. 3:1–6; Mark 1:5; Luke 3:3). Matthew (v. 5) and Luke speak of "all the region about the Jordan," which apparently, although not necessarily, indicates not only the western bank of the river but the eastern one, too. From the fact that the evangelists mention in particular the *desert of Juda* and *the inhabitants of Jerusalem,* we cannot conclude absolutely in favor of the western as against the eastern bank.

As the precise place where our Lord was baptized, Fr. Federlin [66] selected a hillock called Tell el-Medesh, about two miles east of Allenby Bridge, to the left of the road to es-Salt, on the northern side of the Wadi Nimrin and about nine and one-half miles from the Dead Sea, a

---

[64] *In Ioan.* tr. 6. 5: *PL* 35. 1427.

[65] "These things took place at Bethany, *beyond the Jordan* [πέραν τοῦ ᾿Ιορδάνου] where John was baptizing" (1:28). We cannot say that St. John's Gospel should not be taken into account on this point because it does not mention Christ's baptism. Actually, the fourth Gospel is much more precise here than are the Synoptic Gospels. Furthermore, we should take particular note of the fact that St. John remarks further on (3:23) that the Precursor baptized in "Aennon, near Salim," an observation which proves that he had a special interest in pointing out the exact places where events occurred, an interest which the Synoptic authors do not show. Hence, the reason given for leaving aside St. John's Gospel here seems very weak to us.

[66] *Béthanie au delà du Jourdain,* 1908; *RB* (1910), p. 542.

site which various authors have accepted.[67] The pottery found there indicates that there was once some kind of habitation or building on the spot, but there is no tradition to identify the site as the place of Christ's baptism. On the other hand, however, a short distance to the south, in the Wadi el-Kharrar, about five miles from the Dead Sea, very near the Jordan and almost opposite the Greek Monastery of St. John or Qasr el-Yehud, one can still see the remains of an ancient church which was no doubt built there as the result of a tradition that was extant in the Byzantine epoch. In our opinion, although these various circumstances do not point with certainty to this spot as the place of the baptism, they do lend a much greater degree of probability to its claim.[68]

Although we may not be able to calculate the date of our Lord's baptism with precision, we can do so within certain limits. The liturgy commemorates the event on January 6th, but since both the Epiphany and the miracle of the changing of the water into wine are also celebrated on this day, the liturgical feast obviously does not offer a solid foundation upon which to base our choice. However, we must not forget that the date chosen by the Church fits in very well with the impression given by the Gospel narrative. According to John 1:29, 33 and 2:1, 13, the first Passover in our Lord's public life was celebrated not very long after John's testimony to Him as the Messias, and hence not long after His baptism; and since the forty days' fast must be placed between the baptism and the Passover, it follows that our Lord was baptized either in January of the year of the first Passover or at the end of the preceding year.

Why did Jesus receive baptism from John? The Precursor himself gives us the answer: "That he may be known to Israel, for this reason have I come baptizing with water" (John 1:31). John began baptizing precisely in order to provide the occasion for the Messias' revelation of Himself in Israel. Our Lord, then, came to John for baptism in order to accomplish the designs of the Father, who had willed thus to present Him to the world as the Messias. This, of course, does not exclude other reasons such as those pointed out by the Fathers—to give an example of humility, to lend authority to the baptism of His Pre-

---

[67] For example, Barrois in *Dict. de la Bible,* Suppl. I, cols. 968–970.
[68] Cf. Buzy ("Béthanie au delà du Jourdain," in *Rech. de Sc. Rel.,* 21 [1931], 444–462), and Dalman (*Sacred Sites and Ways,* pp. 89 *ff.*), who choose the Wadi el-Kharrar and give very good arguments for their choice. Regarding tradition on the point, see Baldi, *Enchiridion. . . . ,* pp. 211 *ff.*

cursor, to be for us a model of penance, or, as St. Thomas says, to give water its sanctifying power.[69]

Fast and Temptations
(Matt. 4:1–11; Mark 1:12–13; Luke 4:1–13)

The Spirit who descended on Jesus at His baptism moved Him to withdraw into the desert: "Then Jesus was led into the desert by the Spirit. . . ." (Matt. 4:1). There in the solitude, He wished to prepare Himself by fasting and prayer for the great work of preaching His Gospel. All-holy as He was, He did not need any such preparation, yet He wished to give us an example and to show us that union with God, withdrawal from the noise of the world and detachment from created things dispose the soul to play its part in the supernatural world of grace.

The three Synoptic evangelists say that Jesus was led by the *Spirit,* and although they do not qualify the word in any way, it is clear that they are speaking of the Holy Spirit, especially since Luke (v. 1) notes that our Lord was full of the Spirit of God who had just descended upon Him at His baptism. The Fathers and the commentators understand the reference in this way.

The desert to which Christ retired is not specified, yet we naturally conclude that it was the desert of Juda because this was the best-known and also because it bordered on the valley of the Jordan. And although the word "desert" can be interpreted widely, its use here indicates that it refers to an altogether solitary place, and Mark observes (v. 13) that Christ was "with the wild beasts," a phrase which points to a completely uninhabited region. No doubt at that time there were bears and lions in that wild country, for the well-known mosaic of Madaba, which dates from the sixth century, depicts the valley of the Jordan as being infested with lions. Even today jackals and hyenas can be found there.

According to a tradition which dates back to the seventh century at least,[70] the episode took place on the Mount of the Quarantania, Jebel Qarantal, outside ancient Jericho, the present-day Tell es-Sultan,

---

[69] IIIa, q. 39, a. 1; regarding the various reasons for the baptism, see Knabenbauer, *In Matt.* 3, 15. In his book *Jean-Baptiste,* pp. 139–231, Goguel gives a fairly complete interpretation from the rationalist point of view of the account of our Lord's baptism.

[70] Cf. Baldi, *Enchiridion.* . . . , pp. 238 *ff.*

where the monks of the Greek Monastery of St. John take delight in showing pilgrims not only the cave where our Lord probably lived, but even His very footprints! From the Byzantine period onwards, numerous hermits, eager to imitate our Saviour's example of penance, came to live in the forbidding caves with which the mountain is honeycombed.

Later, our Lord was to say: "This kind [of devil] can be cast out only by prayer and *fasting*" (Matt. 17:20); and in the Book of Tobias we read: "Prayer is good with *fasting*. . . ." (Tob. 12:8). For forty days and forty nights Moses remained on the summit of Mount Sinai, without eating bread or drinking water (Exod. 34:28); for forty days and forty nights Elias journeyed, sustained by the bread which the angel had given him, until he reached Mount Horeb (3 Kings 19:8); and for "forty days and forty nights" our Lord fasted (Matt. 4:2) in the desert, for He wished to give practical proof that He approved the conduct of His prophets, to leave us an example of mortification and penance, and to show us, as Suárez says, quoting St. John Chrysostom, that fasting lends wings to prayer and contemplation, and enables the soul to raise itself from earthly to heavenly things.[71]

However, Christ did not go into the desert only to fast and pray and to dwell among wild beasts; the Spirit had another purpose in leading Him thither—to allow Him to be tempted. The three Synoptics speak of the temptations of Christ in such a way as to give them a special importance: "Then Jesus was led into the desert by the Spirit, *to be tempted* by the devil" (Matt. 4:1); "And he was in the desert forty days and forty nights, *being tempted* by Satan" (Mark 1:13); "And Jesus . . . was led by the Spirit about the desert for forty days, *being tempted* by the devil" (Luke 4:1–2). No human mind could conceive such condescension, such profound humility, as the Son of God's allowing Himself to be tempted by Satan! St. Paul gives us the key to the mystery when he tells us that the Heavenly Father decreed that our Lord "should in all things be made like unto his brethren" (Hebr. 2:17), in order that He might know how to "have compassion on our infirmities . . . [being] tried as we are in all things except sin" (*ibid.*, 4:15).

St. Thomas, too, points out several reasons why our Lord allowed Himself to be tempted: to give us strength and assistance in our temp-

[71] *Opera*, XIX, 441.

The Greek Monastery of St. John, on the Mount of the Quarantania.

tations; to put us on the alert and to show us that no one, no matter how holy he may be, can flatter himself that he is immune from temptation; to give us a vivid example of how we should resist the devil's blandishments; and to inspire us with confidence in Christ's mercy.

The life of every true Christian is a battle, a combat without quarter, and the sight of their Captain's glorious triumph over the enemy encourages the soldiers of Christ and makes them confident that they, too, will gain the victory. On the mountain of temptation He showed His followers by His deeds what He later expressed in words to His Apostles: "Take courage, I have overcome the world" (John 16:33).

What was the devil's intention in tempting Christ? He seems to have tempted our Lord to gluttony, to presumption, vanity or boasting, and to ambition or avarice. Suárez, however, observes that the devil did not tempt Christ solely or even principally in order to induce Him to sin, but mainly to see if He were truly the Son of God.[72] And in reality this seems to have been Satan's chief aim. He had seen enough to suspect that this man was the Messias, the Son of God, and he used

[72] *Opera,* XIX, 432.

the temptations in an effort to remove all doubt. It is, of course, obvious that he was able to tempt our Lord only through His senses or imagination and not through concupiscence.[73]

We know of only three concrete, specific temptations, and we know that they occurred at the *end* of the forty days' fast (Matt. 4:2 f.; Luke 4:2 f.). But, we may ask, was our Lord also tempted during the course of the forty days? If we had only St. Matthew's account, we should reply in the negative. But St. Luke's phrasing (πειραζόμενος: "being tempted") seems to imply that the temptations took place during the course of the forty days. This is how Lagrange, B. Weiss and Plummer understand the matter, whereas Knabenbauer, on the contrary, is of the opinion that Luke was anticipating future events and that the present participle ("being tempted") refers to the three temptations which the evangelist goes on to describe. Suárez holds that this interpretation is probably the more correct one.[74] In our opinion, no definite conclusion in favor of either interpretation can be drawn from the Gospel text; however, if we had to choose one of the two alternatives, we should be inclined to accept that favored by Suárez: "I see no adequate reason for asserting that Christ was tempted by the devil during the course of those days." [75]

There has been and there still is much discussion about the true nature of the temptations. Some have wished to give them a purely symbolic value, as if the evangelists merely desired to propose a kind of model of the various temptations that men endure. In that case, of course, the narrative would not be historically accurate. However, the very text itself protests against such an interpretation since the evangelists' intention is clearly to record an objective occurrence and not just to give a symbolic lesson. Others grant that there certainly was an objective reality, but that the temptation was produced solely by internal suggestion. Unlike the hypothesis just mentioned, this theory is not wholly inadmissible since it does retain sufficiently the historical nature of the narrative. However, as Suárez correctly observes, the natural and obvious meaning is that the devil appeared in visible, and probably human, form and that he tempted our Lord with audible words and external acts. This is the impression given by the text, and

---

[73] "Cum ipse non potuerit Christum tentare interna tentatione sed tantum externa per suggestionem" (Suárez, *Opera*, XIX, 445).

[74] *Ibid.*

[75] *Ibid.* Ketter is of the same opinion; cf. *Die Versuchung Jesu, Neutestamentliche Abhandlungen,* VI, Heft 3 (Münster i. W., 1917), pp. 63–67.

Catholic authors in general interpret it in this way. Such an interpretation, however, does not exclude the possibility that some details of the temptations were presented directly to our Lord's imagination.

Matthew and Luke differ as regards the order in which the temptations occurred; in Matthew, the temptation on the pinnacle of the Temple comes second, while in Luke it comes last, and it is not easy to say which order should be preferred. Matthew's arrangement seems more probable, since it follows a kind of gradation of events. Lagrange gives other reasons in favor of Matthew, and, like him, the majority of authors prefer the sequence found in the first Gospel.[76]

In the *first* of the three temptations, Satan, trying to take advantage of the hunger which our Saviour naturally felt after forty days of fasting, suggested to Him that He procure food by working a miracle. The details of the proposed miracle were inspired by the surroundings, for there were many stones lying on the ground and, as often happens, it is likely that several of them roughly resembled loaves. Hence the devil said: "If thou art the Son of God, command that *these stones* become loaves of bread." The action proposed was not bad in itself, nor was the working of a miracle something evil. However, in this case there would have been a certain lack of due order in giving a corporal necessity such importance as to work a miracle to satisfy it. Our Lord replied in the words of Deuteronomy: "Not in bread alone doth man live, but in every word that proceedeth from the mouth of God."

When Moses used these words he was telling the people that God had not required bread to sustain them in the desert, for He had created the manna which had fed them.[77] On our Lord's lips the words of Deuteronomy could have had a twofold meaning: (1) "I do not have to live on bread alone, since God has a thousand ways of sustaining life, either by material means or by His will alone, and by merely willing it He can save Me from growing weak." According to this interpretation, which is that of Knabenbauer, B. Weiss and others, Christ was speaking of bodily life, as the devil had been. (2) But another explanation is possible; the devil was urging Christ to be so anxious to preserve the life of the body that He would go so far as to work a

---

[76] Cf. Ketter, *loc. cit.*, pp. 67 *ff*.

[77] Samuel Driver (*A Critical and Exegetical Commentary on Deuteronomy* [Edinburgh: T. & T. Clark, 3rd ed., 1902], p. 107) holds that the words of Deuteronomy have a wider application and refer to the spiritual life. We believe that they refer only to corporal sustenance, and, if we are not mistaken, this is the opinion of the great majority of commentators.

The southeast corner of the Temple precincts, overlooking the Cedron.

miracle to that end. Replying to this suggestion, one which involved a lack of due order, our Lord reminded the devil that man has another life more noble than that of the body, and that this life is not preserved by bread but by every word that comes from God's mouth. In Deuteronomy, that which came forth from the mouth of God meant everything that He could create by a simple command to feed the people, such as manna, for example. As Christ used the phrase, it meant everything that proceeds from God in the spiritual order, particularly His words or commands, which reflect His will. In this meaning, our Lord's answer is re-echoed in His later reply to the Apostle beside Jacob's well: "My food is to do the will of him who sent me" (John 4:34). Lagrange and Plummer prefer this interpretation, and we, too, regard it as the more probable one.

The scene of the *second* temptation was not the desert, but the city of Jerusalem. The first question that presents itself here is, how did our Lord go from the one place to the other? The words of St. Matthew (4:5) and St. Luke (4:9) appear to leave no doubt on the matter: the devil took Jesus and placed Him on the pinnacle of the Temple. But, as St. Gregory says, the very thought of such a thing is repugnant.[78] Hence in order to get around this difficulty various solutions have been suggested. For example, some say that our Lord had probably gone to the Holy City of His own accord, and that the devil had once more accosted Him there; or, as others believe, Satan had walked with our Lord from the Mount of the Quarantania to Jerusalem; or the devil, without leaving the desert, had represented to Christ a definite place in Jerusalem and had suggested the temptation to Him as if He were really standing in that place.

The idea of Christ's walking side by side with the devil over a distance of more than fifteen miles is also repugnant to us. And the two other solutions do not fit the explicit statements of St. Matthew [79] (". . . took him . . . and set him . . .") and of St. Luke [80] (". . . led him . . . and set him . . ."), both of which indicate positive action by the devil on our Lord. For the rest, St. Gregory, replying to his own objection, which we have quoted above, says: "Why should we wonder at [our Lord's] allowing Himself to be led to the mountain by the devil, when He suffered Himself to be crucified by his minions?" [81] How, actually, was He transported to the Temple? We do not know the answer, but we do know that, if God so permitted it, the fallen angel had the power to carry Him not only to Jerusalem but far beyond. Our Lord, then, had the infinite condescension to allow Himself to be carried by His very adversary, the enemy of all that is good.

Both Matthew and Luke record the exact spot where the second temptation occurred: "The devil . . . set him on the pinnacle of the temple." [82] The Greek word means "wing," "rim," "battlement," "pinnacle," "top"; ἱερόν can mean not only the Temple proper, the ordinary word for which is ναός, but also the whole sacred enclosure, and so it can be understood as referring to one of the porches which surrounded the building. In describing the Royal Porch on the south side of the Temple, Josephus wrote that when one looked down from the top of this porch into the valley below, the height was so great that one grew dizzy.[83] According to tradition, St. James the Less, the

---

[78] "Cum dicitur Deus homo vel in excelsum montem vel in sanctam civitatem a diabolo assumptus, mens refugit, humanae hoc audire aures expavescunt" (*Hom. 16 in Ev.: PL* 76, 1, 135).

[79] παραλαμβάνει αὐτόν . . . καὶ ἔστησεν αὐτόν.

[80] ἤγαγεν δὲ αὐτόν . . . καὶ ἔστησεν.

[81] *Loc. cit.*

[82] ἐπὶ τὸ πτερύγιον τοῦ ἱεροῦ.

[83] *Ant.* xv. 11. 5.

Bishop of Jerusalem, was thrown from this point. It is no wonder, then, that the second temptation should be popularly regarded as having occurred here, too, since it presupposed that our Lord was standing on the brink of a deep abyss.

The second temptation consisted in the devil's urging Christ to prove He was the Son of God by throwing Himself into the valley and escaping unharmed from the fall. As an incentive, Satan again quoted Holy Scripture: "For it is written, 'He will give his angels charge concerning thee; and upon their hands they shall bear thee up, lest thou dash thy foot against a stone' " (cf. Ps. 90 [Hebrew, Ps. 91]: 11 f.). Here we must note two things: first, that the text quoted is not strictly Messianic but refers to every just man; and second, that the devil gives it a meaning which it actually does not possess, since by these words God promises His divine assistance, not to him who rashly puts himself in danger, but only to just men who, through no fault of their own, are exposed to peril. To put oneself in danger without cause and then trust in God for deliverance is to "tempt God" and to be guilty of presumption. Therefore our Lord answered with another text from Deuteronomy: "Thou shalt not tempt the Lord thy God" (Deut. 4:6). It was not God's intention that the Messias should reveal Himself to the world with such a miracle, and therefore to have performed it would have been to go against the divine will.

For the *third* temptation the scene changed again, this time to a high mountain.[84] The remarks we made above about the method of transference from the desert to the Temple apply here also. To which mountain does the Gospel refer? Since the evangelist does not name it, several alternatives have been proposed—Mount Nebo, from which Moses looked upon the Promised Land; the Mount of the Quarantania; Mount Thabor; and Mount Hermon. Because of its height of more than nine thousand feet, Mount Hermon fits the evangelist's description, but it is too far from the general locality in which the temptations occurred. At all events, no matter how high the mountain was, assuredly it was not possible to view "all the kingdoms of the world" from it. We must conclude, then, that we are dealing here with a vision which the devil formed in our Lord's imagination, showing Him the kingdoms in all their splendor or, as the evangelist says, "the glory of them." St. Luke (v. 5) observes that all this took place "in a

---

[84] "in montem excelsum valde": εἰς ὄρος ὑψηλὸν λίαν. (Matt. 4:8.)

Sira Photo

The southeast corner of the Temple precincts, from the so-called
Tomb of St. James.

moment of time," in the twinkling of an eye. On this occasion the
tempter's words were even more daring than before: "All these things
will I give thee, if thou wilt fall down and worship me" (Matt. 4:9).

Luke's formula is more expressive still: "To thee will I give all this power and their glory; for to me they have been delivered, and to whomever I will I give them. Therefore if thou wilt worship before me, the whole shall be thine." It is difficult to imagine how Satan could have had the supreme audacity to make such a proposal. Perhaps driven to despair by his two defeats, he was now not so much tempting our Lord as giving free rein to his terrible pride; or perhaps we ought to say that he now took our Lord for an ordinary mortal and wished to dazzle Him with the sight of so much magnificence. But whatever the reason, we must admit that although his claims were exaggerated, they had some foundation in reality. Just as Christ later proclaimed that He was a king but that His kingdom was not of this world, so we can say that, in a certain sense, the devil is the prince of this world. Our Lord Himself called him by this title in John 12:31 and 14:30: "the prince of the world," while St. Paul named him "the god of this world" (2 Cor. 4:4). To those who adore him, Satan can give power and riches, but only for their eternal damnation.

Christ's answer to His tempter in this instance was brief and categorical and, like His other replies, it was taken from Sacred Scripture (Deut. 6:13). Peremptorily He dismissed His adversary with the words: "Begone, Satan! for it is written, 'The Lord thy God shalt thou worship and him only shalt thou serve.'"

Not daring to continue, the devil withdrew; but St. Luke tells us that he did not depart for good but only "for a while," i.e., until a more opportune moment, until he found another and more suitable occasion. When did this moment come? Later, at the beginning of His Passion, our Lord was to say: "This is your hour, and the power of darkness" (Luke 22:53).

We do not know whether or not the devil attacked Christ again in a visible form but he did assault Him many times invisibly, both directly and indirectly, by means of his servants, the Jews.

When the devil had left our Lord, angels came and ministered to Him.

The Voice in the Desert [85]
(John 1:19–28)

The religious authorities in Jerusalem could not remain indifferent

[85] According to Fr. M. E. Boismard (*Du Baptême à Cana: Jean 1:19–2:11* [Paris, 1956], p. 15), St. John artificially distributes the events recorded in 1:19–2:11

to the powerful spiritual current that was drawing the crowds to John the Baptist. The leaders of the people soon began to inquire into the character of the penitent who was preaching without legal authorization, who came dressed like the prophet Elias, and who had the power to stir the people's conscience so profoundly. However, even the most suspicious of the doctors of Israel could find nothing in his words that was not in perfect harmony with Jewish teaching and with the hope of the approaching appearance of the Messias. Therefore, so far as they could see, there was no motive for forbidding his activities; and it would not have been just to condemn him without a hearing. So the leaders of the people decided on the one reasonable course to remove any doubt they might have had about John: they would ask him to give an account of himself. Accordingly, the Sanhedrin or supreme council of the Jews sent a formal delegation composed of priests, Levites and some of the most notable Pharisees to question the Precursor. The appearance of these great personages at the place of baptism must have aroused lively curiosity in the crowd that was gathered there. In the expectant hush that followed their arrival, the delegation authoritatively asked John: "Who art thou?" as if to say: "Give an account of thyself!"

The Precursor, divining their thoughts, replied categorically and without quibbling: "I am not the Messias."

But the envoys of the Sanhedrin continued to question him: "What then? Art thou Elias?"

According to a popular tradition, based on the prophet Malachias (cf. 3:23 *f.*), Elias was to come as the precursor of the Messias. The question which the Apostles asked of our Lord: "Why then do the Scribes say that Elias must come first?" (Matt. 17:10) was inspired by this tradition. Curtly John replied: "I am not."

"Art thou the prophet?" They meant the prophet foretold by Moses in Deuteronomy 18:15.

over a period of seven days in imitation of the seven days of creation found in Genesis. We believe, rather, that the evangelist was more concerned with historical precision than with strained symbolism. An example of this concern is seen in his remark: "It was about the tenth hour" (1:39), about which Fr. Mollat (*Bible de Jérusalem* [Paris 1953]), beautifully says: "Ce détail infime est comme la signature de l'évangéliste. Dans sa banalité, il confère à toute la scène le caractère d'un témoignage et presque d'une confidance personnelle d'une valeur historique inappréciable." And, in fact, when we accept St. John's account as strictly historical, we find that the events follow each other simply and naturally.

"No."

All John's answers were in the negative, and since the delegation wanted to have some positive information about the mysterious preacher to report to the Sanhedrin, they persisted in their cross-examination: "Tell us then who thou art, that we may give an answer to those who sent us."

Humbly the Precursor explained who he was: "I am the voice of one crying in the desert, 'Make straight the way of the Lord.'"

Surprised, no doubt, by this unexpected reply, they remonstrated with him: "Why, then, dost thou baptize, if thou art not the Messias, nor Elias, nor the prophet?"

And John answered: "I baptize with water," a ceremony for which he did not need to be a prophet, because the ablutions, which could be considered a kind of baptism, were common among the Jews. Although this was answer enough to the delegates' reproach, he went further and added his testimony to the Messias: "In the midst of you"—here in the land of Israel, or rather, in this very region, perhaps in this very audience which is listening to me—"there has stood one whom you do not know." Then he concluded with the humble confession: "He it is who is to come after me, who has been set above me, the strap of whose sandal I am not worthy to loose."

Christ is in our midst today, and how many, more culpable than the Sandhedrists, do not know Him! And even among those who do know Him, how few are animated by His spirit! God, the Holy Trinity, is within us, the soul is His temple; yet how many are they who are virtually ignorant of this mystery. It is in God, in the Holy Trinity, that "we live and move and have our being" (Acts 17:23, 28), and still we do not know Him!

The Lamb of God

The envoys of the Sanhedrin returned to Jerusalem, dissatisfied with their interview with the mysterious penitent, yet without having found in his words or deeds anything that official Judaism could censure.

On the following day, while John was again baptizing in the same place, at Bethany near the Jordan, he saw Christ in the distance coming towards him. Deeply moved, he pointed to the Saviour and exclaimed: "Behold the lamb of God, who takes away the sin of the world!" Then continuing, he said: "After me there comes one who has been set above me, because he was before me. . . . And I did not know him. But he who sent me to baptize with water said to me, 'He upon whom thou wilt see the Spirit descending, and abiding upon him, he it is who baptizes with the Holy Spirit.' And I have seen and have borne witness that this is the Son of God" (John 1:29–34).

Thus did John show that he was a worthy herald of the great King. With ardent zeal, generous love, and deep humility he had prepared and continued to prepare the way for the Messias, who had now come. With what sentiments of loving self-abasement will he call himself simply "the friend of the bridegroom," whom he humbly serves and whose voice he rejoices to hear! Not only that, but he will also say later that the bridegroom must increase and progress in glory while he himself must decrease and disappear! (John 3:29 f.)

In the figure under which John the Baptist presents Jesus to us, there stands out clearly the idea of redemption by the blood of a victim, an innocent victim, an idea that is rooted in the Old Testament, especially in that great poem, chapter 23 of the prophet Isaias.

Because there are very diverse views as to the scope of John's words: "Behold the lamb of God, who takes away the sin of the world," and also because the matter is an important one, we think it best to pause awhile to examine the sentence in question.

The lamb is a symbol of purity and innocence as well as of meekness and patience under suffering. Which of these two qualities did John have in mind? The Greek participle [86] can mean "who *takes away*," or "who *bears*." Which of these meanings is the one intended here? Each interpretation has its supporters as well as its opponents. Some commentators hold that the true sense is: "Behold the lamb of God, who is immaculate, immune from all sin, and who will rid the world of sin." Here there is not the slightest reference to suffering, sacrifice or expiation. Others say that it should be interpreted as meaning: "Behold the lamb of God, meek and patient, who rids the world of sin by taking it upon himself," i.e., by suffering and expiation.

First of all, there is a general argument against this second interpretation, namely, that it does not fit in with the Messianic ideal which John the Baptist had formed during his first period of preaching, for he then spoke of the Messias as a judge who was coming to cleanse

---

[86] αἴρων.

the world as the farmer does his threshing floor (cf. Matt. 3:12; Luke 3:17). Then, too, this second interpretation falls outside the Baptist's horizon; and independent critics consider that this proves that the evangelist attributed to John the conception of the Messias which he himself had formed, namely, that the Messias had been prefigured by the Paschal lamb. There are some who believe that we can avoid this conclusion of the rationalist critics only by appealing to the first interpretation, which, they point out, can be reached by the historical method.[87]

Let us use the historical method to ascertain which of the two meanings corresponds better with the characteristics of the lamb in relation to the Messias as depicted in the Old and New Testaments. Isaias speaks of the Messias as being "dumb as a lamb before his shearer" (Isai. 53:7; cf. Acts 8:32), and Jeremias says of him that he was "as a meek lamb that is carried to be a victim" (Jer. 11:19). St. Peter in his First Epistle speaks of "the precious blood of Christ, as of a lamb without blemish and without spot" (1 Pet. 1:19), while the Apocalypse contains the following references: "The Lamb who was slain. . . ." (5:12); "[They] have made [their robes] white in the blood of the Lamb" (7:14); "They overcame him through the blood of the Lamb" (12:11); "In the book of life of the Lamb who has been slain from the foundation of the world" (13:8; cf. 1:5: "And from Jesus Christ . . . who has . . . washed us from our sins in his own blood"). In each of these passages, which, if we are not mistaken, are the only ones in which the lamb is mentioned in connection with Christ, the characteristic of long-suffering meekness, of victimhood, stands out clearly. Only in 1 Peter 1:19 is there mention of the purity and innocence of the lamb, and even there innocence is not mentioned for its own sake, but only for its relationship with the character of the victim since, as we all know, a lamb or any other animal destined for sacrifice had to be perfect and without blemish, as had the Paschal lamb (Exod. 12:5; cf. Lev. 22:21, which uses the same word as 1 Pet., i.e., ἄμωμος, "without blemish"). Hence, although this passage mentions innocence, it does not present the lamb as a symbol of a just man among sinners.

Even when speaking of the lamb in general and without reference to the Messias, the Old Testament never uses the animal as a symbol of innocence. It is true that in Ecclesiasticus 46:19 we read: "in oblatione

[87] Cf. Lagrange, *Év. selon S. Jean, in loc.*

agni *inviolati*," but we must note that here there is question of a sacrifice offered by Samuel (1 Kings 7:9), and also that the Greek text of Ecclesiasticus uses the word γαλαθηνοῦ exactly as in 1 Kings 7:9 (λαγαθηνόν),where the Vulgate translates it faithfully as *lactantem*. The same is true of the New Testament since in the only text that could be adduced ("Behold, I send you forth as lambs in the midst of wolves." Luke 10:3), the stress is placed, not upon the innocence, but rather upon the unoffending meekness of the lamb as opposed to the daring rapacity of the wolf. Lagrange adduces only one passage in favor of the lamb's characteristic of innocence and even that one text is not from Sacred Scripture but from the apocryphal *Psalms of Solomon:* "The saints of God, like innocent lambs. . . ." (8:28).[88]

Considering this literary background and the prevailing atmosphere, what meaning must we give to "the lamb of God" as used by John, who was undoubtedly familiar with the Scripture? The answer seems obvious: he was speaking of the sins which the lamb was to remove; and he was thinking of the meekness, suffering and victimhood which stand out in all the passages which we have quoted. Certainly he regarded the Lamb of God as innocent, and innocence is presupposed in an expiatory victim, but this was not his main idea. We must conclude, then, that John's phrase "the lamb of God" originated in the text of Isaias (53:7) which represents the Messias as a lamb that is led uncomplainingly to the slaughter.

But we can go even further. The passage from Isaias to which we have just referred speaks of suffering and death, and in verse 10 the idea of expiatory sacrifice is clearly expressed: "if he shall lay down his life for sin he shall see a long-lived seed," i.e., if he offers himself as a *sacrifice of expiation*.[89] Hence we conclude that, in Isaias, the death of the Servant of Yahweh, who is represented by the lamb, is a sacrifice for men's sins, which He took upon Himself (v. 11) and which God placed on His shoulders: "the Lord hath laid on him the iniquity of us all" (v. 6). Thus John's "lamb of God" is not only the Lamb led to death but also the Lamb led to a death that is a sacrifice in expiation for the sins of men.

Whether this conception of the Lamb has any relationship with the lambs offered in the daily sacrifice (Exod. 29:38) or with the immola-

---

[88] Cf. Viteau, *Les Psaumes de Salomon* (Paris, 1911).
[89] With Condamin, Budde and others, and in conformity with the Vulgate, we read the third person masculine.

tion of the Paschal lamb (Exod. 12), is only a secondary question, the answer to which does not affect our main thesis. Without giving this point greater importance than it deserves, we believe that the sacrifices just mentioned could have influenced the formation of the concept of "the lamb of God," since all of them, whatever their nature, had the general theme of sacrifice.[90]

What we have just said gives the solution to the second problem: should the participle αἴρων be translated "qui *tollit:* who *takes away,*" or "qui *portat:* who *bears*"? Does the Lamb simply remove men's sins, or does He take them upon Himself? The word αἴρειν strictly means "to take" or "to take away," and since one often takes something up and carries it, the word can also mean "to carry or bear," as, for example, in Matthew 4:6; 16:24; 27:32.[91] The Hebrew word *nasa'* has both meanings; in Isaias 53:4 it certainly has the connotation of "taking upon oneself," as is evident from the following word, *sabal,* which is repeated in verse 11. But the general sense of the whole chapter is that the Servant of Yahweh, in taking the world's iniquities upon Himself, thereby rids men of them, as it is precisely for this purpose that He wills to carry them upon His own shoulders. Thus the two meanings of taking away and bearing are closely connected, and in this particular case the one includes the other. Hence it matters little whether we translate the Greek as "who takes away" or as "who bears," since the meaning is basically the same in both. However, in the passage in question, the first interpretation seems preferable, for at least it has the advantage of corresponding with the Vulgate and the liturgy. For the rest, the verb *tollo* can and often does mean at once both to take and to burden oneself with, as in John 5:8: *"Tolle grabatum tuum;* take up thy pallet."

The First Disciples
(John 1:35–42)

On the afternoon of the day following his testimony to the Lamb of God, John was standing with two of his disciples, when, seeing Christ

---

[90] See Joüon, "L'Agneau de Dieu (Jean 1:29)," in *Nouv. Rev. Théol.,* 67 (1940), 318–321, where the author, in a brief but effective note, maintains that John the Baptist's words contain the idea of a *redemptive victim;* also J. Leal, "El sentido soteriológico del cordero de Dios en la exégesis católica (Jn. 1:29–36)," in *Est. Ecles.,* 24 (1950), 147–182, where there is a copious bibliography; Eric May, O.F.M.Cap. *Ecce Agnus Dei! A Philological and Exegetical Approach to John 1:29–36* (Washington, 1947).

[91] Str.-Bill., II, 367, n. 3, also cites these very passages.

again as He passed by, he uttered once more the sweet, profound words of the day before: "Behold the lamb of God!"

When, perhaps for the second time, the disciples heard their teacher's declaration, pronounced as it was with so much love and such deep conviction, they were no doubt enlightened and moved by the grace which the Lamb of God Himself communicated to them. Taking their leave of him whom they had hitherto regarded as their master, they prepared to follow Christ. John did not offer the least objection to their going; instead he undoubtedly encouraged them to join the new Teacher.[92]

The Gospel tells us the name of one of these fortunate disciples— Andrew, the brother of Peter; but it does not mention the name of the other. Some believe, and with good reason, that the second was either John the evangelist himself, the future beloved disciple of Jesus, or another follower who did not persevere. And, in fact, if there was question of one of the future Apostles other than John himself, there was no reason why the evangelist should have omitted his name, seeing that he had already recorded that of Andrew. If, on the contrary, the disciple mentioned had decided not to join our Lord and had disappeared from the Gospel scene, there would obviously be no point in the evangelist's telling us who he was. But, actually, this hypothesis seems rather improbable, for since Andrew followed the Messias, it is natural to suppose that the other disciple would have done likewise, and in that case Andrew's companion can have been none other than St. John himself, who, through modesty, forbore to mention his own name.

The two disciples, then, walked towards Jesus. The scene that followed was one of charming simplicity, and the dialogue natural and spontaneous. Out of reverence or bashfulness, they did not dare to speak to Christ but walked a little behind Him, and soon our Lord, knowing that they were there, turned to them and said: "What is it you seek?"

He knew well what they wanted for He could read their hearts, but He wished them to tell Him themselves what they sought. However, they considered that their business was not such as to be dealt with hastily as they walked along the public road, but that it should be talked

---

[92] "Quia talis erat Joannes amicus sponsi, non quaerebat gloriam suam, sed testimonium perhibebat veritati. Numquid voluit apud se remanere discipulos suos ut non sequerentur Dominum? Magis ipse ostendit discipulis suis quem sequerentur." (St. Augustine: *PL* 35. 1441.)

over quietly and in a private place. Therefore, without revealing their wishes, they asked: "Master, where dwellest thou?" In this way they indicated that they desired to speak privately and at some length with Him. "Come and see," said our Lord, issuing a friendly invitation to them to accompany Him to His dwelling.

It is not likely that they walked the rest of the way in silence, for our Lord, reading the deepest secrets of these simple and well-disposed hearts, undoubtedly spoke kindly and familiarly to the two disciples, putting them at their ease and inspiring them with confidence.

Even in his old age the evangelist recalled perfectly the exact time at which the episode occurred, and he adds this delightful touch of realism: "It was about the tenth hour," i.e., about four in the afternoon, counting from six A.M. And since it was towards the end of February, evening was already falling in the deep valley of the Jordan.

They probably arrived at the place where our Lord was staying just as the last rays of the sun were gilding the valley. His habitation must have been a natural cave at the foot of the mountains or in the side of one of the *wadis* that cross the broad valley, or perhaps a little hut made of branches such as can still be seen in the fields there.

How wonderful it would be if we had a record of the sweet and intimate conversation that occupied the rest of the day in that lonely spot! For the Gospel explicitly says that "they stayed with him that day." It is possible and even probable that they spent the night there too, and that our Lord, ever thoughtful and courteous, extended to them the invitation which the two disciples of Emmaus were later to extend to Him: "Stay with Me, for the day is now far spent." The two guests would have needed no urging to accept, and they would have passed the night hanging on our Lord's words, for He did not speak like the other rabbis but "as one having authority" (Mark 1: 22), not, however, an authority that imposed itself by force but rather one that inspired reverence, confidence and love. What a pity that the beloved disciple did not hand down to us an account of this night-long conversation, just as he did that between our Lord and Nicodemus! "What a happy day they spent!" exclaims St. Augustine. "What a happy night! Who will tell us what they heard from the lips of the Lord? Let us, too, build a house in our hearts which He may enter and where He may communicate to us His teachings in sweet conversation." [93]

[93] "Quam beatam diem duxerunt, quam beatam noctem! Quis est qui nobis dicat

"Happy is that soul which hears the Lord speaking within her," says the *Imitation,* "and from His mouth receives the word of comfort. . . . Happy ears which hearken to truth itself teaching within, and not to the voice which sounds without." [94] This was the truth which the two disciples heard that night, and, as St. John Chrysostom says, it was poured out to them in such abundance that they immediately set out to call others to share in their good fortune. Thus it was that Andrew, after taking his leave of Jesus, and no doubt having received permission to visit Him again, hastened away in search of his brother Simon, who had accompanied him from Galilee. When he located him, he could not wait to explain all the circumstances but at once burst out excitedly: "We have found the Messias!" (John 1:41). Simon, despite his rough and impetuous character, was a docile man and allowed himself to be led by his brother to meet the unknown stranger whom Andrew called the Messias.

We can well believe that Andrew introduced his brother to our Lord with a certain air of justifiable satisfaction, for Simon was his first conquest for Christ. His pleasure would have been greater still if he had been able to pierce the veils of the future and see the high office to which the poor fisherman from Galilee was to be elevated. Simon's future greatness was foreshadowed by an event which occurred on this first meeting with Christ. When the usual courtesies had been exchanged, our Lord looked fixedly at His new disciple, a thing He had not done with the others, and solemnly said to him: "Thou art Simon, the son of John; thou shalt be called Cephas," i.e., "rock" (v. 42). Neither Simon nor Andrew understood the significance of this change of name, but they were to see the reason for it when Christ later said to Simon: "Thou art Peter ["rock"], and upon this rock I will build my Church . . ." (Matt. 16:18).

quae audierunt illi a Domino? Aedificemus et nosmetipsi in corde nostro, et faciamus domum quo veniat ille et doceat nos; colloquatur nobis" (*PL* 35. 1442).

[94] Bk. III, chap. 1.

8. Jesus Returns

to Galilee

New Disciples
(John 1:43–51; cf. Map IV)

It was about the beginning of March when our Lord decided to return to Galilee, and probably on the day following His conversation with Andrew and Simon Peter (John 1:42 *f.*). He had been in Judea two months or a little more, and He seems to have spent all of this period in the country about the Jordan. The very configuration of the region suggests the route He undoubtedly took to Galilee—along the Jordan valley to the higher ground at Scythopolis (present-day Beisan), then to the left across the slopes of Little Hermon, past the foot of Mount Thabor and then on for about an hour's journey to His native town of Nazareth. But He could just as well have taken the road through Bethel, which some authors prefer (Fouard, for example) because of His indirect reference to Jacob's vision (John 1:51; cf. Gen. 28:10–22). Or, on arriving at the then recently-constructed city of Phasaelis, He could have left the valley and gone up through Akrabeh to join the great north-south road near Sichem. However, we regard the first route as the most probable one.

It is likely that the two brothers from Bethsaida, Andrew and Simon, had been accompanied from Galilee to Judea by a fellow-townsman of theirs named Philip (v. 44). Jesus met Philip, but St. John, who narrates the episode and who, no doubt, witnessed it himself, does not specify either the time or the place of the encounter. It probably occurred on the day of their departure for Galilee and hence in the valley of the Jordan.

To Philip, Christ simply said: "Follow me," or, at least, these are the only words recorded by the evangelist. Some authors, such as Zahn and B. Weiss, regard them as a mere invitation to return with Him to Galilee, whereas others, for example, Knabenbauer, Lagrange, and Gomá, consider them as a call to the apostolate. The latter is the more probable interpretation. We do not know what Philip's reply was, but at any rate our Lord's words were so efficacious that, with humble and docile promptness, the new disciple joined the little group and followed the Master.

Philip soon had a chance to exercise his apostolate by winning for Christ one of his friends, a man named Nathanael (= "God gives" or "gift of God," the equivalent of our "Theodore"), who was also a Galilean, not, however, from Bethsaida, but from Cana in Galilee (John 21:2). Upon finding his friend, Philip immediately told him about the Messias.

Where and when did our Lord and Nathanael meet? Since Nathanael was from Cana in Galilee and since our Lord went there for the wedding feast, we might be led to suppose that the meeting took place when the party arrived at Cana. Then, too, before Philip had called him, Nathanael had been seated under a fig tree (v. 48), a type of tree which grew in abundance about the town. However, because the marriage feast is not mentioned until later (2:1 *ff.*), whereas the meeting of Philip and Nathanael is related immediately after that of our Lord and Philip, we are inclined to believe that both encounters took place in the valley of the Jordan, and that possibly Philip found Nathanael in the neighborhood of Jericho, where fig trees also grew. Because Philip and Nathanael were acquaintances and probably friends, it is possible that they had come together to Judea and that Philip now invited his companion to return with them to Galilee. Lagrange thinks it unlikely that so many Galileans would have met in Judea, but his objection does not seem very cogent.

As we have already hinted, Fouard places the scene near Bethel.[1] The words "the angels of God ascending and descending . . ." certainly recall the vision which Jacob saw near Bethel (cf. Gen. 28:12),

---

[1] *The Christ, The Son of God,* trans. by F. X. Griffith (New York: Longmans, Green & Co., 1944), I, 135 *f.*

and one of the roads leading to Galilee did pass this way, but there was no reason for Nathanael's being in the region.

The dialogue between Philip and Nathanael is most interesting, and St. John has recorded it for us in all its details. Philip's first words to his friend were very similar to those of Andrew to his brother Simon: "We have found him of whom Moses in the Law and the Prophets wrote, Jesus the son of Joseph of Nazareth." That was the same as saying that Jesus of Nazareth was the Messias, who was indeed mentioned in Genesis 3:15; 12:3; 18:18; 22:18; 49:10; Numbers 24:17; and Deuteronomy 18:15, while the Messianic passages in the prophets are innumerable. It is quite possible that Philip did not know of the mystery of the Incarnation, for he spoke of Christ as He was generally regarded, i.e., as "the son of Joseph," and he did not say that Jesus was from Bethlehem but from Nazareth, since His parents came from that village and He had grown up there.

Nathanael was a somewhat reserved person, little given to sudden enthusiasm. He was well acquainted with the obscure village of Nazareth, for it lay in an isolated valley only a few miles from his own native Cana, and so he replied half skeptically, half disdainfully: "Can anything good come out of Nazareth?"

Was this poor opinion of Nazareth merely Nathanael's own point of view, or was it the judgment which the people in the neighboring towns had formed of the natives of the village? The evangelists' description of the way the villagers treated our Lord (Matt. 13:57 *f.*; Mark 6:6; Luke 4:29) gives us a far from flattering impression of their character. It is not improbable, then, that Nazareth was regarded with a certain contempt, not only because it was small but also, and perhaps even more, because of the character of its inhabitants. It is even possible that this general contempt had crystallized into a kind of proverb.

Nathanael's answer made it clear that he did not share Philip's enthusiasm. Yet Philip was not discouraged, and being a prudent man, he did not wish to argue the point but merely said: "Come and see." To please his friend, Nathanael condescended to go with him, although he was sure that meeting the supposed Messias was not going to change his mind. But how amazed he must have been when, on approaching the little group, he heard Christ saying to those around Him: "Behold one who is truly an Israelite in whom there is no guile."

We should note the precise meaning of this sentence. Our Lord did not say: "Behold a *real Israelite*" (all the sons of Israel were that) nor "a *true Israelite*," but rather: "Behold one who is *truly an Israelite*," i.e., an Israelite worthy of the name. There were many who, although they belonged to the people of Israel, were not truly Israelites. Our Lord gave this title to Nathanael because he was an upright, faithful and sincere man in whom there was no guile.

Surprised, Nathanael said to Jesus: "Whence knowest thou me?"— a natural question since this was the first time they had met.

Jesus replied: "Before Philip called thee, when thou wast under the fig tree, I saw thee."

These apparently ordinary words must have had a hidden and higher meaning, because as they stand they do not account for Nathanael's sudden change of opinion when he heard them. But it is not easy to say what this mysterious meaning was. The expression "I saw thee" can be taken as referring to bodily sight or to intellectual knowledge. If our Lord used the words in the first sense He meant that He had seen Nathanael before Philip had gone to find him, i.e., when he was still far away and not in the range of normal sight. Thus Christ was indicating that He possessed the supernatural power of seeing things at a distance. But several objections can be raised against this explanation. First, our Lord made a simple statement, but gave no proof that it was true. How then could His words have made such a deep impression on Nathanael who had hitherto been so skeptical? Secondly, Christ's answer did not correspond with the question, which obviously dealt with knowledge of Nathanael's moral character, while, if we accept this interpretation, the answer referred to purely material vision. Hence it is very probable that the verb "to see" should be taken in the sense of intellectual sight or knowledge. But here again we meet the same difficulty as before; what guarantee had Nathanael that Christ really had seen into his soul? Our Lord's praise could have been uttered out of courtesy and could have been merely a compliment. In order to get around this difficulty, which is a very real one, more than a few authors hold that the mention of the fig tree reminded Nathanael of something about which he alone could have known and that the reference was incontrovertible proof that Christ had the power of reading his heart. We can only guess at what this secret was. Was it an inner crisis? Had he been asking God to let him know when the

Messias came? Had he received some special favor from God while he was under the fig tree? There are many more hypotheses, all of them just as plausible as these but none of them any more susceptible of positive proof. We are inclined to believe that the main reason for Nathanael's sudden change of attitude towards Christ was a special interior enlightenment. Our Lord, in His mercy, and perhaps to reward Nathanael for his upright life and good will, shed on him a ray of light and gave him a revelation that showed him the truth.

One thing, at least, is certain: Nathanael's mocking skepticism was overcome by living faith and he, who was usually so grave and restrained in speech, burst forth into a glorious confession: "Master, thou art the Son of God, thou art the King of Israel."

From the fact that Nathanael used the definite article we can conclude that he did not mean that Christ was only a man of God, a prophet; i.e., he did not say that Christ was *a* son of God but *the* Son of God, He whom the people of Israel had been expecting. On the other hand, it cannot be asserted that in using this title he wished to bear witness to our Lord's divine Sonship in the strict sense, because that would have presupposed a knowledge of the Holy Trinity on his part. Here the words "Son of God" should be taken instead as a synonym for "the Messias," especially since it was common knowledge and belief that the Messias was to be the King of Israel, precisely the second title which Nathanael gave our Lord. We can then reasonably suppose that since he used the titles "Son of God" and "King of Israel" one after the other, he regarded them as being synonymous. It is true that Nathanael's words are identical with those of St. Peter's glorious confession near Caesarea Philippi, but, as St. John Chrysostom remarks, the meaning was not the same.[2]

To this magnificent confession, Jesus replied: "Because I said to thee that I saw thee under the fig tree, thou dost believe. Greater things than these shalt thou see."

---

[2] "Quamvis eadem verba locuti sunt Petrus et Nathanael, nec tamen eodem uterque sensu. Sed Petrus quidem confessus est eum Filium Dei ut verum Deum, Nathanael vero simplicem hominem" (*In Ioan.* Hom. 2. 1: *PG* 59, 128).

"Although he [Nathanael] calls Jesus the Son of God, he does not use the expression in its strict connotation as indicating natural sonship. Rather he employs this title in the sense given it by popular opinion in reference to the Messias. Or it may be that, having heard from John the Baptist's disciples that their teacher had called Christ the Son of God, he, too, uses the title without understanding its full implications on John the Baptist's lips, and simply as a synonym for the Messianic King of Israel," (Murillo, *Evangelio de San Juan,* pp. 173 f.)

What were these greater things to be? Our Lord Himself explained: "Amen, amen, I say to you, you shall see heaven opened, and the angels of God ascending and descending upon the Son of Man."

Two things stand out clearly in this prophecy: first, it contains an allusion to Jacob's vision at Bethel (Gen. 28:2); and second, Heaven is depicted as being opened as a preliminary condition to the ascent and descent of the angels. But it is difficult to ascertain exactly when and on what occasion this ascent and descent of the angels upon our Lord took place; in other words, it is hard to know what Christ meant by this observation. Various theories have been advanced—that it refers to the appearance of the angels at the Resurrection or at the agony in Gethsemani, or that it refers to angelic visitations not mentioned in the Gospels or to the role of the angels on the Day of Judgment, or else to the miracles which our Lord wrought; or, finally, that the words are to be taken in a purely allegorical sense. For our part, we believe it probable that they refer to the invisible ministry of the angels who were to be always at the disposal and service of the Messias to accomplish the great work which the Father had entrusted to Him and to be messengers, as it were, between Heaven and earth, between the Eternal Father on high and the Son of Man on earth. The Apostles did not see the angels themselves, but they could observe their activity in the miracles wrought by Jesus, and these miracles were to be the "greater things" which Nathanael was one day to see.

There is a very ancient belief, and one which is still quite common, that Nathanael was none other than the Apostle Bartholomew, the former being his first name and the latter his family name, for there was nothing to prevent his being called and known by both. In John 21:2 we find Nathanael mentioned with some of the Apostles, and this fact can be taken as somewhat of an indication that he was one of them. Pilgrims to Cana are still shown the house, or rather the site of the house, in which Nathanael probably lived.[3]

---

[3] See Holzmeister's learned article, "Nathanael fuitne idem ac S. Bartholomaeus apostolus?" in *Biblica,* 21 (1940), 28–39: "Ex his omnibus elucet quanta difficultate laboret sententia hodie a plurimis admissa, quae Nathanaelem eundem virum ac Bartholomaeum apostolum fuisse statuit. Nihilominus tamen omnibus aliis opinionibus, quas collegimus, certo praeferenda est" (p. 39). "Quare omnibus perpensis vix quidquam remanet nisi ut . . . statuamus Nathanaelem verum apostolum evasisse" (p. 34).

Sira Photo

Cana in Galilee.

The Marriage Feast at Cana
(John 2:1–11; cf. Maps II and V)

In Israel marriages were celebrated with great festivities, the principal one being the nuptial banquet. The marriage itself was preceded by a period of betrothal or espousal—twelve months for a virgin and thirty days for a widow.[4] The betrothal was considered as equivalent to marriage, although it consisted only in a *promise* to marry and the betrothed woman continued to live in her parents' house.[5] If the betrothed woman was unfaithful to her fiancé she was regarded and punished as an adulteress. On the day of betrothal the man gave gifts to his intended bride's brothers and other relatives, and to her father he handed the *mohar,* a certain amount of money as compensation for, and to an extent as the price of, the daughter. This custom is still followed by the Arabs, among whom tradition and local usage have exactly determined the number and kind of gifts (clothes, particularly)

---

[4] *Mishnah, Ketuboth* 5:2.

[5] As we have pointed out before, this custom explains the episode in Matt. 1:18–24. When Mary conceived she was already betrothed to Joseph but he had not yet taken her into his house. See pp. 108 *ff.* above; cf. G. Ricciotti, *The Life of Christ,* trans. by A. Zizzamia (Milwaukee: Bruce, 1947), p. 226; Prat, *Jesus Christ,* I, 43–44.

which the man has to give to the woman's female relatives, the value of the gifts being in proportion to the recipient's degree of relationship to the bride.

When the day of the marriage arrived, the bride, crowned with flowers and surrounded by a certain number of virgins who served her as bridesmaids, waited in her parents' house for the arrival of the bridegroom.[6] The latter, accompanied by his *paranymphs* (cf. Matt. 9:15; Judges 14:11), young men of his own age, arrived at the house at night and then he and his bride, both crowned with flowers, set out to return to his house, the bride being carried in a litter if she was a virgin. Accompanied by the virgins and young men, and of course by a large number of guests and also of onlookers who had joined the procession, they wended their way through the streets to the sound of musical instruments and songs. Meanwhile a banquet had been prepared at the groom's house; when the couple arrived there the festivities began, and songs in praise of the newlyweds were sung in the course of the feast.[7]

If the bride was a virgin, the festivities usually lasted for seven days: if she was a widow, for three. According to the *Mishnah,* the marriage of a widow had to be celebrated on a Thursday, and that of a virgin on a Wednesday, the reason being that the tribunal was in session in the cities on Thursdays, and hence the groom could immediately appeal thereto in case of litigation concerning the virginity of his bride.[8] From this some authors conclude that the wedding feast at Cana was celebrated either on Wednesday or Thursday.[9] Such a conclusion is rather doubtful, since we do not know if this law or custom was in force in our Lord's day.

The evangelist speaks only of the marriage feast proper and not of the preparations, which were of no interest to him here. There is no doubt that Mary had close connections with the newly-married couple, but we do not know whether she was a relative of theirs or merely an

[6] Our Lord described this scene in the parable of the wise and foolish virgins (Matt. 25:1–13). It must be noted that the words "and the bride" in verse 1 are not found in the Greek text.

Among the Arabs the bridegroom does not go to seek the bride, but among the Samaritans he does so.

[7] See Str.-Bill., I, 505–517, where all the ceremonies are described in great detail; see also S. Kraus, *Talmudische Archäologie* (Leipzig, 1911), II, 36 *ff*.

[8] *Ketuboth* 1:1.

[9] For example, E. Stapfer, *La Palestine au temps de Jésus-Christ* (Paris, 1908), p. 158.

intimate friend. There is a tradition worthy of some credence that Sephoris was the native city of St. Anne, our Lady's mother; in fact, one can still see the rather well-preserved ruins of a magnificent church which was built there in her honor in very early times. And Cana [10] is only a short distance, about four miles, from Sephoris, while Nazareth is approximately the same distance from Cana. Therefore it is quite possible that one of the newlyweds was related to the Holy Family, or even that both of them were.

It seems that St. Joseph was now dead, and that our Lady was invited as the head of the family, Jesus being asked, too, because of His Mother. At least that is the impression given by the Gospel; and because our Lord was a guest, the disciples who accompanied Him would have been invited too. But be that as it may, we know that Jesus did not refuse the invitation. As St. John Chrysostom says: "He who did not disdain to take the form of a servant, will much less disdain to attend the wedding of servants, and He who associated with publicans and sinners will much less refuse to sit with the guests at the wedding feast." [11]

This episode demonstrates how the disciples of Christ and the imitators of Mary can fulfill legitimate social demands without spiritual loss. Souls who live an intensely spiritual life possess the secret of elevating to a higher plane acts which in themselves are indifferent and ordinary, thereby transforming the base metal of everyday things into purest gold. The incident is of singular importance in other respects, too: first, many authors believe that Christian marriage was instituted at Cana, i.e., that marriage was raised to the dignity of a sacrament; secondly, it was on this occasion that our Lord worked His first miracle; and thirdly, He worked this miracle at the intercession of His holy Mother.

To a certain extent, St. John fixes the date of the marriage feast by telling us that it took place on the third day (v. 1), but since he does not indicate the point from which the days should be counted, this chronological information is rather obscure. Most probably he is alluding to chapter 1, verse 43, i.e., using as a point of reference the day on which Jesus started out on the journey to Galilee and on which He first spoke with Nathanael. This is the way in which many authors, for example, Lagrange and B. Weiss, understand the matter. Actually,

---

[10] See below, pp. 233 *ff.*   [11] *PG* 59, 129.

three days were sufficient for the journey to Cana.[12] Our Lord and His companions could have walked from the neighborhood of Jericho to Beisan (about fifty miles) in two days; and one day was easily enough for the journey from Beisan to Cana, even if they went by way of Nazareth. This presupposes that Jesus attended the banquet held on the first day, which was no doubt the most solemn of the festivities; but since the feasting used to continue for seven days (cf. Judges 14:12), we cannot exclude the possibility that the Gospel may be referring to one of the banquets that were held during the week of celebration.

The words "and the mother of Jesus was there" (v. 1) give us to understand that our Lady was already in Cana when Jesus arrived: it is probable that she had come some time before the date set for the beginning of the wedding feast. However, it is difficult to say how and in what form our Lord received the invitation for Himself and His disciples. If He received it while He was still in the valley of the Jordan, He probably went directly to Cana; if not, then He would no doubt have passed through Nazareth, where he would have been given the young couple's message. We believe it less likely that He went first to Bethsaida, the native town of several of His disciples, met Philip and Nathanael there, and received the invitation there also.[13] On the contrary, it is not unlikely that since Nathanael was a native of Cana, our Lord went directly there with him. Our Lady was already in the town for the wedding and when her Son arrived, He and His disciples were, of course, invited to attend also. Our Lord's coming directly to Cana can be easily explained if we accept the theory advanced by some authors (e.g., B. Weiss), that Mary had taken up residence there some time before, perhaps after St. Joseph's death or following her Son's departure for the valley of the Jordan. But this hypothesis, based on the words quoted above, "and the mother of Jesus was there," is not sufficiently well-founded for acceptance.

Obviously a plentiful supply of wine was necessary for a week-long feast; does not the psalmist say: *et vinum laetificet cor hominis* (Ps. 103:15)?[14] But although provision had been made for the marriage

---

[12] We refer to Kufr Kenna, situated east of Sephoris and about four miles northeast of Nazareth, on the road from Nazareth to Tiberias. See below pp. 233 ff.

[13] This is the view which Prat seems to prefer (*op. cit.*, I, 174).

[14] Then, too, everyone knows how frequently the phrase *cum inebriati fuerint* occurs in both the Old and the New Testaments. These words, however, do not mean that the people concerned were drunk, but only that they had as much wine as they wanted.

feast at Cana, there came a moment when the wine began to run out. We do not know whether the shortage occurred because sufficient wine had not been provided in the first place or, more probably, because a greater number of guests had come than had been expected. It seems that Mary noticed the shortage even before the bridegroom and bride did, perhaps because, due to her close connections with the family, she was alert to ensure that everything went well. As she was tender-hearted and charitable, she wished to save the young couple embarrassment, and so she confidently had recourse to her Son's power and kindness by telling Him the circumstances in a few simple words, equivalent to an appeal: "They have no wine."

Our Lord replied: "What have I to do with thee, woman? My hour has not yet come."

But in spite of this answer, Mary said to the servants: "Do whatever he tells you."

Our Lord's reply to His Mother is perhaps one of the most discussed passages in the whole Gospel, and it certainly is difficult to understand, for He seems to have treated her rather harshly, and at the very moment when she was doing an act of charity. Furthermore, He said that His hour for working miracles had not yet come, and yet He did perform one a few moments later. Thus each part of His answer presents its own special problem.

The expression "What have I to do with thee?" is common enough in both the Old and the New Testaments: Judges 11:12; 2 Kings 16:10; 19:23; 3 Kings 17:18; 4 Kings 3:13; 2 Paralipomenon 35:21; Matthew 8:29; Mark 1:24; 5:7; Luke 4:34. In all these passages without exception it has the general idea of opposition and, we might say, of a certain hostility, i.e., the speaker wants to have nothing to do with his interlocutor; he refuses to have any dealings with him. But this idea can assume very different shades of meaning which are clearly apparent from the written context or, in conversation, from the facial expression, the tone of voice, etc. Thus for example, in Judges 11:12, Jephthe sent a message to the king of Ammon saying that nothing had happened between them to justify the invasion of Israelite territory; in 2 Kings 16:10 and 19:23 David rejects the proposal made to him and protests that *in this matter he has nothing to do with the sons of Sarvia;* in 4 Kings 3:13 the words are equivalent to "I have nothing to do with thee, I want to know nothing about thee," and in 3 Kings 17:18 to "What did I do to thee? What evil did I do thee?", while in 2

Paralipomenon 35:21, Nechao says in effect to the king of Juda: "There is nothing between us two that justifies your attitude." It should be noted that in this last passage, although the expression denies the existence of a point of contact between the king of Egypt and Josias, it does so in the friendly sense that there is no reason for the two monarchs to engage in battle; therefore, in one way, the phrase means "Don't interfere with me; leave me in peace." Thus even when the underlying intention is friendly, the expression still retains overtones of reproach. In the Gospels it is always the devils who use these words when speaking to our Lord, and always in the sense of "Leave us in peace; don't interfere with us." This is especially clear in Mark 5:7 and Luke 8:28, where the devil immediately adds: "I pray thee—do not torment me!" which is just another way of saying: "Leave me in peace." The meaning then is the same here as in 2 Paralipomenon 35:21, with the sole difference that in the latter passage the words are said in a friendly tone, whereas in Mark and Luke the tone is hostile.[15]

Having examined the passages, though it be only briefly, we are now in a position to ascertain the import of our Lord's reply to His Mother. Needless to say, several of the shades of meaning indicated above are excluded by the very context of Christ's words, into which only one meaning will fit, namely, "Leave me in peace; don't interfere with me." But our manner of expressing this thought has a certain brusqueness which is not necessarily present in the Hebrew phrase. Therefore we must seek another formula which has basically the same sense, but which does not give the impression of being a sharp rebuff, as if the speaker were annoyed at being bothered with a request. Such a formula could be: "Don't ask me to do this; don't make this request of me," as if to say: "I should like very much to please you, but it is not possible for me to do so. Therefore I beg you not to insist." This reply does undoubtedly contain a refusal, but there is nothing harsh about it. Hence it is not strictly correct to say that our Lord's words were harsh in themselves, but that they were softened by His facial expression and His tone of voice. His expression and tone were undoubtedly tender, but His words, even when considered in themselves, could have had a meaning that was by no means brusque and repelling.[16]

[15] It is not unusual to hear Arabs using the expression: *"Ma li ulak?*—What have I to do with thee?"

[16] Regarding the meaning of Christ's words, and the whole dialogue in general, see

There was no hint of coldness in our Lord's addressing Mary here as "woman" instead of "mother," as some authors think there may have been in His words to her from the Cross: "Woman, behold thy son." In the case under consideration the use of this title should apparently be attributed to the intimate nature of the conversation: in present-day Spanish the word *"mujer*—woman" is an acceptable, even an affectionate, form of address. Hence we do not think that there is any solid foundation for believing, as many authors do, that by replying thus our Lord wished to stress His independence of flesh and blood in all that pertained to His office as Messias. He did make this point very clear in His answer to Mary when she found Him in the Temple; but, in our opinion, neither the words themselves nor the context here allows of this interpretation.[17] Actually the whole incident can be explained in a perfectly simple and natural way. Mary, moved by charity and benevolence, asked Jesus to perform a miracle, but He besought her not to make such a request of Him, since His hour had not yet come. By His "hour" He did not mean the time of His Passion, as St. Augustine believed,[18] but merely the moment in which the Son of Man was to manifest Himself to the world by working miracles. Thus, in effect, He said to His Mother: "I cannot comply with your request because my time for working miracles has not yet come." What was the precise time fixed by the Eternal Father? Our Lord does not tell us, nor do we need to know it in order to understand the import of the passage.

But if Christ's words were so explicit and His refusal so unmistakable, why did our Lady speak to the servants as if she had received a favorable reply? And why did He work the miracle almost immediately after refusing to do so? Had His hour come in the meantime? In the Gospel narrative, our Lady's words to the servants come right after Christ's reply, but this does not prove that absolutely nothing happened between the Son's refusal and the Mother's command to the servants. The evangelist did not feel obliged to record every little detail. Considering the nature of our Lord's reply, and perhaps the tone in

the interesting article "Les paroles de Jésus à Cana" in *RB* (1897), pp. 405–422. See also J. Enciso's "Quid mihi et tibi?" in *Ecclesia,* VIII (Jan. 1948), 9 *f.;* and E. Power in *Verb. Dom.,* 2 (1922), 129–135.

[17] "Il ne faut donc voir là aucune intention de lui [to our Lady] rappeler la distance entre une femme et le Verbe incarné" (Lagrange, *Ev. selon S. Jean, in loc.*).

[18] Cf. *Breviarium Romanum:* Homilia in Festum Septem Dolorum B.M.V.

which it was uttered, how very natural it would have been for our Lady, with the confidence and holy liberty of a mother, to have urged her Son to hasten the coming of His hour and to spare the young couple embarrassment! [19] By no stretch of the imagination could such conduct on our Lady's part be deemed reprehensible. Jesus, to please His Mother, could have shown by a gesture that He assented to her request—the whole incident could have taken place in a moment, and, thus authorized, Mary would have given the command to the servants. This interpretation accounts for the apparent contradiction between Christ's words and those of His Mother. Although our Lord's reply was not exactly a reproach or a rebuke, it was a real and formal refusal, and there is no reason to try to minimize its impact. Our Lady's order to the servants was not given in spite of this refusal but as a result of a change that took place in Jesus, a change which was brought about by His Mother's intercession. Hence we can say with truth that we owe to Mary the first miracle worked by her Son.

The solution which we have just given [20] seems much more acceptable than any of the numerous other explanations, a few of which we shall mention here. Cajetan interprets the disputed words as meaning: "Of what consequence is the lack of wine to you and me? . . . It is neither your business nor mine to provide what is needed. How does it concern us?" [21] Or as Fouard, who accepts this interpretation, says: "What matters it to you and to Me?" [22]; in other words, "It's not our business to take care of that"—a meaning which at first glance seems reasonable and in perfect harmony with the context, and one which is

---

[19] In a closely-reasoned and very learned article, J. Leal objects: "Some say that by the tone of His voice, by His expression or by something which the evangelist has omitted, our Lord allowed it to be seen that because Mary was His Mother He was acceding to her request by making an exception to the general rule or by advancing His hour. *This solution, however, is only a supposition; it is not in the inspired text as St. John wrote it. Exegesis should be based on the sacred words themselves.*" ("La hora de Jesús, la hora de su Madre" in *Est. Ecles.* [1952], p. 160)—We are at a loss to understand the import of the words we have italicized.

Lagrange has different views on the matter: "Plus attentive peut-être au ton de la voix, au regard à l'accent des paroles qu'à leur sens matériel, elle [Mary] est persuadée qu'il saura concilier son devoir avec le désir de lui plaire" (*op. cit.*, p. 57); as has Simón-Dorado: "Ceterum vultus compositio et vocis sonus non parum sententias emollire consuevere" (*op. cit.*, p. 423).

[20] It is the one put forward by St. John Chrysostom (*PG* 59, 130 *f.*), Maldonatus, Simón-Dorado, and others.

[21] See Knabenbauer, *loc. cit.*

[22] *The Christ, The Son of God*, I, 144.

Native women of Cana in Galilee.

very ancient, for it is found in one of the works falsely attributed to St. Justin, entitled *Quaestiones et responsiones ad orthodoxos*.[23] This translation was also very popular in Maldonatus' day; he says that he found it in many contemporary authors and that, if current usage sanctioned it, it is a fitting and reverent interpretation. It is certainly both reverent and fitting, because on the one hand it excludes any rebuking of the Mother by her Son, and on the other it suits the circumstances perfectly. Unfortunately, although the phrase taken by itself can have this meaning, we cannot translate it here in this manner because contemporary usage did not allow of such an interpretation. In none of the passages quoted above does it have this sense, for in all of them without exception the contrast, or at least the relationship expressed, is between the speaker and his interlocutor, and never between themselves and a third person.

Reuss, Knabenbauer, Fillion, Calmes and others interpret the words as indicative of perfect conformity between Christ and His Mother, as if our Lord had said: "I am in perfect agreement with you: leave it to me": "id meae relinque curae": "laissez-moi faire." But if this was His intention, why did He say: "My hour has not yet come"? He should rather have said the opposite: "I am going to please you by working the miracle because my hour has come." To get around this difficulty some authors hold that our Lord's words were interrogative: "Is it that my hour has not yet come?" which would have been equivalent to an affirmation that His hour had come. However, such a question would have been quite pointless, for if our Lord had said to His Mother: "I am going to work the miracle," where was the need of adding: "My hour has come"? On the contrary, if He had refused her request, His reference to His hour was very much to the point, since it gave His reason for not performing the miracle.[24]

In the interesting article already referred to, Leal writes:

The hour of Jesus has regard to the supreme moment of His return to the Father. . . . The two scenes, at Cana and at Calvary, both recorded by only one evangelist, are intimately related with each other. In

---

[23] *PG* 6, 1390, ad q. 136: "Illud, *Quid mihi et tibi est mulier,* non ad obiurgationem dictum est matri a Salvatore, sed ut ostenderet nequaquam nos esse, inquit, qui vini in nuptiis consumendi curam suscepimus."

[24] See Gächter, "Maria in Kana," in *Zeit. f. kath. Theol.* (1931), pp. 351–402; Schildenberger, "Das Rätsel der Hochzeit von Kana," in *Benediktinische Monatschrift* (1933), pp. 123–130, 224–234.

Cana, our Lady begins to act as mother of the faithful, and Christ says to her that the hour for so acting has not yet come, that it will come at the end of His life. And in fact He does confer this maternal office on her at the end.[25]

And Fr. T. Gallus says:

What hour is Christ speaking about? It is more proper to say that His "hour" is represented as being quite a long time off. . . . Therefore His "hour" is the hour of His redeeming death on the cross, when His mission has been accomplished.[26]

Fr. F.-M. Braun declares: "They [our Lord and the evangelist] always have in mind the hour of the Passion, which is also the hour of Christ's glory, that is, the time of His return to His Father." [27] This is the interpretation given by St. Augustine and, as Knabenbauer remarks, it found favor with many people because of the holy Doctor's authority.[28]

Despite what these authors say, we do not think we should modify the interpretation which we have proposed above as preferable. We hold that Lagrange is correct when he remarks that to regard "my hour" in this simple context as referring to the Passion is to sacrifice the thread of the thought to an unduly erudite and merely verbal relationship.[29]

In deference to His Mother's wishes, Jesus said to the servants: "Fill the jars with water."

The jars referred to were six large earthenware vessels placed there for the frequent ritual ablutions of the Jews, and with great exactness, St. John records the amount of water they could hold; each could contain two or three "measures," and since a "measure" was roughly

[25] See p. 229 above, n. 19; *art. cit.,* pp. 155 and 167.

[26] *Verb. Dom.,* 22 (1942), 48 *f.*

[27] *Revue Thomiste,* 50 (1950), 451. Braun continues to uphold the same interpretation in his *La Mère des fidèles* (Paris, 1953), pp. 55–58 ("Mon heure n'est pas encore venue"), as does Gächter in his *Maria im Erdenleben,* pp. 180–190 ("Noch ist meine Stunde nicht gekommen"). In an article in *Theological Studies* (1956), pp. 1–38, Fr. Christian P. Gercke examines and completely refutes this explanation.

[28] "Celebris est *Aug.* opinio horam illam esse horam mortis: 'ne putes quod te negem matrem; nondum venit hora mea: ibi enim te agnoscam, cum pendere in cruce coeperit infirmitas, cuius mater es'; quae explicatio ob auctoritatem *Aug.* multis placuit" (*In Ioan.,* p. 131).

[29] Cf. *RB* (1932), p. 122. We do, however, believe that "a *merely verbal* relationship" is too strong a term to use here.

equivalent to ten gallons, each jar held from twenty to thirty gallons. The servants obeyed and then, again at our Lord's command, they took some of the contents of the jars to the chief steward who, surprised at the exquisite quality of the wine, called the bridegroom and remonstrated with him because, contrary to the usual custom, he had not served the best wine first, but had kept it until the end of the banquet. The bridegroom must have been no less surprised in his turn at the chief steward's remonstration. The evangelist notes that this was the first miracle worked by our Lord, and that it deepened His disciples' faith in Him.

Kufr Kenna is the place in which the ancient pilgrims venerated the mystery of the marriage feast at Cana. It is a town situated five miles north of Nazareth, near the road that runs from the latter town to Tiberias. The identification of Cana with Kufr Kenna has been and still is hotly contested by some authors who give the preference to a small ruin situated more to the north, at the northern end of Sahel el-Battof, called Khirbet Qana. Professor Alt writes: "As a result of the discussions of the last ten years it can be taken as proved that this expression [Cana of Galilee] does not refer to present-day Kufr Kenna but to Khirbet Qana on the northern edge of the Battof plain." [30] And Dr. Clemens Kopp closes his very erudite monograph, *Das Kana des Evangeliums* (Köln, 1940) with the observation that the identification of the Cana of the New Testament with Khirbet Qana is completely certain ("völlig sicher").

There is no justification for these categorical assertions, which echo the opinion voiced in 1838 by Robinson, who was the first to choose Khirbet Qana as the Cana of the Gospel. Both archaeology and tradition favor Kufr Kenna.

Pilgrims who visited the ancient site of Cana frequently mentioned a *church,* and a *spring* at which water pots were filled. But there is no spring in Khirbet Qana and there is not the slightest trace of an ancient church, two facts that have been explicitly acknowledged by all who have visited the ruin, and to which the present writer can bear witness. On the other hand, however, there is, even today, a free-flowing spring in Kufr Kenna, and excavations have uncovered noteworthy ruins of one or several churches. It is also very interesting to note that the site of an ancient building was discovered under the present Franciscan church here, and that in the mosaic pavement of the old edifice

[30] *Beiträge zur biblischen Landes und Altertumskunde* (1949), p. 62.

there is an inscription in Aramaic which reads: "To the good memory of Joseph, son of Tanhum, son of Butah, and his sons, who have made this *tblh* [a word very difficult to interpret]. May the blessing come upon them." The name Joseph quickly brings to mind the Jewish convert, Count Joseph of Tiberias, who, as we know, received permission from the Emperor Constantine to build several churches, and who actually did build them at Tiberias, Capharnaum, Sephoris and other places. Therefore it is very likely that he would have built one in the place where our Lord worked His first miracle. This archaeological find at Kufr Kenna certainly creates a strong presumption in its favor; yet we abstain from bringing this discovery forward as an additional proof, for there is some discussion as to whether the ancient edifice mentioned was a church or a synagogue.

As regards tradition, there is no clear and explicit textual reference earlier than the second half of the sixth century, not excepting the writings of St. Jerome. In 570 the anonymous Pilgrim of Piacenza wrote that he and his companions went from Ptolemais (Accho) on the coast to Diocaesarea (Sephoris) in Galilee and from there went three miles to Cana, "where the Lord was present at the wedding." [31] If the writer had been speaking of Khirbet Qana, he would certainly have stopped there before going on to Diocaesarea, as it would have been on his route from Ptolemais. Furthermore, there is no spring in Khirbet Qana, while, as we have already said, there is an abundant one in Kufr Kenna. Finally, the Pilgrim gives three miles as the distance between Diocaesarea and Cana, and Diocaesarea is actually only a little more than three miles from Kufr Kenna, while it is nearly five miles from Khirbet Qana. The text therefore refers to Kufr Kenna; as Buhl explicitly says: "There is not the slightest doubt that Antoninus the Martyr (the anonymous Pilgrim of Piacenza) locates the Cana of the Gospel at this town [Kufr Kenna], for he gives three miles as the distance between it and Diocaesarea and indicates that there was a fountain there." [32] None of the other texts up to the end of the thirteenth century can be called absolutely decisive, although they

---

[31] "De Ptolemaida misimus maritimam. Venimus in finibus Galilaeae in civitatem, quae vocatur Diocaesarea. . . . Deinde millia tria venimus in Cana, ubi ad nuptias fuit Dominus . . . ex quibus hydriis duae ibi sunt . . . et in ipsa fonte pro benedictione lavavimus. Deinde venimus in civitatem Nazareth" (Geyer, *Itinera,* p. 161).

[32] *Géographie* (Freiburg i. B. und Leipzig, 1896), p. 219; Clermont-Ganneau expresses more or less the same opinion in *Recueil d'archéologie orientale* (Paris, 1888–1924), IV, 345.

can be said to favor Kufr Kenna. But in 1283 Burchardus of Mount Sion wrote in such a way as to show that he was referring to Khirbet Qana as the location of the marriage feast. We do not know what caused this sudden change of opinion in the literary tradition. Among later writers, some seem to refer to Khirbet Qana, others to Kufr Kenna, but none expresses himself with complete clarity. Quaresimus, in 1626, is the first to make explicit mention of a double tradition; and he leans towards Kufr Kenna, although with a certain reserve.[33] One of the reasons for his preference is that there was no spring in Khirbet Qana and no trace of a church there either, whereas both are present in Kufr Kenna.

Some object to placing Cana at Kufr Kenna because of the expression which St. John uses: "Cana of Galilee" (2, 1, 11; 4, 46; 21, 2), in order to distinguish it from another town of the same name situated seven and a half miles south of Tyre (cf. Jos. 19:28). According to these authors, this indicates that there was in Galilee only one town called Cana and that it was the present-day Khirbet Qana.[34] However, the evangelist merely wished to show that the Cana to which he referred was the one in Galilee and not the one in Phoenicia. He was not concerned with whether or not there was another place of the same name in Galilee, for it was not his aim to give the exact geographical location of the town; he simply wanted to make it clear that it was in Galilee.

Another objection, equally unfounded, is based on Josephus' reference to a village called Cana.[35] Undoubtedly the historian is referring to Khirbet Qana, but this only indicates that the village was still in existence in his day, and not that it was the only one called Cana.

Therefore we conclude that, in view of tradition and archaeology, Kufr Kenna is much to be preferred to Khirbet Qana as the location of the marriage feast.

Capharnaum
(John 2:12–13; cf. Maps II and III)

John's repeated testimony to Jesus as the Messias, our Lord's

---

[33] "Posterior haec sententia mihi valde probabilis videtur, licet alteram rejicere non audeam" (Baldi, *Enchiridion,* p. 262).
[34] Dalman, too, puts forward this argument in favor of Khirbet Qana (*Sacred Sites and Ways,* pp. 101 ff.).
[35] *Life* 16.

power of attracting disciples to Himself, and His manifest ability to read men's hearts were enough to remove any reasonable doubt as to the nature of His mission. But if doubt had remained even after such proofs, the miracle at Cana, so evident and easy to verify, demonstrated clearly that Jesus was more than just the son of a carpenter and that He had a greater mission in life than mending doors and windows, than making carts and yokes. Therefore, St. John very aptly remarks that, in working this miracle, "Jesus . . . manifested his glory, and his disciples believed in him." No doubt they had believed in Him before, but now they began to believe fully and without hesitation in His mission and supernatural authority.

After the marriage feast, Jesus did not return to Nazareth but instead, accompanied by His convinced and resolute disciples, He turned His steps towards Capharnaum, which was to be the center of His apostolate in Galilee. Leaving the plain, Sahel el-Battof, at its eastern end, the party turned to the left a short distance beyond Lubiyeh and then, skirting Qarn Hattin, they descended through the Wadi el-Hammam and came out on to the shores of the Lake of Gennesareth, passed through the pleasant lowland of et-Tabgha, and, after six or seven hours' walking, entered the place that from then on was to be Christ's own town (Matt. 9:1).

It is not difficult to guess why Jesus chose this town and why He abandoned in its favor the hamlet in which He had lived for some thirty years and which was undoubtedly dear to Him. Nazareth was a poor village, hidden at the bottom of a valley, far from the great lines of communication and surrounded by sparsely-populated territory. Therefore it was not suited to be the center of Christ's apostolic activity, for He had come into the world to seek the lost sheep and to announce to men the coming of God's kingdom. Capharnaum (Kefar Nahum), on the contrary, had many qualities to recommend it to our Lord, for it was quite populous and was situated in a densely-inhabited region within the territory of the tribe of Nephtali. Although in the inexorable course of time it lost its prosperity and ceased to exist as a city, one can still see in Tell Hum,[36] about three miles south of the point where the

---

[36] This identification has not always been generally accepted. Some authors located Capharnaum at Khirbet Miniyeh, farther to the south, on the plain of Gennesareth; and not long ago, Mader resurrected this hypothesis as a result of excavations which he performed at Khirbet Miniyeh (cf. *JPOS* [1933], pp. 218–220). However, there are very good reasons for giving the preference to Tell Hum, an opinion which can be regarded as generally admitted nowadays (cf. Dalman,

Murphy Photo

THE PLAIN OF GENNESARETH (EL-GHUWER): *in the background, on the shore of the lake, lies el-Mejdel (ancient Magdala), with the Wadi el-Hammam to the right.*

Jordan enters the lake, its extensive ruins, and in particular the remains of its magnificent synagogue. Lying very close to the *Via Maris*, the great international route that ran from Mesopotamia to Egypt, Capharnaum had easy communication with both the East and the West. Then, too, located as it was on the road from Bethsaida Julias, it received all the trade coming from the tetrarchy of Philip, a fact which explains the existence of a customhouse at the entrance to the city. And in addition it had become the commercial center for many, if not all, of the towns around the lake.

The lake itself went by various names—the Lake of Gennesareth, the Sea of Ginnesar, the Sea of Tiberias, the Sea of Galilee, the Waters of Ginnesar. It is approximately thirteen miles long, eight miles across at its widest point, and about thirty-seven miles in circumference: its maximum depth is 150 feet and its surface is 682 feet below the level of the Mediterranean. In the time of our Lord many vessels sailed upon its waters—according to Josephus, Tarichea alone possessed no

op. cit., pp. 138 *ff.*). In an article in *Est. Ecles.,* 4 (1925), 214–217, entitled "Datos evangélicos sobre la identificación de Cafarnaúm," Bover rejects this theory.

less than 230 [37]—and its western shore was dotted with towns such as
Capharnaum, which we have already mentioned, Bethsaida, Magdala,
Tiberias, Tarichea, some of which, like the last-named, could boast of
a population of 40,000,[38] while on the eastern, less thickly populated
side, and across from Tiberias, half-pagan Hippos, one of the cities of
the Decapolis, stood on its superb site, which was shaped like a
truncated cone. North of Hippos lay Gerasa, some vestiges of which
may perhaps still exist in the ruins of Kursi near the mouth of the
Wadi es Samak.[39]

On the western shore of the lake, between Magdala (el-Mejdel)
in the south and ancient Kinnereth (Tell el-Oreimeh) in the north,
stretches the plain of Gennesareth, known today as el-Ghuwer and
measuring a little more than three miles long and two and one-half
miles across at the widest point. Josephus describes the plain as being
a veritable paradise: "Both its nature and its beauty are wonderful.
The soil is so fertile that all types of trees grow there . . .; its temperature is such and is so well proportioned that it suits trees of the most
diverse kinds, so that vineyards as well as walnut, palm, olive and fig
trees flourish there. It could be said that nature wished to gather
together in this corner of Galilee the most diverse products so that each
season could claim the region for its own." [40] This fertility, perhaps
somewhat exaggerated by the Jewish historian, was partly due to the
plentiful supply of water, derived mainly from the Wadi er-Rabadiyeh,
the Wadi el-'Amud and, in particular, from an abundant spring, En
el-Medauwara.

But today everything is changed; silence and solitude reign over
the lake. No longer do crowds swarm along its shores, or fleets of ships
glide across its waters. Instead of prosperous cities there remain only
the scattered tents of poverty-stricken Bedouins, and the once teeming
ports are no more. However, in spite of the solitude and the ruins, the

---

[37] *Wars* ii. 21. 8.

[38] Josephus *Wars* ii. 21. 4. In the past, Khirbet Kerak, on the southwest end of the
lake, was commonly regarded as the site of ancient Tarichea; but nowadays
there is a well-founded tendency to identify Tarichea with Magdala on the
southern end of the plain of Gennesareth, an identification which we accept as
solidly founded and very probable, although we do not regard it as completely
certain. See Josephus *Wars* iii. 9. 28; 10. 1, 2; Albright, "The Location of
Tarichea," in *Annual of the American School of Oriental Research*, II–III
(1923), 29–46.

[39] Some reputable authors, however, believe that these ruins are of much later
date.

[40] *Wars* iii. 10. 8.

region still presents a picture of peace and love. In itself the lake is a poem, singing of God's condescension to man and His great love for the creatures of His hand. Our Lord sailed these waters, He walked along these shores and climbed these hills: everywhere one looks, one senses the sweet and loving presence of the Saviour. Indeed this is a blessed lake, whose sacred memories could be profaned but not erased by human malice. The cruel Roman solidery stained its waters with the blood of the inhabitants of Tarichea; here, too, the frivolous court of a licentious king indulged in orgies and made the calm air quiver with sensuous music. But despite such cruelty and vice, the lake retained its immaculate purity, and even with its deserted banks, no longer echoing to the shouts of the fishermen at work, and with its ruined cities, it is still what it used to be—the lake of Jesus. The crystal waters reflect His beloved countenance, in the murmuring waves His voice can yet be heard, and on its shores one can still discern the prints left by His feet as He went in search of the sheep that were lost.

The Brethren of Jesus

St. John notes that Jesus went down to Capharnaum accompanied not only by His disciples but also by His Mother and His brethren (John 2:12). There is also mention of His brethren in Matthew 12:46 f., while Matthew 13:55 f. and Mark 6:3 give their names as "James and Joseph and Simon and Jude," and then go on to speak of His "sisters," but without recording their names. From these passages many early heretics and later the Protestants argued against Mary's virginity, at least after Christ's birth. Several of the Fathers and ancient ecclesiastical writers thought that these "brothers" of Jesus were sons of St. Joseph, born to him before his marriage with Mary, a theory apparently derived from some apocryphal gospel, for it is the common opinion of the Church that St. Joseph, too, practiced perpetual virginity. We shall content ourselves with a few brief remarks on this problem since it is frequently discussed by authors and is easily solved when studied with an open mind.

As is well known, the Hebrews and ancient peoples in general used the word "brother" and its plural, "brethren," in a wider sense than we do. The Scriptures contain several examples of this practice. Thus in Genesis 13:8, Abraham says to Lot: "We are brethren," although Lot was his nephew, the son of his brother (Gen. 11:27). In Genesis

29:15, Laban calls Jacob his "brother," whereas he was only his nephew, the son of his sister Rebecca (Gen. 28:2). Again, in Exodus 2:11, we read that Moses returned from the desert to see his "brethren" who were actually only his fellow-Israelites, his compatriots; and in 2 Kings 2:26, Abner calls the Jews of Juda the "brethren" of the other tribes, while in Acts 11:29, we are told that the Christians resolved to send help to their brethren in Judea.

We should note well that no one is ever called "the son of Mary" except Jesus, and that our Lady is never called the mother of anyone but Jesus.

There is no point in discussing here the other passage which is put forward as an argument that our Lord had brothers, i.e., that Mary had other sons, namely, Matthew 1:25: "He did not know her till she had brought forth her *firstborn* son," and Luke 2:7: "And she brought forth her *firstborn* son. . . ." Suffice it to recall that, as St. Jerome remarks, the first-born is "not only he *after whom* other children are born but also he *before whom* no child has been born." [41]

Who, exactly, were these brethren of Jesus? The problem is a difficult and obscure one, and conjecture must necessarily play a large part in any attempt to solve it. Let us begin by assembling all the data that can be derived from the Gospel text.

Four "brethren" of Jesus are mentioned by name: "Is not this the carpenter's son? Is not his mother called Mary, and his brethren James and Joseph and Simon and Jude? And his sisters, are they not all with us?" (Matt. 13:55 *f.*). James and Joseph were the sons of Mary, one of the women who remained at the foot of the Cross: "Among them were Mary Magdalene, and *Mary the mother of James and Joseph,* and the mother of the sons of Zebedee" (Matt. 27:56); "Among them were Mary Magdalene, *Mary the mother of James the Less and of Joseph,* and Salome" (Mark 15:40); "Now, it was Mary Magdalene and Joanna and *Mary, the mother of James* . . . who were with them" (Luke 24:10); "And when the Sabbath was past, Mary Magdalene, *Mary the mother of James,* and Salome, brought spices. . . ." (Mark 16:1); "But Mary Magdalene and *Mary the mother of Joseph* were looking on and saw where he was laid" (Mark 15:47).

James was the son of Alpheus (Matt. 10:3); Jude was the brother of James (Jude 1:1; Luke 6:16), and Mary was the wife of Cleophas

[41] See above, p. 109, n. 7 .

(John 19:25). Hegesippus the historian provides us with two other interesting facts, namely, that Simon was the son of Cleophas, who was St. Joseph's brother.[42]

These are the positive elements at our disposal, and most of them are susceptible of varying interpretations. In our opinion, the following arrangement is the most probable one: Mary, who was at the foot of the cross, is repeatedly named as the mother of James and Joseph, but never of Simon and Jude. Yet she was the wife of Cleophas, and since her son James is called the son of Alpheus (Matt. 10:3), she was also the latter's wife. Not only that, but according to Hegesippus, Simon was the son of Cleophas, and in Luke 6:16 Jude appears as the brother of James the Less, the son of Mary. The theory that best covers these data is that Mary, after bearing James and Joseph to Alpheus, was left a widow by the latter's death and then contracted a second marriage, this time with Cleophas, who had had two sons, Simon and Jude, by his first wife.[43] Simon and Jude were St. Joseph's nephews, and therefore first cousins of our Lord. James and Joseph were also His first cousins, by affinity, as a result of their mother Mary's marriage to Cleophas. James and Jude were Apostles, and Simon (generally called Simeon) became the second bishop of Jerusalem.

Whether Mary, the wife of Alpheus and of Cleophas, was or was not our Lady's sister depends on the interpretation of John 19:25: "Now there were standing by the cross of Jesus his mother and *his mother's sister,* Mary of Cleophas and Mary Magdalene." We believe that "Mary of Cleophas" is not in simple apposition to the phrase "his mother's sister," and that these latter words refer to a different person, someone distinct from "Mary of Cleophas." In our opinion this "sister" of our Lady (either "sister" in the strict sense, or in the general connotation of a female relative) was Salome.[44] Actually, Salome appears twice among the holy women under her own name (Mark 15:40; 16:1), and once as the mother of the sons of Zebedee (Matt. 27:56). It seems probable that when St. John (19:25) speaks of the sister of our Lord's Mother along with Mary, the wife of Cleophas, and Mary Magdalene, he is referring to Salome, the woman who appears in the

---

[42] "Simeon filius Cleopae, illius cuius in Evangeliis fit mentio": "Creditur autem Symeon patruelis fuisse Servatoris; nam Cleopam fratrem fuisse Iosephi testatur Hegesippus" (Eusebius *Hist. Eccles.* iii. 2. 1).

[43] Prat also seems to accept this theory (*op. cit.,* I, 506).

[44] Some hold that our Lady's sister was Mary of Cleophas, and that Alpheus and Cleophas are two names for one and the same person.

accounts left by the other evangelists. It is likely that he, being her son, modestly refrained from inserting his mother's name and even from calling her the mother of the sons of Zebedee as did the other evangelists. If Salome was our Lady's sister (in the strict or in the general sense), then St. James the Greater and St. John were also first cousins or at least relatives of our Lord. But why did not the people of Nazareth mention John and James when they were speaking of Christ's brethren (Matt. 13:55)? Perhaps they did not do so because the sons of Zebedee lived in Capharnaum and not in or near Nazareth, as did the others whom they named.

9. The First Passover in Jerusalem (March-April, A. D. 28)

(Cf. Maps IV and V)

The end of March was approaching and the Passover was drawing near. The Eternal Father had made the solemn presentation of His Son but only before a relatively small group of people and far from Jerusalem, on the banks of the Jordan. Now He was going to present Jesus in the capital itself, in the very center of the civil and religious life of Israel, and during the greatest of the Jewish feasts.

About a score of years had passed since the Child, the Son of Mary, had astounded the doctors of the Law with His questions and answers. Now the young Prophet of Nazareth was going to confront these same doctors and begin His battle with the leaders of Israel.

Later, when standing before Pilate, Jesus was to say that He had come into the world to bear witness to the truth. Now He, the Herald of the truth, was going to proclaim it aloud in the heart of Jerusalem, in the very Temple itself; He was going to speak out against hypocrisy, avarice and abuse. During the course of His whole public life He was to give testimony to the truth and by His direct, candid and straightforward mode of action to teach us, too, to be men of truth. The battle was to be long and hard-fought, and the Champion of truth was one day to suffer an apparent defeat; but He was to turn this defeat into His most glorious victory.

The visit which Jesus paid to Capharnaum after the marriage feast at Cana was a short one (John 2:12: "And they stayed there but a few days"), no doubt because of the nearness of the Passover (15th Nisan=between March 15th and April 15th) which He wished to celebrate in Jerusalem. It is very probable that the group which left Capharnaum with Him also accompanied Him to the Holy City. In order to follow them more easily on their journey, we shall sketch briefly the manner of making these pilgrimages and give a short account of the main feasts which were celebrated in Israel.

The Three Great Feasts: (1) The *Passover* or *Pasch* (*pesah*= passage) commemorated the passing of the avenging angel in Egypt and the sparing of the lives of the Jews' firstborn (Exod. 12:11 *f.*); it was also called "the feast of the unleavened bread" or "azymes" (Exod. 34:18; cf. 12:15–20). (2) *Pentecost* ("the fiftieth day"), or "the feast of weeks," was so named because it was celebrated seven weeks after the Passover; on this occasion the first fruits were offered to God. (3) *The Feast of Tabernacles* was celebrated towards the end of September to give thanks to God for the year's harvest and to commemorate the forty years' wandering in the desert during which the Jews had lived in tents (Lev. 23:39–43). On these three feasts the adult male Jews, i.e., those over thirteen,[1] had to go up to the Temple in Jerusalem (Exod. 23:14:17; 34:23; Deut. 16:16), and hence the Talmud calls them the feasts of the pilgrims.[2] Strictly speaking, the women were not obliged to go to the Temple on these occasions, but many of them did attend out of devotion.

The Road to Jerusalem: Although when speaking of Mary's visit to Elizabeth we briefly sketched the various stages on the road from Nazareth to Jerusalem, it will not be out of place here to describe in more detail the route or routes along which pilgrims were wont to travel to the Holy City for the great feasts.

There were three roads by which the inhabitants of Galilee used to go up to Jersualem; we can call them the eastern, the middle, and the western routes. The western one, which ran along the Mediterranean seacoast through the plain of Saron, has no interest for us now, and therefore we shall limit ourselves to describing the other two.[3]

---

[1] See above, p. 151, n. 2.

[2] For mention of the three feasts together see Exodus 23:14–17; 34:18–23; Deuteronomy 16:1–17.

[3] To go from the plain of Saron to Jerusalem one could cross the mountains by any one of several roads. The most northerly of these was that which ran from

The *eastern* road followed the valley of the Jordan, running along-side the river, possibly on the left bank but more probably on the right, in which case it crossed the district of Aennon, passed through Kerawa at the mouth of the Wadi Far'a, through Phasaelis, the city founded by Herod, and then through Archelais, which was built by Archelaus. On reaching Jericho it turned right, went up the Wadi el-Qelt and, after winding through the desert of Juda, arrived at Jerusalem on the east side. This route was long and inconvenient, but pilgrims often took it to avoid the territory of the Samaritans, who were no friends of the Jews; in this case they followed the eastern bank of the Jordan for some distance.

The *middle road* was the most direct of the three.[4] It was the mountain route and ran along what is usually known as the spine of Palestine. It was the road which Abraham took in traversing the land from north to south, and also the one which travellers usually followed. We know definitely that our Lord passed along it at least twice (John 4:4 *ff.;* Luke 9:22); and Josephus, when speaking about a certain dispute, remarked that "it was the custom of the Galileans to travel through the land of the Samaritans when going to the Holy City for the feasts." [5] This road crossed the great plain of Esdrelon, leaving to the left Little Hermon (Nebi Dahi), the city of Jezrael, which was once the second capital of the kingdom of the north, and the Mountains of Gelboe (Jebel Fuqqu'a), scene of the tragic death of Saul and Jonathan. Then it reached Jenin, the ancient Engannim, near the southern end of the plain and more or less on the border between Galilee and Samaria; here the pilgrims probably spent the first night of their journey. Beyond Jenin, the road continued a little to the left of the present highway, and passed through Qubatiyeh and Sanur, which can possibly be identified with Bethulia; through Geba (Jeba'), near which Holofernes probably encamped; then, leaving the city of

Ras el-'Ain (Antipatris through 'Abud and Bir Zeit: this was probably the road along which St. Paul was brought as a prisoner from Jerusalem to Caesarea. The second route led through Bethoron and Gabaon: this is the way St. Paula and St. Jerome came and it was the one commonly used by the pilgrims. The third road went through Beit Likia, Beit 'Anan and Qubeibeh: the fourth and most southerly ran from 'Amwâs through Bab el-Wad and the Wadi 'Ali, practically coinciding with the present road to Jaffa. It was along this route that the Crusaders passed.

[4] "Those who wish to go to Jerusalem in a *short time* must of necessity pass through this region [i.e., Samaria], for by this road one can reach Jerusalem from Galilee in three days" (Josephus *Life* 52).

[5] *Ant.* xx. 6. 1.

Samaria a short distance to the right, it continued on to emerge between Mounts Ebal and Garizim near Sichem and Jacob's Well of venerable memory for the pilgrims. From here it turned almost at right angles to run south and, passing between Awerta, on the left, and Huwara, on the right, it advanced towards el-Lubban near which, even today, there stands an inn, Khan Lubban, which in all probability is the successor to an ancient caravanserai in which the pilgrims coming from Nazareth and vicinity perhaps spent the second or third night of their journey. From Khan Lubban the present highway winds in great curves up a very steep slope, as did the ancient road. Perhaps the pilgrims followed the valley, which runs to the left, in order to visit the city of Silo, present-day Khirbet Seilun, where they would recall the preservation of the Ark and the delightful infancy of the prophet Samuel (1 Kings 1 *ff.*). If so, they came out on the beautiful plain of Turmus Aya, skirted the Wadi el-Haramiyeh (=valley of thieves) along whose deep bed the present highway twists, and headed practically in a straight line towards Bethel, which would remind them of Abraham's sacrifice and Jacob's ladder (Gen. 12:8; 28:12). Then, bearing somewhat to the right, they went on to spend the night at a town known today as el-Bireh and which many authors believe, not without reason, to be the place where Mary and Joseph first realized that the Child was missing. On the following day the pilgrims easily traversed the ten miles between el-Bireh and Jerusalem, passing many famed towns—Rama, where Rachel's voice was heard "weeping for her children" (Matt. 2:18); Gabaon, where the Ark rested and where Solomon received the divine revelation (3 Kings 3:4–14); and Gabaa of Saul, the first capital of the kingdom (1 Kings 11:4). Finally they arrived at Mount Scopus, from which they first sighted and greeted, with feelings of reverence and love, the Holy City and the magnificent Temple where Yahweh, the Lord God of Hosts, had His Throne.

The Manner of Making the Pilgrimage: The pilgrims travelled in groups, singing psalms, particularly the *gradual* psalms (Ps. 119–133; Hebrew Ps. 120–134), i.e., "the psalms of the ascents," and especially Psalm 121 (Hebrew, 122): "I rejoiced at the things that were said to me: We shall go into the house of the Lord." And, in fact, how great must have been their joy and how fervent their exclamations of happiness, when from Mount Scopus, or from Mount Olivet if they had come by way of Jericho, they had their first view of the Holy City!

The Number of Pilgrims: The number of pilgrims was certainly very great; Josephus says that, one year, as many as 3,000,000 people assembled in Jerusalem for the Passover.[6] He asserts that 256,500 Paschal lambs were sacrificed and that, since each lamb had to be eaten by a group of not less than ten persons, the number of participants in the feast reached as high as 2,700,200. Many authors believe that these figures are exaggerated, and it is likely that they are. But even so, the very fact that Josephus dared to give them presupposes that the number of people must have been very large. Great preparations had to be made to provide travelling facilities and lodgings for such a multiude of pilgrims. The roads were repaired, and the sepulchres in the vicinity of the city were newly whitened to make them clearly visible so that the visitors would not contract legal impurity by unconsciously touching one of them. All available rooms were made ready, yet many of the pilgrims had to find shelter in tents pitched outside the city, and large stores of food were laid in.

The Celebration of the Passover (cf. Exod. 12:1–28): The Passover lasted seven days[7] (Exod. 12:15, 19; 23:15). The first day, an especially solemn one (Exod. 12:16), was the 15th of Nisan (=the end of March), but it actually began on the evening of the 14th (Exod. 12:6, 18). Four days before, on the 10th, a yearling lamb or kid (Exod. 12:3) had been chosen by each family or group, and on the evening of the 14th, which was the beginning of the 15th according to Hebrew reckoning, it was sacrificed, roasted, and consumed, care being taken not to break any of the bones. Work was forbidden on the first day, the 15th, and on the last, the 21st, until sunset. On the 16th the feast of the *omer* or sheaf was celebrated. After sunset on the 15th, three men, each carrying a sickle, went out to the fields, e.g., in the valley of the Cedron, where they cut a sheaf of barley, placed it in a basket and brought it to the Temple. On the following morning the barley was threshed, roasted and ground, and the flour was then mixed with oil to form a dough which was burned on the altar of holocausts.

The pilgrims were free to return home on the morning of the 16th, but many of them remained until the end of the feast.

The ceremonial of the Paschal supper was a complicated one. At least ten people had to participate in it, and the whole lamb had to be

[6] *Wars* ii. 14. 3.

[7] It seems that the rabbis later added an eighth day. Thus, at first, the feast lasted from sunset on the 14th of Nisan to sunset on the 21st, but later it was prolonged until sunset of the 22nd (cf. "Passover," *The Jewish Encyclopedia*, IX, 548–557.)

disposed of. At first the partakers of the meal had to eat standing, each with a staff in his hand (Exod. 12:11), but this custom gradually died out and was no longer observed in our Lord's day. Prayers were recited and hymns sung at intervals throughout the meal. First a cup of wine was passed around, and then bitter herbs dipped in a sharp sauce were eaten to recall the harsh trials suffered in Egypt. A second cup was drunk, after which the roasted lamb and unleavened bread were served. Then a third cup, the cup of benediction, was drunk; it received its name from the prayers of thanksgiving which were recited at this point. If desired, more wine could be taken. At each supper table there was always a leader or head who presided at the ceremony and whose duty it was to cut the bread, dip the pieces in a bitter sauce and pass them to those present. He also began the prayers and recounted the story of the Jewish people's exodus from Egypt.[8]

Nowadays the Jews observe the following ritual: at sunset on the 14th of Nisan they go to the synagogue for public prayer. Upon returning home after nightfall, the members of the family come together, wash their hands and take their seats around the table, upon which dishes of herbs and salt-water have been placed. The father half-sits, half-reclines on a sofa or couch with a cushion under his left arm. Then a cup of wine is placed before each person and some prayers are said. Next, the youngest male member of the family reads the biblical passage describing the flight from Egypt. Then those present ask the father four questions, two of which are: "Why does the father today sit on the couch in a comfortable position and not on a chair as he does during the year? Why are herbs and salt-water placed on the table today?" He replies that the herbs and salt-water are to recall the bitter trials of the Jewish people in Egypt, and that he is reclining on the couch to commemorate their liberation and the comfortable circumstances in which they found themselves after they had regained their freedom. After this, all rise, wash their hands again and begin the supper, during which roast meat, onions, herbs, etc., are served and several prayers are recited.

[8] See below, p. 629, where there is a citation from the *Mishnah* according to which it was obligatory to serve no less than four cups of wine. There were various ceremonies about which the rabbis were not agreed and which, consequently, were continually being changed. Thus it is no wonder that there is some confusion as to the number of cups mentioned. Edersheim's observations in his *Life and Times of Jesus the Messiah* (New York: E. R. Herrick & Co., 1901), II, 492, are very much to the point.

Within the walls of Jerusalem the supper is eaten only on the 14th, whereas outside the city it is also eaten on the 15th.

In order to bring more vividly before the eyes of the reader the scene which we have just briefly sketched, we do not think it will be out of place here to describe more minutely the ceremonies that must be observed according to the ritual, whose title, translated in English, reads: "The Manner of Celebrating the Passover on the First Two Nights Thereof."

On the vigil of the 14th of Nisan, immediately after the evening religious service, the father of the family gathers all the fermented bread in the house, having first recited the prayer: "Blessed art Thou, O Lord, our God, King of the universe, who hast sanctified us by Thy Commandments and who commandest us to remove all leavened bread." All keep silence while he is gathering the bread, and the ceremony ends with another prayer. On the following day, the 14th, at about ten A.M., the leavened bread collected the previous day has to be burned and a prayer is said, proclaiming that any leavened bread that remains in the house as a result of ignorance or carelessness is to be regarded as nonexistent or as so much dust.

The table has to be prepared before sunset, but the ceremony must not begin until after the sun has gone down. Three unleavened cakes are put on a large platter, and a roasted egg, *haroseth*, salted water, the shank-bone of a lamb, bitter herbs, and parsley are arranged above the cakes. The first cup is filled with wine, and the following prayer is said: "Blessed art Thou, O Eternal One, our God, King of the universe, who hast chosen us from among all peoples and hast raised us above all nations, who hast sanctified us with Thy Commandments . . . who hast given us feasts for our enjoyment and especially this feast of the azymes, the commemoration of our liberation and our coming forth from Egypt. . . ." After this prayer, all present wash their hands, the father takes parsley, dips it in vinegar, salt and water, distributes it to the participants, and before eating it, recites this prayer: "Blessed art Thou, Lord, our God, King of the universe, Creator of the fruits of the earth!" He then breaks one of the cakes in two, laying aside one half for after the supper.

It is at this point that the Paschal supper proper begins. The father takes up the egg and shank-bone of the lamb, all present assisting him, and as he does so he recites the prayer: "This is the bread of affliction which our fathers ate in the land of Egypt: let all who are hungry enter and eat of it; let those who are in need come and celebrate the Passover. Now we celebrate it here but *next year we hope to celebrate it in the land of Israel.* This year we are slaves here, but next year we hope *to be free in the land of Israel."*

Then the second cup is filled with wine, the cakes are removed from the table, and the youngest male participant asks: "Why is this night different from all other nights? On other nights we can eat leavened or unleavened bread but tonight only unleavened; on other nights we can eat all kinds of herbs but tonight only those that are bitter; on other nights we do not dip even once but tonight we do so twice; on other nights we eat sitting or reclining, but tonight all re- cline." The platter is then put back on the table and the father answers the questions: "Because we were slaves of Pharaoh, and the Lord, our God, freed us with the strength of His arm . . . ; and if He had not freed us, we and our sons and our sons' sons would still be slaves in the land of Egypt . . . ; therefore we must remember this deed, and those who speak of Him at length are worthy of praise."

Having said this, the father takes a cake from the large plate, shows it to those present, and asked: "Why do we eat these azymes? Because our fathers, in leaving Egypt, had not time to let the bread be leav- ened. . . ." Taking the bitter herbs, he shows them and asks: "Why do we eat these bitter herbs? Because the Egyptians embittered the lives of our ancestors. . . . Each one of us should consider himself as freed from Egypt and should believe that the Lord accomplished the liberation for him."

Then, taking the cup of wine, he says: "Therefore we are obliged to thank, praise, adore, glorify, honor, bless and exalt Him who did all these wonderful things for our fathers and for us, who brought us from slavery to freedom, from the darkness to the light . . .; there- fore let us sing a new canticle: *"Halleluyah!"* Then follow several pas- sages from the Bible in praise of God.

Once more all wash their hands, saying: "Blessed be thou, O Lord, King of the universe, who hast sanctified us by thy commandments and hast commanded us to wash our hands." The father takes the two and a half cakes, eats a piece and recites the prayer: "Blessed be thou, O Lord, etc. . . . who producest bread. Blessed, etc. . . . who com- mandest us to eat unleavened bread." Then he gives a piece of bread to each of the participants, who eat it and recite the same prayer. Next, he takes some of the bitter herbs, dips them in the *haroseth* and says:

"Blessed, etc. . . . who hast commanded us to eat bitter herbs." He distributes the herbs to the others, each of whom repeats the same prayer before eating his portion. The father then breaks the third cake, takes bitter herbs dipped in *haroseth,* and eats both, saying: "Thus did Hillel, while the Temple stood; he ate unleavened bread and bitter herbs all together." This is apparently the end of the supper properly so-called.

Then the father takes the half cake which he had laid aside at the beginning of the meal; he gives a piece to each one present and fills the cup with wine. This is done after the meat has been eaten. A long prayer of thanksgiving follows, which says, in part: "Blessed be our God, whose gifts we have received and by whose goodness we live." The father begins this prayer by saying: "Let us give thanks." And the others answer: "Have compassion on Thy people Israel, on Jerusalem, on Sion, the dwelling place of Thy glory, on the kingdom of the house of David, Thy anointed, on the great and holy Temple. . . . Allow us to see, O Lord, our God, the consolation of Sion, Thy city, and the rebuilding of Jerusalem, Thy city. Grant unto us the remembrance of our fathers, the remembrance of the Messias, the son of David, Thy servant, the remembrance of Jerusalem, Thy Holy City. . . . Rebuild Jerusalem, Thy Holy City, soon, in our days. Blessed art Thou, Lord, our God, King of the universe, our omnipotent Father, King, Fortress, Maker, Redeemer, Creator and our Sanctifier. . . . May the All-Merciful be adored in all generations, and be eternally glorified among us. May He break the yoke of captivity which weighs upon our necks and lead us safely to our land. . . . May He bless my father and my guide, the master of this house, and my mother, the mistress of this house, their children and everything that belongs to them. May He make us worthy of seeing the days of Messias."

Then the door is opened and an invocation recited: "Pour out Thy wrath upon the Gentiles [*haggoim*] that have not known Thee, and against the kingdoms that have not called upon Thy name, because they have devoured Jacob and have laid waste his beautiful abode. Pour out Thy indignation upon them and let Thy wrathful anger take hold of them; pursue them in Thy anger and destroy them from under the heavens of the Lord."

The fourth cup is then filled and the Hallel recited: ". . . What shall I render to the Lord for all the things that he hath rendered to me? I will take the chalice of salvation; and I will call upon the name

JERUSALEM: *The Mosque of Omar, built on the site of the Temple.*

of the Lord. . . . If all the Gentiles surround me, I shall scatter them in the name of the Lord. . . ." Then Psalm 117 is recited: "Give praise to the Lord, for he is good: for his mercy endureth for ever. . . ." Continuing, they pray: "Next year, O, bring us to Jerusalem! . . . Rebuild Thy Holy City, Jerusalem, in our days, and lead us there, and may we be able to eat of Thy fruits and enjoy Thy bounty. . . .

"Omnipotent God, rebuild the Temple soon; rebuild it, Lord, rebuild it, O God; rebuild it, Sovereign of the world; for Thy praise, for Thy glory, rebuild Thy sanctuary! O merciful God, rebuild Thy Temple soon; rebuild it, O God; rebuild it, O Lord; rebuild it, O Sovereign of the world!" The supplication is repeated eleven times: "Rebuild it in our time!" and with it the prayers come to an end.

This finishes the ceremony and for the remainder of the night nothing except water, tea or coffee may be taken.

The Profaners of the Temple [9]

(John 2:14–22; cf. Matt. 21:12–22; Mark 11:15–19; Luke 19:45–48)

[9] There is much discussion as to whether the expulsion recorded by St. John and that narrated by the Synoptic authors are the same episode or completely different incidents. See pp. 573 *ff.* below.

Another view of the Mosque of Omar.

In Psalm 4:5 we read: "Be ye angry, and sin not," a counsel which can be taken in an accommodated sense to mean: "Burn with anger but let there be no sin, no fault, in your wrath." On His first visit to Jerusalem, our Lord gave us a striking example of this teaching.

On the feast of the Passover, many people offered other sacrifices in addition to that of the Paschal lamb. Due to a reprehensible custom, a market for animals to be used in these sacrifices had gradually been set up within the very confines of the Temple, in the Court of the Gentiles. Furthermore, the Jews used to pay their tribute to the Temple at this season, and since only shekels, half-shekels and quarter-shekels were acceptable for this purpose, those who came from the pagan world had to change their drachmas or denarii into this Jewish coinage.[10] Consequently money-changers had set up their tables in the Temple to take advantage of the great demand for shekels, and their noisy transactions caused uproar and confusion and often led to disputes and heated arguments ill-suited to the sanctity of the place.

Such scandalous profanation of God's house filled Christ with holy anger, and making a whip of some cords which He probably found lying about on the ground, He drove animals and traders out of the sacred precincts, and overturned the tables of the money-changers. To those who were selling doves He said: "Take these things away, and do not make the house of my Father a house of business" (John 2:16), words which recall those of Jeremias (7:11): "Is this house then, in which my name hath been called upon, in your eyes become a den of robbers?" (cf. Matt. 21:13). In this action of Chist's, His disciples beheld the fulfillment of the psalmist's declaration: ". . . The zeal of thy house hath eaten me up" (Ps. 68:10). And in reality, what we may call His outburst of indignation was but the expression of the noblest sentiments of love and respect for the Father. He did not allow Himself to be carried away by passion, but rather controlled and channeled it, retaining perfect self-control always and in every circumstance.

The traders were too stunned to offer any resistance, for Christ's commanding and resolute bearing struck them with awe. But His action wounded the pride of the priests and chief officials of the Temple. What right had this stranger to set Himself up as a reformer of other people's lives and to assume an authority which He did not possess? Yet their consciences pricked them for their culpable inertia.

---

[10] A shekel was worth about $1.40 in our money. (Translator.)

Interior of the Mosque of Omar, showing the "sacred rock" which once formed the foundation of the altar of holocausts in the Temple of Jerusalem.

and perhaps even more for their own profitable part in the sacrilegious abuse; and, much against their wills, they were forced to admit that the intruder's action had been right and praiseworthy. Therefore, not daring to condemn Him outright, they asked Him angrily and resentfully for His credentials: "By what authority dost thou do this?"

Because of their evil disposition, Christ did not deem them worthy of a clear answer. Calmly and serenely He replied with an enigmatic pronouncement: "Destroy this temple, and in three days I will raise it up."

He was referring to His own Body, which He would raise up on the third day after the Jews had killed it. The Apostles came to understand the real meaning of His words after the Resurrection.

Conversation With Nicodemus [11]
(John 3:1–21)

As Lebreton rightly remarks, this dialogue is "one of those passages in St. John's Gospel which open up some of the widest vistas of theological science where it touches the new life in the Christian soul, and the part played by the Holy Spirit in bringing it about." [12] It took place during the time our Lord remained in Jerusalem for the first Passover. Some authors have tried to prove that it occurred during the last Passover, but their arguments lack solid foundation. [13]

In order to place the episode in its proper setting, we shall have to explain the last verses (23–25) of the preceding chapter in St. John. During the time covered by these verses Jesus had worked several miracles in Jerusalem (John 2:23) which had attracted great attention (cf. John 4:45), and which had caused many to believe in Him. But we should notice particularly our Lord's attitude towards the new converts. The evangelist says that "Jesus did not trust himself to them." The same verb is used in both the Greek text and the Vulgate to express the convert's belief and our Lord's distrust ($\epsilon\pi\iota\sigma\tau\epsilon\upsilon\sigma\alpha\nu$; $o\upsilon\kappa$ $\epsilon\pi\iota\sigma\tau\epsilon\upsilon\epsilon\nu$: *crediderunt; non credebat semetipsum*), but, as is obvious,

---

[11] U. Holzmeister, "Grungedanke und Gedankengang im Gespräche des Herrn mit Nikodemus," in *Zeit. f. kath. Theol.*, 45 (1921), 527–548.

[12] Jules Lebreton, S.J., *The Life and Teaching of Jesus Christ Our Lord*, trans. by Francis Day (New York: The Macmillan Company, 1949), I, 58.

[13] Among others, M.-J. Lagrange, O.P. in *The Gospel of Jesus Christ*, trans. by the English Dominicans (Westminster, Md.: The Newman Press, 1943), p. 98, n. 2, whose arguments are refuted by Lebreton, *op. cit.*, I, 57, n. 1; cf. also *Rech. de Sc. Rel.*, 19 (1929), 336, n. 8.

the meaning is not completely identical. They *believed* in Jesus, i.e., they recognized Him as a man sent by God; if they took Him for the Messias, the text does not say so, and it may well be that their faith did not go that deep. But Jesus did not *believe in them,* i.e., He did not trust Himself to them, an expression which seems to indicate that He did not trust them and that therefore He did not confide fully in them but maintained a certain reserve in their regard.[14]

Why did Jesus adopt this attitude? St. John explicitly tells us the reason: "in that he knew all men"; our Lord saw into the depths of their hearts and He did not have to be told what went on in their minds, for He knew perfectly "what was in man" (John 2:25). There was some imperfection in their faith, but what it was we can only guess. Some, like Knabenbauer, think that they acknowledged Him as a Messias but as a worldly Messias, a great conqueror who would free the people from their oppressors, a saviour from whom they expected political rather than spiritual liberation. Others, like Lagrange, believe that they lacked the proper moral dispositions; they regarded Jesus as a man sent by God but they were not disposed to surrender themselves generously to Him; they were prepared to be His followers up to a certain point only, and not unconditionally; and so, because they practiced a certain reserve with Jesus, He had to do so with them, for they gave only half their hearts to Him.

As we have seen, Jesus had attracted attention and had started a trend of popular opinion and support in His favor, particularly among the common people. However, the Temple officials were still hostile to Him because of what they regarded as His highhanded action in driving the vendors out of the sacred precincts. It is only against this historical background that the episode of Nicodemus appears in its true light.[15]

Nicodemus (="conqueror of the people," like our "Nicholas") was a leading personage, "a leader of the Jews," i.e., a member of the Sanhedrin, and a Pharisee. He appears on two other occasions in the

---

[14] Olivieri's interpretation of this passage is a strange one: he holds that our Lord adopted an attitude of reserve not towards those who, according to John 2:23, believed in Him, but towards the priests and Pharisees who were hostile to Him, and that St. John is indicating here that, from this moment on, Jesus "had to take precautions to guard against an attack on His life" (*RB* [1926], p. 390). In our opinion, such an interpretation is in open conflict with the text.

[15] The Gospel account can be divided into three parts: (1) introduction (vv. 1–2); (2) spiritual rebirth (vv. 3–15); (3) the reception which the world gave to the Son of God (vv. 16–21).

fourth Gospel—in 7:50, a particularly interesting passage which tells us that he remained a *hidden* disciple of our Lord, and which allows us to see his good judgment and discretion, and in 19:39, where he and Joseph of Arimathea bury Jesus.

Nicodemus had seen the miracles wrought by Christ and was convinced that He came from God. But being a prudent man, he wished to become better acquainted with the Miracle-worker before committing himself. A personal interview and heart-to-heart talk would surely remove his last doubts. But what would his friends and colleagues say? Would they not reproach him and laugh at his credulity? Yet he was determined to speak with Jesus, and so he resolved to go to Him by night so that no one would know of his visit. His first words to our Saviour breathe sincerity, humility and reverence: "Rabbi, we know that thou hast come a teacher from God, for no one can work these signs that thou workest unless God be with him."

Although Jesus was a relatively young man, Nicodemus gave Him the honorific title of "rabbi" or doctor, thereby frankly acknowledging that our Lord's miracles were a guarantee that He had come from God, and that He had come to teach. Nicodemus' use of the title also implied that he had come to be taught the doctrine of the young Master. When we remember the great opinion that the doctors of the Law had of themselves, we can but admire and wonder at the humble simplicity of Nicodemus.

We might have expected Jesus to reply to His visitor with some general and rather vague sentences such as one of the formulas of courtesy so common among oriental peoples; or He might have invited Nicodemus to ask some definite question and then have given him the appropriate answer. But nothing like that happened, or if it did we do not know of it, since we have no means of telling whether the evangelist recorded the whole conversation or handed down to us only a summary thereof, as Maldonatus and others presuppose. According to the text, our Lord began without preamble: "Amen, amen, I say to thee, unless a man be born again, he cannot see the kingdom of God."

This answer on Christ's part is somewhat surprising, the more so because it was pronounced with such force and solemnity. It could be regarded as rather premature, but in fact it is not so. We must not forget that Jesus could read His guest's thoughts and that He was replying to them, although Nicodemus had not yet put them into words. But even if we prescind from our Lord's ability to see into men's hearts, we can easily understand His mode of reply if we remember the historical background of His words. The kingdom of God had been preached by John the Baptist, and it was moreover a concept already known from the Old Testament, which contained also the fundamentals of the whole Messianic economy. And our Lord, too, was preaching the kingdom of God. Therefore, it was a common concept, and many people must have asked themselves what they had to do to enter this kingdom.

The uncompromising tone of the reply may perhaps be explained by Christ's intention to rid Nicodemus' mind of the ideas which the doctors of the Law had formed of the kingdom of God. His words meant that the kingdom was like a new and superior life, one that was divine, and that therefore a rebirth, a divine regeneration, was essential. That is the basic intent of our Lord's declaration.

It should be noted that the Greek word ἄνωθεν has a twofold meaning: "again," and "from on high." It is used in the latter sense in John 3:31; 9:11, 23; Origen, St. Cyril of Alexandria, and St. Thomas, and, among the exegetes, Calmes, Lagrange, Joüon, and Lebreton prefer to give it this meaning in our passage, while Knabenbauer, Durand, Plummer, B. Weiss, Zahn, Murillo, Bover, Gomá and Prat lean towards the first interpretation. Prat gives three reasons for his preference: (1) Nicodemus' reply; (2) the regeneration is represented as a *second birth* (cf. Tit. 3:5; 1 Pet. 1:3, 23); (3) the Vulgate and the other ancient versions translate the word in this sense. And actually, as B. Weiss correctly observes, if Nicodemus had taken our Lord's words to refer to a birth from on high, he would not have made the objection: "How can a man be born when he is old? Can he enter a second time into his mother's womb and be born again?" [16] Therefore, we regard as more probable the first of the two meanings referred to, i.e., ". . . unless a man be born *again*. . . ."

Nicodemus' answer was a natural one, and Jesus no doubt was waiting for it in order to use it as a starting point for clarifying His first statement. The new birth was to be accomplished by water and the Spirit: "Amen, amen, I say to thee, unless a man be born again of water and the Spirit, he cannot enter into the kingdom of God. That which is born of the flesh is flesh; and that which is born of the Spirit is spirit."

[16] On this point see Knabenbauer, Prat and B. Weiss.

In Mark 1:8 a contrast is drawn between the baptism of water and that of the Spirit, but here our Lord unites the two; water will be the external sign of that which the Spirit effects internally. Theologians are agreed that Jesus is speaking here of Christian baptism, as in fact He is, no matter how much some (B. Weiss, for example) may deny it. Even in the very first verses of Genesis water and the Spirit are united: "The Spirit of God moved over the waters." Our Lord is drawing a contrast between birth in the flesh and birth in the spirit (". . . Who are born not of blood, nor of the will of the flesh, nor of the will of man, but of God": John 1:13), since, as St. Paul says (1 Cor. 2:14), the flesh is incapable of understanding the things of the spirit.

Nicodemus must have shown some surprise at our Lord's answer to his objection, for Jesus went on to say: "Do not wonder that I said to thee, 'You must be born again' " (v. 7). Then, to give His questioner some understanding of the Spirit's action on man, our Lord used a comparison taken from the wind and proposed in the form of a parable: "The wind blows where it will, and thou hearest its sound but dost not know where it comes from or where it goes. So is everyone who is born of the Spirit."

These words of our Lord have created no small difficulty for commentators. Verse 6 definitely refers to the Holy Spirit ("That which is born of the flesh is flesh; and that which is born of the Spirit is spirit"), as does the second half of verse 8, which we have just quoted ("So is everyone who is born of the Spirit"). It would seem, then, that the first part of verse 8 should be understood in the same sense (translating "Spiritus ubi vult spirat, etc.," as "The Spirit breathes where He wills, etc."), and all the more so since it would be perfectly true to say that the Spirit breathes where He wills and that no one knows whence He comes or whither He goes, whereas the wind has no will and we know perfectly well whether it is blowing from north to south, for example, or vice versa. Hence a good number of the Fathers, St. Augustine in particular, interpret this passage as referring to the Holy Spirit.[17] However, if the context is examined closely, there seems to be no doubt that the word *spiritus:* πνεῦμα, should be understood as meaning the natural element which we call the wind. The particle *sic,* οὕτως ("so"), indicates that in the second part of verse 8, where *spiritus* definitely refers to the Holy Spirit, our Lord is applying the parable

---

[17] St. Augustine explicitly denies that it refers to the wind (*In Ioan.* tr. 12. 7: *PL* 35, 1487 *f.*).

that is evidently contained in the first part of that verse (cf. Mat. 13: 40). And it is obvious that in any parable there must be two terms distinct from each other. In our case these terms are the wind and the Holy Spirit, which share a certain similarity of characteristics. Then, too, the parable is rendered more pointed by the fact that its terms, in reality so distinct from each other, are both expressed by the same word. Our Lord used the parable to show Nicodemus that his inability to understand the nature of the new birth was no reason for denying it, provided that it gave some sign of its existence, since even in the merely natural order we acknowledge the reality of things, such as the wind, whose properties we do not know. The phrase "the wind blows where it will" should be taken as a *personification,* a common figure of speech; or else it may refer to the spontaneous strength with which the wind blows, which nothing can resist and which we cannot change.[18] As regards our Lord's reference to our ignorance of the wind's direction, St. Thomas gives the following explanation, which Lagrange also adopts: "We know whether the wind comes from the north or the south, but we do not know in which part of the world it began to blow or where it will cease, in the same way as, when we see somebody go by, we know perfectly well the direction he is taking, but we do not know either his point of departure or his destination." This use of the wind in a simile was not new, for we find it in Ecclesiastes 11:5:

> "As thou knowest not what is the way of the wind,
> nor how the members are joined together in the
> womb of her that is with child:
> so thou knowest not the works of God, who is the
> maker of all." [19]

Although the two expressions employed by our Lord may have had primarily a general application, it is probable that, in using them, He wished to hint at the way in which the Holy Spirit operates in souls. There is no question here of the grace necessary to do good, which is

[18] St. John Chrysostom, who interprets the word *spiritus* as "the wind," says: "Medium aliquid corporeum inter et incorporeum invenit, venti nempe impetum; indeque illum instituit. De vento namque dicit: *Vocem eius audis; sed nescis unde veniat aut quo vadat.* Cum dicit *Ubi vult spirat,* non significat ventum arbitrio suo ferri, sed naturalem eius impetum et vim sine impedimento latam" (*In Ioan.* Hom. 26. 1: *PG* 59, 154).

[19] This translation seems preferable to that of "spirit of life" which Podechard gives: "As thou knowest not the way in which the *spirit of life penetrates into* [*beth* instead of *kaph*] the members in the womb. . . ." Allgeier and Crampon are correct in upholding the Massoretic Text.

never denied to anyone, but rather of those more specific inspirations and illuminations which the Holy Spirit is accustomed to give, which are not absolutely necessary for salvation but which greatly assist us to practice virtue with more facility and perfection. The Holy Spirit is sovereignly free in bestowing these graces; He confers them on whom He wills and as He wills, and we cannot complain at His choice, since we have no right to them. However, we know that if we dispose ourselves properly, He will give them to us because, as the saints say, He is more desirous of bestowing them upon us than we are of receiving them. But we must prepare ourselves by removing the impediments within us, because, since the Holy Spirit is not flesh but a most pure spirit, and since everyone tends to unite himself with those who are like him, we must strive to empty our souls of everything that is coarse, gross, earthly and carnal. Moreover, although the Holy Spirit sometimes communicates Himself in the manner of a rushing wind, as happened on Pentecost—for in this too He is perfectly free to do as He chooses—yet He more ordinarily comes like a gentle breath. Therefore the soul must try to cultivate an habitual state of *silence*. If there are noise and tumult within it, it will not hear the whispered words of God.

Nor do we know at times whence the Spirit comes or whither He goes. The breathing of the Spirit is not always preceded by conscious preparation. Sometimes He comes suddenly and in circumstances which do not seem very favorable, while at other times, when we apparently have reason to expect Him, He does not allow His presence to be felt.

Our Lord's explanation gave Nicodemus to understand that He was not speaking of a material but of a spiritual rebirth, a rebirth of whose positive nature Nicodemus had not yet been able to form any exact idea. The Jewish doctor did not deny the possibility of such a spiritual rebirth, but simply inquired: "How can these things be?"

It is not likely that he was pretending to be ignorant; rather, he openly admitted that he did not understand Christ's words and asked to be enlightened. However, his ignorance was, to a certain extent, culpable. The prophets (e.g., Ezech. 11:19; 36:25-26; [20] Zach. 13:1; Isai. 44:3; Joel 3:1) had spoken of a spiritual regeneration, and since Nicodemus was "a teacher in Israel," he should have known this doctrine. Hence Jesus answered him, not exactly ironically, but still in

[20] "And I will give you a new heart and put a new spirit within you."

a tone of gentle reproach: "Thou art a teacher in Israel and dost not know these things?"

Then followed a long discourse (vv. 11–21), and we should note that in it our Lord did not explain spiritual rebirth, but insisted solely on the obligation of giving credence to His words.

The formula "Amen, amen, I say to thee" lent greater solemnity to what He was going to say, and it is probable that these words were accompanied by an expressive gesture. Christ here used the first person plural, "we know . . . we have seen . . ."; this is the only time He employed it. What was the reason for this unusual mode of expression? Many explanations have been suggested: that Jesus was speaking in the name of the Three Divine Persons (St. Thomas); that He was including John the Baptist (B. Weiss) or His disciples (Fillion); that He was referring to His two kinds of knowledge, divine and human (Cajetan). However, the most probable solution is that He was using the royal "We" to give greater emphasis to His words (Schanz), or else that the evangelist alone was responsible for the plural (cf. John 21:24), as Knabenbauer believes.

Not only did Jesus assert that He knew (His knowledge could have come by hearing), but also that He had seen—with His own eyes, we would say—that which He was declaring and to which He was formally bearing witness. And yet, he added: "our witness you do not receive." This reproach was clearly addressed to Nicodemus, but not to him alone, for it was also directed against those who had been included in his words "we know" in verse 2, and who, in a sense, were his colleagues. Hence the reproof was not levelled exclusively at Nicodemus' difficulty in believing, but referred also to those occasions on which others had adopted a similar attitude. It was as if Jesus had said: "I have other and much more sublime things to tell you, things which are found in heaven alone, such as the mystery of the Most Holy Trinity, and the relationship between the Three Divine Persons. But how will you be able to believe these heavenly truths if you cannot bring yourself to believe things which are earthly in comparison, though still supernatural, such as rebirth through grace, and which take place in men's hearts?"

Then Christ stated that He, and He alone, knew these sublime things, since they could be known only by one who had ascended to Heaven and had come down on earth to communicate them to men. The ascent to Heaven mentioned here is not the Ascension itself, although some authors have understood it thus. The verb "to ascend" can be considered here as a synonym for "to be," and certainly the Word had been in Heaven for all eternity and had come down from there to assume human nature. Maldonatus and others, including Simón, understood it to refer to Christ's human nature which, through what is called the *communicatio idiomatum,* an effect of the hypostatic union, ascended to Heaven in the sense it was in Heaven because the Person of the Word was there. However, the first explanation seems to us more acceptable.

Thus far the young Rabbi, as Nicodemus had called Him, had placed before His questioner two great mysteries, that of spiritual rebirth through baptism and that of the Incarnation, although the timid doctor of the Law had not understood the new doctrine. In verses 14–15, our Lord went further still, and spoke clearly to him about the purpose of His own earthly sojourn, which was to win salvation for men, to obtain eternal life for them (cf. John 19:29) through His death on the cross. To express this idea, Jesus used an episode from the Old Testament with which Nicodemus was doubtless familiar, the episode of the brazen serpent (Num. 21: 4–9): "And as Moses lifted up the serpent in the desert, even so must the Son of Man be lifted up, that those who believe in him may not perish, but may have life everlasting."

The Jews already knew that the brazen serpent had a spiritual significance and that it was a symbol of something higher, for the Book of Wisdom (16:6) calls it "a sign of salvation," and adds that those who turned their eyes towards it were healed, not by what they saw, but by God, the Saviour of all (v. 7). In the same way, the Son of Man was to be lifted up, a reference both to His *Crucifixion* and to His being *raised on high* so that all might look upon Him. In fact, when Jesus spoke of His being lifted up (John 8:28, and particularly 12:32, where the evangelist adds his own commentary), He was certainly referring to His death. Nevertheless we can say that in this lifting up— which to the Jewish mind must have seemed ignominious—the idea of glory was also included, since Christ Himself said: "And I, if I be lifted up from the earth, will draw all [men] to myself"; i.e., all men, both Jews and pagans, will hasten to the cross, acknowledging Him who hangs upon it as the true Messias and the Son of God. The Church has enshrined this idea in that vigorous phrase of her liturgy:

"Regnavit a ligno Deus," and even Pilate proclaimed it in the title which he caused to be affixed to the cross.

The mystery of death which Jesus revealed here to Nicodemus is closely connected with the mystery of baptism, because in baptism we die with Christ and are buried with Him, as St. Paul teaches in the beautiful and profoundly significant words: "Do you not know that all we who have been baptized into Christ Jesus have been baptized into his death? For we were buried with him by means of Baptism into death . . ." (Rom. 6:3 *f.*); elsewhere the same Apostle writes: "For you were buried together with him in Baptism . . ." (Col. 2:12).

Christ died for the salvation of men, but if men are to be saved they must believe in Him: "Without faith it is impossible to please God . . ." (Heb. 11:6). But, obviously, this faith must be a living faith, i.e., it must be accompanied by good works and consequently by charity.

In order to confirm Nicodemus in his faith, which no doubt was still wavering, Jesus showed him, as it were, the Heart of God, and revealed to him the depths of God's love for men, a love so great that He willed to give them His own Son: "For God so loved the world that he gave his only-begotten Son, that those who believe in him may not perish, but may have life everlasting."

The Divine Teacher closed His discourse by showing the Son of Man's attitude towards the judgment of the world (vv. 17–21).[21] The Word did not become flesh in order to judge the world, but rather to save it; His mission, then, was not one of justice but of mercy. Nevertheless, if man is to be saved he must cooperate by believing in the Son of God. And he who possesses this faith, accompanied, of course, by charity—as St. Paul also teaches—will not be judged. But he who rejects this faith is already judged, i.e., he has already made himself worthy of being condemned, and if he dies in this state he will be damned.

This unfolding of God's plan and of His loving designs offers no

[21] More than a few authors, Belser among them, attribute to the evangelist all this passage from v. 13 inclusive. It would be beside the point to discuss the matter here. Bover-Cantera (*Sagrada Biblia* [Madrid, 1951]) believe that the whole passage was uttered by our Lord. Murillo (*Evangelio de San Juan,* p. 203) is of the same opinion in regard to vv. 13–17; of the following verses he says: "For our part we believe that the discourse is wholly our Lord's up to v. 17, and that only vv. 18–21 have any solid basis for being regarded as the evangelist's own contribution." Lagrange, Braun and others attribute vv. 16–21 to the evangelist, while Knabenbauer, Fillion and others attribute them to our Lord.

difficulty. There are, however, two points which require some explanation: why is the judgment limited to the evil, and why is it spoken of as if it took place in this world and not after death?

Judgment is an act of the intellect whereby one proclaims, internally or externally, that something is or is not such and such. The judge pronounces a verdict declaring the accused guilty or innocent; his judgment, then, may be favorable or unfavorable. And although punishment and liberation do not pertain to the essence of judgment, they are closely connected with it, and so the verdict may be called condemnatory or absolving. Now in the passage under consideration, the evangelist, or rather our Lord Himself, used the words "judgment" and "to judge" in the unfavorable, condemnatory sense; and this is the reason why the judgment is here restricted to the evil. As regards the second point, the time of the judgment, Christ declared that whoever does not believe in the Son of God is by that very fact already judged, and therefore the passage refers to a judgment in this world. And indeed, by knowingly rejecting the faith that is offered, man makes himself an enemy of God, and therefore the judgment which he passes on himself must necessarily be unfavorable. However, this judgment is not irrevocable, since man can always repent while he remains on earth.

In verse 19, our Lord explained in what the judgment consists. However, He did not deal with judgment properly so-called which, as we have remarked above, is an act of the intellect. He was speaking of the deeds which are the cause of an unfavorable and condemnatory judgment. The light came into the world (John 1:9), that is, the Word made flesh came on earth, and men preferred darkness to the light (John 1:10) because they were doing evil and, wishing to go on doing it, they sought the darkness as a cloak for their iniquity. But those who act according to the truth [22] have no reason to hide; instead, they love the light, since the glory of God is reflected in their works.

---

[22] The expression used in the original text is stronger and more vigorous: "he who *does* the truth: he who *practices* the truth": ὁ δὲ ποιῶν τὴν ἀλήθειαν (v. 21). This is a surprising turn of phrase because truth is the object of the *intellect,* and, consequently, we usually say that one *knows* the truth. We must remember, however, that the Hebrew concept of truth is not completely identical with the Greek, which is also ours. The Hebrew word *'emet* connotes firmness, solidity, fidelity, uprightness, and goodness, while the Greek ἀλήθεια signifies exact knowledge of reality or reality itself. In the fourth Gospel all these various shades of meaning are concentrated and combined in the word ἀλήθεια which therefore acquires such a wide range of significance that it can be used in cases and circumstances in which our narrow concept would not be wholly suitable: "Every-

Twice in this dialogue with Nicodemus Jesus called Himself "the Son of Man" (v. 13 *f.*), a title very frequently used in the Gospels; we find it thirty-one times in St. Matthew, fourteen in St. Mark, twenty-five in St. Luke and twelve in St. John, but always on our Lord's lips alone, and never referring to anyone but Himself. In itself the phrase simply means "man," as can be clearly seen in Job 25:6, where the two expressions form a parallel and are used as perfect synonyms. We also find it used in an identical sense in other passages, e.g., Ezech. 2:1, 3, 8; 3:1, 3, 4; Isaias 51:12; 56:2. But in Daniel 7:13 *f.* the words "son of man" indicate a supernatural being definitely superior to man, and, as a consequence of this passage, the title came to be regarded as Messianic, i.e., the title "son of man" was to be one of the names of the Messias, as is clearly evident from the *Book of Henoch (Ethiopic)*, written in the first century B.C.[23] Nevertheless the title did not spread and become popular among the Jews. If we keep these circumstances in mind, we shall not find it difficult to see why our Lord used it in preference to others. First of all, on the Divine Master's lips it did not mean simply "man," nor was it a substitute for the personal pronoun "I," nor was it inspired exclusively by humility; it had a much more sublime meaning, one which was closely related to Christ's dignity and the Messianic economy. The two principal mysteries which our Lord wished to reveal to men were His character as Messias and as Son of God. But there were great obstacles in the way of such a revelation. The name "Messias" evoked in the Jewish mind the idea of a national hero who would break the yoke of Roman domination and restore the ancient freedom of the Chosen People. Therefore, if Christ had proclaimed that He was the Messias, He would have stirred up patriotic feeling and raised on high the banner of independence. On the other hand, the title of "Son of God" would have been in direct conflict with the strict monotheism of the Jews; to them a man-God was inconceivable. But the expression "Son of Man" contained, in a veiled manner, both the concept of the Messias and that of the Son of God. Hence it was eminently suited to serve as a vehicle for a discreet and prudent revela-

---

one who is of the truth hears my voice" (John 18:37); ". . . the truth is not in us" (1 John 1:8); ". . . that we may be fellow-workers for the truth" (3 John 8). Cf. M. Zerwick, *Verb. Dom.*, 18 (1938), 338–342, 373–377.

[23] Bonsirven (*Le Judaïsme palestinien au temps de J.-C.* [Paris, 1935], I, 373) maintains that the passages in this work which refer to the Son of Man are genuine, as against Lagrange who regards them as Christian interpolations (*Le Judaïsme avant Jesus-Christ* [Paris, 1931], pp. 372 *ff.*).

tion of the truth, one which could be used without fear of violent reactions. That such indeed was Christ's intention is clear from His answer to Caiphas, where, referring to the prophet Daniel, He said: ". . . You shall see the Son of Man sitting at the right hand of the Power and coming upon the clouds of heaven" (Matt. 26:64). Thus while on the one hand the title "Son of Man" expressed our Lord's human nature (and under this aspect it can be regarded as inspired by humility), on the other hand it referred to His Messianic character and His Divine Nature.[24]

---

[24] It is scarcely worthwhile even to mention the opinion of those who deny that the title was used by Christ and attribute it to tradition, which they regard as the source from which the evangelists drew it.

There is a copious literature on the words "Son of Man." See Bonsirven, *Les Enseignements de Jésus-Christ* (Paris, 1946), pp. 56–67, where many authors are cited; also Dalman, *Die Worte Jesu* (Leipzig, 1930); Rosbaniec, *Sensus genuinus et plenus locutionis "Filius Hominis"* (Rome, 1920); Simón-Dorado, *Praelectiones Biblicae,* Nov. Test., I, pp. 478–480; L. de Grandmaison, *Jesus Christ,* II, 27–31.

10. Ministry in Judea

John the Baptist's Testimony
(John 3:22–36; cf. Map IV)

Having cast the seed, the Divine Sower thought it prudent to give it time to germinate and bear fruit, and so, when the cycle of the Passover closed, He left Jerusalem. It is also quite possible that the atmosphere then prevailing in the capital was partly responsible for His sudden departure. The enmity of the priests and leaders of the Temple had not died down, and, since they did not acknowledge that the new Prophet had been sent by God, they were doing everything in their power to discredit Him in the people's eyes. Jesus had indeed worked miracles and won followers, but this initial success had only served to increase the anger of His adversaries. The result was that Jerusalem had split into two parties, and Christ judged it better to withdraw and allow the tempest to abate.

The Master, then, departed with His Apostles; He did not return immediately to Galilee, however, but remained in Judea. The evangelist has not specified the place to which our Lord went. It does not seem that He turned south towards Hebron, as Fouard believes. We find a slight clue to His destination in John 4:4 where we read that Jesus "had to" ($\check{\epsilon}\delta\epsilon\iota$) pass through Samaria in order to reach Galilee, no doubt a reference to the road which traversed Palestine from north to south

'Ain Beda, one of the numerous springs in Aennon-Salim.

across the mountains and which ran through the city of Sichem. Consequently it is probable that our Lord stayed at some spot in the mountain region where there was plenty of water for baptisms. Prat suggests the neighborhood of Bethel, where there was a gushing spring with a large reservoir which can still be seen. Of course, the banks of the Jordan were the most appropriate place for baptisms and therefore it is no wonder that several authors, Lagrange among them, locate His ministry there. If this were the case, then in returning to the north He would probably have gone through the Wadi Fasail and Akrabeh, following the road that was later to be a Roman highway. But then it would be difficult to explain the words "had to" in John 4:4, since He would not have had to go north through the mountain region and it would then have been easier and more practical to follow the Jordan valley and enter Galilee through Beisan, which was no doubt the route He had taken in the other direction when going from Nazareth to the place where John was baptizing. The words "had to" could also refer, not to a necessity imposed by our Lord's location at the time, but to His plan to meet the Samaritan woman; however, this interpretation seems a little strained. At all events, we know that He exercised His ministry in the region north of Jerusalem.

John 3:22 tells us that Jesus was baptizing, although later, in 4:2, he qualifies his first statement by saying that it was not Jesus Himself but His disciples who were doing so. Several of the Fathers and early commentators believed that this baptism was a sacrament, and that it conferred grace and remitted sins, i.e., that it was baptism "with the Holy Spirit" (1:33).[1] And some think that our Lord baptized His Apostles before they began to administer the sacrament themselves. But the great majority of modern authors—Knabenbauer, Lagrange and Prat, for example—hold that this baptism was not true Christian baptism. As a matter of fact, the disciples did not then know of the mystery of the Holy Trinity; and, furthermore, if this baptism conferred grace, how explain the fact that it is not mentioned again? Finally, St. John's explicit statement that Jesus did not baptize, but only His disciples (4:2), seems to indicate that the rite in question was not the baptism instituted by our Lord. Basically the ceremony did not differ from John the Baptist's; it merely moved the recipients to do penance and created a closer relationship between them and Christ.

While the disciples of Jesus were baptizing, John was doing likewise, not, however, at the Jordan opposite Jericho, but farther north. Why did the Baptist change to a new territory? Perhaps he left Bethabara or Bethany beyond the Jordan because this region was under the rule of Antipas, who may even then have been trying to imprison him. It is also possible that he wished to move away from Jerusalem in order to be farther from the reach of the Scribes and Pharisees. At any rate we know definitely that he was baptizing at Aennon ('Ayyun=fountains) near Salim, which was probably situated about six miles south of Beisan. There, within a comparatively small area, six or eight springs rise, the principal and certainly the most abundant of which are 'Ain ed Deir, where one can still see the remains of an ancient monastery, and 'Ain er-Ridgha. It is noteworthy that near the latter spring, which rises at the foot of Tell er-Ridgha, there is a *weli*, i.e., a kind of Moslem sanctuary, consisting simply of a tree which the Bedouins of the district

---

[1] Not, however, St. John Chrysostom, who says: "Quod si quis percontetur quid plus habuerit discipulorum quam Ioannis baptisma, dicemus, nihil. Nam utrumque baptisma Spiritus gratia vacuum erat." (*In Ioan.* Hom. 20. 1: *PG* 59, 167.)

call Sheikh Salim, a name which evidently echoes the one mentioned in the Gospel.

While the Precursor and the disciples of Jesus were baptizing, some of John's followers happened to fall in with a certain Jew (the singular is found in important manuscripts) and the conversation turned to purification, or, in other words, to baptism. As we would expect, the baptisms of Jesus and of John were compared and the numbers each was attracting were discussed. It would appear that the Jew was more favorable to, or at least showed a leaning towards, the baptism of Jesus; and it is not unlikely that he himself had received it. John's disciples took his partiality badly, and no wonder, since Christ Himself had been baptized by their master, who therefore had acted as the superior, and whom many of his followers were now abandoning in favor of the new Prophet. So strongly did they feel about the turn of events that they complained about it to John.

"Master," they said, "he who was with thee beyond the Jordan, to whom thou hast borne witness, behold he baptizes and all are coming to him" (v. 26).

Their zeal for the glory of their master had more than a little self-interest in it, for if the people's esteem for John lessened, then their standing would suffer too.

How magnificently did the Precursor show his humility and his greatness of soul in his last testimony to Christ! To his disciples he said: "No one can receive anything unless it is given him from heaven."

With these words he put a stop to their complaints and pointed out to them that when Jesus gave proof of possessing unusual powers and drew the people after Him, He was doing so with God's help. And if God wished things to be so, what right had they to complain? They should have known better, for had he not declared publicly that he himself was not the Messias but was far inferior to Him? Then, using a beautiful image drawn from contemporary marriage customs, he said: "He who has the bride is the bridegroom; but the friend of the bridegroom, who stands and hears him, rejoices exceedingly at the voice of the bridegroom. This my joy, therefore, is made full."

This is a reference to the Hebrew custom of giving the bridegroom an escort composed of a number of young men of his own age. Thus, for example, when Samson went down to Thamnatha to marry the Philistine woman, he was given no less than thirty companions (Judges

14:11). These young men were usually called "friends of the bride-groom" (1 Mach. 9:39) or "children of the marriage" (Matt. 9:15; Mark 2:19; Luke 5:34)—the latter phrase being a Hebraism. These attendants or pages were not supposed to seek glory for themselves but for the bridegroom, and were to rejoice in the marks of honor shown him.

Having proposed the comparison, John the Baptist proclaimed: "He must increase, but I must decrease." This declaration must have sounded strange to his disciples, for it was directly contrary to what they wished for and deemed proper. John's words referred to the future glory of Christ; St. Augustine applies them to the fact that the Precursor suffered bodily decrease by being decapitated, while Christ was exalted by being lifted up upon the Cross.[2]

Then in verses 31–36 there follows a wonderful eulogy of Jesus.[3] He is the Son of God, who is above all men because He came from on high, from Heaven, while others belong to the earth (v. 31). He bears witness to what He has seen and heard, and only He can give such testimony, because He is the only one who has been in Heaven. And since He received this testimony from God, anyone who accepts it and acknowledges it as true testifies thereby that God is true. There is good reason for accepting this testimony because the Messias, having been sent by God, speaks only the words of God, who gave Him the Spirit without measure (vv. 32–34). The Father loves the Son and placed all things in His hands. He who believes in the Son will have life eternal; he who rejects Him shall perish (vv. 35–36): "He who believes in the Son has everlasting life; he who is unbelieving towards the Son shall not see life, but the wrath of God rests upon him."

The Champion of Chastity
(Mark 6:17 ff.)

In Judea, where Jesus was exercising His ministry and His disciples

[2] "Haec testimonia et hanc veritatem, etiam passionibus suis, significaverunt Christus et Ioannes. Nam Ioannes capite minutus, Christus in cruce exaltatus." And applying John's words to men, he aptly says: "Antequam veniret Dominus Iesus, homines gloriabantur de se: venit ille homo ut minueretur hominis gloria, et augeretur gloria Dei. . . . Ipse [homo] in se minuatur, ut in Deo augeatur" (*PL* 35, 1504).

[3] Many authors (Patrizi, Calmes, Belser, Tillmann, Lagrange, Prat) regard these verses as a development of the Precursor's thought written by the evangelist, St. John, whose theological ideas they claim to recognize therein. But Schanz, Knabenbauer, Zahn and Fillion attribute the passage to John the Baptist.

were baptizing, storm clouds had begun to gather; an atmosphere charged with anger and resentment surrounded the Penitent of the Jordan and the Prophet of Nazareth. John's biting words: "Brood of vipers! . . ." had cut the Scribes and Pharisees to the quick, and the wound still smarted. Nor had the proud priests forgotten that they had been put to shame by the noble, forthright action of Jesus in expelling the profaners of the Temple. Impatiently they were awaiting their hour of revenge, and it was not long in coming.

As we have already seen, Herod the Great had left Galilee and Perea to his son Antipas, who then assumed control of these territories with the title of tetrarch. Antipas had married a daughter of Aretas, king of the Nabateans, whose capital was the famed city of Petra. His brother bore their father's name, Herod; St. Mark calls this man Philip (6:17), but he is not to be confused with Philip the Tetrarch, who had founded Caesarea Philippi. This Herod Philip had married his own niece Herodias, daughter of Aristobulus and granddaughter of Herod the Great and Mariamne, the noble Hasmonean, and by her he had a daughter named Salome. Unlike his brothers, he lived in Rome as a private person, a state in life which did not satisfy his haughty wife's ambitions. Antipas, paying a visit to the capital of the Empire, stayed at Herod Philip's house and repaid his brother's hospitality by seducing his wife. She made a pact with her lover that when he had returned to his tetrarchy, she would leave her husband and join him there. There was one obstacle in the way—Antipas' lawful wife—but he had made up his mind to give her a bill of divorce; she, however, discovered her husband's plan and forestalled him. She asked him for permission to spend some time in the fortress of Machaerus which was perched like an eagle's nest on the mountain to the east of the Dead Sea. Once there it was easy for her to escape to the nearby territory of her father, Aretas. As can be guessed, her flight did not displease Antipas, and it delighted Herodias, who, with her daughter Salome, came to live with her paramour, who was also her uncle and her brother-in-law. At this time the mother was about forty years of age and the daughter about fifteen.[4] This adulterous alliance caused great scandal, and John the Baptist voiced the opinion of the people on the matter (Matt. 14:1–5; Mark 6:17–20; Luke 3:19 ff.). With apostolic frankness, he flung the monarch's crime in his face (Mark 6:18): "It is not lawful for thee to have thy brother's wife."

---

[4] Cf. *Ant.* xviii. 5. 1.

We do not know where or in what circumstances these words were uttered. It could well be that the great penitent presented himself in person before the tetrarch, as Nathan had before David (2 Kings 12: 1–15) and Elias before Achab (3 Kings 21:17 *ff.*), and had made the halls of Tiberias or the palace of Livias [5] ring with his indictment. But it is also possible that he pronounced the condemnation before the crowds near the banks of the Jordan, from which spot it would soon have reached the tetrarch's ears.

How did Antipas react to John's censure? It appears that, either designedly or through fear, he did not immediately seize the austere preacher.[6] Perhaps he wished to avoid giving the impression that he was imprisoning John for personal reasons and consequently from a manifestly unjust motive. Instead, he would wait for or engineer a set of circumstances that would give his seizure of the Baptist at least some semblance of justice. Josephus has some interesting observations to make in this regard:

[John] was a good man who exhorted the Jews to practise virtue, to be upright in their dealings with each other and to be devout towards God. . . . Many came in crowds about him for they were greatly moved at hearing his words. Herod [Antipas] feared that his powers of persuasion would start a rebellion since the people seemed ready to follow his counsels in everything. He decided, therefore, to seize him in order to forestall any seditious movements and also so that he [Herod] might not have to repent later for having exposed himself to danger. As a result of these suspicions of Herod's, John was sent as a prisoner to Machaerus, where he was put to death.[7]

Thus, according to the Jewish historian, John was imprisoned as a political measure, and some authors have maintained that the evangelists are partial, or even lying, when they attribute the Precursor's

---

[5] This city, the present Tell er-Rameh, was situated at the foot of Mount Nebo, about six miles north of the Dead Sea. Buzy (*Saint Jean Baptiste*, p. 272) believes that John confronted Antipas there.

[6] Prat holds this opinion (*Jesus Christ*, I, 192), whereas Buzy (*op. cit.*, p. 273) and Huby (*Év. selon S. Marc* [Paris, 1924], p. 140) believe it more probable that the tyrant imprisoned John immediately after he had uttered the condemnation.

[7] *Ant.* xviii. 5. 2. Machaerus was the palace-fortress described by Josephus in *Wars* vii. 6. 1, 2: "[Herod the Great] built a wall . . . and . . . raised a palace magnificent in its grandeur and the beauty of its halls." Alexander Janneus (103–76 B.C.) had already built a castle there. For a description of the ruins see *RB* (1909), 386 *ff.*; G. Ricciotti, *Il cantiere di Hiram* (Torino, 1936), pp. 99–113, which contains many photographs. See also p. 402 below.

incarceration to a religious cause (Mark 6:17; Luke 3:19 *f.*). The truth is that, as Schürer correctly observes, the one motive does not exclude the other.[8] The Precursor's powerful personality had started a fervent religious movement, and his vehement protests against the scandalous concubinage must have stirred up popular aversion to the adulterous tetrarch. Hence by the very nature of things, the political and religious aspects of the matter were closely connected and both could have influenced the decision of the guilty, suspicious ruler.[9]

Josephus does not say how John was taken prisoner, but the phrase employed by St. Matthew: ". . . John had been delivered up . . ." (Matt. 4:12) seems to imply that the Precursor had been betrayed, doubtless by the Pharisees.[10]

Antipas' action is in perfect accord with that masterpiece of psychological insight, the description of his character left us by St. Mark (Mark 6:19 *f.*). It is likely that St. Mark's account of the tetrarch's feelings towards John applies both to the period before the Precursor's imprisonment and to the actual imprisonment itself.

Herodias, a vengeful woman whose pride had been deeply wounded, nursed in her heart an implacable hostility [11] towards John, and tried by every means in her power to bring about his death. Driven on by her pride and lust, she no doubt urged her lover to murder John. But her efforts were in vain, for Antipas would not consent, and the evangelist tells us why: the tetrarch, perhaps much against his will, regarded John with a reverence that bordered on fear, for he was well aware of the austere penitent's sanctity. Consequently he defended and protected [12] the Precursor against the attacks and machinations of his vicious consort. When John spoke with him—most likely in private interviews—he felt distressed and anguished,[13] as if tortured by remorse; yet he did not cease to converse with his prisoner but rather listened to him with pleasure, as the evangelist expressly says: "and he liked to hear him." The tetrarch's moral sense had not been com-

---

[8] Schürer, I, 438.

[9] Even Goguel acknowledges that Antipas could have been influenced by this double motive (cf. *Jean-Baptiste*, p. 293).

[10] Cf. Prat, *op. cit.*, I, 193, n. 4.

[11] This is the exact meaning of ἐνεῖχεν, which the Vulgate translates as *insidiabatur;* however, the latter can easily be reduced to the former.

[12] The Vulgate's *custodiebat* can be understood in this sense.

[13] This is the meaning of the reading πολλὰ ἠπόρει, which, although less well confirmed by the codices, is admitted by many authors (Knabenbauer, Lagrange, B. Weiss, and others) who prefer it to the more common πολλὰ ἐποίει, which the Vulgate translates as *multa faciebat.*

pletely blunted, nor had passion altogether silenced the voice of his conscience as it had that of his partner in adultery. He acknowledged the justice of John's reproaches, but his will was weak and he could not bring himself to break the chains that bound him.

At first glance, St. Matthew appears to give a very different account of Antipas' state of mind. In fact, the evangelist says that "he [Herod] would have liked to put him [John] to death, but he feared the people, because they regarded him as a prophet" (Matt. 14:5). Thus the tetrarch is represented as wishing to kill John, and as being deterred only by his fear that the people would rebel against a crime of such magnitude. However, if we examine the matter more closely, we shall see that it is not difficult to harmonize the two accounts of the tetrarch's attitude towards his prisoner. Undoubtedly the austere prophet's outspoken and insistent reproaches must at times have exasperated the adulterous ruler. It would be no wonder, then, if at such moments he actually did resolve to put an end to the Baptist's denunciations with the sword, but was restrained by the thought of the possible consequences. However, when these fits of anger had died down, he had time to reflect, his basic reverence for the Precursor once again came to the fore and he desisted from his bloodthirsty purpose. In a word, he was not so much depraved as weak, not so much cruel as sensual, and it is this combination of characteristics that explains his apparently contradictory attitudes towards John.

A short while after the Precursor had been imprisoned, and therefore about the beginning of May, our Lord left Judea and returned to Galilee. The evangelists give two reasons for His departure. According to John 4:1, He left Judea because the Pharisees were daily becoming more envious of, and angered by, His growing popularity. Perhaps they were already plotting to seize Him, but since His hour had not yet come, He judged it prudent to withdraw from the sphere of their influence by retiring to Galilee. St. Matthew gives another reason for our Lord's departure—the imprisonment of John the Baptist. These two causes were probably interrelated, since it is not unlikely that John was put into prison at the instigation of the Pharisees (". . . John had been delivered up. . . ." Matt. 4:12),[14] and consequently Jesus had reason to fear that they might treat Him likewise. Hence His withdrawal to Galilee was not a flight from Herod Antipas, to whom

---

[14] Cf. Prat, *op. cit.,* I, 193, n. 26. Buzy (*op. cit.,* p. 272) believes that the expression simply means that he was seized.

Galilee was subject, but rather from the Pharisees. Perhaps our Lord had a third motive for leaving the south, namely, the desire to avoid jealousy and quarreling between His own disciples and those of John the Baptist.

The Samaritan Woman
(John 4:5–42; cf. Maps I–IV)

The episode of the Samaritan woman is an outstanding example of the power of grace, and a perfect model of supernatural prudence and delicacy in the exercise of the apostolic ministry.

About midday—"it was about the sixth hour," counting from 6:00 A.M.—our Lord, accompanied by His disciples, came to Jacob's well.[15] The time of year was the end of April or the beginning of May.[16] After a journey of about five or six hours over rough and dusty roads, beneath the burning rays of the spring sunshine (which can be strong in Palestine), our Saviour was thirsty and fatigued, as the evangelist expressly says—"wearied as he was from the journey." Accordingly, while the disciples went into the nearby town of Sichar[17] to buy food, He sat alone on the curb of the well, which was perhaps shaded by a tree.

"I sleep and my heart watcheth" (Cant. 5:2), said the spouse in the Canticle of Canticles. With greater reason could Jesus have said:

[15] It is not easy to ascertain their route thither. The road they took depends principally on their point of departure, which was most probably the place where the disciples had been baptizing, i.e., the banks of the Jordan, according to some authors. If this was so, then we can suppose that they came through the city of Phasaelis into the Wadi Fasail, crossed the Acrabataneh region and came out on the great north-south road near Sichem. See what we have said above, pp. 270 f., about the place where our Lord's disciples had been baptizing.

[16] On this point see below, p. 284, n. 23.

[17] Was this the wretched present-day village of Askar, north of Jacob's Well and on the edge of the plain, Sahel el-Askar? Some think so because of the similarity between the two names, Askar and Sichar or Sychar. But it is difficult to harmonize this opinion with the text of St. John, which expressly mentions a *city* (πόλιν). It is much more probable that the evangelist was referring to ancient Sichem, which excavations, begun in 1913 and carried on for several years, have identified with Tell Balata at the eastern entrance to the valley in which the city of Nablus stands today. Near Tell Balata lies the little town of Balata, from which the *tell* derives its name, and where there is a good spring. Some authors ask skeptically why the Samaritan woman went to get water from the deep well when there was a spring so close at hand. The answer is that she may have been living in an isolated cottage near the well; or, as some suggest, despite her evil life, she may have come out of devotion to draw water from the well of Jacob, her father; or she may have believed that the well-water had some curative power.

*Present-day Nablus, between Mounts Ebal (right) and Garizim (left).
Jacob's Well is in the foreground.*

"My body is wearied but my spirit is on watch." The Good Shepherd had not stopped merely to rest; He was awaiting the arrival of a wandering sheep which He intended to bring back to the fold. And before long a woman came from the nearby town with pitcher and rope to draw water. She glanced at the stranger and immediately saw that He was a Jew. Without a word she drew a pitcher full of water and made ready to depart.

But Jesus said to her: "Give me to drink."

She broke her hostile silence with a discourteous refusal: "How is it that thou, although thou art a Jew, dost ask drink of me, who am a Samaritan woman? Knowest thou not that Jews and Samaritans have no dealings with each other?" [18]

[18] The Jews and the Samaritans had been bitter enemies since the destruction of Samaria about 721 B.C. The king of Assyria, in order to replace the great number of inhabitants whom he had carried away as captives, sent new settlers, who were pagans and adored their own gods. But a short while later the whole region was infested with lions, and the king, attributing the invasion to the fact that his settlers did not adore the God of the Samaritans, sent a Jewish priest to teach them the Law (4 Kings 17:25-28). The settlers, however, combined the practice of the Law with their idolatry (4 Kings 17:29-41), thereby provoking the wrath of the Jews, who were faithful adherents of the Law and adorers of the one true God. Hence arose the enmity between the two peoples, an enmity which was made more bitter still when the Jews, upon their return from exile,

Crypt of the Greek church, showing Jacob's Well in the center.

The stranger was not put out of countenance by the woman's curtness. Without taking offence and without reproaching her, He answered calmly and kindly: "If thou didst know the gift of God, and who it is who says to thee, 'Give me to drink,' thou, perhaps, wouldst have asked of him, and he would have given thee living water."

Our Saviour was alluding to the gift of grace which He was ready to give her, but since "living water" means water that flows from the ground, from a well or a spring, as distinct from water gathered in cisterns (Gen. 26:19; Jer. 2:13), and since therefore Jacob's Well contained living water, the adjective conveyed no special meaning to the Samaritan woman. She merely took the stranger's somewhat mysterious words to refer to some unusual method of drawing the water from the well. Therefore, without hostility and even with a certain air of respect she answered: "Sir, thou hast nothing to draw with, and the well is deep. Whence then hast thou living water? Art thou greater

refused to allow the Samaritans, whom they regarded as idolaters, to assist in the rebuilding of the Temple (1 Esd. 4:1 *ff.*). Years later, a priest who had been cast out of the Jewish community took refuge with the Samaritans. They built him a temple on Mount Garizim, which they claimed was the place where the true God had to be adored. For further details see A. Fernández, *Comentario a los Libros de Esdras-Nehemías* (Madrid, 1950), pp. 62 *ff.*

than our father Jacob who gave us the well, and drank from it, himself, and his sons, and his flocks?"

Our Lord replied: "Everyone who drinks of this water will thirst again. He, however, who drinks of the water that I will give him shall never thirst; but the water that I will give him shall become in him a fountain of water, springing up unto life everlasting."

Her curiosity now thoroughly aroused, the woman burst out with childlike spontaneity: "Sir, give me this water that I may not thirst, or come here to draw."

Now that the ground was prepared and the woman better disposed, our Lord said to her in tones of authority and without further preamble: "Go, call thy husband and come here."

The command was totally unexpected and must have shaken the woman; but because she was not lawfully married at the moment she replied curtly: "I have no husband."

Although she was a hardened sinner, her conscience must have been troubled at Christ's words; but she was far from suspecting that the stranger was reading the deepest secrets of her heart.

"Thou hast said well, 'I have no husband,' for thou hast had five husbands, and he whom thou now hast is not thy husband. In this thou hast spoken truly."

The unhappy sinner was thunderstruck—should she turn on her questioner? Try to deny His accusation? Or simply run away? But the hand that had hurled the thunderbolt had healed at the same time. The Divine Physician, having opened the wound, poured in the living water that softened her heart and disposed her to repent. With sincere admiration she exclaimed: "Sir, I see that thou art a prophet."

And then, partly to settle a doubt, and partly, perhaps principally, to change the subject, she pointed to Mount Garizim, the Samaritan's place of worship, and brought up the ancient dispute between her people and the Jews: "Our fathers worshipped on this mountain, but you say that at Jerusalem is the place where one ought to worship."

Her words implied the unspoken question: "You are a prophet; what have you to say about this matter?"

Jesus saw her intention, and He could have kept her to the subject by replying: "Leave that dispute aside for a while and think instead about improving your conduct." But the kind Master, who had not come to quench the smoking flax (cf. Isai. 42:3), condescended to the unhappy sinner's weakness and deigned to give her a sublime lesson in

*Nablus (ancient Neapolis), between Mounts Ebal (right) and Garizim (left).
At the foot of Ebal is Tell Balata, the ancient Sichem.*

theology: "Woman, believe me, the hour is coming when neither on this mountain nor in Jerusalem will you worship the Father. You worship what you do not know; we worship what we know, for salvation is from the Jews. But the hour is coming, and is now here, when the true worshippers will worship the Father in spirit and in truth. For the Father also seeks such to worship him. God is spirit, and they who worship him must worship in spirit and in truth."

Thus our Lord did answer her unspoken query, though He did not confine Himself to its terms. Instead, He went much further and in a few brief phrases expounded the true nature of the New Covenant and of the new kingdom which He had come to establish. However, the wretched woman, sinner and Samaritan that she was, understood little or nothing of this profound doctrine, and she continued her train of thought as if she attached no importance to our Lord's answer: "I know that Messias is coming (who is called Christ), and when he comes he will tell us all things."

Then, as if to reward her for her docility and good dispositions, Jesus gave her the clear and blinding revelation: "I who speak with thee am he."

This time the woman understood. The gift of "living water" had washed the scales from her eyes and allowed her to recognize in the despised Jewish stranger the Messias who was to teach her all things. And so well did she understand that, forgetting her pitcher and rope,

Sira Photo

At its right is the village of Askar. The wide plain is the Sahel el-Askar.

she turned and ran to the town as quickly as she could to spread the good news. But although she was almost beside herself with excitement and joy, she still acted with great good sense. As St. John Chrysostom says:

We must admire the woman's prudence. She did not exclaim: "Come and see the Christ," but, with calculated caution, she invited her fellow-citizens, saying: "Come and see a man who has told me all that I have ever done." Nor was she ashamed thus to recall her evil life. She could well have said: "Come and see a prophet." But no; when a soul is aflame with the divine fire, it takes no account of earthly things, nor of good- or ill-fame: the sacred flame alone inspires it. And the woman added: "Can he be the Christ?" Here again her great prudence is evident. She neither affirmed nor denied. She did not claim that they should believe her, but only asked that they see and speak with the man and convince themselves that He was truly the Messias.[19]

In the meantime the disciples had come back with their purchases, and St. John, who was the only evangelist present, for St. Matthew had not yet been called, notes that they wondered at their Master's speaking to a woman alone. But none of them dared to ask Him the reason for the conversation; their great respect for Him did not permit them to take such liberties. The disciples' surprise at seeing Christ

[19] *PG* 59, 143.

speaking to the woman can be explained in the light of the Jewish customs prevailing at the time. According to the *Mishnah,* a woman was to be punished "if she goes out with her hair unbound, or spins in the street, or speaks with any man." [20]

Our Lord was still fasting and the disciples offered Him some of the food they had brought, probably some bread, dried figs, raisins and olives.

"Rabbi, eat."

But He, wishing to give them a different and more substantial food, replied: "I have food to eat of which you do not know."

In whispers, the disciples asked each other: "Has someone brought him something to eat?"

They did not understand Christ's words, and as St. Augustine remarks: "What wonder was it that the woman had not understood the meaning of the water, when here we see that the disciples did not yet understand the meaning of the food?" [21]

However, the kind Master immediately explained. "My food is to do the will of him who sent me, to accomplish his work."

The fulfillment of God's will is the sum of all good and so it is the *summum bonum* of this life, an anticipation of beatitude, a paradise on earth, a glory in this valley of tears. "The salvation of men is here called [Christ's] food in order to show us how much He had it at heart. He desires our salvation as much as we long for food." [22]

At that moment His food was the salvation of the Samaritans whom He saw coming to Him, promising to provide an abundant spiritual harvest. Taking an image from His immediate surroundings, as He so often did, He spoke to His disciples about this harvest. The time was the beginning of May, when the grain fields of the extensive and fertile plain, Sahel el-Askar, were turning white. Accordingly He said to them, using what was apparently a proverb: "Do you not say, 'There are yet four months, and then comes the harvest?' " [23] And

---

[20] *Ketuboth* 7:6. There is a curious story told about Rabbi Joseph the Galilean. While travelling, he met a woman, the wife of another rabbi, and he asked her: "By what road does one go to Lydda?" The woman replied: "You stupid Galilean, don't you know that our teachers say that a man should not tarry overmuch when speaking to a woman? You should have said: 'Which way to Lydda?' " What fantastic scruples!

[21] *PL* 35, 152.

[22] St. John Chrysostom, *PG* 59, 194.

[23] There has been much discussion as to whether these words of our Lord should be taken in a real or a symbolical sense, i.e., were there really four months to go before the harvest (in which case the incident took place in December or Janu-

Raad Photo

White-robed Samaritan priests reciting the prayers which precede the celebration of the Passover. The high priest kneels in the center, beside the block of stone.

then, indicating the broad fields of waving wheat, He added: "Well, I say to you, lift up your eyes and behold that the fields are already white for the harvest."

These fields were a symbol of the Samaritans who were already ripe for the kingdom of God. And having begun to speak of the harvest

ary), or was He only quoting a proverb, and using the following phrase, "behold that the fields are already white for the harvest," to refer to the fact that the crops were already ripe? We prefer this second interpretation, as do Maldonatus, Lagrange, Murillo, Prat, Lebreton and others. For the other opinion, see the interesting article by Bover in *Biblica*, 3 (1922), 442–444, and another more recent article in *Est. Ecles.*, 26 (1952), 78–82. For our part, we think that the second interpretation harmonizes much better with the Gospel chronology. Then, too, this is not the only time our Lord uses a proverb (cf. Matt. 13:57; Luke 9:6–, 62). See above, pp. 66 *f.*, where we have treated the matter at greater length.

of souls, Christ, with a few deft strokes, painted a beautiful picture of the work of the apostolate and of the relations between those who labor in the great field of their Father. Some gather what others have sown, but both sowers and reapers rejoice together. The sower is not discouraged because he does not see the fruit of his labor, for he knows that the crop will be harvested later. And the reaper is not puffed up with pride, for he knows that the merit of the harvest belongs mainly to those who tilled and sowed. They, the disciples, were about to gather now that which they had not sown, for a crowd of Samaritans from the town had come in haste to the well, eager to see with their own eyes the stranger about whom the woman had told them such wonderful things. So well disposed were they that they besought Jesus to stay with them. And our Lord, always kind, always merciful, acceded to their request, not only to please them but also to instruct and confirm them in faith.

He remained for two days, days which were undoubtedly filled with intense apostolic work and during which He reaped an abundant harvest. Finally, the good Samaritans, full of admiration for Him, said to the woman who had met Him first: "We no longer believe because of what thou hast said, for we have heard for ourselves and we know that this is in truth the Saviour of the world."

The Official's Son
(John 4:43–54; cf. Map IV)

After staying two days with the Samaritans, our Lord left Sichar and continued His journey towards Galilee, no doubt through Sanur, Qubatiyeh, Jenin, the plain of Esdrelon and, finally, without touching Nazareth, on to Cana where He had worked His first miracle. We do not know the reason for this second visit to Cana; perhaps He wished to call on the young married couple or other people whom He knew there.

He was very well received in Galilee: many of the inhabitants of the region had been in Jerusalem during the last Passover and still remembered vividly the wonders He had worked in the capital. In particular, they must have been struck by the air of authority with which He had expelled the profaners of the Temple. As a consequence, they showed Him every mark of reverence and esteem, all the more so since

His fame redounded to their own glory, for they regarded Him as their fellow countryman.

But if this was the Galileans' attitude towards our Lord, how can St. John first tell us that Jesus went to Galilee and then add in the very same sentence, "for Jesus himself bore witness that a prophet receives no honor in his own country" (4:44)? This seems in open contradiction to the fact that Christ had been received with great honor in His homeland, Galilee.

On this point, we should note that when the three Synoptic authors (Luke 4:24; Matt. 13:57; Mark 6:4) speak of the hostile reception given Jesus by the people of Nazareth, they quote the very words which we find in St. John, and there is no doubt that in this case Christ's own country is the town of Nazareth. Hence some authors understand the passage from St. John in this sense: "Jesus went into Galilee, *but without stopping at Nazareth* because a prophet receives no honor in his own country." This interpretation certainly makes clear the meaning of the phrase under discussion, but if that was the evangelist's underlying thought it is rather strange that he did not express it more clearly. There is another solution, more probable than the foregoing, but still not wholly satisfactory. The words "his own *country*" can be applied to the place where the prophet was *born,* the region in which he *habitually lives,* or the *nation* to which he belongs. Thus Christ's country could be the town of Bethlehem, or the province of Judea in which the town lay. And so the evangelist could say that Jesus left His own country, Judea, where, as a matter of fact, He had been persecuted by the Scribes and Pharisees.

Once again Cana was to be the scene of a miracle (John 4:46–54). Hardly had our Lord returned to Galilee when the news of His arrival spread rapidly and quickly reached Capharnaum. In this city there was a prominent personage whom the Vulgate calls *"regulus:* a ruler," but who was in reality only an official employed by the tetrarch Herod Antipas, who was popularly given the title of king. We do not know what this man's office was or whether it was civil or military, nor do we know his name. Perhaps he was the "Chuza" referred to in Luke 8:3, or the "Manahen" mentioned in Acts 13:1; but these are only conjectures. At all events, he had an only son who had fallen ill, and when he heard that Jesus was at Cana, he immediately set out thither. The distance between Caparnaum and Cana is about nineteen miles and hence about a six hours' journey. Leaving his home city, the

The Heptapegon or "seven fountains": in the center background one can see the Wadi el-Hammam, behind which rises Qarn Hattin.

official crossed the fertile lowland which pilgrims later called the *Heptapegon*, then traversed the plain of Gennesareth, went along the Wadi el-Hammam or "Valley of the Doves," to Qarn Hattin, near Lubiyeh. Here he turned right and followed for some distance the caravan route which later became a Roman road and which, crossing Sahel el-Battof, emerged onto the plain of Ptolemais or Accho, as the ancients called it. A good part of his journey was uphill because Cana is almost 2,650 feet higher than Capharnaum.

The grieving father, when brought before our Lord, besought Him to come down and heal his son who was at death's door. But Jesus answered reproachfully: "Unless you see signs and wonders, you do not believe."

Our Lord's reply to the request is somewhat surprising. So far as we know, the official had never witnessed a miracle being worked by Christ, although he had undoubtedly heard of many; and yet he had believed, for otherwise he would not have appealed to Jesus to save his son. Certainly his faith was not perfect; he seems to have thought that the miracle of healing could not be performed at a distance; yet he did have faith. The most probable explanation of the difficulty is that Christ was addressing these rather severe words to the Jews in general, who were attracted more by His miracles than by His doctrine, and that He also wished to test the petitioner's faith. The official was not offended by the answer he had received; instead he repeated his plea, and Christ granted him more than he had asked. There and then He healed his son: "Go thy way, thy son lives."

From elsewhere in the narrative we learn that our Lord said these words "at the seventh hour," i.e., at 1:00 P.M., as we would say, and that at that very moment the fever left the invalid. Several of the official's servants were dispatched to bring the good news to their master, and perhaps to tell him that there was no need to trouble Jesus by having Him come down to Capharnaum. If the evangelist is referring in verse 51 ("even as he [the official] was going down . . .") to the rapid descent from Lubiyeh to the plain of Gennesareth through the Wadi el-Hammam, we could calculate with almost mathematical precision the spot where servants and master met. However, St. John is probably using the verb here in the same general sense as the official did in verse 49 when he said to our Lord at Cana: "Sir, come down . . ." i.e., in reference to the whole journey and not to any particular part of the route.

When the official met his servants and heard the good news of his son's recovery, he asked them at what time the improvement had occurred. His question was motivated either by general curiosity or perhaps by a desire to see if the cure had coincided with Christ's words, as indeed it had, for the servants answered: "Yesterday, at the seventh hour, the fever left him."

This chronological reference creates some difficulty. When, actually, did the meeting between the official and his servants take place? Some commentators hold that scarcely had the loving father heard our Lord's consoling words than he immediately set out for Capharnaum to embrace his son and to see for himself the reality of the miracle. Then, too, it is very easy to see how the official's family would have wished to let him know of the sudden recovery of the boy by at once dispatching the servants to bring him the joyous news. Thus the meeting between master and servants probably occurred that same evening, but since the Hebrews regarded sunset as the beginning of a new day, the messengers could have said with perfect truth "yesterday at the seventh hour" although, according to our manner of reckoning, the meeting took place on the same day.

This solution is in perfect harmony with the feelings of the father and the members of his household. Yet, in our opinion, there is a grave objection to it. Cana, where the official received our Lord's assurance that his son was safe, was six hours' journey from Caphar-naum. Therefore if both the official and his servants had started out soon after the seventh hour (i.e., 1:00 P.M.) they would have met approximately halfway, after a three hours' journey, that is, between 4:00 and 6:00 P.M. Hence the servants could not have said with truth that the healing had occurred "yesterday at the seventh hour" because, even according to Hebrew reckoning, the new day had not yet begun when they met their master, for it was still only late afternoon on the day of the miracle. We would say, therefore, that the official, eager though he was to return home, had not been able to start before nightfall or very early next morning, either because he had to rest his horses, as some authors say, or because of some circumstance unknown to us. Thus when his servants met him "as he was now going down" to Capharnaum, they were speaking literally when they said: "Yesterday, at the seventh hour. . . ."

We can surmise the official's joy as he embraced his son, now restored to health. And it is no surprise to read in the Gospel that he and all his household became faithful disciples of Christ.

11. From Galilee

to Jerusalem

The Cure of the Paralytic at Bethesda
(John 5 [1]; cf. Map I)

ifty days after the Passover, the feast of Pentecost,[2] or "the feast of weeks" (cf. Exod. 34:22; Deut. 16:10) came around again and Jesus wished to pay a second visit to Jerusalem for the celebration. On this occasion, as before, the young Master taught His sublime doctrine in the capital, not, however, in secret, by night, and to a single doctor of the Law, but publicly, in broad daylight, to the leaders of the synagogue and to great crowds, expounding to them clearly His close and unique relationship with the Father, and pointing out to them incontrovertible proofs of His having been sent by God.

His magnificent revelations were occasioned by the miraculous cure of a sick man on the Sabbath. In the northeast corner of the city, near the Probatic Gate (the Sheepgate),[3] there was a pool with five porches

---

[1] Some authors place this chapter between Chapters 6 and 7. See below, pp. 296 ff., where the matter is discussed.

[2] The evangelist does not specify the feast, but simply says that "there was a feast [or "the feast"] of the Jews" (5:1). Some codices have the article (ἡ ἑορτή =*the* feast), in which case the reference is very probably, although not necessarily, to the Passover. But other no less authoritative codices, as well as the *textus receptus,* omit the article (ἑορτή =*a* feast), and so the feast referred to obviously cannot be the Passover. We prefer to read ἑορτή without the article, and identify the feast with Pentecost. For further details see the commentaries and pp. 66 *f.,* above.

[3] The Probatic Gate is mentioned in 2 Esdras 3:1, 31; 12:39

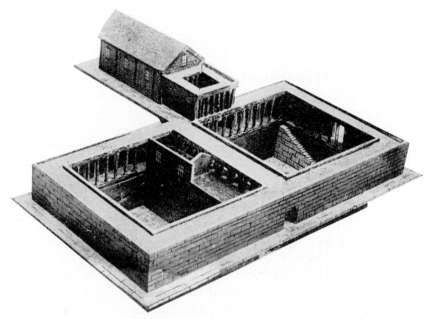

Jerusalem: *Reconstruction of the Pool of Bethesda with its five porches (north, south, east, west, and center), made by the White Fathers in the Sanctuary of St. Anne, in the north-east of the city. At right angles to the pool lies the Basilica of St. Mary, which is, naturally, of much later date than the pool.*

which went by the name of Bethesda,[4] and which has been correctly identified with the ancient pool discovered near the Church of St. Anne. The excavations made here by the White Fathers showed that the pool had been 394 feet long and 197 feet wide, divided into two equal parts by a wall with a gallery built on top which, along with

(Vulgate, v. 38), where it is called "the flock gate," probably due to the fact that the animals destined for the Temple sacrifices entered through it, or else because there was a cattle market in that locality. According to the Vulgate, it was the pool and not the gate that bore the name Probatic ("est . . . probatica piscina"), but with the majority of Greek codices we should read "in the probatic" (ἐπὶ τῇ προβατικῇ), the word "gate" being understood. It should be noted that St. Jerome's translation read: "Est autem Hierosolymis, super probatica [porta, understood], piscina. . . ."

[4] This name is found in several forms: *Bethesda* (=house of mercy); *Bethzatha* or *Bethzaitha* (=house of the olive trees, because the pool lay at the foot of a hill which was covered with these trees); *Bezetha* or *Bezatha* (=a cutting, from the verb *baza'*, to cut: the hill was separated from the Fortress Antonia by a ditch; cf. *Wars* v. 4 .21); or, finally, *Bethsaida* (=house of fishing): this last form is certainly erroneous. Although it is difficult to decide between the first and third forms, the first is more probably the correct one.

the four other galleries that ran along the sides of the pool, comprised the five porches.[5] These archeological findings have confirmed the identification of this pool with that referred to in John 5:1. Some authors, like L. B. Paton and P. Mickley, identified this pool at the Church of St. Anne with the pool of Siloe.[6] The only reason for this view is that the Gihon spring, from which the pool of Siloe is supplied, flows intermittently, a fact which, according to these authors, explains the movement of the waters referred to by St. John. But Professor Jeremias has brought forward cogent arguments against this theory,[7] which need not be restated here.

Around the pool lay crowds of sufferers, the blind, the lame, the paralytic, who hoped to be cured by the wonderful power of the water.[8] Our Lord, moved by His merciful charity, went to visit this temple of pain, and among the sufferers He saw a man who had been afflicted for thirty-eight years. Standing before this invalid, He asked him: "Dost thou want to get well?"

Christ knew without asking what the man's feelings were on the point; what other reason had he for coming to the pool but to be cured? But our Saviour wished to arouse still further his desire for health and to dispose him to make an act of faith. Sorrowfully the

[5] Cf. H. Vincent and F.-M. Abel, *Jérusalem Nouvelle* (Paris, 1914–1922), pp. 669 *ff.*; Van der Vlit, *"Sainte-Marie, où est-elle née?" et la Piscine Probatique* (Jerusalem, 1938).

[6] L. B. Paton, *Jerusalem in Bible Times* (Chicago, 1908), pp. 41 *ff.*; P. Mickley in *PJB*, 7 (1911), 58 *f.*

[7] J. Jeremias, *Die Wieder-entdeckung von Bethesda* (Göttingen, 1949), pp. 9 *ff.*

[8] At the end of verse 3 we read that the sick were waiting for the moving of the waters; and in verse 4 we are given the cause of the movement and the curative power of the waters: "For an angel of the Lord used to come down at certain times into the pool, and the water was troubled. And the first to go down into the pool after the troubling of the water was cured of whatever infirmity he had." This verse presents a difficult problem of textual criticism which has been a bone of contention among exegetes from ancient times. The verse is lacking in many Greek manuscripts, including the uncials S,B,C,D, and in several ancient versions; therefore quite a few authors, even Catholics like Schanz, Calmes, Belser, Lagrange, Prat, Braun and Durand, do not regard it as authentic, an opinion which apparently be held as the most probable one since the addition is more easily explained than the suppression. If the passage was in the first manuscripts, it is difficult to imagine how anyone would have conceived the idea of eliminating it, because it fits perfectly into the context. On the other hand, it is not hard to visualize how a copyist might have tried to explain the mysterious movement of the waters by attributing it to the activity of "an angel of the Lord," thereby making explicit what he believed was contained implicitly in the text.

The recently discovered Bodner Papyrus II (see above, p. 66, n. 29) does not contain the passage referred to here, that is, it does not mention the intervention of the angel.

sick man replied: "Sir, I have no one to put me into the pool when the water is stirred; for while I am coming, another steps down before me."

Christ said to him: "Rise, take up thy pallet and walk."

The invalid was immediately cured, and taking up his pallet, he began to walk. The evangelist then expressly tells us that it was the Sabbath, a circumstance which occasioned the superb discourse that St. John heard from our Lord's lips and transmitted to us with loving fidelity.

Some of the Scribes and Pharisees saw the man carrying his pallet, and being zealous for the observance of the Law as they understood it, they stopped him, saying: "It is the Sabbath; thou art not allowed to carry thy pallet."

The former cripple, whose common sense told him that anyone who had the power to cure him could also give him permission to carry his bed on the Sabbath, replied ingenuously: "He who made me well said to me, 'Take up thy pallet and walk.' "

Their curiosity aroused, and perhaps suspecting that the young Prophet from Galilee had had a hand in the matter, they asked: "Who is this man who said to thee, 'Take up thy pallet and walk'?"

The poor man could not answer them, for he did not know who his Benefactor was and could not even point Him out because, immediately after the miracle, Jesus had retired from the crowd swarming near the pool. A short while later, when our Lord came across the man again, this time in the Temple, He gave him a severe warning: "Behold, thou art cured. Sin no more, lest something worse befall thee."

Physical ills are not necessarily the effect of some sin, as can be seen from the case of the man born blind (John 9:1–3); but in certain instances they are, and this was one of them. After Jesus had spoken to him in the Temple, the man, in all innocence, hastened to tell the Jews who it was that had cured him. No doubt he did so out of respect for the authority of the Scribes and Pharisees, never thinking that he might be harming his Benefactor.

He could not have brought the Jewish leaders better news. Since the day on which Jesus had cast the vendors out of the Temple (John 2:44 ff.) they had looked with hostility upon the young Rabbi from backward Galilee who had arrogated to Himself supreme authority in the very capital city of the land, thereby implicitly condemning their negligence or greed. With increasing alarm they had watched His popularity growing greater day by day (cf. John 4:1), but much as they longed to take action against Him, they could find nothing in His conduct to censure. Now, however, when they had least expected it, they were given a chance to avenge themselves. He who had set Himself up as an ardent defender of the glory of God had trampled on that glory by breaking the sacrosanct law of the Sabbath; not only that, but He also caused others to violate it. What more did they need to accuse the hypocritical Prophet and strip Him of all authority in the eyes of the people?

They wasted no time in confronting our Lord. Pretending great zeal for the observance of the Law but in reality goaded on by hatred and a desire for revenge, they upbraided Him for what they chose to regard as His flagrant violation of the Sabbath, a violation all the more grave for having been perpetrated publicly, and for having scandalized all the people.

Jesus did not try to excuse Himself but answered tranquilly: "My Father works even until now, and I work." That is to say: "My Father, who is God, works continually, without interrupting His work even on the Sabbath." If God ceased to exercise His power for one moment the whole world would fall back into nothingness. "And so, I simply do as my Father does; consequently the law of the Sabbath cannot interfere with my work, nor have you any right to reproach me on that account."

The Jews fully understood the meaning of His brief answer; they realized that He was placing Himself on a level with God, making Himself equal to the Most High. Their rage increased to the point of frenzy and they wanted to put Him to death without more ado, for not only was He a violator of the Sabbath but a blasphemer who invested Himself with divinity.

In the face of His enemies' furious invectives, our Lord did not minimize the import of His words, but rather added to and confirmed what He had already said: "Amen, amen, I say to you, the Son can do nothing of himself, but only what he sees the Father doing. For whatever he does, this the Son also does in like manner."

Jesus thus let it be understood that His action was identical with the Father's, that one and the same action proceeded from both Persons, the Father and the Son: He could not have affirmed His divinity more clearly. And since He, the Son, is God, it is essential "that all men . . . honor the Son even as they honor the Father. He who does not honor the Son, does not honor the Father who sent him."

In order to prove the truth of what He had said, He appealed to His works: "For the works which the Father has given me to accomplish, these very works that I do bear witness to me, that the Father has sent me."

And because the Father had sent Him, the testimony of His works was, in a certain sense, the Father's own testimony to Him: "And the Father himself, who has sent me, has borne witness to me."

But they, His enemies, had refused to believe the evidence, and so He referred them to the Holy Scriptures: "You search the Scriptures, because in them you think that you have life everlasting. And it is they that bear witness to me. . . ."

But the Jews were blind to all this light that He was shedding on them, the basic reason for their blindness being a depravity of soul which sought its own interests and not those of God: "How can you believe who receive glory from one another, and do not seek the glory which is from the only God?"

Finally, our Lord brought His crushing argument to a close by telling them that Moses himself, in whom they hoped, would become their accuser because they would not believe what he had written about the Messias: "For if you believed Moses you would believe me also, for he wrote of me."

Instead of being converted by Christ's words, these Jews only became more obdurate. They did not dare put Him to death as they had planned, nor even to lay hands on Him, because the people, who had witnessed the great miracle, would have sided with Him. Perhaps, too, their hands were stayed by the majestic bearing of the young Teacher who had told them things never heard before. But be that as it may, they refused to open their eyes to the light which He shed upon them, and they hardened their hearts in the face of His terrible indictment. Our Lord's subsequent visits to Jerusalem showed that their resentment and thirst for revenge went on increasing and would be satisfied only with the blood of their innocent Victim.

This chapter (John 5) contains several elements which would seem to harmonize better with others in the two following chapters, 6 and 7, if it were taken from its present position and placed between these two chapters, so that the order would then be 6, 5, 7.[9] This idea

9 The system of transposing, begun with chapters 5 and 6, has been gradually

of inversion is an ancient one: it appears in Tatian's *Diatessaron,* and in the fifteenth century in Ludolph of Saxony's *Life of Christ;* later it was upheld by the German Catholic, Cassell (1851), and the English Protestant, Norris (1871), while in our day a good number of authors accept it (e.g., Olivieri, Lagrange, Prat, Lebreton, Joüon, Meinertz, Sutcliffe, and others). Prat [10] supports the inversion with arguments which are identical with those of Bernard,[11] and which are basically the same as those which the other authors bring forward: (1) the end of chapter 5, where Jesus is in Jerusalem, fits in badly with the beginning of chapter 6, where we are told that He crossed to the other side of the Jordan, a statement which implies that He was already in Galilee; (2) on the contrary, the end of chapter 5, where the Jews wanted to kill Jesus, harmonizes perfectly with the beginning of chapter 7, where we read that our Lord did not wish to go to Judea because the Jews were seeking to kill Him; (3) in 7:21–23 there is a reference to 5:8, and in 7:25 to 5:18, which implies that only a short space of time elapsed between the events of chapter 5 and those of chapter 7; (4) John 5:35 implies that John the Baptist had been beheaded a long time before, and from Matthew 14:13 and Mark 6:29–30 we learn that the multiplication of loaves described in John 6 followed close upon the death of the Precursor.

These arguments are certainly not to be lightly brushed aside, and when we consider them we can readily understand how the theory of inversion has won the support of numerous authors. However, one great obstacle to their acceptance is the fact that in all the codices and versions we find chapters 5 and 6 in that order, which is undoubtedly

extended to many other passages in the fourth Gospel. The history of these inversions and a critical examination of some of them, particularly of chapters 5 and 6, can be seen in N. Uricchio's "La teoria delle trasposizioni nel Vangelo di S. Giovanni," in *Biblica,* 31 (1950), 129–163. The article, occasioned by F. R. Hoare's book *The Original Order and Chapters of St. John's Gospel* (London, 1944), closes with the following words: "La storia della questione, l'inconsistenza delle prove, soprattutto quel procedere acrobatico di supposizione in supposizione pur di giungere ad erigere un edificio di apparenze suggestive ma niente affatto salde, ci han condotto a concludere che nella teoria delle inversioni, al suo stato attuale, vi è molto di soggettivo e ben poco di oggettivo" (p. 163). On pp. 138 *f.* the writer gives a long list of Catholic and non-Catholic authors who have advocated one or other of the aforementioned transpositions. In *Razón y Fe,* 134 (1946), 344 *f.,* there is a short review of Hoare's book by Fr. Puzo, who reaches this sober and well-considered verdict: "The history of these [transpositions] during the last fifty years plainly demonstrates the subjectivism to which the transposers are liable."

[10] *Jesus Christ,* I, 526 *f.*

[11] See the latter's *Gospel According to St. John* (Edinburgh, 1928), pp. xvii-xix.

the actual chronological sequence of the events described by the evangelist. Therefore very weighty reasons indeed are required to warrant the inversion of the chapters; and we doubt if the arguments given above are sufficiently cogent. To the *first* of these arguments we reply: as B. Weiss correctly remarks in his commentary on St. John, the evangelist considered the visit to Jerusalem in chapter 5 as merely a temporary interruption of our Lord's ministry in Galilee, and therefore there is nothing strange in his speaking of crossing the lake without first telling us that Jesus had returned from Jerusalem to Galilee. To the *second* and *third* arguments we answer: our Lord's words in 7:21–23 certainly refer to the curing of the paralytic in 5:8, but it is no less certain that such a reference would be perfectly normal even after a long lapse of time. We must not forget that Jesus was still well remembered by the people of Jerusalem because the miracle at the pool of Bethesda had been widely talked about, it had provoked a lively dispute with the Pharisees, and the doctors of the Law had regarded it as a grave violation of the Sabbath which they could, and in fact did, use as a weapon against the young Rabbi from Galilee. We have several clear indications that our Lord was very much in the news in Jerusalem both before and after the incident at the pool. In Luke 5:17 we read that among the Scribes and Pharisees who were listening to Christ's preaching there were some who had come from Jerusalem, and who had, no doubt, been sent to spy on Him; and on the feast of Tabernacles, even before our Lord appeared in the Temple, there was widespread interest in Him, some being in favor of Him, others against Him (John 7:12). Considering these circumstances, is it any wonder that when He appeared during the feast the people flocked around Him, and the Scribes and Pharisees lost no time in accusing Him again of having broken the Law by curing a man on the Sabbath and of causing him also to break the Sabbath, as everyone knew? It is very likely that they again resolved to kill Him, a resolve to which our Lord refers in John 7:20. Therefore, in view of the atmosphere which prevailed in the capital, there is nothing strange in what St. John says of Christ in 7:1: ". . . He did not wish to go about Judea because the Jews were seeking to put him to death."

To the *fourth* argument quoted above we reply: our Lord's words concerning John the Baptist: "He *was* the lamp, burning and shining . . ." certainly imply that the Precursor's public ministry had come to an end, but do not justify Lagrange's conclusion ("The imperfect

$\hat{\eta}\nu$ shows that John was already dead"), nor that of Sutcliffe ("That is to say, he was dead"). It would perhaps be more true to say with Durand that "John's light was quenched, or at least hidden behind the walls of a prison," and with Knabenbauer that "he was no longer engaged in public preaching, and that therefore he was imprisoned before the second Passover of Christ's public life"; and with B. Weiss in his commentary on St. John that "[The imperfect] means that the Baptist's activity had ended either because he had been imprisoned or because he was dead." Although John, as a prisoner, was allowed to communicate with his disciples, there is no doubt that once he had been thrown into the dungeons of Machaerus, he was no longer a burning light placed on high and casting its rays far and wide.

In addition to all these objections, there is a positive difficulty arising out of the inversion of chapters 5 and 6. If we place chapter 6 first, we find that the incident at Bethesda took place immediately after the discourse on the Bread of Life; this is how Lagrange, Prat, Lebreton and others arrange the events. But it seems to us very unlikely that Jesus would have gone to Jerusalem to confront His worst enemies immediately after the great crisis in which many of His disciples had abandoned Him. We would expect instead that He would retire from public life for a while as, according to our view of the sequence of events, He actually did, withdrawing to the region of Tyre and Sidon.

Finally, the proponents of the inversion must give a satisfactory explanation of the way in which the chapters came to be in their present order, and that is not an easy thing to do. Of course, if the Gospel was originally written on separate pages and not on a roll of parchment, the displacement of chapters is possible and can be admitted, provided that very cogent exegetical reasons are given for the order that is put forward as the primitive sequence.[12] However, in

---

[12] The possibility of the two chapters having been displaced, and the various ways in which the inversion could have occurred, are discussed by Sutcliffe, *A Two Year Public Ministry* ("The Bellarmine Series," I; London: Burns, Oates & Washbourne, 1938), pp. 92–105; Brinkman, "Zur Frage der ursprünglichen Ordnung im Johannesevangelium," in *Gregorianum*, 20 (1939), 55–82, 363–369; 22 (1941), 503–505; and in *Verb. Dom.*, 21 (1941), 155 *f.* Cf. Zerwick, *Verb. Dom.*, 19 (1939), 219-224. On this very argument, see Uricchio, *loc. cit.*, pp. 146–154. We must confess, however, that we find it difficult not to feel skeptical when confronted with such complicated calculations and ingenious combinations.

Some observations made by Fr. F.-M. Braun in *Ephemerides Theologicae*

spite of all the arguments, it still seems odd that not the least trace of the inverted order is found in either codices or versions.

The arrangement found in the *Diatessaron* has no probative value. First of all, this work contains many other inversions which are generally recognized as being unjustified and which no critic accepts. Moreover, the author's transpositions were not made in accordance with the order of events as depicted in the codices which he consulted, but rather are the result of his preoccupation with Gospel chronology. As Father Sutcliffe correctly remarks: "Tatian . . . does invert the order of the two chapters; but no serious argument could be based on this fact to prove that the inverted order was that of the codices he followed. His inversions and rearrangements are so numerous that it is not possible from his order to demonstrate the original order of any of the Gospels." [13]

To sum up: although we do not in the least wish to minimize the force of the arguments in favor of the inversion of chapters 5 and 6, yet in view of the absolute unanimity with which the codices and versions support the present sequence, and bearing in mind the historical and psychological background, within which, in our opinion, the various elements appear in perfect harmony, we must say with Father Levie that "we cannot bring ourselves to accept the solution that transposes chapters 5 and 6 of St. John"; [14] and, with Father Allo, that the reasons brought forward in support of the thesis "do not seem convincing. Would the transposition help us to follow more easily the development of ideas or history? We do not think so." [15]

We conclude that, although new arguments may be found in the future, as the matter stands today it is more scientific and critical to retain the existing sequence of chapters.

Lovanienses, 32 (1956), are of interest here: "Dodd et Barrett, Strathmann et Bent Noak en conviennent, l'Évangile johannique doit être traité comme une oeuvre originale, solidement construite à ce qu'il semble, et dans laquelle *aucune transposition ne s'impose*" (p. 538). And farther on, speaking on his own account, he says: "Après la première guerre mondiale, la fièvre mandéenne sévissait dans la plupart des écoles; elle est tombée. Hier encore, la théorie des dislocations et des transpositions accidentelles inspirait les constructions les plus variées; *la voici au point mort*" (546). The italics are ours.

It should be noted that in the recently discovered *Bodner Papyrus II,* which dates back to the end of the second century and which we have already mentioned (see above, p. 66, n. 29), the chapters follow the traditional order.

[13] *Op. cit.,* pp. 92 f.
[14] *Nouv. Rev. Théol.* (1939), 603.
[15] *Dict. de la Bible,* Suppl., Fasc. **XXI**, 824. J. Bover writes against the transposition in *Est. Bibl.,* 2 (1931), 81–88.

12. Ministry in Galilee

The Gospel of the Kingdom
(Mark 1:14; 2:27)

Jesus had visited Jerusalem twice, once at the Passover and again at Pentecost, and both visits had resulted in a conflict with officialdom, with the religious leaders of the capital. Full fifteen months were to pass before our Saviour was to set foot again in the Holy City, months during which He exercised His ministry in Galilee and Perea with greater intensity than before. He did not go up to Jerusalem for the next Passover, the one of 29; we find Him there again only for the feast of Tabernacles in the first part of October in the third year of His public life, i.e., towards the end of 29. This long withdrawal from the capital may seem strange, but it was due to the hostility of the Jewish leaders, whose envy, hatred and wounded pride made them thirst for revenge. There was still another and deeper motive for the Jews' hostility: they felt that the young Prophet of Nazareth was animated by a spirit that was not theirs. Instinctively they knew that, although the Galilean was a member of their race, He was not Jewish in the same way as they were. Even at this early stage, they must have felt that if the young Rabbi's day of triumph ever came, it would spell doom for the Judaism of the Scribes and Pharisees, the representatives of official religion. Nor were they mistaken. In order to save their brand of Judaism, one from which the marrow of Israel's true religion had been extracted, leaving only the dry bones, they were one day to kill the new Prophet. But the Prophet's death was also to be the death of the Judaism they were trying to save.

Having returned from Jerusalem, Jesus began His Galilean ministry properly so called. Of the three Synoptic authors, St. Mark seems to be the one who narrates the beginning of this ministry with the greatest chronological exactness. The interesting and varied scenes which the evangelist describes took place in and around Capharnaum, and are preceded in 1:14 *f.* by an extremely important introduction stating the theme of our Lord's preaching: ". . . Jesus came into Galilee preaching the gospel of God. . . ."

This general outline is immediately made more specific by Christ Himself: " 'The time is fulfilled, and the kingdom of God is at hand. Repent and believe in the gospel.' "

Because the sacred text is here dealing with the preaching of God's own Son, it is vitally important for us to ascertain the exact meaning of each word recorded by the evangelist.

"The gospel" always means the "good tidings," whose object was the Messianic era announced by the prophets, the New Covenant with all the spiritual riches contained therein. But the word "gospel" is frequently used with some qualifying phrase, e.g., "the gospel of the kingdom" (Matt. 4:23; 9:35; 24:14); "the gospel of God" (Mark 1:14; Rom. 15:16; 1 Thess. 2:2, 8); "the gospel of Jesus Christ, the Son of God" (Mark 1:1); "the gospel of Christ" (2 Cor. 2:12; 9:13; Gal. 1:7); "the gospel for the uncircumcised . . . for the circumcised" (Gal. 2:7); "the gospel of peace" (Eph. 6:15).

The grammatical construction in these phrases is always the same, but the relationship between "the gospel" and its qualifying phrase varies. Thus "the gospel of God" does not mean the Gospel that speaks of God or in which God is announced, but that which *comes from* God, whereas, on the contrary, "the gospel of the kingdom, of Jesus Christ" means the good tidings announcing the kingdom and Jesus Christ. "The gospel for the uncircumcised . . . for the circumcised" has a special meaning, i.e., the Gospel as preached to the Gentiles and to the Jews, respectively.

The first of the three elements that go to make up the preaching of the Gospel is: "The time is fulfilled, and the kingdom of God is at hand," two distinct concepts which, however, express the same basic idea. The prophets had foretold that the kingdom of God would come in due course, in the fullness of time; hence, the phrases "the time is fulfilled" and "the kingdom of God is at hand" mean one and the same thing.

"The fullness of time" of which St. Paul speaks (Gal. 4:4) had arrived. With the baptism of Jesus the new kingdom had been, as it were, publicly and solemnly inaugurated. But our Lord did not then say, "The kingdom is here," for the new day was only dawning and the new kingdom had not yet even been preached, much less established in men's hearts. And when He did speak of the kingdom as beginning, He said that it was "at hand," as if He wished to describe its slow advance down the centuries as it daily approached nearer and nearer to the fullness of time.

But in what exactly does this kingdom consist? As in the case of "gospel," the word "kingdom" sometimes appears alone, e.g., in the Our Father: "Thy kingdom come" (Matt. 6:10; Luke 11:2); "My kingdom" (John 18:36): at other times it appears with a qualifying phrase, e.g., "The kingdom of heaven" (Matt. 3:2; 4:17; 5:3; 10; 11:12; 13:24, 31, 33, 44, 45, 47, etc.)—this phrase appears very frequently; "the kingdom of God" (Matt. 12:28; Luke 11:20; Mark 1:15)—also very commonly used; "the kingdom of Christ and God" (Eph. 5:5); "the kingdom of his beloved Son" (Col. 1:13). All these various phrases have the same meaning, but many different interpretations of this meaning have been advanced, some of which must be rejected as false or incomplete, such as (1) a purely spiritual, interior, and therefore invisible kingdom; (2) a temporal kingdom, such as the Jews hoped for, in which they would shake off the Roman yoke and rule over the Gentiles; (3) an eschatological kingdom which would be inaugurated at the second coming of Christ, i.e., the doctrine of millenarianism. The first interpretation is that of the Protestants, who deny the visible character of the Church. The second and third are those preferred by modern rationalists. None of these three meanings of the word is acceptable.

On many occasions our Lord explained the nature of the kingdom, and He did so especially in Matthew 13, where He repeatedly used the phrase "The kingdom of heaven is like . . ." and where He expounded the doctrine of the kingdom in seven parables.

The kingdom which Christ preached was "the kingdom of heaven" because it came from, and led back to, Heaven; in this sense it "is not of this world," as He Himself said (John 18:36). It is a *spiritual* kingdom because it is founded, preserved and consolidated by spiritual means. It is *internal* because it is the kingdom of souls, but since it must be known by men it also appears externally. Such is the kingdom proclaimed by Christ.[1]

But if one is to become a member of this kingdom, one must repent: penance, the transformation of the old man and rebirth to a new life, are the second element of our Lord's preaching.

Finally, men must "believe in the gospel," i.e., believe the "good tidings"; they must have faith.

One would be inclined to think that the Jews would have welcomed promptly and joyously this good news which their prophets had stressed so insistently down through the ages. But no; their prejudices, their erroneous interpretation of the prophecies, and their nationalistic pride blinded their eyes and hardened their hearts. They dreamed of a dazzling, glorious earthly kingdom, and they could not see that the fulfillment of their hopes lay in the humble, spiritual preaching of Christ.

The Calling of the Four Great Apostles
(Matt. 4:18–22; Mark 1:16–20; Luke 5:1–11; cf. Map II)

Although Jesus had been in Capharnaum only a short while, He was already well known there as a result of what the Galileans had seen Him do in Jerusalem and the first miracle at Cana, but perhaps most of all because of the curing of the official's son. Therefore it is no wonder that the people followed Him and wished to hear His teaching.

While our Lord was near the lake, a great crowd of people thronged about Him, pressing close to Him in their eagerness to hear the word of God: "Now it came to pass, while the crowds were pressing upon him to hear the word of God. . . ." (Luke 5:1). Not far from where He was standing there were two boats moored in the shallow water just offshore. He wished to speak to the people, but it was difficult for Him to do so since He was hemmed in by them and on the same level as they. Therefore, in order to get a better vantage point from which to address them, He went on board one of the boats,

---

[1] There is a full study of "El Reino de Dios in la Sagrada Escritura" by J. A. Oñate in *Est. Bíbl.*, 3 (1944), 343–382; see also J. Bonsirven, *Les enseignements de Jésus-Christ* (Paris, 1946), pp. 43–56, where there is a copious bibliography.

Raad Photo

LAKE OF GENNESARETH: *with Mount Hermon in the background.*

the one belonging to Simon Peter, and asked the owner to push out a little way from the shore. From this improvised pulpit, the Divine Orator, seated as became His dignity as Teacher of the world, instructed the crowds which thronged the waterside: "And sitting down, he began to teach the crowds from the boat."

In Christ's selection of Peter's boat in preference to the other vessel, the Fathers have seen His loving intention of bestowing the primacy on Peter. The boat was a symbol of the future Church from which Jesus was to preach through the mouth of His Vicar.

The incident probably took place in the morning, for the lake-fishermen usually plied their trade during the night hours. Even today the boats put out from Tiberias shortly after sunset, and return at dawn. The various methods of fishing mentioned in the Gospel are still in use on the lake: (1) fishing with a line and *hook* (ἄγκιστρον: cf. Matt. 17:26: ". . . Cast a hook . . ."; it was thus that Peter caught the fish with the tribute money in its mouth); (2) fishing with the *shabakeh* (ἀμφίβληστρον; Matt. 4:18; cf. Mark 1:16), a fan-shaped net with a rope at the center; (3) fishing with the *jarf* (σαγήνη: Matt. 13:47), a long net, sometimes 440 yards in length; it is thrown into the water, and the fishermen, standing on the shore, then draw it in by hauling on its two extremities; (4) fishing with the *mbattem* (δίκτυον; Luke 5:4: "Put out into the deep, and lower your nets . . ."

LAKE OF GENNESARETH: *hauling in the nets.*

τὰ δίκτυα); this was a combination of three nets of varying mesh placed one behind the other and tied to the same rope; the fishermen let down the triple net into deep water, drew away some distance, and slowly came back, beating the surface of the lake to drive the fish before them towards the nets; the fish that eluded the first net were caught in one or other of the remaining two. Apparently this was the method which the Apostles had been using but without success, for they had been fishing all night and had caught nothing.

When our Lord finished speaking to the crowd, He said to Peter: "Put out into the deep, and lower your nets for a cast."

Peter replied that they had been toiling all night without catching anything, the implication being that it was useless to let down the nets again. "But," he went on, "at thy word I will lower the net."

His faith and obedience were rewarded with so large a catch that they could not haul the net ashore without running the risk of tearing it. They therefore signalled to their friends in the other boat to come to their assistance. As the evangelist tells us a little later (v. 10), these friends were James and John, the sons of Zebedee. Doubtless the four were partners in trade, having pooled their money to buy the expensive nets, and sharing among them the profits from the catches.

At the sight of the miracle a holy fear descended upon them all, and Peter, already showing signs of his impetuous nature, cried out to Jesus: "Depart from me, for I am a sinful man, O Lord!"

He considered himself unworthy to be in the company of such a wonder-worker. But our Lord did not depart; instead He told Peter of the sublime destiny that was in store for him: "Until now thou hast been a fisherman, drawing up fish from the sea: thou shalt continue to be a fisherman, but henceforth thou shalt catch men."

Our Lord's words lent inspiration to the Christian artists of the first centuries. In the catacombs, Christ is depicted as a fisherman and the faithful as little fish born in the waters of baptism. Furthermore, the fish came to be looked upon as a symbol of Christ Himself because the Greek word ἰχθύς (fish) is made up of the initials of the phrase Ἰησοῦς Χριστὸς Θεοῦ Υἱὸς Σωτήρ: "Jesus Christ, Son of God, Saviour"; hence the frequency with which the fish appears on ancient Christian monuments.

The conversation had been carried on only by Jesus and Peter, but in the very next sentence the evangelist says that, when they had brought the boats to land, *they* followed Him (Luke 5:11), i.e., not only Peter but the others too.

St. Luke speaks only of Peter and the sons of Zebedee, James and John, but St. Matthew and St. Mark also mention Andrew, Simon's brother, and both evangelists note that James and John were with their father. We are told that as soon as they were called, all four, Peter, Andrew, James and John, left their families and their nets and followed Jesus (Matt. 4:19, 22; Mark 1:18, 20). As St. John Chrysostom so beautifully says:

Consider their faith and obedience, for, hearing the invitation of Jesus amid their occupations, they did not delay or show themselves remiss and slothful. They did not say: "Let us first return home and tell our relatives"; instead, leaving all, they followed Him. . . . This is the obedience which Christ requires of us: He demands unhesitating obedience even though we may be occupied with things that seem necessary.[2]

The Gospel narrative here, taken by itself, would lead one to believe that this calling of the Apostles at the Lake of Gennesareth was the first invitation they had received to follow Christ. But we know from the fourth Gospel (1:33–42) that Andrew, John and Peter had already been with Jesus on the banks of the Jordan, that

[2] *In Matt.* Hom. 14. 2: *PG* 57, 219.

they had followed Him to Galilee, and had attended the wedding feast at Cana with Him. How then could He call them here as if they had never followed Him before?

The solution is simple; at first the disciples followed Jesus on their own initiative and accompanied Him to Galilee because they had to go there anyway, since it was their home. But their adherence to Him was only a passing one without any obligation on their part, so that, once they had arrived home, they did not consider themselves bound to follow Him, each going back to his old trade. Their first meeting and conversations with our Lord were but the beginning of their vocation: it was at the Lake of Gennesareth that they received the formal call to the apostolate.

There is another difficulty, however, which is not so easily solved, namely, whether, in addition to the invitation mentioned by St. John (1:33–42), there were one or two other occasions on which our Lord called the first Apostles. The narratives of St. Matthew and St. Mark are identical, but St. Luke's account differs notably in details. If St. Luke is speaking of an incident distinct from that related by the other evangelists, then we must admit three invitations. This is the interpretation that is mirrored in the three stages of the following of Christ found in the *Spiritual Exercises* of St. Ignatius: first, a certain interest in Christ; second, a partial adherence to Him, with the intention of repossessing what they had left; third, total and unconditional allegiance to Him.

This interpretation is not an improbable one and is upheld by some authors, e.g., Fouard; [3] in that case St. Matthew's and St. Mark's account would be chronologically first. However, the theory that the three Synoptic authors are describing the same incident is more probably the correct one, and is followed by Prat, Knabenbauer and others. The two narratives can be harmonized thus: our Lord came to the lake shore where the future Apostles Peter and Andrew were casting their nets; He went aboard Peter's boat and preached to the people; the boat put out into deep water and the crew caught the miraculous draught of fishes; He called Peter and Andrew to follow Him, and, a short while later, also called John and James, who were preparing their nets. Neither of the two accounts gives all the details; instead, they are mutually complementary.

[3] *The Christ, the Son of God,* I, 246–255.

Preaching and Miracles

The intensity of our Lord's apostolic activity was increasing day by day. Frequently He preached in the synagogue and spoke so convincingly and with such assurance that His listeners were moved to exclaim: "This man teaches as one having authority, and not as the Scribes and Pharisees" (cf. Matt. 7:29). This does not mean, as Strack-Billerbeck maintain,[4] that He spoke with authority received from God and not with His own, i.e., that He, like the prophets, was merely passing on to men what He had received from God. The sense is rather that there was a note of assurance and certainty in His manner of speaking which the Scribes lacked, and that, when the occasion arose, He solved difficulties on His own authority, breaking clean away from the teaching of the Scribes with those words which He used so frequently: ". . . But I say to you. . . ." Because of this reassuring certainty and also because of the miracles He worked, the people followed Him, and went seeking Him when He was absent (cf. Mark 1:37): they flocked to His lodgings in such great numbers that the evangelist could say: "The whole town had gathered together at the door."

One Sabbath morning, between nine and ten o'clock, our Lord was preaching in the synagogue at Capharnaum when suddenly a man possessed by the devil stood up and began to shout: "What have we to do with thee, Jesus of Nazareth? Thou hast come to destroy us. I know who thou art, the Holy One of God."

Thus the devil acknowledged Christ's sanctity and proclaimed that it was proper and exclusive to Him alone. But Jesus, in ringing tones of authority, commanded him: "Hold thy peace and go out of the man."

Our Lord did not need Satan's testimony, nor did He wish His character as Messias to be manifested out of due course. Forthwith, the unclean spirit left the man, howling as it went; and we can imagine the fear and awe that fell upon those present.

Accompanied by Simon and Andrew, James and John, the four Apostles whom He had so lately called, Jesus then left the synagogue and went to the house of Simon and Andrew, where he was probably staying. On arriving there, they were greeted with bad news: Simon's mother-in-law was confined to bed with one of those severe attacks of

[4] I, 470.

fever which are not uncommon in Capharnaum and elsewhere along the lake shores. Of course the members of the household discussed the matter with Jesus, and He, without waiting to be asked to heal the sick woman, entered the room where she lay and took her by the hand. Immediately, her fever abated; in fact, so rapidly did the illness leave her and so complete was her cure that the good woman felt well enough to serve them a meal with her own hands.

The news about the casting out of the devil during the morning meeting at the synagogue had already spread through the city, and it was followed in the afternoon by an account of the miracle wrought in Simon's house. As a result the whole populace was seething with excitement, and at sunset, when the Sabbath had ended, the people came swarming about the door of Simon's dwelling, carrying their sick to be cured by the Wonder-worker. To reward their faith Jesus "cured many who were afflicted with various diseases, and cast out many devils. . . ." (Mark 1:34).

It was to be expected that the scene of the previous evening would be repeated in the morning. Therefore our Lord rose long before daybreak, left the house quietly while the others were still asleep, and retired to a solitary place to pray. Scarcely had day dawned when the crowds came knocking at the door of Simon's house. Simon, finding that Jesus was gone, went out with his companions to seek Him, but they must have known where He would be, for they soon found Him and said worriedly: "They are all seeking thee."

That fact was soon self-evident, for the people who had come crowding around Simon's house had seen him and his companions leave, and had followed them to where Jesus was. Now these, coming up, begged Him to stay and "tried to detain him that he might not depart from them" (Luke 4:42). But this time He did not yield to the wishes of the crowd: "To the other towns also I must proclaim the kingdom of God, for this is why I have been sent."

This may not have been the only reason for His refusal. He probably judged it prudent to absent Himself for some time to allow the wave of enthusiasm which had swept over the city to die down. Therefore He departed with His Apostles to announce the "good tidings" throughout the land of Israel.

One day, during His travels, there came to Him a leper who, kneeling down before Him, said without preamble: "If thou wilt, thou canst make me clean."

The unhappy man's resolute and confident attitude pleased the Divine Master, and He stretched out His hand, touched him and said: "I will; be thou made clean."

Immediately the leprosy disappeared: faith had appealed to kindness, and kindness had responded.

Then Christ said to the man: "See thou tell no one; but go, show thyself to the high priest, and offer for thy purification the things that Moses commanded, for a witness to them."

The Law (Lev. 14:1 ff.) commanded that a person who had been cleansed of leprosy should offer a lamb and two pigeons. The man whom Christ had cured resolved to present himself to the priest and offer the prescribed sacrifices so that he would be officially declared clean and be allowed to mingle once more with his fellows. But he could not restrain himself from expressing the joy, wonder and gratitude which filled his heart, and the evangelist records that he "began to publish and to spread abroad the news of his healing" (Mark 1:45).

Although we know nothing of this first missionary journey made by our Lord except the curing of the leper, there is no doubt that it was very fruitful in results and rich in incidents which attracted the people's attention to the young Prophet from Nazareth. The crowds, drawn to Him by His kindness, fascinated by His doctrine and His manner of teaching, and awe-struck by the wonders which He was working, crowded into the synagogues where, as St. Luke puts it, He "was honored by all" (Luke 4:15). They followed Him through the streets, so that His entry into each town became a triumphal procession. Perhaps it would not be an exaggeration to say that this missionary journey was the one on which He received the warmest reception and aroused the most fervent enthusiasm. In fact, the people's response reached such a pitch that Jesus, in order to avoid their acclamations, began to enter the towns incognito and, as it were, in secret. Frequently, too, He purposely sought out deserted places where He gave Himself up to prayer. But He was not allowed to enjoy solitude for long, because as soon as the crowds found out where He was they came from all quarters to see and hear Him (Mark 1:45).

It was in Galilee that our Lord's activity developed most freely, for there it was unhampered by the continual, hostile spying of the Jewish leaders who ruled in Judea and particularly in Jerusalem.

Then, too, the Galileans, although uncultured, were simple, spontaneous and goodhearted people, well-disposed to receive Christ's doctrine; they were fertile soil in which to plant the seed of the Gospel. Moreover, religious fervor could spread all the more easily in this province because it was thickly populated: in fact, according to Josephus, all Galilee was dotted with cities and towns, the smallest of which contained no less than fifteen thousand inhabitants.[5]

The Messianic Secret

We may be surprised that our Lord forbade the leper to tell anyone of the miraculous cure, and that He repeated a similar prohibition on many other occasions and in many different circumstances during His apostolic ministry. He imposed silence on the devils and unclean spirits (Mark 1:34; 3:12); on Jairus and his wife (Mark 5:43); on those who were present at the curing of the deaf-mute (Mark 7:36); on the Apostles, commanding them to tell no one that He was the Christ (Mark 8:30); and on Peter, James and John, forbidding them to speak of what they had seen during the Transfiguration (Mark 9:9). The other two Synoptic authors also record identical commands, but not so frequently as St. Mark (cf. e.g., Matt. 16:20; 17:9; 9:36; Luke 9:21).

Jesus certainly wished to be acknowledged as God's envoy and the promised Messias; He severely censured the Jews who refused to regard Him as such and, in order to convince them, He pointed to the miracles He had wrought. Why, then, did He forbid others to broadcast His miracles, and why did He never refer to Himself in public as the Messias?

The explanation of these two apparently contradictory attitudes is to be found in the intellectual and religious atmosphere in which He was exercising His ministry. The Jews had formed the idea of a glorious Messias who would break the yoke of foreign domination, restore Israel's independence, and bring back the glory which the nation had known in the days of David and Solomon. Therefore, if Jesus had openly declared that He was the Messias, He would have run the risk of inflaming the nationalistic passions of the people and awakening the suspicions of the Roman authorities. Thus, even during the last year—and almost during the last months—of His

[5] *Wars* iii. 3. 2: but see above, p. 12.

public life, during the feast of Dedication, the Jews gathered round Him in Solomon's Porch, and besought Him: "How long dost thou keep us in suspense? If thou art the Christ, tell us openly."

He could have answered simply: "Yes, I am the Messias." He did not; but the words He used instead are very significant: "I tell you and you do not believe. The works that I do in the name of my Father, these bear witness concerning me" (John 10:24 f.).

His reply shows clearly how discreet, one could almost say how cautious, He was in letting His character as Messias be known. He had already revealed Himself as such, not by using the word Messias, but by the works He had done in the name of His Father. And He did not even wish these works, these miracles, to be indiscriminately noised abroad because, under certain circumstances, they could have aroused premature enthusiasm. Only once did He explicitly proclaim that He was the Messias, and that was in private conversation with the Samaritan woman (John 4:25 f.). Again, in praising Peter's confession, He acknowledged that He was the Messias, but immediately, "he strictly charged his disciples to tell no one that he was Jesus the Christ" (Matt. 16:13–20).

Hence, when we take into consideration the prevailing conditions, our Lord's mode of action is not only not surprising, but rather is perfectly adapted to objective reality and dictated by the sublimest wisdom and prudence.[6]

As would be expected, the rationalists and others who deny the divinity of Christ give a totally different interpretation of His actions. It is not our purpose here to refute them. We know that Christ was God and that consequently, from the very first moment of His life, He had full knowledge of His office of Messias. Therefore it would be superfluous to discuss here the much-argued question of when exactly Jesus acquired His Messianic consciousness.

The Holy Women

Among the various aspects and details of our Lord's public life, there is one which we might never have suspected if the evangelists

---

[6] Cf. L. de Grandmaison, *Jesus Christ,* I, 276–291; Bonsirven, *op. cit.,* pp. 377–389. Both of these authors, especially the latter, cite numerous Protestant writers, such as Wrede, Holtsmann, Mundle, and Sanday, as representative of the various interpretations of the Messianic secret and the Messianic consciousness of Christ.

had not revealed it to us. St. Luke (8:1–3) tells us that during His apostolic ministry Jesus was accompanied by a group of devout women, three of whom are named in the third Gospel. One of these women was Mary Magdalene, out of whom Christ had cast seven devils,[7] as the evangelist tells us. "Magdalene" means "from Magdala," a city on the shores of the Sea of Galilee, on the southern end of the plain of Gennesareth (el-Ghuwer). The former city is now reduced to a small group of miserable huts, but it retains its ancient name in the Arabic form, el-Mejdel. The two other women to whom St. Luke refers were Joanna, the wife of Chuza, Herod's steward, and Susanna ("lily"), of whom we know nothing but her name. We also know the names of some of the other holy women—Mary, the mother of James the Less and Joseph (Mark 15:40), and Salome, mother of the sons of Zebedee, i.e., John and James the Greater (Matt. 27:56). Besides those just mentioned, there were other women who accompanied our Lord and who must have been numerous, if we are to judge by St. Matthew's words (27:55): "And many women were there, who had followed Jesus from Galilee, ministering to him," and by what St. Mark tells us (15:41). These women followed Jesus either out of gratitude, for several of them had been freed from evil spirits or cured of some illness (Luke 8:3), or because they had a son or relative among the Apostles (Matt. 27:56; Mark 15:40), or, finally, because of the esteem they had for Jesus and their devotion to Him.

In general, the holy women performed the ordinary domestic tasks for our Lord and His disciples. In addition, since several of them were of high social position (e.g., the wife of Chuza, Herod's steward), they helped to defray the very modest living expenses of the party. We read in rabbinical literature that "a widow with seven sons provided for the support of a rabbi," [8] and presumably this was not an isolated case. Obviously not all the holy women accompanied our Lord at the same time: some would go with Him on one occasion, others on another, in such a way that the party would never be very large.

In the absence of any indication on the part of the evangelists, it is not easy to say exactly what concrete form the ministry of the holy women assumed. We can conjecture that, when Jesus and His

---

[7] For the exact import of this phrase, see below, pp. 362 f.
[8] Cf. Str.-Bill., III, 164.

Apostles had to stop at a town to eat and rest, and particularly when they had to stay overnight, the devout women went ahead of them to find lodgings and to prepare a frugal meal. From Luke 9:53 we know that on one occasion, when Jesus had to pass through Samaria, He sent James and John ahead to arrange for lodgings for the night. It is not improbable that the task given here to the two Apostles was usually performed by the holy women. And this is all the more likely when we consider that some of the women in the party would no doubt often have a relative or friend in the town to which Christ was coming who would help them greatly in executing their commission.

It is probable that all the women were Galileans: certainly the ones whose names we know were from our Lord's own province. And we are told expressly that those who stood at the foot of the cross "had followed Jesus from Galilee, ministering to him" (Matt. 27:55).

It is not easy to tell if any of them took part in the first apostolic journey through Galilee, about which we have just spoken. St. Luke's passage referring to the holy women (8:1–3) comes immediately after the episodes of the widow's son at Naim, the disciples of the Baptist, and the anointing of Jesus by the repentant sinner, and although the passage is rather vague and therefore of little value in fixing dates, it still seems to indicate that the women were present during the first year, and even at the very beginning of our Lord's public life. At all events, their devoted service was not merely an occasional thing but rather an ordinary procedure, for we find the mother of the sons of Zebedee with Jesus and the Apostles near Jericho on His last journey up to Jerusalem (Matt. 20:20), while at the foot of the cross there were "many women . . . who had followed Jesus from Galilee, ministering to Him" (Matt. 27:56; Mark 15:40). Nevertheless, ordinary though the procedure was, it should not be regarded as permanent and uninterrupted.

Here the question naturally arises as to whether or not our Lord's Mother was among the holy women who accompanied Him. During the public life, the Blessed Virgin appears only twice: at the wedding feast at Cana (John 2:1 *ff.*), and on the occasion of her distressful visit to her Son while He was preaching in a town whose name we do not know (Luke 8:19). In the first case, it is evident from the context that our Lady did not accompany Jesus to Cana but was already there when He arrived. And in the second, we are told explicitly that Mary went with some relatives to visit Jesus. Therefore at the time this incident occurred, probably during the second year of the public life, our Lady was not accompanying her Son on His missionary journeys. But did she do so at other times? Due to the lack of positive evidence, it is not possible to give a definite answer. We know that Mary was in Jerusalem at the time of the Passion, but when and how did she come to the Holy City? Seven or eight days before His death, Christ came to Bethany from Perea, and we do not think that His Mother had been with Him in that region. It is not rash to suppose that when, as a result of the raising of Lazarus, the hostility of Christ's enemies was growing more acute with each passing day, the alarming news of an approaching crisis reached our Lady in Galilee, whether at Capharnaum or Nazareth we cannot say, since we do not know where she was residing then. Thus warned, the Blessed Virgin would have set out for Jerusalem, accompanied by some holy women. In conclusion, we are inclined to believe that, except perhaps for some isolated occasions, our Lady did not go with Jesus on His missionary journeys. Instead, she probably lived a retired life, silently contemplating the mysteries of her Divine Son. We shall see her on Calvary at the foot of the cross, but after that, she appears no more, and in the days following the death and Resurrection of Jesus, when the holy women were anxiously bustling about, Mary remained in retirement, closely united in spirit with her Divine Son, as no doubt she had done during the years of His public life.

The Paralytic of Capharnaum
(Matt. 9:2–8; Mark 2:1–12; Luke 5:17–26)

When our Lord finished His missionary journey, He returned to Capharnaum. In passing through cities and villages He had gathered an abundant harvest of souls; but His success had excited, or rather increased, the jealousy of the Scribes and Pharisees, who were to make their hostility felt on every possible occasion.

The news of the Wonder-worker's return spread quickly through the city, so that soon there was an unending procession of people to Simon Peter's house, where Christ was probably staying. So great was the crowd that they could not all fit into the house, many being compelled to stand around the door, which perhaps opened onto a small yard and not directly onto the street.

Our Lord took advantage of the excellent opportunity offered by the gathering to teach and to speak of the kingdom of God. But while He was expounding His doctrine, a paralytic was laid before Him to be cured. The episode is of particular interest both from the purely archeological and from the dogmatic points of view. In order to understand the circumstances of the event, it is necessary to remember the manner in which houses were ordinarily built in those days. One frequently sees the villages of that period depicted as if they were the same as those of present-day Arabs, each house with a domed roof of stone and mortar looking, from the outside, like a small cupola. The artists may think that they are faithfully reproducing the village architecture of our Lord's time, but actually their conception is a pure anachronism. In reality the village houses of that period were roofed with heavy beams, the ends of which were embedded in two opposite walls. Across the spaces between the beams, small transverse joists were fixed and upon these a thick layer of reeds or branches was placed, covered with earth and tamped down. Sometimes slabs of stone, large bricks or flat tiles were laid over the clay roofing as an added protection against the elements.[9] In his account of the incident, St. Luke (5:19) mentions the tiles which were removed to allow the sick man's bed to be lowered into the room where Jesus was teaching.

Josephus refers to an episode in which an opening was made in a roof, just as in the Gospel incident. In the town of Isana ('Ain Sinia, near Jifna), "because the houses were filled with armed men, many of whom had climbed up on the flat roofs, Herod first took possession of the roof tops and then, breaking in the roofs of the houses and thus ascertaining that the rooms below were in fact filled with soldiers, he had stones thrown in to kill the defenders." [10]

In houses of this type the roof top was reached from outside, as is the case today in many of the houses in the towns and even in some of the cities of Palestine.

The assembly which the Gospels describe was an especially solemn one. Besides people from Capharnaum, there were Pharisees and doctors of the Law from different parts of Galilee and Judea, and, most surprising of all, even from Jerusalem—a clear indication that the Prophet of Nazareth was now well-known, not only because of

---

[9] In regions where wood was scarce, several parallel arches were built close to each other, and upon them large slabs of stone were laid. In Sbeitha, an ancient city in the Negeb, the southern portion of Palestine, we saw one of these buildings dating back to the Byzantine period. Cf. *RB* (1926), p. 588.

[10] *Ant.* xiv. 15. 12.

His visits to the Holy City, but also because, as St. Luke tells us (4:44), He had been preaching in the synagogues of Judea (if we admit this reading, which a large number of exegetes prefer, instead of "Galilee"). The presence of the doctors of the Law was significant. They had not come to Capharnaum to be instructed by Jesus; they had other reasons. They had not begun their open battle with our Lord; as yet, their attitude was one of secret hostility and distrustful vigilance.

After sketching in the general background, St. Luke briefly remarks: "And the power of the Lord was present in him in order to heal" (5:17),[11] in contrast to the intentions of the Scribes and Pharisees. They had come to surprise, accuse and confound the hated Rabbi; but instead, God was going to throw them into confusion by showing that His power dwelt in the young Prophet.

While Jesus was speaking to the gathering, there was a disturbance near the door, with many whispered appeals, refusals, and protests being exchanged before peace was restored. Soon, however, something else happened which obliged our Lord to break off His discourse. A group of men carrying a paralytic on a litter had tried to enter the house through the door, but because the crowd would not move to let them pass, they climbed the outside staircase onto the roof, lifted the tiles, removed the clay covering, broke through the layer of reeds that lay across the roof beams, and began to lower the sick man on his litter through the large hole they had made.

The people gathered in the room below were amazed at the unusual sight. Some of them cried out in surprise, others became frightened, while those beneath the hole in the roof fought to get out of the way when they saw the litter being lowered upon them. The whole house was in an uproar, our Lord alone remaining calm and tranquil. Finally the litter reached the floor with its pitiful burden, a paralyzed man who turned beseeching eyes upon Jesus. A hush of expectation fell upon those present, each one holding his breath in suspense, wondering what the Miracle-worker was going to do. Our

---

[11] The Vulgate translates: "et virtus Domini erat ad sanandum eos." Some Greek codices have αὐτούς = "eos," others have αὐτόν = "eum." In the first case it is a question of healing (morally, of course) the Pharisees and doctors of the Law; in the second, the subject of ἰᾶσθαι is Jesus, and the evangelist would then mean that God (Κύριος here does not refer to our Lord, as in many other passages, but to Yahweh) would show His divine power by the cure which Jesus was about to perform. In common with many other authors, we prefer the second reading.

Lord did what no one expected; as if He did not realize that the sick man wanted to regain his health, Christ simply said to him: "Take courage, son; thy sins are forgiven thee."

The faces of many of the onlookers must have registered disappointment and surprise at these words, whose meaning in the circumstances they did not understand.

It could very properly be pointed out that, while the sick man had asked for one thing, he had received another and much more precious gift. However, it is more likely that there was a close connection between Christ's words and the bodily affliction. It was a common belief at the time that illness was a punishment for sins committed, as can be seen from the Apostles' question concerning the man born blind (cf. John 9:1). Sometimes the belief was justified; for example, our Lord said to the paralytic whom He had cured on the Sabbath: "Behold, thou art cured. Sin no more, lest something worse befall thee" (John 5:14); at other times, sickness was not due to past sin, as, for example, in the case of the man born blind (cf. John 9:3). Therefore, Christ's announcing to the paralytic that his sins were forgiven was, in a certain sense, an intimation that he was going to be cured of his disease.

Our Lord's words greatly scandalized the Scribes and Pharisees, since they regarded Him as a mere man, but they did not dare show their wrath. Their hearts were filled with rage at what they considered the blasphemy of this Galilean who dared to claim a power that belonged exclusively to God, and they murmured within themselves: "Who is this man who speaks blasphemies? Who can forgive sins, but God only?"

Our Lord read their thoughts, and, far from modifying the declaration that had scandalized them, He challenged them bluntly: "Why are you arguing in your hearts? Which is easier, to say, 'Thy sins are forgiven thee,' or to say, 'Arise and walk'? But that you may know that the Son of Man has power on earth to forgive sins"—He turned to the paralytic—"I say to thee, arise, take up thy pallet and go to thy house."

Instantly, the man got up, put his pallet across his shoulder and pushed his way through the onlookers. At first the crowd was struck dumb with amazement and holy fear, but they soon recovered and burst out enthusiastically: "Never did we see the like. We have seen wonderful things today" (Mark 2:12; Luke 5:26), "and [they] glorified God who had given such power to men" (Matt. 9:8).

In the face of such a demonstration, the Scribes and Pharisees had no choice but to withdraw as unobtrusively as possible. They had been overcome but not converted by our Lord's incontrovertible proof of His divinity. They would appear again, maintaining their hostility to Him with a perseverance that was worthy of a good cause.

This episode is a clear proof of Christ's divinity. The Scribes and Pharisees understood that He forgave sins on His own authority: He Himself confirmed this impression by saying: "That you may know that the Son of Man has power on earth to forgive sins. . . ." Since only God has power to forgive sins, our Lord here wished to show that He *was* God.

The Calling of Levi
(Matt. 9:9–17; Mark 2:13–22; Luke 5:27–39)

A short while after curing the paralytic, Jesus was walking along the shore of the lake, when He passed by the place where the taxes were taken up. This "tax collector's place," as the Gospel calls it, was not situated on the *Via Maris,* which ran a short distance to the northwest of Capharnaum, but rather on the road which connected the tetrarchy of Antipas with that of Philip and which, after passing through Bethsaida Julias, skirted the lake.

One of the tax collectors there was a man called Levi, the son of Alpheus. Pausing before him, our Lord said: "Follow me."

Immediately Levi arose, and, leaving everything, followed Him. Porphyrius and Julian the Apostate, commenting on Levi's prompt obedience to the call, mockingly observed that no one would follow a perfect stranger so readily. But, as St. Jerome aptly remarks, Jesus was not unknown in that region; Levi had certainly seen or heard about several of the miracles worked in Capharnaum, and therefore He was not unacquainted with Christ, at least by reputation. Then, too, one cannot discount the influence of the grace he received, which enlightened his mind and moved his will. Finally, as St. Jerome also points out, we must take into account the aura of majesty and sanctity which surrounded our Lord, attracting and gently winning to Him souls of good will.

To show his gratitude and joy at having been chosen, Levi, who was also called Matthew ("gift of God"), gave a banquet in honor of his new Master. Besides the Apostles who were with Jesus, he invited many of his friends, publicans like himself and therefore shunned by the people. He also extended invitations to others whom he himself calls sinners, either because they were so in the sight of God or because they were commonly regarded as such. These, then, were the guests with whom our Saviour dined.

There were no Scribes or Pharisees at the feast, for Levi had no friends among them. Even if they had been invited, they certainly would not have come to the banquet, which was an abomination in their eyes. But, always on the alert as they were to catch our Lord breaking the Law, they were watching Levi's house, no doubt murmuring among themselves and to the bystanders about the great scandal that Jesus was giving by associating and even eating with publicans and sinners. Impatiently they waited for the feast to end so that they could accuse Christ to His face: but when the time came their courage failed them, and not daring to confront Him directly, they accosted His disciples with the words: "Why does your master eat with publicans and sinners?"

Our Lord heard what they said although He was some distance from them, and without giving His disciples time to reply (they were, perhaps, embarrassed by the question), He confronted His accusers and said firmly: "It is not the healthy who need a physician, but they who are sick. But go, and learn what this means: 'I desire mercy, and not sacrifice.' For I have come to call sinners, not the just."

The Pharisees, though momentarily silenced by this firm answer, did not admit defeat but, as St. Luke seems to indicate (v. 33), immediately shifted the argument to the question of fasting. On this point they were not alone; they could count on the support and added authority of John the Baptist's disciples, who, like themselves, observed in a spirit of penance fasts over and above those imposed by the Law.[12] If we are to judge by the way St. Mark expresses himself (2:18: "And the disciples of John and the Pharisees were fasting"), the Pharisees and John's disciples were fasting on that very day, while our Lord and His friends were feasting, a circumstance that made the

---

[12] In St. Matthew's Gospel it is John the Baptist's disciples who speak to our Lord about fasting; in Luke it is the Pharisees; and in Mark it is a group who are not identified. But the three accounts can easily be harmonized with each other.

discussion more timely and more tensely dramatic.[13] The Pharisees and John's disciples, now united in a common cause, no longer addressed the Apostles, but spoke directly to Jesus: "Why do we [i.e., the disciples of John] and the Pharisees often fast, whereas thy disciples do not fast?"

Our Lord replied: "Can the friends of the bridegroom mourn as long as the bridegroom is with them? But the days will come when the bridegroom shall be taken away from them, and then they will fast."

Then, in order to make His point clearer and more general in application, He proposed an allegory: "And no one puts a patch of raw cloth on an old garment, for the patch tears away from the garment, and a worse rent is made. Nor do people pour new wine into old wineskins, else the skins burst, the wine is spilt, and the skins are ruined. But they put new wine into fresh skins, and both are saved."

It would be difficult to find words that throw into sharper relief the glaring contrast between the spirit of the Old Law and that of the New. An old garment is not strong enough to hold a patch of new, unworn cloth and the result is that instead of being improved by the mending, it is torn worse than before; or, as St. Luke says with greater precision, if a patch is cut from a new garment, it will not match the old, and the new garment is spoiled. Thus there was no way of reconciling the Mosaic Law, as understood by the Scribes and Pharisees, with the New Law which Jesus had come to preach. The New Law was life, profound, exuberant life, energetic and forceful; it could not be constrained to follow the narrow, twisting channels of a dying Law any more than new, fermenting wine could be confined in old wineskins.

But whoever wanted to taste the new wine had to renounce the old. This is what our Lord meant by that rather enigmatic declaration which St. Luke has recorded for us (5:39): "No man after drinking old wine immediately desires the new; for he says, 'The old is good.' " [14] The Pharisees were devoted to their accustomed external

---

[13] The sentence "And the disciples of John and the Pharisees were fasting" can indeed be understood in a general sense. However, the interpretation we give here is more probably the correct one.

[14] The proper reading here is "good" and not "*melius:* better," as the Vulgate has it. The meaning is that a person drinking wine does not compare old wine with new; he simply tastes the old, and finding it to his liking, does not bother with the new.

practices, and their taste for the old wine of routine had made them incapable of savoring the sweetness and strength of the stimulating new wine which was being offered to them. These few short words of our Lord contain a profound lesson which transcends the limits of His discussion with the Pharisees. In effect, Jesus was pointing out that when a man takes pleasure in lower things, he bars the way to the higher, and that a delight in frivolous and childish affairs renders him incapable of aspiring to great and manly enterprises.

Before narrating the two, or if one prefers, the three short parables referred to above, our Lord had said something which the Apostles did not understand at the time and which concerned a subject that was very much in their Master's mind: "The days will come when the bridegroom shall be taken away from them. . . ." He did not say: "when the bridegroom will *leave* them," or "when he will *go away*." Therefore He was speaking of a violent separation, a clear allusion to the cruel, ignominious death which He was to suffer at the hands of His compatriots and which was ever present to His mind. There is nothing strange, then, in His referring to His Passion here at the beginning of His public ministry, and there is no reason to reject this reference as unauthentic or out of place.

The Choice of the Apostles
(Matt. 10:1–4; Mark 3:13–19; Luke 6:12–16; cf. Acts 1:13)

Not long after His return from Jerusalem to Galilee, Jesus formally, and, in a certain sense, solemnly, chose His Apostles. Several of them had already been called and were following Him; now He confirmed these in their vocation and extended the summons to others.

St. Luke tells us that, before selecting His Apostles, our Lord spent the night in prayer: "He . . . continued all night in prayer" (6:12). The Divine Master thereby wished to show us that we ought to prepare ourselves for important events and decisions by praying, and this for two reasons: first, in order to obtain God's special help, and second, because prayer clears our mind and calms our will, thus enabling us to know what is best and to choose it with greater facility.

Jesus retired to a mountain to pray, evidently in order to find solitude, because external silence is an aid to that interior quiet which is so necessary for speaking with God. Both Luke and Mark mention a mountain, but neither of them gives any further details that would enable us to identify it. Some of the ancient pilgrims thought that it was Qarn Hattin, a hill with two peaks like horns, situated near Tiberias. Nowadays, however, the general preference is for another hill very near Capharnaum, overlooking the *Heptapegon* and having on its eastern slope a small Byzantine church which was most likely built there to commemorate a Gospel incident, either the choice of the Apostles or the Beatitudes.

We should note that St. Mark says: "He called to him men of his own choosing . . . ," words which show the gratuitous nature of the call, which was given, not because of the merits of the recipient, but out of the goodness of Him who bestowed it: "You have not chosen me, but I have chosen you . . ." (John 15:16). The Fathers point out that our Lord did not choose men who were wise and rich, but rather ones who were poor and ignorant, so that no one would think that the conversion of the world was due to human knowledge or riches. St. Mark goes on to say: "And he appointed twelve that they might be with him and that he might send them forth to preach," i.e., He made them His companions and Apostles, to be with Him continually so that they could come to know and be imbued with His spirit, and then, thus prepared, go out to preach. This close contact with Christ and participation in His spirit is especially necessary for those who preach the word of God, but it is also of vital importance for other men, because each one is bound to work for the good of his brother; and it is absolutely essential for those who profess the religious life, because they must live close to Jesus and impregnate themselves with His spirit if they are to communicate it to others.

The three Synoptic evangelists record that there were *twelve* Apostles. The Fathers and ecclesiastical writers have discussed the reason why our Lord selected this particular number of Apostles and no other. The most obvious answer is that it corresponds to the twelve sons of Jacob who were the founders of the twelve tribes of Israel, because, in a sense, the Apostles were to be the fathers of the whole Christian people. Other reasons, or rather comparisons, have been proposed: the Apostles have been likened to the twelve springs of Elim (Exod. 15:27; Num. 33:9), the twelve jewels on the high priest's breastplate, the twelve loaves of proposition, and the twelve stones set in the Jordan; for the Apostles were to pour forth their doctrine in a copious stream, they were to shine like jewels with knowledge and virtue, nourish the souls of the people with spiritual food, and be firm as rocks in their faith.[15]

The names of the Apostles are found in all three Synoptic authors and in Acts 1, 13. There are some interesting features about the arrangement of the names in the four lists, in each of which they are set down in three groups of four names. All four lists place Peter at the head of the first group, a fact which indicates that he was acknowledged as possessing a certain superiority over the others. The second group begins with Philip and the third with James, the son of Alpheus (James the Less), while the other names are always found in the same group, but in varying order. The first group, for example, reads as follows in the four sources:

Matthew	Mark	Luke	Acts
Peter	Peter	Peter	Peter
Andrew	James	Andrew	John
James	John	James	James
John	Andrew	John	Andrew

Judas Iscariot always appears last, and the three evangelists note that he was the traitor.

Our Lord changed the names of three of the Apostles. He called Simon (=obedient) Κηφᾶς (=rock, Peter); to the two brothers John and James, the sons of Zebedee (Zabdi, an abbreviation of Zebadyah =gift [zebed=gift] of Yahweh), He gave the title Boanerges (benê regesh, "sons of the tumult," "the tumultuous ones," which the Vulgate translates as "Sons of Thunder"; cf. Mark 3:17), perhaps in reference to the ardor of their zeal, which they showed when they wished to bring fire down from Heaven to consume the Samaritans (cf. Luke 9:54).

The other Apostles were:

Andrew ('Ανδρέας), a Greek name meaning "man"; Philip (Φίλιππος), another Greek name, meaning "lover of horses"; Thomas (Θωμᾶς), a Hebrew name (teom=twin; "qui dicitur Didymus" [Δίδυμος] =twin; John 11:16); Bartholomew (Βαρθολομαῖος =bar tolmai=son of Tolmai), who is probably none other than Nathanael (in Arabic, Atallah,=gift of God), a native of Cana of Galilee; Matthew (Ματθαῖος =Mathathias=Matthias=gift of Yahweh) or

---

[15] Cf. Knabenbauer, In Matt., I, 429.

Levi, the publican; James, the son of Alpheus,[16] (Ἰάκωβος Ἀλφαίου) or St. James the Less (Mark 15:40), "the brother of the Lord" (Gal. 1:19; 2:9), whose mother's name was Mary; Thaddeus (Θαδδαῖος [Matt. 10:3]; *tod,* Hebrew *shod*=a breast) or Lebbeus (Λεββαῖος: *leb* =a heart) or Jude of James (Ἰούδας Ἰακώβου: Luke; Acts), i.e., he who was the brother of James the Less; Simon the Cananean (Σίμων ὁ Κανανίτης; Matt.), so called not because he was either a Cananean or a native of Cana in Galilee, but from the Aramaic *qanani* (from *qana*=to be zealous; cf. Exod. 20:5; 34:14), whence comes the Greek ζηλωτής ("Zelotes": Luke, Acts), an observer of the Law (cf. Num. 25:7); lastly, Judas Iscariot (=*ish qeriot*), i.e., man from Qeriot, perhaps the district in the territory of the tribe of Juda (cf. Jos. 15:25: "Carioth").[17]

In the case of some of the Apostles, the Synoptic Gospels give only their names, e.g., Philip, Thomas, Bartholomew or Nathanael, and Jude. St. John, however, supplies some details: on *Philip*—1:44–49, his conversation with Jesus and Nathanael; 6:5–7, the question which our Lord asked him before multiplying the loaves, and his answer; 14:8–9, he said to Jesus: "Lord, show us the Father. . . ." On *Thomas*—11:16, "Let us also go, that we may die with him"; 14:5, "Lord, we do not know where thou art going. . . ."; 20:24–28, at first he was incredulous that the others had seen the Risen Christ, but later he believed; 21:2, he was present at the scene by the Lake of Gennesareth. On *Nathanael*—1:45–49, Philip brought him to Jesus; 21:2, he also was present at the scene by the lake. On *Jude Thaddeus*—14:22, after the Last Supper he asked our Lord: "Lord, how is it that thou art about to manifest thyself to us, and not to the world?"

Authors have often asked themselves why Christ chose Judas Iscariot, when He knew he would become a traitor. The same question could also be asked in regard to those priests and religious whom the Lord called to His special service even though He knew that they would one day abandon their vocation and perhaps even apostatize.

---

[16] As we said above, p. 241, this Alpheus was probably the first husband of Mary, who bore him two sons, James and Joseph. After the death of Alpheus, Mary married Cleophas, who had had two sons, Simon and Jude, by his first wife.

[17] If this is so, then Judas was the only non-Galilean Apostle. Other etymologies of varying degrees of probability, as well as some fantastic ones, have been suggested.

St. Augustine says that Judas was not chosen imprudently but "providentially," i.e., that his selection was a part of the designs of God's providence. Others (Prat, for example) [18] suggest that the calling of Judas may have been meant to serve as a norm of conduct for superiors who, since they cannot foresee the future, must judge by their subjects' present dispositions. Perhaps we can also say that God wished to show by Judas' example the depths of degradation into which an unbridled passion can plunge even those who at one time possessed a more than usual degree of sanctity; for it is reasonable to suppose that, at the time of his selection, Judas was not unworthy of the apostolate.

[18] *Jesus Christ,* I, 235.

13. The Sermon

on the Mount

(Matt. 5–7; Luke 6:17–49; cf. Map VI)[1]

St. Luke places the Sermon on the Mount immediately after the choice of the Apostles (6:12–16), whereas St. Matthew records several episodes between the two incidents (Matt. 10:1–4). If there was an interval between the two events, it does not seem to have been a long one.

It has been said with truth that in proclaiming the Beatitudes on the mount, our Lord was like a divine singer pouring out His heart in a glorious melody, for the Beatitudes are so many sweet yet strong and vibrant notes of music springing from the lips and heart of Christ, enchanting to those who possess His spirit, ominous to those who follow the maxims of the world.

The Sermon on the Mount has been called the *Magna Charta* of Christianity. However, it is neither a complete code of civil or religious law, nor a compendium of Christian doctrine, since it contains nothing about the Redemption, the sacraments, the Church, etc. Nor is it a treatise on moral theology: it is very incomplete, and does not fix precisely the limits of obligation, or distinguish sufficiently between precepts and counsels. Yet it can truly be regarded as the charter of Christianity because it lays down the great principles upon which Christianity is founded; it reveals the true Chris-

[1] Cf. Buzy, *S. Matt.*, pp. 48 *ff.*; Prat, *Jesus Christ*, I, 255–280,

tian spirit in contradistinction to the spirit of the Jews and that of the world. Moreover, it is so rich in doctrine that St. Augustine could well say:

He who devoutly meditates upon the sermon which our Lord Jesus Christ preached on the mount, as found in the Gospel of St. Matthew, will, I believe, find in it everything that pertains to good habits, for it is a perfect model of the Christian life.[2]

The Sermon on the Mount is indeed the quintessence of Christ's doctrine, yet it would be wrong to interpret everything in it literally. Our Lord was not a professor lecturing to a learned society, framing sentences with meticulous care, and making distinctions and sub-distinctions. He was speaking to the people, to an unlettered oriental crowd. Therefore He clothed His doctrine in language designed to hold their attention and convey His meaning. He used vivid imagery, striking phrases, hyperbole so bold that at times it bordered on the unlikely and even on the impossible. Take for example the sentence spoken elsewhere: "It is easier for a camel to pass through the eye of a needle, than for a rich man to enter the kingdom of heaven" (Matt. 19:24);[3] or that maxim from the Sermon on the Mount itself: "So if thy right eye is an occasion of sin to thee, pluck it out and cast it from thee. . . . And if thy right hand is an occasion of sin to thee, cut it off and cast it from thee. . . ." (Matt. 5:29–30). The people were accustomed to this mode of expression, and their common sense enabled them to grasp the lesson it contained. Thus it was that when the great penitents of the Thebaid or the desert of Juda retired from the world to practice their awesome corporal penances and wage their titanic warfare on the rebellious flesh, they never dreamed of taking Christ's words literally and plucking out an eye, cutting off a hand, or mutilating any part of their hated bodies.[4] Later there came others who lived in an atmosphere different from that of the early Christian ages, and who were unable to distinguish between the spirit that vivifies and the letter that kills. Consequently they held up Christ as a communist or an implacable enemy of the rich. But that was not how He was regarded by the immense army of Christian ascetics who,

---

511–512; Gomá, *El Evangelio explicado,* II, 155–212; Pirot, "Béatitudes," in *Dict. de la Bible,* Suppl. I, cols. 927, 950.

[2] *De sermone Domini in monte* i. 1. 1: *PL* 34, 1229 *f.*

[3] See below, p. 549, n. 16.

[4] The well-known case of Origen is exceptional, perhaps unique.

down through the ages, embellished with their virtues the garden of the Church, for although these heroic followers of His practiced fully their Lord's basic doctrines, they did not plunge into excesses inspired by the form of words in which those doctrines were expressed.

From the literary point of view, the Sermon on the Mount is not, strictly speaking, a formal discourse with an introduction, a body divided into parts, and a conclusion;[5] nor can the Beatitudes be properly regarded as a prologue or prelude, as they are sometimes called. Although the Sermon opens with them, they are not a mere introduction but form the nucleus of the whole discourse; they are, as it were, its displaced center, displaced because the Divine Teacher went without preamble to the heart of the matter, striking these verbal hammer blows which, coming as they did one after the other without interruption, must have produced a deep impression on His audience.

When we compare St. Matthew's account with St. Luke's, the first question that comes to mind is whether the evangelists are recording the same discourse or two different ones. St. Augustine was struck by the differences between the two accounts and concluded that there were two sermons, whereas St. John Chrysostom, influenced by the obvious similarities between the narratives, favored the view that there was only one. In general, modern commentaries follow the latter opinion, which seems the more probable one.[6]

But even when it has been established that the two discourses are identical, another problem arises—which is the original form, St. Matthew's or St. Luke's? In other words, did our Lord deliver the Sermon all at once, as St. Matthew records it, and did St. Luke extract parts of it and place them in another context? Or were the various parts of the Sermon spoken at different times and in different places, and did St. Matthew then weld them together into a single

---

[5] In *Verb. Dom.,* 27 (1949), 257–269, S. Gallo studies the structure of the Sermon on the Mount and divides it into three parts: the *exordium,* i.e., the Beatitudes (Matt. 5:1–16); the *peroration* (7:24–29); and the *body of the sermon* or the *treatise,* i.e., the part between the exordium and the peroration. He subdivides the body of the Sermon into four sections, which, he claims, are so closely interconnected that "est . . . in eo [the Sermon] perfectio unitatis," a unity which, however, is "Semitic," i.e., a unity of concentric circles (p. 258).

This division is ingenious, but we suspect that it will seem somewhat artificial to more than one reader.

[6] The audience is the same in both cases, the beginning is the same (the Beatitudes), each account closes with the same parables, and, we may say, the substance of each is basically the same. Cf. *RB* (1894), pp. 94–109, for an article which deals minutely and from several points of view with the arguments for each opinion.

discourse? There is still another possibility: several sections of the Sermon may have been spoken by our Lord more than once, an eventuality that is by no means improbable since He undoubtedly expounded some of His doctrines on more than one occasion.

Without prejudice to the other hypotheses, we think it more probable that St. Matthew incorporated into one continued discourse sentences spoken on different occasions and in different places. The principal reason for our preference is the method which the first evangelist employs several times elsewhere. Thus in chapters 8 and 9 our Lord is presented as a Miracle-worker; His pastoral doctrine is summarized in chapter 10; His parables are brought together in chapter 13, and in chapter 24 His eschatological teaching is set down.[7] It is therefore probable that St. Matthew has joined together into one discourse doctrines which our Lord taught on different occasions. Hence we can say that the greater part of the Sermon found in Matthew 5–7 was preached on the mount and in the circumstances indicated by the evangelist, but that our Lord spoke several of the sentences found therein at the times and in the places mentioned by St. Luke.[8]

When we come to examine the first part of the Sermon, i.e., the Beatitudes, we find that St. Luke mentions only four, whereas St. Matthew records eight. Some authors, such as Harnack, believe that our Lord uttered only four and that St. Matthew added the others on his own account, although he did draw the inspiration for his additions from his Master's teaching. But it is difficult to see how St. Matthew would, of his own accord, have placed on Christ's lips sentences so solemn and so unexpected in the circumstances of time and place. Therefore the difference in the Gospel accounts must be explained otherwise.

We propose the following explanation: in the handing down of the doctrine contained in the Sermon on the Mount, primitive oral tradition assumed two forms. In some circles all eight Beatitudes were proposed, while in others it was thought more opportune to limit the teaching to the ones which touched more closely on the lives of the people, or, at any rate, to the ones which left the greatest impression

[7] Cf. Buzy, *op. cit.*, p. 49.

[8] Prat (*op. cit.*, I, 512) attempts to ascertain more closely the parts actually spoken on the mount, but as he himself admits, there is a great deal of theorizing in his reflections.

on the listeners, i.e., those which were, as we might say, less spiritual in character. And it is precisely this type of Beatitude that we find in St. Luke—"Blessed are you poor . . . you who hunger . . . you who weep. . . . Blessed shall you be when men shall hate you. . . ." The third evangelist did not eliminate the others—there was no reason why he should—but just handed down to us those which he found in one of the currents of oral tradition. We should note, too, that there are several very characteristic differences even in the Beatitudes common to both evangelists. St. Matthew does not speak simply of the poor, but of "the poor *in spirit*," nor of those who merely suffer hunger, but of those who "hunger and thirst *for justice*." He uses these qualifying phrases to indicate the kind of poverty and hunger blessed by Christ. However, in our opinion, St. Luke's formulae are the original ones spoken by our Lord, for the evangelist had no reason to eliminate elements which complete and, to a certain extent, explain the Beatitudes. Did St. Matthew introduce the qualifying phrases himself, or did he find them in tradition? It is not possible to give a categorical answer to this question, although we are inclined to believe that he found them in tradition. We can, however, state definitely that the phrases in question are inspired by Christ's teaching, and that therefore they do not alter but rather complete and clarify our Lord's words.

As regards the *place* in which the Sermon was preached, there seems to be a difference and even a contradiction between St. Matthew, who speaks of a mountain (5:1: ". . . he went up the mountain"), and St. Luke, who says that Jesus delivered His discourse on a level place (6:17: "And coming down with them, he took his stand on a level place. . . .": ἐπὶ τόπου πεδινοῦ). The difficulty vanishes if one holds that there were two different discourses, one spoken on the mount and the other on the plain, but as we have already said, we are inclined to believe that both accounts deal with the same sermon. St. Augustine solves the problem by explaining that there was a sort of bench or level place in the side of the mount, so that a person standing there could say he was on a mountain and also on a level place. This is probably the correct solution, and Buzy accepts it.[9] As a matter of fact, the hill near the *Heptapegon* has a level place on one of its slopes, and it is quite possible that this was the reason for the erection in this particular spot of the little Byzan-

[9] *Op. cit.*, p. 50.

tine church whose ruins, including parts of the original mosaic work, are still preserved today.[10]

But whether the Sermon was preached on the mount or on the plain, it is certain that both evangelists mention a mountain. The question is, which mountain? According to St. Jerome, some "rather simple people" said it was Mount Olivet, probably because St. Matthew's account contains the Our Father, which, according to St. Luke (10:38; 11:4), is connected with this mount. St. Jerome himself preferred Mount Thabor. From the twelfth and thirteenth centuries on, general opinion favored Qarn Hattin, near Tiberias, on the road from Nazareth. But the most likely site seems to be the hill near et-Tabgha upon which one can still see the above-mentioned ruins of an ancient Byzantine church, probably erected to commemorate the proclamation of the Beatitudes.[11]

Christ had come to establish on earth the kingdom of God, the heavenly kingdom (*regnum caelorum*), the kingdom of the spirit, as opposed to the kingdom of the flesh, the earthly kingdom, whose citizens place all their happiness in riches, pleasures and honors. In vainglorious Babylon, in cultured Athens and mighty Rome, in fact all over the world, amid the smoke of sacrifice, the clash of arms, and the applause of the multitude, the constant cry went up from men's hearts: "Blessed are the rich! Blessed are they that rejoice! Blessed are they who reach the heights of fame!" Against these maxims accepted by everyone and never questioned until now, our Lord launched the most explicit and absolute condemnation, proposing in their stead other axioms which summed up the teaching of the Cross, "to the Jews indeed a stumbling block and to the Gentiles foolishness," but to the citizens of the new kingdom, "the power . . . and the wisdom of God" (cf. 1 Cor. 1:23 *f.*):

"Blessed are the poor in spirit, for theirs is the kingdom of heaven. Blessed are the meek, for they shall possess the land. Blessed are they who mourn, for they shall be comforted. Blessed are they who hunger and thirst for justice, for they shall be satisfied. Blessed are the merci-

---

[10] In 1935 Fr. Bagatti, O.F.M. carried out some excavations here: cf. the interesting account of his findings in *La Terra Santa* (1936), pp. 65–69. The discoveries fit in perfectly with the account of the Spanish pilgrim, Etheria (Petrus Diaconus): "Inde in montem, qui iuxta est, est specula [grotto or cave] in qua ascendens beatitudines dixit Salvator" (cf. Baldi, *Enchiridion*, p. 354).

[11] Cf. *Dict. de la Bible,* Suppl. I, cols. 940–950, art. by Heidet. Gomá, too, prefers Qarn Hattin.

Murphy Photo

The Little Valley of Et-Tabgha (the Heptapegon): *1. The Mount of the Beatitudes; 2. Ruins of the small Church of the Beatitudes; 3. Basilica of the Multiplication; 4. Octagonal ruins in the center of which rises the most abundant of the seven springs; 5. Road to Capharnaum, which is about 1¼ miles from et-Tabgha; 6. Sanctuary of the Mensa Christi or the Primacy of Peter; 7. The Wadi es-Samak, the country of the Gerasenes; 8. The Lake of Gennesareth.*

ful, for they shall obtain mercy. Blessed are the clean of heart, for they shall see God. Blessed are the peacemakers, for they shall be called children of God. Blessed are they who suffer persecution for justice' sake, for theirs is the kingdom of heaven. Blessed are you when men reproach you, and persecute you, and, speaking falsely, say all manner of evil against you, for my sake. Rejoice and exult, because your reward is great in heaven; for so did they persecute the prophets who were before you."

Then, in contrast to these eight blessings, Jesus uttered what may be termed four curses (Luke 6:24–26):

"But woe to you rich! for you are now having your comfort. Woe to you who are filled! for you shall hunger. Woe to you who laugh now! for you shall mourn and weep. Woe to you when all men speak well of you! In the selfsame manner their fathers used to treat the false prophets."

The almost stereotyped formula which our Lord used in the Beatitudes is an echo from the Old Testament. The best-known passage in which it is found therein is Psalm 111:1: "Blessed is the man that feareth the Lord," but it also occurs with some frequency elsewhere in the Psalms, e.g., Psalms 1:1; 31:1; 40:2, etc., as well as in the sapiential books, e.g., Proverbs 3:13; 8, 34, etc.; Ecclesiasticus 14:1; 28:23, etc., and it is used in rabbinical literature. Rabbi Yochanan ben Zakkai (c. A.D. 80) exclaimed: "Blessed art thou, O Abraham, our father, who hast had Eleazar as a descendant. . . . Blessed are ye [two of the Rabbi's disciples], and blessed are the mothers who bore ye; and blessed are these eyes of mine which have seen ye." [12]

A more or less close parallel to the central idea of each Beatitude can be found in the Old Testament: e.g., for the first Beatitude, Psalm 11:6; for the second, Psalm 36:11, etc. Thus the Beatitudes have their roots in the Old Testament, but when set forth all together in a schematic form as they are in the Gospel, they are uniquely impressive, focusing as they do the scattered rays of light into a beam that illuminates and captivates the hearts of men. [13]

The Poor in Spirit:—In itself, the phrase "the poor in spirit" can mean those who keep their hearts detached from riches, whether in the midst of abundance or in the grip of poverty. [14] However, in the context of the Beatitudes, the words refer to those who are poor in material things, those who are the outcasts of fortune and who, because of their modest and humble state in life, often have to suffer injustice and tyranny. They are the ones who are poor and love their poverty, or are at least completely resigned to it. They are the imitators of Him who, for love of us, willed to be born, to live and to die poor. This Beatitude does not condemn riches: the rich whose hearts are detached from the goods of earth possess the spirit of poverty and are beloved of God; but, strictly speaking, the Beatitude does not refer to them.

Not only *will* the kingdom of heaven belong to the poor in spirit,

[12] Str.-Bill., I, 189.

[13] Cf. F. Asensio, "Las bienaventuranzas en el A. Testamento," in *Estud. Bibl.*, 4 (1945), 241–258; L. Pirot, "Béatitudes évangéliques," in *Dict. de la Bible*, Suppl. I, cols. 292 *f.*

[14] Considered in itself, the phrase can also be interpreted as meaning those who are spiritually poor, i.e., those who realize their spiritual poverty. But in the context here, this interpretation is unsatisfactory, and even more so is the explanation proposed by those who take the phrase to mean dullness of intellect or lack of courage.

it is already theirs. They will possess it fully only in the next life, but even now they have entered into their inheritance, because by virtue of their good dispositions they already form part of the kingdom, and if they persevere they will possess it perfectly in heaven.

The Meek:—The meek are those who restrain their anger, bear contradictions patiently and are kind and indulgent to others. Obviously, meekness is closely connected with humility, but it is not strictly correct to substitute the word "humble" for "meek" in this Beatitude, as some do, because the two virtues, although very similar, still have their own individual characters. In one and the same sentence, our Lord has proposed Himself as a model of both virtues: "Learn from me, for I am meek and humble of heart" (Matt. 11:29). The land which Christ promised to the meek is the Promised Land, the land of Canaan, but since this country possessed a certain sacredness as the earthly abode of God and the cradle of the Messias, it was regarded as a symbol of Messianic joy, that joy which begins in this world and is completed in the next. This was the land which was repeatedly promised in Psalm 36 (Hebrew Ps. 37): "They that wait upon the Lord, they shall inherit the land. . . . But the meek shall inherit the land . . ." (vv. 9, 11, 29, 34).

The reward promised to the meek is basically the same as that of the poor in spirit, but expressed in different terms. In the accommodated sense, the meek shall possess the inner land of their own and other men's hearts, because they are masters of themselves and shall win the friendship and love of others by their gentle and agreeable manner.

They who mourn:—A more accurate rendering of the Greek text would be "they who are afflicted." However, the meaning is the same because mourning is caused by some affliction or sorrow weighing on the heart. But if mourning is a sign of sorrow, how can one who mourns be called blessed or fortunate? Because misfortune leads man to reflect, detaches him from earthly things, and makes him turn to God, while the very hope of being consoled and of enjoying eternal bliss is a consolation in itself, for the day will come when "God will wipe away every tear from [his] eyes. And death shall be no more; neither shall there be mourning, nor crying, nor pain any more . . ." (Apoc. 21:4).

They who hunger and thirst for justice:—As we have already said, our Lord, in pronouncing this Beatitude, seems to have used the formula recorded by St. Luke (6:21): "Blessed are you who hunger now, for you shall be satisfied." However, as we have also pointed out before, St. Matthew's version, although different from St. Luke's, was inspired by our Lord's teaching. Moreover, it is very probable that at one time or another Christ used the concrete and explicit terms recorded by St. Matthew and taken by him from one of the currents of primitive oral tradition.

Here "justice" does not mean the justice of God, or the justice to which we have a right in our relations with our fellow men. In this context the word means sanctity or perfection, i.e., it is used in the same sense in which St. Joseph was called a "just man." Those who really desire this justice and who take the means to procure it will obtain it from God, partially in this life and fully in the next.

The Merciful:—The virtue of mercy is not here limited to a specific category of good works, but includes all the works of mercy. The Beatitude probably refers primarily to the corporal works of mercy, but it also includes the spiritual. Thus the merciful are those who do not egotistically close their hearts to their unfortunate fellows but who, instead, know how to sympathize with others in their physical or spiritual distress. In the parable of the cruel servant (Matt. 18:23–35) and in that of the good Samaritan (Luke 10:30–37), our Lord showed how greatly God esteems this virtue. The merciful, in their turn, will obtain clemency in the Messianic kingdom on the day of judgment: "Come, blessed of my Father . . . for I was hungry and you gave me to eat; I was thirsty and you gave me to drink; I was a stranger and you took me in . . ." (Matt. 25:24 *ff.*).

The Pure of Heart:—Obviously the purity referred to is not that merely legal, external purity against which the Divine Master launched His anathemas: "Woe to you, Scribes and Pharisees, hypocrites! because you clean the outside of the cup and the dish, but within they are full of robbery and uncleanness" (Matt. 23:25). Instead, it is interior purity, the source from which all good outward actions spring. Certainly this Beatitude includes the virtue of chastity, which, by keeping the body pure, cleanses the eyes of the soul and enables it to see God more easily. But here purity of heart has the wider meaning of innocence and uprightness; it signifies freedom from inordinate affections which darken the mind and obscure its vision of God here below. The Beatitude promises this vision of God on earth to the clean of heart in a degree corresponding to their inner purity, and it assures them of the Beatific Vision in Heaven if they persevere.

The Peacemakers:—Here the word is not employed in the usual sense of those who reconcile enemies, but in the wider one of those who promote, diffuse and radiate peace all around them. The peacemakers are those who are at peace within themselves and who, by their gentle, disarming ways, bring their fellow men closer together. But their gentleness does not degenerate into spinelessness, and when necessary they can show a holy firmness in fulfilling their obligations. It is no wonder then that our Lord honors them with the title "sons of God," for God is "the God of peace and love" (2 Cor. 13:11), while the Messias, who was foretold as "the Prince of Peace" (Isai. 9:6), greeted His disciples with the words: "Peace to you!" (Luke 24:36).

They who suffer persecution for justice' sake:—After praising justice, mercy, innocence and peace so sublimely, our Lord seems to strike a harsh, discordant note by referring to persecutions, insults and calumnies, things which wound men deeply and which the worldly-minded hate and avoid. Yet those who bear such things are truly blessed, not only because they are promised the kingdom of heaven as a reward for their suffering, but also because these contradictions, although they wound and bruise the heart, can become a source of purest joy, as in the case of the Apostles who "departed from the presence of the Sanhedrin, rejoicing that they had been counted worthy to suffer disgrace for the name of Jesus" (Acts 5:41). Suffering for Christ and for justice is the suffering which makes men blessed; it is the suffering that filled the martyrs' hearts with joy and rendered sweet the penances of the anchorites, for, like the Apostles, these martyrs and hermits counted themselves blessed to be allowed to suffer for their Lord.

Jesus placed such emphasis on this Beatitude that, not content with having simply announced it as He had the others, He added a commentary on it: "Blessed are you when men reproach you, and persecute you, and, speaking falsely, say all manner of evil against you, for my sake. Rejoice and exult, because your reward is great in heaven; for so did they persecute the prophets who were before you."

When He had finished proclaiming these maxims of the kingdom of heaven, our Lord addressed the disciples, who were gathered around Him: "You are the salt of the earth. . . . You are the light of the world."

He warned them that, just as salt must preserve its full savor and a light must shine from a lampstand, they were to season and illuminate the world with their good works so that their example would bring men to give glory to the Heavenly Father.[15]

Turning back to the crowd, our Lord drew a sharp contrast between the Law of the Jews and the New Law which He was giving to the world. But because the Scribes and Pharisees were already accusing Him of despising the Mosaic Law, He began by stating formally and solemnly that He had not come to destroy the Law (Matt. 5:17–19): "Do not think that I have come to destroy the Law or the Prophets. I have not come to destroy, but to fulfill. For amen I say to you, till heaven and earth pass away, not one jot [16] or one tittle shall be lost from the Law till all things have been accomplished. Therefore whoever does away with one of these least commandments, and so teaches men, shall be called least in the kingdom of heaven; but whoever carries them out and teaches them, he shall be called great in the kingdom of heaven." Or, as St. Luke records in another context (16:17): "It is easier for heaven and earth to pass away than for one tittle of the Law to fail."

The Law to which our Lord refers here is taken by some to mean the *moral* element in the Mosaic Law, an element which cannot cease to exist.[17] Others believe that Christ was speaking instead about the whole Mosaic Law, but only as united with the law of the Gospel and forming an indivisible unit with it.[18]

---

[15] In reference to the salt, Knabenbauer writes: "Quaerunt fiatne sal revera fatuus? affirmant pauci, plerique negant." Actually, if salt is not completely pure it becomes useless when allowed to get damp. In *ZDPV*, 59 (1936), 133 *f.* there is a record of the interesting example of some slabs of salt which, after being used by the Arabs to line the bottom of an oven, were then thrown into the street because they had become useless as salt.

[16] This is the Hebrew letter *yod*, the smallest consonant in the so-called square script.

[17] Cf. Lagrange: "Comment concilier celà avec l'abrogation de la loi mosaïque? C'est d'abord que Jésus n'a en vue que la loi morale que ne passe pas" (*Év. selon S. Matt.*, p. 94); "C'est donc que la loi se perpétue dans son sens profond, la loi morale étant éternelle" (*Év. selon S. Luc*, p. 440). Marchal, *S. Luc.* p. 200: "Le contexte permet de la préciser, en l'entendant de la loi morale."

[18] Cf. Buzy, who says: "Désormais la Loi et l'Évangile ne se séparent plus. Ils constituent une seule réalité indivisible et intangible. . . . C'est cette Loi unique que ne passera pas" (*op. cit.*, p. 61).

There are some authors who regard the aforementioned verses from St. Matthew as being absolutely opposed to other pronouncements of our Lord, and therefore they arbitrarily eliminate them from the text; or else they agree with Allen that "Christ is here represented as speaking in the spirit of Alexandrine

It must be admitted that the Divine Master's words are somewhat obscure; hence it is not surprising to find a diversity of interpretation. For our part, we believe that Christ was referring to the *whole* Mosaic Law and to it *alone,* i.e., the Law with all its moral and ritual precepts, down to the most insignificant regulation. When in verse 17 He drew a distinction between the Law and the Prophets, He certainly used the word "Prophets" to mean the part of Sacred Scripture that went by that name in the Hebrew canon. Hence, when He spoke of "the Law," He wished to signify the entire section of the holy books known by that title, without drawing a distinction of any kind as regards the precepts contained therein. As Lebreton rightly observes: "There is nothing in the present passage or in the Gospel story to authorize any distinction of this kind," i.e., between the moral and ritual laws of the Old Dispensation.[19] Even less can it be said that Christ was referring to an indivisible unit composed of the Old Law and the Gospel.

When He went on to add that not one jot or tittle would be lost from the Law until all things were accomplished, He was definitely speaking about the Law which He came not "to destroy but to fulfill." But how could He say that the Old Law would not cease or be abrogated, when it would surely have to disappear in face of the New? The solution to this apparent contradiction must be sought in the special and peculiar nature of the Mosaic legislation. St. Paul, in his Epistle to the Romans (10:4), writes: "Christ is the consummation of the Law . . . ," and in his Epistle to the Galatians (3:24 *f.*), he says: "The Law has been our tutor in Christ, that we might be justified by faith. But now that Faith has come, we are no longer under a tutor." The Law, as a whole, led towards Christ; it was *in via,* as it were, towards its divinely appointed goal. Every part of it, even the most insignificant, looked to Christ, as if yearning and pleading to be completed by Him and brought to the degree of perfection decreed for it by God. The Mosaic Law was an unfinished thing which our Lord completed and raised to the fullness of its being. And because this elevation extended to all parts of the Law, great and small, Christ could say that not one tittle thereof would pass, that is, would fail to be completed.

and Rabbinical Judaism" (W. C. Allen, *A Critical and Exegetical Commentary on the Gospel According to S. Matthew,* p. 45).
[19] *Life and Teachings of Jesus Christ,* I, 154.

Thus it can be seen how the doctrine of Paul, the disciple, harmonizes perfectly with that of his Divine Master, and how, when Christ had come, the Old Law ceased to be a tutor to men. Although it may seem a contradiction in terms, we may say that the Mosaic Law was abrogated and yet remained in force, for when it was completed and brought to perfection in the New Dispensation it ceased to be what it was before, but did so only to become something better.[20] Yet we cannot properly say that the moral or ceremonial precepts of the Mosaic Law were abrogated; rather they were complemented because, as we have pointed out, the *whole* Law led towards Christ, by whom that which was imperfect was to be perfected, and that which was a shadow was to be turned into a reality—"These are a shadow of things to come, but the substance is of Christ" (Col. 2:17): "For the Law [has] but a shadow of the good things to come . . ." (Hebr. 10:1). In this sense the precepts of Moses ceased to exist, for as St. Paul again writes: "When that which is perfect has come, that which is imperfect will be done away with" (1 Cor. 13:10). We can truly say that the full-grown tree is the seed from which it grew; but there is no less truth in the statement that the tree and the seed are two distinct things.[21]

To illustrate the relationship between the Mosaic Law and the Law of the Gospel, our Lord enumerated several of the old precepts which He had come to perfect. He declared that His disciples must not only avoid murder, but also insults, disparaging words, and even purely interior feelings of resentment and anger, and that they were not to offer sacrifice without first being reconciled with those whom they had offended.

[20] "Haec enim quae veluti figurae ac typi considerentur oportet, implentur cum adest veritas, cum adest id quod illa adumbratione portendebatur; inde autem clarum est quomodo *hac ipsa sua impletione abrogentur*" (Knabenbauer, *In Matt.*, I, 260); "Ce sont deux aspects divergents d'une seule et même réalité" (A. Durand, *Évangile selon S. Matthieu* [Paris, 1927], p. 70).

[21] Cf. Fernández, *Est. Ecles.*, 12 (1933), 444–446. In regard to Matthew 5:19, we shall merely remark that the "least commandments" are those which are compared to a "tittle" in verse 18; and that the verb λύσῃ should be taken in the sense of καταλῦσαι in verse 17. That is how Knabenbauer, Durand, B. Weiss and Schanz view the matter. The presence of the verb ποιήσῃ does not invalidate this interpretation; each of the verbs, λύσῃ and ποιήσῃ, should be taken in its proper sense. The meaning then is: "Whoever *denies,* or *does not acknowledge the force* of one of these least commandments . . .; but whoever *acts* in conformity with them *as a consequence of having recognized their force.* . . ." The verb λύσῃ denotes intellectual judgment, while ποιήσῃ refers to the *actions* which follow in *virtue* and as a consequence of this judgment.

Speaking of chastity, He declared that not only was the act of adultery forbidden but also the inner desire to commit it, even if this desire was not manifested externally; and also that the granting of a bill of divorce was no longer allowed, for marriage was indissoluble. As regards oaths, He said that it is better to abstain from using them and to limit oneself to a simple "Yes" or "No." Generosity was to be substituted for the *lex talionis,* "an eye for an eye and a tooth for a tooth": "But I say to you not to resist the evildoer; on the contrary, if someone strike thee on the right cheek, turn to him the other also; and if anyone would go to law with thee, and take thy tunic, let him take thy cloak as well. . . ."

These words need some explanation. They are general maxims and must be taken in the sense in which they were proposed. Our Lord did not intend to enjoin on us absolute nonresistance to evil and such complete passivity in the face of injustice that we would not be allowed to claim our rights. Instead, He meant that we ought not always to push our demands to the limit of the law, that the children of the new kingdom should treat each other as brothers, and that at the proper times we should show detachment and meet harshness and hatred with gentleness and love, thus putting into practice what St. Paul advises: "Be not overcome by evil, but overcome evil with good" (Rom. 12:21).

St. Luke reverses the order of the words: "From him who takes away thy cloak, do not withhold thy tunic also" (6:29). This seems to be the more natural sequence since the cloak was worn over the tunic and if it were taken away the tunic would then be exposed. The difference between St. Luke and St. Matthew on this point is explained by the diversity of the circumstances visualized by each. Luke is speaking of a robber who suddenly attacks the wayfarer and snatches his cloak, which he wears over his tunic, whereas Matthew is referring to a lawsuit over the ownership of a tunic.

Then our Lord gave His listeners the great precept of love: "You have heard that it was said, 'Thou shalt love thy neighbor, and shalt hate thy enemy.' But I say to you, love your enemies, do good to those who hate you, and pray for those who persecute and calumniate you. . . ."

These are wonderful words, new to the ears of the Gentile world, yet they create a difficulty because there is no passage in the Old

Testament which reads: "[Thou] shalt hate thy enemy." In what sense, then, must we understand our Lord's statement? In Leviticus 19:18 there is a sentence which the Vulgate translates: "Thou shalt love thy friend as thyself." The Hebrew word for "friend" can mean "friend" or simply "neighbor"; the Jews, taking it in the first sense, concluded that they were not commanded to love their enemies and so could hate them. It was to this twisted interpretation, current among the rabbis, that our Lord referred. Even Strack-Billerbeck admit that the words which Christ quoted "must have been a popular saying of the time, in accordance with which the Israelites regulated their attitude towards their friends and enemies." [22]

Vanity and ostentation in the practice of virtue were very common faults of the day, particularly among the Scribes and Pharisees. Christ severely condemned this vice of vainglory, which corrupts every good work, and to do so He chose several of the cases in which it was most apparent.

"Take heed not to do your good before men, in order to be seen by them; otherwise you shall have no reward with your Father in heaven." Therefore when they gave alms they were not to do it to the sound of a trumpet and on the public street, but quietly and in such a way that their left hand would not know what the right was giving away. And when they prayed, they were not to do so standing up ostentatiously in the synagogue or at the street-crossings in the city so that everyone would see them; rather were they to withdraw from the sight of men and, in the presence of God alone, to pray to the Father from whom they were to look for their reward. When they fasted they were not to appear melancholy and sad like those hypocrites who made their faces unsightly in order to let others see that they were fasting; instead, they were to anoint their heads, wash their faces and show no outward signs of penance, and their Father, who sees in secret, would reward them (cf. Matt. 6:18).

Our Lord's warning about this form of vainglory led up to His condemning another defect in prayer, namely, verbosity, for God need not be addressed in many words. Then, in order to teach His listeners how to pray, He proposed the formula of the Our Father. According to St. Luke (11:1–4), Jesus taught the Our Father in other circumstances of time and place (see below, pp. 595 *ff*. for a

[22] I, 353; cf. Fernández, *Verb. Dom.*, 1 (1921), 27 *f.*, 39–42.

discussion of the various problems that arise out of the collation of these two passages).

Then, continuing in the same conversational tone that He had been using all along, Christ gave several admonitions regarding different subjects:

Contempt for earthly things and esteem for those of heaven: "Do not lay up for yourselves treasures on earth, where rust and moth consume, and where thieves break in and steal; but lay up for yourselves treasures in heaven, where neither rust nor moth consumes, nor thieves break in and steal. For where thy treasure is, there also will thy heart be." [23]

Trust in Providence: "Do not be anxious for your life, what you shall eat; nor yet for your body, what you shall put on. Is not the life a greater thing than the food, and the body than the clothing? Look at the birds of the air: they do not sow, or reap, or gather into barns; yet your heavenly Father feeds them. Are not you of much more value than they? . . . See how the lilies of the field grow; they neither toil nor spin, yet I say to you that not even Solomon in all his glory was arrayed like one of these. . . . Therefore . . . seek first the kingdom of God and his justice, and all these things shall be given you besides."

Charity in judging: "Do not judge, that you may not be judged. . . . Why dost thou see the speck in thy brother's eye, and yet dost not consider the beam in thy own eye? . . . Thou hypocrite, first cast out the beam from thy own eye, and then thou wilt see clearly to cast out the speck from thy brother's eye."

The efficacy of prayer: "Ask, and it shall be given you; seek, and you shall find; knock, and it shall be opened to you. For everyone who asks, receives; and he who seeks, finds; and to him who knocks, it shall be opened."

The path to life and the path to perdition: "Enter by the narrow gate. For wide is the gate and broad is the way that leads to destruction, and many there are who enter that way. How narrow the gate and close the way that leads to life! And few there are who find it."

[23] Several sentences follow (Matt. 6:22 f.), the sense of which is: The eye is to one's body what the heart is to one's moral life. If the eye is healthy, it guides one's steps, and one's whole body is bathed in light; but if the eye is diseased, the whole body is enveloped in darkness. So also if a man's heart is not swayed by evil desires, it will guide his moral life along the right paths and he will walk in the full light of day.

False prophets: "Beware of false prophets, who come to you in sheep's clothing, but inwardly are ravenous wolves. By their fruits you will know them. . . . Every good tree bears good fruit, but the bad tree bears bad fruit. . . . Every tree that does not bear good fruit is cut down and thrown into the fire. . . . Not everyone who says to me, 'Lord, Lord,' shall enter the kingdom of heaven; but he who does the will of my Father in heaven shall enter the kingdom of heaven. Many will say to me in that day, 'Lord, Lord, did we not prophesy in thy name, and cast out devils in thy name, and work many miracles in thy name?' And then I will declare to them, 'I never knew you. Depart from me, you workers of iniquity!' "

Hearing this new doctrine and the tone of authority in which it was preached, so unlike that of the Scribes and Pharisees, the crowds were spellbound, and no doubt voiced their sincere enthusiasm and admiration. But the Divine Teacher went on to use a beautiful parable as a warning to them that they had to do more than merely listen to His doctrine; they also had to put it into practice:

"Everyone who hears these my words and acts upon them, shall be likened to a wise man who built his house on rock. And the rain fell, and the floods came, and the winds blew and beat against that house, but it did not fall, because it was founded on rock. And everyone who hears these my words and does not act upon them, shall be likened to a foolish man who built his house on sand. And the rain fell, and the floods came, and the winds blew and beat against that house, and it fell, and was utterly ruined."

Gomá comments on this parable in the following words:

As St. Basil remarks, the rock, the cornerstone, is Christ; and he who takes his stand on it by faith and good works is immovable in every storm that comes, whether from man or from God. Paul's steadfastness in the midst of the cares, dangers and toils of his apostolate; the martyrs' constancy; the perseverance of the confessors who spent long years in sanctifying themselves and making their souls pleasing to God—all this came from the cornerstone of human life, our Lord Jesus Christ.[24]

Having proposed the image of the house and its foundations, our Lord ceased speaking and came down from the mount, while the

[24] *Op. cit., in loc.*

crowds slowly made their way homeward, turning over in their minds the new heavenly message they had heard.

The Sermon on the Mount had opened a new era in the history of humanity. The proud peak of Mount Sinai, the mountain of thunder and lightning, and the lowly hill of Gennesareth, the pulpit of holy peace and heavenly meekness, were the milestones that marked the passage of God; the former witnessed the justice of Yahweh and the imparting of His stern laws; on the latter men were allowed to see the infinite mercy of the Word made flesh and to glimpse the sweet and ineffable depths of divine love.

The Centurion's Servant
(Luke 7:1–10; Matt. 8:5–13)

Coming down from the mount, Jesus re-entered Capharnaum. This relatively populous city had a custom house and a small port, and was guarded by a garrison of one hundred soldiers under the command of a centurion. Some authors believe that the garrison was really a military post charged with watching Herod Antipas and putting a check on whatever ambitions he might entertain. Most commentators, however, are of the opinion that the soldiers were in the tetrarch's own employ and directly under his command. But however that may be, we do know that the centurion was a Gentile (Luke 7:5, 9), and probably a Roman. There was nothing unusual in Antipas' hiring foreigners to fill responsible posts such as that of a garrison commander; and anyway the centurion, although he was a pagan, was well-disposed towards the Jews.

Those who professed the Jewish religion were divided into two classes, the Jews properly so called, i.e., the descendants of Abraham, and the proselytes, i.e., Gentiles who, as a result of the intense proselytism of the sons of Israel, had embraced the Jewish religion, such as, for example, the eunuch of Queen Candace, and Helen, Queen of Adiabene, who built the sepulchre in Jerusalem known as the Tomb of the Kings. It does not seem as if the centurion was a proselyte, although Fouard believes he was; instead, he was a Jewish sympathizer or Judeophile, as we would say today, and he showed his love for the Chosen Race by building at his own expense the synagogue at Capharnaum. Some authors, such as Orfali,[25] believe

[25] *Capharnaüm et ses ruines* (Paris, 1922).

that the ruins at Tell Hum are the remains of this synagogue, but others, apparently with greater probability, think that these ruins date back only to the second century A.D. At all events, the site is the same.[26]

The centurion had a servant or slave who was dear (ἔντιμος) to him because of faithful service or personal affection or a combination of both factors. This servant had fallen ill, and the fact that the illness was causing the centurion deep concern is a clear indication of his kindness of heart. St. Matthew says that the servant was "paralyzed" (8:6), but the term then had a wider application than now and could mean a general loss of strength in the limbs, or a disease of the bones or spinal column. But whatever his illness was, the sick man was in severe pain and near death.

The centurion knew of the wonders which Jesus had worked, and he undoubtedly had heard about the curing of the official's son, for the father may have been a member of his own garrison. He decided, therefore, to have recourse to our Lord, but not daring to approach Him personally because he was a pagan and perhaps also because he wished the better to ensure a favorable reply by having influential mediators, he asked the elders of the city, that is, the most respected men in Capharnaum, to beseech the Master to grant the favor he desired. He had every right to expect that the leading citizens would do as he requested, not only because of his position as commander of the garrison, but also and especially because of the debt of gratitude which the whole city owed him. Nor was the centurion disappointed in his hopes, for the city elders willingly agreed to present his petition and went to Jesus entreating Him to go to their benefactor's house. The evangelist notes that their request was earnest and insistent (σπουδαίως), and that they reminded Jesus of the centurion's zeal for the worship of God and his having built them a synagogue, thus meriting the favor he sought.

Our Lord was not slow in acceding to their wishes: no sooner had He heard their petition than He started out with them to the garrison commander's house. In comparing Christ's reaction on this occasion with His attitude towards the official when the latter besought Him to come and cure his son, the Fathers remark that our Lord did not wish to go in person to heal the son, whereas He did go

26 Cf. Kohl and Watzinger, *Antike Synagogen in Galilaea* (Leipzig, 1916).

to cure the poor slave, as if to make clear that He was no respecter of persons and that virtue and not social position was what counted in His eyes. St. John Chrysostom, however, says that by going to the house Christ wished to give the centurion a chance to manifest his great faith to all those present.[27]

As soon as Jesus had started towards the house, someone ran ahead to tell the centurion that the Master was coming and would soon be there. On hearing this the soldier, moved by profound humility, besought some of his friends who were present to go to meet Jesus and to tell Him in his name that he did not deem himself worthy to receive the Master under his roof. Was he concerned because, since he was a pagan, our Lord would contract legal uncleanness by entering his house? Or was he motivated only by a sense of his own unworthiness? The latter seems more probable.

In the message which he gave his friends to deliver to Jesus, the centurion added another reason why our Lord should not come to his house. In effect he said: "There is no need for you to come closer, because you can cure at a distance," thus expressing his deep humility and firm faith. The Church has immortalized his words by placing them daily on the lips of the priest before his own and the people's Communion: *"Domine, non sum dignus. . . ."*

Still speaking through his friends, the centurion went on to explain the motives behind his faith. In so many words he said: "I am just a low-ranking officer with many superiors over me ["subject to authority"], and yet I have power to command those who are subject to me and they obey me. Surely, then, you who have supreme power can command my servant's illness to depart and it will obey, no matter how far away you are when you give the order."

"Now when Jesus heard this, he marvelled," i.e., His experimental knowledge of the centurion's faith produced in Him the effect which we call wonder, and He was moved to declare that He had found livelier faith in this pagan than in the sons of Israel. Then, as St. Matthew tells us (8:11), He added that many Gentiles would be received into the kingdom of heaven while the children of the kingdom would be cast into the darkness outside.

When we compare St. Luke's account with St. Matthew's, we are apparently faced with a grave difficulty. According to St. Luke, the

[27] *In. Matt.,* Hom. XXVII, 1: *PG* 57, 333.

centurion did not come in person to Jesus, either to ask for the cure in the first place or to dissuade our Lord from coming to his servant; instead, he sent the elders with his request and dispatched some of his friends to meet Jesus before He reached the house. St. Matthew, on the contrary, says that it was the centurion himself who went to our Lord to ask the favor, and that it was also he who dissuaded Christ from entering his abode.

There are three possible solutions to the difficulty: Matthew attributes to the centurion in person the actions which he performed indirectly through others (St. Augustine); [28] or Luke introduces the elders and friends in order to throw the centurion's humility into sharper relief; or, finally, that when he had dispatched his friends, he changed his mind and decided to go in person. The first solution is not very probable, since the relatively long considerations spoken by the centurion would not sound well on the lips of his friends. The second can hardly be accepted, for it is inconceivable that St. Luke, on his own initiative, introduced the elders and friends; and all the more so since it would have been simpler and just as effective to say that the centurion had gone in person. The third solution is probably the correct one, for it is more likely that he first sent the elders to ask for the cure, then sent his friends, and later decided to follow them and speak personally with Jesus. [29]

But even in Luke's narrative itself there is a certain inconsistency. First the centurion, through the agency of the elders, asks Jesus to come (ἐλθών) and heal his servant (v. 3), and later (v. 6) he protests that he is not worthy that our Lord should enter his house. The simplest and most likely explanation is that the soldier changed his mind. Some authors, including Knabenbauer, say that ἐλθών expresses the way the elders understood the centurion's request and that it was they and not he who used the word. Others, such as Schegg, believe that the phrase "come and save" was a kind of idiom which simply meant "save." At all events, the centurion showed such a high degree of virtue that he merited a glorious tribute of praise from Christ's own lips.

---

[28] For example, we can say with truth that it is the king who performs an act when his ambassador does it in his name.

[29] St. John Chrysostom deals expressly with this point: the centurion intended to go in person to Jesus but the Jews dissuaded him; his good will, however, was taken for the deed (*PG* 57, 335 *f.*).

The Son of the Widow of Naim
(Luke 7:11–17; cf. Map II)

About this time (it is not possible to fix the date more exactly), Jesus started out on one of His usual missionary journeys, accompanied by His disciples and a large crowd of people, as the evangelist tells us: "and a large crowd went with him." The great increase in the number of His immediate followers was due to the Sermon on the Mount, preached a few days before (cf. Luke 7:1 f.). On that occasion He had said: "Blessed are the poor. . . . Blessed are they who suffer. . . ." There were so many poor and so many sufferers! The unfortunates who had heard His words felt that Jesus loved them; they had heard Him use a new language such as they had never heard from the lips of the rabbis. No wonder, then, that they were attracted to the young Prophet of Nazareth and followed Him whom they knew in their hearts to be the gentle, compassionate friend of the poor.

Our Lord's way probably led through the *Heptapegon,* across the plain of Gennesareth, up the Wadi el-Hamman, through Lubiyeh and along the road near which was later built Khan Tujjar, whose ruins are still in existence. Then skirting the slopes of Mount Thabor, He and His followers came out on the plain which was dominated by the holy mount and which was an extension of the great plain of Esdrelon. Then, leaving the *Via Maris* and bearing slightly to the left, the party headed for the small city called Naim, which in Hebrew means "the beautiful," a title probably derived from the beauty of the surrounding countryside. Naim is situated a short distance up the slope of Nebi Dahi or Little Hermon, overlooking the fertile valley and facing the majestic bulk of Mount Thabor. Today the ancient city is reduced to an insignificant huddle of miserable little houses. Nearby, one can still see a large number of sepulchres, one of which may well have been the proposed burial place for the widow's son.

As Jesus approached the gate of the city, He met a funeral procession in the middle of which walked four men carrying on their shoulders the corpse of a young man wrapped in a white sheet and laid on an open bier. The sorrowful cortège drew nearer, preceded and followed by the mourners, who, with hair unbound, were reciting in a sad monotone a refrain from Jeremias (22:18): "Alas, my brother! Alas, my brother!" It was a heart-rending scene, made all the more poignant by the fact that they were "mourning . . . an only son" (Jer. 6:26), for the young man was "the only son of his mother, and she was a widow" (Luke 7:12). The bereaved woman was there, overcome with grief and lamenting her son, the sole support of her old age. Little did she suspect that her bitter sorrow was soon to be changed into radiant joy.

The merciful heart of Jesus being deeply moved at the sight of the mother's sorrow, He "had compassion on her," and said to her with gentle reassurance: "Do not weep."

Jesus was true God but He was also true Man, and as such His heart could be touched by every lawful human emotion; and compassion is one of the most ennobling and worthy of these emotions. The God-Man was now about to put His divine omnipotence at the service of His compassion.

Approaching the litter, He touched it, and the pallbearers halted. Then in a tone of great solemnity He said: "Young man, I say to thee, arise."

Immediately the dead man came to life, sat up and began to speak, and Jesus, taking him by the hand, gave him to his mother.

At the sight of the miracle a holy fear fell upon the onlookers, and they all began to glorify God, saying: "A great prophet has risen among us," and "God has visited his people."

John the Baptist's Deputation
(Matt. 11:2–19; Luke 7:18–35)

During all this time, John, the defender of chastity and the flayer of vice, had remained shut up in the dungeons of Machaerus, the palace-fortress of Herod Antipas. However, he was allowed to receive visits from his disciples, who, now quite numerous, were not convinced that Jesus of Nazareth was really the Messias.

During our Lord's brief ministry in Judea shortly after the first Passover of His public life, they had voiced their distrust (cf. John 3:26), and they had not been able to resign themselves to seeing their own teacher's glory eclipsed by that of the new Prophet. Later, they took scandal from Christ's conduct in mingling freely with sinners and eating at their table instead of observing the fast which they themselves were keeping; and to a certain extent they even gave the impression of making common cause with the Scribes and Pharisees

against Jesus (cf. Matt. 9:14 *ff*.). They doubtless had seen the
miracles which the young Rabbi worked, but never having heard
Him declare openly that He was the Messias, they regarded His
silence on the point as very significant; and they went to their master
in the fortress of Machaerus, bringing him "word of all these things"
(Luke 7:18).

Did John the Baptist share his disciples' doubts? Did the young
Prophet's inexplicable silence about His Messianic character, and His
strange intimacy with publicans and sinners cause the Precursor to
waver in his first steadfast faith and confidence? Did he not at least
feel some impatience and annoyance when the Prophet whom he had
announced so clearly and confidently did not stand forth before the
people in a blaze of heavenly light? If, as some authors claim, that
had been his state of mind, we can imagine how he would have
decided to remove, once and for all, the doubt that was gnawing at
him by forcing Jesus to declare openly whether He was or was not
the Messias.

But these were not the Precursor's feelings. He had seen the
wonderful happenings at the baptism of Jesus, and even before the
young Rabbi had performed any miracles, he had unwaveringly
pointed Him out as the Messias. He had uttered a sublime hymn in
praise of Jesus, declaring that he himself was unworthy even to loose
the strap of His sandals (John 1:27). It is not possible, then, that in
the space of a few months he would have changed his outlook so
radically, or that he would have begun to doubt. John did not expect
a spectacular show of power and glory, as perhaps the Apostles did.
To him, Jesus was the Lamb of God who was to be sacrificed for the
sins of the world and whose role therefore was a purely spiritual one.
Nor can it be said that he thought it inopportune for Christ to
maintain unbroken silence regarding His Messianic character. How
could he, the lowest of God's servants, dare to stand in judgment on
the conduct of his Lord? Did not Jesus, whom the Eternal Father had
presented to the world as His dearly beloved Son, know well the way
in which He was to perform the task which the Father had committed to Him? Finally, we must not forget that, as Precursor, John
enjoyed an especially close relationship with the Messias and that,
consequently, he must have received special enlightenment on the
true nature and character of the Messianic plan. It is true that great
saints have at times undergone severe trials of faith, and have even

felt that their whole spiritual life was crumbling into ruins. But there is not the slightest indication in the Gospel that John the Baptist experienced anything of the kind.

It cannot be maintained that the darkness of the dungeons of Machaerus and the enervating inactivity and isolation to which John was subjected had had such a depressing and disheartening effect on him that he had become an easy prey to doubt and discouragement. In the first place, he was not as isolated as some authors seem to believe, for he was allowed to receive visits from his disciples, and we know that the tetrarch himself had frequent interviews with him. Furthermore, great souls only become stronger in the crucible of suffering, and solitude tends to bring them closer to God, in whom they find their support and from whom they gather new strength. And John was indeed a great soul.

Thus when his disciples came to him with reports about Jesus, he sent two of them to our Lord to ask Him: "Art thou he who is to come, or shall we look for another?" In doing so he had but one object—to strengthen his disciples' faith in Jesus as the Messias. He had always striven to plant this faith in the hearts of his followers; he, the friend of the Bridegroom, had constantly guided them towards the Bridegroom, but false prejudices, the attitude of the most prominent Jews, and their own love for him, their teacher, had held them back and made them hesitate to abandon their old way of life and embrace the new. Now John was convinced that only an explicit and definitive declaration on the part of Jesus would dissipate their doubts and overcome their vacillation.

Accordingly, the two messengers presented themselves to Jesus and asked: "Art thou he who is to come, or shall we look for another?" "He who is to come" referred to him who the prophets had said would come in the fullness of time: thus using this phrase was equivalent to saying "the promised Messias."

The envoys expected that Jesus would give a clear, categorical and definitive answer to their blunt, point-blank question, which almost amounted to a challenge. But He did not. Deeds being more convincing than words, Christ appealed to His works: "In that very hour," records the evangelist (Luke 7:21), "he cured many of diseases, and afflictions and evil spirits, and to many who were blind he granted sight."

Referring, then, to these miracles, Jesus said to the two messengers: "Go and report to John what you have heard and seen: the blind see, the lame walk, the lepers are cleansed, the deaf hear, the dead rise, the poor have the gospel preached to them."

The miracles which He wrought as a testimony to His Messianic character were His answer to their inquiry, an answer all the more convincing because the miracles were the fulfillment of a prophecy concerning the Messianic era (cf. Isai. 29:18 *f.;* 35:5 *f.;* 61:1).

He ended His reply with an admonition that referred to the lack of faith, not on John's part, but on the part of his disciples who had been scandalized by His own way of acting and His humble bearing: "And blessed is he who is not scandalized in me."

John's deputation was pleasing to Jesus, inspired as it was by the desire that all should recognize Him as the Messias. Our Lord knew that His Precursor was suffering for truth and justice, and He took this opportunity to utter a magnificent panegyric of the Baptist. John was not a reed that bent with every wind: he was the valiant herald of justice who did not fear to confront the adulterous tetrarch and to stand firm and inflexible in the face of the tyrant's power. He was not a soft effeminate who decked himself out in fine clothes like those of the courtiers who lived luxuriously in the palaces of kings; instead, he wore a tunic of camel's hair and a belt of leather. He was the greatest of the prophets, the angel of the New Testament (cf. Mal. 3:1); he was Elias, the prophet who was to come.[30]

Then, after eulogizing John the Baptist, Jesus reproached the people of the day with their inconsistent behavior. They rejected John's message because he was austere and said that "he [had] a devil" because he neither ate bread nor drank wine. But when He Himself came, eating and drinking like everyone else, they refused to credit Him and said: "Behold a man who is a glutton, and a wine-drinker, a friend of publicans and sinners!"

To point up their capriciousness and inconsistency, our Lord used a picturesque simile taken from everyday life: ". . . The men of this generation . . . are like children sitting in the market place, calling to one another and saying,

'We have piped to you, and you have not danced;

we have sung dirges, and you have not wept.' "

That is to say, the children did not wish to play either at weddings or

---

[30] See pp. 176 *ff.* above for the explanation of some of the difficult phrases in this passage.

at funerals; they did not wish to take part in joyful games or in sad ones.

Although exegetes are not agreed as to whether we should regard the children as being divided into two groups or as forming but the one, the meaning of the parable, or, if you will, the allegory, is clear: the children who refused to take part in the games represented the Jews, who did not wish to follow either John or Jesus. That is the central idea of the parable. But we can apply it even further provided that a perfect correspondence between the terms of the comparison is not looked for; and in reality such an undeviating parallelism is foreign to the nature of parables. We can say that the children who invited their companions to play represented, to a certain degree, Jesus and His Precursor, because our Lord and John, each in his own way, invited their compatriots to partake in a moral rebirth; but the Jews in general, and the Scribes and Pharisees in particular, rejected their invitation.

There were, however, some Jews who were wiser and less stiffnecked than their fellows and who did accept Christ's invitation. Our Lord, therefore, closed His description of His compatriots' obstinate resistance with the consoling words: "And wisdom is justified by all her children." [31]

By this our Lord meant that there were many who recognized that He and John had been sent by God and who saw and venerated in their different methods the providence of God and the plans of His wisdom. It was on such men as these that Christ conferred the title "children of wisdom."

The Sinful Woman in the Pharisee's House
(Luke 7:36–50)

When questioned by John the Baptist's messengers, Jesus had pointed to His miracles as irrefutable proof of His Messianic character. It was about this time, too, that He had an opportunity of showing that He possessed also the Messianic qualities of mercy and

[31] This is the reading found in Luke 7:35 (τέκνων). In Matthew 11:19, several codices have ἔργων ("works") instead of τέκνων ("children"), the meaning being that our Lord's and John's works were such that wisdom shone forth in them, and that by means of these works wisdom came to be acknowledged and justified. It seems that each reading should be preserved in its own place. Cf. Bover-Lagrange in *Biblica,* 6 (1925), 323–325, 461–465.

forgiveness in contrast to the proud, unbending severity of the Pharisees. For it was now that He strikingly demonstrated the infinite kindness of His heart, first by allowing a sinful woman to anoint His feet, and then by pardoning her sins.

About halfway between Tiberias and Capharnaum, at the southern end of the plain of Gennesareth, there is a village called el-Mejdel huddled on the right-hand side of the road, beside the lake. It is composed of a few small, squat hovels with mud walls and flat roofs. During the summer months the inhabitants sleep on the roofs of their houses under rude shelters formed of reeds supported by four poles, one at each corner of the house.

This miserable hamlet is all that remains of ancient Magdala,[32] the home of Mary Magdalene; more accurately still, the town was known as *Magdala Nunaiya,* "Magdala of the fishes," and perhaps it also went by the Greek name, Tarichea, of sad renown, for the blood of the inhabitants of this town was spilled in such profusion that it stained the waters of the lake.[33] In its heyday it had been prosperous, deriving its riches from the surrounding fertile soil and from its trade in salted fish: it had been one of the three cities which, according to the rabbis, sent immense treasures to Jerusalem.[34] But with prosperity had come luxury and frivolity, and through the streets of the town there used to pass young women answering Isaias' description of the daughters of Sion, with heads held high and haughty glance, bedecked with earrings, bracelets and tiaras and tripping along with jingling anklets (cf. Isai. 3:16 *ff.*). In such an atmosphere, as one would suspect, base passions flourished and sinful women lived in open luxury. In fact morals reached such a low ebb that the rabbis asserted that the city had been destroyed by its own scandalous corruption.[35]

One of these public sinners, whose name the evangelist does not mention, gave the city and the world a wonderful example of contrition and humility. How did this lost sheep find her way back to the fold of the Good Shepherd? Did she know Him only by reputation,

---

[32] Many authors believe that the incident of the sinful woman in Simon's house took place here, while others believe that it occurred at Naim or Capharnaum. However, due to the lack of Gospel data, it is not possible to fix the site with certainty.

[33] *Wars* iii. 10. 9.

[34] Neubauer, *La géographie du Talmud* (Paris, 1868), p. 217.

[35] Cf. *Ibid.*

Magdala (el-Mejdel) on the Lake of Gennesareth.

having heard of His kindness and mercy to sinners? Had she seen one
of His miracles or been present at the Sermon on the Mount? Or had
she caught a glimpse of His serene and holy countenance and been so
impressed, so conscience-stricken, that she felt moved to cast herself
at His feet? We do not know the answer; all we can say is that, urged
on by grace, she ran to Jesus, who had opened the wound of remorse
in her heart, so that He might heal her.

A banquet was being held in the house of Simon the Pharisee, and
among the guests was the young Prophet of Nazareth. In oriental
fashion, the doors of the banquet-hall were wide open and a crowd
had gathered on the threshold to peer in curiously at the feasters.
Suddenly a young woman pushed her way through the onlookers
and entered the room. At first her appearance there merely surprised
the guests, but when they saw who she was their eyes blazed with
anger. What had this notorious courtesan come for? To tempt them
with her beauty? How dared she thus profane the house of an austere
Pharisee? But before Simon the host could order his servants to
remove her, she, the haughty sinner who had insolently paraded her
beauty in the streets of the city, had thrown herself humbly at
Christ's feet, and had begun to wash them with her tears, wipe them
with her flowing hair, kiss them and anoint them with costly perfume.

Simon was almost beside himself with anger and shame at the intruder's boldness; but what particularly exasperated the proud Pharisee was the fact that the young Prophet of Nazareth was allowing the impure woman to touch Him. Not daring to reproach Jesus openly, he thought to himself: "This man, were he a prophet, would surely know who and what manner of woman this is who is touching him, for she is a sinner" (Luke 7:39).

Jesus could have guessed at Simon's thoughts from the expression on his face; but He did more, for He read the Pharisee's mind as if it were an open book. With that delicacy which put a divine seal on all that He did, He turned to Simon and, as it were, asked him as host for permission to speak: "Simon, I have something to say to thee."

"Master, speak."

"A certain moneylender had two debtors; the one owed five hundred denarii, the other fifty. As they had no means of paying, he forgave them both. Which of them, therefore, will love him more?"

Simon answered and said, "He, I suppose, to whom he forgave more."

And he said to him: "Thou hast judged rightly." And turning to the woman, he said to Simon, "Dost thou see this woman? I came into thy house; thou gavest me no water for my feet; but she has bathed my feet with tears, and has wiped them with her hair. Thou gavest me no kiss; but she, from the moment she entered, has not ceased to kiss my feet. Thou didst not anoint my head with oil; but she has anointed my feet with ointment. Wherefore I say to thee, her sins, many as they are, shall be forgiven her, because she has loved much. But he to whom little is forgiven, loves little." And he said to her: "Thy sins are forgiven. . . . Thy faith has saved thee; go in peace."

What a moving scene the evangelist has depicted in recording this incident—the once proud sinner, conquering all human respect, forcing her way into the crowded room and throwing herself at our Lord's feet to wash them with her tears of contrition and wipe them with her silken hair; and Jesus, the Good Shepherd, gazing with tender forgiveness on this sheep that had wandered far but had returned at last to find shelter and rest at His feet!

Our Lord's chain of reasoning on this occasion has created no small difficulty for commentators, for it seems to beg the question. On the one hand, He spoke of the forgiveness of sin as an *effect* of love ("Her sins, many as they are, shall be forgiven her, because she has loved much"), while on the other hand He represented forgiveness as the *cause* of love ("He to whom little is forgiven, loves little").

Numerous and widely varied explanations of the difficulty have been proposed by authors. However, we believe that if we take into account the Pharisee's outlook and the purpose of our Lord's words, we can give a simple, but none the less satisfactory, interpretation of the passage.

Forgiveness of sins involves two types of love: contrite love, which is present before forgiveness is granted and which *disposes* the soul to receive pardon, and grateful love, which the soul feels as a result or *effect* of having been forgiven. The sinful woman had both these types of love; her contrite love was evident from her conduct in the banquet-hall (vv. 44–46), and her grateful love is taken for granted and is implied in Simon's answer (v. 43) and in our Lord's words: "He to whom little is forgiven, loves little." If the passage is viewed in that light, the difficulty vanishes.

In our Lord's dialogue with Simon the Pharisee, contrite love and grateful love are so interwoven as to seem at first glance to be confused one with the other. But if we do not concentrate so much on the material order of the sentences as on our Lord's thought, we shall see that there is not the slightest trace of confusion. Simon, the scrupulous observer of the Mosaic Law, regarded himself as greatly superior to the sinful woman; and Jesus wished to prove to him that the contrary was true, by his own admission. It was for this purpose that He proposed the parable of the two debtors. Immediately after narrating it and receiving Simon's answer (vv. 41–43), He could simply have said to the woman: "Thy sins are forgiven." The implied conclusion was evident: more had been forgiven to the woman than to Simon, therefore she had greater love than he, i.e., she had a higher degree of grateful love. That was the central idea of the parable.

But our Lord wished to drive home his argument by contrasting the Pharisee's coldness with the woman's loving homage (vv. 44–46). Consequently these verses are not an application and continuation of the parable, but rather a new element introduced for the same purpose as the parable and containing a description of the contrite love that had earned the woman the promise: "Her sins . . . shall be forgiven her, because she has loved much" (v. 47). The last sentence in the passage: "He to whom little is forgiven, loves little" was not meant to be an antithesis to the preceding sentence: "Her sins, many as they are, shall be forgiven her, because she has loved much." The former sentence is wholly unconnected with the latter, for the one speaks of contrite love, the other of grateful love. Instead, when our Lord said: "He to whom little is forgiven, loves little," He was referring back to the parable and gently reproaching the Pharisee who was so assured of his own justice that he thought he had little to be forgiven.

The "Problem of the Three Marys"

The common opinion of the faithful today, which is reflected in the Latin liturgy, identifies the anonymous sinner with Mary Magdalene and Mary the sister of Lazarus. But Greek tradition favors a distinction between the three women, and in this it is more in harmony with Gospel data. Even from the first centuries of the Christian era much has been written on what is usually called the question of "the three Marys," although we know the names of only two of the women concerned. One thing is certain, however: tradition cannot be invoked in favor of their identity. Holzmeister has pointed out this fact in two long and very learned articles.[36]

From the exegetical point of view, we believe that the distinction between the "three Marys" must be regarded as much more probable than their identification. The way the Gospels speak of the sinful woman, Mary Magdalene, and Mary the sister of Lazarus, leads us to believe that the evangelists are referring to three different persons. We regard as very probable the distinction between Mary Magdalene and the sinful woman, and that between Mary Magdalene and Mary the sister of Lazarus as morally certain.

We shall indicate briefly the reasons for our conclusions. We find both Mary Magdalene and Mary, the sister of Lazarus, mentioned

[36] "Die Magdalenenfrage in der Kirchlichen Überlieferung," in *Zeit, f. kath. Theol.*, 46 (1922), 402–422, 556–584: "Aus der ganzen Untersuchung ergibt sich ganz klar das eine Ergebnis: die Frage nach einer einheitlichen Tradition ist gewiss nicht im affirmativen Sinne zu beantworten" (p. 584). Lagrange has come to the same conclusion: "La première conclusion qu'on peut tirer de ce rapide examen des écrivains ecclésiastiques c'est qu'il n'existe pas sur l'unité ou la pluralité de la ou des myrophores ce qu'on pourrait nommer une tradition exégétique des Pères. Ils ne sont pas d'accord, et presque aucun n'est très affirmatif" (*RB* [1912], pp. 529 *f.*).

four times in the Gospels. Mary Magdalene appears among the holy women who accompanied our Lord on His apostolic journeys (Luke 8:1); she was on Mount Calvary at the death of Christ (John 19:25); she ran to the Holy Sepulchre (Luke 24:10); and it was she who was favored with the appearance of the Risen Lord (John 20:11). We see Mary, the sister of Lazarus, at our Lord's feet (Luke 10:39); in John 11:1, she is named along with Lazarus and Martha, and in the same chapter she is present at the raising of her brother, while in John 12:2 she is described as anointing Christ's feet at the banquet in Bethany.

As can be seen, in all of these passages the names of the women concerned are clearly indicated: one woman is always called Mary, the sister of Lazarus and Martha, while the other is always referred to as Mary Magdalene. In addition, the circumstances of time and place are different. Mary the sister of Lazarus came from Bethany, and every incident in which she appeared occurred in that town. Mary Magdalene came from Magdala, and we find her first accompanying Jesus, and later in Jerusalem during the Passion and Resurrection. It is clear, therefore, that Mary of Bethany and Mary Magdalene must be regarded as two distinct persons. The sole foundation for the identification of Mary of Bethany with the repentant sinner is the passage from St. John 11:2: "Now it was Mary who anointed the Lord with ointment," [37] in which the aorist of the Greek verb "to anoint" is taken as referring to the past and not to the future. The whole passage reads: "Now a certain man was sick, Lazarus of Bethany, the village of Mary and her sister Martha. Now it was Mary who anointed the Lord with ointment, and wiped his feet dry with her hair, whose brother Lazarus was sick. The sisters therefore sent to him, saying, 'Lord, behold, he whom thou lovest is sick.' "

Now, say the proponents of the identification theory, when the two sisters sent the news of Lazarus' illness to Jesus, the anointing at Bethany had not yet taken place, but the anointing by the penitent woman, described in Luke 7:36–50, had already occurred, and therefore St. John must be referring to the latter episode. Consequently,

---

[37] With Knabenbauer, Lagrange, de la Torre, Colunga, Braun, Mollat, Fillion, Crampon, and others, we translate the verb in the past tense, "anointed," and not in the pluperfect "had anointed."

Mary of Bethany must be the unnamed repentant woman of Luke 7:36–50.

Actually, from St. John's point of view, the aorist in this sentence does refer to the past and not to the future. When the evangelist was writing this passage, all of the events which he was narrating had happened in the distant past, and the mere fact that he mentions the anointing by Mary before describing the feast at Bethany does not mean that Mary anointed Jesus twice, once at some point of time before the feast and again during it. His real meaning was that "it was Mary who *later* anointed the Lord with ointment.[38]

Nor is there any indication that Mary Magdalene and the unnamed sinful women were one and the same person. We know Mary Magdalene's name and her native city, but we do not know what the sinful woman was called, nor where she was from, nor where the anointing took place.[39] The Gospels provide no possible line of argument in favor of the identification of the two women. Some authors do indeed invoke the passage from St. Luke (8:1–3) in which, immediately after the penitent woman's anointing of our Lord, the evangelist mentions Mary Magdalene among the women who accompanied Him on His missionary journeys. These authors say that St. Luke thereby intended to point out, discreetly and delicately, that Mary Magdalene and the sinful woman were one and the same person. The evangelist's intention is made all the more clear, they maintain, by the fact that Jesus had cast seven devils out of Mary Magdalene, an obvious indication of the disorderly life she had led in the past.

We must point out, however, that diabolical possession can be, and sometimes is, permitted without any fault on the part of the possessed person. When mentioning demoniacs, the Gospels never say, or even hint, that their unhappy state was a consequence or an indication of a sinful life. And a number of authors (e.g., Knabenbauer, Marchal, Colunga, and others) hold that Mary Magdalene's being possessed by seven devils was neither a sign of, nor a punishment for, an evil life. But even if she had been possessed as a result of her sins, this fact would not prove that she was the repentant sinner. There

[38] Cf. Zerwick, *Analysis philologica Novi Testamenti graeci* (1953), p. 232: "Αλείψασα . . . tempus praeteritum, non relate ad tempus narrationis (unctio tunc futura erat) sed relate ad tempus scriptionis: 'erat illa quae, ut notum est, unxit. . . .' " Cf. Lagrange, *Évangile selon S. Jean*, 3e éd. (Paris, 1927), p. 296.

[39] See above, p. 356, n. 32.

could have been, and undoubtedly there were, many sinful women in the towns and cities of Galilee at the time.

It is difficult to see any indication of St. Luke's intention in his mention of Mary Magdalene immediately after the incident of the sinful woman. And it would be arbitrary to say, without any positive evidence, that he thereby meant to show that the one was identical with the other. Not only that, but, as Prat correctly observes, a comparison of the two passages from St. Luke seems rather to support the distinction between Mary Magdalene and the repentant sinner.[40]

Plucking the Ears of Wheat:
The Man With the Withered Hand
(Matt. 12:1–37; Mark 2:23–28; 3:1–6, 20–23; Luke 6:1–11; 11:14–26)

The proud Pharisees deeply resented our Lord's kindness and candor, and in the days following the scene in Simon's house their resentment grew. The great struggle had begun—legalistic Pharisaism pitted against the freedom of the Gospel, hypocrisy against sincerity, the death-dealing letter against the life-giving spirit, a struggle in which the people, guided by their common sense and sure instinct, sided with Jesus, whom they acknowledged as their Teacher and whom they faithfully followed, eager to drink in His divine doctrine.

One Sabbath day in June, Jesus and His disciples were crossing a wheat field not far from Capharnaum. The crop was ripe for the harvest, and the disciples, who perhaps had not yet broken their fast, plucked some ears of wheat and rubbed them between their hands to extract the grain.

At that moment some Pharisees happened to be passing and, scandalized at what the Apostles were doing, said to them: "Why are you doing what is not lawful on the Sabbath?"

In reality their reproach was not directed against the disciples, but against their Master. On hearing it, Jesus, who was standing a little apart, defended His Apostles: "Have you not read what David

---

[40] "Magdalene is here introduced as an unknown person, one of the women whom Jesus had cured of various maladies and freed from unclean spirits. This fact does not seem to fit in with the story of the unnamed sinner of whom St. Luke has just spoken" (*op. cit.*, I, 292).

"Immediately after having told of the anointing by the unnamed sinner, St. Luke mentions Mary Magdalene without seeming to suspect the least link between the two women. . . ." (*ibid.*, II, 485).

did when he and those with him were hungry? How he entered the house of God, and ate the loaves of proposition which neither he nor those with him could lawfully eat, but only the priests?" (cf. 1 Kings 21:4 *ff.*).

He said this to show the Pharisees that there were circumstances which dispensed from the observance of the Law. But He then went on to give a deeper and more radical justification of His disciples' actions: "The Son of Man is Lord even of the Sabbath." Consequently, He had power to dispense from the Law of the Sabbath.

A short while later, in a tensely dramatic scene, Jesus again had occasion to show His power, not only over the Sabbath precept, but also over the bonds of disease.

On another Sabbath day when He entered the synagogue to preach, there was in the congregation a man with a paralyzed hand who very likely expressed by gestures his desire to be cured. Present also were some Scribes and Pharisees who, being persons of importance, occupied the first places, and who watched Jesus intently to see if He would heal the afflicted man, thus giving them a chance to accuse Him.

Our Lord, reading their inmost thoughts, took the offensive and said to the man with the withered hand: "Arise and stand forth in the midst."

A hush of expectation fell on the assembly, and all eyes were riveted on the Wonder-worker. Then, confronting His unrelenting enemies, He flung a challenge at them in the form of a question: "Is it lawful on the Sabbath to do good, or to do evil? to save a life, or to destroy it?" But no one answered. Then Jesus said to them: "What man is there among you who, if he has a single sheep and it falls into a pit on the Sabbath, will not take hold of it and lift it out? How much better is a man than a sheep! Therefore, it is lawful to do good on the Sabbath."

Then, after fixing them with a look of indignation tinged with sadness at their hardness of heart, He said to the crippled man: "Stretch forth thy hand."

The man did as he was commanded, and his hand was completely cured.

Such an obvious miracle, wrought with such solemnity, should have enlightened the minds of the Scribes and Pharisees and melted their stubborn hearts. But the contrary was the case. Furious at their humiliating defeat, for that was how they viewed it, they plotted with the Herodians, the supporters of the Idumean dynasty of Herod, and swore to put an end to the matter by killing Jesus. Their resolve was at once proof of their hatred and of their powerlessness. Hitherto they had spied on Him, accused Him before the people, and opposed Him at every step. Scribes had gone down from Jerusalem to support their fellows in Galilee in their fight against the hated Rabbi (cf. Mark 3:22). But the serene majesty of the young Prophet, His unanswerable arguments, and the evidence of His miraculous power, had made Him impervious to all their attacks. Therefore, having failed to defeat Him in open combat, they resolved to resort to violence and do away with Him.

Their defeat was all the more galling and their anger all the more bitter because they saw Christ's popularity increasing every day. The crowds flocked continually to the house where He was staying, keeping Him so occupied in ministering to their needs that He had no time even to eat (cf. Mark 3:20). The news of this intensive activity in Capharnaum passed from mouth to mouth until it reached Nazareth, considerably augmented and distorted, so that "when his own people had heard of it, they went out to lay hold of him, for they said, 'He has gone mad' " (Mark 3:21).

Our Lord's relatives had become alarmed at what they regarded as His senseless behavior, and their alarm was increased by the fact that they had always been uneasy about His missionary wanderings. Only a short time before, He had been just "the carpenter's son" who had lived most of His life in the village working with chisel and saw. But suddenly He had abandoned His workshop, left Nazareth, and, although He had had little education, had begun to preach, going from town to town and stirring up the crowds. He had even dared to set Himself up against the respected teachers of Israel. Obviously He had lost His mind and had become a crazy rabble-rouser. Accordingly, a family council was held at which His relatives decided that they would have to go in search of Him at once, seize Him and try to bring Him to His senses. They concluded that the best thing to do would be to get Him back to His carpenter's bench and have Him live quietly making yokes and ploughs. Therefore, without losing any time, they made ready to start out on the trail of their troublesome Kinsman.

To us, the attitude of our Lord's relatives seems strange and their proposal harsh, and the splendor of twenty centuries of Christianity makes it difficult for us to understand the psychology of these kinsmen of our Lord who had lived and worked with Him for thirty years, treating Him merely as an equal and failing to see in Him even the smallest indication of a special divine mission.

Other interpretations of St. Mark's rather enigmatic passage (3:21) have been suggested. Some authors say that it was not our Lord's relatives but His friends and supporters [41] from Capharnaum who set out to take Him in hand because they said (or because it was being said [42]): "He is beside himself." [43]

Or perhaps the sense is that those who were in the house with Jesus went out into the street to restrain the crowd of which they said; "It [i.e., crowd] is beside itself" with enthusiasm. This interpretation, quoted by Knabenbauer [44] and very learnedly upheld by G. Hartmann,[45] considerably simplifies the problem because, according to it, our Lord's relatives do not enter the picture at all, and there is no reference to His psychological state. However, despite its advantages, it is, in our opinion, unacceptable, and we regard the first explanation as more probable.

Meanwhile the enthusiasm of the citizens of Capharnaum had not abated but had, instead, continued to grow daily. But the contrast between our Lord's popularity with the crowds and the hatred which the Scribes and Pharisees bore Him, had created an atmosphere of tension from which He judged it prudent to withdraw in the interests of peace. Therefore He left the city, but could not prevent many people from following Him (Matt. 12:15). Yet even in His place of retirement He was confronted with His enemies.

Among the sick who were brought to Him to be cured, there was "a possesssed man who was blind and dumb." The unhappy wretch had therefore three burdens to bear, but the Divine Wonder-worker cast out the devil from him, and he immediately recovered his sight and began to speak. At the sight of the miracle the onlookers were

---

[41] Absolutely speaking this can be the sense of the expression οἱ παρ' αὐτοῦ, "his own people" (cf. 1 Mach. 9:44; 11:73; 12:27 etc.).

[42] ἔλεγον can be understood in the impersonal sense: "it was being said."

[43] In itself, ἐξέστη need not necessarily mean frenzied or insane. In many passages, e.g., Mark 2:12; 5:42, etc. it simply means to be beside oneself with admiration, amazement or some other emotion. But we believe that here, on the lips of our Lord's relatives, it is employed in a derogatory sense.

[44] In Marc., p. 107.

[45] In Bibl. Zeit., 11 (1913), 249–279.

amazed, and wonderingly asked each other: "Can this be the Son of David [i.e., the Messias]?"

The people's reaction cut the Scribes and Pharisees to the quick, and not being able to explain away the miracle which had been wrought before their eyes, some Scribes from Jerusalem made the monstrous accusation: "He has Beelzebub. . . . By the prince of devils he casts out devils" (Mark 3:22).

Such a specious claim was easy to refute. "How can Satan cast out Satan?" Jesus inquired of them; "And if a kingdom is divided against itself, that kingdom cannot stand. . . . And if Satan has risen up against himself, he is divided and cannot stand, but is at an end" (Mark 3:23–26). "And if I cast out devils by Beelzebub, by whom do your children cast them out? Therefore they shall be your judges. But if I cast out devils by the Spirit of God, then the kingdom of God has come upon you" (Matt. 12:27–28).

The issue was now clear-cut and unmistakable; it was open war between the army of Christ and that of Satan. In terse words Jesus summed up the situation: "He who is not with me is against me,[46] and he who does not gather with me scatters."

In this war, every man was a combatant; there was no such thing as neutrality.

The Scribes and Pharisees had sinned against the light, against the known truth, and had maliciously attributed to Satan the works of God. They had sinned against the Holy Spirit, and Jesus warned them that such a sin would not be forgiven: "Whoever speaks against the Son of Man, it shall be forgiven him; but whoever speaks against the Holy Spirit, it will not be forgiven him, either in this world or in the world to come."

That is, it will be forgiven only with difficulty, not because God is lacking in mercy, but because the sinner, by closing his eyes to the light, obstructs his own path to salvation and, insofar as he blinds himself, renders himself incapable of repentance.

Our Lord then closed His scarifying denouncement with the biting words: "You brood of vipers, how can you speak good things, when you are evil? For out of the abundance of the heart the mouth speaks."

The malice of the Scribes and Pharisees must indeed have been

---

[46] This seems to contradict Mark 9:40: "For who is not against you is for you." See p. 454 below for the explanation.

great to have wrung such harsh words from the lips of the Good Shepherd.

Moved by Christ's triumphant reply to His adversaries and by the majesty of His bearing, a woman in the crowd cried out: "Blessed is the womb that bore thee, and the breasts that nursed thee" (Luke 11:27).

To which Jesus modestly replied: "Rather, blessed are they who hear the word of God and keep it."

As the Fathers pointed out, these words are very consoling for us. It is within our own power to be called blessed by our Lord, for we can hear and keep the word of God; and the most blessed of all, therefore, was Christ's own Mother who had so lovingly listened to God's word and kept it to the full.

The crowds gathered around Jesus had grown bigger, and were pressing closer to Him to hear the heated debate between Him and His accusers. Some of the Scribes and Pharisees, being unable to answer our Lord's arguments, suddenly shifted their ground and issued Him a veiled challenge: "Master, we would see a sign from thee."

They had already seen many signs, but they had closed their eyes to them. Now they wanted to behold some spectacular portent such as fire coming down from Heaven as happened in the time of Elias (cf. 3 Kings 18:38), or a sudden storm with thunder and lightning as in the days of Samuel (1 Kings 12:18).

Jesus, reading their thoughts and angered at their obstinacy and hypocrisy, exclaimed: "This generation is an evil generation: it demands a sign, and no sign shall be given it but the sign of Jonas. For even as Jonas was a sign to the Ninevites, so will also the Son of Man be to this generation" (Luke 11:29–30). "For even as Jonas was in the belly of the fish three days and three nights, so will the Son of Man be three days and three nights in the heart of the earth" (Matt. 12:40).

By this He did not mean that He would work no more miracles, but only that He would not perform the spectacular feats which the Scribes and Pharisees wanted to see. Just as Jonas, by his preaching and miraculous escape, had been a sign of God's power to the Ninevites, so Jesus, too, by His preaching and the miracles He had worked, should have been recognized as the Messias. But, over and above the wonders He had already wrought, He would perform one which would crown all the rest and which would be the final proof of His divine mission—His Resurrection.

As a matter of fact, Jesus was to be in the tomb only one day and two nights; how then could He refer to three days and three nights as the length of His burial? The explanation is that the Jews reckoned even part of a day as a full one; and our Lord was in the tomb for part of Friday, all Saturday and part of Sunday. Thus, although He was to be there for only two nights, He used the common phrase for designating three days, "three days and three nights."

The Mother and Brethren of Jesus
(Matt. 12:46–50; Mark 3:31–35; Luke 8:19–21)

Our Lord's relatives did not delay in putting into effect their resolution to seek Him out and take Him in hand. No doubt they came from Nazareth to Capharnaum, and not finding Him there they followed Him to the place to which He had retired shortly before. Mary went with them, but not because she shared her kinsmen's misgivings, for she was perfectly aware of her Son's divine mission and knew that, in making His journeys, He was only doing His Father's will. Yet in such circumstances, how could she have helped being deeply anxious about the fate of her Son? Moreover, the search party may even have compelled her to accompany them; and there is the possibility that she herself wished to be present in order to prevent insult or injury being done to Jesus.

Our Lord was addressing the crowd when the unexpected visitors arrived. The newcomers wished to speak to Him, but not being able to get near Him because the house was filled with people, they had a message passed in to Him: "Behold, thy mother and thy brethren are standing outside seeking thee."

Jesus knew full well the holy sentiments which had animated His beloved Mother, but He wished to demonstrate again His sovereign independence of and detachment from the ties of flesh and blood. Therefore, in answer to the message, He said, "Who is my mother and who are my brethren?" Then, looking around on the assembly, He pointed to His disciples, and exclaimed, "Behold my mother and my brethren! For whoever does the will of my Father in heaven, he is my brother and sister and mother."

The beautiful commentary of St. Gregory the Great on this passage is well known:

Jesus deigned to call His faithful disciples brothers. . . . But if by embracing the faith, one becomes the brother of Jesus, how can one also be His mother? The explanation is that he who becomes, through faith, the brother and sister of Christ, can also become His mother through preaching. For we can truly say that we beget the Lord when we cause Him to be born in the hearts of our hearers.[47]

---

[47] *Hom. 3 in Evangelia.*

14. On the Shores
of the Lake

The Parables

Returning from His apostolic journey, Jesus once more entered Capharnaum, but not to rest; His zeal for the glory of His Father and the salvation of men urged Him on and allowed Him no repose. Therefore He did not remain long in the city, but soon left it, accompanied by His Apostles and followed by a crowd. After walking a short distance He stopped by the shore of the lake at a place where one or two boats were moored to the land in one of the small semicircular bays which are so common in this part of the lakeside. Seeing that the crowds were eager to hear Him preach, and being no less eager to teach them, our Lord went on board one of the boats so that He could face His audience and be heard by all. From this improvised pulpit, in the center of that unusual amphitheatre, He began to speak to the multitude.

From the mount a short while before, He had proclaimed the Beatitudes, the charter of the new kingdom. Now, from the sea, He was going to explain in more detail the nature and true character of this kingdom, and He was going to do so in parables, using a method that was, to a certain extent, new. Of course, the use of parables was not unknown to the authors of the Old Testament,[1] the Jews at the time of Christ, and even to

---

[1] Nathan used a true parable to bring home David's crime to him (2 Kings 12:1–4); but Joatham's lesson to the inhabitants of

profane writers. Our Lord's use of parables was new only in the sense that this seems to be the first time He employed them in His preaching.[2] At any rate, His speaking in parables was apparently so unusual that it caused His disciples to ask in surprise: "Why dost thou speak to them in parables?" (Matt. 13:10). The disciples' question is hard to explain unless there was something new in our Lord's use of this mode of preaching.[3]

A *parable* is a more or less short narrative in which words are employed in their proper sense but which is used to convey thoughts other than those that appear on the surface. It is distinct from the *allegory*, which is based on an extended metaphor, and from the *fable*, which deals with a fantastic world in which, for example, animals speak, while the parable keeps within the bounds of probability.

Not all the details of a parable have a special meaning, some being included simply to provide literary adornment or to lend vividness and flexibility to the narrative. Thus, for example, in Luke 15:4, a *hundred* sheep means only a considerable number, the specific figure being quoted simply to catch the imagination of the listeners. This point is of some importance for the correct interpretation of the parables.[4]

Sichem was conveyed by means of a fable (Judges 9:8–15). In the Old Testament the Greek word παραβολή ordinarily corresponds to the Hebrew *mashal*, but the latter has a wider meaning and is often applied to a simple proverb, e.g.: "Therefore it became a proverb. Is Saul also among the prophets?" (I Kings 10:12).

[2] He had already used images and similes in His preaching, e.g.: "You are the salt of the earth. . . . You are the light of the world. . . ." (Matt. 5:13, 14); "Do not give to dogs what is holy, neither throw your pearls before swine. . . ." (Matt. 7:6), etc. But He had not used parables properly so called, and there is not one to be found in the Gospels before the parable of the sower (Matt. 13, Mark 4, Luke 8). Certainly, in the episode of the sinful woman in Simon's house, we read what has been called the "parable" of the two debtors. But the chronological position of this incident is uncertain, and the story of the debtors scarcely deserves to be called a parable when compared with the later ones.

[3] "Talem eius docendi modum eousque fuisse insolitum, admiratione et interrogatione discipulorum satis declaratur" (Knabenbauer, *In Marc.*, p. 107).

"Here we regret to have to differ from Lagrange in the view he has expressed in *RB* (1910, p. 10). . . ," says Lebreton. "[The Apostles'] question [is] only to be understood if there had been some change in the methods employed by Him [Jesus]" (*Life and Teachings of Jesus Christ*, I, 243). Buzy is of the same opinion: "Les paraboles font leur apparition dans l'enseignement évangélique à la journée du lac" (*S. Matt.*, p. 169).

[4] Cf. *Institutiones Biblicae* (Romae, 1951), I, 455–460. Salmerón, in his treatise on the parables, *Commentarii in Evangelicam Historiam et in Acta Apostolorum*, Vol. VII, *De parabolis Domini Nostri Jesu Christi* (Coloniae Agrippianae, 1613), 16 f., makes some very apt observations on this point: "Quarto statuendum est ex doctrina B. Chrysostomi homil. 16 in ep. ad Rom. non opus esse nimia cura in

How are we to weigh the various elements of each parable and allot to each element only the scope and value which belongs to it? It is indeed a difficult task, as can readily be seen from the great variety of opinions on the exegesis of the parables. Of course, it is possible to settle upon certain principles as a norm of exegesis; [5] but actually, in the last analysis, common sense and mature reflection are the best guarantees of a correct interpretation.

Since the parables are extremely rich in content, they are usually divided systematically into several classes: *dogmatic, moral, eschatological,* parables of *mercy,* and parables of the *kingdom,* the last named category being the principal one because therein we find explained, with an abundance of detail, the character and properties of the new Kingdom, the Church which Christ came to found.

Why did our Lord teach so much of His doctrine by means of parables? If we confined ourselves solely to the concept of the parable as a pedagogical device, we could say unhesitatingly that He used it because its simplicity was well suited to the mental level of His audiences; because its concrete and tangible terms, being taken from nature, appealed to the imagination and conveyed His message very vividly; and finally because He could thereby present indirectly truths which, if proposed openly, would perhaps have been wrongly interpreted. For the people were so taken up with their material concept of the Messianic kingdom and were so easily aroused in this matter that it would not have been prudent to expound clearly the doctrine of the kingdom; therefore our Lord judged it wiser to soften the blinding light of truth with the veil of parables. That is to say, He taught in parables so that the people would more easily understand His doctrine: He adapted His teaching to their level of intelligence, thereby showing His kindness and condescension.

But some of our Lord's declarations in the Gospels regarding the parables seem to reflect more of a spirit of harshness and strict justice than one of kind condescension. The usual way to state the problem

---

singulis parabolarum verbis anxium esse; neque in singulis eius partibus adaptationem et accommodationem ad rem ipsam spiritalem et intentam investigare." He goes on to illustrate what he has said with several appropriate examples, one of which is that of the sword, which cuts only with its edge, and he concludes: "Ita in parabolis multa adferuntur quae, etsí per seipsa sensum spiritalem non efficiant, conducunt tamen ut parabola per eam partem scindat et secet, ad quod praestandum ab auctore proposita fuerat."

[5] Cf. those which Bover has listed in *Est. Bíbl.* (1944), pp. 241–246, under the title "Criterio para la interpretación de las parábolas."

presented by this contrast is to offer a choice between the theory of *justice* and the theory of *mercy*. We, however, prefer to prescind from the contrast between these two divine attributes, and to listen attentively to the spontaneous voice of the Gospel text, taking account, as far as possible, of its slightest modulations. And perhaps it would not be out of place to recall that in the solution of this difficult question we must frankly recognize the rights of philology as well as those of history and theology, and not favor one more than the others. The divine attributes of mercy and justice are not, nor can they ever be, opposed to each other, but it is possible that we may not be able to see clearly the bond that unites them.

First of all, it is certain and beyond discussion that, while the Gospel parables are well fitted to facilitate the understanding of the truth, this truth does not reach the hearers in all its splendor, but only in a veiled, semi-obscured form. Our Lord's own words to His disciples on this point are explicit: "To you it is given to know the mysteries of the kingdom of heaven, but to them it is not given" (Matt. 13:11). And to those who were closest to Him (Mark 4:11, 34) He explained fully the same truths which He had proposed in parable form to the crowds.

Why this difference in His attitude towards the people at large and His close associates? In other words, why did He speak to the crowds in parables? He Himself gives us the answer, which the three Synoptic authors have recorded: "And the disciples came up and said to him, 'Why dost thou speak to them in parables?' And he answered and said, 'To you it is given to know the mysteries of the kingdom of heaven, but to them it is not given'" (Matt. 13:10–12). "And when he was alone, those who were with him and the Twelve asked him about the parables. And he said to them, 'To you it is given to know the mystery of the kingdom of God; but to those outside, all things are treated in parables, that seeing they may see, but not perceive; and hearing they may hear, but not understand; lest perhaps at any time they should be converted, and their sins be forgiven them'" (Mark 4:10–12). "But his disciples then began to ask him what this parable meant. He said to them, 'To you it is given to know the mystery of the kingdom of God, but to the rest in parables, that seeing they may not see, and hearing they may not understand'" (Luke 8:9–11).

It is hard not to see in these texts some more or less culpable resistance to our Lord's teachings.[6] In reaction to this resistance on the part of the Jews, our Lord could have given them more light or He could have left them in their blindness. But He did neither the one nor the other. With fatherly kindness and condescension He suited His method of preaching to His hearers' dispositions, and He did so by using parables.

In His secret designs Jesus did not grant them more light—they already had sufficient—and this was an act of justice on His part. He did not abandon them, however, but went on teaching them in a way eminently suited to their psychological state; and this was an act of mercy. Therefore in His use of parables justice and mercy were mingled: there was justice in His procedure but it was tempered by mercy. We should note, however, that the element of justice consisted in His not granting the people a greater degree of light and not in His use of parables, which of themselves and in our Lord's intention tended to enlighten their minds and move their wills. The Divine Teacher did not wish to blind and harden, but rather to enlighten and convince them.[7]

However, in the Gospel passages just quoted there is one point, regarding the *object* of the parables, which should be clarified. In St. Mark we read ". . . that 'Seeing they may see, but not perceive; and hearing they may hear, but not understand; lest perhaps at any time they should be converted, and their sins forgiven them' " (4:12);

---

[6] Lagrange recognizes the Jews' culpability: "Jésus parle en paraboles parce que les Juifs n'ont pas compris et ne comprendraient pas an enseigement plus claire, *dont ils se sont d'ailleurs rendus indignes.* . . . Mais le peuple, du moins lorsqu'il subissait l'empire de ses chefs religieux, *ne s'était pas soumis de bon coeur à sa doctrine.* . . . Mais il pouvait arriver ceci, que le peuple, qui *avait fermé les yeux à la lumière,* prendrait encore moins de goût à l'enseignement des paraboles." (*Év. selon S. Matt.,* pp. 260, 262; italics are ours.) And Durand paraphrases our Lord's words thus: "Quant aux autres, ceux du dehors, adversaires ou indifférents, je leur parle en paraboles, parce que jusqu'ici ils ont regardé sans voir, ils ont entendu sans comprendre. C'est faute de bonne volonté et de sympathie qu'ils n'ont pas pris vis-à-vis de ma doctrine et de ma personne l'attitude qui fait de vous mes disciples" (*Év. selon S. Matt.,* p. 222).

There seems to be no doubt that on numerous occasions the people showed that they were unwilling to accept and follow our Lord's doctrine. As proof of this, one need only recall His words: "Woe to thee, Corozain! Woe to thee, Bethsaida!", His terrible pronouncement on Capharnaum (Matt. 11:20–24), and His sorrowful apostrophe of Jerusalem (Matt. 23:37; Luke 13:34).

[7] It is obvious that God could have given them greater internal light to enlighten their minds and greater grace to move their wills. But He did not, and who will dare to call Him to account for His mode of action?

Here we touch upon the profound mystery of Divine Providence and grace, which we are not allowed to penetrate.

while St. Luke says ". . . that, 'Seeing they may not see, and hearing they may not understand' " (8:10). In St. Matthew (13:14 *f.*) we see the fulfillment of a prophecy in Christ's use of parables:

"In them is being fulfilled the prophecy of Isaias,
    who says,
'Hearing you will hear, but not understand;
    and seeing you will see, but not perceive.
For the heart of this people has been hardened,
    and with their ears they have been hard of hearing,
And their eyes they have closed;
Lest at any time they see with their eyes, and hear
    with their ears, and understand with their mind,
And be converted, and I heal them' " (cf. Isai. 6:9 *f.*).

Therefore it will help us to interpret the Gospel text correctly if we ascertain the meaning and scope of God's words to the prophet. The Greek text of St. Matthew follows the Septuagint translation, but the original is more expressive and vigorous. God says to Isaias: "Go and say to that people: 'Hear and do not understand; see and do not recognize.' Harden the heart of that people, stop their ears, close their eyes, lest they see with their eyes, and hear with their ears, and understand with their heart, and be healed anew."

These are severe words, and some authors endeavor to soften them. In our opinion, to regard them merely as a stern admonition or as biting irony is to miss the basic intent of the passage.[8] Instead, the words were originally used in an atmosphere of justice: in the preceding chapter of Isaias (5:19) we read that the people had become so perverse that they had had the effrontery to challenge Yahweh Himself, and that He had declared: "Woe to you . . . that say: Let him make haste, and let his work come quickly, that we may see it: and let the counsel of the Holy One of Israel come that we may know it." God had sent Isaias to these people who had become so completely wrongminded that they called "evil good, and good evil . . . put darkness for light, and light for darkness" (5:20). Therefore the historical background clearly shows that the passage was concerned with retributive justice. Must we, then, interpret it to mean that God

---

[8] As do Durand (*Études,* 107 [1906], 760) and Ricciotti (*Life of Christ,* p. 375). The passage is interpreted with greater insight by Knabenbauer (*In Isaiam*), Skrinjar (*Biblica* 11 [1930], 291–321, 426–499; 12 [1931], 27–40), Condamin (*Le livre 4 d'Isaïe* [Paris, 1905]), and Feldmann (*Das Buch Isaias* [Münster, 1925–26]).

willed the damnation of His people? By no means, for God sent the prophet, not to blind and harden, but to enlighten and convert them. However He foresaw that, because of their evil will, the preaching of His prophet would only make them more obstinate than before. But since the Semitic mentality and the character of the Hebrew language make no distinction between *willing* and *permitting,* this lamentable effect of Isaias' preaching was expressed in the form of a command, so that God seemed to be positively willing that which He was merely permitting. God could certainly have changed the hearts of the people by the power of His grace, but in His inscrutable designs He did not do so; and His not doing so, His punishment of their sins by withholding from them the efficacious grace that would have converted them, justifies to some extent the use of the imperative in His instructions to Isaias, as if He Himself had positively and directly intended the effect which was to follow on the prophet's preaching. As we have already said, we here touch upon the profound and impenetrable mystery of grace; but the profundity of the mystery is no reason for diluting the true meaning of the biblical text in order to bring it down to the level of our puny minds.

In the light of this passage from Isaias, quoted explicitly by Matthew and implicitly by Mark and Luke, the real meaning of the Gospel text stands out clearly. The people had not corresponded, as they could and should have done, with the light which Jesus was giving them in the veiled form of parables. He did not use this new method of teaching for the purpose of preventing them from seeing, and it would not only be inexact but would be a very grave and impious error to say that Christ intended to blind and harden His listeners. Rather, His intention was wholly kind and merciful. He wished to enlighten them; if He had not so desired, He had only to remain silent, as St. John Chrysostom remarks. Therefore He used parables, and the subdued light which they contained was sufficient for His purpose. But His listeners were ill-disposed and refused to be enlightened and converted, thereby making themselves more culpable. Their hearts were as clay in the sun; the greater the light He shed upon them, the harder they became. Thus our Lord's use of the parables was merciful in intent and not vindictive. The particle ἵνα ("*that seeing they may see . . .*") offers no difficulty since it can still be regarded as expressing an intention (which we believe is its true sense in the text) provided that we understand it as the evangelist did, i.e., in conformity with the Semitic mentality which looked upon the *permitted* effect as really *willed,* and which therefore used words expressive of intention where we would employ terms denoting a mere *consequence.* But we ought not, nor have we the right, to modify the meaning of Semitic expressions in order to adapt them to our manner of thinking.

As we have seen, our Lord's use of parables can be viewed under the double aspect of justice and mercy; under the aspect of *justice,* not because the parables in themselves were a punishment, but because He used them as a consequence of a punishment: He denied to the Jews a greater degree of light to chastise them for their lack of co-operation with that which they had already received, but, so that they would not be left in complete darkness, He spoke to them in parables. His use of parables was *merciful* because it was a condescension to the people's weak spiritual perception and their bad dispositions, and it was, at the same time, a very effective method of imparting knowledge.

Therefore it is not exact to say that Jesus spoke in parables in order to blind and harden, nor is it any more exact to affirm that all idea of retributive justice is to be excluded from His use of parables in such a way that only mercy remains. In our opinion, both of these concepts are too one-sided. It may be difficult, and perhaps impossible, to fix precisely the border line between justice and mercy, but we maintain that both of these divine attributes intervened, and that each played its part in our Lord's decision to speak to the people in parables.

To sum up what we have said:

(1) The people had not corresponded with the clear and direct teaching of Jesus. As a punishment God had not given them a greater degree of light and grace, thereby exercising His justice.

(2) But He did not abandon them. Jesus continued to teach them, but in parables, i.e., in a veiled, semi-obscure way, in harmony with their inner dispositions, not to blind them or harden their hearts, but to enlighten and convert them. We can therefore say that in this God exercised His kindness and mercy.[9]

---

[9] The punitive character of the parables is upheld by Durand, "Pourquoi Jésus-Christ a-t-il parlé en paraboles?" *loc. cit.,* 256–271; Prat, "Nature et but des paraboles évangéliques," in *Études,* 135 (1913), 198–213. But see Prat, *Jesus Christ,* I, 320–327, where divine mercy is stressed; Fillion, *Life of Christ,* II, 687 *ff.;* Skrinjar, "Le but des paraboles sur le règne," in *Biblica* 11

Another point, of minor importance, upon which authors are not agreed, is whether some parables contain *two* or *more* truths (or morals as we would call them) which Jesus wished to inculcate, or whether, on the contrary, it should be stated as a general rule that each parable, regardless of length, contains only *one* lesson that the Divine Master desired to give us. L. Baudiment argues in favor of the second theory,[10] while Buzy discovers in the parable of the prodigal son three truths which our Lord wished to stress, and in the parable of the rich man and Lazarus he sees one main and one secondary or complementary truth, the latter being contained in Luke 16:27-31.[11] Baudiment proves his thesis mainly from the example of the tellers of fables (Aesop, Phaedrus, La Fontaine, Fénelon, and others), who never present more than one lesson or moral at a time. He also points out the advantages of this practice, the principal one being that it makes for more concentrated and lively attention on the part of the listeners. But we do not believe that the example of the fable-tellers is a sufficiently solid foundation upon which to base a judgment of our Lord's parables. One cannot reach a decision from a consideration of the parable in general as a literary form, but must examine carefully each one individually, weighing the manner in which it is formulated, its context, its aim, and the harmonious proportion of its parts. Yet even when exegetes thus dissect the individual parables, they are by no means always in agreement as to which elements are merely incidental and which are essential. Hence elements which some commentators regard as purely ornamental, are taken by others to be truths which our Lord wished to stress.

We are of the opinion that, strictly speaking, each parable con-

(1930), 291-321, 426-449; 12 (1931), 27-40—a very complete study. In favor of the so-called "mercy thesis," see Lagrange in *RB* (1910), pp. 5-36, and his commentaries; José Manuel Diaz, *Anotaciones sobre las Parábolas del Evangelio* (Bogotá, 1949), pp. 33-55; and many others.

Salmerón discusses the problem with great clarity in his magnificent treatise already referred to above (p. 372, n. 4). He defends the thesis of justice and answers the objections brought against it. See also the learned and closely-reasoned article by Holzmeister, "Vom angeblichen Verstockungszweck der Parabeln des Herrn," in *Biblica*, 15 (1934), 321-368, which provides a copious bibliography, and Buzy, *Introduction aux paraboles évangéliques* (Paris, 1912), pp. 231-413; *S. Matt.*, pp. 169 *ff*.

[10] *RB* (1946), pp. 47-55: "Les paraboles évangéliques, spécialement les plus longues, comportent-elles une ou plusieurs leçons? . . . Nous pensons donc pouvoir conclure cette étude en disant: Il semble plus conforme à la pensée de Notre-Seigneur de chercher une seule leçon dans chacune des paraboles."

[11] *Les paraboles* (Paris, 1932), pp. 203, 397 *f*.

tains only *one* lesson. But we do not thereby mean to exclude the possibility that, in driving home the principal point towards which all parts of the parable converge, Christ may have chosen to use certain elements both as background material and as secondary lessons. The parable of the prodigal son is a case in point. The climax of the story is certainly the open-armed reception given by the father to his repentant son; all the rest is aimed towards this welcome, and therefore we can truly say that the story is a perfect unit. However, this does not militate against our Lord's wishing to show also how the sinner, by turning his back on God, plunges himself into profound wretchedness, and to teach that the just should not complain but rather rejoice at the loving welcome extended to the repentant sinner. Thus it can be seen that there is no need to strive to fit all the parables into a rigid framework. By their very nature they are susceptible of a certain flexibility, and it is not an undue liberty to take this flexibility into consideration when interpreting them.

In the parable of the rich man and Lazarus, it may well be that the last section (Luke 16:27-31) is a secondary or complementary truth, but it is equally possible that it is only a prolongation of the parable intended to stress the terrible pains of hell and to throw into sharper relief the rich man's unhappy lot.

In the parable of the sower (Matt. 13:18-23; Mark 4:13-20; Luke 8:11-15), at first glance there seems to be a certain multiplicity, since our Lord Himself makes many applications of the elements contained therein. However, on closer examination, the perfect unity of thought can be discerned, for all the parts of the parable are employed to inculcate the one truth.

According to the three Synoptic Gospels, our Lord seems to have spoken eight parables on this occasion, when He was preaching from the boat on Lake Gennesareth. But it is quite possible that St. Matthew has included several which were spoken in other circumstances. Even granting that this is what happened, we have absolutely no way of knowing when and where these other parables were used, and therefore the best thing for us to do is to follow the order in which they occur in St. Matthew's Gospel. According to the first evangelist, Jesus appears to have spoken the parables on two successive days since, after the first four, He returned to the house in which He was staying (Matt. 13:36). But we may ask if this return is narrated in its proper chronological position, for immediately after the parable of the sower St. Mark (4:10) says that, Jesus being alone (i.e., alone with His disciples and apart from the crowd; Matt. 13:10 and Luke 8:9 also presuppose this), His disciples asked Him about the meaning of the parable; yet authors commonly admit that this latter episode is out of its due chronological position. Hence it is not clear whether Jesus preached from the boat for two days or only for one. The second alternative is very possibly the true one, and St. Mark (4:35) seems to hint at it.

We can say with assurance that all these parables are closely interlinked, and that they are aptly called "the parables of the *kingdom*." In fact, the expression "the kingdom of God" or "the kingdom of heaven" is found at the beginning and serves as a title for all of them except the first, that of the sower, in connection with which, however, "the kingdom of heaven" is mentioned also (cf. Matt. 13:11). Moreover, in these eight parables our Lord speaks about the founding of the kingdom, its development, the things that promote its growth and those that hinder it.

The parable of the sower (Matt. 13:1–23; Mark 4:1–20; Luke 8:4–15) enumerates the various causes which render the preaching of the Gospel unfruitful and which, consequently, hinder the establishment or the spreading of the kingdom of God:—

"Behold, the sower went out to sow. And as he sowed, some seeds fell by the wayside, and the birds came and ate them up. And other seeds fell upon rocky ground, where they had not much earth; and they sprang up at once, because they had no depth of earth; but when the sun rose they were scorched, and because they had no root they withered away. And other seeds fell among thorns; and the thorns grew up and choked them. And other seeds fell upon good ground, and yielded fruit, some a hundredfold, some sixtyfold, and some thirtyfold."

The whole parable is a beautiful picture drawn from everyday life and corresponding very closely to the condition of the soil of Palestine, particularly of the region which Jesus had in mind when narrating it. The last part, i.e., the prodigious increase of the seed that fell on good soil, is no exaggeration. For instance, in the fertile land near the Lake of Gennesareth one seed has been known to grow into four ears, each of which contained from sixty to seventy grains, so that the single seed increased between 240 and 280 times: this, however, is not the general rule.[12]

The Apostles found the parable obscure, and so, when they were alone with Jesus, they asked Him for an explanation. He told them that the seed is the word of God and that the wayside represents those who hear the word of God, but soon Satan comes and plucks away what has been sown in their hearts. The stony ground stands for the fickle, superficial souls who fall away when they meet the smallest difficulty or contradiction. The thorns are riches and excessive worldly preoccupations, which stifle the divine word. Finally, the good ground represents those who listen to God's word with sincerity, guard it carefully, and valiantly overcome all obstacles and opposition.

The parable of the slow-germinating seed (Mark 4:26–29) shows us how the kingdom of God is established in silence, and grows slowly, almost imperceptibly. The lesson to be learned here is that we must wait and hope and avoid over-impatience. "Thus is the kingdom of God; as though a man should cast seed into the earth, then sleep and rise, night and day, and the seed should sprout and grow without his knowing it. For of itself the earth bears the crop, first the blade, then the ear, then the full grain in the ear. But when the fruit is ripe, immediately he puts in the sickle because the harvest has come."

Like the seed, the kingdom of God grows in silence and in hope. God's work is not done with the speed of a lightning-flash or with the noise of an earthquake. Most of the time it is accomplished gradually and in obscurity. There is no need for us to make ill-advised and feverish efforts to hasten artificially the growth of the seed. God's hour will come and then the ripe harvest will be gathered in.

In the parable of the weeds (Matt. 13:24–30; Mark 4:33–34), which is, as it were, a confirmation of the one just quoted, we are warned not to be surprised that there are both good and evil people in God's kingdom. In our rash zeal, which is often plain impatience, we would like to expel the evildoers at once. But this parable teaches us to be long-suffering in their regard, because they may be converted as time goes by. And even if they go on doing evil to the end, the hour will come when they will be punished as they have deserved.

[12] Cf. *Biblica*, 8 (1927), 84 *f.* where several very curious cases in point are quoted. An interesting article by Dalman in *PJB*, 22 (1926), 120–132, provides an excellent commentary on the parable; cf. pp. 129–131 in particular.

Here our Lord compared the kingdom of heaven to a man who sowed good seed in his field, but while he slept his enemy came and sowed weeds among the wheat. When the blades sprang up and bore fruit, the weeds appeared also. The householder's servants, seeing the weeds, said to him: "Sir, didst thou not sow good seed in thy field? How then does it have weeds?" He replied: "An enemy has done this." Then they asked him: "Wilt thou have us go and gather them up?" "No," he said, "lest in gathering the weeds you root up the wheat along with them. Let both grow together until the harvest; and at harvest time I will say to the reapers, Gather up first the weeds, and bind them in bundles to burn; but the wheat gather into my barn."

The disciples asked our Lord for an explanation of this parable also, and He kindly gave it to them. He who sowed good seed is the Son of Man; the field is the world; the good seed represents the children of the kingdom; and the weeds are the children of the evil one (i.e., the devil). The enemy who sowed the weeds is the devil, the harvest is the end of the world, and the reapers are the angels. The Son of Man will send His angels, who will gather up from His kingdom "all scandals and all those who work iniquity and [will] cast them into the furnace of fire, where there will be the weeping and the gnashing of teeth. Then the just will shine forth like the sun in the kingdom of their Father." Jesus ended His lesson with the grave admonition: "He who has ears to hear, let him hear."

In the parable of the grain of mustard seed (Matt. 13:31–32; Mark 4:30–32; Luke 13:18–19), our Lord foretold how the kingdom of God would, from humble beginnings, reach magnificence and splendor:—

"The kingdom of heaven is like a grain of mustard seed, which a man took and sowed in his field. This indeed is the smallest of all the seeds; but when it grows up it is larger than any herb and becomes a tree, so that the birds of the air come and dwell in its branches."

The parable of the leaven (Matt. 13:33; Luke 13:20–21) shows us the power of the kingdom of heaven to transform all things, just as the parable of the grain of mustard seed demonstrates its power of expansion. It could be said that the former refers to quality, and the latter to quantity. "The kingdom of heaven is like leaven, which a woman took and buried in three measures of flour, until all of it was leavened." (A "measure," Vulgate *"satum,"* was equal to about twelve quarts.)

The two parables of the hidden treasure and the pearl of great price (Matt. 13:44–46) point out how precious and desirable is the kingdom of heaven, and they teach us that we ought to seek it with all our strength, sacrificing everything else for it. The lesson is practically the same as that of Luke 14:33: "Every one of you who does not renounce all that he possesses, cannot be my disciple"; "The kingdom of heaven is like a treasure hidden in a field; a man who finds it hides it, and in his joy goes and sells all that he has and buys that field. Again, the kingdom of heaven is like a merchant in search of fine pearls. When he finds a single pearl of great price, he goes and sells all that he has and buys it." Or as our Lord said elsewhere: "Only one thing is needful" (Luke 10:42); "For what does it profit a man, if he gain the whole world, but suffer the loss of his own soul? Or what will a man give in exchange for his soul?" (Matt. 16:26).

Finally, the parable of the net (Matt. 13:47–50), confirming that of the weeds, shows us that good men and evil live side by side in the world, but that in the end each type will meet a very different fate: "The kingdom of heaven is like a net cast into the sea and gathering in fish of every kind. When it was filled, they hauled it out, and sitting down on the beach, they gathered the good fish into vessels, but threw away the bad. So will it be at the end of the world. The angels will go out and separate the wicked from among the just, and will cast them into the furnace of fire, where there will be the weeping, and the gnashing of teeth."

When He had finished speaking these parables, Jesus turned to His disciples, who were near Him, and asked them: "Have you understood all these things?"

And they answered: "Yes."

Jesus said to them: "So then, every Scribe instructed in the kingdom of heaven is like a householder who brings forth from his storeroom things new and old," that is, as Maldonatus says, he is like a man who has an abundance of everything or like one who has at his disposal new garments and old. Thus the disciples, who were one day to be teachers skilled in the doctrine of the kingdom, would instruct the faithful, harmonizing the old teachings, which would continue to be true, with the new lessons of the Gospel.

Calming the Tempest: The Gerasene Demoniac
(Matt. 8:23–34; Mark 4:35; 5:20; Luke 8:22–39; cf. Maps III and IV)

Evening was already falling when Jesus dismissed the crowd which for many hours had been hanging on His words as He spoke from the boat. Without returning to land,[13] He commanded the Apostles to set sail for the eastern shore of the lake, towards the territory of the Gerasenes. This region certainly lay on the eastern side of the lake, but it is very difficult, though not impossible, to define its position more closely. There is scarcely a place on the whole eastern shore that has not been suggested by some author or other as the home of the Gerasenes. Some commentators, taking their stand on the reading "Gadarenes" which is found in some manuscripts,[14] locate it at Gadara, the present small town of Umm Keis, situated on a spur of the hills on the southern side of the Wadi Yarmuk. This identification has little probability since Gadara (Umm Keis) is far from the lake (about 7½ miles), from which it is separated by a deep valley through which runs a turbulent river, the Hieromax of the ancients. Others prefer Qal'at el-Hosn, farther to the north and overlooking the lake: this was ancient Hippos, where even today one can see numerous tombs which may well be those referred to in the Gospel.[15] Still others favor the place known as el-Hammi Moqa'edlo,

---

[13] Prat (op. cit., I, 331) and Fouard (The Christ, I, 308) presuppose that Jesus returned to Capharnaum for a short while before crossing the lake. But St. Mark (4:35) gives the impression that He did not go ashore, but dismissed the crowd there beside the lake and not in the city: "And sending away the crowd, they took him just as he was, in the boat." That is how Fillion, Lagrange, and Lebreton understand the matter.

[14] The name of the region presents a thorny problem of textual criticism. Generally speaking, the accepted readings are: in Matthew 8:28, "Gadarenes"; Mark 5:1, "Gerasenes"; Luke 8:26, "Gergesenes." Lagrange studies the problem in Év. selon S. Marc, pp. 132–135, and discounts the reading "Gergesenes" as being due to the influence of Origen. Bover deals with the same question in Sefarad 12 (1952), 275–280, and decides in favor of "Gergesenes," a reading which he admits in Matthew and Luke: of Mark he says that "the variant, 'Gerasenes,' accepted by almost all the critics, is founded on documentary evidence that is too weak to support it" (p. 280).

In our humble opinion, the documentary evidence on the whole question is too intricate and confused to allow of a definite and well-founded decision, while the topographical data available do not seem to offer a sufficiently solid basis for a really satisfactory conclusion. All we can say with certainty is that, if the variant "Gadarenes" is connected with the city of Gadara (present-day Umm Keis), then it must be discarded, since this city cannot be the one referred to in the Gospel.

[15] Thus Neumann, followed by Lagrange, in RB (1895), pp. 520 f. Refuted by Dalman in PJB (1911), p. 22.

Raad Photo

LAKE OF GENNESARETH: *a storm.*

about two miles farther north, where there is a small spring of
sulphurous water and where, probably, unclean animals were disposed of by being thrown into the lake. It is very probable that our
Lord disembarked at the mouth of the Wadi es-Samak, which lies
about 1¼ miles north of el-Hammi Moqa'edlo, across from Magdala
and closer to Capharnaum than the Wadi ed-Jamusiyeh and the
Wadi en-Negeb.[16] It is very easy to see how Jesus, having landed here,
could have ascended the gentle slope on the southern side of the Wadi
es-Samak and come out on the promontory which reaches almost to
the water and from which the swine could have been precipitated into
the lake. No great importance need be attached to the fact that this
headland does not fall sharply, but levels off towards the water; if the
swine were driven headlong down the steep slope by the unclean
spirits, their momentum would have been sufficient to plunge them
into the lake. This topogaphical evidence is confirmed to some extent

---

[16] Many authors hold this view, e.g., Guérin, Dalman, Prat, Buzy. Lagrange at first
   rejected (*RB* [1895], 519), but later accepted it (*The Gospel of Jesus Christ,*
   I, 185).

by the archaeological fact that at the entrance to the valley there are some ancient ruins, whose date unfortunately cannot be precisely fixed. These ruins are known as Kursi, a name that could be a corruption of Gergesa or Gerasa since the consonants are similar. Therefore this could be the site of the ancient town.

When Jesus and his disciples set sail towards the land of the Gerasenes, the lake was calm and their little vessel glided swiftly and silently over the smooth waters. The Apostles talked quietly together, confident that within two hours, before night had fallen, they would put into port on the opposite shore, for the distance was only about 7½ miles. They were very far from suspecting that a sudden storm would put their faith and confidence to the test and would give their Divine Master an opportunity to show striking proof of His sovereign power.

Beneath its smiling, tranquil appearance, the tiny Sea of Galilee always carries the threat of a raging storm. Situated as it is 680 feet below the level of the Mediterranean, and hemmed in by an almost continuous belt of high hills, it lies at the mercy of the winds that sweep down on it from the snowy peak of Mount Hermon, turning its waters into a witch's cauldron and making the waves rear up like fiery steeds at the cut of the whip. That is what now happened to the lake which had been so peaceful, without the least sign of the approaching storm, when the Apostles and their Master had set out from the little bay.

During the first part of the crossing, Jesus had taken advantage of the quiet interval to rest after the toils of the day. He had lain down in the stern of the boat, with His head on the cushion, as St. Mark observes (4:38). This cushion probably consisted of a soft leather case stuffed with wool, which was used by the sailors themselves or reserved, perhaps, for the comfort of any distinguished passenger who happened to be on board. Apparently it was a part of the ordinary equipment of the boat, for the evangelist uses the definite article ("on *the* cushion": τὸ προσκεφάλαιον), as if referring to something that everybody knew about and would expect to find on board. How lovingly the angels must have contemplated their King and Lord as He who watches from all eternity lay sleeping on the hard wood, as He who holds the entire universe in the palm of His hand lay spent with fatigue!

Suddenly the Apostles stopped speaking and scanned the horizon with anxious eyes. From long experience they knew that a storm was brewing fast, and they were not wrong, for a squall swept down on them with lightning speed, threatening to swamp the boat. But Jesus slept on undisturbed. At first they let Him sleep while they lowered the sail, got out the oars, and used all their seafaring skill to avert the danger that threatened them. But the lake grew wilder every moment and the boat ran the risk of being swallowed by the waves. It was only then, as a last resort, that they had recourse to Jesus, crying: "Lord, save us! we are perishing!"; or, in the more vivid expression of St. Mark: "Master, does it not concern thee that we are perishing?" Their words reveal how frightened they were and how they had almost lost hope of escaping alive. But was not He with them, He who had said: "I have set the sand a bound for the sea. . . . And the waves thereof shall toss themselves and shall not prevail: they shall swell, and shall not pass over it" (Jer. 5:22)?

Upon being so rudely awakened, Jesus asked them reproachfully: "Why are you fearful, O you of little faith?" Then rebuking the wind and the sea, He said, "Peace, be still!"

At once the wind fell and there came a great calm, so that all who were in the boat said to each other: "Who then is this, that even the wind and the sea obey him?"

Night had long since fallen when they finally came to land, tired and worn out by the storm, so that they were content to cast anchor close inshore and spend the remaining hours of darkness sleeping in the boat as they had so often done before. At dawn the next day they landed, but scarcely had they begun to walk up the sloping shore than they met a man possessed by an evil spirit, of whose ferocity the evangelist has painted a fearsomely realistic portrait. This poor demoniac spent his life wandering among the tombs howling and gashing himself with stones, and was so fierce that no one could restrain him, for he could break fetters and chains as if they were so much thread. "And when he saw Jesus from afar, he ran and worshipped him, and crying out with a loud voice, he said:

" 'What have I to do with thee, Jesus, Son of the most high God? I adjure thee by God, do not torment me!'

"For he [Jesus] was saying to him, 'Go out of the man, thou unclean spirit.'

"And he [Jesus] asked him [the spirit], 'What is thy name?' And he said to him 'My name is Legion, for we are many.' And he entreated him [Jesus] earnestly not to drive them out of the country."

On the slopes of the mountain leading down to the lake, a large herd of some two thousand swine was feeding. The spirits besought Jesus to let them enter these swine. When He gave them permission to go, the unclean spirits, leaving the man, entered the swine, which then rushed headlong down the steep slope and were drowned in the sea.

The amazement and terror of the swineherds can readily be imagined. Half-crazed with fear, they took to their heels and brought the news to the nearby city. When, as was to be expected, a large crowd of curiosity seekers came out to view the scene of the miracle, they found the former demoniac sitting at the feet of Jesus, clothed and in his right mind. The sight convinced them that some supernatural power had been at work, and they were filled with fear. But instead of recognizing the power and kindness of Jesus and inviting Him to stay with them as had the Samaritans, the wretched Gerasenes, dismayed at the loss of their swine, begged Him to leave their district. Jesus, acceding to their boorish request, made ready to depart, but just as He was boarding the boat, the man whom He had delivered from the devils and who had followed Him down to the shore, begged to be allowed to go with Him. But the good Master, wishing him to be an apostle in his own country, said kindly to him: "Go home to thy relatives, and tell them all that the Lord has done for thee. . . ."

The man did as he was bid, going through the city and relating in the Decapolis the wonders Jesus had done for him, so that everyone marvelled.

Diabolical Possession

To judge by the numerous occasions on which our Lord cast out devils, diabolical possession must have been surprisingly common in Israel at the time. Some authors maintain that there was really no question of possession, but only of simple physical ailments whose effects or symptoms were sometimes so bizarre that they were popularly regarded as signs of diabolical intervention. It is, of course, possible that the symptoms of merely natural diseases were at times taken to be manifestations of the devil's presence. But it is wrong to hold that such erroneous diagnosis was the rule and that all the cases of possession recorded in the Gospel were simply due to natural sickness. The abundance of concrete details which accompanied our Lord's expulsion of the devils leaves no room for doubt that He was dealing with true diabolical possession. For example, the words which the man in the synagogue at Capharnaum cried out to our Lord (Luke 4:31–37) could not have been spoken by a madman or an epileptic. Instead, they clearly reveal the presence of a superior being who was using the wretched man as a mouthpiece. Again, in the episode at Gerasa (Luke 8:26–39; Matt. 8:28–34), why did our Lord ask, "What is thy name?" if the man was not a victim of possession? And how else can one explain why the herd of swine plunged down the cliff into the lake?

The partisans of the *Formgeschichte* school will have no difficulty in finding an answer to these questions of ours. They will simply say that the Gospel account is the fruit of the Christian community's gradual elaboration on the actual facts, and that it does not describe an historical reality. This is not the place to refute the *Formgeschichte* theory, which opens the way to all kinds of arbitrary assertions and which would require many pages of refutation. We have already dealt briefly with the matter before.[17] Suffice it to say that St. Matthew was an eyewitness of the episode at Gerasa and has left us a detailed description of it. The circumstances of the incident were such that they must have remained clear in his memory, so that when he came to write his Gospel, he described the episode as he saw it happen and not as the Christian community might have elaborated upon it.

In an attempt to eliminate the probative value of our Lord's procedure at Gerasa, some may hold that He adapted His actions to popular opinion and treated as diabolical possession an affliction which He knew was purely natural. But such an hypothesis is rendered untenable by certain details of the incident which would not be affected even if our Lord had accommodated Himself to popular ignorance, e.g., the devil's reply, the swines' rushing down into the lake. Then, too, not only in the presence of the crowds, but also in private conversation with His Apostles, Christ clearly showed that He acknowledged the fact of possession; for example, on the occasion

[17] See above, pp. 59 *ff*.

of the curing of the possessed boy at the foot of Mount Thabor, He said to the Apostles: "This kind [of devil] can only be cast out by prayer and fasting" (Matt. 7:20).

Why were there so many cases of possession precisely in our Lord's day? Before attempting to answer this question we must point out that even though no particular cause for the frequency of the phenomenon could be found, there would still be no grounds for denying the reality of so many well-proven incidents. There is no doubt that the powers of darkness never waged fiercer war against God than when the Incarnate Word came on earth. With the coming of Jesus, "the prince of this world" saw that his domination over men was gravely threatened. The subsequent battle between good and evil, light and darkness, Christ and Belial is vividly and constantly portrayed in the pages of the Gospel. Hardly had Christ begun His immediate preparations for His public ministry than the devil launched three subtle but nonetheless mortal attacks against Him in the desert. And only a few hours before His death, at the Last Supper, our Lord put His Apostles on their guard against His and their implacable enemy: "Simon, Simon, behold Satan has desired to have you, that he may sift you as wheat" (Luke 22:31). During His earthly life He repeatedly referred to the unrelenting conflict which was to end in Satan's defeat: "I was watching Satan fall as lightning from heaven" (Luke 10:18); "Now will the prince of the world be cast out" (John 12:31).

When reviewed in this light, the frequency of diabolical possession in our Lord's day seems less surprising. The devil, feeling Christ's overwhelming strength and realizing that he was powerless to resist it, turned the full force of his despairing wrath on men. But here, too, he met defeat and was compelled to acknowledge Jesus as "the Holy One of God" (Luke 4:34).

15. Return to

Capharnaum

The Daughter of Jairus:
The Woman With the Issue of Blood
(Matt. 9:1, 18–26; Mark 5:21–43; Luke 8:40–56)

The three Synoptic Gospels give the impression that Jesus did not spend the night in the district of the Gerasenes but returned to Capharnaum the same day. However, as we have pointed out above, the cure of the demoniac took place, not on the evening of His arrival, but on the following morning.

Upon disembarking at Capharnaum, Jesus was given a reception very different from the one He had received from the ungrateful, fear-ridden Gerasenes. The crowd to which He had preached from the boat had followed Him with their eyes as He sailed away to the other side of the lake; and it is probable that many of them had either remained where they were, patiently awaiting His return, or had come back the following day in the hope of seeing Him again. When they finally caught sight of His boat drawing near, they no doubt sent news to their friends, so that a large crowd soon gathered to greet Him as He stepped ashore. As St. Luke tells us: "the crowd welcomed Him, for they were all waiting for him." When He and His Apostles disembarked they were greeted joyfully, and the people crowded around Him to express their welcome, each one trying to get as near Him as possible. But suddenly the throng fell back to make way for a person of great importance who had come to ask Jesus for a favor. The newcomer was none other than Jairus, a leader of the synagogue or *archisynagogus,* who straightway fell at our Lord's feet, begging: "My daughter is at the point of death; come, lay thy hands upon her, that she may be saved and live."

The heart of Jesus was moved by the anguished father's tears, and granting him his request, He started to return with him to his house. Naturally, the whole crowd followed them, both out of love for Jesus and out of curiosity to see the miracle that was about to be wrought. While they were making their way to the house, our Lord suddenly stopped and, turning around, said with an air of surprise: "Who touched me?"

Everyone who heard wondered at His question, not knowing what to think, because many people must have touched Him, some even thoughtlessly crowding close to Him. Nobody dared answer Him at first; but then Peter, with his resolute character and the freedom which he derived from the confidence his Master reposed in him, said with a tinge of reproach in his voice: "Master, the crowds throng and press upon thee, and dost thou say, 'Who touched me?' "

Well could the evangelist have added here the observation which he later made on the occasion of the Transfiguration, that Peter asked this question "not knowing what he said."

Jesus, however, insisted and reiterated gravely: "Someone touched me." Then He told them how He knew: "For I perceived that power had gone forth from me."

Many people had touched Him, but casually and by chance: only one had done so deliberately. The crowd waited expectantly for something to happen, for they sensed a mystery here. The Apostles did not know what to think, and Peter must have felt somewhat chagrined, as our Lord continued to stand where He was, as if waiting for someone to confess. No longer did the people press about Him; reverently they had drawn back to a respectful distance. For a long moment nothing happened, but finally a woman detached herself from the throng and came timidly towards Him. For twelve years she had been afflicted with an issue of blood, and although she had undergone many painful treatments at the hands of physicians, and had spent all her money, she had obtained no relief. However, she had heard what the people were saying about Jesus, and had made her way through the crowd so that she could touch the hem of His cloak, for she was confident that mere contact with His clothing would cure her. Now that her plan was discovered, she fearfully approached our Lord, and throwing herself at His feet, told Him why she had touched Him and how her affliction had been healed the moment she had done so. But Jesus reassured her kindly: "Daughter, thy faith hath saved thee; go in peace."

He had scarcely finished speaking when one of Jairus' servants came running up to his master with the sad news: "Thy daughter is dead; do not trouble him [Jesus]."

They had hoped that He would cure the girl, but now they either did not dare to ask Him to raise her from the dead, or perhaps the thought never even occurred to them. But the Sacred Heart gives more than is requested. Turning to the sorrowing father, Jesus said: "Do not be afraid; only have faith and she shall be saved."

As they drew near the house, they could hear the sound of flutes, the wails of the mourners, and the noise of the crowd that had gathered. When finally they arrived, Jesus said to the bystanders: "Why do you make this din, and weep? The girl is asleep, not dead."

But they laughed scornfully at Him, for they well knew that she was dead. Yet their expectation and curiosity were aroused and they all wanted to go into the house to see what He would do. However, He allowed only His three beloved disciples, Peter, James, and John, and the girl's parents to go with Him to the room where she lay. Taking the dead child by the hand, He said: *"Talitha, cumi!*—Girl, arise!"

Immediately the child sat up and held out her arms to her mother. What a tableau of majestic power and tender love!

At Nazareth
(Luke 4:16–30; cf. Matt. 13:54–58; Mark 6:1–6; cf. Maps II and V)

On His journeys, Jesus must often have passed through Nazareth, the village which held such sweet memories for Him, and in which He had passed the tranquil years of His childhood and youth. But it was only now, almost at the end of His second year of public life, that He came to pay a protracted visit to His own village.[1]

---

[1] We do not know whether His coming was only a part of another long missionary journey or whether He went there directly from Capharnaum. If the latter was the case, then He probably crossed the plain of Gennesareth, ascended the Wadi

The small church which has been in the hands of the Greek Uniates since 1741 is pointed out as the site of the synagogue where Jesus read the passage from Isaias (61:1 f.). This tradition is a recent one, apparently dating back only to Burchard of Mount Sion (1283), who writes: "One can still see in [Nazareth] the synagogue, now converted into a church, where the Book of Isaias was handed to Jesus, who was teaching there." [2] However, since the spot is situated in what was undoubtedly ancient Nazareth and since there is no positive reason to question this identification, we may accept the tradition as probably correct.[3] It was this place, then, that formed the stage for the dramatic scene recorded by the Synoptic writers and described with a wealth of vivid detail by St. Luke in particular.

Strange though it may seem, our Lord was in a very delicate situation in His own home town. The inhabitants of Nazareth probably shared by now the enthusiasm which His preaching and miracles had aroused in the rest of Galilee, and they were doubtless very proud of Him and regarded His glory as their own or at least as redounding to their credit, since they were His fellow townsmen. But their natural self-satisfaction was offset by a certain resentment which at the slightest provocation could turn into open hostility. For had not Jesus, the great Worker of miracles, left Nazareth to take up residence in Capharnaum just when He had begun to show Himself to the world? And had He not wrought many miracles in and around Capharnaum, but had not deigned to perform even one in His own town? Thus His reception at Nazareth must have been somewhat

el-Hammam and, bearing to the right, towards the west, passed through Cana of Galilee, and from thence on to Nazareth, a seven or eight-hour walk in all.

[2] "Et est adhuc in ea [Nazareth] synagoga, sed in ecclesiam commutata, in qua Ihesu docente traditus est liber Ysaie. . . . " (cf. Baldi, *Enchiridion*, p. 12). The anonymous Pilgrim of Piacenza (A.D. 570) speaks of a synagogue, but gives no identifying details. For other writers see *ibid*.

[3] Dr. Klement Kopp in his *Nazareth und seine Heiligtümer* in *Das Heilige Land in Vergangenheit und Gegenwart* (1950), pp. 63–95, first reviews the available tradition and then concludes that the present Greek Uniate church could not be the successor to the synagogue because the site it occupies lies outside the old town (pp. 81–84). He locates Jewish Nazareth (the Nazareth of Jesus) beside Mary's Well and says that the town began to occupy its present site only during the Byzantine period. He points out that there are many caves and underground passages marking the location of the primitive town, which, he asserts, dates back to 2000 B.C and beyond (cf. *loc cit.*, pp. 63 f., and *JPOS* [1938], pp. 189 ff.). But Dalman (*Sacred Sites and Ways*, pp. 260 f.) believes that Nazareth already occupied its present site in the time of Christ, and he regards as solidly probable the identification of the synagogue with the Greek Uniate church (*ibid.*, p. 68). We, too, accept this identification as probable, but not as certain.

cool, although the people probably rejoiced at His arrival because they hoped to see a demonstration of His miraculous power.

While He was in the little town, the Sabbath day came around and, as was His custom, He went to the synagogue. The usual service was made up of two parts: the first and less important one consisted in the saying of various prayers; the second and principal part was the reading of the five books of Moses; these were divided into sections so that the whole would be read over a certain period, which in Palestine, at least in later times, was three years. Sometimes the reading of the Prophets was omitted; but we know that it was still observed in the New Testament era (cf. Luke 16:31; Acts 13:15, 27). The readers were not self-elected but were designated by the ruler of the synagogue, the *archisynagogus,* and were handed the scroll by the *hazzan,* who was a kind of sacristan. No prescriptions were laid down regarding instruction or commentary on the Law or the Prophets; it was given only when someone in the congregation was skilled enough to undertake it. In Acts 13:15 we read how, during the services in the synagogue, Paul and Barnabas were invited to speak, although they were only visitors in the place. The service usually ended with the blessing by the priests, the descendants of Aaron.[4]

We can picture the friendly curiosity which our Lord's presence must have excited in the congregation, many of whom had doubtless either seen or heard of the miracles He had worked. Naturally, they marvelled how the young Tradesman, the Son of Mary, whose relatives were well known to them, could do and say the wonderful things He was credited with; and they could scarcely wait to hear Him speak. Therefore when the prayers, the *Shema'* and the *Tefillah* [5] had been said, and the reading of a *parasha,* or section of the Torah, was finished, it was only to be expected that Jesus should be invited to read and comment upon a *haftarah,* or passage from the Prophets. He accepted the invitation, and mounting the pulpit, opened the scroll of Isaias, from which He read the well-known Messianic passage (61: 1 *f.*):

---

[4] Cf. *Mishnah, Megillah* 4:1 *ff.* where many detailed prescriptions for the readings are laid down; Dalman, *Jesus-Jeshua,* pp. 38–55; and in particular, the excursus entitled "Der altjüdische Synagogengottesdienst" in Str.-Bill., IV, 153–188, which is followed by another dealing with the *Shema'* (pp. 189–207), and a third, on the *Shemoneh 'Esreh,* i.e., the *Tefillah* or *Eighteen (Blessings)* (pp. 208–249).
[5] Cf. pp. 501 *f.* below.

The Spirit of the Lord is upon me;
because he has anointed me;
To bring good news to the poor he has sent me,
to proclaim to the captives release, and
sight to the blind;
To set at liberty the oppressed, to proclaim
the acceptable year of the Lord,
and the day of recompense.

When He had finished reading, He rolled up the scroll, returned it to the *hazzan,* and sat down. With bated breath and eyes fixed intently upon Him, the congregation waited to hear His commentary. Simply, but with great authority, He announced: "Today this Scripture has been fulfilled in your hearing."

Then He went on to comment on the prophecy with such skill and sublime simplicity that His listeners were vociferous in their approval, and they marvelled at hearing such wisdom from one whom they had known as a lowly tradesman: "Is not this Joseph's son?" they asked each other in amazement.

With His majestic yet modest bearing, and His profound yet clear teaching, Jesus had won their hearts. Their prejudices seemed to have vanished and they appeared lost in admiration of their compatriot who had spoken such things to them. But some of them were not wholly satisfied and maintained their attitude of reserve, bordering on hostility. They still deeply resented His preference for Capharnaum; they thought and perhaps murmured to each other that if He wanted them to believe Him, then He ought not merely to speak to them but should perform some of those miracles which He had worked in the city by the lake. Moreover, did not they, His fellow-townsmen, have a prior claim on Him?

Jesus, answering their innermost thoughts, or perhaps even their spoken complaints, said to them: "You will surely quote me this proverb, 'Physician, cure thyself! Whatever things we have heard of as done in Capharnaum, do here also in thy own country.' . . . Amen I say to you, no prophet is acceptable in his own country."

He meant that their having known and lived with Him before He had done anything to distinguish Himself was to a certain extent an obstacle to their believing in Him. Continuing, He said:

"In truth I say to you, there were many widows in Israel in the days of Elias, when heaven was shut up for three years and six

NAZARETH: *The Church of the Maronites, probably on the site of the "Precipice."*

months, and there came a great famine all over the land; and to none of them was Elias sent, but only to a woman, a widow in Sarepta of Sidon (cf. 3 Kings 17:19; 18:1). And there were many lepers in Israel in the time of Eliseus the prophet; and not one of them was cleansed, but only Naaman the Syrian (cf. 4 Kings 5:9 *ff.*)."

His meaning was quite clear: Elias and Eliseus, unacknowledged in their own country, had worked miracles for foreigners. The listeners understood the implication and regarded it as an insult. The malcontents among them were loud in their protests and they suc-ceeded in swinging the rest over to their side. The old resentment flared up again, and they cried out with indignant contempt: "Where did he get this wisdom and these miracles? Is not this the carpenter's son? Is not his mother called Mary, and his brethren James and Joseph and Simon and Jude?[6] And his sisters, are they not all with us? Then where did he get all this?" Neither His eloquence nor His virtue counted for anything with them now, inflamed as they were with wrath. Indeed, they lashed themselves into such a fury that they finally seized Him and dragged Him out of the town to a high place

[6] See what we have said above, pp. 239–242, about these brethren of Jesus.

on the side of the mountain from which they intended to cast Him down. But His hour had not yet come, and "he, passing through their midst, went his way." His serenity and majestic calm stayed their hands and none of them dared to commit the intended sacrilege.

In Nazareth there is still to be seen a sanctuary which is venerated as the site of the *Precipice*. In the *Commemoratorium de casis Dei* (*c.* A.D. 800) [7] we read that, a mile from Nazareth, there was a church dedicated to our Lady at the place of the Precipice; and in *De situ urbis Jerusalem* (A.D. 1130) we are told that: "a mile from Nazareth, to the south, is the place which is called *the precipice*." [8] These two documents are referring to Jebel el-Qafseh, overlooking the plain of Esdrelon 1¼ miles from Nazareth, on the slope of which one can still see an apse cut into the rock and traces of an ancient monastery. But this identification does not seem to fit in with St. Luke's description (4:29) in which he relates that the crowd led Jesus out to the brow, or height, or peak (ἕως ὀφρύος) of the mountain on which their town was built.[9] Therefore the mountain could not be 1¼ miles from Nazareth. A site which is in perfect accord with the Gospel text is the rocky precipice near the Maronite church, which stands on higher ground than the Greek Uniate church. This precipice forms part of Jebel es-Sikh and is located on the outskirts of the town.

Sending the Apostles to Preach
(Matt. 10:1–42; Mark 6:7–13; Luke 9:1–6)

It was about this time that Jesus sent His Apostles on an experimental missionary journey: however, we do not know exactly where the event took place.[10] Up to that moment they had been constantly with their Master, accompanying Him on His apostolic journeys and never leaving His side for long, for they were, so to speak, doing their apprenticeship, their novitiate. But now Jesus

---

[7] Cf. Tobler, *Descriptiones Terrae Sanctae ex saeculo VIII, IX, XII et XV* (Leipzig, 1874), p. 81.

[8] Cf. Baldi, *Enchiridion,* p. 12.

[9] It is true that the word ὄρος which St. Luke uses can, in itself, be understood of a group of mountains. However, in view of the configuration of the country about Nazareth, it is very difficult to see how this could have been the evangelist's meaning.

[10] Prat (*Jesus Christ,* I, 351) believes that it occurred on or just before His arrival at Nazareth. From St. Mark (6:1) we know that the Apostles went with Jesus to His home town; but the evangelist does not say that they stayed there.

decided that the time had come for them to stand on their own feet and work by themselves.

St. Mark (6:7) has preserved for us the interesting detail that the Apostles went out in pairs to preach, and from St. Matthew, who lists them all by name (10:2–4), we can perhaps deduce the order in which they were sent, namely, Peter and Andrew, James and John, Philip and Bartholomew, Thomas and Matthew, James, the son of Alpheus, and Thaddeus, Simon the Cananean and Judas Iscariot.

Before they went, Jesus outlined for them the theme for their preaching—*the kingdom of God;* He bestowed on them the power to cast out devils and heal the sick, and gave them a series of practical directions, which we find set down at length in St. Matthew (10:5–16), telling them *to whom* they were to preach, the *poverty* they were to observe, and the *way* in which they were to receive hospitality:

"Do not go in the direction of the Gentiles, nor enter the towns of Samaritans; but go rather to the lost sheep of the house of Israel. And as you go, preach the message, 'The kingdom of heaven is at hand!' Cure the sick, raise the dead, cleanse the lepers, cast out devils. Freely you have received, freely give. Do not keep gold, or silver, or money in your girdles, no wallet for your journey, nor two tunics, nor sandals, nor staff; [11] for the laborer deserves his living.

"And whatever town or village you enter, inquire who in it is worthy; and stay there until you leave. As you enter the house, salute it. If then that house be worthy, your peace will come upon it; but if it be not worthy, let your peace return to you. And whoever does not receive you, or listen to your words—go forth outside that house or town, and shake off the dust from your feet. Amen I say to you, it

---

[11] St. Mark (6:8–9) permits a *staff* in the hand and *sandals* on the feet. Several ways of harmonizing St. Matthew's and St. Mark's accounts have been suggested: (1) Jesus gave each set of instructions on a different occasion (cf. Knabenbauer); (2) a staff for carrying a bundle of clothing, and shoes in the strict sense, were forbidden, but a staff for walking and simple sandals were allowed (Prat, *op. cit.,* I, 349, n. 8, c); (3) shepherds used to carry two sticks, one, a club or bludgeon, for defense, the other, a simple staff for walking or for guiding the sheep; the first was forbidden, while the second was allowed (Power, *Biblica,* 4 [1923], 241–266); (4) the two evangelists are really saying the same thing since they merely wish to indicate that the Apostles were commanded to practice extreme poverty, a state which certainly allows the carrying of a staff and the wearing of sandals; thus Knabenbauer, following Maldonatus, who writes: "Contrariis verbis eandem uterque sententiam eleganter expressit; uterque enim non Christi verba, sed sensum exponens voluit significare Christum apostolis praecepisse ne quid haberent praeter ea quae essent in praesentem usum necessaria." Durand, Buzy, Pirot and others are of the same opinion.

will be more tolerable for the land of Sodom and Gomorrah in the day of judgment than for that town."

To these rules concerning the manner in which the Apostles were to bear themselves on their missionary journeys, our Lord added several warnings which only the first evangelist has recorded for us. These admonitions were meant to put them and all their successors on their guard against certain dangers, and to point out to them how they should act in definite sets of circumstances which would arise. The Apostles were to realize that they were venturing among wolves, but that they themselves were to act like sheep by meeting violence with meekness, and ferocity with gentleness and kindness. Their struggle with the world was to be fought with arms other than those used against them, for they were to fight what was human with what was divine; they were to meet the weapons of earth with those of heaven. Only thus would they gain the victory. In practicing meekness, however, they were not to be foolish or simple-minded. Jesus wishes the ministers of the Gospel to be simple as doves yet prudent as serpents, the ideal being to harmonize the two extremes.

He warned them that persecutions would arise, not only from strangers and enemies, but even from relatives and friends. But they were not to fear for the ultimate victory of their doctrine, because their Heavenly Father was watching over them. For the rest, the most their enemies could do would be to kill their bodies, for they could not touch their souls. The Apostles were not to wonder at persecution, since it was part of the cross which He Himself carried and which had to be borne by anyone who wished to follow Him. The disciple is not above his teacher: "If they have persecuted me, they will persecute you also" (John 15:20). How could they hope that the world would leave them in peace when He had come on earth not to bring peace but war, a holy war that would lead to true peace? As the proverb says: "If you desire peace, prepare for war."

Finally, for all, Apostles and faithful alike, Jesus stressed the need of confessing Him publicly and the generous renunciation of all earthly things, even those most cherished, if the service of God so demanded: "He who loves father and mother more than me is not worthy of me; and he who loves son or daughter more than me is not worthy of me. . . . He who finds his life will lose it, and he who loses his life for my sake, will find it," i.e., he who saves his bodily life by denying Christ will lose eternal life; and he who sacrifices himself for love of Christ, will gain eternal life.

Thus instructed and encouraged by their Master, the Apostles zealously set forth to preach in the towns and cities, calling men to do penance, casting out devils, and healing the sick by anointing them with oil.

The Death of John the Baptist
(Matt. 14:2–12; Mark 6:17–29; cf. Map V)

The struggle between John, the austere prophet, and his bitter enemy, the shameless courtesan Herodias, was about to draw to its tragic close. The adulteress had succeeded in having the Precursor shut up in the dungeons of Machaerus, but her hate had not been assuaged, nor would it be with anything less than his death. She was only waiting for a chance to strike the final blow, and at last her opportunity came, perhaps when she least expected it.

In the spring of 29 Herod Antipas celebrated his birthday with great pomp, as was the custom of monarchs from very ancient times, for example, the Pharaohs of Egypt (cf. Gen. 40:20). For some reason of which we know nothing, the tetrarch wished to have the festivities in Machaerus and not, as one would expect, in Tiberias, his capital. If he had tried, he could not have chosen a better stage for the twofold drama which was about to be enacted, a drama which began with a scene of sensual pleasure and ended in one of savage cruelty. The fortress was perched on a rocky eminence high above the Dead Sea, and was surrounded by deep gullies which made it both inaccessible and impregnable. The district was an arid one, broken by steep ravines and jagged ridges in its descent to the Dead Sea. On the site of the castle built here by Alexander Janneus (103–76 B.C.), Herod the Great had erected a superb edifice with high towers and massive walls. Within these walls he had constructed a palace which, as Josephus remarks, was magnificent in the size and beauty of its halls and the great wealth of its ornamentation.[12] It was to this palace-fortress that Antipas invited the high officials of his court and the military leaders and aristocracy of the land to partake in his birthday festivities. When we consider the tetrarch's sensual, self-indulgent character, we can imagine the sybaritic excesses com-

---

[12] *Wars* vii. 6. 1–2; cf. above, p. 275, n. 7.

mitted at the banquet, excesses which were all the more likely to occur since the women were not permitted to eat with the men. At the end of such great feasts it was customary to bring in professional dancers, women of easy virtue whose lascivious gyrations entertained the guests and added fuel to the fires of lust already kindled by wine. But on this occasion it seems that no dancing girls were available, perhaps because of the isolated position of the fortress, which was far from any important center of population. However, in order to provide the usual entertainment, the fifteen-year-old Salome, daughter of Herodias and her lawful husband, Herod Philip, appeared in the banquet hall and danced before the guests.

We do not know if the girl had been invited to perform by Antipas himself, or if her mother had suggested the move and encouraged her to appear. Some authors suspect that the arrangement was a scheme concocted by Herodias, who foresaw the tetrarch's offer and meant to take advantage of it to wreak her vengeance by asking for John the Baptist's head. But we do not think that this opinion is well-founded, for we cannot see how the evil woman, consumed with hatred though she was, could have even dreamt that the feast would offer her a chance of bringing about the death of the hated prophet. It is more likely that the opportunity came unexpectedly and that she was quick to take advantage of it. Her enmity towards John had never abated, so that when her daughter told her of Herod's unlimited offer of reward, the image of her fiery accuser sprang to her mind and, without a thought for John's standing with the people or the feelings of the guests, she asked for his head—and got it!

Thus sacrilege, lust and cruelty, all the lowest passions and sins, united in a fearsome alliance to snatch the life of the valiant defender of justice, purity and truth.

The Gospel narrative is starkly tragic in its unadorned simplicity:

"And a favorable day came when Herod on his birthday gave a banquet to the officials, tribunes and chief men of Galilee. And Herodias' own daughter having come in and danced, she pleased Herod and his guests. And the king said to the girl, 'Ask of me what thou willest, and I will give it to thee.' And he swore to her, 'Whatever thou dost ask, I will give thee, even though it be the half of my kingdom.' Then she went out and said to her mother, 'What am I to ask for?' And she said, 'The head of John the Baptist.' And she came in at once with haste to the king, and asked, saying, 'I want thee right away to give me on a dish the head of John the Baptist.' And grieved as he was, the king, because of his oath and his guests, was unwilling to displease her. But sending an executioner, he commanded that his head be brought on a dish. Then he beheaded him in the prison, and brought his head on a dish, and gave it to the girl, and the girl gave it to her mother."

As St. Peter Chrysologus says, our inmost being quakes, our heart trembles and we are benumbed at the sight of the contrast between Herod's cruelty and John's virtue. John, the model of virtue, the teacher of life, the mold of sanctity, the norm of justice, the mirror of purity, the example of chastity, is surrendered to an adulteress and sacrificed to a dancer. Herod, the violator of the Law and of all morality, an enemy of all religion, an assassin, a thief and a murderer, though he had soaked the land in blood, still thirsted for more. But now he lies in the shadows of death while his victim John, whom he sacrificed, enjoys the fullness of life. He has lost a mantle of purple, while John triumphs in the glorious crimson raiment of his own blood. His guests are now sharers in his pains, while John is seated at the heavenly table with the chorus of angels. John, whose head was claimed as a reward by Herod's adulterous consort and her dancing daughter, now enjoys an eternal reward in the kingdom of heaven, while the tetrarch is receiving in the depths of hell the recompense for his promise to Salome.[13]

Merx regards the whole episode as a pure legend, and solemnly asserts that "only a person who has not seen oriental solo dances [Solotänze] could believe it"; then he goes on to say that it is inconceivable that "a haughty Herodian princess would have permitted her daughter to do such a thing." [14] Imagine appealing to the dignity of Herodias, the public concubine! Dalman, who knows the Orient well, denies Merx's assertion and brings forward concrete evidence to support his opinion. He tells of a feast which he attended in the region of Merj'Ayun in the north of Palestine. After the banquet, at which the men and women ate apart from each other, the former gathered in the salon, where they were entertained by a dance performed by the young daughter of the house and executed with irreproachable modesty and appealing grace.[15]

[13] Cf. PL 51, 549 f., 655.
[14] Die vier kanonischen Evangelien, I, 228.
[15] Cf. PJB, 14 (1918), 44–48.

16. The Bread of Life

(March-April A. .D 29)

The First Multiplication of the Loaves
(Matt. 14:13–36; Mark 6:30–56; Luke 9:10–17;
John 6:1–24; cf. Map VI)

The Apostles' return from their first missionary journey coincided with the beheading of John the Baptist. They joined their Master at Capharnaum, and St. Matthew's words (14:12–13) seem to indicate that, to a certain extent, the news of John's death led Jesus to decide to cross to the other side of the lake. We say "to a certain extent" because, according to St. Mark (6:31), the primary cause of His journey was His desire to get away from the importunity of the crowd, thus giving Himself and His disciples a chance to rest after their preaching.

"Come apart into a desert place," He said, "and rest a while." For in silence and solitude the soul replenishes its strength and prepares itself to undertake once more the work of the apostolate.

From St. John (6:4) we know that the Passover was near, and that consequently the time was the end of March or the beginning of April. St. Mark (6:39) confirms this by saying that Jesus made the people sit down on "the green grass," thereby indicating that it was springtime. St. Luke tells us that our Lord and His Apostles withdrew to Bethsaida (9:10). The Vulgate and several Greek manuscripts read "to a *desert place, which belongs to Bethsaida*"; but with Knabenbauer,

Lagrange and others, we prefer the first reading. However, St. Luke definitely did not mean to say that they went to the city itself, for in verse 12 he notes that they were in a desert region, and in verse 10 itself the expression "he withdrew apart" gives us to understand that they retired to a secluded place; the evangelist simply meant, therefore, that they withdrew to the district about Bethsaida. And both Matthew 14:13 and Mark 6:31, 32, say that their destination was a *desert place*.

Northeast of the lake, on the plain known today as el-Batiha and in the place now called Khirbet el-'Araj, a short distance east of the Jordan and near the lake shore, lay the small town of Bethsaida, which was the home of several of the Apostles and which in our Lord's day was under the dominion of Philip the Tetrarch.[1]

Philip, wishing to enlarge and embellish the old town, chose a new site a little farther inland and northeast of the lake, probably the spot where the ruins of et-Tell can still be seen. He called the reconstructed town Julias in honor of Julia, the daughter of Augustus, and the old town of Bethsaida came to be regarded merely as a suburb or satellite of the new city.[2] The southeast end of the plain and the adjacent mountains were uninhabited, and no doubt the evangelists are referring to this region when they speak of a desert place. And since St. John (6:3) mentions a mountain which Jesus ascended, the scene of the multiplication of the loaves was very probably located in this mountainous region between the plain of el-Batiha and the Wadi es-Samak. The fact that our Lord afterwards told the Apostles to cross the lake towards Bethsaida (Mark 6:45) [3] is sufficient indication that the spot where the multiplication of the loaves occurred was situated some distance from the plain.

The Apostles did not get their well-deserved rest, for when the people saw them leave in the boat, they guessed where they were going and followed them, some perhaps sailing after them and others walking around the end of the lake, a journey of some 7½ miles which entailed fording the Jordan near its mouth or crossing it by boat. Thus when Jesus arrived at the other side of the lake, He was met by a large crowd (Matt. 14:14; Mark 6:34). Mark expressly says that "many . . . got there ahead of them," possibly due to the

---

[1] According to Josephus (*Wars* ii. 9. 1), this town lay in the territory of lower Gaulanitis. However, the Jews who lived there regarded themselves as Galileans.

[2] Cf. Dalman, *Sacred Sites and Ways*, pp. 161 ff.; Prat, *Jesus Christ*, I, 406.

[3] See below, pp. 409 ff.

fact that an unfavorable wind had forced the Apostles to tack or even to take to the oars.

They had left Capharnaum to escape the crowd, and here was the crowd waiting for them in the desert. Would Jesus send them away? No, for His merciful heart "had compassion on them, because they were like sheep without a shepherd" (Mark 6:34), and abandoning His first intention of withdrawal, He began to teach them about the kingdom of God and to heal their sick.

Our Lord spoke to the people at length and they, hanging on His words, did not seem to notice the passage of time or the pangs of hunger. But the Apostles, worried because the hour was late and night was not far off, decided to bring the fact to the notice of their Master. Approaching Him, they said with some anxiety: "This is a desert place and the hour is already late; send the crowds away, so that they may go into the villages, and buy themselves food."

Jesus answered them: "You yourselves give them some food."

His command surprised them, for where were they to find food for so many people? To stress the absolute impossibility of carrying out His orders, they asked Him rhetorically: "Are we to go and buy two hundred denarii worth of bread and give them to eat?"

"How many loaves have you? Go and see."

They did so, and Andrew, the brother of Simon Peter, returned with the answer: "There is a young boy here who has five barley loaves and two fishes. . . ." And he added: "But what are these among so many?"

Then Jesus, without heeding Andrew's very natural objection, said: "Bring them here to me, and make the people sit down on the grass."

The Apostles promptly obeyed and began to divide up the crowd into groups of fifties and hundreds. There was great bustle and confusion as the people sorted themselves out into sections, each person trying to make sure that he would be in the same group as his relatives and friends. But when at last they were all seated and silent, Jesus took the five loaves and two fishes into His sacred hands, raised His eyes to heaven, blessed and broke the food, and gave it to His disciples to distribute among the crowd, which numbered five thousand men, without counting women and children. With what good appetite the crowd must have eaten the food which, one could say, had fallen from heaven! And with what love and joy Jesus must have watched them as they partook of the fruit of His bounty! He who had given them nourishment for their souls had also taken care to provide for the needs of their bodies. When all had eaten as much as they wanted, the Apostles were able to fill twelve baskets with the fragments that remained.

The miracle was so great, so obvious, and so far beyond the people's wildest dreams that, impulsive Galileans that they were, they spontaneously acclaimed our Lord with the cry: "This is indeed the Prophet who is to come into the world."

They were referring to the great Prophet foretold in Deuteronomy 18:15. The more impetuous among them, carried away by the magnitude of the miracle and seeing in Jesus the promised Messias, wanted to take Him by force and proclaim Him their king, a king who, according to their nationalistic ideas, was to break the chains that bound the Jews and bring Israel to the heights of glory.

But the humble Master's ideas did not coincide with theirs. He was indeed the great Prophet; He was a King, as He would later declare to the Roman procurator: "Thou sayest it; I am a king" (John 18:37), but He was not such a king as the Jews visualized and the enthusiastic Galileans were now seeking, for His kingdom was not of this world (cf. John 18:36). Therefore because the crowd's acclamations showed no signs of dying down, and since His disciples, too, still shared the popular misconceptions concerning the Messias, He judged it prudent to take them aside from the multitude. Accordingly, He immediately told them to get into the boat and cross the lake ahead of Him. But they could not bring themselves to leave without Him, so that He was compelled to command them formally to go, as St. Matthew and St. Mark record (Matt. 14:22; Mark 6:45): "he *made* his disciples get into the boat." Obediently they cast off, and Jesus, disengaging Himself from the crowd, retired alone to the mountain to pray.

The Apostles would have been even more reluctant to leave if they had foreseen what was awaiting them. A short while after they had put out from land, a strong head wind sprang up, slowing them down so much that at the fourth watch of the night, about three o'clock in the morning, they had covered only twenty-five or thirty stadia (i.e., between three and four miles, a stadium being about 200 yards); not only that, but turbulent waves were buffeting the little vessel so fiercely that it was in danger of foundering. But their kind

Master took pity on them and came to their assistance, walking on the water. As He drew near the boat, they could discern through the darkness only a mysterious shape moving over the waves towards them. They were terror-stricken at the sight and cried out: "It is a ghost!"

But a well-known voice came out of the night to reassure them: "Take courage; it is I, do not be afraid."

The Apostles' terror left them, and Peter, always impulsive, shouted above the storm: "Lord, if it is thou, bid me come to thee over the water."

Again the beloved voice spoke, saying: "Come!"

Leaping from the boat, Peter began to walk over the waves towards his Lord. But an especially violent gust of wind swept down upon him, causing him to lose courage. Feeling himself beginning to sink, he cried out: "Lord, save me!"

Taking him by the hand, Jesus said to him: "O thou of little faith, why didst thou doubt?"

Then together they got into the boat, and immediately the wind dropped. Amazed at all that had happened, and overcome with reverential fear, the Apostles threw themselves at our Lord's feet, proclaiming fervently: "Truly thou art the Son of God."

Then, with Jesus in the boat, they swiftly came to land.

Meanwhile, most of the crowd which had eaten the miraculously-provided food on the eastern shore of the lake had dispersed to their homes. But there were some who stayed to spend the night there, either because they knew that Jesus had not gone away with the Apostles and wanted to see Him again, or else because they did not wish to travel during the hours of darkness. But early the next day, while these people were debating what they should do, several boats from Tiberias put in to shore close by. Concluding that there was no longer any hope of seeing Jesus there, they took advantage of the chance to go aboard the boats and sail across the lake to seek Him in Capharnaum.

One or Two Bethsaidas?
(Cf. Map VI)

At the time of our Lord's public life, the city of Bethsaida Julias, built by Philip the Tetrarch, stood about two miles northeast of the

Lake of Gennesareth. And southwest of this city, beside the lake, there was a group of dwellings on the spot now known as el-'Araj. Did this group of houses form a small town that went by the name of Bethsaida and that had been in existence before the founding of Bethsaida Julias, or was it rather only a kind of suburb of the city, an outpost in which the fishermen of the lake lived for greater convenience because it was near the scene of their labors? It is not possible to give an assured answer to this question. We are inclined, however, to favor the view that the group of dwellings did form the town of Bethsaida, and that it was in existence before Bethsaida Julias.[4] Consequently when we refer to Bethsaida we mean the town which was situated beside the lake shore and from which Peter, Andrew and Philip came.

The account of the Apostles' return from the desert place to Bethsaida gives rise to the problem commonly called "the problem of the two Bethsaidas." The principal passages bearing on the question are: Mark 6:45; Luke 9:10; John 6:17 and 12:21.

We are told that Jesus commanded the Apostles to cross the sea towards Bethsaida (Mark 6:45; cf. Matt. 14:22), and that on the following morning they came to the land of Gennesareth (Mark 6:53; Matt. 14:34), or more precisely to Capharnaum (John 6:17), which St. John tells us was "the land towards which they were going" (6:21). From this it would seem to follow that Bethsaida was in the district of Gennesareth and therefore on the western shore of the lake.

Some authors give great weight to a phrase found in St. Mark (6:45). After the multiplication of the loaves, our Lord commanded the Apostles to get into the boat and "*cross the sea* ahead of him" to Bethsaida ("ut praecederent eum *trans fretum*": εἰς τὸ πέραν). And, say these authors, since the place in which the Apostles received the command lay on the eastern shore of the lake, it follows that the Bethsaida to which our Lord told them to go must have been on the western shore.

St. John, too, seems to imply this when he says (12:21) that the Apostle Philip was from "Bethsaida of Galilee." This Bethsaida apparently could not have been the town east of the lake because the district in which it stood, present-day el-Batiha, did not lie in Galilee but in Gaulanitis.[5]

---

[4] See above, p. 406.

[5] *Wars* ii. 9. 1: "the city Julias, in lower Gaulanitis." See Prat, *op. cit.,* I, 367.

For these two reasons many authors uphold the existence of a town called Bethsaida situated on the *western* shore of the lake, between Capharnaum and Magdala, that is, on the plain of Gennesareth, or else at the *Heptapegon,* the "seven fountains." But in our opinion the Gospel narrative can be satisfactorily explained by the hypothesis of only *one* Bethsaida, northeast of the lake.

There would be nothing unusual in the Apostles' setting sail for one place and then, because of the contrary wind and the storm, putting in to shore at another port. That happens frequently with boats that depend on sail. Therefore no conclusion can be drawn from the fact that they disembarked at Capharnaum although they had been told to go to Bethsaida, particularly since their journey to the latter was no doubt only for the purpose of taking Jesus on board before continuing on to Capharnaum. Consequently, it was quite natural that, since the storm had abated and they already had Jesus with them in the boat, they should have gone direct to Capharnaum. Thus St. John (6:21) can say with truth that Capharnaum was the place towards which they were headed, because it actually was their destination after the storm and their meeting with Jesus on the lake.

In regard to the phrase "to cross the sea" ("ut praecederent eum *trans fretum*": εἰς τὸ πέραν), we should recall what Fr. Abel remarks about a passage from Josephus,[6] namely, that the people used to speak of "crossing" from Tiberias to Tarichea although both cities were on the same side of the lake.[7]

And close examination shows that the argument from John 12:21, "Bethsaida of Galilee," is very weak, not to say futile. Our Bethsaida, beside the northeast shore of the lake, was almost on the borders of Galilee, and because the province of Galilee was much better known than that of Gaulanitis, it is no wonder that St. John, who was not writing a textbook on geography, referred to "Bethsaida of Galilee," not to distinguish it from another town of the same name, but merely to give his readers some idea of its location. In the circumstances, it would have been somewhat pedantic for him to have said "Bethsaida of Gaulanitis."

Therefore we do not believe that there is sufficient reason for

---

[6] *Life* 59.
[7] *Géographie de la Palestine* (Paris: 1933–38), II, 280: "pour aller de Tibériade à Tarichée qui sont du même bord on disait διαπεραιοῦν."

postulating the existence of a second Bethsaida, situated on the western shore of the lake.

Other solutions have been proposed which, in our opinion, have little to recommend them but which, nevertheless, we shall mention briefly: (1) the particle πρὸs (our "*to* Bethsaida" in Mark 6:45) should be translated as "opposite"; thus our Lord commanded the Apostles to go to the other side of the lake to a place *opposite* Bethsaida (Lagrange): we reply that, in itself, the particle can mean "opposite," but that the context in this particular case excludes that meaning. In point of fact, both Capharnaum and the land of Gennesareth were too well known to make it necessary to define their position. It is inconceivable that Jesus, when telling the Apostles to go to the other side, would have added "opposite Bethsaida": instead, He would simply have said "to Capharnaum." In addition, it should be noted that Capharnaum was more strictly speaking opposite the place where the Apostles were than it was opposite Bethsaida. (2) The words εἰς τὸ πέραν: "to the other side," lacking in some codices, should be eliminated from the text (Pirot): [8] to this we object that there is no textual justification for the proposed suppression. (3) Bethsaida was only an intermediate point at which the Apostles had to put in to take Jesus on board, their final destination being Capharnaum; it is to this destination, Capharnaum, and not to Bethsaida that "to the other side" refers. To this we say that although the interpretation is possible, it seems strained. It is true that Bethsaida, as we stated above, was only an intermediate point at which the Apostles were to stop to take our Lord on board; but since "to the other side" is followed immediately by "towards Bethsaida," we believe that it must refer to the latter town.

The Bread of Life
(John 6:22–72; cf. Map III)

Our Lord delivered the magnificent discourse on the Bread of Life on the day of His return to Capharnaum, and, as appears from

---

[8] An almost identical solution is proposed by L. Vaganay, who, in a long article in *RB* (1940), pp. 5–32, arrives at the conclusion that in Mark 6:45 we should read εἰς Βηθσαϊδάν ("to Bethsaida") instead of εἰς τὸ πέραν πρὸς Βηθσαϊδάν ("to the other side towards Bethsaida"). This modification of the text removes every difficulty and cuts away the foundation for the hypothesis of two Bethsaidas. However, despite the great erudition displayed in the article, we do not believe that the author's conclusion is justified.

the context, His words arose out of the multiplication of the loaves on the day before. The discourse itself was spoken in the synagogue, as St. John explicitly tells us (6:60), but Christ's dialogue with the Galileans who had come from the other side of the lake (vv. 25–40) probably took place on the lake shore and on the way to the synagogue.[9] It is doubtful if the second dialogue arising out of the sermon on the Eucharist (vv. 61–66) occurred in the synagogue too, while it is probable that our Lord's conversation with His Apostles (vv. 67–72) took place elsewhere and perhaps on a subsequent day, for it is likely that the disciples who afterwards left Him did not all do so at once but only gradually, a few at a time.

When those who had just arrived from the scene of the multiplication met Jesus, they asked Him with surprise and childlike curiosity: "Rabbi, when didst thou come here?"

Their question was pointless and did not deserve an answer. Our Lord, perceiving the real motive behind their search for Him, took advantage of the occasion to instruct them: "Amen, amen, I say to you, you seek me, not because you have seen signs, but because you have eaten of the loaves and have been filled."

Continuing, He exhorted them to raise their thoughts and desires to a higher level: "Do not labor for the food that perishes, but for that which endures unto life everlasting, which the Son of Man will give you. For upon him the Father, God himself, has set his seal."

The Galileans did not understand the profound meaning of these words, but they did realize that Jesus was speaking of something higher than corporal food, and that to obtain it they would have to perform certain actions pleasing to God. Despite their lack of perfection they felt that they were disposed to do whatever was necessary, and therefore they asked Him: "What are we to do in order that we may perform the works of God?"

The answer was no doubt very different from the one they were expecting: "This is the work of God, that you believe in him whom he has sent."

His interrogators knew that He was referring to Himself, but because they did not consider that they had sufficient motive for the act of faith which He required, they inquired further: "What sign,

---

[9] Some authors, e.g., Fouard and Fillion, believe that these people met Jesus in the synagogue itself.

then, dost thou, that we may see and believe thee? What work dost thou perform?"

This was a surprising question to ask, for had they not just witnessed the great miracle of the multiplication of the loaves? But even this did not appear to them sufficient to warrant belief in Jesus. Had not Moses done greater things? Therefore they added: "Our fathers ate the manna in the desert, even as it is written, 'Bread from heaven he gave them to eat.' "

Jesus corrected their error, pointing out that what Moses gave was not the true bread from heaven. Only His Father could bestow the true bread, which gives life to the world. It is unlikely that the ignorant Galileans understood the nature of this bread; yet they did perceive that it was something precious and exalted, for they exclaimed: "Lord, give us always this bread."

Seeing that the moment had come to expound His teaching fully, Jesus said clearly and explicitly: "I am the bread of life. He who comes to me shall not hunger, and he who believes in me shall never thirst. . . . For I have come down from heaven. . . . This is the will of my Father who sent me, that whoever beholds the Son, and believes in him, shall have everlasting life, and I will raise him up on the last day."

These were indeed unambiguous words, leaving no room for doubt, and for that very reason they scandalized the listeners. Some Scribes and Pharisees who were in the crowd and whom St. John designates by the name "Jews," began to murmur among themselves: "Is this not Jesus the son of Joseph, whose father and mother we know? How, then, does he say, 'I have come down from heaven'?"

Our Lord was well aware of their objections. But far from watering down the meaning of His words, He confirmed what He had said, repeating and even amplifying it: "Do not murmur among yourselves. . . . Amen, amen, I say to you, he who believes in me has life everlasting. I am the bread of life. . . . I am the living bread that has come down from heaven. If anyone eat of this bread he shall live forever; and the bread that I will give is my flesh for the life of the world."

To the Jews this seemed the height of insanity. Jesus, the son of Joseph, was the *living bread? His very flesh* was the bread of life? Such a breath-taking assertion, particularly the last part, provoked a heated dispute among the Jews. Perhaps some of them claimed that

Christ's declaration was to be taken in a purely metaphorical sense, while others insisted that His words were clear and unequivocal and interpreted them, as Salmerón says, "most carnally and literally": "How can this man give us his flesh to eat?"

But Jesus did not retract or correct the assertion that had caused the dissension:

"Amen, amen, I say to you, unless you eat the flesh of the Son of Man and drink his blood, you shall not have life in you. He who eats my flesh and drinks my blood has life everlasting, and I will raise him up on the last day. For my flesh is food indeed, and my blood is drink indeed."

There cannot be the slightest doubt that our Lord was speaking here of the august mystery of the Eucharist. We know that He was not using merely symbolic language because, although His words had scandalized many of His hearers, He did not soften them or explain that they were to be understood in a purely spiritual sense. On the contrary, He reaffirmed what He had said and insisted that it be taken literally, even though He knew that many of His listeners would turn away from Him as a result.

In point of fact, our Lord's announcement of the doctrine of the Holy Eucharist caused a painful crisis in His life. Now the Scribes and Pharisees were not the only ones hostile to Him, for many of His own disciples turned against Him, murmuring: "This is a hard saying. Who can listen to it?"

One by one they left Him, and St. John (6:67) tells us that "from this time many of his disciples turned back and no longer went about with him."

We can glimpse the extent of this desertion in the sorrowing question which Jesus asked His Apostles: "Do you also wish to go away?"

To which Peter answered with characteristic earnestness and conviction: "Lord, to whom shall we go? Thou hast words of everlasting life, and we have come to believe and to know that thou art the Christ, the Son of God."

Or as Salmerón paraphrases it:

We have followed Thee, O King and Messias. Whom besides Thee shall we find possessing the words of eternal life? Thou art the true Saviour, who does not promise the passing goods of this world but who has words which promise eternal life to all who receive those words with true faith.[10]

Peter certainly intended to speak in the name of all the Apostles; but Jesus read the depths of the future traitor's heart and there escaped from His lips the loving lament and terrible condemnation: "Have I not chosen you, the Twelve? Yet one of you is a devil."

He had selected them all to be His faithful disciples, but one of them had not corresponded with the grace of his high vocation and in the depths of his soul was already an enemy of Christ, a devil.

St. John adds his own commentary on our Lord's anguished words: "Now he was speaking of Judas Iscariot, the son of Simon; for he it was, though one of the Twelve, who was to betray him."

[10] *Opera,* VIII, 288.

17. To the Land of Tyre and Sidon

The Canaanite Woman
(Matt. 15:21–29; Mark 7:24–31)

Our Lord's discourse on the Bread of Life, and the desertion of a large number of His disciples, produced in Capharnaum, and no doubt in a good part of Galilee, disquiet and turmoil in men's minds, filling the air with marked hostility. This was the critical point in the missionary life of Christ.

From the time of His first miracle at the wedding feast at Cana, our Lord's popularity had been growing with ever-increasing speed. The people had listened to Him with interest; they had followed Him enthusiastically, brought Him their sick, and besieged Him on all sides. Finally they had come to acknowledge Him as the great Prophet and had even wished to proclaim Him king. Certainly there had been a discordant note in this growing hymn of praise. The inhabitants of Nazareth had maintained an attitude of reserve towards Him, a coolness which turned to hostility and culminated in violence. But this was an exceptional case, due to very special circumstances. The episode related by Mark (3:20 f.), far from revealing animosity or even coldness on the people's part, reflects instead a fervent and even exalted enthusiasm; and the very attitude of His relatives, which in this context appears somewhat strange and disrespectful, was not caused by ill will but rather by lack of intelligence and good judgment.

Thus we can say with truth that, from the beginning of His ministry at the end of 27 to March–April of 29, the young Rabbi of Nazareth had been constantly sought after and admired by the people, and that during this time His triumphal progress had met with no reverses.

Undoubtedly the people had not always been docile to the Divine Master's admonitions, nor had they conformed their lives wholly to His teachings. Indeed, He had had to reproach them severely on many occasions for their torpor and lack of correspondence with grace. But in spite of their moral lethargy, their resistance and continual disobedience, they had retained their esteem, admiration and enthusiasm for the Prophet of Nazareth; they had followed Him and listened gladly to His doctrine, even though they had afterwards failed to put it into practice. Thus it can be said that Galilee as a whole sided constantly with Jesus, and that neither the opposition of the respected Pharisees nor the specious arguments of the Scribes and doctors of the Law succeeded in shaking the Galileans' fidelity to their Fellow Countryman. On the contrary, Jesus had more than once been obliged to put a check on their enthusiasm. In short, from the very beginning of His public life two currents had been set in motion and had run parallel to each other at a constantly increasing rate: on the part of official Judaism there was a current of suspicion, envy and hatred; on the people's part there was an outpouring of confidence, admiration and love. The people of Judea in general, and of Jerusalem in particular, may sometimes have shown themselves undecided or even hostile; but this was due to the powerful influence wielded by Christ's unrelenting enemies, the official leaders of Judaism.

The sudden, profound change in the people's attitude had its origin in the synagogue at Capharnaum, shortly after the Passover of 29. The discourse on the Bread of Life produced a violent reaction in those who heard it; it dried up the current of good will and withered the bloom of confidence. Our Lord's popularity had reached its zenith, for from this point on it began to decline. Now, in addition to the Scribes and Pharisees, the ordinary people turned their backs on Him. They did not become positively hostile to Him like their leaders, but they did complain about His doctrine, object to His demand for faith, and finally desert Him. They began to feel that they had been deceived and that their enthusiasm for the Prophet of Nazareth had been a mistake. And His enemies were not slow to foster the people's doubts and fancied disillusionment. The net result was that those who had acclaimed Jesus only a few days ago now studiously avoided Him, as if they were ashamed of their former devotion to Him.[1]

In the three or four months (May–August) following this painful crisis, which must have deeply wounded our Lord's tender heart, His apostolic activity was less intense than before. He took advantage of the lull to devote Himself instead to the intellectual and spiritual formation of the Apostles; and in the meantime He decided to retire from the scene for a while to allow the storm to die down and men's minds to grow calm.

His route of withdrawal from Capharnaum probably ran through Safed, then northwest through ed-Jish or ancient Gamala and through Yarun, to come out on the coast not far from Tyre. Apart from the flight into Egypt, this was the first and last time He left the land of Israel. St. Mark (7:24) supplies an interesting detail: although Jesus was travelling incognito, as we would say, ("he . . . wanted no one to know it"), the people came to hear of His arrival ("but he could not keep it secret"). He had scarcely entered the house where He intended to stay when a pagan Syro-Phoenician woman, no doubt accompanied by other people from the district, came to Him and cast herself at His feet, crying out: "Have pity on me, O Lord, Son of David! My daughter is sorely beset by a devil."

We need not be surprised at the woman's using the title "Lord, Son of David." The fame of the great Jewish Prophet had reached

---

[1] According to Goguel (*La Vie de Jésus-Christ* [Paris, 1932], pp. 357 *ff*.), the crisis came about as a result of the multiplication of the loaves and not after the discourse at Capharnaum, which, he claims, is not at all historical: "Ce discours expose la théologie d'une époque bien postérieure; il est d'une importance capitale pour l'analyse de la pensée johannique, il n'y a pas à en tenir compte pour l'interprétation de la pensée de Jésus" (p. 358). He goes on to say that the cause of the crisis was exclusively political. According to him, the struggle between Jesus and Herod had become more acute, and the people, who had wholeheartedly sided with the great Prophet of Nazareth, were hoping that He would gather His followers around Him to fight and conquer the tetrarch and establish the kingdom of God which He had been proclaiming. But when they saw that their chosen Leader refused to join battle and instead drew back, they suffered a bitter disillusionment, lost all confidence in Him and abandoned Him.

This is not interpreting the Gospel: it is merely replacing the objective reality with a subjective fantasy that can take any one of a thousand different forms to suit the whim of each reader.

these lands and more than a few of the inhabitants must have known Him personally, for, as St. Mark tells us concerning an earlier occasion: "of those about Tyre and Sidon, a large crowd, hearing what he was doing, came to him" (3:8), and it is obvious that these people would have heard Jesus referred to as the Son of David. No doubt the poor Gentile woman did not understand the full meaning of the expression, but at least she knew that she was appealing to one who could work miracles.

When our Lord did not reply, she reiterated her plea, but to no avail. Seeing that she was not succeeding with the Master, she turned to the disciples, telling them of her need, of her daughter's affliction, and begging them to intercede for her. Moved to compassion, or perhaps merely desiring to rid themselves of her importunity, the Apostles approached their Master and said: "Send her away [i.e., give her what she asks], for she is crying after us."

Jesus finally broke His silence, but only to repulse the woman: "I was not sent except to the lost sheep of the house of Israel."

He had indeed come to save all men, but it was His Father's will that He should personally evangelize Palestine alone, while the rest of the world was to receive the Gospel from His Apostles. We do not know whether or not the Syro-Phoenician woman heard our Lord's discouraging reply; but we do know that, undeterred by the Miracle-worker's cold and apparently hostile attitude, she threw herself once more at His feet with the plea: "Lord, help me!"

This time Jesus did speak directly to her, but in a severe tone of voice: "Let the children first have their fill, for it is not fair to take the children's bread and cast it to the dogs."

These were indeed harsh words, but Jesus uttered them with a kindly intention, for He wished to provide both Jews and Christians with an example of heroic humility on the part of a pagan woman. Instead of being insulted by His cutting rebuff, the supplicant only humbled herself the more and replied: "Yes, Lord; for even the dogs under the table eat of the children's crumbs."

As St. Jerome says: "How admirable is the faith, the patience, the humility of this woman!: her faith, in believing that her daughter can be cured; her patience in persevering in her pleading, so often rebuffed; her humility, in comparing herself not even to the full-grown dogs but rather to the pups who feed under the table."

Her heroism caused our Lord to voice the feelings which He, as it were, had hitherto suppressed: "O woman, great is thy faith! Let it be done to thee as thou wilt."

Her perseverance and humility had won, and her daughter was healed from that moment. Upon returning to her house, she found the girl resting peacefully upon the bed, and the devil gone.

Some authors arrange the various parts of this episode differently. Taking their stand upon St. Matthew's words (15:22): "And behold, a Canaanite woman came out of that territory . . ." they hold that she went to meet Jesus before He had entered the region of Tyre and Sidon, or, as Fillion thinks, that she encountered Him in a house within the borders of Galilee, and followed Him and the Apostles along the road, pleading all the time (cf. Matt. 15:23). Others (e.g., Gomá) believe that she met Him on the road and accompanied Him to the house in which He intended to stay, which stood in Phoenician territory. We, however, are of the opinion that our interpretation corresponds exactly to St. Mark's text, with which St. Matthew's can easily be harmonized. Fouard gives an unusual version of Matthew 15:22: "A Chanaanean of these parts, coming out of the city, from the house she dwelt in. . . ." [2]

St. Matthew (15:29) and St. Mark (7:31) both tell us that Jesus returned from the land of Tyre to the Sea of Galilee, but there are several opinions as to the route followed. Wellhausen changes St. Mark's "Sidon" to "Bethsaida," and supposes that our Lord returned directly to the latter town. If this is what happened, then it is probable that He went south to the plain of el-Huleh and followed the Jordan down to the plain of el-Batiha, upon which Bethsaida stood. [3] However, the suggested change of text is completely arbitrary. Consequently we must hold that, as we read in St. Mark, Jesus went north from the land of Tyre and passed through Sidon, a distance of about twenty-two miles; and He may have gone through the city of Sidon itself and not merely through the district.

According to other authors, our Lord probably travelled still farther north, turned right across the Anti-Lebanon, the territory of Damascus, and from there, walking parallel to the great Hermon range and perhaps through the neighborhood of Kuneitra, arrived on the eastern coast of the Sea of Galilee. [4] Such a roundabout route is

[2] *The Christ, The Son of God,* II, 9.
[3] Cf. Dalman, *Sacred Sites and Ways,* pp. 200 f.
[4] Thus, for example, Knabenbauer: "A Sidone per Libanum et Antilibanum

possible, but in our opinion very improbable. It is more likely that upon leaving Sidon, our Lord would have turned southeast and, passing near the springs of the Jordan on the southern slope of Mount Hermon, would have turned right and continued south to the lake.

We know that Jesus entered the territory of the Decapolis: "And departing again from the district of Tyre, he came by way of Sidon to the sea of Galilee, through the midst of the district of Decapolis" (Mark 7:31). The Greek phrase, however, can be taken to mean either "through the midst of" or simply "to" the district of Decapolis. In the first sense the territory of the Decapolis was the "terminus *per quem*"; in the second, it was the "terminus *ad* quem." The former is the meaning found in the Vulgate and is the one accepted by Knabenbauer, Dausch, Fillion, Prat, Lebreton, and B. Weiss; the latter is preferred by Lagrange and by Gould, who gives a strange reason for his preference, for he holds that Jesus came *to* and not *through* the Decapolis, since He went by boat to the western shore of the lake after having fed the multitude.[5]

The first interpretation, "through the midst of the district of Decapolis," is much the more probable one. In the last analysis, however, both translations come to practically the same thing, since "through the midst of" does not mean that Jesus penetrated deep into the territory of the Decapolis and crossed it exactly in the middle, but only that He *passed through* it. The itinerary which we have described above takes account of this fact inasmuch as the whole region east of the lake belonged to the Decapolis.

The Second Multiplication of Loaves
(Matt. 15:29–39; Mark 8:1–9; cf. Map III)

As we have said before, the Decapolis was a kind of confederation, or rather group, of ten cities, whence it derived its name, although the number was not a fixed one and sometimes went as high as thirteen or fourteen. These cities were scattered over an extensive territory reaching from Damascus in the north to Philadelphia ('Amman) in the south. All of them, including Hippos, Gadara and Gerasa, were

montes profectus est in regionem decapolitanam" (*In Marc.,* 7, 31); Fillion, *Life of Christ,* II, 520 *f.;* B. Weiss in his commentary on St. Mark.
[5] Ezra P. Gould, *A Critical and Exegetical Commentary on the Gospel According to St. Mark* (New York: Charles Scribner's Sons, 1901), p. 138.

east of the Jordan; only one, Scythopolis (Beisan), lay west of the river. Conquered first by Alexander Janneus, they were freed in 64 B.C. by Pompey who, however, placed them under the direct rule of Rome. The vast majority of the inhabitants were pagans, mostly Graeco-Romans, with a good many Jews scattered unevenly throughout the territory.

Our Lord was known in this region, and hence as He journeyed through it He attracted a large crowd, not only of Jews but also of pagans who were eager to hear His teaching, but who were doubtless even more desirous of being cured of their ills. The kind Master fully satisfied their wishes, for He healed many who were dumb, blind, lame, maimed or suffering from other infirmities, thereby causing the crowds to marvel at His power and to glorify the God of Israel. The words of St. Matthew, "the God of Israel," seem to indicate that the majority of those present were Gentiles.

Among those cured by Jesus at this time we should perhaps number the deaf-mute whose healing St. Mark describes so vividly. When the afflicted man was brought to Him, our Lord took him aside from the crowd, put His fingers into his ears, placed spittle on his tongue and then, looking up to heaven, sighed and said: "Ephpheta . . . Be thou opened."

Immediately, the man regained his hearing and began to speak. On seeing the miracle the people gave vent to an enthusiastic cry: "He has done all things well. He has made both the deaf to hear and the dumb to speak."

The crowd had now been with Jesus three days, but they were so carried away by His miracles and enchanted with His words that they did not realize that there was little left of the few cakes of bread and handfuls of olives or raisins which they had brought with them. Nor did they seem to advert to the fact that every step was taking them farther from home. But the loving providence of the Father took care to make up for the distracted improvidence of His children. Calling His disciples, our Saviour said to them: "I have compassion on the crowd, for behold, they have now been with me three days, and have nothing to eat; and if I send them away to their homes fasting, they will faint on the way, for some of them have come from a distance."

The Apostles followed their Master's thoughts and, forestalling

Him, they objected: "Where then are we to get, in a desert, enough loaves to satisfy so great a crowd?"

For the multitude numbered four thousand men, apart from women and children. Jesus asked them: "How many loaves have you?"

"Seven, and a few little fishes."

He told the people to sit on the ground, and taking the seven loaves, He gave thanks, broke them, and gave them to His disciples, who distributed them among the crowd. He blessed the little fishes, too, and they were given out in like manner. All ate as much as they wanted, and yet the fragments that remained filled seven baskets.

As can be seen from the context, this multiplication, like the first one, took place in the region east of the lake. Because of this and other similarities, many exegetes, particularly non-Catholic ones, admit only one multiplication. But, as St. Jerome has pointed out, there are also many differences between the two episodes.[6] Furthermore, since both St. Matthew and St. Mark place each of the two episodes in different circumstances of time and place, it is only good criticism to conclude that each evangelist wished to describe two multiplications, and even aside from the question of inspiration there is no reason to reject their testimony.[7]

Dalmanutha
(Matt. 16:1–12; Mark 8:10–26; cf. Map III)

St. Matthew (15:39) and St. Mark (8:10) tell us that immediately after the multiplication of the loaves Jesus got into the boat and went "into the district of Magedan," as St. Matthew puts it, while St. Mark says that He went "into the district of Dalmanutha." In all probability, both evangelists are referring to the same place, but there is much doubt as to its location. Several good codices have Μάγδαλα

---

[6] "Ibi quinque panes erant et duo pisces; hic septem panes et pauci pisciculi. Ibi super foenum discumbunt, hic super terram. Ibi qui comedunt, quinque millia sunt, iuxta panum numerum quos comedunt; hic quatuor millia. Ibi duodecim cophini replentur de reliquiis fragmentorum; hic septem sportae" (*Comm. in Matt.: PL* 26, 112).

[7] As Prat aptly remarks: "Whenever there is question of a meal, a blessing must be pronounced, guests must be fed, food must be distributed, and the fragments must be collected. But all the rest of the details are different" (*Jesus Christ,* I, 401).

tell us.[11] It would be interesting to know why they had come to Gennesareth. Perhaps the recent crisis at Capharnaum had some-thing to do with their being there, for it is possible that having heard about the incident, the leaders in the capital had hurriedly sent their emissaries to exploit it to the full. It was the first time the people had shown a lack of confidence in Jesus, and His ever-watchful adversaries were not going to let such a golden opportunity pass.

When the visitors from Jerusalem saw Jesus, they quickly gathered around Him and began a lively dispute on the subject of ablutions. In itself, the point under discussion was of secondary im-portance, but it came to assume such proportions that finally the very principles of the Jewish religion, as it was understood and practiced by the Pharisees, were called into question.

St. Mark (7:3 f.) describes in detail the practice of ablutions among the Pharisees: "The Pharisees and all the Jews do not eat without frequent washing of hands, holding the tradition of the ancients. And when they come from the market, they do not eat without washing first. And there have been handed down to them many other things to observe: washing of cups and pots, and brazen vessels and beds." The evangelist is not exaggerating the case: rabbini-cal literature provides even more surprising examples of the lengths to which the practice of ablutions was carried.

Having observed that some of our Lord's disciples ate without first washing their hands, the Scribes and Pharisees confronted Him and asked accusingly: "Why do not thy disciples walk according to the traditions of the ancients, instead of eating bread with defiled hands?"

Christ's reply was a clear-cut and biting rejoinder in which He did not limit Himself to the particular concrete matter proposed but raised the discussion to the level of principles. He began by casting up against them the superficiality and emptiness of their religion, a Judaism which concerned itself solely with external practices and cared nothing for interior dispositions. They were doing exactly what Isaias had prophesied they would: "This people honors me with their lips, but their heart is far from me; but in vain do they worship me, teaching for doctrines precepts of men" (29:13).

His adversaries had appealed to tradition; but He turned their

[11] St. Matthew seems to refer to both the Scribes and the Pharisees, and St. Mark to the Scribes alone.

own charge against them and condemned the sacrilegious abuse they were committing in sacrificing the divine precepts to their man-made laws: "Well do you nullify the commandment of God, that you may keep your own tradition!"

To drive home His point, He gave a concrete example of their perversion: "For God said: 'Honor thy father and thy mother' [a command which of course includes helping them in their need]. . . . But you say, 'Whoever shall say to his father or mother, "Any support thou mightest have had from me is dedicated to God," does not have to honor his father or his mother' " [i.e., is not bound to help them with his possessions]. He was referring to the legal ruse by which bad sons, under the pretext of religion, defrauded their parents of the assistance due to them by divine law.

Our Lord did not merely confound and silence His enemies; He wished also to lay down a principle containing the germ of the new religion that was so much in contrast to the system which the Pharisees had elaborated and defended with such zeal. Solemnly and with authority, He spoke to the crowd that surrounded them. "Hear, and understand. What goes into the mouth does not defile a man; but that which comes out of the mouth, that defiles a man."

It is not food that makes men pure or impure; it is the thoughts, desires, words and works that spring from the depths of their hearts. Men are not sanctified by external formalism but by their acts of will.

Then His disciples said to Him: "Dost thou know that the Pharisees have taken offense at hearing this saying?"

His answer was like the crack of a whip: "Every plant that my heavenly Father has not planted will be rooted up. Let them alone; they are blind guides of blind men. But if a blind man guide a blind man, both fall into a pit."

The disciples were not scandalized at their Master's words, but they did not understand them, so that when they were alone with Him in the house, Peter said to Him: "Explain to us this parable."

"Are you also even yet without understanding? Do you not realize that whatever enters the mouth passes into the belly and is cast out into the drain? But the things that proceed out of the mouth come from the heart, and it is they that defile a man. For out of the heart come evil thoughts, murders, adulteries, immorality, thefts, false witness, blasphemies. These are the things that defile a man; but to eat with unwashed hands does not defile a man."

In order to explain to His still-unformed disciples the lofty doctrine contained in His somewhat enigmatic words, our Lord had to use very realistic language. Thus He drew a clear and definite line between two kinds of religious conceptions—scrupulous external ablutions concerned with bodily cleanliness, and inner cleanliness, purity of heart.

Despite their humiliating rout His enemies did not accept defeat, but returned to the attack. This time the Pharisees and Sadducees, although they were bitter enemies, joined forces against the hated Prophet of Nazareth. They knew that Jesus claimed that He was the Christ, the Messias, and they asked Him to prove His claim by a sign from heaven such as the miracle which Josue had wrought in stopping the sun in its course (cf. Jos. 10:12 f.) or such as Elias had performed in opening the cataracts of heaven after three years of drought (cf. 3 Kings 17:1; 18:5). Their intention was evil; they did not want to be enlightened, for their sole aim was to force Jesus into an untenable position.

Looking into their hearts and seeing their malice and willful blindness, He gave a deep sigh of pain. Then leaving their challenge unanswered, He took the offensive once more:

"When it is evening you say, 'The weather will be fair, for the sky is red.' And in the morning you say, 'It will be stormy today, for the sky is red and lowering.' You know then how to read the face of the sky, but cannot read the signs of the times!"

Our Lord meant that they could not read the signs of the Messianic era, the many proofs He had given to show that He was the Messias. Then closing the discussion with the terrible words: "An evil and adulterous generation demands a sign, and no sign shall be given it but the sign of Jonas"—an allusion to His Resurrection—He left them and went away.

Boarding the boat, He commanded His Apostles to sail once more to the eastern shore of the lake. During the crossing a delightfully ingenuous dialogue took place between Master and disciples. Their departure had been so rushed that they had forgotten or had not had time to make provision for the journey, and they realized their omission only when it was too late to turn back. As it was, they had only one loaf in the boat, and they were worried about what they would say to Jesus when mealtime came around and their lack of foresight became known. Suddenly their Master, recalling sadly the malice of

His enemies, broke the silence He had hitherto maintained: "Take heed and beware of the leaven of the Pharisees and Sadducees!"

That is, the Apostles were to beware of the Pharisees' doctrine and hypocrisy, which affected all who came in contact with them, as leaven spreads through dough. St. Mark (8:15) adds "and [beware] of the leaven of Herod!" no doubt meaning that they should be on their guard against being infected with the worldly, cunning spirit of the tetrarch and his party, the Herodians.

When the Apostles, preoccupied as they were with the question of provisions, heard the word "leaven," they thought Jesus was referring to bread, and they whispered to each other: "He says this because we have brought no bread." They were under the impression that He had discovered their omission and was reproving them for it; and perhaps they argued among themselves as to who was to blame.

Hearing them whispering, and knowing why they were doing so, Christ said to them: "Why do you argue among yourselves that you have no bread? Do you not yet understand, nor remember the five loaves among five thousand men . . . nor the seven loaves among four thousand?"

It was as if He said: "Why are you so worried? Haven't you seen how easily I can remedy your omission?" They understood then that He had been referring to the doctrine and way of life of the Pharisees and Sadducees.

The Blind Man of Bethsaida

When they landed at Bethsaida, the people brought a blind man to Jesus and besought Him to touch him. The merciful Saviour, taking the man by the hand, led him outside the village. Then, placing spittle on the man's eyes, He laid His hands upon him and asked him if he saw anything. As if desperately trying to see, the man replied: "I see men as though they were trees, but walking about."

Again Jesus laid His hands upon the man's eyes, whereupon he was cured and was able to see everything plainly. Then our Lord sent him away, saying: "Go to thy house, without entering the village." [12]

This implies that the man must have been living on the outskirts

[12] According to the best Greek reading.

of the village. It is difficult to say why Jesus cured him only gradually rather than all at once. The Fathers see a symbolic meaning in our Lord's procedure, e.g., that the action of grace allows itself to be felt gradually and progressively, or that great effort is needed to bring men from the darkness of error to the light of truth.

18. In Caesarea Philippi:
Thabor

Peter's Confession: Foretelling the Passion
(Matt. 16:13–28; Mark 8:27–39; Luke 9:18–27; cf. Maps III, V)

From Bethsaida Jesus went north along the Jordan towards the small lake, el-Huleh, beside which lay a fertile oval-shaped plain, with the majestic bulk of Mount Hermon rising in the background. At the foot of Mount Hermon, near the sources of the holy river, lay Caesarea Philippi, about twenty-five miles or a two-days' journey from Bethsaida. Philip the Tetrarch had founded this city, naming it Caesarea in honor of Augustus.[1] It was some two and one-half miles from the ancient Dan (formerly Lais; cf. Judges 18:27–29), the present-day Tell el-Qadi. Nearby there is a spacious cave which, three centuries before Christ, the Greeks dedicated to Pan, whence came the name Paneas, today preserved in the name of the miserable little Moslem town of Baniyas. Josephus speaks of a magnificent marble temple which Herod the Great, Philip's father, built there in honor of Augustus.[2] This place was the beautiful and imposing stage upon which Jesus chose to enact one of the principal scenes of His public life.

[1] *Ant.* xviii. 2. 1; *Wars* ii. 9. 1.
[2] *Ant.* xv. 10. 30; *Wars* iii. 10. 7.

Here it was that one day, after spending a long time in prayer, and while He was walking with His disciples, He suddenly asked them: "Who do men say the Son of Man is?"

They answered: "Some say, John the Baptist; and others, Elias; and others, Jeremias, or one of the prophets."

It is surprising that by this time, the beginning of our Lord's third year of preaching, there had not yet arisen among the people the idea that He was the Messias, especially after the glorious manifestations which we find recorded in St. John and the Synoptic Gospels. John the Baptist had declared that Jesus was greater than he, so much greater that he was not worthy to loose the strap of His sandals (Mark 1:7); the devils had proclaimed Him "the Holy One of God" (Mark 1:24), "Son of the most high God" (Luke 8:28), and "the Son of God" (Mark 3:11); and He had claimed for Himself the power to forgive sins (Luke 5:24). Is it conceivable, then, that such clear, repeated proofs would have failed to give the people at least some faint glimmering of the Messianic character of Jesus?

Some authors believe that the people actually had recognized our Lord's Messianic dignity, but that they had lost faith in Him as a result of the discourse on the Eucharist, while the Apostles had remained steadfast. But we do not think that this is the correct solution to the problem. The painful crisis at Capharnaum was only a passing phase; we have seen how enthusiastically Jesus was received upon His return from Phoenicia. Furthermore, it would be arbitrary to say that, when the Apostles replied to our Lord's question concerning the people's opinion of Him, they took into account only the period of time that had elapsed since the discourse on the Eucharist.

It must be remembered that the disciples' answer to Christ's question was unprepared and spontaneous, and did not make any pretension of going into details: it merely echoed the opinions that were generally current among the populace. Consequently, it would be premature to conclude therefrom that no one had acknowledged that He was the Messias. On the other hand, there would be nothing strange in the fact that only a few accepted Him as such, for the humble Prophet of Nazareth was very different from the popular conception of the Messias as a warlike, glorious conqueror, a conception that was still deeply impressed on the minds of the Jewish people.

Having heard the Apostles' answer, Jesus asked them in a tone of unusual solemnity: "But who do you say that I am?"

To which Simon Peter, with his characteristic promptness and

One of the sources of the Jordan, at the foot of Mount Hermon.
Above, the grotto of the god Pan.

wholeheartedness, replied with deep conviction: "Thou art the
Christ, the Son of the living God." [3]

[3] Mark 8:29 has only "the Christ," and Luke 9:20, "the Christ of God." Because these two evangelists refer only to the *Messianic character,* the majority
of non-Catholic and some Catholic authors, like Le Camus and Battifol, claim
that St. Matthew's expression "the Son of the living God" is synonymous with
"the Christ." But the immense majority of Catholic commentators (Maldonatus,
Calmet, Fillion, Knabenbauer, Durand, Lagrange, Gomá, Médebielle, Prat, Buzy,
and others) correctly understand the expression to refer to the Divine Sonship
in the strict sense.

If the words "Son of God" have no more meaning on Peter's lips than they
had as the disciples used them in the boat (Matt. 14:33), or even as the unclean spirits used them (Mark 3:11), there is no explanation why Jesus should
have so solemnly and particularly called Peter blessed, for he would have been
merely repeating a confession already made by so many others. Nor would Peter
have needed a special revelation from the Father before he could bear witness
to a truth which so many others, devils included, had already acknowledged.

If we remember how fragmentary and incomplete the evangelists' accounts
really are, we shall not wonder at the silence of Mark and Luke on this point,
and we must not forget that these two evangelists may have had to depend on a
current of tradition that laid particular stress on our Lord's Messianic character.
Cf. W. Goossens, *Collationes Gandavenses,* 27–28 (1940–45), 61–85, who upholds the strictly Messianic nature of Peter's confession, and the refutation of
his arguments by D. J. Sanders in "The Confession of Peter," in *Theological
Studies,* 10 (1949), 522–540. Goossens supplies a very copious bibliography.

The tenor of Peter's words and the solemn nature of the formula which he used indicates that he wished to bear witness to Jesus not only as the Messias, but also as the true Son of God. And our Lord immediately rewarded his faith by declaring: "Blessed art thou, Simon Bar-Jona, for flesh and blood has not revealed this to thee, but my Father in heaven." Then followed the great promise:

"And I say to thee, thou art Peter, and upon this rock I will build my Church, and the gates of hell shall not prevail against it. And I will give thee the keys of the kingdom of heaven; and whatever thou shalt bind on earth shall be bound in heaven, and whatever thou shalt loose on earth shall be loosed in heaven." [4]

Peter's confession and our Lord's great promise constitute one of the peak points of the public life, for on this occasion the founding of the Church was announced, and Peter was told that he was to be the rock upon which it would be built. The words are clear and unambiguous, admitting of only one interpretation, the obvious one. But the Protestants cannot bring themselves to acknowledge this fact, and choose instead the following explanation: Jesus did pronounce the words recorded in the Gospels and He did first address Peter, saying: "Thou art a rock"; but when He went on to add, "and upon this rock I will build my Church," He pointed to Himself, thereby indicating that He Himself and not Peter was to be the foundation stone of the Church. Such an interpretation is not only puerile but actually borders on the ridiculous. Why would our Lord have so solemnly called Simon "Peter, a rock," if the rock was not going to be used for anything? And how did the Protestants get to "know" that Jesus pointed to Himself as He spoke?

This interpretation is so unlikely that modern Protestants have

---

[4] Doubts have been raised as to whether our Lord spoke these words in the circumstances of time and place indicated by St. Matthew, i.e., at Caesarea Philippi on the occasion of Peter's confession (see Oscar Cullmann, *Peter, Disciple, Apostle, Martyr: An Historical and Theological Study*, trans. by Floyd V. Filson [Philadelphia: The Westminster Press, 1952], pp. 206 *ff*.). And in reality, it is surprising that in the parallel passages in the two other Synoptic authors (Mark 8:27–30; Luke 9:18–21) there is not the slightest reference to our Lord's reply.

Undoubtedly it is quite possible that here, as elsewhere, St. Matthew recorded Christ's words in a framework of time and place different from that in which they were actually spoken. Such an hypothesis would explain why the passage is lacking in Mark and Luke although both of them record Peter's confession. Still, the connection between Peter's confession and Christ's promise of the Primacy is so intimate and spontaneous that we have a right to demand more cogent reasons for disassociating the one from the other.

abandoned it and acknowledge that all of our Lord's words refer to Peter. However, they maintain that it was not Peter himself but rather his faith that was to be the foundation stone of the Church. But this explanation does not take into account the fact that it was Peter himself, and not his faith, that received the title of "rock." Consequently it was he, in person, who was to be the foundation of the Church, his faith, his confession, being the reason that he was thus singled out, as all Catholic authors admit.

Finally, the rationalists, appealing to literary and textual criticism, claim that St. Matthew never wrote the passage, and therefore they eliminate it from the text as a later interpolation; or else they agree that the evangelist wrote the words, but deny that Jesus ever uttered them; instead, they hold that the passage is merely the product of the faith of the first Christian community.

The whole manuscript tradition protests against the assertion that the evangelist did not write the passage, for it appears in all the manuscripts without exception and in all the ancient versions. Hence to delete it would be to violate all the canons of textual criticism. As regards the rationalists' second assumption, we need only point out that it is based exclusively on their arbitrary conception of the evolution of dogma, the theory of the *Formgeschichte* school, which, as we saw, regards the Gospels, not as records of real events, but as the end product of the community activity of the Christians, whose religious faith transformed historical facts and gave them a character quite distinct from that which they possessed in reality.[5]

In violent contrast to Peter's magnificent confession and the wonderful promises of Jesus, there followed a prophecy of events which the Apostles would never even have dreamed possible—the foretelling of the humiliation and mortal sufferings of the Messias. Our Lord told them "that he must go to Jerusalem and suffer many things from the elders and Scribes and chief priests, and be put to death, and on the third day rise again."

Being Jews and children of their times, the Apostles shared the idea which the great majority of Israelites had formed of the coming

[5] See above, p. 59. On the authenticity of Matthew 16:18, see the very complete article by Scheppens in *Rech. de Sc. Rel.*, 10 (1920), 269–302; on the authenticity and exegesis of the same passage see Médebielle's magnificent study in *Dict. de la Bible*, Suppl. II, cols. 545–585. In cols. 687 *f.* of the same work, there is a very copious bibliography. L. Fonck deals more briefly with the matter in *Biblica*, 1 (1920), 259–263.

Messias and which was reflected in the petition made by the mother of the sons of Zebedee (Matt. 20:21; Mark 10:37) and plainly implied in the question which the disciples asked shortly before our Lord's Ascension: "Lord, wilt thou at this time restore the kingdom to Israel?" (Acts 1:6). The Apostles, in common with their countrymen, thought of the Messias as a glorious liberator who would conquer Israel's enemies, restore the ancient kingdom and subject all nations to it. How was it possible to reconcile this conception with that which Jesus now set before them, with the thought that He would one day be persecuted and rejected by the Jewish authorities themselves, who would end by condemning Him to an ignominious death? It is no wonder then that our Lord's words left the Apostles aghast; and the shock they received was all the greater because He spoke "openly" (Mark 8:32) and for the first time (Matt. 16:21; Mark 8:31) about His Passion; or at least because this was the first time He had spoken so clearly about it.[6] The impact of the announcement was so stunning that Peter, impetuous by nature and further emboldened by his Master's marked predilection for him, took Jesus aside and said resolutely to Him: "Far be it from thee, O Lord; this will never happen to thee."

But Jesus rebuked him severely: "Get behind me, satan, thou art a scandal to me; for thou dost not mind the things of God, but those of men."

Although He had told the Apostles plainly that His ignominious death would be followed by His glorious Resurrection, they apparently had not fully realized the import of His words, so bewildered were they by His prophecy of the treatment He would receive at the hands of the elders and chief priests. Peter's reaction leaves no doubt that they understood perfectly that Jesus was speaking about suffering, insult and death. But if that is so, how explain the fact that when He afterwards referred several times to the same matter, the evangelists note that it was a mystery to the Apostles?[7]

The explanation of the apparent contradiction is to be found in

---

[6] Matthew 16:21 says "From that time [ἀπὸ τότε] Jesus began to show . . ." an expression which seems to indicate that He had not hitherto manifested His future Passion, and that from then on He continued to refer to it. Mark 8:31 reads: "And he *began* to teach them. . . ."

[7] Mark 9:31: "But they did not understand the saying, and were afraid to ask him"; Luke 9:45: "But they did not understand this saying, and it was hidden from them, that they might not perceive it; and they were afraid to ask him about this saying."

the psychology of the Apostles. Peter, and no doubt his companions, too, thought that the sufferings prophesied were to come solely and exclusively from the malice of the Jews. They did not understand that, in accordance with the divine plan, Jesus would freely give Himself into the hands of His enemies. By his vehement protest, Peter wished to assure his Master that what He had foretold would not come to pass because he and the other disciples would defend Him against the wiles of the Jews, and would see Him safe through any danger that threatened Him.[8] It is clear, therefore, that neither Peter nor the other Apostles had the least conception of a suffering Messias.[9] But when their Master insisted again and again on His prophecy of suffering, they began to suspect the truth, yet they were unable to harmonize the new idea being presented to them with their ingrained hope of a glorious Messias, and thus they found our Lord's predictions mystifying. But they did get a glimpse of the somber reality behind His words, with the result that they were beset by vague, uneasy doubts, yet were afraid to ask Him to explain (Mark 9:30 f.; Luke 9:44 f.; Matt. 17:21 f.).

Jesus first foretold His Passion to His Apostles alone, but, immediately afterwards, He addressed a brief discourse to them and the people together, a discourse which was certainly related to His prophecy and which was in fact a compendium of Christian asceticism.[10]

To His Apostles He had said that He would tread a painful path to His death; now He warned them and the crowd that those who wished to be His disciples would have to follow in His footsteps along that path. His words were another blow to the general concept of a worldly, powerful Messias. His followers, His courtiers, could not look forward to honors, riches and material prosperity as could the courtiers of the kings of this world. Instead, they were to anticipate quite the contrary—pain, humiliation and death. With rare unanimity, the three Synoptic authors express this thought (Matt. 16:24; Mark 8:34; Luke 9:23): "If anyone wishes to come after me, let him deny himself, and take up his cross, and follow me."

To deny oneself means to despoil oneself, and since this spoliation

---

[8] Cf. Knabenbauer *In Matt., in loc.*

[9] "Adeo longe itaque Petrus aberat a notione Messiae patientis" (*Ibid.*).

[10] Mark 8:34: "And calling the crowd together with his disciples. . . ."; Luke 9:23: "And he said to all. . . ."

is not possible without great effort in overcoming natural self-love, it implies a positive struggle with self and with all that stands in the way of self-denial. Hence denying self means conquering self; it is the *Vince teipsum* of Christian asceticism. Taking up the cross is a metaphor derived from the custom according to which those who had been condemned to death by crucifixion were made to carry their crosses to the place of execution. Doubtless our Lord's listeners were familiar with the practice, for, after the death of Herod the Great, Varus had had two thousand Jews crucified,[11] and Quadratus had crucified all those whom Cumanus had taken prisoner,[12] while Titus had condemned so many to death by the same method that there had not been enough wood for the crosses.[13]

Denying oneself and taking up one's cross are two indispensable conditions for following Christ. But what is meant by "and follow me"? Is this a third condition? Does it mean something different from "If anyone wishes to come after me. . . ."? Knabenbauer thinks so [14] and so does Plummer,[15] who holds that our Lord meant: "and follow me *faithfully*," so that there are three conditions to be fulfilled if one wants to be a disciple of Christ: self-denial, carrying the cross, and obedience. In our opinion, however, the third condition does not exist. In Mark 8:34, many manuscripts have "follow" (ἀκολουθεῖν) instead of "come after" (ἐλθεῖν ὀπίσω), i.e., the same verb at the beginning and end of the verse. But even if we keep "come after," the two phrases should be understood in the same sense. Thus, for example, Jesus said to Simon and Andrew: "Come after me" (δεῦτε ὀπίσω μου; Mark 1:17), and the two brothers, leaving their nets, "followed him" (ἠκολούθησαν αὐτῷ; 1:18); and we are told that the two sons of Zebedee, when called by Jesus, "went after him" (ἀπῆλθον ὀπίσω αὐτοῦ; 1:20), i.e., they *followed* Him. It seems evident, therefore, that the two verbs "to come after" and "to follow" mean the same thing. Both of them are understood in the figurative sense, the metaphor being taken from the physical act of going after or following someone, two completely identical ideas; the real sense is that of becoming someone's disciple. Consequently Plummer's distinction, mentioned

[11] *Ant.* xvii. 10. 10.
[12] *Wars* ii. 12. 10.
[13] *Wars* v. 11. 1.
[14] *Loc. cit.*
[15] *A Critical and Exegetical Commentary on the Gospel According to St. Luke* (New York: Charles Scribner's Sons, 1901), *in. loc.*

above, is quite arbitrary. As we see it, the passage in Mark (and the ones in Matthew and Luke also) should be interpreted thus: our Lord represents Himself as walking with the cross on His shoulders, and saying: "If anyone wishes to come after me, let him follow me [or 'come after me,' which means the same thing] by denying himself and taking up his own cross." Thus the two conditions for a proper following of Christ are self-denial and the cross. We must remember that our Lord was speaking throughout in terms of the metaphor He had chosen. There were two ways of following a condemned man bearing his cross to execution: one could walk after him unburdened, or one could follow him bearing one's own cross. In either case one would be following the condemned man, but in what different ways! Consequently, the words "follow me" at the end of the verse refer not so much to the actual following of Christ as to the *way in which* we are to follow Him, namely, bearing our cross.

But why did not our Lord merely say, "let him deny himself, and take up his cross"? This would have been more than sufficient; He could even have said simply: "let him deny himself," since self-denial necessarily involves taking up the cross. But, we repeat, Christ had in mind the condemned man carrying his cross on his shoulders towards the place of execution. Now, if one of the spectators at such a scene took up a cross but remained standing in the one spot, he could not be said to be following the condemned man. Therefore, continuing the image, Jesus added "and follow me," although, in the moral order, anyone who really takes up his cross by that very fact follows in our Lord's footsteps.

In order to encourage His disciples to follow Him along the hard road of suffering, Jesus revealed to them the punishment that was in store for him who did not do so (the loss of his soul), and the reward awaiting him who did (salvation): "He who would save his life will lose it; but he who loses his life for my sake will find it. For what does it profit a man, if he gain the whole world, but suffer the loss of his own soul?"

It should be remembered that the Greek word ψυχή, like the Hebrew *nefesh*, can mean "soul," "person" or "life" (natural, mortal life, or spiritual, eternal life). The context makes it clear that the life referred to was not only mortal but also eternal life, for our Lord immediately goes on to say that when He will come in glory with His angels He will mete out due punishment to those who were ashamed to acknowledge Him. He wished to impress upon His listeners that they would have to be prepared to suffer anything, even death itself, in order to save their souls, and that it profits a man nothing to gain the whole world if in the end he loses his soul, i.e., if he fails to attain eternal salvation.[16]

According to the three Synoptic Gospels, our Lord closed His discourse with a sentence that can well be called mysterious, for He said that some of His listeners would not die before seeing "the kingdom of God" (Luke), or "the Son of Man coming in his kingdom" (Matt.), or "the kingdom of God coming in power" (Mark).

The Fathers believe that He was referring either to the Transfiguration, which was to follow six days later, to the Resurrection, the Ascension, the coming of the Holy Spirit, the destruction of Jerusalem, the founding of the Church, which is the kingdom of God, or, finally, to the second coming of the Son of Man at the end of the world. This last interpretation must be excluded, since none of those present were to see it. Some authors, such as Gomá and Vilariño, take our Lord's words to refer to the growth and power of the Church. But Knabenbauer, Lagrange, Fillion, Prat, Buzy, Pirot and many others prefer to regard the text as alluding to the manifestation of God's power in the destruction of Jerusalem in the year 70; however, we think that this interpretation is not very probable. Lebreton is of the opinion that our Lord was speaking both of His Transfiguration and of the expansion of the Church. Pirot holds that the sentence in question was spoken in circumstances different from those in which it appears in the Gospels. That is possibly true, but we believe that the perfect agreement between the three Synoptic authors renders this opinion improbable.

None of the interpretations just mentioned is wholly satisfactory, but if we had to choose one of them, we should say that the expansion of the Church corresponds least imperfectly to our Lord's mysterious words, because the Church is the kingdom of God on earth and its expansion is truly the work of God's power.

[16] In a decree dated July 1st, 1933, the Biblical Commission has declared that this is the true meaning of the passage, and that it is not lawful to say that the words "sensu litterali non respicere aeternam salutem animae, sed solam vitam temporalem hominis, non obstantibus ipsorum verborum tenore eorumque contextu, necnon unanimi interpretatione catholica." Cf. *Biblica*, 14 (1933), 435–447.

The Transfiguration

(Matt. 17:1–9; Mark 9:1–9; Luke 9:28–36; cf. Maps V, II)

Centuries before the coming of Christ, Mount Thabor had been immortalized by the triumphant canticle which Debbora, the prophetess of Israel, had sung from its peak in praise of Israel's resounding victory over the armies of the tyrant Jaban, led by his general Gisara (Judges, chaps. 4–5). But infinitely more glorious was the halo which the Prophet of Nazareth cast around the mount by illuminating it, if only for a moment, with the splendors of His divinity.

The announcement of the Passion had struck the Apostles a hard blow. Therefore, our Lord resolved to allow them to see a ray of His heavenly glory to raise their hearts and dissipate their gloomy forebodings, and at the same time to make them understand that if the Messias was going to face ignominy and death, it was not because any man compelled Him to do so, but solely because He chose that course of His own sovereignly free will.

The three Synoptic writers and St. Peter, who was an eyewitness of the event (cf. 2 Peter 1:18), say that it occurred on a mountain, but none of them gives its name or any indication as to its geographical position. Some authors believe that Mount Hermon was the scene of the Transfiguration because it is situated near Caesarea Philippi, where Jesus was at the time, because it is very high and solitary, and because the whiteness of the snow that covers its summit almost all year round offers an obvious analogy with the whiteness of Christ's garments during the awesome event. However, these reasons do not appear strong enough to offset the tradition already existing in the fourth century and represented especially by St. Jerome [17] and St. Cyril of Jerusalem,[18] who locate the great mystery on Mount Thabor.

This mountain stands in the extreme northeast of the great plain of Esdrelon, about 6½ miles from Nazareth. It rises 1,844 feet above sea level, and though only about 990 feet above the plain, it seems higher, due to its isolated position; thus it fits in well with the evangelists' description of a "high mountain." Hence there is no need to have recourse to Mount Hermon's great height of more than 9,000 feet to justify the Gospel expression. There were solitary places on Thabor's summit and slopes, for although Antiochus the Great had

[17] *Epist.* 46. 12; 108. 13: *PL* 22, 491, 889.
[18] *Catech.* 12. 16: *PG* 33. 744.

Mount Thabor.

built a wall around its peak in 218 B.C. and Josephus did likewise in A.D. 66, there is no mention in history of a settled population on the mountain; and Josephus always distinguishes it from the surrounding towns.[19] But even if there were some dwellings there, the mountain was extensive enough to contain many unfrequented spots as well.

Standing as it does in majestic isolation, Mount Thabor gives a singular impression of grace and dignity, and seems an ideal stage for the manifestation of our Lord's celestial splendor. One could say that the Heavenly Father, who was one day to make His august voice heard here, had taken pains to prepare a fitting background for the future glorification of His Son.

The evangelists give us no hint as to the path Jesus followed from Caesarea Philippi to Thabor. The simplest route between the two points is along the *Via Maris,* across the plain of Gennesareth by the side of the lake, up the Wadi el-Hammam, leaving Qarn Hattin on the right and continuing on to Lubiyeh, from which the mount is easily reached. The distance between Caesarea Philippi and Thabor is about forty-four miles, and so Jesus could have covered it in three days even if He had stopped at places along the road or gone a more roundabout way.

[19] Cf. *Wars* ii. 20. 6; iv. 1. 8.

MOUNT THABOR: *The Basilica of the Transfiguration.*

The evangelists record the space of time that intervened between the foretelling of the Passion and the Transfiguration: "after six days" (Matt. 17:1; Mark 9:2); "about eight days after" (Luke 9:28). The fact that they mention the interval seems to indicate that they saw a close connection between the two episodes, and as we have already pointed out, Jesus may have wished to allow His Apostles to catch a glimpse of His glory in order to counterbalance, as it were, the painful impression which His prophecy of suffering and death must have made on them.

Thus when He went up the mountain to pray, He took with Him His three favored disciples, Peter, James and John. From the fact that Luke (9:37) says that they came down on the following day, we gather that they spent the night on the mountain, a detail which makes it easier to understand how the heavenly radiance of our Lord's garments would have shone through the darkness and why the Apostles were "heavy with sleep" (Luke 9:32). Hence they must have begun the ascent late in the evening.

"And as he prayed, the appearance of his countenance was changed, and his raiment became a radiant white. And behold, two men were talking with him. And these were Moses and Elias, who,

Interior of Basilica of the Transfiguration.

appearing in glory, spoke of his death, which he was about to fulfill in Jerusalem."

The Law and the Prophets had referred clearly to the future Messias, as He Himself was to point out to His Apostles after the

Resurrection (Luke 24:44); now, by their presence on the mountain, the great legislator of Israel and the prophet who was the champion of God's glory, gave witness to the Messianic character of Jesus. And we should note particularly that it was amid all the splendor of the celestial radiance that Jesus spoke with Moses and Elias about the Passion and death which He was going to suffer in Jerusalem. For in God's designs for the Messias, glory and contempt, triumph and humiliation were closely connected: "Did not the Christ have to suffer these things before entering into his glory?" (Luke 24:26). That was precisely what the Apostles had not yet succeeded in understanding.

The vision was so awe-inspiring that Peter exclaimed: " 'Lord, it is good for us to be here. If thou wilt, let us set up three tents here, one for thee, one for Moses, and one for Elias.'

"As he was still speaking, behold, a bright cloud overshadowed them, and behold, a voice out of the cloud said, 'This is my beloved Son, in whom I am well pleased; hear him.'

"And on hearing it, the disciples fell on their faces and were exceedingly afraid. And Jesus came near and touched them, and said to them, 'Arise, and do not be afraid.'

"But lifting up their eyes, they saw no one but Jesus only."

St. John Chrysostom comments:

Happy, thrice happy were the Apostles, especially those three who had the good fortune to be enveloped in the cloud with the Lord! But we, too, if we wish, can see Christ, not as they saw Him on the mountain, but much more resplendent. For on that occasion He adapted the vision to His disciples' capacity and radiated only as much splendor as their weakness could bear. But on the last day He will come in the very glory of the Father, accompanied, not by Moses and Elias, but surrounded by an immense army of angels, archangels and cherubim, who will form His glorious crown.[20]

As He was coming down from the mountain the following day, Jesus gave the three Apostles a command: "Tell the vision to no one, till the Son of Man has risen from the dead."

They turned these words over in their minds, and as they descended the mountain, they whispered together, discussing what their Master could have meant by "till the Son of Man has risen from the

[20] *PG* 58, 554.

dead." They certainly believed in the resurrection of the body at the end of time, as did all the Jews except the Sadducees. Jesus, however, was speaking of His own personal Resurrection, and had referred to it as something that would occur within a comparatively short space of time. But resurrection involves death, and the Apostles could not understand how the Messias whom they had just seen resplendent and glorious could possibly be subject to death. It is true that Jesus Himself had spoken of His death only six days before in Caesarea Philippi, and that they had again heard Him refer to it only a few hours ago on the mountain. However, their national prejudices had so blinded them that not even one ray of light could penetrate their minds. In their bewilderment they felt urged to ask Jesus what He meant, and perhaps James and John tried to get Peter to act as spokesman, but he, having learned his lesson at Caesarea Philippi, had no desire to risk a second reprimand.

Besides the matter of resurrection and death, there was another point that puzzled them, and this they did venture to propose to Jesus for solution: "Why then do the Scribes say that Elias must come first?"

The Jews had a deep-rooted tradition, based on Malachias 4:5 *f.* (Hebrew 3:23 *f.*; cf. Ecclus. 48:10), that Elias was to reappear at the end of time to prepare for the coming of the Messias. Therefore the Apostles could not understand why Elias had appeared on the mountain, not before, but after the Messias' coming, and why his appearance had been so short, lasting as it did only a few moments.

Our Lord replied kindly to their question: "Elias indeed is to come and will restore all things." These words can be regarded as a confirmation of the Jewish tradition. Jesus then went on: "But I say to you that Elias has come already, and they did not know him, but did to him whatever they wished. So also shall the Son of Man suffer at their hands."

There seems to be a contradiction between our Lord's two declarations: "Elias . . . is to come and will restore all things," and "Elias has come already, and they did not know him." However, the apparent discrepancy disappears when we remember that in the first sentence, Jesus was referring to Elias the prophet, and in the second to John the Baptist. Both men were precursors of the Messias, John preparing for His first coming in the fullness of time, and Elias making ready for His second advent at the end of time. It was thus that the Apostles understood Christ's words: "Then the disciples understood that he had spoken to them of John the Baptist."

This interpretation seems to be suggested by the way in which the author of the Book of Ecclesiasticus (48:10) and St. John in his Apocalypse (11:3, 6) speak of Elias. Nevertheless, in view of our Lord's words as reported by St. Matthew (11:14): "He [John the Baptist] is Elias who was to come," and St. Mark (9:12): "But I say to you that Elias has come, and they did to him whatever they wished . . . ," we may perhaps say with many authors [21] that Jesus was referring solely to John, whom He called Elias because he possessed the characteristics which Malachias (4:5–6) attributed to the great prophet of the Old Testament.

Yet we must admit that it is not easy to ascertain whether our Lord understood Malachias' phrase "Elias the prophet" to refer to John the Baptist alone, or, rather, whether He conferred that name on John because, at the first coming of the Messias, the Precursor had performed the task which Elias, the Old Testament prophet, will perform at the second coming of Christ.[22]

In His reply to the Apostles' question Jesus did not simply answer what they had asked. Instead, He used His reference to the ill-treatment received by John the Baptist as a basis for repeating the prophecy of His Passion, thereby replying perhaps to their unspoken question, and certainly reiterating the truth which they found so hard to understand: "So also shall the Son of Man suffer at their hands."

Seeing that the Transfiguration was such an extraordinary and patently supernatural occurrence, we need not be surprised to find that the rationalists have attacked it with all the destructive power at their command. Some of them flatly deny that it ever occurred, and relegate it to the realm of myths and legends. Of course, it is very easy to deny that an event took place, but it is not so easy to explain away a sober account of an incident complete with concrete details. This is particularly true in the case of the Transfiguration, which is described, not once, but three times, in the Gospels. There are undoubtedly several circumstantial differences between the three ac-

---

[21] For example, Pirot, Buzy, Prat, Benoit, and others.

[22] As the angel had foretold to Zachary even before John's birth, namely, that John was to precede the Messias "in the spirit and power of Elias" (Luke 1:17).

counts, but these minor variations only serve to enhance the historical value of the Gospel narratives.

Other rationalists, while admitting the reality of the event, explain it in a purely natural way. They claim that while Jesus and the Apostles were on the mountain a sudden storm broke out, a flash of lightning lit up the Master's face, and the Apostles took the rolling of thunder for the voice of the Father. Then, presupposing that the incident took place on Mount Hermon, these critics hold that Christ's garments were made radiant by the light reflected from the snow that covered the mountaintop. Still others say that this fantastic explanation offers more difficulties than the miracle it seeks to eliminate. They maintain, instead, that everything happened as described, but *only in the minds of the Apostles,* whose imagination had been inflamed at Caesarea Philippi by the violent contrast between the glory of the Messias, as proclaimed by St. Peter, and the great humiliations foretold by Jesus.

We do not think it necessary to stop and show how unfounded, how puerile even, are these hypotheses. Actually, they are so unlikely that they refute themselves. We should like to point out, however, that the evangelists knew very well how to distinguish between dreams and reality, for they speak elsewhere about the revelations made in dreams to Joseph at Nazareth and Bethlehem. And they were even more capable of discerning the difference between objective reality and visions. This certainly applies to the three Apostles who saw the Transfiguration, one of whom later described it in explicit terms (cf. 2 Peter 1:15 *ff.*). As regards the light reflected from the snow, the rolling of thunder and the flashing of lightning—all that is sheer fantasy.[23]

The Boy Possessed by the Devil
(Matt. 17:14–20; Mark 9:13–28; Luke 9:37–44)

While Jesus was coming down from Mount Thabor engaged in peaceful conversation with His three beloved and privileged Apostles, a very different scene was being enacted at the foot of the mountain.

An anguished father, hearing of our Lord's arrival in the district,

[23] These rationalistic attempts at interpretation are listed and refuted in E. Dabrowski's *La Transfiguration de Jésus* (Romae, 1939), pp. 113–156.

had brought his son to be freed from the devil that possessed him. Since he and his demoniac son were well known to the people of the place, a crowd had accompanied them to see the anticipated miracle, and in the group were several Scribes. When the suppliants arrived, our Lord had already ascended the mountain, to the dismay of the poor father and the disappointment of the crowd, who felt cheated out of a sensation. But recovering, they said to themselves, are there not still nine disciples here, who surely share their Master's power? The unhappy father turned to the Apostles, appealing to them to cure his son, and they, remembering that they had once been given the power to cure the sick and cast out devils, saw no reason why they should not be able to rid the boy of the evil spirit that was tormenting him. Then, too, if they worked the miracle it would redound to the credit of their Master. So, with great authority, they commanded the devil to go out of the boy. But nothing happened. The evil spirit did not obey, and the boy remained as before. Most likely they repeated the command, but with the same lack of result. The crowd began to whisper among themselves, and the Scribes, gloating over the Apostles' defeat, began to argue with them, no doubt throwing in their faces their lack of power and using it to cast a slur on their Master. Meanwhile the crowd, curious as ever, were milling around the Apostles and the mocking Scribes.

At this point Jesus appeared and saw the altercation. When the crowd realized that He had returned, they ran forward to meet Him, and He, having calmed them somewhat, asked them: "What are you arguing about among yourselves?"

The Apostles, mortified at their failure, kept silent, while the Scribes, no longer bold now that Jesus was there, did not dare answer. But the father of the boy approached our Lord, and falling on his knees before Him said: "Master, I have brought to thee my son, who has a dumb spirit; and wherever it seizes him it throws him down, and he foams and grinds his teeth; and he is wasting away. And I told thy disciples to cast it out, but they could not." And he repeated his anguished petition: "Master, I pray thee to look at my son, for he is my only child: have pity on him."

The whole combination of circumstances—the lack of faith on the part of His own disciples, the malice of the Scribes, the inconstancy of the people always eager to see miracles and never really converted, the imperfect dispositions of the father, who did not yet believe—all these things begot deep sadness and holy anger in our Lord's heart, causing Him to exclaim poignantly: "O unbelieving and perverse generation, how long shall I be with you? How long shall I put up with you?" Yet He wished to give the crowd still another proof of His goodness and power: "Bring him here to me," he said.

They brought him, but as soon as the evil spirit saw Jesus, it threw the boy into convulsions so that he fell down on the ground and rolled around foaming at the mouth. Our Lord asked the father: "How long is it since this has come upon him?"

"From his infancy. Oftentimes it has thrown him into the fire and into the waters to destroy him. But if thou canst do anything, have compassion on us and help us."

Then Jesus said: "If thou canst believe, all things are possible to him who believes."

And the good man, with the tears streaming down his face, cried out fervently and humbly: "I do believe; help my unbelief."

Meanwhile, the crowd had grown larger and was pushing closer and closer about our Lord to see what was happening. When He had questioned the father and elicited his act of faith, Jesus rebuked the unclean spirit: "Thou deaf and dumb spirit, I command thee, go out of him and enter him no more."

The devil could not stand against the voice of the Master as it had against the command of the disciples. Crying out and violently convulsing the boy, it left him apparently lifeless, so that many of the onlookers exclaimed: "He is dead!" But Jesus, taking him by the hand, raised him from the ground and gave him to his father; and those who saw the miracle were astounded at such a display of power.

While all this was going on, the Apostles had stood pensively by, wondering why they had not been able to cast out this devil as they had so many others. Therefore, as soon as they got a chance to speak to Jesus alone, they asked him: "Why could we not cast it out?"

To which Jesus answered: "This kind can be cast out only by prayer and fasting."

This sad yet ultimately consoling episode is generally thought to have taken place in the little town of Daburiyeh (the Dabaritta of Josephus and rabbinical literature) which lies at the foot of Mount Thabor.[24]

24 Cf. *Wars* ii. 21. 3.

A Lesson in Humility: Forgiveness of Injuries
(Matt. 17:21–18:35; Mark 9:32–49; Luke 9:44–50; cf. Map II)

After His glorious Transfiguration, Jesus returned from Thabor to Capharnaum, accompanied by His Apostles. From St. Mark's manner of speaking (9:29), it would appear that our Lord did not go directly to Capharnaum, which was only one long day's walk from Mount Thabor, but journeyed about Galilee. However, the second evangelist gives no other indication of the route the party followed. We do know one thing from St. Mark's account—that Jesus travelled incognito: "and he did not wish anyone to know it," i.e., that He was passing through, no doubt because He wanted to speak undisturbed with His disciples.[25]

As they walked along at their ease, unmolested by crowds, Jesus made use of the peripatetic method of instruction and engaged in close conversation with His Apostles. From the Gospel narrative we gather that, as usually happens when a large party is travelling on foot, the Apostles split up into small groups. It even seems that some of them left the main body and went by different routes, perhaps to avoid attracting attention. This custom of dividing up the party would appear to be the reason for our Lord's question when they came together in the house at Capharnaum: "What were you arguing about on the way?" Apparently He had not taken part in the conversation, but had heard it at a distance without their knowing that He was doing so. The custom also explains the incident of St. John's rebuking the man who was casting out devils in Christ's name, for if our Lord had been present, the Apostle would certainly not have assumed such authority.

We can visualize Jesus walking first with one group and then with another, conversing intimately with two or three Apostles at a time, and giving the remainder an opportunity of speaking freely among themselves and of digesting what He had taught them, so that they would be all the more eager to receive further lessons. And these lessons fell on the Apostles' hearts like gentle rain upon fertile soil. But, good pupils though they were in other things, they still did not succeed in understanding the Passion of the Son of Man, although on this occasion our Lord foretold it for the third time. St. Luke (9:45)

---

[25] Mark 9:30 seems to hint at this: "For he was teaching his disciples. . . ."

expressly says that "they did not understand this saying" and were afraid to ask Him about it. No doubt a vague uncertainty, a degree of embarrassment and perhaps the instinctive fear that they would be disquieted by what they would hear, made them reluctant to request an explanation. For the rest, the evangelist remarks that their incomprehension was part of God's plan, for if they had seen clearly the lowering clouds of the Passion advancing over the horizon, and had been fully aware of the future agonizing and ignominious death of their Master, they would perhaps have lacked the courage to follow Him and would have abandoned Him.

When they all finally arrived at the house in Capharnaum, probably the home of Peter's family, Jesus reprimanded them severely. St. Mark describes the episode so vividly and in such detail that we can almost see it being enacted before our very eyes. No sooner had they reached the house than Jesus, addressing the groups nearest Him, asked with an air of natural interest: "What were you arguing about on the way?"

It is quite possible that the dispute had become heated and that the Apostles' ruffled composure gave our Lord an opening for His inquiry. They, however, were ashamed of themselves and did not answer. But Jesus, knowing the reason for their confusion, did not persist in His demand for an explanation. Instead He sat down as if to rest (in reality He must have been tired after the journey), waited until the others arrived and then summoned them all about Him. A child happened to be there also, and Jesus called him too, placing him in the midst of the Apostles, who were standing around in a circle. They looked at each other in surprise, wondering what their Master intended to do. Jesus drew the child to Him, embraced him and said to the Apostles: "Amen I say to you, unless you turn and become like little children, you will not enter the kingdom of heaven" (Matt. 18:3). "If any man wishes to be first, he shall be last of all, and servant of all" (Mark 9:34).

At this point, presuming on the liberty which the good Master allowed His disciples in general, and perhaps His beloved disciple in particular, John broke in on our Lord's discourse with the words: "Master, we saw a man who was not one of our followers casting out devils in thy name, and we forbade him."

Probably the young Apostle thought he had done a very laudable deed and, hoping to receive well-merited praise, was eager to let his

Master know about it. Great indeed must have been his disappointment when Jesus not only did not praise him but expressed evident
disapproval, concluding with a general maxim: "He who is not
against you [26] is for you."

By this the Divine Master meant that we ought always to be more
inclined to think good rather than evil of our neighbors, as against
the cynical adage: "Think the worst and you'll be right." At first His
words seem to contradict what He had said before (Matt. 12:30;
Luke 11:13): "He who is not with me is against me." But there is
really no contradiction, because in the latter case our Lord was speaking of a man's true feelings about Him; and since Christ and Beelzebub
have nothing in common, everyone who is not with Christ is with Beelzebub and therefore against Christ: neutrality in this matter is impossible. On the other hand, in Mark 9:39 and Luke 9:50, as the context
sufficiently proves, He is dealing with a subjective judgment of other
men's inner dispositions: if we do not discover in others evident signs
that they are against Christ, we are to assume that they are for Him.
This is simply an application of the axiom: "Every man is innocent
until proved guilty," not merely out of charity, but in all justice and
prudence.[27]

When our Lord, with kind condescension, had dealt with His
zealous disciple's somewhat indiscreet interruption, He resumed His
discourse, or, as we had better say, His conversation, for His counsels
and replies alternated with His disciples' questions, a fact which
explains a certain lack of unity between the various parts of His
address on this occasion. As we all know, in such circumstances a
phrase or even a word is sufficient to change the current of conversation to a completely different subject. The Gospel narrative is
simply a faithful painting from life wherein we see the disciples being
taught by their Divine Master. Kindly and with fatherly patience,
never showing displeasure at their impertinence and always replying
gently, He allowed them to voice their doubts and ask questions
freely.

Returning to the subject of children, He continued: "Whoever
causes one of these little ones who believe in me to sin, it were better

---

[26] ἡμῶν is the most probable reading in Mark 9:39: but that of Luke 9:50, ὑμῶν,
seems more in harmony with the context.

[27] There are other interpretations which we need not pause to mention. The one
which we have given seems the most satisfactory and is accepted by Lagrange,
Lebreton and others.

for him to have a great millstone hung around his neck, and to be drowned in the depths of the sea." Then, broadening the scope of His discourse on scandals, He added: "Woe to the world because of scandals! For it must needs be that scandals come, but woe to the man through whom scandal does come! And if thy hand or thy foot is an occasion of sin to thee, cut it off and cast it from thee! It is better for thee to enter life maimed or lame, than, having two hands or two feet, to be cast into the everlasting fire." As if He could not stop thinking about His beloved little ones, He returned to them once more, saying: "See that you do not despise one of these little ones; for I tell you, their angels in heaven always behold the face of my Father in heaven." [28]

Then, so that no one should think himself at liberty to pay little regard to children just because they are children, our Lord proposed a beautiful parable which shows how valuable each soul is in God's eyes:

"What do you think? If a man have a hundred sheep, and one of them stray, will he not leave the ninety-nine in the mountains, and go in search of the one that has strayed? And if he happen to find it, amen I say to you, he rejoices over it more than over the ninety-nine that did not go astray. Even so, it is not the will of your Father in heaven that a single one of these little ones should perish."

Just as God is the Good Shepherd who tries to bring the lost sheep back to the fold, so also the Apostles, and the faithful in general, were to strive to put the sinner back on the right road; [29] and in order that they should do so prudently and charitably, Jesus marked out three stages of approach, as it were. First of all, they were to correct the sinner in secret, to spare him embarrassment. If he remained obstinate, they were to remonstrate with him in the presence of one or two witnesses. But if even that failed to move him, they were to appeal to the Church, as the last resort. Then if he refused to heed the Church, all that remained to do was to regard him as a heathen and a publican. Such a procedure takes it for granted that the Church has judicial power, as is also clearly indicated by the words that follow:

---

[28] The following phrase, Matthew 18:12: "For the Son of Man came to save what was lost," is of doubtful authenticity.

[29] It should be noted that the *in te* of the Vulgate (Matt. 18:15:"But if thy brother sin *against thee*"), which also appears in Greek codices, does not seem to be authentic. Hence our Lord was not speaking of a personal offense, but simply of sin in general.

"Amen I say to you, whatever you bind on earth shall be bound also in heaven; and whatever you loose on earth shall be loosed also in heaven." Then, as if He wished to emphasize the unity which ought to reign among the faithful and the great advantages of that unity, Jesus pronounced these consoling words: "If two of you shall agree on earth about anything at all for which they ask, it shall be done for them by my Father in heaven. For where two or three are gathered together for my sake, there am I in the midst of them."

By an association of ideas, our Lord's teaching on fraternal correction presented Peter with a problem. His brother's sin might consist in a personal injury, and although he knew the basic law of pardoning offenses, the Apostle was not sure about its extent. Therefore he asked: "Lord, how often shall my brother sin against me, and I forgive him? Up to seven times?"

No doubt Peter considered seven a large number of times to forgive. But Jesus replied: "I do not say to thee seven times, but seventy times seven," i.e., indefinitely, without limitation. It would be intolerable if man, a miserable creature, were to refuse forgiveness to anyone who injured him, while God, the Creator, always pardons the penitent sinner. To show how absurd and contemptible such conduct would be, Jesus related the beautiful parable of the generous king and the cruel debtor. The monarch, moved to compassion, forgave one of his servants a debt of ten thousand talents, an enormous sum, about twenty-one million dollars in our money. But almost immediately after he had been released from his obligation, the debtor met one of his fellow servants who owed him a hundred denarii (about thirty-five dollars), and seizing him by the throat, he demanded payment in full at once. The poor man pleaded for time to obtain the money, but his aggressor would not listen and had him thrown into prison. When the king heard what had happened, he summoned the cruel servant, and said to him: "Wicked servant! I forgave thee all the debt because thou didst entreat me. Shouldst not thou also have had pity on thy fellow servant, even as I had pity on thee?" The monarch then angrily handed him over to the torturers until he should pay all he owed.

With a grave warning, Jesus concluded the parable: "So also my heavenly Father will do to you, if you do not each forgive your brothers from your hearts."

It was as if He had said: "Do you wish to be forgiven by God?

Then forgive other men, your brothers, from your heart, for if you do not do so, then you pronounce sentence against yourself every day when you say: 'Forgive us our trespasses as we forgive those who trespass against us.' "

The Coin in the Fish's Mouth
(Matt. 17:23–26)

About this time, shortly after the Apostles' return to Capharnaum, the Temple taxgatherers met Peter on the street and asked him if his Master was not going to pay the didrachma, i.e., two drachmas, equivalent to half a shekel,[30] about seventy cents in our money. In Exodus 30:12–14, God had commanded Moses, when he was taking the census of the children of Israel, to have every man of twenty years and over pay a half-shekel. Nehemias (2 Esdras 10:33 f.) had ordered everyone to contribute a third of a shekel each year for the support of the Temple. Later (it is not possible to fix the date more exactly), the practice of offering a half-shekel was introduced, as Josephus bears witness;[31] and this custom was still in force in our Lord's day.

Unhesitatingly Peter answered "Yes" to the tax collectors' question, and upon returning to the house, he was about to tell his Master of their demand when Jesus forestalled him by proposing a parable: "What dost thou think, Peter? From whom do the kings of the earth receive tribute or customs; from their own sons, or from others?"

Peter replied: "From others."

"The sons then are exempt."

Of course the king's sons would not have to pay tribute to their father; and because Jesus was the Son of God, the Son of the true King of Israel, He was not obliged to pay the tax.

Yet He added: "But that we may not give offense to them, go to the sea and cast a hook and take the first fish that comes up. And opening its mouth thou wilt find a stater;[32] take that and give it to them for me and for thee."

Among the many kinds of fish in the Sea of Galilee there is one called *Chromis Simonis* which has a peculiar property: "At the end of

---

[30] *Ant.* iii. 8. 2.

[31] *Ant.* xviii. 9. 1.

[32] Equivalent to four Greek drachmas or one Hebrew shekel. (About $1.40 in our money.—Translator.)

May or the beginning of June, the female lays her eggs in the slime among the reeds. Shortly afterwards, the male *Chromis* gathers up the eggs in his mouth and in the space of a few days, the metamorphosis is complete. The young fish, which grow rapidly, are packed together like seeds in a pomegranate, and the mouth of the male fish becomes so full that he can scarcely close it." [33] Some authors say that the males of this species of fish are so used to carrying their young in the manner just described that when their mouths are empty they feel an urge to fill them, which they do by picking up pebbles. Thus the *Chromis* which St. Peter caught had picked up a lost stater along with its mouthful of small stones. In that case, the miracle would consist in our Lord's supernatural knowledge of the fact that the fish had the coin in its mouth and that it would be the first to take Peter's hook.

The Hostility of the Samaritans: Three Callings
(Luke 9:51–61; Matt. 8:19–22; John 7:2–10; cf. Maps V and IV)

Summer was drawing to a close, and since Jesus wished to celebrate the approaching feast of Tabernacles in Jerusalem, He left Galilee to go to the capital. With this departure, He practically abandoned Galilee forever; we say "practically" because it is probable that He paid His home province one more visit, but only a short and flying one. St. Luke (9:51) begins his account of the journey to the Holy City with a certain solemnity: "Now it came to pass, when the days had come for him to be taken up, that he steadfastly set his face to go to Jerusalem. . . ."

For the third evangelist, this was the beginning of that series of missionary journeys which was to end finally in the fatal dénouement in Jerusalem, the Passion and Death of Christ, which in turn were to be followed by the glorious Resurrection and Ascension. St. Luke had this divine tragedy before his eyes as he wrote, and for him the six months that were to pass were but the preparation for the great sacrifice and triumph.[34]

[33] Z. Biever, *Conférences de Saint-Étienne* (Paris, 1910–1911), pp. 295 *f.* See also E. Masterman, *Studies in Galilee* (Chicago: University of Chicago Press, 1909), pp. 43 *f.* Father Täper, the director of the hospice at et-Tabgha, told the present writer that, on more than one occasion, he had seen the young of this species take refuge in their father's mouth when frightened by the presence of a large fish.

[34] In three different places St. Luke says that Jesus was going to Jerusalem: 9:51:

The announcement of our Lord's going to Jerusalem (Luke 9:51) begins the much-discussed "Lucan section"—so called because it is almost wholly proper to Luke—which extends to Luke 18:14. It is not easy to co-ordinate these chapters with the narratives of the other two Synoptic authors or St. John, and as a result, numerous hypotheses have been advanced concerning this Lucan section, each possessing a greater or lesser degree of probability, but none being completely certain.

The crucial problems in the Lucan section are: (1) Is Luke 9:51 parallel to John 7:2, 10, where Jesus goes to the feast of Tabernacles, or to Matthew 19:1 and Mark 10:1, where He leaves Galilee for the last time? (2) If Luke 9:51 is parallel to John 7:2, 10, did Jesus return to Galilee after the feast of Tabernacles? (3) Is the Lucan section a closely-knit account of events that took place in uninterrupted chronological sequence, or is it, rather, a collection of incidents which belong to different periods and which St. Luke brought together in a continuous narrative, without regard, perhaps, for the precise circumstances of time and even of place in which each incident occurred?

Without pausing to review the many interpretations that have been suggested, and recognizing the fact that each theory presents its own difficulty, we believe it most probable that: (1) Luke 9:51 is parallel to John 7:2, 10; [35] (2) When the feast of Tabernacles was over, Jesus returned for a very short time to Galilee and most probably to Capharnaum or its environs.[36] We are led to this conclusion by

"He steadfastly set his face to go to Jerusalem"; 13:22: "And he was passing . . . making his way towards Jerusalem"; 17:11: "As he was going to Jerusalem . . . he was passing between Samaria and Galilee." Several authors, Levesque, for example, find in these three passages indications of three distinct journeys, and they support their claim by pointing to the chronological positions of the passages and their correspondence with the events narrated in the other three Gospels. But in our opinion the three passages refer to so many stages of one and the same journey, which had Jerusalem as its aim. See p. 504 below.

[35] Godet (cf. Lebreton, *Life and Teachings of Jesus Christ,* II, 4–5; Bover, *Est. Bibl.,* 4 [1943], 3–10) opposes this identification by pointing out that in St. John our Lord's departure was secret, while in St. Luke it must necessarily have been public, since it must have taken place in connection with the sending of the seventy disciples (Luke 10:1), an event that could not fail to be known. This objection can be eliminated if we simply accept the very plausible supposition that the sending of the disciples took place *after* the feast of Tabernacles.

[36] Some may object that, if Jesus had to return to Galilee, why does St. Luke employ, in 9:51, a formula so solemn that it seems to indicate a definitive and final action? In our opinion, this objection is easily answered: our Lord's visit was so fleeting that the evangelist scarcely takes it into account; then, too, this

the fact that the anathema which Christ hurled against Corozain, Capharnaum and Bethsaida (Luke 10:13–15) is more easily understood if it was pronounced within sight of these cities rather than from a great distance, in Judea. It is true that our case falls to the ground if the incident is placed before the feast of Tabernacles: but since we think it most probable that Luke 9:51 is parallel to John 7:2, 10, there is then no reason to disrupt the chronological order of Luke 9:51—10:1–20.

(3) It is very difficult to give a sound verdict on the nature of the Lucan section. We are inclined to believe that it is a record of events that are, in general, closely linked together. But, we repeat, the reasons that can be adduced for and against this opinion are almost evenly balanced. As regards the journeys narrated by St. Luke, we are convinced that the evangelist did not intend to record three distinct journeys but only the one, namely, that which he announced with some solemnity in 9:51, and which was made up of several parts, each of which can, to a certain extent, be regarded as a stage on the road to Jerusalem and the Passion. The other two passages (13:22; 17:11) deal with this one journey, which was prolonged and extended through several regions, but which was always directed towards the Holy City as its final goal.[37]

Jesus had not gone up to Jerusalem for the Passover of that year; since the second multiplication of loaves and, particularly, since the discourse on the Bread of Life in the synagogue at Capharnaum, He had led a retired life, taken up principally with instructing His Apostles. His relatives, or brethren, as they were commonly called, were not pleased with His retirement, and wanted Him to show Himself more in public and to make a greater display of His power. However, they were not motivated by solicitude for Jesus or for His doctrine, but only by the thought of the glory that would redound to themselves.

St. John (7:5) notes that His relatives did not believe in him, a fact which may seem surprising after His two years of public ministry, but which, in reality, is easily accounted for. They, like their compatriots in general, had deep-rooted convictions that the Messias

---

visit, like the other incidental journeys of this period, was only part of the one great journey whose final aim was Jerusalem, the scene of the great dénouement, the Passion and Death of our Lord.

[37] See above, pp. 70 ff.

would be a glorious conqueror, whereas Jesus was a model of humility and modesty. Furthermore, the people's enthusiasm for Him had cooled considerably since His promise of the Bread of Life, and it is probable that since then the prevailing atmosphere in Capharnaum had been, perhaps, not one of positive hostility, but certainly one of cold reserve. And His relatives, though they could scarcely escape being influenced by this general attitude, still believed that He could win glory and renown by using His power of working miracles.[38] Consequently, they urged Him to go up to Jerusalem for the approaching feast of Tabernacles: "Leave here," they said to Him, "and go into Judea that thy disciples also may see the works that thou dost. . . . If thou dost these things, manifest thyself to the world."

But He answered: "My time has not yet come. . . . As for you, go up to the feast, but I do not go up to this feast, for my time is not yet fulfilled."

Our Lord's reply is enigmatic because He apparently contradicted it by His subsequent action. First He said clearly: "I do not go up," giving as His reason the fact that His time had not yet come; but then, when His brethren had left, He did go to Jerusalem.[39] A little thought, however, will show how easily our Lord's words and actions can be harmonized. By saying He was not going, He meant that He was not prepared to travel in a caravan with the Galilean group and to enter Jerusalem openly, because the opportune moment for Him to do so had not yet come.[40] They could go any way they wished because they had no enemies to fear, whereas He had to be on His guard, for His foes were spying on Him, and He had to avoid a clamorous appearance in the capital. His "time," the opportune moment for participating in the feast, came when His brethren had left and He could quietly and unostentatiously start out with His small group of disciples for Jerusalem.

---

[38] But see above, pp. 365 f., where we describe how our Lord's brethren came to seize Him because they thought He was insane. Apparently they had changed their minds somewhat with the passage of time; yet, as we have said, St. John (7:5) remarks that "not even his brethren believed in him."

[39] A large number of authoritative manuscripts have οὔπω, "not yet," instead of οὔκ, "not," in itself a very desirable reading since it does away with the difficulty. But its very desirability leads one to fear that it was purposely introduced into the text, and that consequently it has no right to be considered authentic.

[40] More than a few authors understand the words "my time" to refer to His Passion and subsequent glorification.

As we have already indicated, there were two routes from Capharnaum to Jerusalem—one along the River Jordan, and the other, more direct, through Samaria, which was the one Jesus now chose. He was accompanied by His disciples and it would have been difficult to find lodging if they all came unannounced to an inn at nightfall. Therefore the prudent Master sent some of His companions ahead to arrange for accommodations.

They had to spend the first night in Samaritan territory. We are not told the name of the town to which the messengers went, but it must have been between Jenin, on the northern border of Samaria, and Sichem. Perhaps it was either Qubatiyeh, Sanur or Geba (Jeba'), towns which lay along the route that Jesus followed. At any rate, the travellers were refused hospitality, not because there was no room for them, but because they were going to Jerusalem. In the face of such ill will and fanaticism, the two "Sons of Thunder" became indignant and, perhaps recalling what Elias had done (4 Kings 1:10), wanted to call down fire from heaven to avenge the insult to their Master: "Lord, wilt thou that we bid fire come down from heaven and consume them?"

Their misguided zeal, however, earned them a severe reproach and a stern lesson on the spirit of meekness that impregnated the New Law: "You do not know of what manner of spirit you are; for the Son of Man did not come to destroy men's lives, but to save them."

Without punishing the insolence of these Samaritans, Jesus and His disciples set out for another village.

According to St. Luke (9:57–62), it was on this journey that Jesus met the three men who offered to follow Him. It is possible and even probable that the three meetings occurred at different times and in different places (cf. Matt. 8:19–22), and that the evangelist brings them together here because of their similarity to each other, for they form a short practical treatise on vocation, that is, on the conditions required for the following of Christ. It should be noted that the first man and the third offered themselves spontaneously, while the second received an explicit invitation from Jesus. Our Lord did not reject the first one (who, according to Matthew 8:19, was a Scribe), but merely pointed out to him the consequences of following the Son of Man: "The foxes have dens, and the birds of the air have nests, but the Son of Man has nowhere to lay his head," i.e., following Jesus meant accepting privations and labors. It is probable that the Scribe, when confronted with this somber future, abandoned his noble resolve.

Again according to St. Matthew (8:21), the second was one of our Lord's own disciples who was probably already following Him. This man, having just received the news that his father had died, requested permission to go home to bury him. But our Lord answered: "Leave the dead [i.e., the men of the world, those who do not follow a special divine vocation] to bury their dead." [41] This reply may sound harsh, but He was using this particular, concrete case to teach all men in general that at times even the most legitimate desires and affections must be sacrificed in God's service, and that the preaching of the kingdom of God must take precedence over all personal interests.

The third man lacked generosity and alacrity, for the divine call must be followed without delay, and he who looks back is not worthy to become an apostle of the kingdom of God: "No one, having put his hand to the plow and looking back, is fit for the kingdom of God."

[41] Our Lord used the word "dead" first in its figurative, and then in its literal sense.

19. From the Feast of Tabernacles to the Feast of Dedication (29 A.D.)

The Feast of Tabernacles
(John 7:11—8:59)

The feast of Tabernacles was celebrated from the 15th to the 22nd of the month of Tishri, which corresponds to the end of September and the beginning of October, so that the celebration lasted roughly from September 30th to October 7th. It had been instituted to commemorate the Israelites' wandering in the desert and to give God thanks for the harvest (cf. Lev. 23:33–43; Deut. 10:13–16). Hence the custom of erecting bowers of branches in the courtyards of the houses, in the gardens and on the flat roof tops to recall the tents in which the Chosen People had lived for forty years. Even today in Jerusalem during the feast of the Tents, one can see on all sides small huts made of branches and decorated inside with various kinds of fruit. It is customary for the members of each family to spend a good part of the day in their arbor. This used to be one of the most solemn feasts, yet at the same time one of the most joyous. It was the occasion for a great gathering, for the crowds that came to celebrate it were larger than for any other feast. In fact, Jews and proselytes used to flock to Jerusalem from the most distant territories to partake in the festivities and to pay their Temple tax.

The solemnity and drama of the religious ceremonies were as breath-taking as the crowds were numerous. At midnight of the first day, the gates of the Temple were opened wide, and all the sacred precincts were ablaze with lights. On the fifteen steps of the staircase that led down from the Court of Israel to the Court of the Women, the Levites made their harps, lyres and cymbals resound joyfully. At cock-crow, the priests, standing at the top of the staircase in the Gate of Nicanor (the Beautiful Gate), blew three blasts on their trumpets, one sustained blast, one quavering and the third sustained. Then they descended to the tenth step and once more sounded the trumpets three times. They then came down the remaining steps, and upon reaching the Court of the Women, they blew a third series of blasts on their trumpets. Advancing to the Eastern Gate, they halted there, and turning to face the Temple building, they pronounced the following solemn words, which seemed like a profession of faith: "Our fathers when they were in this place turned with their backs toward the Temple of the Lord and their faces toward the east, and they worshipped the sun toward the east; but as for us, our eyes are turned toward the Lord." And they ended by repeating: "We are the Lord's, and our eyes are turned to the Lord." [1] Such a solemn, dramatic scene could not fail to leave a deep impression on all who saw it.

Although it had been a long time since Jesus had allowed Himself to be seen in Jerusalem, the people of the city had not forgotten Him. Apart from everything else, the Galileans who had preceded Him to the feast (cf. John 7:10) probably refreshed the citizens' memory. But be that as it may, we do know that at that moment in the capital, and particularly in the environs of the Temple, there was lively interest in Him and a diversity of feelings about Him.

St. John (7:2–10:21), to whom we owe the narrative, paints a masterly series of pictures which allows us to sense vividly the atmosphere which surrounded Jesus, the inner dispositions of those who came in closest contact with Him, the diversity of opinion and feeling about Him, and, in particular, the marked contrast between the cold, often actively hostile attitude of the Jewish leaders and the favorable, even enthusiastic temper of the people. The clash between the forces of good and evil, the alternation of brilliant light and deep shadow, make this period a tensely dramatic one.

[1] There is a detailed description of these ceremonies in the *Mishnah, Sukkah* 5:4.

The religious leaders had hoped that Jesus would come to the feast, not because they wished to listen docilely to His teaching, but because they wanted to spy on Him and find some pretext for accusing Him. Therefore, disappointed at not finding Him among the pilgrims, they asked one another: "Where is he?"

The people at large were of two minds concerning Jesus, some saying, "He is a good man," while others protested, "No, rather he seduces the crowd." There were also those who, upon hearing His teaching and recalling the miracles He had worked, declared themselves openly on His side: "When the Christ comes will he work more signs than this man works? . . . This is truly the Prophet."

When the feast was already half over, Jesus entered the Temple and began to teach. But His enemies interrupted Him constantly, and there ensued a lively exchange of argument and rebuttal.

Certain Scribes and Pharisees who had joined our Lord's audience in order to spy on Him, murmured aloud in feigned, ironical surprise: "How does this man come by learning since he has not studied?"

To which Jesus replied: "My teaching is not my own, but his who sent me." Fully aware of their evil intentions, He asked: "Why do you seek to put me to death?"

Some of the crowd answered: "Thou hast a devil. Who seeks to put thee to death?" Others murmured: "Is not this the man they seek to kill? And behold, he speaks openly and they say nothing to him. Can it be that the rulers have really come to know that this is the Christ?" But they added: "Yet we know where this man is from; but when the Christ comes, no one will know where he is from."

They passed these last remarks among themselves, not intending Jesus to hear them. But He replied as if their observations had been addressed to Him directly: "You both know me, and know where I am from. Yet I have not come of myself, but he is true who has sent me, whom you do not know."

On hearing this, His enemies wished to seize Him there and then, but no one laid hands on Him, for His hour had not yet come.

Yet not everyone was against Him, for many of the people believed in Him, admired Him and spoke in His favor. The fact that they did so gave the priests and Pharisees new cause for alarm, so that they decided to strike the final blow, and sent their guards to seize Him immediately. When the guards returned without Him, the Jewish leaders demanded angrily: "Why have you not brought him?"

The guards replied: "Never has man spoken as this man."

In angry frustration, the Pharisees asked sarcastically: "Have you also been led astray? Has any one of the rulers believed in him, or any of the Pharisees? But this crowd, which does not know the Law, is accursed."

At this point Nicodemus, who was present, observed sagely: "Does our Law judge a man unless it first give him a hearing, and know what he does?"

The remark was a very just one, and the others could find no answer except the ironic rejoinder: "Art thou also a Galilean? Search the Scriptures and see that out of Galilee arises no prophet."

On this note of obstinate ill will, they dispersed, each one returning to his house.

The Woman Taken in Adultery
(John 8:3–11)

The incident of the adulterous woman is lacking in numerous manuscripts; the Greek Fathers do not mention it, and apparently some of the Latin Fathers, St. Cyprian, for example, did not know of it, although others among them, such as St. Ambrose and St. Augustine, regarded it as authentic. At all events, whether or not the passage comes from the pen of St. John, a point upon which critics and exegetes are divided, it is certainly canonical and, consequently, it is inspired and forms an integral part of Sacred Scripture.[2]

After the intense apostolic labor of the day, rendered all the more fatiguing by the constant attacks of His enemies, Jesus retired to the Mount of Olives, while His listeners returned to their homes. It does not seem that He went as far afield as Bethany, for the evangelist would very likely have mentioned it if He had done so. Instead, He probably spent the night in a tent or a cave, perhaps in the grotto which many regarded as the place of the Agony, or in the one near the top of the mount, which tradition has venerated as the scene of

---

[2] Quite a few authors hold that the narrative is part of the authentic Gospel tradition, but say that it was incorporated into St. John's Gospel only at a later date. Cf. L. de Grandmaison, *Jesus Christ,* II, 363, n. Z; Lagrange, *Év. selon S. Jean, in loc.*

His teaching, and over which St. Helena built a basilica. From either place, He could reach the Temple in a short time through the Eastern Gate.

At dawn the following day, He was again in the Temple. Soon He was surrounded by a crowd, and, sitting down, He began to teach, as was His custom. The Scribes and Pharisees, always on the lookout for a chance to accuse Him, came to ask His opinion on the interpretation of the Law in a problem of moral theology. The case was concerned with Moses' command that an adulterous woman be condemned to death (Deut. 22:22; Lev. 20:10), and that a betrothed woman who had yielded to seduction be stoned (Deut. 22:23 f.).

The Scribes and Pharisees had brought with them a woman who, a short while ago, had been taken in adultery, and placing her before Jesus, they said to Him: "Master, this woman has just now been caught in adultery. And in the Law Moses commanded us to stone such persons. What, therefore, dost thou say?"

On the surface their question was a respectful one, and they seemed to be honoring Christ by asking His opinion, but in reality they were trying to trap Him. If He favored punishing the woman according to the letter of the Law, they would accuse Him of harshness, and if He advocated letting her go unpunished, they would say that He was breaking the Law. The trap seemed so escape-proof that, behind their obsequious demeanor, they were already gloating over their victory. But Jesus did not answer their barbed question. Seated as He was, He was easily able to reach the ground without changing position, and, bending down, He began to write in the dust with His finger. Impatiently, His enemies continued to insist on an answer. Straightening up, He said indifferently to them: "Let him who is without sin among you be the first to cast a stone at her." Then stooping down again, He continued to write as before. Such an unexpected reply disconcerted them; they suddenly found themselves changed from accusers to accused. No longer did they have the courage to insist, but with heads lowered in shame and acutely conscious of the crowd's mocking glances, they slipped away as unobtrusively as possible, beginning with the eldest, as the evangelist tells us.

What did our Lord write on the ground? St. Jerome thinks that He wrote the sins of the woman's accusers; [3] Eisler suggests that He

[3] *Adv. Pelagium* ii. 17: *PL* 23, 553.

wrote the passage from Jeremias (17:13): "They that depart from thee shall be written in the earth: because they have forsaken the Lord, the vein of living waters." Perhaps the most probable opinion is the one favored by Maldonatus,[4] Prat and Gomá, namely, that He did not write letters or words but only drew meaningless designs, as a man does when he is thinking over something, or does not wish to grant a request that has been made, or has no interest in what is going on around him. It was as if He wished to show the woman's accusers that He had nothing to do with the case and that it was not His business to pass sentence.[5]

When He finally broke silence, His words were very consoling. Turning to the woman, he said: "Woman, where are they? Has no one condemned thee?"

"No one, Lord."

"Neither will I condemn thee. Go thy way, and from now on sin no more." [6]

What a perfect example of how our compassionate and most holy Lord deals with sinful men, showing Himself merciful to the sinner but implacable to the sin!

The Fountain of Living Water, and the Light of the World

In His magnificent discourse to the people during the feast of Tabernacles, Jesus referred to Himself as "the light of the world" and the "fountain of living water." It was very fitting that He should have stressed these two Messianic characteristics precisely during the feast of Tabernacles, for water and light played an important part in the solemnities.

---

[4] "Mihi valde placet quod quidam dicunt, nihil scripsisse quod legi posset; nullos enim formasse characteres, sed incertas nihilque significantes figuras delineasse, quales homines meditabundi solent facere" (*Comm. in Joh., in loc.*).

[5] In *Biblica*, 2 (1921), 54–57, Fr. Power cites some interesting parallel cases from Arabic writers. We shall quote two of them here. Qasim, son of Ummayya, wishing to praise highly the generosity of his tribe, said: "When they are asked for gifts, they do not start writing on the ground with their sticks, seeking excuses." One day Ibrahim, son of Al-Mahdi, was asked by his nephew to improvise some verses of song; for a few moments he wrote on the ground with his stick, and then began to sing. As these two examples show, writing on the ground was a way of deferring or avoiding the necessity of giving an answer, or a device to gain time to think and decide what to say.

[6] See the interesting article by Dr. Bartolomé Pascual, "Una demostración de la divinidad de Cristo en la fiesta de los Tabernáculos," in *Analecta Sacra Tarraconensia*, 2 (1926), 407–426.

The *Mishnah's* description of this feast is very interesting. On each of the seven days there was a procession down through the Tyropoeon valley to the pool of Siloe. There the priest filled a golden vessel with water, and the procession reformed to ascend to the Temple. When they arrived at the Water Gate, three blasts, one sustained, one quavering and the third sustained, were blown on the *shofar* or trumpet, and entering the Temple, the priest sprinkled the altar with the water from the pool. In conformity with the prescriptions of Leviticus 23:40, during the procession to and from the pool everyone carried a *lulab,* a palm frond entwined with branches of myrtle and willow, in his right hand, and a citron fruit in his left. As they walked they waved the branches and the fruit in the air, and sang the *Hallel,* i.e., our Psalms 112–117. As can be seen, the whole ceremony centered around the water which was brought from the pool and sprinkled on the altar.

The same prominence was given to the symbolism of light. On the evening of the first day of the feast, a procession went down from the Court of Israel to the Court of the Women, where huge golden candlesticks had been placed. Four young men of the priestly caste ascended four ladders to fill and light the lamps on the candlesticks, and the resultant radiance was so intense that "there was not a court-yard in Jerusalem that did not reflect the light," as the *Mishnah* says. Singing hymns and songs of praise and holding lighted torches in their hands, devout Jews danced around the candlesticks, while a great number of Levites, standing on the fifteen steps that led from the Court of Israel to that of the Women, accompanied them with harps, lyres, cymbals and trumpets.[7]

When we consider this historico-liturgical background, we can see how appropriate and striking were the two symbols of light and water which Jesus used when speaking of Himself. It was as if He said to the people: "You light your torches and candelabra to illuminate the Temple and the city: but I am the true light, not only for Jerusalem, but for the whole world. I am the light of life which illuminates, not the eyes of the body, but those of the soul. You go to seek water at the pool of Siloe, but I am the true fountain of living water, the only one capable of quenching thirst."

The people's wonder, curiosity and admiration at the young

[7] See the *Mishnah, Sukkah* 4:9—5:4.

Prophet's new doctrine are well brought out in the vivid dialogue which St. John has recorded for us.

On the last day of the feast, Jesus stood and cried out in a loud voice: "If anyone thirst, let him come to me and drink. He who believes in me, as the Scripture says, 'From within him there shall flow rivers of living water.' " [8]

He was referring to the Holy Spirit, whom those who believed in Him would receive, and His words made such a deep impression on some of the crowd that they exclaimed, "This is truly the Prophet," while others said, "This is the Christ." But there were also skeptics who met their companions' enthusiasm with the objection: "Can the Christ come from Galilee? Does not the Scripture say that it is of the offspring of David, and from Bethlehem, the village where David lived, that the Christ is to come?"

Thus there arose dissensions and disputes among the people concerning Him, some being for Him, others against Him. Some of the more fanatical even wished to seize Him, but in the end no one dared lay hands on Him.

Again He spoke to the crowd: "I am the light of the world. He who follows me does not walk in the darkness, but will have the light of life."

The Pharisees, always ready to contest any statement of His, retorted: "Thou bearest witness to thyself. Thy witness is not true."

Jesus replied: "Even if I bear witness to myself, my witness is true, because I know where I came from and where I go. But you do not know where I came from or where I go. . . . It is I who bear witness to myself, and he who sent me, the Father, bears witness to me."

---

[8] Notice the striking parallelism between the words our Lord uses here and those He spoke to the Samaritan woman: "He . . . who drinks of the water that I will give him shall never thirst; but the water that I will give him shall become in him a fountain of living water, springing up unto life everlasting" (John 4:14).

Some authors, such as Lagrange, Braun, and others, change the punctuation in John 7:37 thus: "If anyone thirst, let him come to me; and let him drink who believes in me. As the Scripture says, 'From within him there shall flow rivers of living water.' " According to this interpretation, therefore, the rivers of living water flow, not from within him who believes in Jesus, but from our Lord Himself. It is in this sense that Pius XII uses the passage in his Encyclical *Haurietis Aquas,* on devotion to the Sacred Heart of Jesus (*Acta Ap. Sedis,* Vol. 48, 370). Fr. Hugo Rahner, S.J. defended this interpretation in two long articles in *Biblica,* 22 (1941), 269–302, and 367–403, and more briefly in *Cor Salvatoris* (Freiburg, 1954), pp. 19–45.

When they heard the Father mentioned, the Pharisees asked Him: "Where is thy father?"

"You know neither me nor my Father," replied Jesus. "If you knew me, you would then know my Father also. . . . I go, and you will seek me, and in your sin you will die. Where I go you cannot come."

The Jews, disconcerted, whispered to each other: "Will he kill himself, since he says, 'Where I go you cannot come'?"

Without taking any heed of the whispering, Jesus continued, revealing further His true Nature: "You are from below, I am from above. You are of this world, I am not of this world. Therefore I said to you that you will die in your sins; for if you do not believe that I am he [i.e., he who is to come, the Messias; cf. Mark 13:6], you will die in your sin."

Spontaneously there burst from His hearers' lips the vital question: "Who art thou?"

"Why do I speak to you at all! I have many things to speak and to judge concerning you; but he who sent me is true, and the things that I heard from him, these I speak in the world. . . . When you have lifted up the Son of Man, then you will know that I am he, and that of myself I do nothing: but even as the Father has taught me, I speak these things. And he who sent me is with me; he has not left me alone, because I do always the things that are pleasing to him."

This was indeed a sublime exposition of the intimate union between Jesus and His Eternal Father, an implicit affirmation of His divinity.

Then addressing the Jews who had believed in Him, He said: "If you abide in my word, you shall be my disciples indeed, and you shall know the truth, and the truth shall make you free."

His hearers resented these last words, which, they thought, made them out to be slaves who needed liberation, and they protested: "We are the children of Abraham, and we have never yet been slaves to anyone. How sayest thou, 'You shall be free'?"

In clarification of what He had said, our Lord went on: "Amen, amen, I say to you, everyone who commits sin is a slave of sin. . . . I speak what I have seen with the Father; and you do what you have seen with your father."

The Jews retorted: "Abraham is our father."

"If you are the children of Abraham," Jesus answered, "do the works of Abraham. . . . The father from whom you are, is the devil, and the desires of your father, it is your will to do. He was a murderer from the beginning, and has not stood in the truth. . . ."

Indignantly, they exclaimed: "Are we not right in saying that thou art a Samaritan, and hast a devil?"

"I have not a devil," answered Jesus, "but I honor my Father, and you dishonor me."

The interchange had been getting sharper all the time, and our Lord's questioners were becoming more wrathful with every word He spoke. But He did not take back one syllable of what He had said. Instead, He went further: "Amen, amen, I say to you, if anyone keep my word, he will never see death."

The Jews, now thoroughly enraged and scandalized, shouted: "Now we know that thou hast a devil. Abraham is dead, and the prophets, and thou sayest, 'If anyone keep my word he will never taste death.' Art thou greater than our father Abraham, who is dead? And the prophets are dead. Whom dost thou make thyself?"

Serenely Jesus replied: "If I glorify myself, my glory is nothing. It is my Father who glorifies me, of whom you say that he is your God. And you do not know him, but I know him. . . . Abraham your father rejoiced that he was to see my day. He saw it and was glad."

With heavy sarcasm the Jews inquired: "Thou art not yet fifty years old, and hast thou seen Abraham?"

Tranquilly and with great solemnity, He assured them: "Amen, amen, I say to you, before Abraham came to be, I am."

That was the last straw! The Galilean had arrogated a divine attribute to Himself; therefore He had committed blasphemy and deserved to be stoned. Accordingly the people took up stones to cast at Him, but with the same serene majesty which He had shown while speaking, Jesus withdrew from them and from the Temple, leaving His enemies standing with the stones in their hands.

On which days of the feast and in what place did Christ speak to the people? It is impossible to give an assured and well-defined answer to this question, but we can reach solidly probable conclusions. Let us begin by fixing certain points: (1) the discourse of 7:14–36 was delivered, all at once or at several different times, between the fourth or fifth and the last day of the feast; (2) that of 7:37–8:1, occurred on the last day, the most solemn day of the feast (7:37).

Some authors, such as Lagrange, Braun and others, believe that this discourse was pronounced on the seventh day, which, strictly speaking, was the last day of the feast; while others, such as Prat, Fillion, Knabenbauer and Gomá, are of the opinion that it was spoken on the eighth day, on which, according to Leviticus 23:36, there was to be a holy assembly to close the feast, and which was to be a day of rest just as the first day had been. Strack-Billerbeck discuss the question at length and conclude, somewhat indecisively, that the evidence seems to favor the seventh day.[9] We agree with this conclusion, but not without some reserve. It is very probable that the discourse of 8:21 *ff.* should be separated from the preceding one, since in 8:20 we are told the precise place in which the latter was given. It is very doubtful if 8:12–20 is a continuation of 8:2–11, and 8:31 of 8:21–30.

In our opinion, the following scheme is quite possibly the true one:

(1) 7:14–36, spoken before the seventh day;

(2) 7:37–81, on the seventh day;

(3) 8:2–11 and 8:12–20, on the eighth day, but perhaps at different times during that day;

(4) 8:21–59, after the eighth day, at one or at several different times: in all this discourse, the people's voice is not heard once.

The Man Born Blind [10]
(John 9:1–38)

St. John's account of the healing of the man born blind is a masterpiece of dramatic description in which each actor plays his part with captivating verve and spontaneity. The merciful kindness of Jesus, the blind man's shrewdness and spirit, his parents' caution, the Pharisees' anger and spite, the vigorous dialogue—all contribute to the mounting interest of the plot.

It was probably near the Temple, on the south side, that Jesus came across the blind man as he sat and begged one Sabbath day. The disciples noticed the beggar and asked: "Rabbi, who has sinned, this man or his parents, that he should be born blind?"

[9] II, 490 *f.*

[10] Cf. J. M. Bover, "Crítica de un milagro: El ciego de nacimiento," in *Razón y Fe,* 73 (1925, III), 152 *ff.*

THE POOL OF SILOE: *in the upper background one can see part of the ruins of the basilica built by Eudoxia.*

Their question stemmed from the conviction, common among the Jews and ancient peoples in general, that every physical affliction was an effect of, or a punishment for, sin. The argument between Job and his friends is a case in point. It was also generally believed that children were punished for the sins of their parents, and the Apostles, on seeing the blind young man, concluded immediately that some sin had caused his affliction; the only doubt they had was whether he himself or his parents had committed the sin that had cost him his sight. Our Lord's reply was in flat contradiction to this false conception, which the prophet Ezechiel had already vigorously opposed: [11] "Neither has this man sinned, nor his parents, but the works of God were to be made manifest in him. . . ." Then, spitting on the ground, He mixed His saliva with the dust to form clay, which He spread over the man's sightless eyes. When He had done this, He said to the blind man: "Go, wash in the pool of Siloe. . . ."

The pool was not far from the Temple, and the man was easily able to make his way thither by going down the Tyropoeon valley, or along one of the streets that then crossed the now-deserted hill of Ophel. The pool had been built by King Ezechias at the end of the seventh century B.C.; it was, and still is, supplied with water by the Fountain of Gihon (now called the Fountain of the Virgin), through a channel which St. John calls "sent" and which we would term a conduit. In commemoration of the miracle of the blind man's regaining his sight, the Empress Eudoxia built there, in the fifth century, a basilica whose ruins are still preserved. The pool built by Ezechias was the successor to another which was, perhaps, the work of the Jebusites, and which today has been converted into a garden.

The blind man, doing as Jesus told him, went to the pool, washed the clay from his eyes, and returned with his sight restored. Then followed a delightful scene which St. John has recorded for us, complete with vivid dialogue. When the cured man returned, his neighbors, who had so often seen him begging alms, exclaimed in wonder: "Is not this he who used to sit and beg?"

Some said: "It is he," while others disagreed: "By no means, he only resembles him."

The man himself settled the dispute by interjecting: "I am he!"

[11] Cf. A. Fernández, *El problema de la responsabilidad individual en el profeta Ezequiel (Florilegio Bíblico, VIII).*

Immediately, he was besieged with questions: "How were thy eyes opened?"

He replied very simply: "The man who is called Jesus made clay and anointed my eyes, and said to me, 'Go to the pool of Siloe and wash.' And I went and washed, and I see."

"Where is he?"

"I do not know."

Because the occurrence was so extraordinary and had some bearing on religious affairs, the crowd decided to bring it to the notice of the doctors of the Law, who would determine how the matter should be regarded. Therefore the beggar's neighbors brought him to the Pharisees, who asked him how he had regained his sight. Ingenuously he replied: "He put clay upon my eyes, and I washed, and I see."

Completely disregarding the obvious miracle, some of the Pharisees seized on the one point that seemed to give them a case against Jesus. "This man is not from God, for he does not keep the Sabbath." But others, less prejudiced, objected: "How can a man who is a sinner work these signs?" Turning again to the once-blind man, they asked: "What dost thou say of him who opened thy eyes?"

Unhesitatingly he answered: "He is a prophet."

If the facts of the case were as they had been represented, then an evident miracle had occurred. There was, however, the possibility that the man had never really been blind at all, and the Pharisees eagerly grasped at the chance to escape their dilemma. Summoning the man's parents, they asked them: "Is this your son, of whom you say that he was born blind? How then does he see?"

The cautious parents did not wish to compromise themselves, for they knew that the Scribes and Pharisees hated Jesus, and had threatened to excommunicate anyone who showed favor to Him. Therefore they kept out of danger by answering only the first question, and neatly side-stepping the second: "We know that this is our son, and that he was born blind; but how he now sees we do not know, or who opened his eyes we ourselves do not know. Ask him; he is of age, let him speak for himself."

The irrefutable testimony of the man's own parents put an end to the Pharisees' hopes of an easy escape and drove them to resort to intimidation. They would still save face if they could frighten the man into denying the miracle. Calling him before them again, they brought the full force of their authority to bear on him: "Give glory to God! We ourselves know that this man is a sinner."

This they meant as a denial of Christ's power to work miracles. But the young man did not retreat from his position. Pointedly, and not without a touch of irony, he answered: "Whether he is a sinner, I do not know. One thing I do know, that whereas I was blind, now I see."

His reply was so unexpected that it left even the crafty Pharisees at a loss. Not knowing what to say, they took to repeating themselves: "What did he do to thee? How did he open thy eyes?"

The question was completely superfluous, and the young man, perceiving the embarrassing position in which his judges found themselves, answered impudently: "I have told you already and you have heard. Why would you hear again?" Then, with gleeful malice, he added: "Would you also become his disciples?"

His shaft struck home, enraging the pompous Pharisees, and stinging them into bandying insults with him: "Thou art his disciple, but we are disciples of Moses. We know that God spoke to Moses; but as for this man, we do not know where he is from."

The beggar, instead of backing down before their anger, took up the challenge implied in their words. If the haughty doctors had unbent so far as to argue with him, then he would show himself a worthy opponent.

"Why, herein is the marvel, that you do not know where he is from, and yet he opened my eyes. Now we know that God does not hear sinners; but if anyone is a worshipper of God, and does his will, him he hears. Not from the beginning of the world has it been heard that anyone opened the eyes of a man born blind. If this man were not from God, he could do nothing."

The Pharisees had had enough of the exasperating beggar's insolence; but what galled them most was that they were unable to answer him. Boiling with rage and at a complete loss for a reply, they gave vent to their anger and wounded pride by shouting at him: "Thou wast altogether born in sins, and dost thou teach us?"

And with that, they turned him out. But this scene of violence and hate was to have a sequel full of peace and love. When Jesus came across the young man who had proved himself such a spirited and skilled apologist for Him, and who had been excommunicated for his pains, He asked him: "Dost thou believe in the Son of God?"

With touching obedience, the man replied: "Who is he, Lord, that I may believe in him?"

And Jesus said: "Thou hast both seen him, and he it is who speaks with thee."

The fortunate young man, enlightened from on high, cried out: "I believe, Lord."

And prostrating himself before Jesus, he worshipped Him.

The Good Shepherd
(John 9:39—10:21)

When the passers-by, some Pharisees included, saw Christ again speaking to the cured man, they gathered around Him, and He, seeing Himself surrounded by this audience, said: "For judgment have I come into this world, that they who do not see may see, and they who see may become blind."

His reference was obvious: the beggar, blind in body and soul, had received both corporal and spiritual sight, while the Pharisees, regarded by all as wise and learned in the things of God, had been blinded by their stubborn pride. The Pharisees who were present caught the allusion and demanded indignantly: "Are we also blind?"

To which our Lord replied sternly: "If you were blind, you would not have sin. But now that you say, 'We see,' your sin remains."

These words of Christ's silenced them; and when they did not answer, He proposed to them a parable to show them that they were false guides of the people and that their conduct was unjust and cruel, as was evident from the case of the poor blind man whom they had excommunicated and cast off. He charged them with being mercenaries, while He, who had received the wretched beggar with loving solicitude, was the true shepherd, the Good Shepherd.

This parable of the good shepherd is closely connected with the preceding episode of the cure of the man born blind, as can be seen from John 10:6, where Jesus is depicted as addressing the same audience (αὐτοῖς), and from verse 21 in the same chapter, where explicit reference is made to the miracle. Although at first glance the line of thought in the parable seems totally distinct from that of chapter 9, a closer examination shows that the parable is really a spontaneous continuation of the incident of the blind man. Then, too, as Prat rightly remarks, the expression "Amen, amen" used in chapter 10, verse 1, never occurs in St. John at the beginning of a discourse but is employed only to insist on something already said, a fact that goes to show further that chapter 10 is a continuation of chapter 9.

The parable unfolds simply and naturally in three short phases: (1) the telling of the narrative itself (vv. 1–5), which the crowd did not understand (v. 6); (2) elaboration and explanation of the parable (vv. 7–18); (3) its effect on the listeners, who had been growing more numerous all the time and who now began to argue among themselves, some saying that Jesus was possessed by the devil and was mad, to which others replied that His words were not those of a demoniac, and that the devil could not restore sight to a blind man (vv. 19–21).

Our Lord's beautiful description of the good shepherd is a faithful picture of the prevailing customs, which have remained almost unchanged down to the present day.

At nightfall the flocks are driven to a common fold surrounded by a low stone wall surmounted by thorn-branches and used by several shepherds at a time. Each fold has but one gate, purposely made narrow so that the sheep may be the more easily counted as they enter one by one.[12]

One of the shepherds remains on guard during the night to defend the flock from thieves and wolves. In the morning, when the other shepherds arrive to start the day's work, the gate of the sheepfold is opened by the night watchman, and each shepherd calls to his sheep. The animals know their keeper's voice, and upon hearing it, they break away from the others and gather around him. Then, when his flock has assembled, each shepherd starts down the road towards the pasture, and his sheep follow him docilely.

---

[12] Jeremias (33:13) makes a clear reference to this custom. Speaking about the future restoration of Israel and foretelling that the day would come when the pastures, then deserted, would be covered with flocks, the prophet says: ". . . and in the cities of Juda shall the flocks pass again under the hand of him that numbered them, saith the Lord." He was alluding to the diligent shepherd who, standing in the evening at the entrance to the sheepfold, touched each of the sheep with his crook to make sure that none was missing. In Ezechiel (20:37), where the prophet is foretelling the return of the exiles and the separation of the good from the bad, there is an even more explicit reference when Yahweh says: "I shall make you pass under my crook." And in Leviticus 27:32, in connection with the tithes, we read that, "Of all the tithes of oxen, and sheep, and goats, *that pass under the shepherd's rod,* every tenth that cometh shall be sanctified to the Lord."

A characteristic of the good shepherd, that is, of him who owns the flock he tends, is the interest he takes in them: because they are his own, he will defend them even at the risk of his life. But when the hireling sees the wolf coming, he thinks only of seeking his own safety in flight, leaving the flock unprotected.

"Amen, amen, I say to you, he who enters not by the door into the sheepfold, but climbs up another way, is a thief and a robber. But he who enters by the door is shepherd of the sheep. To this man the gatekeeper opens, and the sheep hear his voice, and he calls his own sheep by name and leads them forth. And when he has let out his own sheep, he goes before them; and the sheep follow him because they know his voice. But a stranger they will not follow, but will flee from him, because they do not know the voice of strangers. . . .

"I am the good shepherd. The good shepherd lays down his life for his sheep. But the hireling, who is not a shepherd, whose own the sheep are not, sees the wolf coming and leaves the sheep and flees. And the wolf snatches and scatters the sheep. . . .

"I am the good shepherd, and I know mine and mine know me, even as the Father knows me and I know the Father; and I lay down my life for my sheep. And other sheep I have that are not of this fold. Them also I must bring, and they shall hear my voice, and there shall be one fold and one shepherd. For this reason the Father loves me, because I lay down my life that I may take it up again. No one takes it from me, but I lay it down of myself. I have the power to lay it down, and I have the power to take it up again. Such is the command I have received from my Father."

Our Lord's words, clear and consoling though they were, started a new argument among His hearers, many of whom shouted, "He has a devil and is mad. Why do you listen to him?" while others defended Him by retorting, "These are not the words of one who has a devil. Can a devil open the eyes of the blind?"

For us who are His followers, Christ's words are light for the mind and balm to the heart, for in them we find His lofty teaching on the Church. The shepherd is he who has been lawfully delegated to give the faithful the nourishing food of true doctrine; the gate is Christ; the sheep are the faithful, and the sheepfold is the Church.[13]

---

[13] Cf. the interesting article by Leal, "La Eucaristía y la Parábola del Buen Pastor" in *Est. Ecles.*, 27 (1953), 317–324.

Sending Out the Seventy-Two Disciples
(Luke 10:1–24; cf. Matt. 11:20–30)

After the feast of Tabernacles had ended, Jesus remained several days in Jerusalem and then left the Holy City, going, very probably, in the direction of Galilee. We know little or nothing about the two months that intervene between this journey and the feast of Dedication, when we find our Lord once again in Jerusalem (John 10:22 *ff.*). Yet it seems that the sending of the seventy-two disciples [14] should be placed in this period, although it is not possible to tell exactly either where the incident took place, or which district was visited by the disciples. We do know, however, that they must have covered an extensive territory, for we are told that they went in pairs, and therefore, considering their number, we can conclude that they preached in many towns and villages.

The instructions which Jesus gave to the seventy-two disciples are very similar to, and, in the main, even identical with, those He gave the Apostles (cf. Matt. 10:1 *ff.; Mark 6:7 ff.; Luke 9:1 ff.*). But this is not reason enough for regarding the two sendings as one and the same incident. Furthermore, St. Luke speaks of the two as completely distinct episodes. And seeing that the purpose and conditions were the same in each case, it is not surprising that our Lord's two sets of instructions were almost identical.

Yet there is one prominent part of the sending of the seventy-two disciples that does not appear in that of the Apostles. After having declared that it would go easier with Sodom on the day of judgment than with any town that refused to receive His disciples, Jesus launched a terrible anathema against Corozain, Bethsaida and His own adopted city, Capharnaum, all of which had rejected the good tidings:

"Woe to thee, Corozain! woe to thee, Bethsaida! For if in Tyre and Sidon had been worked the miracles that have been worked in you, they would have repented long ago, sitting in sackcloth and ashes. But it will be more tolerable for Tyre and Sidon at the judgment than for you. And thou, Capharnaum, shalt thou be exalted to heaven? Thou shalt be thrust down to hell." Then, addressing His

---

[14] A good many manuscripts give seventy as the number of the disciples. But it should be noted that since seventy was, to a certain extent, regarded as a sacred number, "seventy-two" was more likely to have been changed to "seventy" than vice versa.

disciples directly, He concluded: "He who hears you, hears me; and he who rejects you, rejects me; and he who rejects me, rejects him who sent me."

We do not know where our Lord received the seventy-two upon their return from their missionary expedition, but we are told about the happy outcome of their apostolate. In particular, the wonders they had worked filled them with enthusiasm, not unmixed with some self-complacency, as was to be expected in men who were still imperfect. Thus it was that on returning to report to Jesus, they burst out joyfully: "Lord, even the devils are subject to us in thy name."

But according to the interpretation given by many Fathers, our Saviour dampened their enthusiasm a little by giving them a grave warning which could well have been directed against vainglory: "I was watching Satan fall as lightning from heaven. Behold, I have given you power to tread upon serpents and scorpions, and over all the power of the enemy; and nothing shall hurt you. But do not rejoice in this, that the spirits are subject to you; rejoice rather in this, that your names are written in heaven."

However, it seems that the first sentence, "I was watching Satan fall as lightning from heaven," should be taken as referring to the triumphant expansion of the kingdom of God, symbolized by the power of the name of Jesus over Satan.

Then, as if in an ecstasy of gratitude to the Eternal Father, and overflowing with joy in the Holy Spirit, our Lord exclaimed: "I praise thee, Father, Lord of heaven and earth, that thou didst hide these things from the wise and prudent, and didst reveal them to little ones. Yes, Father, for such was thy good pleasure. All things have been delivered to me by my Father; and no one knows who the Son is except the Father, and who the Father is except the Son, and him to whom the Son chooses to reveal him."

Turning once more to His disciples, He said lovingly to them: "Blessed are the eyes that see what you see! For I say to you, many prophets and kings have desired to see what you see, and they have not seen it; and to hear what you hear, and they have not heard it."

As St. John Chrysostom paraphrases:

·· The Scribes and the wise men, who thought themselves prudent, had ended by falling into miserable blindness on account of their pride. If, then, such great mysteries were hidden from them for that reason, you ought to fear for yourselves and be careful to remain always among the "little ones." [15]

Then, penetrating the future and contemplating humanity groaning under the pressing weight of the world's sin and pain, Jesus tenderly invited all sufferers to have recourse to Him in their affliction: "Come to me, all you who labor and are burdened, and I will give you rest. Take my yoke upon you, and learn from me, for I am meek and humble of heart; and you will find rest for your souls. For my yoke is easy, and my burden light."

St. John Chrysostom again paraphrases beautifully:

I do not call only one or two, but *all* of you who groan beneath the weight of anxiety, sorrow or sin. Come, not in order that I may exact from you the penalty that you have deserved, but so that I may free you from sin. Come, not because I need your praise, but because I thirst for your salvation. . . . Do not be afraid when you hear me mention a yoke, for it is easy; nor need you fear when I speak of a burden, for it is light.[16]

To Perea
(Matt. 19:1; Mark 10:1; cf. Map IV)

Jesus remained but a short time in Galilee. It could be said that He had gone there merely to say His last farewells, for after only a few weeks, probably in the month of November, He left Galilee for Perea, never to return again during His mortal life.

This journey from Galilee to Perea is the one mentioned in Matthew 19:1 and Mark 10:1: "He departed from Galilee and came to the district of Judea beyond the Jordan." The evangelists, however, give not the slightest hint as to the route He took, but it is probable that He went south along the Jordan valley, either following the right, or western, bank of the river, passing by the springs of Aennon and through the cities of Phasaelis and Archelais, or more probably, perhaps, along the left bank, skirting the height upon which stood the city of Pella, later the refuge of the Christians when Titus besieged Jerusalem, and crossing the valley "Amethan" (=Tell 'Ammata) and the mouth of the Jabbok (=Nahr ez-Zerqa), the river at which Jacob stopped on his return from Mesopotamia. From

[15] *PG* 57, 430.
[16] *Ibid.*

there Jesus could have ascended into the mountainous region, or gone farther south along the Wadi Nimrin, but perhaps He remained on the plain, which formed part of the territory of Perea.

From this point on, He confined His ministry to this district, leaving it only twice; once to go to Jerusalem for the feast of Dedication, and once to make the short journey to Bethany to raise Lazarus from the dead. We know nothing of His work between the time of His arrival in Perea and the feast of Dedication, for the narrative found in Matthew 19:2 *ff.* and Mark 10:1 *ff.* is concerned with the period subsequent to the feast.

The Good Samaritan
(Luke 10:25–37; cf. Map IV)

The feast of Dedication, or the Encoenia, lasted for eight days, beginning on the 25th of the ninth month, Kislev (=November-December), i.e., about December 10th. Consequently, our Lord probably left Perea during the first days of the month, and travelled either along the route that crossed the Jordan at the ford of el-Ghorani, where Allenby Bridge now stands, or perhaps crossed the river a little farther south, at a place which the Madaba mosaic map of Palestine marks with a small boat. Then, passing through Jericho, He ascended the steep side of the Wadi el-Qelt and came down the Tal'at ed-Dam, the biblical "ascent of Adommin" (Jos. 15:7), where the Good Samaritan Inn (Khan el-Hatrur) stands. Proceeding along the course of the Wadi es-Sikkeh and the Wadi el-Hod, He arrived at Bethany.

It is very likely that He related the parable of the good Samaritan (Luke 10:25–37) during the course of this journey, which followed in part the route taken by the unfortunate man who fell among robbers on his way down from Jerusalem to Jericho. The road was a desolate one, winding tortuously through the rocky hills of that region which is known in Sacred Scripture by the very apt name of "the desert of Juda"; it was therefore an eminently suitable place for bandits and highway robbers to ply their nefarious trade. St. Jerome bears witness to the frequency of these robbers' forays in his own day when, in explaining the meaning of "the ascent of Adommin," he says that it could be called "the ascent of the red ones" because of the blood that was shed so frequently there by murderous bandits.[17] However, it is not possible to ascertain the exact spot our Lord had in mind when narrating the parable of the good Samaritan. Probably He did not intend to refer to any particular place on the road, but was only speaking in general. He did specify that the passers-by were a priest and a Levite, men who, by their very office, were more strictly obliged than others to practice charity, while He depicted the traveller who stopped to help the wounded man as being a Samaritan, a stranger who, because of his people's traditional enmity towards the Jews, apparently had some excuse for ignoring the unfortunate Jew as he lay bleeding by the roadside. In this way, Christ heightened the contrast between the indifference of the two who passed by and the kindheartedness of the one who stopped to help. The use of a mixture of oil and wine in the treatment of wounds was common in our Lord's day, and is still practiced. Fr. M. Jullien relates the following episode: a Franciscan Father was going down from Jerusalem to Jericho, accompanied by a Bedouin, when the latter tore his leg on his stirrup. The Bedouin had a small bottle of oil with him, and he asked the priest: "Have you any wine?" Taking the wine and oil, he mixed them, washed the wound with the mixture, and remounted his horse.[18]

The parable of the good Samaritan arose out of the apparently respectful but really malicious question which a Scribe, a doctor of the Law, asked our Lord: "Master, what must I do to gain eternal life?"

In His turn, Jesus asked him a question: "What is written in the Law? How dost thou read?"

The Scribe answered: "Thou shalt love the Lord thy God with thy whole heart, and with thy whole soul, and with thy whole strength, and with thy whole mind; and thy neighbor as thyself."

There was nothing more to say; and so Jesus commended him: "Thou hast answered rightly; do this and thou shalt live."

The Scribe should have been satisfied with Christ's reply, but he was not. He had wanted to embarrass and create difficulties for our Lord, but he now found that in answering his own question, he had

---

[17] *In Ier. III. 2: PL* 24, 726: "Latine appellari potest ascensus ruforum sive rubrantium, propter sanguinem qui illic creber a latronibus funditur." Actually, the place takes its name from the red soil of the region, a color that is easily discernible from the road.

[18] *L'Égypte* (Lille, 1891), p. 276.

left himself without an opening. Therefore, in order to create another opportunity for debate, he asked further: "And who is my neighbor?"

Instead of expounding the theory of the matter, Jesus related a parable which clearly brought out the fact that not only Jews but all men, even traditional enemies such as the Samaritan, were the Scribe's neighbors, and that love for one's neighbor ought to be shown in a practical way: "A certain man was going down from Jerusalem to Jericho, and he fell in with robbers, who after both stripping him and beating him went their way, leaving him half-dead. But, as it happened, a certain priest was going down the same way, and when he saw him, he passed by. And likewise a Levite also, when he was near the place and saw him, passed by. But a certain Samaritan as he journeyed came upon him, and seeing him, was moved with compassion. And he went up to him and bound up his wounds, pouring on oil and wine. And setting him on his own beast, he brought him to an inn and took care of him. And the next day he took out two denarii and gave them to the innkeeper and said, 'Take care of him; and whatever more thou spendest, I, on my way back, will repay thee.' "

Our Lord concluded with the question: "Which of these three, in thy opinion, proved himself neighbor to him who fell among the robbers?"

The Scribe had no choice but to reply: "He who took pity on him."

Jesus gravely advised him: "Go and do thou also in like manner."

Martha and Mary
(Luke 10:38–42; cf. Map IV)

A little more than halfway along the main road from Jericho to Jerusalem, which was later a Roman highway, a side road ran south to Bethany. Our Lord turned aside along this route, for He wished to visit friends in the town before going on to the capital.

The present-day traveller who follows the modern road from Jerusalem to Bethany finds his eye caught by some prominent ruins which stand on the western edge of the village and which the inhabitants point out as the house of Martha and Mary. In reality these ruins are the remains of the convent which Queen Melisenda built so that the daughters of the heroic Crusaders could continue Mary of Bethany's humble and loving contemplation of the Divine Master.

Bethany.

But a day came when these pure souls had to flee before the Mohammedan wave that again swept over the land of Christ's birth. Centuries later, however, their place was taken by the daughters of St. Teresa of Avila who came from distant lands to settle on the summit of Mount Olivet, within sight of Bethany, there to drink in their Master's teachings in loving silence.

Late one morning at the beginning of December, our Lord arrived at the charming little town of Bethany that lay on the eastern slope of Mount Olivet, about two miles from Jerusalem. St. Luke, to whom we owe the narrative, does not give us its name, but we know from St. John (11:1) that Martha and Mary and their brother Lazarus lived in Bethany, a name probably derived from *Beit Anania,* i.e., the house of Ananias.

The town of our Lord's time lay a short distance, about two or three hundred yards, southwest of the present village, which the Arabs call el-'Azariyeh, after the *Lazarion,* the name of the town of the Byzantine epoch which was built around the tomb of Lazarus. Fortunately, there is no positive reason to doubt the authenticity of Lazarus' tomb. We should also like to know the site of the house in which the two sisters received our Lord, but although the villagers claim to be able to point it out, there is no trustworthy tradition regarding it.

On this occasion Bethany was not our Lord's main destination, as it was to be later when He came to raise Lazarus; the principal object of this journey was to celebrate the feast of Dedication in Jerusalem. But since Bethany lay so near His route to the capital, He took advantage of the opportunity to visit the house where He was always received with such sincere and respectful attention. There, in the peace and joy that reigned in the home of Martha and Mary and their brother Lazarus, and in the company of these close friends, He found temporary rest from the unrelenting hostility and continual scheming of His implacable enemies.[19]

When He and His disciples arrived at the house, no doubt unexpectedly, Martha solicitously set about preparing a meal for them, for the morning was already far advanced. Meanwhile, our Lord, tired after a hard journey of five or six hours, had taken a seat, perhaps beneath the vine arbor at the side of the house, for in Palestine the weather can be beautiful even in December. And Mary, the gentle Mary of Bethany, had seated herself humbly and peacefully at her Lord's feet. As the Divine Master spoke, the disciple drank in His words in silence, her gaze fixed upon Him.

Martha bustled about, never pausing for a moment in her preparations; but from time to time she glanced meaningfully at her sister, trying to get her to come and help to serve the guests. Mary, however, hanging on our Lord's words, either did not see Martha's glances or did not catch her meaning. Finally, when Martha saw that she was being left to do the work alone, and because she was in a hurry to feed the hungry guests, she stopped before our Lord and in a tone of thinly-veiled reproach, said to Him: "Lord, is it no concern of thine that my sister has left me to serve alone? Tell her therefore to help me."

Mary remained silent, looking half-timorously, half-confidently at her Divine Master's face, wondering if He would command her to rise and go to help her sister.

Our Lord's answer was grave, yet affectionate: "Martha, Martha, thou art anxious and troubled about many things; and yet only one thing is needful." [20]

[19] Cf. A. Fernández, *En Betania y Betfage (Florilegio Bíblico,* III), pp. 37 *f.*
[20] The Greek manuscripts have three different readings: (1) ἑνὸς δέ ἐστιν χρεία

Then, pointing to the younger sister, who was anxiously awaiting His reaction, He added: "Mary has chosen the best part, and it will not be taken away from her."

Thus, after admonishing Martha for her perturbation and impatience, our Lord went to Mary's defense. Although He did not say so explicitly, He was really comparing Mary's occupation with Martha's, and implying that the former was to be preferred to the latter. The whole context shows clearly what these two occupations were: Mary's part was to sit at our Lord's feet listening to His teaching ("Blessed are they who hear the word of God and keep it": Luke 11:28); [21] Martha's was to prepare a meal for Him and His disciples. But there is an obvious difficulty here, for, as St. Teresa says, if both sisters had sat spellbound at their Master's feet, there would have been no one to prepare food for the Divine Guest.[22] Hence it seems that Martha's activity could be regarded as more perfect and more meritorious than Mary's contemplation, since the elder sister had sacrificed her own wish to be at our Lord's feet so that she might serve Him and His Apostles.

We must not forget, however, that Christ's words were uttered to defend Mary against her sister's reproach, and that to do so He spoke

("only one thing is needful"); (2) ὀλίγων δέ ἐστιν χρεία ("few things are needful"); (3) ὀλίγων δέ ἐστιν χρεία ἢ ἑνὸς ("few things are needful or only one"). Plummer says that the first two are corruptions of the third, which is the one he prefers. We, on the contrary, believe that the third results from the combination of the first two, for the copyists always tend more to amplify than to shorten. There are numerous instances of composite readings, especially in Lucian. And because the second reading is regarded as the less well-founded, critically speaking, of the remaining two, it follows that the first should be taken as the most probably correct of the three.

Some authors interpret the word ἑνὸς in a material sense, as if Jesus wished to say that it was not necessary to prepare many dishes for the meal since one was sufficient. But as Prat aptly remarks: "The ancient and modern commentators who interpret thus: a few dishes or only one are needed to appease hunger, seem to us to be substituting a puerile idea for a sublime teaching" (Jesus Christ, II, 25).

Some of those who prefer the third reading and make the word ὀλίγων refer to the dishes which should be served at the meal, presuppose that when our Lord had said to Martha that she was busy about many things and had pointed out that few things were needful, He paused and, looking at Mary with love, drew attention to her, and added: "Yet only one thing is needful," in reference to Mary's occupation, namely, her listening attentively to His words (cf. Zerwick, Verb. Dom., 27 [1949], 294–298). We suspect, however, that more than a few readers will regard this exegesis as artificial and strained.

[21] Cf. Zerwick, loc. cit.

[22] Cf. St. Teresa of Jesus, The Way of Perfection, Vol. II, The Complete Works, trans. by E. Allison Peers (New York: Sheed and Ward, 1946), p. 70.

of both their occupations regarded in themselves. Now there is no doubt that, absolutely speaking, it is a much more exalted thing to listen to Christ's words and drink in His teaching than to busy oneself among the pots and pans. And that is what our Lord meant by His reply to Martha. She had asked Him to command her sister to rise and help her, but He answered that Mary's part would not be taken away from her, that He wished her to remain seated at His feet. And not only that: His words, "it will not be taken away from her," did not refer merely to the existing circumstances. They went much further, for they meant that listening to God's word and paying close attention to His doctrine was an occupation that Mary could continue in the future and even through all eternity.

The two sisters are usually regarded as symbols of the *active* and *contemplative* lives. The symbolism is legitimate and very appropriate, yet the ideal is to combine action with contemplation, to do the work of both Martha and Mary at the same time—*in actione contemplans*—to animate and vivify one's action by contemplation.[23]

---

[23] Regarding the distinction between Mary of Bethany and Mary Magdalene, see above, pp. 360 *f.*

20. The Feast of Dedication
(December A. D. 29:)
The Our Father

The Feast of Dedication
(John 10:22–39)

Three years after Antiochus IV Epiphanes had profaned the Temple (cf. 1 Mach. 1:22–54; 2 Mach. 5:15–21; 6:2; *Ant.* xii. 5. 4), Judas Machabeus purified it, devoting eight days to its re-dedication, beginning on the 25th of Kislev (=November–December) of the year 164 B.C.; and he decreed that in the future a feast was to be celebrated at that time each year (1 Mach. 4:52–59; 2 Mach. 2:20; 10:1–8). The feast was called the Encoenia (τὰ ἐγκαίνια; John 10:22) because worship had been resumed, or Dedication (in Hebrew, *hanukkah*) because the Temple had been re-dedicated, or the feast of Lights [1] because many lamps were lighted in the synagogues and private houses as a sign of rejoicing. It was an occasion of great happiness; palm fronds and green branches were carried, the psalms of the *Hallel* (our Ps. 112–117) were sung to the sound of flutes, and the people answered the Levites' chant with shouts of "Glory to Yahweh!"

After visiting Martha and Mary, our Lord continued His journey to Jerusalem, where He presented Himself in the Temple. No doubt He had several arguments with the Jews, who were always ready to set traps for Him so that they might find some grounds for accusing

[1] *Ant.* xii. 7. 7.

Him. St. John has preserved for us one of these disputes in all its dramatic intensity.

One day when, perhaps because of the inclemency of the weather (it was the middle of December), Jesus was walking and teaching in Solomon's Porch, which ran along the eastern side of the great courtyard of the Temple, a group of Jews, that is, of Scribes and Pharisees, approached Him and asked Him with resolute aggressiveness: "How long dost thou keep us in suspense? If thou art the Christ, tell us openly."

As we have already pointed out, our Lord had never publicly called Himself the Messias because He did not wish to stir up nationalistic fervor and incur the suspicion of the Roman authorities. Yet He had shown in a thousand different ways, by His words and works, that He was the Christ. Consequently, He did not now satisfy His questioners' demand by declaring plainly that He was the Messias, but simply said: "I tell you and you do not believe. The works that I do in the name of my Father, these bear witness concerning me. But you do not believe because you are not of my sheep. My sheep hear my voice, and I know them and they follow me. And I give them everlasting life; and they shall never perish, neither shall anyone snatch them out of my hand. My Father, who has given them to me, is greater than all; and no one is able to snatch anything out of the hand of my Father." And He concluded by proclaiming solemnly: "I and the Father are one."

This was a categorical affirmation with only one possible meaning —that Jesus was one with the Father. The Jews fully understood what He meant, and considering His words blasphemous, they took up stones to cast at Him. But He asked them unflinchingly: "Many good works have I shown you from my Father. For which of these works do you stone me?"

"Not for a good work do we stone thee," they retorted, "but for blasphemy, and because thou, being a man, makest thyself God."

Far from repudiating their interpretation of His words, He replied: "Is it not written in your Law, 'I said you are gods'? If he called them gods to whom the word of God was addressed (and the Scripture cannot be broken), do you say of him whom the Father has made holy and sent into the world, 'Thou blasphemest,' because I said, 'I am the Son of God'? If I do not perform the works of my Father, do not believe me. But if I do perform them, and if you are not willing to believe me, believe the works, that you may know and believe that the Father is in me and I in the Father."

Despite His reasoning with them, or perhaps because of it, the Jews wished to lay hold of Him, but He eluded them, because His hour had not yet come.

Among the Baptist's Disciples
(John 10:40–42; cf. Map IV)

After the lively discussion in Solomon's Porch, where the Jews had wanted to seize Him, our Lord left Jerusalem and returned to Perea, to the place where John was at first baptizing (John 1:28), a chronological note that distinguishes this spot from the other location, Aennon, near Salim, where the Precursor had baptized later (cf. John 3:23). Jesus therefore halted in the valley of the Jordan, east of the river, in the region of Beit Nimra and Livias (=Tell er-Rameh). Here, very close to the Jordan, and across from the Greek Monastery of St. John (Qasr el-Yehud), one can still see the ruins of an ancient church of the Byzantine period, which very probably marks the site of Bethabara or Bethany beyond the Jordan (John 1:28), where John baptized. The evangelist notes that Jesus remained in this place (John 10:41), and it is probable that He spent here the three or four months that passed between the feast of Dedication and the raising of Lazarus. It is very likely, however, that He did not remain constantly in the one location for such an extended period of time. Perhaps He went up along the Wadi Nimrin into the mountain region of Perea, but we can make no definite assertions in this regard because, although St. Luke has left us a rich store of incidents and parables from this period, he is so sparing with topographical and chronological data that it is very difficult, not to say impossible, to fix the exact locations and time sequence of the individual episodes. But at any rate, we do know that this period included many miracles and many beautiful lessons, including several of the most touching parables of the Gospel, such as those of the prodigal son, the rich man and Lazarus, and the Pharisee and the publican. Hence the evangelist more than compensates for his sparsity of references to time and place by providing us with a rich store of doctrine.

The inhabitants of the region beyond the Jordan received Jesus warmly. The memory of John the Baptist was still green among them and they had continued to venerate him, so that when our Lord came to stay with them they said: "John indeed worked no sign. All things, however, that John said of this man [i.e., Jesus] were true."

Their words reflected a marked and very justified interest in the honor of the man whose preaching they had doubtless heard and by whom they may have been baptized. They acknowledged the fact that John had not worked any miracles, but they saw that what he had said about Jesus was true. This made them honor John the more, since it showed that he was a prophet, and it also disposed them to believe in Jesus, as many of them subsequently did (John 10:41 *f.*). The receptive atmosphere thus generated among the people of Perea gave our Lord a welcome respite from the bitter attacks of the obstinate citizens of Jerusalem.

The Our Father
(Luke 11:1–4; Matt. 6:9–13)

St. Luke paints a beautiful picture of the circumstances surrounding the teaching of that truly divine prayer, the Our Father (Luke 11:1).

Motionless, with His eyes fixed on heaven, Jesus was praying, while His disciples stood respectfully by, not wishing to interrupt Him. But when He had finished His prayer, one of them approached Him with the request: "Lord, teach us to pray, even as John also taught his disciples." [2]

In answer to the petition, Jesus taught them the Lord's Prayer, as we call it, a prayer that is sublime in its simplicity, the prayer of a son addressing his Father, whom he loves, in whom he has implicit confidence, and from whom he hopes to receive all things:

"Our Father who art in heaven,
        hallowed be thy name.
Thy kingdom come, thy will be done
            on earth, as it is in heaven.
Give us this day our daily bread.
And forgive us our debts,
        as we also forgive our debtors.

---

[2] It would be interesting to know the prayer which the Precursor taught his disciples, but unfortunately the Gospels are silent on the matter, and tradition has handed down nothing in its regard.

And lead us not into temptation,
but deliver us from evil."

Where did this moving scene take place? St. Luke tells us only that it occurred "in a certain place" (11:1), a phrase which, although it reveals nothing positive concerning the location, still seems to hint that the episode did not stem from the one recorded immediately before, i.e., our Lord's stay in Bethany, but that it happened some time later (Knabenbauer). We are inclined to believe that Jesus was in Perea at the time, in the Jordan valley, to be more precise. The petition, "Lord, teach us to pray, *even as John taught his disciples,*" harmonizes well with the atmosphere of the place where John had baptized, and it would sound appropriate on the lips of one of the inhabitants who had venerated the Precursor and had been one of his followers before becoming a disciple of Christ. The chronology here offers no difficulty if we place the incident of Martha and Mary first (Luke 10:38–42), then the feast of the Dedication, and immediately after that, our Lord's return to Perea (John 10:40).

There is, of course, a tradition which places the teaching of the Our Father on Mount Olivet on the site of St. Helena's basilica, formerly known as Eleona but now called the Church of the Paternoster. But the ancient pilgrims speak only in general terms,[3] or else they mention explicitly our Lord's teachings about the end of the world.[4]

To find even an obscure reference to the Our Father, we must come down as far as the ninth century,[5] and there is no explicit mention of the prayer until the end of the eleventh century.[6] Consequently, we do not believe that a tradition of this type can be regarded as very valuable, especially since it is so easy to pass from speaking about our Lord's teaching in general to the doctrine con-

---

[3] ". . . Spelunca illa, in qua *docebat* Dominus": Etheria (or Eucheria), fourth century (Geyer, *Itinera,* p. 82).

[4] ". . . Et cum suis discipulis in eius montis cacumine mysteria de *consummatione* tradidit": Eusebius, third century (*PG* 22, 457; Baldi, *Enchiridion,* p. 484).
". . . In spelunca in qua cum discipulis suis Dominus de *consummatione saeculi* disputavit": *Vita S. Melaniae Junioris,* fifth century (Baldi, *Enchiridion,* p. 492).

[5] ". . . In qua servatur scriptura in lapide marmoreo, quam Dominus scripsit in terra": Bernardus Monachus, A.D. 870 (Baldi, *Enchiridion,* p. 508). Here there is obvious confusion with the incident of the woman taken in adultery.

[6] ". . . Inde ad orientem est mons Oliveti, unde Dominus caelos ascendit et ubi discipulis suis *Pater noster* scripsit": *Qualiter sita est Ierusalem,* A.D. 1095 (Baldi, *Enchiridion,* p. 509).

tained in the Our Father. Another possible explanation of the tradition is that the incident of the prayer is narrated immediately after Christ's visit to Bethany, which is situated on the slope of Mount Olivet itself.[7]

St. Matthew (6:9–13) incorporates the Our Father in the Sermon on the Mount, which had been preached a long time before. The question therefore arises, who puts the prayer in its correct place, Matthew or Luke? It is not impossible that Jesus repeated the same prayer twice, but if He taught it only once—and that seems most probable—there is scarcely any doubt that St. Luke's chronology is the true historical one, since St. Matthew frequently brings together instructions and incidents that originally occurred at different times. Furthermore, the insertion of the Our Father in the Sermon on the Mount (Matt. 6:7–15) seems to disrupt the harmony of the three parallel passages (6:1–4, 5–6, 16–18), each of which ends with the words, "and thy Father, who sees in secret, will reward thee."

There is another problem, more important than the placing of the Our Father, and that is the difference between St. Matthew's and St. Luke's versions of the prayer. St. Luke's is the shorter, for it lacks three phrases found in St. Matthew—"Our [Father] who art in heaven," "thy will be done on earth, as it is in heaven," and "but deliver us from evil"; and instead of "forgive us our *debts*" as in St. Matthew, St. Luke has "forgive us our *sins*." Which of the two texts is the authentic one? Some authors say that both are, and that our Lord used the words recorded in St. Matthew when speaking to the crowd, while He employed the version given by St. Luke when speaking privately to His disciples. Obviously this theory is tenable, but we may ask, if Jesus had already taught the Our Father, why did one of His disciples ask Him to instruct them how to pray? A possible answer is that the petitioner was a new disciple, one of those who had joined our Lord in Perea, as we have indicated above (p. 496), and

---

[7] See Lebreton's remarks (*Life and Teachings of Jesus Christ,* II, 61). He places the teaching of the Our Father in the Garden of Gethsemani. In support of the view that the incident took place on Mount Olivet, more than a few authors (e.g., Lagrange, Prat) bring forward the text of Mark 11:23–26, in which our Lord, in the course of a brief instruction on Mount Olivet shortly before His Passion, refers to pardoning enemies and to "your Father in heaven." But these are concepts which by their very nature could easily have been repeated on different occasions, and therefore we do not believe that this text has any value in fixing the scene of the Our Father.

who therefore had not heard His previous teachings. Thus the objection loses much of its force.

But even if Christ taught the prayer only once, the diversity can be readily explained by the fact that the two evangelists may have drawn from two different currents of oral tradition, of which there were several, substantially the same but differing in details, as we pointed out when discussing the eight Beatitudes in St. Matthew as compared with the four in St. Luke.

In that case, which of the two versions of the Our Father is to be preferred? Some authors favor the shorter one, i.e., St. Luke's,[8] but the majority of exegetes, particularly the Catholic ones, rightly give the preference to St. Matthew's version, which is the one adopted by the liturgy and of which St. Luke's is a summary.

Almost all the ancient Latin commentators follow St. Augustine in distinguishing *seven* petitions in the Our Father,[9] while the Greek Fathers and the majority of modern authors count only *six*, and, in our opinion, correctly so since the last two phrases, "lead us not into temptation" and "deliver us from evil," really ask for the same thing.[10] The latter enumeration gives a perfect parallel between the first series of three petitions directed to the glory of God, and the second series of three, whose object is the fulfilling of our needs. All six petitions are fittingly introduced by the invocation: "Our Father who art in heaven," which, as St. Augustine says, serves to win for us the divine benevolence so that our prayer may be favorably received.[11]

The second petition, "thy kingdom come," is a consequence of the first, "hallowed be thy name," for if God is glorified, by that very fact His kingdom is established in us;[12] and the third, "thy will be

---

[8] Thus, for example, C. Votaw in *Hastings' Dictionary of the Bible* (New York: Charles Scribner's Sons, 1904), V, 32 *ff.* This author makes a fairly complete study of the collation of the two texts.

[9] *De sermone Domini in monte (PL* 34, 1,285): "Sed harum septem petitionum consideranda et commendanda distinctio est."

[10] See below pp. 500 *f.*

[11] "Cum in omni deprecatione benevolentia concilianda sit eius quem deprecamur, deinde dicendum quid deprecemur; laude illius ad quem oratio dirigitur solet benevolentia conciliari, et hoc in orationis principio poni solet; in quo Dominus noster nihil aliud nos dicere iussit nisi *Pater noster, qui es in caelis*" (*Ibid.,* col. 1,275).

[12] Some authors, following the example of more than a few of the Fathers, understand the kingdom of God here in the eschatological sense of the glorious *second coming* of Christ. Yet although this meaning may perhaps not be excluded from the prayer—in fact, we can even say that it is included as the

done," is concerned with the means by which the first two are to be accomplished, namely, the doing of God's will.

To hallow God's name means to acknowledge Him as infinitely holy and to venerate and glorify Him as such. The kingdom of God is established and extended on earth when men, respecting His sovereign rights, render Him fitting homage and do His bidding. The third petition, "thy will be done," can have two meanings: it may be regarded as asking that God's plans be carried out, or else that men may do His will and act in accordance with His law. The second interpretation seems to fit in better with the preceding petitions. However, since the carrying out of God's plans and the doing of His will by men are so closely connected, perhaps it would be more correct to say that the somewhat vague formula includes both meanings.[13]

The second series of petitions, the fourth, fifth and sixth, look to the present, the past and the future respectively. The fifth, "forgive us our debts . . .," offers no difficulty, but the other two do, particularly the first, "Give us this day our daily bread."

The words "our daily bread" have been interpreted in three ways to mean our bodily food, the Holy Eucharist, and the word of God. St. Augustine excludes the first two interpretations and declares himself in favor of the third.[14] Some may think it simplest to say that our Lord had all three things in mind when He spoke of "bread." Obviously He could have had, but there is no positive reason for affirming that He actually did intend to use the word in that way. In view of all the circumstances, the great majority of modern authors believe that in this passage, "bread" refers to bodily food, the part being taken for the whole as, for example, in Genesis 3:19: "In the sweat of thy face shalt thou eat *bread*."

It is more difficult to fix the precise meaning of the adjective ἐπιούσιος, which the Vulgate translates as *supersubstantial* in St. Mat-

---

final end—the primary sense is certainly God's reign over men from this moment on: "Regnum Dei intra vos est" (Luke 17:21), i.e., the kingdom of God is *in* each of us, in our souls, or else, and more probably, it is *among* us.

[13] Cf. *Ephemerides Theologicae Lovanienses* (1949), pp. 61–76.

[14] "Panis quotidianus aut pro iis omnibus dictus est, quae huius vitae necessitatem sustentant. . . , aut pro sacramento corporis Christi quod quotidie accipimus. . . , aut pro spirituali cibo. . . . Sed horum trium quid sit probabilius, considerari potest." Then after setting forth the difficulties presented by the first and second meanings, he concludes: "Restat igitur ut quotidianum panem accipiamus spiritualem, *praecepta* scilicet *divina,* quae quotidie oportet meditari et operari" (*PL* 34, 1,280).

thew and as *daily* in St. Luke, while the Peschitto version has *our needful bread;* several other versions have *perpetual bread,* the Ethiopian gives *the food of each day,* and the Georgian, *the bread of our sustenance.*[15]

The adjective ἐπιούσιος appears nowhere in the Bible outside of these two passages, and it occurs only once in profane literature,[16] whence the great difficulty in ascertaining its exact meaning. Its etymology, a possible source of light on the question, can be twofold: (1) the word may come from ἡ ἐπιοῦσα (ἡμέρα being understood), i.e., "the coming day, tomorrow," or "the day that is beginning, today": (2) it may be derived from οὐσία, "sustenance," "means of subsistence" (cf. Luke 15:12), so that the bread we ask for is the sustaining bread we need, that which is *necessary* for our bodily nourishment. This sense is quite acceptable, but we prefer the first derivation, bread for "the day that is beginning," i.e., for today, because the other meaning, "the coming day, tomorrow," does not seem to harmonize well with the words of Christ in Matthew 6:34: "Therefore do not be anxious about tomorrow. . . ." Thus in the Our Father we ask God to give us each day (Luke) the bread necessary for the current day, a petition that is in perfect accord with abandonment to Divine Providence.[17]

In the last petition, the word "temptation" (πειρασμός) means a situation or set of circumstances that, considering our weakness, could be an occasion of sin for us. Hence when we say, "lead us not into temptation," we are asking God not only to help us to avoid succumbing to temptation, but, what is more, to preserve us from it, not because temptation is evil in itself, but only because we are conscious of our frailty.

In St. Matthew there is a final phrase, "but deliver us from evil," which is lacking in St. Luke, probably because it was not present in the source, oral or written, from which he drew his information. It is doubtful whether the Greek word used for "evil" (τοῦ πονεροῦ) is masculine, in which case it would mean "the evil one, the devil," or

---

[15] Cf. Zorell, *N.T. Lexicon Graecum.*

[16] In a papyrus which Flinders Petrie found at Fayum in Egypt, and which contains a list of things pertaining to the kitchen. Cf. Zorell, *Biblica,* 6 (1925), 321 *f.*

[17] Cf. Zorell, *op. cit.,* for a clear and concise explanatoin of the various etymologies; cf. also *Theologisches Wörterbuch zum Neuen Testament* (Stuttgart, 1932), II, 587–595.

neuter, evil in general, which is the more common interpretation.[18] But in either case, the petition is simply an extension of the preceding one, as if we said: "O God, do not place us in such circumstances; but if Thou dost, preserve us from evil." Therefore we do not regard the last words in St. Matthew as a seventh petition, but only as a continuation of the sixth.

Is there any analogy to be drawn between the Our Father and the customary prayers of the Jews? The two best-known prayers among the Jews were the *Shemoneh 'Esreh,* or *Eighteen (Blessings),* also called the *Tefillah* or prayer *par excellence,* which every Jew had to recite three times a day,[19] and the *Kaddish,* which was twofold, liturgical and rabbinical. The liturgical version of the *Kaddish* begins: "May the great name of Him who created according to His will be praised and blessed. May He establish His kingdom"; and the rabbinical version also begins with the same phrase: "May His great name be praised and blessed." Thus there is an obvious similarity between these ideas and terms from the *Kaddish* and the first two petitions of the Our Father. But the resemblance stops there, and there is no particular likeness between the remainder of the two prayers. Then, too, the liturgical use of the *Kaddish* goes back no further than the seventh century A.D., although certain parts of it may be of much more ancient date.

The *Tefillah* seems to have been already in use in the second half of the first century A.D., after the destruction of Jerusalem. Two of its petitions run as follows: "Give us, Our Father, knowledge . . .": "Forgive us, Our Father, for we have sinned; pardon us, Our King, for we have transgressed; for thou dost pardon and forgive. Blessed art Thou, O Lord, who art gracious and dost abundantly pardon." These beautiful and fervent phrases are very reminiscent of the beginning of the Our Father, and of the fifth petition, "forgive us our debts," but apart from them, no other portion of the *Tefillah* finds an echo in the Our Father.

---

[18] This is how Knabenbauer, Lagrange, Prat, Colunga, and others understand it; we, too, regard this interpretation as the more probable one.

[19] See the original in Dalman, *Sacred Sites and Ways,* p. 35. There was also the *Shema'* which had to be said twice a day; in the morning, preceded by two benedictions and followed by a third, and in the evening, preceded and followed by two benedictions. However, since this prayer was composed of three passages from Scripture (Deut. 6:4–9; 11:13–21; Num. 15:37–41), it contains nothing that recalls the Our Father. The name *Shema'* was taken from the beginning of the first passage (Deut. 6:4), *"Shema', Israel:* Hear O Israel." Cf. *Mishnah, Berakoth* 1–3.

We believe that only a prejudiced mind will regard the aforementioned resemblances as proof that the prayers of the Jews exercised a positive and direct influence on the Our Father. Furthermore, the nationalistic, restricted character of the Jewish prayers is totally different from the universality of the Our Father. For the rest, we need not wonder at the resemblances between the prayer our Lord taught and the Jewish prayers, because when composing the Our Father, Jesus drew on the Old Testament as the Jews had when devising their formulae.

21. Ministry in

Perea

After his account of the Our Father, St. Luke has a long section (11:5–18:14) which is almost completely exclusive to him. And since he gives practically no chronological or topographical data, it is very difficult to fix the time and place of the incidents he records, with the result that there are numerous opinions as to the sequence and location of the events. Our theory, which we advance modestly and reservedly, is as follows: we divide the section referred to into two parts, the second of which (17:11–18:14) we place after the raising of Lazarus, for reasons which we shall give later, while we place the first part (11:5–17:10) before the raising of Lazarus and in Perea, at least in the main.

We base our opinion on Luke 13:22, 31: "And he was passing on through towns and villages, teaching and making his way towards Jerusalem. . . . Certain Pharisees came up, saying to him, 'Depart and be on thy way, for Herod wants to kill thee.' "

From John 10:40, we know with certainty that, immediately after the feast of Dedication, Jesus returned to Perea where, in our opinion, the episode of the Our Father took place (Luke 11:1–4). Now, from Luke 13:31 we know that our Lord was in the territory of Herod Antipas, and since we cannot suppose that He was in Galilee at the time, we must therefore conclude that He was in Perea. And because there is no positive evidence to the contrary, it seems only reasonable to believe that the events between Luke 11:5 and 13:31 occurred in that region. Of course, Luke 13:22 does mention a journey to Jerusalem, but we think that this was not a new, special journey, but only the continuation of the great one which Luke announced in 9:51, and to which he refers again here because he is about to speak of the capital (13:33 *ff.*). Then, too, our Lord's stay in Perea is clearly indicated in 13:31, after the reference to the journey in 13:22.

As regards the events of the following chapters (13:34–17:10), there is no reason to locate them in another region. It is clear that during His stay in Perea, Christ did not remain in one place, for St. Luke tells us explicitly (13:22) that "he was passing on through towns and villages. . . ." But we cannot be sure whether He remained on the eastern side of the Jordan valley, which was not uninhabited then as it is now, for it had a considerable population along the river, as is evident from the numerous *tells;* or whether He penetrated the mountain region, ascending the Wadi Nimrin to the ancient city of Gador, now known as es-Salt; or, finally, whether He followed the Wadi ez-Zerqa and passed through ancient Mahanaim, the present-day Tulud ed-Dahab.

Since, as we have said, there is no certainty about the exact chronological sequence of the events of this period, we have judged it best to group together similar parables and instructions which the evangelist records separately.

The Efficacy of Persevering and Humble Prayer

THE IMPORTUNATE FRIEND
(Luke 11:5–13)

The great charm of this parable lies in its simplicity and its trueness to the everyday life of the people. A hard-working peasant has retired for the night, and he and his family are asleep on their pallets, which are probably only thin mats laid on the floor. At midnight, however, he is roused from deep slumber by loud knocks on the door. Startled, he sits up, wondering what is wrong. But it is only his neighbor, a poor man like himself, who has just had an unexpected guest arrive, tired and hungry. Unfortunately the neighbor has no food in the house, and has come to borrow three loaves to feed his guest, the urgency of his need being his excuse for the untimeliness of his request. Ordinarily the householder would have unhesitatingly given his friend what he asked, for neighbors are usually happy to render each other such small services; but he is unwilling to leave his warm bed, particularly because he is afraid he will disturb his children, who are sleeping beside him under the same bedcoverings. Therefore he calls out to his friend: "Do not disturb me; the door is now shut, and my children and I are in bed; I cannot get up and give to thee."

But the neighbor will not be put off and continues to knock, so that the householder, anxious to get rid of him and be allowed to go back to sleep, rises from his bed and gives him the loaves.

Jesus concluded His parable with the consoling words: "Ask, and it shall be given to you; seek, and you shall find; knock, and it shall be opened to you. For everyone who asks receives; and he who seeks finds; and to him who knocks, it shall be opened."

THE UNJUST JUDGE AND THE POOR WIDOW
(Luke 18:1–8)

The evangelist himself tells us the lesson which Jesus wished to teach in this parable: "they must always pray and not lose heart" (v. 1). We are to keep on praying without becoming discouraged; we are to persist in our request, convinced that in the end we shall obtain our petition.

In two telling phrases our Lord sketches the character of the unjust judge "who did not fear God nor respect man," and who therefore had nothing to restrain him.

In the town where the judge officiated, there was a certain widow who came to him seeking redress for an injustice she had suffered. For a long time he paid no heed to her, but finally, since the widow kept insisting on being heard, he said to himself: "Although I do not fear God, nor even respect man, yet because this widow bothers me, I will do her justice, lest by her continual coming she finally wear me out."

And our Lord concluded: "Will not God avenge his elect, who cry to him day and night? And will he be slow to act in their case? I tell you that he will avenge them quickly."

St. Luke then records an unexpected and, we could almost say, a wholly displaced sentence, apparently completely unconnected with the one immediately preceding: "Yet when the Son of Man comes, will he find, do you think, faith on the earth?"

This thought seems to have so little bearing on the parable that a good number of authors regard it as completely foreign to the context; some (e.g., Jülicher) hold that it is the evangelist's own reflection, while others (e.g., Buzy) take it to be "a relic of a longer discourse." [1] We believe that, although the sentence is not strictly speaking one of the elements of the parable, it is still part of it, and was spoken by our Lord in the circumstances in which the evangelist presents it.

The parable and the sentence are linked by an association of ideas. Before relating the parable, Christ had been speaking about the coming of the Son of Man (Luke 17:20–37), and now, when He is promising that God will hear the persevering supplication of the faithful and will wreak vengeance on their oppressors, He is thinking of the last day, the day of retribution. Pausing in reflection upon the condition of the world on that fateful day, He asks, as if speaking to Himself, what the moral disposition of men will be when the Son of Man comes to judge and to give each one his just deserts. The sentence, therefore, is decidedly eschatological; but we doubt that the same can be said of the parable itself. We do not deny that certain parts of it, for example the expression "quickly," may be susceptible of such an interpretation, but we do not believe that this is sufficient reason for concluding that the parable as a whole is eschatological. [2]

THE PHARISEE AND THE PUBLICAN
(Luke 18:9–14)

Our Lord could scarcely have chosen two characters more suited to the purpose He had in relating this parable "to some who trusted in themselves as being just and despised others."

The Pharisee observed the Law down to its minutest details: "O God, I thank thee that I am not like the rest of men, robbers, dishonest, adulterers, or even like this publican. I fast twice a week; [3] I pay tithes of all that I possess."

---

[1] *Les Paraboles* (Paris, 1932), p. 574.
[2] See the detailed study by Puzo in *Est. Ecles.*, 19 (1945), 273–334.
[3] "Bis in sabbato": "sabbatum" was sometimes taken to mean a week.

In itself, such strict observance of the Law was praiseworthy, but in the Pharisee's case it was vitiated by self-complacency and contempt for others, with the result that his prayer was not acceptable to God. The publican, on the other hand, was a member of a class which the people had good cause to hate, and he was perhaps weighed down with the burden of the many injustices he had done them; yet his prayer was a model of humility and sincere repentance. Without even daring to raise his eyes to heaven, he struck his breast again and again, repeating as he did so: "O God, be merciful to me the sinner."

And because his heart was contrite and humble, God accepted his prayer: "I tell you, this man went back to his home justified rather than the other; for everyone who exalts himself shall be humbled, and he who humbles himself shall be exalted."

Although the Pharisee and the publican are both depicted as praying, prayer is not the principal element of the parable, but is only the background for the lesson which our Lord wished to teach. The evangelist's introduction, and the conclusion which Jesus drew from the narrative, clearly show that the central theme is humility. The parable also stresses the idea that our prayer will not be acceptable to God unless we pray with humility.

The Hypocrisy of the Scribes and Pharisees
(Luke 11:37–54)

On a certain occasion when our Lord was speaking to the crowds, one of the Pharisees who lived in the town approached and politely invited Him to dine at his house. There is reason to believe that the invitation was given with evil intentions and perhaps as the result of a conspiracy between the host and the other Pharisees of the place, who, apparently, were also invited. Our Lord's enemies wished to get Him alone, away from the crowds which were so favorable to Him, so that they might observe Him at close quarters and try to find something in His words with which to accuse Him.

Jesus accepted the invitation, but upon entering the Pharisee's house, instead of going first to wash His hands at the place prepared for the ritual purification, He immediately took His place at table. The Scribes and Pharisees who were present were shocked and angered by His action, but none more so than the host. Jesus read their secret thoughts, and answered their unspoken reproach by mercilessly flaying their hypocrisy: "Now you Pharisees clean the outside of the cup and the dish, but within you are full of robbery and wickedness. . . . Woe to you Pharisees! because you pay tithes on mint and rue and every herb, and disregard justice and the love of God. But these things you ought to have done, while not leaving the others undone. Woe to you Pharisees! because you love the front seats in the synagogues and greetings in the market place. . . ."

Although Christ had mentioned only the Pharisees, one of the Scribes present felt that he and his fellows were included in the condemnation, and he complained: "Master, in saying these things, thou insultest us also."

But his objection only served to elicit a direct attack on the Scribes: "Woe to you lawyers also! because you load men with oppressive burdens and you yourselves with one of your fingers do not touch the burdens. . . . Woe to you lawyers! because you have taken away the key of knowledge; you have not entered yourselves and those who were entering you have hindered."

We can imagine the effect that Christ's biting words had on His proud enemies. The evangelist notes that from that moment on, they never left Him in peace; they followed Him about constantly, besieging Him with questions in the hope of goading Him into saying something that would give them a hold on Him and provide them with an opportunity of repaying Him for His searing condemnation of them and their ways.

The Importance of Salvation: Loving Abandonment to Providence
(Luke 12:1–13:9)

On leaving the Pharisee's house, Jesus was met by a large crowd which had been waiting for Him to emerge. It is likely that when He had been invited to dine, His audience had followed Him and remained outside in hope of seeing Him again. While they waited, so many others had joined them that the evangelist could say, not without a touch of hyperbole, however, that "immense crowds had gathered together, so that they were treading on one another." Seeing their good will and eagerness to learn, Jesus began to speak to them about the importance of salvation, preparation for death, and loving abandonment to Divine Providence (Luke 12–13).

This discourse, besides being notable for the importance and variety of the doctrine it contains, is also remarkable for the fact that, as our Lord spoke, He first addressed His disciples (vv. 1–12), then the people (vv. 13–21), then His disciples again (vv. 22–53), and finally the people once more (vv. 12:54–13:9). This alternation, combined with the circumstance that a large part of the material is found dispersed through St. Matthew's Gospel, seems to suggest that here St. Luke has simply gathered together into one group lessons that our Lord originally taught at different times and in different places. Moreover, how could Jesus have singled out His disciples, mingled as they were with a large and densely packed crowd?

However, a close examination of the text will show that it is not as difficult as it appears to vindicate the objective reality of the chronological and topographical details of St. Luke's account. First of all, Peter's question in Luke 12:41, "Lord, art thou speaking this parable for us or for all alike?" presupposes that Jesus had spoken first to the disciples and then to the crowd, a procedure that is also clearly indicated by the word "first" ("he addressed his disciples *first*," 12:1); and there is no reason to believe that the evangelist used this word or made Peter ask his question merely as a literary device. Again, the opening words of the chapter, "in the meantime" (i.e., while Jesus was dining in the Pharisee's house), link our Lord's discourse with what went before. But why would the evangelist have given us this chronological indication if it did not correspond to reality? As regards Christ's addressing His disciples in particular, this did not entail taking them aside from the crowd; He simply spoke to them as they stood, surrounded by the people, who heard everything He had to say to the disciples.

The links between the different parts of the discourse do seem weak, yet we must remember that it is more a dialogue than an extended address. Thus, for example, in verse 13 we find one of the crowd interrupting Jesus, and it would not be rash to suppose that this was not the only time that someone broke in on Him as He was speaking. And even though He deals with a great variety of subjects in this address as it is recorded by St. Luke, it would be an exaggeration to say that His discourse lacks cohesion, for there is a certain logical bond between the subjects treated.

These are the reasons, then, that incline us to retain the chronological and topographical framework within which St. Luke presents our Lord's instructions.

The disciples had witnessed the scene in the Pharisee's house, and Jesus, addressing them in particular (although all present could hear His words), put them on their guard against the hypocrisy of the Pharisees: "Beware of the leaven of the Pharisees, which is hypocrisy. . . . Do not be afraid of those who kill the body, and after that have nothing more that they can do. But . . . be afraid of him who, after he has killed, has power to cast into hell. . . . Are not five sparrows sold for two farthings? And yet not one of them is forgotten before God. Yes, the very hairs of your head are all numbered. Therefore do not be afraid, you are of more value than many sparrows."

While He was speaking, a man approached with a request: "Master, tell my brother to divide the inheritance with me."

But Jesus replied: "Man, who has appointed me a judge or arbitrator over you? . . . Take heed and guard yourselves from all covetousness, for a man's life does not consist in the abundance of his possessions."

To drive home His lesson, our Lord recounted the following parable: "The land of a certain rich man brought forth abundant crops. And he began to take thought within himself, saying, 'What shall I do, for I have no room to store my crops?' And he said, 'I will do this: I will pull down my barns and build larger ones, and there I will store up all my grain and my goods. And I will say to my soul, Soul, thou hast many good things laid up for many years; take thy ease, eat, drink, be merry.' But God said to him, 'Thou fool, this night do they demand thy soul of thee; and the things that thou hast provided, whose will they be?' So is he who lays up treasure for himself, and is not rich as regards God."

Continuing the same line of thought, but addressing Himself now to His disciples, He gave a series of beautiful lessons on detachment from worldly goods, on filial abandonment into the arms of Divine Providence, and the necessity of continual preparedness for death: "Do not be anxious for your life, what you shall eat; nor yet for your body, what you shall put on. The life is a greater thing than the food, and the body than the clothing. Consider the ravens: they neither sow nor reap, they have neither storeroom nor barn; yet God feeds them. . . .

"Consider how the lilies grow; they neither toil nor spin, yet I say to you that not even Solomon in all his glory was arrayed like one of these. . . .

"But seek first the kingdom of God, and all these things shall be given you besides. . . .

"Let your loins be girt about and your lamps burning, and you yourselves like men waiting for their master's return from the wedding; so that when he comes and knocks, they may straightway open to him. . . .

"You also must be ready, because at an hour that you do not expect, the Son of Man is coming."

It was at this point that Peter interrupted Him with the question:

"Lord, art thou speaking this parable for us or for all alike?"

Without answering the query directly, Jesus said: "Who, dost thou think, is the faithful and prudent steward whom the master will set over his household to give them their ration of grain in due time? Blessed is that servant whom his master, when he comes, shall find so doing. Truly I say to you, he will set him over all his goods. . . .

"I have come to cast fire upon the earth, and what will I but that it be kindled? But I have a baptism to be baptized with; and how distressed I am until it is accomplished! Do you think that I came to give peace upon the earth? No, I tell you, but division."

The fire which Jesus brought on earth is the fire of charity, whereby hearts are purified and the dross of sin is burned away. His most ardent desire is that men be inflamed by this holy fire, and that it spread across the face of the earth. Thus will the kingdom of God, which He came to found, be established and propagated. But in the designs of the Father, the realization of this high ideal demanded that Jesus Himself should undergo the painful baptism of His Passion. And the fire which He cast on earth was to cause division among men, some giving themselves to it, others resisting it, with the result that there would be two opposing camps engaged in deadly combat, the sons of darkness against the sons of light. Then would be fulfilled Simeon's prophecy: "Behold, this child is destined for the fall and for the rise of many in Israel" (Luke 2:34).

This is the most obvious interpretation of our Lord's rather enigmatic words, particularly those in Luke 12:47. But there is another interpretation which seems preferable in view of the context.

The fire which Jesus came to cast on earth is not specifically charity or the Holy Spirit, but is instead a symbol of the spiritual upheaval, the powerful revolutionary movement which His new doctrine would bring about. He desired to start this movement, this struggle between good and evil, because from it the kingdom which He had come to found would emerge triumphant, as a result of the grace which God would pour out on souls. But in order that this victory might be realized, it was God's will that Christ should undergo His Passion, the thought of which had kept His soul in anguish since the first moment of His life.

Then addressing the crowd, our Lord said: "When you see a cloud rising in the west, you say at once, 'A shower is coming,' and so it comes to pass. And when you see the south wind blow, you say, 'There will be a scorching heat,' and so it comes to pass. You hypocrites! you know how to judge the face of the sky and of the earth; but how is it that you do not judge this time?"

At that same period, perhaps on that very day (the Greek expression in 13:1, ἐν αὐτῷ τῷ καιρῷ, is vague), while Jesus was speaking, some people came to Him with the news that Pilate had slaughtered a group of Galileans while they were offering sacrifice in the Temple, a massacre that probably had resulted from a clash between the rebellious Galileans and the cruel Roman governor. From the horrifying news Christ drew a striking lesson on the true nature of physical calamities, and the necessity of doing penance: "Do you think that these Galileans were worse sinners than all the other Galileans, because they have suffered such things? I tell you, no; but unless you repent, you will all perish in the same manner."

And stressing the same point still more, He recalled another disaster that had also occurred in Jerusalem: "Or those eighteen upon whom the tower of Siloe [4] fell and killed them; do you think that they were more guilty than all the other dwellers in Jerusalem? I tell you, no; but unless you repent, you will all perish in the same manner."

Then, in order to throw into sharp relief the necessity of prompt repentance on the one hand, and the merciful long-suffering of God on the other, our Lord related the following parable: "A certain man

---

[4] In 1914, excavations uncovered the base of a tower near the old channel through which the water ran from the Fountain of Gihon (now called the Fountain of the Virgin) to the pool of Siloe. This tower could well have been the one to which Jesus was here referring.

had a fig tree planted in his vineyard; and he came seeking fruit thereon, and found none. And he said to the vinedresser, 'Behold, for three years now I have come seeking fruit on this fig tree, and I find none. Cut it down, therefore; why does it still encumber the ground?' But he answered him and said, 'Sir, let it alone this year too, till I dig around it and manure it. Perhaps it may bear fruit; but if not, then afterwards thou shalt cut it down.' "

The Stooped Woman
(Luke 13:10-21)

In Perea our Lord preached in the synagogues on the Sabbath days, as He had done in Galilee (Mark 1:21). And it was in one of the synagogues that another incident occurred which showed the great contrast between His kindness and the unbending rigorism of the Jews in interpreting the Law.

In the congregation on this occasion there was a woman who for eighteen years suffered from an illness that kept her stooped over, so that she could not even look upwards. When our Lord saw her, He called her to him and said: "Woman, thou art delivered from thy infirmity."

Having spoken these words, He laid His hands upon her and she immediately straightened up and gave praise to God.

The ruler of the synagogue, angered because Jesus had cured on the Sabbath, but not daring to confront Him directly, vented his wrath on the crowd by saying: "There are six days in which one ought to work; on these therefore come and be cured, and not on the Sabbath."

Upon hearing this hypocritically pious admonition, our Lord turned to the ruler of the synagogue and severely reprimanded him and his fellows: "Hypocrites! does not each one of you on the Sabbath loose his ox or ass from the manger, and lead it forth to water? And this woman, daughter of Abraham as she is, whom Satan has bound, lo, for eighteen years, ought not she to be loosed from this bond on the Sabbath?"

"And as he said these things," continues St. Luke, "all his adversaries were put to shame; and the entire crowd rejoiced at all the glorious things that were done by him."

The Number of Those Saved
(Luke 13:23–30)

Another day, when Jesus was perhaps preaching to the crowd, one of His listeners asked Him: "Lord, are only a few to be saved?"

This point, the greater or lesser number of the elect, was much discussed by the rabbis.

Our Lord, however, did not answer the question, for it was inspired by mere curiosity. Instead, He profited by it to exhort His audience to strive with all their strength to make themselves worthy of entering the kingdom of heaven: "Strive to enter by the narrow gate; for many, I tell you, will seek to enter and will not be able. But when the master of the house has entered and shut the door, you will begin to stand outside and knock at the door, saying, 'Lord, open for us!' And he shall say to you in answer, 'I do not know where you are from.' "

Then He went on to warn them that it would not be enough to have heard His teaching, or to have lived or even eaten with Him: all that would count for nothing if it had not been accompanied by good works. Furthermore, it could well happen that some of the Gentiles whom they despised, but who had led good lives, would be admitted to the kingdom and given preference over the very Jews themselves: "And they will come from the east and from the west, from the north and from the south, and will feast in the kingdom of God. And behold, there are those last who will be first, and there are those first who will be last."

Our Lord said that the gate ($\theta\acute{v}\rho a$) is *narrow,* and precisely because it is so, one can enter it only by exerting oneself. This is obviously an allusion to a doctrine which He had explained more fully elsewhere, and which St. Matthew has preserved for us among the lessons of the Sermon on the Mount (Matt. 7:13 *f.*): "Enter by the narrow gate. For wide is the gate and broad is the way that leads to destruction, and many there are who enter that way. How narrow the gate and close the way that leads to life! And few there are who find it."

The basic idea in the two passages is clear and unmistakable: the path to heaven is a difficult one, and those who walk it are few; the path to perdition is easily travelled, and many follow it. Our Lord expressed this concept by placing before us a picture of two cities, the city of life and the city of eternal death, each one with a gate and a road leading to that gate. Both these images, that of the gate and that of the roads, are to be found in the Old Testament and in rabbinical literature. For example, God commanded Jeremias: "And to this people thou shalt say: Thus saith the Lord: Behold I set before you the way of life and the way of death" (Jer. 21:8); and Rabbi Akiba used to say: "God set two roads before Adam. One led to life, the other to death; and he chose the road of death," while we read in a *midrash:* "Lord of the world, give me to know the gate that opens upon the life of the world to come." [5]

While the symbolic meaning of the two images is quite clear, the relationship between them is not. Does the road *begin* at the gate, as Lagrange believes? In that case, the gate would be somewhat like one of those triumphal arches which used to be erected some distance from a city, such as can still be seen today at Gerasa. Or did the road *end* at the gate? If so, the gate could only be that of the city.[6] Or, finally, did the road *pass through* the gate? [7]

Be that as it may, in our opinion our Lord did not conceive or intend to propose the two images as linked together, but as independent of each other,[8] although they both mean the same thing, namely, the difficulty of observing the Commandments, represented by the narrow gate and the close way, and the ease with which the Commandments can be broken, symbolized by the wide gate and the broad way.

Did Christ mean that all who walk the broad way and enter by the wide gate are damned? We know that if they keep travelling that road and do not turn back, they will end by being damned; but they can, at any moment, leave the broad way and take the narrow one that leads to life.[9] Yet our Lord was not, on that account, speaking of

---

[5] Cf. Str.-Bill., I, 460–464. A *midrash* is a rabbinical commentary on the Hebrew Scriptures.

[6] This would seem to be the most likely arrangement: one approaches the city along the road and gains entrance to it through the gate in the walls.

[7] Loisy, *Les Évangiles Synoptiques,* II, 120 *ff.* Joüon interprets "gate" in the sense of a defile, or narrow pass, through which the road runs (*L'Évangile de N.S. J.-C.* [Paris, 1930], *in loc.*), but we believe that this meaning is improbable in the present passage.

[8] This is the view favored by B. Weiss, Buzy, and others.

[9] Perhaps some may object that such a change of direction is easily understood in the metaphor of the road, but not in that of the gate, for once a traveller has

man's final and irrevocable destiny, but of his mode of action, good or bad, which would lead him to the city of life or the city of death. He was not referring to those who, in the end, are lost or saved, but to the world at large, where the majority of men walk, not in the narrow path of virtue, but along the broad way of sin.

But the last sentence in St. Matthew (7:14): "And few there are who find it" (i.e., the narrow path that leads to life), seems to indicate that many do not find the path, never walk in it, and therefore never arrive at the city of life. In addition, if, ordinarily, many walk the broad path and few the narrow, then the damned outnumber the saved, even though some of those on the broad road turn back. Hence it would appear that our Lord declared, if only indirectly, that more souls are damned than are saved. We believe, however, that the passage should be interpreted in the sense that Jesus was only expressing forcibly the general impression left by the spectacle of a world given over to the satisfaction of its passions, and that He was not making a pronouncement on the ultimate consequences of such widespread iniquity. There is no doubt that this interpretation is in perfect accordance with the general drift of the Gospel text.

Jerusalem, Jerusalem!
(Luke 13:31–35)

While Jesus was still speaking to the crowd, some Pharisees came hurriedly up to Him and, with every evidence of good will, warned Him that He would have to leave the district quickly if He did not want to fall into Herod's hands: "Depart and be on thy way," they urged, "for Herod wants to kill thee."

Was their concern for Him sincere? Some authors think so; and actually it is not impossible that, just as there was a Nicodemus among the Pharisees of Jerusalem, so also there were some in Perea

passed through the gate, he is inside the city of life or the city of death, as the case may be, and he cannot turn back. We must remember, however, that a symbol does not always correspond in every particular with the thing symbolized. The observance of God's law leads to life; it requires effort; and this effort must be continuous and may last for long years. This last condition, *continuous* effort, is not necessarily fulfilled in the symbol of the narrow gate, which, however, does faithfully represent the first two conditions, since the gate leads to life and demands an effort if one is to enter by it. And these two points of correspondence are sufficient to justify the use of the image. The same observations hold good for the wide gate.

JERUSALEM: *On the right is the Cedron, on the left is the Valley of Ben-Hinnom, which coming together form the Wadi en-Nahr. 1. Gethsemani; 2. the Mosque of Omar on the site of the Temple; 3. Calvary and the Holy Sepulchre; 4. Basilica of the Dormition and Cenacle on Mount Sion; 5. Palace of Herod at the Jaffa Gate; 6. the Pontifical Biblical Institute; 7. the Basilica of St. Stephen.*

who admired and respected Jesus and sincerely wished to save Him from being seized by the tetrarch. Other writers take the opposite view and hold that the threat of death at Herod's hands was a sheer invention on the part of the Pharisees, who wished thereby to rid themselves of the young Prophet's unwelcome presence by causing Him to retire to Judea, where He would be within reach of their powerful colleagues in Jerusalem. But if that was so, it is strange that in His reply, Christ did not make the slightest reference to the base stratagem. Therefore it is more probable that Herod really was hatching some plot against our Lord and that the Pharisees, hearing about it, took advantage of the information to attempt to strike fear into Him and thus, by feigning friendship for Him, rid themselves of His hated presence. Several authors believe that the Pharisees were in collusion with Herod, but we are inclined to think that they were acting solely on their own account. Yet our Lord's clear and biting answer shows that the tetrarch's hostility was no mere figment of the

Pharisees' imagination, but a stern reality: "Go and say to that fox, 'Behold, I cast out devils and perform cures today and tomorrow, and the third day I am to end my course. Nevertheless, I must go my way today and tomorrow and the next day, for it cannot be that a prophet perish outside Jerusalem.' "

These are mysterious words. The sense seems to be that, by way of reply to the crafty tetrarch's machinations, our Lord made it clear that God had fixed the course of His earthly life, and that He would not depart a hairsbreadth from His Father's plan out of fear of Herod. He would go on exercising His ministry and working miracles day by day until the time appointed for His death, which was to take place in Jerusalem, the city that had already witnessed the death of so many prophets.

The thought of the Holy City aroused in Christ's heart a feeling of poignant regret for the ingratitude and rebellion of that capital whose future ruin He foretold with deep sorrow: "Jerusalem, Jerusalem, thou who killest the prophets, and stonest those who are sent to thee! How often would I have gathered thy children together, as a hen gathers her young under her wings, but thou wouldst not! Behold, your house is left to you. And I say to you, you shall not see me until the time comes when you shall say, 'Blessed is he who comes in the name of the Lord!' " [10]

God's abandonment of the Temple was a fearful punishment, for without His presence the sacred edifice, the heart of Israel and the center of the nation's spiritual life, would no longer have any reason for existence. The Jewish people would cut themselves off from the Messias; they would no longer see Him, nor would they even wish to do so. Yet their alienation was not to be final, for the day would come when they would go to meet Him whom they had rejected, crying: "Blessed is he who comes in the name of the Lord!" What a day of rejoicing that would be! Our Lord, then, was not here referring to His triumphal entry into Jerusalem before His Passion, or to His second coming at the end of time, but to the conversion of the Jews, which St. Paul also foretold in his turn (Rom. 11:25 f.).

[10] This same apostrophe is found in almost identical terms in Matthew 23:37-39, where it occurs in a highly dramatic context, namely, after our Lord's terrible prophetic indictment of the Scribes and Pharisees (see below, pp. 594 ff.). Therefore there is not sufficient reason for regarding Luke's passage as a duplicate of Matthew's or vice versa.

Curing the Man With Dropsy: The Great Supper
(Luke 14:1–24)

Some time later our Lord went to dine at the house of one of the most influential Pharisees. This may appear strange in view of His scathing denunciation of the party on a similar occasion shortly before (cf. Luke 11:37–54). But we must remember that not all the Pharisees came under Christ's condemnation, for there were probably some of them whom He esteemed for their virtue and who, in turn, respected and showed their friendliness towards Him. It is also possible that this invitation was inspired by another motive, not altogether disinterested, yet not really reprehensible, for the host may have wished to gain favor with the people, who, as he was well aware, held Jesus in high regard. And it is likely, too, that he wanted to observe our Lord at close quarters, as subsequent events seem to indicate. Consequently there is no compelling reason for placing the incident earlier in the Gospel narrative. We must remember, too, that our Saviour readily accepted invitations of this kind because they gave Him an opportunity of exercising His ministry and of leading back to the Father the lost sheep of Israel.

The evangelist observes that this banquet also took place on the Sabbath; and it was probably centered around the midday meal. The Jews, of course, were forbidden to cook on the Sabbath, but this did not mean that the guests at a Sabbath banquet would have to be content with cold dishes, for the food was prepared the evening before and kept warm until needed.[11]

A number of Scribes and Pharisees had also been invited, whether to honor Jesus or to spy on Him we do not know. Present also was a man afflicted with dropsy, who may have been brought in by the Scribes and Pharisees for the express purpose of testing Christ to see if He would heal on the Sabbath, or who may have pushed his way into the banquet hall to beg our Lord to heal him. But St. Luke's remark, "when [Jesus] entered the house . . . they were watching him," seems to indicate that the others had arranged the meeting between Him and the sick man to see what He would do.

Our Lord did not need to examine the faces of His fellow guests

---

11 The *Mishnah* discusses this matter at great length in the treatise *Shabbath*. In Tiberias, and in other places, too, the food was prepared on the eve of the Sabbath and brought to the public oven, in which it was kept warm for the morrow.

in order to read their thoughts, for He saw deep into their hearts as they waited in expectant silence. But His first words took them by surprise: "Is it lawful to cure on the Sabbath?"

The direct attack so disconcerted them that they either did not know what to say, or did not dare answer. Taking the sick man by the hand, Jesus cured him and sent him away. Then, fully aware that they were murmuring against Him in their hearts although their lips were silent, He asked: "Which of you shall have an ass or an ox fall into a pit, and will not immediately draw him up on the Sabbath?"

But none of them could answer Him.

Observing how the guests vied with each other to occupy the places of honor at table, Jesus took the opportunity to give them a lesson in humility, which He concluded by saying: "Everyone who exalts himself shall be humbled, and he who humbles himself shall be exalted."

Turning to His host, He admonished him to show unselfishness and a spirit of generosity in issuing invitations, not giving them to his friends and rich neighbors so that they would invite him in return, but to the poor, the crippled, the lame and the blind, who had nothing wherewith to repay him. Then he would be truly blessed because he would receive his reward at the resurrection of the just.

One of the diners, deeply impressed by our Lord's doctrine and echoing the word "blessed," which He had used, exclaimed fervently: "Blessed is he who shall feast in the kingdom of God."

The exclamation gave Jesus an occasion for narrating a parable on the call of God, on the different ways men correspond with it, and the fate that awaits those who reject it:

"A certain man gave a great supper, and he invited many. And he sent his servant at supper time to tell those invited to come, for everything is now ready. And they all with one accord began to excuse themselves. The first said to him, 'I have bought a farm, and I must go out and see it; I pray thee hold me excused.' And another said, 'I have bought five yoke of oxen, and I am on my way to try them; I pray thee hold me excused.' And another said, 'I have married a wife, and therefore I cannot come.'

"And the servant returned, and reported these things to his master. Then the master of the house was angry and said to his servant, 'Go out quickly into the streets and lanes of the city, and bring in here the poor, and the crippled, and the blind, and the lame.'

And the servant said, 'Sir, thy order has been carried out, and still there is room.' Then the master said to the servant, 'Go out into the highways and hedges, and make them come in, so that my house may be filled. For I tell you that none of those who were invited shall taste of my supper.' "

Such is the fearsome destiny that awaits those who ungratefully refuse to accept God's invitation to the eternal banquet.[12]

The Following of Christ
(Luke 14:25–35)

Despite the unrelenting hostility of the Scribes and Pharisees, our Lord's preaching had awakened great interest and enthusiasm among the people of Perea. One day as He was walking along, He turned to the crowd that was following Him and, lest anyone should be laboring under a misapprehension, He made clear to them the conditions which had to be fulfilled by those who wished to be His disciples: "If anyone comes to me and does not hate his father and mother, and wife and children, and brothers and sisters, yes, and even his own life, he cannot be my disciple. . . . Every one of you who does not renounce all that he possesses, cannot be my disciple."

The following of Christ demands great sacrifice and is not to be undertaken lightly, with the consequent danger of turning back. Hence Jesus warned His listeners that they must imitate the man who, desiring to build a tower, estimates the cost with great care to ensure that he has enough money to complete the work. Or they were to act like a king who, before engaging his enemy in battle, carefully weighs his chances of defeating an army of twenty thousand when he has only ten thousand men under his command. Therefore mature reflection, and not mere impulsive enthusiasm, was to be their guide, for it would be a shameful thing to undertake a life of perfection and then abandon it. Those who thus fell away from their high resolves are like the salt that has lost its strength and is no longer good for anything: "Salt is good; but if even the salt loses its strength, what shall it be seasoned with? It is fit neither for the land nor for the manure heap, but must be thrown out. He who has ears to hear, let him hear."

[12] Concerning the relationship between this parable and that of the wedding feast prepared for the king's son, see below, pp. 587 f.

The Parables of Mercy
(Luke 15)

As before in Galilee, so now in Perea there were publicans and sinners among our Lord's followers. The fact that He mingled freely with such people angered the Scribes and Pharisees, who were the Puritans of those days, as scrupulous about external cleanness as they were careless about purity of heart. They criticized His conduct, doing everything they could to lessen His authority and popularity and complaining among themselves: "This man welcomes sinners and eats with them."

In answer to His enemies' criticism, Jesus narrated three parables which are appropriately called "the parables of mercy," because they demonstrate very strikingly God's infinite mercy towards the sinner. Taken from everyday life, they are charmingly simple and contain many vividly human touches. The first tells the story of the shepherd in search of a lost sheep, the second that of the woman who lost a coin, and the third is the moving tale of the prodigal son and his loving father. The three stories are so beautiful in content and structure that, even if they did not contain divine doctrine, they would still be literary gems.

The good shepherd, having lost one of his hundred sheep, leaves the ninety-nine in the desert and goes in search of the one that has strayed. When he finds the lost sheep, he lays it upon his shoulders and brings it home. Then calling his friends and neighbors he says to them: "Rejoice with me, because I have found my sheep that was lost."

Having related the parable, our Lord pointed out its consoling lesson: "I say to you that, even so, there will be joy in heaven over one sinner who repents, more than over ninety-nine just who have no need of repentance."

The parable of the lost coin tells how a woman who had ten drachmas,[13] lost one of them. Lighting the lamp, she swept out her house, looking carefully in every corner for the lost coin. When at last she found it, she called in her friends and neighbors and said: "Rejoice with me, for I have found the drachma that I had lost."

Again our Lord drew the moral from His parable: "Even so, I

---

[13] A drachma was worth about thirty-five cents in our money. (Translator.)

say to you, there will be joy among the angels of God over one sinner who repents."

The parable of the prodigal son tells the story of a headstrong young man who persuaded his father to advance him his inheritance, and then went off to a foreign land where he squandered the money in loose living. Driven by poverty to take a job as a swineherd, he suffered such pangs of hunger that he even envied the swine their feed. Sadly he began to think of home, where even the servants were better off than he was now: "How many hired men in my father's house have bread in abundance, while I am perishing here with hunger!" The thought decided him: "I will get up and go to my father, and will say to him, 'Father, I have sinned against heaven and before thee. I am no longer worthy to be called thy son; make me as one of thy hired men.' And he arose and went to his father.

"But while he was yet a long way off, his father saw him and was moved with compassion, and ran and fell upon his neck and kissed him. And the son said to him, 'Father, I have sinned against heaven and before thee. I am no longer worthy to be called thy son.' But the father said to his servants, 'Fetch quickly the best robe and put it on him, and give him a ring for his finger and sandals for his feet; and bring out the fattened calf and kill it, and let us eat and make merry; because this my son was dead, and has come to life again; he was lost, and is found.' "

Instead of punishing his erring son with lashes, the father embraced him. Love is blind to past sin, and thus the father requited his son's offenses with the kiss of peace and a tender embrace.[14]

The parable could have ended here with this happy scene which completes a story that illustrates vividly God's ineffable kindness to the repentant sinner. But surprisingly enough, this tender drama of paternal love goes on to include a third act, which at first sight seems only an epilogue, but which is really an integral part of the story.

"Now his elder son was in the field; and as he came and drew near to the house, he heard music and dancing. And calling one of the servants he inquired what this meant. And he said to him, 'Thy brother has come, and thy father has killed the fattened calf, because he has got him back safe.' But he was angered and would not go in.

"His father, therefore, came out and began to entreat him. But he answered and said to his father, 'Behold, these many years I have

[14] Cf. St. Peter Chrysologus, *PL* 52, 192.

been serving thee, and have never transgressed one of thy commands; and yet thou hast never given me a kid that I might make merry with my friends. But when this thy son comes, who has devoured his means with harlots, thou hast killed for him the fattened calf.'

"But he said to him, 'Son, thou art always with me, and all that is mine is thine; but we are bound to make merry and rejoice, for this thy brother was dead, and has come to life; he was lost, and is found.' "

Obviously the elder son represents a certain class of people. But which class? The just in general, or the Pharisees in particular? The answer is not easy to find, and, as Buzy remarks, this is "one of the most discussed passages in the exegesis of the parables." [15]

In this parable, as in the two preceding ones, our Lord undoubtedly had in mind the attitude of the Scribes and Pharisees who "murmured, saying, 'This man welcomes sinners and eats with them!' " (Luke 15:2). We take this reaction of the Jews to be a clear indication that in describing the elder son's complaint, Jesus was alluding to the Scribes' and Pharisees' unending criticism of His actions in this regard. Some may object to our interpretation by asking how God could say to the Pharisees, as the father said to his eldest son: "You are always with me, and all that is mine is yours," or how the Pharisees could say with the elder son: "We have never transgressed one of thy commands." [16] This objection, however, overlooks the very nature of parables, which does not demand that every detail find a parallel in reality. Yet our interpretation does not mean to say that our Lord was not thinking also of the just in general. We believe that He had them in mind, too. Therefore there is no reason to regard the problem as a dilemma and say that He was thinking either about the just or about the Pharisees. The one concept does not exclude the other. Christ was referring to the Pharisees, but He also had the just in mind.

The Unjust Steward: The Rich Man and Lazarus: Avoiding Scandal
(Luke 16:1—17:10)

Without being able to fix the exact time and place, we know that

[15] *Op. cit.*, p. 191.
[16] Cf. Prat, *Jesus Christ*, II, 124 *f.*

during this period in Perea Jesus narrated a parable which contrasted the diligence and foresight of evil men with the negligence and improvidence of the good. He was speaking particularly to His disciples (16:1; 17:1), who included many others besides the Apostles; some of his enemies were also present, and heard what He said (cf. 16:14): "There was a certain rich man who had a steward, who was reported to him as squandering his possessions. And he called him and said to him, 'What is this that I hear of thee? Make an accounting of thy stewardship, for thou canst be steward no longer.'

"And the steward said within himself, 'What shall I do, seeing that my master is taking away the stewardship from me? To dig I am not able; to beg I am ashamed. I know what I shall do, that when I am removed from my stewardship they may receive me into their houses.' And he summoned each of his master's debtors and said to the first, 'How much dost thou owe my master?' And he said, 'A hundred jars of oil.' [17] He said to him, 'Take thy bond and sit down at once and write fifty.' Then he said to another, 'How much dost thou owe?' He said, 'A hundred kors of wheat.' [18] He said to him, 'Take thy bond and write eighty.' "

The steward's procedure was, of course, fraudulent and reprehensible, but it was also a clever ruse to win favor with his employer's debtors. And it was the steward's cleverness, not his deceit, that our Lord praised in closing the parable: [19] "And the master commended the unjust steward, in that he had acted prudently; for the children of this world, in relation to their own generation, are more prudent than the children of the light."

This last observation of our Lord's is, and always has been, only too true.

Developing the thought expressed in the parable, Christ went on to give His disciples various counsels—that they should use riches to gain the friendship of the poor, who would later receive them into the everlasting dwellings of heaven; that if they were faithful in small things, i.e., in the administration of earthly goods, they would be faithful also in what is great, i.e., in the things of the spirit. He con-

[17] The "jar" (Hebrew *bath*) was equivalent to 9.8 gallons (Translator). The quantity of oil was therefore a considerable one; however, all the measurements in the parable are purely secondary elements.
[18] A *kor* was equivalent to 10.48 bushels (Translator).
[19] In the text it is actually the master who commends the steward and not Jesus, at least not directly.

cluded with a statement which many do not even wish to understand, let alone practice: "No servant can serve two masters; for either he will hate the one and love the other, or else he will stand by the one and despise the other. You cannot serve God and mammon."

Among those present were some Pharisees who, upon hearing Jesus say these words, looked at each other and began to laugh derisively at Him. In their opinion, riches, far from being a danger to God's service, were a clear sign of His favor. Perhaps they thought that the young Prophet was speaking against riches because He did not possess any. But their sarcastic mirth did not disconcert our Lord. He knew their clique well and treated them as they deserved, calling them hypocrites and condemning them for regarding themselves as just men, while in reality they were an abomination in God's sight: "You are they who declare yourselves just in the sight of men, but God knows your heart; for that which is exalted in the sight of men is an abomination before God." [20]

To show what the ill-use of riches can lead to, and how those who bear poverty with patience will be rewarded in the next life, our Lord told the parable of Lazarus and the rich man, which in all probability He did not mean to be historical, although more than a few authors regard it as a true story: "There was a certain rich man who used to clothe himself in purple and fine linen, and who feasted every day in splendid fashion. And there was a certain poor man, named Lazarus, who lay at his gate, covered with sores, and longing to be filled with the crumbs that fell from the rich man's table; even the dogs would come and lick his sores."

The picture painted here by Christ is starkly realistic, and unfortunately still has its counterpart in our own days. There are still rich men who live in palaces, dress luxuriously and feast every day, without a thought for the emaciated, half-naked poor who inhabit the slums of the cities, crowded together in bleak tenements or living in hovels not fit for cattle. But the day will come when the roles will be reversed: "And it came to pass that the poor man died and was borne away by the angels into Abraham's bosom; but the rich man also died and was buried in hell. And lifting up his eyes, being in torments, he saw Abraham afar off and Lazarus in his bosom. And he cried out

---

[20] Then follow (Luke 16:16–18) several sentences which seem to be fragments of a discourse or discourses spoken here or in other circumstances of time and place.

and said, 'Father Abraham, have pity on me, and send Lazarus to dip the tip of his finger in water and cool my tongue, for I am tormented in this flame.'

"But Abraham said to him, 'Son, remember that thou in thy lifetime hast received good things, and Lazarus in like manner evil things; but now here he is comforted whereas thou art tormented."

Thus is the justice of God fulfilled in the next life. As St. Peter Chrysologus puts it, the rich man, out of the abundance of his wealth, did not help the beggar, nor did he contribute anything to the worship of God. But the beggar, rich in pain, poor in money, weak in body and covered with sores, continually offered to God the sacrifice of his soul, the only healthy part of his being. Therefore he now receives rest in exchange for his pains, honor instead of insults, immortality for his sufferings, a fount of refreshing water for his thirst, and the eternal delights of the heavenly table for his hunger. And the rich man, who in his lifetime wore purple garments, is now covered with filth; he has exchanged his soft bed for eternal torments; instead of dainty dishes he now sups on pains; and all this he has deserved for spurning the poor man at his gate.[21]

Turning once more to His disciples (Luke 17:1), our Lord gave them several instructions, apparently disconnected one from the other, as often happens in familiar conversation: "It is impossible that scandals should not come; but woe to him through whom they come! It were better for him if a millstone were hung about his neck and he were thrown into the sea, than that he should cause one of these little ones to sin. [No doubt there were some children in the crowd.]

"Take heed to yourselves. If thy brother sin, rebuke him; and if he repent, forgive him. And if seven times in the day he sin against thee, and seven times in the day turn back to thee, saying, 'I repent,' forgive him."[22]

The Apostles then besought Jesus: "Increase our faith."

To which He answered: "If you have faith even like a mustard

21 Cf. *PL* 52, 388.
22 These two admonitions about scandal and forgiveness of injuries have parallels in Matthew 18:6-9, 15-17, and in Mark 9:42-50, where they are more fully developed. It is hard to know whether these passages were spoken in the same circumstances of time and place, or whether our Lord repeated them during His ministry. See pp. 454 *ff*. above.

seed, you will say to this mulberry tree, 'Be uprooted and be planted in the sea,' and it will obey you."

With a simple parable drawn from the most ordinary domestic tasks, He inspired them with feelings of humility, rooting out any tendrils of vainglory that might be starting to grow in their hearts and showing them that no matter how much they did for God, they were only fulfilling their obligations: "But which of you is there, having a servant plowing or tending sheep, who will say to him on his return from the field, 'Come at once and recline at table!' But will he not say to him, 'Prepare my supper, and gird thyself and serve me till I have eaten and drunk; and afterwards thou thyself shalt eat and drink'? Does he thank that servant for doing what he commanded him? I do not think so. Even so you also, when you have done everything that was commanded you, say, 'We are unprofitable servants; we have done what it was our duty to do.' "

22. From Perea

to Bethany

The Raising of Lazarus
(John 11:1–44; cf. Map IV)

Everything our Lord did was, of course, directed towards the glory of God and the good of men. But the miracle at Bethany was also inspired by His love for His friends. Thus He went to Bethany so that the Father might be glorified, but also in order that He might bring comfort to Martha and Mary, whom He loved.

St. John has left us a moving description of the loving confidence with which the two sisters appealed to Jesus for help, our Lord's weeping at the death of His friend, and His divine power in recalling him from the grave.

When Lazarus fell sick, Jesus had been in Perea about three months. Martha and Mary, seeing that their brother's illness was growing worse, sent a message to their Divine Friend: "Lord, behold, he whom thou lovest is sick." They did not say "Come and heal him," because they knew that it was enough to state the fact of his illness. It was as if they had said, "It is sufficient that you know; you do not abandon those whom you love." [1]

One would think that, upon receiving the alarming news, our Lord would have hastened to Bethany to cure His friend and relieve the sisters' anxiety. But he did not

[1] Cf. St. Augustine, *PL* 35, 1749.

do so; instead, He remained two days longer in Perea. How different are God's thoughts from those of men, and how hidden are His designs, yet always directed towards our good! If Jesus had gone immediately to Bethany and found Lazarus alive, He would have been moved by friendship and by the sisters' tears to save him from death; and the cure of a sick man would have rendered far less glory to God than the raising of one already dead.

When two days had passed since the arrival of the news, our Lord said to His disciples: "Let us go again into Judea."

They, however, remembered only too well how, during the last feast of Dedication, they had had to leave Jerusalem to escape being stoned, and so they replied anxiously: "Rabbi, just now the Jews were seeking to stone thee; and dost thou go there again?"

Quieting their fears by pointing out that nothing happens apart from God's will, He told them the reason for the journey: "Lazarus, our friend, sleeps. But I go that I may wake him from sleep."

But the Apostles, having no desire to return to Judea, were quick to point out: "Lord, if he sleeps, he will be safe."

They meant that a healthy sleep was a sign of improvement. Why should they go to wake the sick man? It would be much better to let him sleep peacefully on.

Then Jesus said to them plainly: "Lazarus is dead; and I rejoice on your account that I was not there, that you may believe. But let us go to him."

His resolute tone of voice silenced any objections the disciples may have had to offer. Wordlessly they resigned themselves to their fate, convinced that they were going to their death. With an air of courage, assumed perhaps to conceal his fear, Thomas, who was also known as Didymus, the Twin, said to his companions: "Let us also go, that we may die with him."

So it was that, on the fourth day after receiving the message, Jesus set out with His disciples for Bethany. After crossing the Jordan and passing through Jericho they went up the Wadi el-Qelt to the top of Tal 'at ed-Dam, "the ascent of Adommin" (Jos. 15:17), and from there, turning left off the road that led to Jerusalem, they penetrated a short distance into the Wadi es-Sikkeh and its continuation, the Wadi el-Hod, as far as the spring of the same name, now called the "Fountain of the Apostles" and known in the Bible as "the fountain of the Sun" ('Ain Shemesh; Jos. 15:7), one of the boundary marks

Tomb of Lazarus, present entrance.

between the territories of Juda and Benjamin. From here, it would take the party only a few minutes to ascend the steep slope and come out on the height. The present small chapel belonging to the Greek Orthodox Church probably marks the spot where Jesus was met by

Martha, who, as soon as she heard He was coming, ran to meet Him without even pausing long enough to tell her sister. The sepulchre in which Lazarus had been buried lay between this meeting place and the town, which in those days was situated a short distance to the southwest of its present location, as we have already seen.

Throwing herself at our Lord's feet, Martha expressed her sorrow in a gentle reproach: "Lord, if thou hadst been here my brother would not have died."

How many times during the last four days must not the two sisters have said the same words to each other! But there was still a ray of hope, for Jesus had the power to raise their brother from the dead. Yet in her humility, Martha did not dare to ask for the stupendous miracle of bringing back to life a corpse that had already begun to decay. She contented herself with hinting timidly: "But even now I know that whatever thou shalt ask of God, God will give it to thee."

Our Lord's reply was categorical: "Thy brother shall rise."

But even such a definite statement was open to two interpretations: it could refer either to immediate raising from the dead, or to the general resurrection at the end of the world, a belief common among all Jews, with the exception of the Sadducees. Martha took Christ's words in the second sense, for she could not imagine that He would have announced the stupendous miracle so suddenly and so simply: "I know that he will rise at the resurrection, on the last day."

Yet she had hoped for something more. Then Jesus said in a tone of great solemnity: "I am the resurrection and the life; he who believes in me, even if he die, shall live; and whoever lives and believes in me, shall never die. Dost thou believe this?"

With sincere faith Martha answered: "Yes, Lord, I believe that thou art the Christ, the Son of God, who hast come into the world."

At this point our Lord probably asked for Mary, and Martha ran home to call her. Finding her sister still seated amid the relatives and friends who had come to offer their condolences, Martha whispered to her: "The Master is here and calls for thee."

How Mary's loving heart must have leaped with joy at the news! Swiftly she arose and ran to Jesus, throwing herself at His feet, weeping and repeating her sister's words: "Lord, if thou hadst been here, my brother would not have died."

Seeing Mary and her companions in tears, "Jesus wept." The

tears of God! What a miracle of condescension! What a miracle of love!

When those present saw Him weeping, some of them said: "See how he loved him."

But not all of those present were moved by our Lord's tears. Sinful hearts have the unfortunate ability to turn good into evil, medicine into poison. Thus some of those who were there complained: "Could not he who opened the eyes of the blind, have caused that this man should not die?"

Such persons as these always look for the bad side of things; they judge everything according to the standards evolved by their own narrow minds; they are self-righteous and despise everyone else. No doubt these were the ones who, instead of opening their eyes to the light shed on them by the great miracle, maliciously ran to the Pharisees to report all that Jesus had done. St. John's summing up of the whole event is terrible in its brevity: "Many therefore of the Jews who had come to Mary, and had seen what he did, believed in him. But some of them went away to the Pharisees, and told them the things Jesus had done" (11:45 f.). The evangelist's words are an echo of Simeon's fateful prophecy: "Behold, this child is destined for the fall and for the rise of many in Israel, and for a sign that shall be contradicted" (Luke 2:34). Although in the raising of Lazarus our Lord's wondrous power shone forth in all its splendor, yet, while some of those who witnessed it were enlightened and believed in Him, others only became more obstinate in their unwillingness to see. The same ray of light that softens wax only makes clay harder.[2]

When Mary had thrown herself at our Lord's feet and had tearfully repeated her sister's words, He asked those present: "Where have you laid him?"

They replied: "Lord, come and see."

Accompanied by the crowd, He approached the sepulchre and,

---

[2] Several other interpretations of John 11:45–46 have been proposed: (1) those who maliciously reported Christ's actions to the Pharisees had not been in Bethany at the time of the miracle; (2) they had been in Bethany at the time of the miracle but had not witnessed it; (3) those who reported to the Pharisees had seen the miracle and went to tell them about it with the idea of dissipating or lessening their hostility to Jesus. Without denying a certain amount of probability to the first and third explanations, we believe that the most obvious meaning of the whole passage favors the interpretation which we have given above and which is the one preferred by Calmet, Cornelius a Lapide, Fouard, Fillion, Lebreton and others. Durand, also, is inclined to accept this explanation.

TOMB OF LAZARUS: *This is the antechamber or vestibule to which access was originally gained from the eastern side through a door which is now blocked up (1). When the adjoining church was taken over by the Moslems a new entrance (2) had to be made. This entrance is the one used today: twenty-four steps lead from ground level down to the tomb. The burial chamber proper is reached through a rectangular opening (3); it was in this chamber (St. John's "cave") that Lazarus' body was laid. The opening was covered by a horizontal stone slab. The bench at the right (4) is used for saying Mass on the feast of St. Martha.*

passing through the door which then opened from the eastern side, He entered a cave cut out of the rock. Moving to the left of the doorway, He turned with His back to the south wall and faced the entrance to the tomb proper, which St. John (11:38) describes as "a cave, and a stone was laid against it." The actual receptacle for the corpse was therefore quite different in form from the common type of burial vault or sepulchre, the entrance to which was usually covered by a simple perpendicular slab or a large circular stone somewhat like a millstone.[3]

"Take away the stone," commanded Jesus.

But Martha intervened, protesting: "Lord, by this time he is already decayed, for he is dead four days."

Lazarus had died the very day his sisters had sent word to Jesus, and because our Lord had remained two days longer in Perea, this was now the fourth day since His friend's death.

Gravely, Jesus reproached her: " 'Have I not told thee that if thou believe thou shalt behold the glory of God?'

"They therefore removed the stone. And Jesus, raising his eyes, said, 'Father, I give thee thanks that thou hast heard me. Yet I knew that thou always hearest me; but because of the people who stand round, I spoke, that they may believe that thou hast sent me.' When he had said this, he cried out with a loud voice, 'Lazarus, come forth!' And at once he who had been dead came forth, bound feet and hands with bandages, and his face was tied up with a cloth. Jesus said to them, 'Unbind him and let him go.' "

There is no mention nor even the slightest hint of this great miracle by the three Synoptic authors, whose silence has been used to impugn the historical reality of the event and give it a purely symbolic significance. The solution to this difficulty depends in great part upon the investigator's opinion of the character of the fourth Gospel. If he, like rationalist critics in general, denies the historical validity of St. John's Gospel, he will be inclined to regard the raising of Lazarus as a mere symbol. But if, on the contrary, he takes into account the precise topographical and chronological data found in the fourth Gospel, and the author's own assertions (20:30 *f.*; 21:24 *f.*), he will see that St. John set out to record actual, concrete events.

[3] In 1949–50 the Franciscans made some excavations near the sepulchre and uncovered the remains of the ancient Byzantine church (*La Terra Santa*, 25 [1950], 30, 87, 186).

Consequently, he will have an indisputable right to accept the raising of Lazarus as truly historical, even if he cannot give positive reasons for the silence of the Synoptic authors.

Yet there is a probable explanation of the other three evangelists' failure to record the miracle. It is well known that, for one reason or another, the Synoptic tradition disregards almost completely our Lord's ministry in Jerusalem: it contains not one word about the feasts of the Passover, Tabernacles or Dedication. It is no wonder, then, that the first three evangelists do not mention the raising of Lazarus, which, due to the circumstances in which it occurred, belongs in a way to the ministry in Jerusalem. There is another explanation, one which Father Lagrange says is that of Catholic exegetes and which he makes his own, namely, that the Synoptic authors omitted the raising of Lazarus from their narratives so as not to expose Martha, Mary and their brother to the anger of the Sanhedrin, whereas when St. John wrote his Gospel the danger had passed.[4]

Withdrawal to Ephrem
(John 11:45–54; cf. Map IV)

As a result of the raising of Lazarus, the Jews who had come to Bethany [5] and who had been eyewitnesses of the miracle, were filled with enthusiasm and believed in Jesus. However, there were some among them, perhaps those very ones who had murmured against our Lord for not having healed Lazarus (v. 37), who were blinded even more than before by the miracle. These were the malicious gossips who hurried off to tell the Pharisees everything that had happened.

The Pharisees and the chief priests were alarmed at the news of the miracle, which, instead of opening their eyes and moving them to believe in Jesus, only blinded and hardened them still further. Priests

[4] Cf. Lagrange, *Év. selon S. Jean,* p. 312.

[5] Authors translate John 11:45 in two different ways: (1) "Many among the group of Jews who had come to Mary . . ."; (2) "Many of the Jews, those who had come to Mary . . ." Knabenbauer, Lagrange and Bernard prefer the second interpretation, i.e., that *all* those who had come to Bethany and had seen the miracle believed in Jesus. In our opinion, the context (vv. 45–46) gives the impression that only the *majority* and not all of those who came and saw, believed. The Jews who went to report to the Pharisees undoubtedly did so with malicious intentions, and it seems very probable from the context that these troublemakers had been among those present at Bethany.

and Pharisees met together in council and angrily demanded of each other: "What are we doing? for this man is working many signs. If we let him alone as he is, all will believe in him, and the Romans will come and take away both our place and our nation."

The people's enthusiasm for Jesus could readily become political agitation which would provoke the Romans into taking cruel repressive measures. The Jewish leaders did have some reason to fear reprisals, but their hatred and envy of Christ led them to exaggerate the danger and to seize upon it as a good excuse for proceeding against the young Rabbi. But although all were agreed that something had to be done quickly, there was apparently some argument as to the actual measures to be adopted. Caiphas, the high priest, peremptorily cut short the dispute: "You know nothing at all; nor do you reflect that it is expedient for us that one man die for the people, instead of the whole nation perishing."

And the evangelist observes: "This, however, he said not of himself; but being high priest that year, he prophesied that Jesus was to die for the nation; and not only for the nation, but that he might gather into one the children of God who were scattered abroad."

Caiphas did not prophesy in the sense that he was invested with the gift of prophecy, or that the Holy Spirit exercised a special influence on him at that moment. He prophesied only in the sense that God so disposed matters that he should use words which contained a meaning higher than the one he intended to convey. Thus it came about that, in voicing his own thoughts, Caiphas, all unwittingly, expressed the thoughts of God. The high priest's pronouncement, therefore, contained a twofold meaning: a human one, which he conceived and intended to express, and a divine one, which God Himself wished to convey.[6]

The Sanhedrin's decision was what one would expect: "So from that day forth their plan was to put him to death."

Our Lord judged it prudent to withdraw for the moment from the storm center; His hour had not yet come. He left the neighbor-

---

[6] Incidentally, we should note that there is no question here of a plurality of literal meanings such as is dealt with in hermeneutics, for all such meanings are regarded as coming at once from God as the principal Cause and from the sacred writer as the instrumental cause. There is certainly a plurality of meanings in Caiphas' words, one sense being purely human and the other divine. But the high priest had nothing to do with the latter meaning, not even as a simple instrument. However, he is said to have prophesied because he spoke words which in reality were the expression of a divine prophecy.

hood of the capital, where passions were seething, and retired to Ephrem, present-day et-Taiybeh, an isolated town on the edge of the desert, about twelve miles north of Jerusalem as the crow flies. On His way thither, He probably followed the eastern slope of Mount Olivet to Anathoth, the birthplace of Jeremias, and then descended the path (which still exists) to Hizmeh, the Azmaveth of 2 Esdras 12:29. From there His most likely route was on to Geba (Jeba'), crossing the Wadi es-Sweinit to Mikhmas, and continuing north through Ramman, the rock of Remmon, where the six hundred Benjamites took refuge (Judges 20: 45 ff.), He would have arrived at the small city of Ephrem after a journey of four or five hours.

The modern visitor to et-Taiybeh may at first find it hard to see how the town can be identified with the Ephrem of the Bible because the surrounding district, far from being a desert, is rich in flourishing olive groves, particularly to the south. It must be remembered, however, that the Gospel does not say that Ephrem was *in* the desert, but in "the district near the desert," a description that fits exactly, since a considerable portion of the mountainous terrain that separates et-Taiybeh from the Jordan valley really is a desert, in the same sense in which we speak of the desert of Juda. As a matter of fact, a section of land which lies only a short distance east of the town is known today as *el-barriyeh*, "the desert." [7]

The town is magnificently located on the slope of a mountain, and seems to dominate the whole vast region. To the east lie the ranges of the Transjordan; to the south the top of Mount Olivet with its two high towers can be discerned in the distance, and beyond it, a little to the east, rises the truncated cone of Herodium; while to the southeast lies the oasis of Jericho, and farther off, the flat calm waters of the Dead Sea, over which looms the imposing bulk of the Mountains of Moab.

How blessed this town was, to have been allowed to shelter the Saviour of the world and provide Him with a sure refuge against the anger and schemes of His enemies! The ruins of an ancient church, which are still to be seen there, provide a lasting reminder of our Lord's visit.

---

[7] The present writer has heard the inhabitants call the spot by this name. Regarding the identification of et-Taiybeh with Ephrem, see A. Fernández, *Problemas de topografía palestinense*, pp. 134–138.

23. Again in

Perea

The Ten Lepers
(Luke 17:11–19; cf. Map IV)

Our Lord must not have stayed long in Ephrem, for the last days of His life were fast approaching, and He no doubt wished to spend the short time left to Him in diligently seeking the sheep that were still wandering afar. The most obvious route from Ephrem to Perea was the one which still goes down to Jericho; this path undoubtedly existed in our Lord's day, and later became a Roman road, as is clear from the numerous traces that remain. This route runs towards the southeast, leaving Ramman to the right, and then, skirting the Wadi el-Lubeit and passing through 'Ain en-Nueimeh and 'Ain ed-Doq (which was probably the Naaratha of Josue 16:7, and where a mosaic from a later synagogue was uncovered), it passes near the site of ancient Jericho. From there Perea was easily reached by crossing the Jordan.

However, our Lord, it seems, did not follow that route, but turned to the north instead. Leaving the peaceful little city, He first bore to the west to join the great highway that traversed the country from end to end, and then followed it north to the plain of Esdrelon. There He turned south, either going down along the valley of Jezrael and through the city of Beisan, or else, bearing a little more to the south, He crossed the Mountains of Gelboe and came out into the valley of the

Jordan near Aennon, where His Precursor had baptized. Perea then lay just across the river. St. Luke seems to hint at this roundabout journey when he says that Jesus "was passing between Samaria and Galilee," for the borderline between the two provinces crossed the plain of Esdrelon.[1]

If our Lord took the route which we have just described, the episode of the ten lepers probably took place in Jenin, the ancient Engannim ("fountain of gardens"), since, according to Josephus, this city, which he calls Ginea, was "on the borders of Samaria and the great plain" (i.e., of Esdrelon).[2] And this topographical reason is in a way corroborated by a reliable tradition which, however, is not very ancient, since it dates back only to the fourteenth century.[3] This location would account for the fact that there were both Jews and Samaritans among the lepers.

Therefore it was probably here in Jenin that Jesus was accosted by ten lepers who, being forbidden to come close to any healthy person, cried out to Him from a distance: "Jesus, master, have pity on us."

Our Lord, touched by their plea, said to them: "Go, show yourselves to the priests."

And it came about that, as they were on their way to do his bidding, they were cleansed. We would expect that after such a miracle all of them would hasten back to give thanks to their Benefactor. But only one did so, and he was a Samaritan. The loving heart of Jesus felt keenly the ingratitude of the other lepers, and He was moved to ask sadly: "Were not the ten made clean? But where are the nine? Has no one been found to return and give glory to God except this foreigner?"

The Coming of God's Kingdom
(Luke 17:20–37)

Jesus had probably already entered Perea when the Pharisees came to challenge Him with a new question: "When is the kingdom of God coming?" Their query is not a surprising one considering that, from the very beginning of His public life, Jesus had announced the

[1] Cf. *Wars* iii. 3. 4; ii. 12. 3; *Ant.* xx. 6. 1; Dalman, *Sacred Sites and Ways,* pp. 210 *ff.*
[2] *Ant.* xx. 6. 1.
[3] Cf. Baldi, *Enchiridion,* pp. 307 *ff.*

kingdom of God, declaring that it was already at hand. For example, in Mark 1:14–15, we read that "After John had been delivered up, Jesus came into Galilee, preaching the gospel of the kingdom of God, and saying, 'The time is fulfilled, and the kingdom of God is at hand.' " From ancient times this kingdom had been foretold and described at length by the prophets, and eagerly expected by the whole Jewish people. Hence the question: "When is the kingdom of God coming?" was in itself a very natural one. But in this particular case, did the Pharisees ask it, not out of a sincere desire to be enlightened, but rather in a hostile and perhaps ironical spirit? In view of their habitual attitude towards our Lord, it is not only possible but even probable that their inquiry was an inimical and sarcastic one.

The Jews had a deep-rooted belief that the kingdom of God would be inaugurated ostentatiously, in glory and splendor, an idea which seemed to be implied in the brilliant figures of speech which the prophets used to describe the longed-for Messianic age. The same thought is contained also in later rabbinical documents, in one of which we read, for example, that "just as the sun and the moon can be plainly seen as they run their courses, so also when the kingdom of the Messias appears it will be visible to the world." [4]

In His answer to the Pharisees, Jesus referred to the twofold preoccupation of the Jews, namely, the time of the kingdom's advent and the form in which it would come: "The kingdom of God comes unawares. Neither will they say, 'Behold, here it is,' or 'Behold, there it is.' "

Therefore, the kingdom of God will not come as a blinding apparition, accompanied by cosmic upheavals. Instead its advent will be so lacking in show, so little perceptible, that no one will be able to point it out and say, "Here it is!" or "There it is!"

Our Lord then went on to declare openly: "The kingdom of God is within you."

It was not to come in the future, for it was already present, but the Pharisees, because of the malice which blinded their eyes, did not recognize it.

After speaking to the Pharisees about the kingdom which the Messias was to establish (or, rather, which He actually had established at His first coming), our Lord addressed His disciples, in whom He saw all the faithful who, down through the centuries, were to

[4] Cf. Str.-Bill., II, 236.

make up the kingdom of God on earth. With bold strokes, He drew a vivid picture of the vicissitudes through which the Church was to pass before the end of time: "The days will come when you will long to see one day of the Son of Man, and will not see it.[5] And they will say to you, 'Behold, here he is; behold, there he is.' Do not go, nor follow after them. For as the lightning when it lightens flashes from one end of the sky to the other, so will the Son of Man be in his day. But first he must suffer many things and be rejected by this generation.

"And as it came to pass in the days of Noe, even so will it be in the days of the Son of Man. They were eating and drinking, they were marrying and giving in marriage, until the day when Noe entered the ark, and the flood came and destroyed them all. Or as it came to pass in the days of Lot. They were eating and drinking, they were buying and selling, they were planting and building; but on the day that Lot went out from Sodom, it rained fire and brimstone from heaven and destroyed them all. In the same wise will it be on the day that the Son of Man is revealed. In that hour let him who is on the housetop and his goods in the house, not go down to take them away; and likewise let him who is in the field not turn back. Remember Lot's wife. Whoever tries to save his life will lose it; and whoever loses it will preserve it. I say to you, on that night there will be two on one bed; one will be taken, and the other will be left."

Upon hearing that some would be taken and, consequently, brought to join the Son of Man, the disciples asked curiously: "Where [will they be taken], Lord?"

Jesus replied with a comparison drawn from nature. Just as eagles, or rather, vultures,[6] quickly gather about their prey, so too the elect, as if impelled from within, will hasten to group themselves about the Son of Man in His glory: "Wherever the body is, there will be the eagles gathered together."[7]

---

[5] "One day of the Son of Man" does not refer to the period of Christ's life on earth, which the disciples would recall with yearning. Our Lord was looking to the future, not the past. This is the interpretation given by Knabenbauer, Lagrange, Prat, and others.

[6] The Greek word can mean either eagles or vultures, but the circumstances of the passage seem to point more to the latter than the former.

[7] This was probably a sort of proverb. Therefore, it is not right to say that our Lord was comparing Himself to a corpse and the faithful to vultures. Nor does there seem to be any objective foundation for applying His words to the gathering of the faithful around His dead body on the cross. In Matthew 24:28 we find the same metaphor employed.

The Indissolubility of Marriage
(Matt. 19:3–12; cf. 5:31 *f.*; Mark 10:2–12)

It was not long before our Lord was confronted by another group of Pharisees whose intentions in accosting Him were certainly evil, for St. Matthew (19:3) explicitly tells us that they meant to test Him, that is, to set a trap for Him.

Their test question was concerned with the matter of divorce: "Is it lawful for a man to put away his wife for any cause?"

No one disputed the legality of divorce itself, for it was clearly authorized by the Law, which laid down that: "If a man take a wife, and have her, and she find not favor in his eyes, for some uncleanness: he shall write a bill of divorce, and shall give it in her hand, and send her out of his house" (Deut. 24:1). But there was a difference of opinion about the interpretation of the phrase "some uncleanness": *'erwat dabhar,* giving rise to a dispute about the causes for which it was lawful to write a bill of divorce. According to the school of Hillel, the slightest cause was sufficient: for example, a man could divorce his wife because she put too much salt in the soup. The school of Shammai, however, was much stricter, holding as it did that adultery by the wife was the only legitimate reason for divorcing her. Our Lord's interrogators probably belonged to the latter school. If, in His answer to their question, He followed their own teaching, He would further antagonize the adherents of Hillel, whereas if He favored the latter's interpretations, His questioners would accuse Him of laxity.

Jesus avoided both pitfalls by disregarding the rabbinical discussions entirely, and by recalling the divine command (Gen. 2:24). Going straight to the heart of the matter, He plainly affirmed the indissolubility of marriage as laid down by God Himself: "What therefore God has joined together, let no man put asunder."

But the Pharisees had a ready objection to this categorical statement: "Why then did Moses command to give a written notice of dismissal, and to put her away?"

And, in point of fact, our Lord seemed to be contradicting Moses, the legislator of Israel. But He answered: "Because Moses, by reason of the hardness of your heart, permitted you to put away your wives; but it was not so from the beginning. And I say to you, that whoever puts away his wife, except for fornication, and marries another, commits adultery; and he who marries a woman who has been put away commits adultery."

The listening disciples understood perfectly that their Master was affirming the indissolubility of marriage. Struck by the grave responsibility undertaken by the contracting parties in binding themselves with an unbreakable tie, they exclaimed: "If the case of a man with his wife is so, it is not expedient to marry."

Under such conditions they considered it would be better to remain celibate than to run the risk of becoming involved in an unhappy marriage. Our Lord replied: "Not all can accept this teaching; but those to whom it has been given. For there are eunuchs who were born so from their mother's womb; and there are eunuchs who were made so by men; and there are eunuchs who have made themselves so for the sake of the kingdom of heaven. Let him understand who can."

Few indeed are they who understand the excellence of virginity and are ready to practice it. But even so, in the Church there will always be radiant choirs of virgins who will abstain voluntarily from the pleasures of the flesh in order to live like angels on earth.

Our Lord's statement that marriage, once validly contracted, could not be dissolved, was clear and categorical, but it was followed by a phrase which has been and still is the subject of much discussion by theologians and exegetes. At first glance, St. Matthew's expression (19:9), "if it be not for fornication," or rather, "except for fornication," [8] appears to indicate that in the case of infidelity on the woman's part, the husband is authorized to give her a bill of divorce. If that is so, then marriage is not indissoluble.

If we follow closely the dialogue between Jesus and the Pharisees we shall see that in His answer to their question: "Is it lawful for a man to put away his wife for any cause?" (Matt. 19:3) our Lord, rising above rabbinical disputation and the differences between schools, went back to the very origin of marriage and proved from Sacred Scripture its unity and indissolubility. Then He confirmed the divine law with His own authority by declaring: "What therefore God has joined together, let no man put asunder" (Matt. 19:6).

---

[8] Both readings, each with the same sense, appear in the codices. Matthew 5:32 has the second reading only, "except [παρεκτός] for fornication." Apparently this latter passage should be interpreted in conformity with the sense of Matthew 19:9, where the excepting phrase occurs in circumstances which allow us to estimate its scope with more precision.

With this firm, uncompromising declaration, Jesus placed Himself in open conflict with the Mosaic Law, which explicitly authorized divorce. The Pharisees understood Him perfectly and objected: "Why then did Moses command to give a written notice of dismissal, and to put her away?" [9] In reply our Lord said: "Because Moses, by reason of the hardness of your heart, permitted you to put away your wives; *but it was not so from the beginning*" (Matt. 19:8).

Then, leaving the high plane of principles and taking His stand on the same level as His interrogators, the level of the Mosaic Law, He replied to their original question: "Is it lawful for a man to put away his wife for any cause?" Thus when He declared: "And I say to you, that whoever puts away his wife, except for fornication, and marries another, commits adultery. . . ." (Matt. 19:9), He was speaking *solely in terms of the Mosaic Law* and was settling the dispute between the schools of Hillel and Shammai by stating that the latter was right in maintaining that, under the Mosaic Law, marriage could be dissolved *only on account of adultery* and not for any trivial cause, as the school of Hillel taught.

It should be noted that our Lord was not approving, either definitively or provisionally, the divorce permitted in the Mosaic Law. He had already set forth His own teaching on the indissolubility of marriage by declaring: "What therefore God has joined together, let no

---

[9] Deuteronomy 24:1–4 permitted a man to give his wife a bill of divorce, but a woman had not the right to do likewise with her husband. When recording that Salome, sister of Herod the Great, sent a bill of divorce to her husband Costobar, Josephus remarks (*Ant.* xv. 7. 10) that her action was not in conformity with the law of the Jews. But our Lord's words in Mark 10:12 seem to presuppose just the opposite: "And if the wife *puts away her husband,* and marries another, she commits adultery."

The contradiction disappears if we read, as do several codices: "if the woman *leaves* her husband," for then it would be only a question of desertion and not of divorce. However, we regard this reading as an intentional modification of the primitive text. Some authors resolve the difficulty by saying that Mark, taking account of Graeco-Roman customs and convinced that he was interpreting the mind of Christ, added the sentence of his own accord (Prat, *Jesus Christ,* II, 82). But we are not inclined to accept this solution, and we believe that another and more satisfactory one can be given. It is very probable that, to a greater or lesser degree, Roman usage had been introduced into the Jewish world, as is indicated by the text from Josephus to which we referred above. After remarking that Salome had not acted according to Jewish law, the historian adds that she had availed herself of the law then in use, an undoubted allusion to the Roman custom that had begun to creep into Palestine. Therefore there was sufficient reason for our Lord to have spoken the sentence recorded in Mark and to have been referring thereby, not to simple desertion, but to actual divorce on the wife's part.

man put asunder" (Matt. 19:6); and by His words "except for fornication" He was neither approving nor disapproving of divorce, but was simply pointing out the true interpretation of the Law.[10]

We find the indissolubility of marriage, so solemnly affirmed in Matthew 19, clearly expressed in Mark 10:11–12, Luke 16:8, and in 1 Corinthians 7:10–11, 39 where St. Paul says explicitly: "A woman is bound as long as her husband is alive, but if her husband dies, she is free. Let her marry whom she pleases, only let it be in the Lord" (v. 39). "And let not a husband put away his wife" (v. 11).

Numerous other interpretations of the phrase "except for fornication" (Matt. 19:9) have been proposed, some of which we shall mention here.

St. Jerome's solution is very tempting and has been adopted by many authors, for it is simple and cuts the difficulty off at the root. He held that our Lord was permitting separation *quoad thorum,* that is, the cessation of *cohabitation,* with the bond of marriage remaining intact. The husband could put away his wife but neither he nor she could contract a new marriage.[11] But this explanation meets with a grave difficulty. The Jews certainly intended to speak of the *bond* of marriage, because the breaking of that bond was the essence of the dispute between the schools of Hillel and Shammai. Our Lord's reply also makes that clear: "Moses, by reason of the hardness of your hearts, permitted you to put away your wives; but it was not so from the beginning." Furthermore, there were other causes, besides adultery, for simple separation.

Other authors interpret πορνεία ("fornication") in the sense of *concubinage* or an *invalid marriage* (invalid because it was incestuous or for any other reason). Therefore our Lord meant that "whoever repudiates his wife, except because his marriage is *invalid* or is simply *concubinage,* and marries another, commits adultery."[12] In our

---

[10] This solution is not a new one. In its essentials it was proposed by J. Grimm in *Das Leben Jesu* (3d ed. [Regensburg, 1919], V, 256 *f.*), and before him by others such as Hug and Adalbert Maier. It was accepted by Sickenberger ("Die Unzuchtsklausel in Matthaüsevangelium," in *Theologische Quartalschrift,* 123 [1942], 189–206), and it was upheld by A. Tafi in *Verb. Dom.,* 26 (1948), 18–26.

[11] St. Jerome, *In Matt.* 19. 9: *PL* 26, 135, followed by Knabenbauer, Fillion, Ricciotti, Buzy and others. This interpretation has been refuted by Fr. Vaccari ("Il divorzio nei Vangeli," in *Civiltà Cattolica,* II [1956], 350–359, 475–484; see especially p. 358), who gives good reasons for his stand.

[12] Cf Patrizi; Prat, *op. cit.,* II, 81, n. 5; Bonsirven, *Rech. de Sc. Rel.,* 35

opinion, there are several objections to this solution. The word πορνεία, since it is a general term, could in itself mean an invalid marriage.[13] But the Pharisees were definitely speaking to our Lord about normal, valid marriage, for otherwise their question would have been meaningless. Therefore, as one would expect, in His reply He was referring to lawful marriage. Furthermore, assuredly every good Jew believed that a man living in concubinage not only could, but ought to send away the woman. Hence the Pharisees' question would have been pointless if it had referred to concubinage.[14]

To sum up: in the three Synoptic Gospels Jesus affirmed the indissolubility of marriage clearly and decidedly, but in St. Matthew He added the true interpretation of the Mosaic Law regarding divorce, a point which was the source of much discussion among the Jewish schools.[15]

Jesus and the Children
(Luke 18:15–17; Matt. 19:13–15; Mark 10:13–16)

From this same period of our Lord's life the Gospels record a delightful and touching episode. Jesus was in the house of a certain family, speaking no doubt to a small audience, when some children edged timidly up to Him, and mothers began bringing their babes in arms to Him so that He might touch and bless them. The disciples objected to what they deemed an annoyance to their Master, but He admonished them: "Let the little children come to me, and do not hinder them, for of such is the kingdom of God."

Then, embracing the children, and laying His sacred hands on their heads, He blessed them (Mark 10:16).

Raphael has immortalized this charming scene in which we see

(1948), 442–464; *Le divorce dans le Nouv. Testament* (Paris, 1948); Vaccari, *loc. cit.*, etc.

[13] The Hebrew word *zenut* can signify an invalid marriage, but this is not its only meaning.

[14] There are other solutions which we shall merely summarize: the phrase in St. Matthew is to be taken (1) in an *inclusive* sense: *"even* in the case of fornication" (Ott, Vogt, Staab, Allgeier); or (2) in a *prescinding* sense: *"leaving aside* the case of fornication" (St. Robert Bellarmine, Lagrange); or (3) as an *interpolation* (cf. R. Leconte, *Mélanges de Science Religieuse,* 8 [1915], 284).

[15] A list of the various interpretations, with a criticism of each can be found in Holzmeister, "Die Streitfrage über die Ehescheidungstexte bei Matthäus 5:32, 19:9," in *Biblica,* 26 (1945), 133–146; and in A. Tafi, *loc. cit.* Regarding the Fathers' interpretations, see Bonsirven, *Le divorce dans le Nouv. Testament,* pp. 61–90.

depicted our Lord's love for children—His love not only for those who are young in years, but also for those who, although burdened with the weight of age, still retain their spiritual childhood.

Voluntary Poverty
(Luke 18:18–30; Matt. 19:16–30; Mark 10:17–31)

No sooner had Jesus left the house where He had blessed the children, and started on his way, than a young man rushed up to Him. The stranger, who, as it turned out, was a rich man, fell on his knees before our Lord and asked Him earnestly: "Good Master, what shall I do to gain eternal life?"

The young man's fervor and humility were all the more admirable because of the fact that he must have been well known to everyone in the district. In view of the fact that his intention was certainly pure and his desire for guidance sincere, Christ's answer to his question was a surprising one: "Why dost thou call me good? No one is good but God only."

It would seem from this retort that He was rejecting the title which His petitioner had conferred on Him. And there was no need for Him to point out to the young man that the one true good, the *summum bonum,* is God, for he must have known that already. Yet there is no doubt that our Lord had a reason for answering as He did.

It should be remembered that, among the Jews, the word "good" was applied only to God and the Law. Apart from our passage, we do not find it used of our Lord anywhere else in the Gospels. Therefore, it may be regarded here as a device to gain favor, a form of flattery, which was not, however, base and insincere. If this was the speaker's intention, then Christ's answer is perfectly understandable. He was declining an honor which was really due Him, a gesture of modesty that is not infrequently employed by humble souls. Consequently, His words were not, as some heretics and rationalists would have us believe, a denial that He possessed divine attributes.

Continuing, He gave the young man the advice he sought: "If thou wilt enter into life [that is, if thou wilt be saved], keep the commandments."

"Which?"

"Thou shalt not kill, thou shalt not commit adultery, thou shalt not steal, thou shalt not bear false witness, honor thy father and mother, and, thou shalt love thy neighbor as thyself."

"Master, all these I have kept ever since I was a child."

On hearing this, Jesus looked at him lovingly, and said: "One thing is lacking to thee; go, sell whatever thou hast, and give to the poor, and thou shalt have treasure in heaven; and come, follow me."

In His replies, our Lord plainly marked out the two paths to heaven, the path of the divine Commandments, and that of the evangelical counsels. The second is more perfect than the first, but Jesus did not make it obligatory; He merely invited men to follow it: "If thou wilt be perfect. . . ." (Matt. 19:21). And blessed are they who accept the divine invitation to do so.

But the rich young man was not among those who chose the higher life; on hearing that he would have to give up everything he owned in order to do so, "he went away sad, for he had great possessions." Sorrowful at the young man's failure to accept the divine call, Jesus exclaimed to His disciples: "With what difficulty will they who have riches enter the kingdom of God! For it is easier for a camel to pass through the eye of a needle,[16] than for a rich man to enter the kingdom of God."

The disciples, astonished at His words, murmured among themselves: "Who then can be saved?"

Our Lord, noting their amazement, gazed steadily at them and said: "With men it is impossible, but not with God; for all things are possible with God."

The discussion about riches and their renunciation, and the wealthy young man's unwillingness to sacrifice his possessions, inspired Peter to ask in the name of all the disciples: "Behold, we have left all and followed thee; what then shall we have?"

---

[16] Some authors have thought this comparison so absurd that they take the "eye of a needle" to mean the small door that was to be found beside the large gate of a city, or else they resort to other explanations to avoid what they regard as an insuperable difficulty. But actually, no such difficulty exists. Our Lord was simply using hyperbole. Similar figures of speech appear in rabbinical literature: for example, a certain rabbi reproved one of his confreres for over-subtlety by saying, "Thou art indeed from Pumbeditha, where they make an elephant pass through the eye of a needle" (cf. Str.-Bill., I, 828). In Georg Aicher's *Kamel und Madelöhr* (*Neutestamentliche Abhandlungen* [Münster i. W., 1908], Band 1, Heft 5, pp. 1–64), the reader will find many strange interpretations of these words, which, considered in their proper context of time and place, are quite simple and clear. Our Lord was referring to nothing more or less than the eye of a sewing-needle.

To which Jesus replied: "Amen I say to you that you who have followed me, in the regeneration when the Son of Man shall sit on the throne of his glory, shall also sit on twelve thrones, judging the twelve tribes of Israel. And everyone who has left house, or brothers, or sisters, or father, or mother, or wife, or children, or lands, for my name's sake, shall receive a hundredfold, and shall possess life everlasting."

The sacrifice of worldly goods will have its reward even in this life, not only in exclusively spiritual, but also in temporal advantages. He who despoils himself of everything in order to follow Christ will receive from Divine Providence, in generous and superabundant measure, whatever he needs to sustain him. He who leaves father and mother will find fathers and mothers who will treat him as a beloved son. The maidens who, in the flower of their youth, renounce the joys of motherhood, will be made mothers of innumerable children, upon whom they can lavish all the tenderness of a truly maternal heart.

In St. Mark, the enumeration of the rewards promised includes an interesting note: "along with persecutions." This is a reminder of the distinguishing mark of Christ's followers: "If they have persecuted me, they will persecute you also" (John 15:20). But these trials will not be an obstacle to the enjoyment of the rewards promised to generous souls. These promises are indeed wonderful, but they have a condition attached—perseverance. It is not enough for us to set out on the path trodden by our Lord: we must continue to follow Him, for if we do not, we shall lose the first place in His favor and fall to the last, as He Himself pointed out immediately after enumerating the rewards: "But many who are first now will be last, and many who are last now will be first."

The Laborers in the Vineyard
(Matt. 20:1–16)

Jesus ended His instruction of the disciples with the mysterious words about the first becoming last and the last first, a statement which He then went on to explain by means of a parable. At the end of the parable He repeated the statement, a clear indication of the connection between it and the parable.

"The kingdom of heaven is like a householder who went out early in the morning to hire laborers for his vineyard. And having agreed with the laborers for a denarius a day, he sent them into his vineyard. And about the third hour, he went out and saw others standing in the market place idle; and he said to them, 'Go you also into the vineyard, and I will give you whatever is just.' So they went. And again he went out about the sixth, and about the ninth hour, and did as before. But about the eleventh hour he went out and found others standing about, and he said to them, 'Why do you stand here all day idle?' They said to him, 'Because no man has hired us.' He said to them, 'Go you also into the vineyard.' But when evening had come, the owner of the vineyard said to his steward, 'Call the laborers, and pay them their wages, beginning from the last even to the first.' Now when they of the eleventh hour came, they received each a denarius. And when the first in their turn came, they thought that they would receive more; but they also received each his denarius. And on receiving it, they began to murmur against the householder, saying, 'These last have worked a single hour, and thou hast put them on a level with us, who have borne the burden of the day's heat.' But answering one of them, he said, 'Friend, I do thee no injustice; didst thou not agree with me for a denarius? Take what is thine and go; I choose to give to this last even as to thee. Have I not a right to do what I choose? Or art thou envious because I am generous?' "

Our Lord then closed the parable with the words He had spoken before in Matthew 19:30: "Even so the last shall be first, and the first last."

This conclusion aptly sums up the whole parable, in which the last laborers to be hired were made equal to the first, and vice versa.[17]

The parable was taken from real life, and even today laborers gather every morning near the Jaffa Gate in Jerusalem, hoping to be hired. But the details of the story do not correspond so closely to the reality. For example, it is not usual to send a laborer to work in the fields just before sunset. However, in conformity with the nature of parables, our Lord took some liberty in arranging the details to throw into higher relief the lesson which He wished to teach. "Early in the

---

[17] We do not think Fr. Buzy's remark is wholly justified: "C'est une conclusion apparente, un appendice" (*S. Matt.*, p. 262, n. 4), and his reasons for making it do not seem convincing. The very fact that all the laborers received the same wage for varying amounts of work shows that the last ones to come received preferential treatment over the first. There follows a short phrase: "for many are called, but few are chosen," which certain authors, perhaps not without some foundation, reject as unauthentic. It is repeated, however, in Matthew 22:14. See p. 587 below.

morning," the "third," "sixth," "ninth" and "eleventh hour" were
reckoned from 6:00 A.M., and therefore corresponded to our 6:00
A.M., 9:00 A.M., twelve noon, 3:00 P.M. and 5:00 P.M. respectively.
Thus the last laborers hired had to work only one hour, since work
ceased at sundown, about 6:00 P.M. The point of doctrine enshrined
in the parable is that no one has a right to complain about the way
God distributes His gifts, for they are His own and therefore He can
dispose of them as seems best to Him. Of course, it goes without saying
that in allotting these gifts, God will never, indeed can never, be unjust.

We must also remember that in relating this parable, Jesus had
in mind the future fate of the Gentiles and Jews: the latter, who
looked upon themselves as the first, would, through their own fault,
be placed after the former; and in like manner, the proud Pharisees
would find themselves preceded by the humble sinners whom they
had despised.

Going Up to Jerusalem for the Great Sacrifice
(Luke 18:31–19:28; Matt. 20:17–34; Mark 10:32–52;
cf. Map IV)

Once more the month of Nisan (March–April) had come around,
and the Passover was drawing near, that Passover during which our
Lord, the Lamb of God, knew He would be sacrificed. Therefore at
the beginning of the month, perhaps between the fifth and seventh of
Nisan (March 20th–22nd), He left Perea for the last time, and took
the road to Jerusalem.

This journey was somewhat unusual; Jesus was accompanied by
the Twelve and by a group of disciples, among whom were the holy
women and perhaps some pilgrims who were going to the Holy City
for the feast. The Apostles noticed that their Master, instead of
walking and talking with them, went out ahead of them (Mark
10:32), as if pushing on eagerly towards His goal and urging them,
by His example, to make haste. Then, too, the Twelve had not forgotten that, not long before, as a result of the raising of Lazarus, He
had had to leave the neighborhood of Jerusalem so as not to fall into
the hands of the chief priests, who had decreed that He was to die.
Now He was returning to the dangers of the capital, and they had no
hope of persuading Him otherwise, for He was obviously bent on
reaching His chosen destination. Because of all these circumstances,

the Apostles were astonished and dismayed (ἐθαμβοῦντο; Mark 10:32). The rest of the company shared their feeling that there was something mysterious about the journey; they, too, were aware of the hostility and malevolence of the Scribes and Pharisees towards Jesus, and therefore they were beset by fear (ἐφοβοῦντο), especially the holy women.[18]

With a few sure strokes, St. Mark has drawn for us an impressive picture. He describes our Lord as *going up* to Jerusalem, not only because the road from the Jordan to Jericho really does climb, but also, and particularly, because he is thinking of Christ's destination, the Holy City whose dignity so elevated it above all the cities of the earth that, by force of custom, the expression "to *go up* to Jerusalem" had become classic. He tells us that Jesus walked *on in front* of His small group of followers, like a captain leading His soldiers into battle. And what a battle that was to be! Although our Lord knew the forces which the prince of darkness was going to hurl against Him, He went forward resolutely and with calm assurance; and the evangelist contrasts the Master's courage with the discouragement, uneasiness and fear that gripped the disciples, who, although they were willing to follow their Lord, were still disquieted and troubled by their gloomy forebodings of what was going to happen in the capital, where, as they well knew, His enemies were lying in wait for Him.

Another Prophecy of the Passion
(Matt. 20:17-19; Mark 10:32-34; Luke 18:31-34)

At one point on the road to Jerusalem, our Lord slackened His pace, and finding a means of taking the Apostles aside (κατ᾽ ἰδίαν; Matt. 20:17), revealed to them for the fourth time (cf. Luke 9:22, 44; 17:25) the mystery of the Passion—the insults, the cruel tortures, and

---

[18] Not all authors give this interpretation of Mark 10:32, where we find these interesting details. The *textus receptus* has καὶ ἀκολουθοῦντες ("and following Him"), and refers it back to the subject of the preceding verb, "they were astonished": this is how Rösch, Crampon, Gomá and de la Torre understand it, i.e., "They [the disciples] were astonished and, *following Him,* were afraid." But the great majority of authors, with the support of good manuscripts, read οἱ δὲ ἀκολουθοῦντες ("but those who were following Him"), and hold that those who followed Jesus were a group distinct from the Apostles (or disciples), who were astonished. Still other writers (e.g., Fouard, Gould) believe that some of those who set out on the journey with our Lord were so overcome by fear that they turned back, while the rest continued on despite their fear; and it is to the latter that the evangelist is referring.

the agonizing death He was about to undergo. But at the same time He gave them a glimpse of His glorious Resurrection: "Behold, we are going up to Jerusalem, and the Son of Man will be betrayed to the chief priests and the Scribes; and they will condemn him to death, and will deliver him to the Gentiles to be mocked and scourged and crucified; and on the third day he will rise again."

St. Luke observes (18:34) that, despite their clarity and precision, our Lord's words seemed obscure to the Apostles, who understood none of the things He told them. Bewildered, they were unable to reconcile their Master's prophecy with their ingrained prejudices, and their confusion was increased by the uneasiness and apprehension which were weighing on them. How was it possible, they asked themselves, that He who had so often shown His power over nature, should be finally conquered by His foes? How could the Messias, whom the prophets had foretold as the Liberator of Israel, the Victor over His enemies, and the glorious and triumphant Heir to the throne of David His father—how could such as He be subjected to insult, much less to death itself? But it is possible that, in their own way, they understood something of what Jesus had foretold. Maybe they thought that their Master would actually have to suffer at the hands of His enemies, but that He would triumph over them and would then establish the glorious kingdom which they were so eagerly expecting.

The Mother of the Sons of Zebedee
(Matt. 20:20–28; Mark 10:35–45)

It is only in the light of the Apostles' misconceptions that we can explain the episode of the sons of Zebedee, which St. Matthew and St. Mark, the two evangelists who record it, place after the prophecy of the Passion.

The holy women had not heard what our Lord had said to the Apostles; but James and John, convinced that their Master's glorification was approaching, probably shared His prophecy with their mother, Salome (cf. Matt. 27:56; Mark 15:40), who decided that the moment had come to make a request which she had doubtless long desired to see fulfilled. She was encouraged by the knowledge that her two sons were dearer to Jesus than the other Apostles; and she thought it only proper that they should be especially privileged in the kingdom that was soon to be established. The good woman therefore approached Christ respectfully, her two sons at her side, with all the appearances of a person about to ask a favor.

Forestalling her, Jesus asked: "What dost thou want?"

"Command that these my two sons may sit, one at thy right hand and one at thy left hand, in thy kingdom."

Our Lord, seeing that the request was more the sons' than the mother's, said curtly to the two Apostles: "You do not know what you are asking for." He paused a moment, then added: "Can you drink of the cup of which I am about to drink?"

"We can," they replied stoutly, hoping perhaps that this answer would influence Jesus to grant their request. But it had no such effect.

"Of my cup you shall indeed drink; but as for sitting at my right hand and at my left, that is not mine to give you, but it belongs to those for whom it has been prepared by my Father."

He meant that the granting of reward in heaven was a function of Divine Providence which is usually attributed only to God the Father.

When the other Apostles heard of the request which the mother of James and John had made, they knew that the two brothers had had a hand in the matter, and they were angry with them. Our Lord took advantage of the incident to give all of them a lesson in humility: "You know that the rulers of the Gentiles lord it over them, and their great men exercise authority over them. Not so is it among you. On the contrary, whoever wishes to become great among you shall be your servant; and whoever wishes to be first among you shall be your slave."

He concluded by giving them the most telling of all examples— His own: "Even as the Son of Man has not come to be served but to serve, and to give his life as a ransom for many."

The Apostles needed the lesson, for even now, on the very eve of the Passion, they were still far from possessing the spirit of Christ.

Zacchaeus

(Luke 19:1–10)

In due course the party arrived at Jericho, the town which Herod had greatly embellished, and which lay to the south of the ancient Canaanite city of the same name (today known as Tell es-Sultan) and to the west of present-day er-Riha, at the exact spot where the

Matson Photo

Modern Jericho.

Wadi el-Qelt opens onto the plain. The hill (Tell Abu 'Alaiq) which today rises beside the road, covers the ruins of Herod's magnificent palace near which, to the south, lay the city in the heart of a green oasis. Josephus praises the extraordinary fertility of the district, which was so covered with palms, cypresses, aromatic plants and countless beautiful gardens, that the historian was moved to exclaim: "It would not be a mistake to call the place divine." [19]

Jericho was an important city, lying as it did at the junction of the road from Perea and that which came from the north along the Jordan valley. Consequently, it counted among its citizens a considerable number of publicans or tax collectors, under the orders of a leader. At the time about which we are speaking, the head tax collector was a rich man named Zacchaeus (Hebrew *Zakkaî*=pure; cf. 1 Esdras 2:9) whom the evangelist calls "a leading publican." This Zacchaeus was hated by the Jews, not only because of his office, but also because they all knew that he was not overscrupulous in the means he took to add to his wealth. He had heard of Jesus, and when he saw the people of the city running to crowd around the young

[19] *Wars* iv. 8. 3.

Prophet, he also hastened to catch a glimpse of Him, probably out of curiosity mixed, perhaps, with some reverence and respect. We get an idea of his simple and somewhat childlike character from the fact that, without a thought for his dignity and social standing, he joined the crowd, and "because he was small of stature," did not hesitate to climb up into a sycamore or wild fig tree (there are still some to be seen in Jericho) to get a good view of Jesus as He passed.

When our Lord, surrounded by the multitude, came to the foot of the tree in which Zacchaeus was perched, He looked up and said to him: "Zacchaeus, make haste and come down; for I must stay in thy house today."

How startled the publican must have been to hear Jesus address him by name! And his joy was no doubt even greater than the bad humor of the crowd who, on seeing Christ enter the house of the hated taxgatherer, complained aloud: "He has gone to be the guest of a man who is a sinner."

But Jesus paid no heed to their murmuring. As the Good Shepherd who had come into the world to search for the lost sheep, He had accepted the invitation of Levi the publican, and had allowed the sinful woman to kiss His feet, so that He might bring them both into His fold. He knew, too, that the murmurers' apparent delicacy of conscience was nothing more than refined pride and cruel egotism.

Zacchaeus, the wandering sheep of Jericho, obeyed the Good Shepherd's voice: "Behold, Lord," he proclaimed, "I give one-half of my possessions to the poor, and if I have defrauded anyone of anything, I restore it fourfold."

Moved by the publican's good will, detachment and generosity, Jesus exclaimed: "Today salvation has come to this house, since he, too, is a son of Abraham. For the Son of Man came to seek and save what was lost."

The Parable of the Gold Pieces

(Luke 19:11–28)

With our Lord's arrival in Jericho and the spreading of the news that He was going up to Jerusalem, the fervor of the citizens increased, for they suspected that the final struggle was at hand, and they were sure that the great Wonder-worker would emerge triumphant. They even thought it possible that the glorious reign of the

Messias would be inaugurated during the approaching feast of the Passover. But wishing to dissipate their false hopes and put a check to their fantasies, Jesus told them a parable full of local color and particularly appropriate in Jericho, for in 40 B.C. Herod the Great, and in A.D. 4 his son Archelaus, had both gone to Rome to receive royal investiture. Furthermore, in the case of Archelaus, a delegation had hastened to the capital of the Empire to protest that they did not want him for king.[20]

"A certain nobleman went into a far country to obtain for himself a kingdom and then return. And having summoned ten of his servants, he gave them ten gold pieces and said to them, 'Trade till I come.'

"But his citizens hated him; and they sent a delegation after him to say, 'We do not wish this man to be king over us.' And it came to pass when he had returned, after receiving the kingdom, that he ordered the servants to whom he had given the money to be called to him in order that he might learn how much each one had made by trading.

"And the first came, saying, 'Lord, thy gold piece has earned ten gold pieces.' And he said to him, 'Well done, good servant; because thou hast been faithful in a very little, thou shalt have authority over ten towns.'

"Then the second came, saying, 'Lord, thy gold piece has made five gold pieces.' And he said to him, 'Be thou also over five towns.'

"And another came, saying, 'Lord, behold thy gold piece, which I have kept laid up in a napkin; for I feared thee, because thou art a stern man. Thou takest up what thou didst not lay down, and thou reapest what thou didst not sow.' He said to him, 'Out of thy own mouth I judge thee, thou wicked servant. Thou knewest that I am a stern man, taking up what I did not lay down and reaping what I did not sow. Why, then, didst thou not put my money in a bank, so that I on my return might have gotten it with interest?' And he said to the bystanders, 'Take away the gold piece from him, and give it to him who has the ten gold pieces.' But they said to him, 'Lord, he has ten gold pieces.'

"I say to you that to everyone who has shall be given; but from him who does not have, even that which he has shall be taken away.

[20] *Ant.* xiv. 14. 3 *ff.*; xvii. 9. 3 *ff.*

But as for these my enemies, who did not want me to be king over them, bring them here and slay them in my presence."

The meaning of the parable is clear. Authors commonly regard the nobleman as a figure of Christ, leaving earth for heaven to receive the kingdom there, and giving each man the graces necessary for the working out of his salvation. At the end of time, on the day of the last judgment—and before that, in the particular judgment after death—He will demand an account of the way in which each one has used the graces he received, and He will give each the reward he has earned or the punishment he has deserved. We should note that the good use of graces obtains further graces for us, while the abuse thereof renders us liable to lose them.

It would be easy to construct two parables from the elements contained in this one narrative: the parable of the nobleman who went to obtain a kingdom and, upon his return, punished his enemies; and that of the householder who, being compelled to go away, entrusted various sums of money to his servants, each of whom he rewarded later according to his merits. But that is no reason for affirming that there were originally two distinct parables which were later combined into one.[21] In the parable as it stands, every one of the elements has its purpose, each fits perfectly into place, and all combine to form a harmonious whole.

The Blind Men of Jericho
(Matt. 20:29–34; Mark 10:46–52; Luke 18:35–43)

As our Lord, followed by a large crowd of people, was leaving Jericho, there were two blind men seated by the roadside begging alms. When these beggars heard that Jesus of Nazareth was passing by, they began to cry out: "Jesus, Son of David, have mercy on us!"

The crowd angrily tried to silence them, but they only cried out all the louder: "Lord, have mercy on us, Son of David!"

On hearing their plea, Jesus stopped and commanded them to be summoned to Him. St. Mark tells us the name of one of them—

---

21 In Les Paraboles, pp. 542–548, Fr. Buzy upholds the duality. However, we believe that he exaggerates the difficulties presented by the interpretation of the parable as found in the present text. J. Pirot, Paraboles et allégories évangéliques (Paris, 1949), pp. 366 ff., argues in favor of one parable, as does Diaz, Anotaciones sobre las parábolas del Evangelio (Bogotá, 1949), p. 385.

Regarding the identification of this parable with that of the talents, see below, p. 617, n. 20.

Bartimeus, i.e., the son of Timeus. To him, and no doubt to the other beggar also, the crowd said: "Take courage. Get up, he is calling thee."

The blind men did not have to be told a second time. Throwing off their cloaks to give themselves more freedom, they sprang to their feet and made their way to Jesus.

When they stood before Him, our Saviour asked: "What will you have me do for you?"

With piteous eagerness, they answered: "Lord, that our eyes be opened."

Mercifully granting their request, Christ touched their eyes and restored their sight.

From our description of the episode, the reader can guess the solution which we give to the long-discussed problem of the blind men of Jericho. St. Luke speaks of only *one* blind man who cried out to our Lord as He was *entering* or nearing Jericho; St. Mark also mentions only *one* blind man, but says that he made his plea as Jesus was *leaving* the city; and St. Matthew tells us of *two* blind men, both of whom begged our Lord to cure them as He was *departing* from Jericho.

Most commentators admit that the evangelists, and St. Matthew in particular, do not always follow the chronological order of events but sometimes combine incidents and discourses which took place at different times and in different circumstances. Therefore St. Luke may have deliberately anticipated the episode of the blind men by placing it before the conversation with Zacchaeus and narrating it as if it had occurred as our Lord was nearing or entering the city, although it really happened during His departure. Thus we agree with Fillion when he says: "It is likely that St. Luke purposely anticipated, because he had to relate afterwards the episode about Zacchaeus, to which he attached greater importance." [22] Therefore each of the three Synoptic evangelists is speaking about an episode which occurred as Christ was *leaving* the city. There is no difficulty in the fact that Luke and Mark each mention only one blind man, whereas Matthew refers to two. Either Luke and Mark are speaking about the same blind man, Bartimeus, who was one of Matthew's two beggars, or else Mark alone is referring to Bartimeus, while Luke is speaking about the second of Matthew's two beggars, whose name we

[22] *The Life of Christ*, III, 218.

do not know. Therefore we hold that there were *two* blind men, both of whom our Lord cured as He was *leaving* the city.

Several other solutions to the problem have been proposed: (1) one blind man at our Lord's entrance into Jericho and another as He left the city; St. Matthew combines both in the one narrative; (2) a blind man begged to be cured as our Lord was entering the city, but his petition was not granted until later, when he and another blind man were both cured as Jesus left the city; (3) "to draw near" and "to be near" are synonymous; hence, when St. Luke says that Jesus "drew near" to Jericho, we can understand his words to mean that our Lord was *leaving* Jericho, since then also He was *near* the city; (4) Jesus was coming from ancient Jericho (Tell es-Sultan) and approaching the Jericho of Herod; Bartimeus and his companion were begging by the roadside between the two cities; hence it can be said that our Lord met them as He was leaving the old city and entering the new; this is Fouard's solution.

This last interpretation is very farfetched, and the third is impossible. The second must be regarded as unlikely unless one holds, as some authors do, that the first three verses of St. Luke's account (vv. 35–37) come before our Lord's entry into Jericho, while the next three (vv. 38–43) come after His leaving the city. No serious objection can be made to the first solution, since there is nothing improbable in Christ's encountering one blind man as He entered the city and another as he left. However, we still prefer the answer which we have proposed above.[23]

---

[23] Cf. Ketter, "Zur Lokalisierung der Blindenheilung bei Jericho," in *Miscellanea Biblica,* I (1934), 291–298.

24. Preludes to the Passion (April, A. D. 30)

The prolonged journey described by St. Luke had lasted several months, and was now coming to an end. Our Lord had travelled through and exercised His ministry in many different regions, but He always had His eyes fixed on the final goal, Jerusalem, the city in which He was to suffer ignominy, torture and death before He rose triumphantly from the tomb.

He now had only a short time left to Him, and He seems to have intensified His activity as if eager not to lose a moment out of the fleeting days. In order to make it more easy to follow the events of this period, we shall note some chronological and topographical data derived from a collation of the Gospels.

The three Synoptic authors give the impression that the triumphal entry into Jerusalem followed immediately upon our Lord's leaving Jericho; but we know that the feast at Bethany intervened, although St. Matthew (chap. 26) and St. Mark (chap. 14)—St. Luke does not mention it—seem to place the banquet after the eschatological discourse. Actually, St. John (12:1) says that Jesus went to Bethany six days before the Passover, i.e., the Saturday before the Passover, which was celebrated on Friday, and he also notes that the entry into Jerusalem took place on the next day, i.e., Sunday (12:2).

The chronological succession of the three days, Monday, Tuesday and Wednesday, is vague and indeterminate in Matthew and Luke. Matthew gives only one concrete indication when he tells us that, after the triumphal entry, our Lord returned to Bethany the same (Sunday) evening, and that on the next day He returned again to Jerusalem (21:17 *f.*). But St. Mark gives us more details on the subject. On Sunday evening Jesus retired to Bethany, and, on the following day, Monday, He left there and re-entered Jerusalem (11:11, 12, 15). On Monday evening He left the city (11:19), and no doubt went again to Bethany, or at least to Mount Olivet (cf. Matt. 21:17); on the following day, Tuesday, He returned to the Temple (Mark 11:20, 27). Since He seems to have left the Temple the same day (13:1), Tuesday, and there is no other chronological indication given, we conclude, as many other authors do, that He did not go to the Temple on Wednesday.

On the first day, Monday, St. Mark mentions only the episode of the fig tree (11:12–14) and the cleansing of the Temple (11:15–18); and he records all the rest as happening on the following day, Tuesday. We shall adhere to this arrangement, although we are aware that it may perhaps be somewhat artificial.

In Jerusalem, the atmosphere was heavy with the threat of the coming storm. The members of the civil and religious aristocracy were thirsting for revenge on the Prophet of Nazareth, whose popularity both angered and, at the same time, restrained them. The people at large knew how their leaders felt, and were wondering what was going to happen to Jesus. He and His possible fate were the talk of the day, and those who had come up from the country for the feast stood about in the Temple inquiring of each other: "What do you think, that he is not coming to the feast?"

It is no wonder that the crowds discussed Jesus so much, for the chief priests and Pharisees had given orders that, "if anyone knew where he was, he should report it, so that they might seize him" (John 11:56). Our Saviour heard the rumbling thunder of the approaching storm, but He was not afraid. Even considered from a merely human point of view, His bearing in the circumstances displayed a tragic greatness. He knew how His enemies hated Him; He knew also that they were resolved to seize Him, and that their thirst for vengeance would be satisfied only by His death. Yet despite His awareness of all this, He calmly appeared in the Temple, fearlessly confronted His adversaries, and launched terrible anathemas against them and their doctrine. This, more than any other period of His life, was the time of battle; it was the climax of the gigantic struggle between innocence and malice, truth and falsehood, justice and iniquity.

The Feast at Bethany
(Matt. 26:6–16; Mark 14:3–11; John 12:1–11)

It is probable that, out of respect for the Sabbath rest, our Lord did not undertake the journey from Jerusalem to Bethany on Saturday, but traveled on Friday afternoon, reaching His destination before sunset.

The inhabitants of Bethany, remembering the great miracle of the raising of Lazarus, wished to honor Jesus with a banquet, or rather a supper (δεῖπνον), given on Saturday after sundown, i.e., when, according to Jewish reckoning, the Sabbath was over and the next day had begun.

The supper was not a private affair, arranged and attended only by the beloved family at Bethany, who surely would have preferred to have had our Lord dine with them alone in the intimacy of their home. It was, instead, a kind of public function, organized in the name of the whole town. Consequently it was held in the house of an important personage, a leading citizen named Simon the leper. Perhaps Simon had been cured of his disease by Jesus, and was now showing his gratitude by holding the public celebration at his house. Doubtless Lazarus was present at the banquet, and was stared at by everyone; in fact, St. John (12:9) says that many Jews came to Bethany, "not only because of Jesus, but that they might see Lazarus, whom he had raised from the dead."

The two sisters were also there, each perfectly in character, Martha being busily engaged in directing the catering, while Mary [1] lovingly took precious ointment, poured it on our Lord's head, anointed His feet with it and then wiped them dry with her flowing hair. All this Mary did without uttering a word, but her silence was eloquent and her actions proclaimed the love that burned in her pure heart. As St. Augustine says:

[1] For the distinction between this Mary (Mary of Bethany) and Mary Magdalene, see pp. 360 f. above.

If you wish to be a faithful soul, anoint the feet of the Lord with precious ointment, as Mary did. . . . Anoint the Lord's feet by following in His footsteps, that is, by living a good life. Dry His feet with your hair by giving what you can to the poor.[2]

St. John tells us that "the house was filled with the odor of the ointment" (12:3). But although everyone smelled the perfume of the ointment, not all perceived the fragrance of the devoted love that inspired Mary to pour out the precious unguent so lavishly. For some of those present, the fragrant odor was life, for others it was death: "Woe to thee, miserable man!" exclaims St. Augustine, "The beautiful odor kills thee." [3] The miserable man to whom St. Augustine refers was, of course, Judas Iscariot, who regarded Mary's generosity as sheer prodigality, even waste, and complained to those about him: "Why was this ointment not sold for three hundred denarii, and given to the poor?"

What vile hypocrisy! St. John, who understood the high motives that inspired Mary to act as she did, reveals the true reason for the traitor's querulous complaint: "Now he said this, not that he cared for the poor, but because he was a thief, and holding the purse, used to take what was put in it" (12:6). The corrupting power of bad example can be seen in the effect that Judas' words had on those who stood near. Some of the disciples, whose hearts certainly were not evil, also began to look askance at Mary's display of love and reverence, and to grow angry with her even to the extent of murmuring aloud: "To what purpose is this waste? (Matt. 26:8). Their complaint implied that Jesus was at fault for allowing the precious ointment to be lavished upon Him.

If Mary heard the disciples' criticism, she gave no sign, but remained, humble and silent, at our Lord's feet. As before, Jesus defended her, this time not against the well-meant complaint of her sister but against the malevolent slur of the vile traitor and those whom he had influenced: "Why do you trouble the woman? She has done me a good turn. For the poor you have always with you, but you do not always have me. For in pouring this ointment on my body, she has done it for my burial.[4] Amen I say to you, wherever in the

[2] *In Ioan.* tr. 50. 6: *PL* 35, 1760.
[3] "Vae tibi miser! bonus odor occidit te": *ibid.: PL* 35, 1761.
[4] Mary's anointing was a symbol of, and a prelude to, the final anointing of our Lord's body for burial.

whole world this gospel is preached, this also that she has done shall be told in memory of her."

What glowing praise and what a magnificent promise!

In St. Matthew (26:14–16) and St. Mark (14:10–11), the betrayal of our Lord by Judas follows hard upon Mary's anointing of His head and feet. There is indeed a frightening contrast between the two episodes—in one we see an angel of light, in the other a devil from the dark pit of hell; Mary portrays the innocence of a dove, while Judas displays the savagery of a tiger. The traitor had already begun to plan his unspeakable crime, but the anointing at Bethany and our Lord's gentle yet resolute attitude on that occasion brought matters to a head. Judas would wait a few days before putting his plot into effect; yet he had already resolved to commit the horrifying sacrilege. As St. Luke says (22:3), Satan had entered his heart, and would not leave him until he had hanged himself from a tree.

The Triumphal Entry Into Jerusalem
(Matt. 21:1–17; Mark 11:1–11; Luke 19:29–44; John 12:12–19)

Looking into the future and contemplating the Messianic era, the prophet Zacharias had exclaimed jubilantly (9:9), "Rejoice greatly, O daughter of Sion, shout for joy, O daughter of Jerusalem: behold thy King will come to thee, the just and the saviour. He is poor and riding upon an ass and upon a colt, the foal of an ass." [5]

Now the time had come for this prophecy to be fulfilled. Laying aside for a moment His customary reserve and aversion to adulation, our Lord prepared to enter gloriously and triumphantly the city of David, His father. He was going to present Himself as the Heir of the royal house of Juda, and to show Himself publicly and solemnly as the longed-for Messias.

Thus it was that, on the day after the banquet at Bethany, He made ready to return to Jerusalem. With Him went His disciples, and also, presumably, more than a few of those who had come to Bethany to see Him and had spent the night with their friends and relatives in the town. Most probably, the route which He followed is the same one which today goes up Mount Olivet, skirts the Carmelite convent, and descends the western slope. On reaching the Benedictine

---

[5] It should be noted that, in this prophecy, which St. Matthew quotes (21:4 f.), there is mention of only one animal and not two, since "an ass" and "the colt, the foal of an ass" are simply parallel expressions.

Sira Photo

*Palm Sunday procession leaving Bethphage, in the background, to ascend
to Mount Olivet and then to enter Jerusalem.*

convent, the road forks, and in the Byzantine period, the path to the
right was formed of steps cut into the rock, some of which are still
preserved on the property belonging to the Russian Orthodox
Church, near Gethsemani. This fork leads directly down into the
Valley of the Cedron. A tradition which apparently dates back no
further than the fourteenth century has fixed the site of the *Dominus
flevit,* the spot where our Lord wept over Jerusalem, about halfway
down this path. Yet it is difficult to see how Jesus could have
descended such a steep slope riding on the ass, particularly since in
those days the path was really a staircase cut into the side of the hill.
Consequently it is much more likely that He took the left fork of the
road, which passes by the so-called Tomb of the Prophets and
descends by a much gentler declivity into the valley.

It was probably when the party had walked a little more than a
quarter of a mile from Bethany that Jesus told two of His disciples
to go on to Bethphage and bring Him a colt upon which no one had
yet sat, as well as an ass which they would find tied there, no doubt
beside one of the houses of the village.[6]

[6] Mark (11:2, 4, 5, 7) and Luke (19:30, 33, 35) speak only of the colt, while

Bethphage ("house of figs") must have been a little village a short distance off the route which our Lord was following, between Bethany and the summit of Mount Olivet, and consequently in the vicinity, if not on the very site of, the small chapel built by the Franciscans about half a mile from Bethany. In 1876 the foundations of an ancient church were discovered here. This church could very well have been the one which Etheria saw when going "from Jerusalem to Lazarium" at the end of the fourth century,[7] or else the one which was later rebuilt by the Crusaders. Also discovered on this site was a cube of stone bearing half-effaced paintings, one of which referred to the episode at Bethphage, as well as a description which read in part, "Bethphage . . . cum asina ductus ad Hierosolimam."

Out of deference to their Master, the Apostles wished to caparison His mount, and having nothing better, used their cloaks for the purpose. Seated on this improvised saddle, our Lord rode up the eastern slope of Mount Olivet, accompanied by His party. As He rode, some of His followers threw their cloaks on the ground in front of Him, while others carpeted the road with leaves and branches as a sign of honor to the great Wonder-worker who had performed the astounding miracle of raising Lazarus from the dead.

Matthew (21:2, 7) mentions an ass also, an addition which must have been inspired by the passage from Zacharias; neither of the other two Synoptic authors quotes this passage. St. John does quote Zacharias' prophecy (12:15) but mentions only the colt (v. 14). There is a difficulty in Matthew 21:7: "And they brought the ass and the colt, laid their cloaks on them, and made him sit thereon": καὶ ἐπέθηκαν ἐπ' αὐτῶν τὰ ἱμάτια καὶ ἐπεκάθισεν ἐπάνω αὐτῶν. Various solutions to the difficulty have been proposed:

(1) If αὐτῶν refers in both places to the animals (as Allen believes), then the disciples laid their cloaks on the two asses and Jesus sat on both beasts.

(2) The first αὐτῶν refers to the animals and the second to the cloaks (Durand, Merk, Knabenbauer, Buzy, Bover), in which case Jesus mounted only one of the asses, the colt, and sat on the cloaks which the disciples had placed on its back.

(3) Some authors (e.g., B. Weiss, Lagrange, Joüon) change the first αὐτῶν to the singular, αὐτὸν, a reading which appears in one codex and a few versions and which eliminates the difficulty at the source: thus the disciples laid their cloaks on the colt, which Jesus then mounted. From an exegetical point of view this last interpretation is the most satisfactory of the three; but critically speaking, the reading αὐτὸν is less probable than αὐτῶν. At all events, both the second and the third explanations solve the problem satisfactorily.

This difficulty does not exist in the Hebrew text, for the particle wau, which the Vulgate translates as et, is not copulative here but explanatory (i.e., it means "that is to say"), so that there are not two different objects ("the ass and the colt") in question but only one ("the ass, that is to say, the colt"), expressed in two different ways.

[7] Cf. Baldi, *Enchiridion*, pp. 455 f.

Sira Photo

Palm Sunday procession near Gethsemani.

But this display of enthusiasm was as nothing to that which occurred when the procession crossed the brow of the hill and began to descend the other side. This side of Mount Olivet was covered with the tents of the pilgrims who had come for the Passover. Many of the visitors were Galileans who knew of Jesus, and all of them had heard about the miracle at Bethany, so that when they saw the procession and found that the great Prophet was being escorted triumphantly to Jerusalem, they, too, cut branches from the palm and olive trees and went to meet Him, waving the branches in the air. Then all who were there, those who went before our Lord and those who followed behind Him, burst into a hymn of jubilation: "Hosanna [8] to the Son of David! Blessed is he who comes in the name of the Lord! Hosanna in the highest!"

What a stirring spectacle our Lord's exultant approach to Jeru-

[8] This is a Hebrew word, *hôshi'ah   na'* (cf. Ps. 117:25) meaning "Save, we beseech thee!" (cf. Ps. 19:10: "Yahweh, save [hôshi'ah] the king.") Therefore it was originally a formula of supplication, but in time it came to be a cry of praise and was used as an interjection in somewhat the same way as our "Hurrah!" As St. Augustine says: "Vox autem obsecrantis est, hosanna, sicut nonnulli dicunt qui hebraicam linguam noverunt magis affectum indicans quam rem aliquam significans, sicut sunt in lingua latina quas interiectiones vocant" (*In Ioan.* tr. 51: *PL* 35, 1764 *f.*). In the *Journal of Biblical Literature,* 65 (1946), 91–122, there is an article entitled "Hosanna in the Gospels," which reviews the numerous interpretations of the word that have been proposed.

salem must have been! And yet, in the midst of all the acclamation, Jesus wept! "When he drew near and saw the city, he wept over it."

Looking down sadly at the city that was going to kill Him, its God, He allowed the pain He felt to find expression in words: "If thou hadst known, in this thy day, even thou, the things that are for thy peace! But now they are hidden from thy eyes. For days will come upon thee when thy enemies will throw up a rampart about thee, and surround thee and shut thee in on every side, and will dash thee to the ground and thy children within thee, and will not leave in thee one stone upon another, because thou hast not known the time of thy visitation."

A fearful prophecy, indeed, and one which must have torn at our Lord's Sacred Heart as He pronounced it.

As the procession approached, the whole city was stirred by the unusual sight, and many of those who saw it, probably strangers from among the Diaspora, asked: "Who is this?"

Their question was answered most likely by the Galileans in the crowd, since they were our Lord's closest neighbors: "This is Jesus the prophet from Nazareth of Galilee."

But as usual, not all shared the general enthusiasm. The upsurge of feeling in favor of Jesus which had resulted from the raising of Lazarus had already so angered the Pharisees that they had resolved to kill the young Man. And this fresh acclamation must have made them boil with new rage, so that some of them, unable to contain themselves any longer, demanded sharply of Christ: "Master, rebuke thy disciples."

But He replied firmly: "I tell you that if these keep silence, the stones will cry out."

Again, when He had entered the Temple, the children began to shout: "Hosanna to the Son of David."

Further goaded by this new ovation, the chief priests and Scribes asked Him indignantly: "Dost thou hear what these are saying?"

"Yes; have you never read, 'Out of the mouth of infants and sucklings thou hast perfected praise'?" [9]

Finally, seething with impotent rage, the Pharisees said to each other: "Do you see that we avail nothing? Behold, the entire world has gone after him!"

[9] Psalm 8:2.

We do not know if Jesus preached in the Temple that day: the evangelists give us no information on the point. It is possible that, seeing how excited the people were, He judged that they were not then properly disposed to listen quietly and calmly to a spiritual discourse. But on the other hand, the crowd which had accompanied Him into the city must have been eager to hear Him preach in the Temple, and so He might well have taken advantage of their good will and satisfied their laudable desire. It is because of this uncertainty that we are unable to say definitely whether the triumphal entry into Jerusalem took place in the morning, as would seem most likely, or in the evening, as St. Mark appears to indicate (11:11) when he says that our Lord entered the Temple, "and when he had looked round upon all things, then, as it was already late, he went out to Bethany with the Twelve."

It is, however, a solid probability that the cleansing of the Temple did not take place on the same day as the entry into the city, as St. Matthew and St. Luke seem to imply, but on the following day, as St. Mark explicitly tells us.

The Barren Fig Tree
(Matt. 21:18–22; Mark 11:12–14; 20–26)

Our Lord spent that night in Bethany, presumably at the house of Lazarus and his two sisters, and on the following morning, Monday, He returned to the Temple with His disciples, most likely by the same route they had taken the day before.

It is very possible that, before leaving Bethany in the early morning, Jesus had not been hungry and had left without breaking His fast. But once on the road and walking in the invigorating morning air, He regained His appetite and felt the pangs of hunger. In Palestine it is a recognized custom that a wayfarer, when passing by a vineyard or an orchard of fig trees, may take a bunch of grapes or a handful of figs, provided he eats them there and then (cf. Deut. 23:24 f.). Today there are only a few fig trees to be seen along the road from Bethany to Jerusalem, but in our Lord's day there must have been many of them, if we are to judge by the name of the village, Bethphage ("house of figs"), which the party had to pass.

A short distance from the road along which Jesus and His disciples were walking, there stood a green, thick-foliaged fig tree such as one can see in the valley of Siloe, the site of the ancient gardens of the king. Turning aside for a moment, our Lord approached the tree to pick some of its fruit. It is true that, as St. Mark points out, it was not the season for figs; but the tree had such abundant foliage and, since the time was the beginning of April when early figs appear, it was possible that the tree might offer some fruit which, though still green, could yet be eaten. On nearing the tree and seeing that it bore no fruit, but only an abundance of beautiful leaves, Jesus cursed it, saying: "May no one ever eat fruit of thee henceforward forever."

Obviously our Lord's principal aim in this episode was not so much to satisfy His hunger as to give His disciples a lesson by means of what we may call a parable in action. He wished to show that the Jews, with their multitude of purely external practices, lacked good works and were therefore rejected; and, in a wider and more general sense, He wanted to point out that we must strive to acquire solid virtues and not be content with the mere appearance of holiness. However, this lesson, which, according to the Fathers, is contained implicitly in the episode, does not take away from the likelihood that Jesus actually was hungry and went to the tree to get something to eat. Some people may object, first, that, as St. Mark points out, "it was not the season for figs," and second, that our Lord knew beforehand that there was no fruit on the tree. To the first objection we reply that, as we have already noted, although it was not properly speaking the time for figs, there was a probability that there were some early ones on the tree, still green, of course, but edible nevertheless. To the second objection we answer that our Lord did not always use His infused knowledge, but sometimes acted on His experimental knowledge alone.

The Cleansing of the Temple
(Matt. 21:12–13; Mark 11:15–19; Luke 19:45–48)

Our Lord's prompt and resolute action in casting the vendors and money-changers out of the Temple at the beginning of His public life (cf. John 2:13–16) had temporarily suppressed the sacrilegious abuse of God's house. But the profaners had returned again, so that when He came to the Temple on this occasion, He found the Court of the Gentiles converted into a huge, clamorous market where victims for the sacrifices, lambs, oxen and doves, were being bought and sold.

To add to the din and confusion, the money-changers had also set up their tables once more and were doing a thriving business in exchanging half-shekels for didrachmas.

For the second time Jesus was fired with holy anger and zeal for the house of His Father, which was being profaned. Without regard for the priests who had authorized the abuse, no doubt for the sake of personal profit, He drove out the merchants and their customers, proclaiming with divine authority as He did so: "It is written, 'My house shall be called a house of prayer'; but you have made it a den of thieves."

The chief priests who were present raged inwardly, but did not dare hinder Jesus because they were cowed by His resolute air of authority, and perhaps also because they were conscious of their guilt in permitting the abuse. Hence they remained silent for the moment, biding their time for revenge.

Is the cleansing of the Temple which St. John describes at the beginning of his Gospel (2:13 *ff.*) the same as the one recorded by the Synoptic authors towards the end of their narratives (Matt. 21:12 *f.*; Mark 11:15–19; Luke 19:45–48)? In other words, were there two cleansings, or only one? The problem is an ancient one, and has not yet been satisfactorily solved. The great majority of Protestant and a good number of Catholic authors, e.g., Calmes, Lagrange, Braun and Buzy, admit only one cleansing, which they commonly place at the beginning of our Lord's public life, as St. John does in his Gospel. But most Catholic exegetes, among them Belser, Tillmann, Knabenbauer, Dausch, Prat, Durand, Simón-Dorado and Gomá, as well as some Protestants, such as Zahn, Godet and Plummer, hold that there were two, one at the beginning and the other towards the end of the public life. The general similarity between the episodes favors their identity, but the differences in detail seem to point to a distinction between them. The similarity is easily explained, because both St. John and the Synoptic authors are describing how Jesus drove vendors from the Temple. The differences, however, are another matter. As Durand correctly remarks, there are sufficient divergences here to discredit the hypothesis of only one cleansing.[10] The Protestant author, Plummer, puts the case more strongly when he says: "That this is a second cleansing, and not identical with John ii, 14–22, may be regarded as

[10] Cf. *Évangile selon S. Jean* (Paris, 1927), p. 541.

reasonably certain." And he adds: "What is gained by the identification, which involves a gross chronological blunder on the part of either John, who places it [the cleansing] at the beginning of Christ's ministry, or of the others, who place it at the very end?" [11] The numerous reasons advanced by Buzy in his commentary on St. Matthew's Gospel [12] and by Braun [13] are far from convincing.

From Death to Life
(John 12:20–36)

Our Lord remained all day in the Temple, and it was probably late in the evening when some Greeks who wished to be presented to Him approached Philip and said politely: "Sir, we wish to see Jesus."

These strangers (we do not know their number) were either proselytes or God-fearing Gentiles who, like the centurion at Capharnaum (cf. Luke 7:2 *ff.*) and the other centurion, Cornelius (cf. Acts 10:1 *ff.*), were sympathetic towards the Jewish religion without embracing it, and came up to the great feasts out of devotion. Perhaps they approached Philip because he was the first one of the Apostles they met. Philip went and told Andrew, and both of them informed Jesus of the strangers' request. It may well have been that the newcomers wished to receive some instruction, but it is also probable that their wish to meet Christ was inspired by devout and, on the whole, legitimate curiosity.

We do not know what reply Jesus made to their request, but at all events the brief discourse which He delivered on this occasion was well suited to teach them the true character of the Messias, the nature of His mission, and the rewards reserved for those who resolved to follow Him. As He spoke, our Lord revealed the inmost feelings of His heart and painted a moving word-picture in which light alternated with shadow, life with death, and humiliation with glory: "The hour has come for the Son of Man to be glorified"—the hour which Jesus always had before Him and of which He had spoken earlier (cf. John 7:6, 30; 8:20), a time of suffering and triumph, the one being, as it were, the condition for the other. Therefore He added: "Amen, amen, I say to you, unless the grain of wheat fall into the

---

[11] Alfred Plummer, *A Critical and Exegetical Commentary on the Gospel According to St. Luke,* p. 453.
[12] p. 273.
[13] *RB* (1929), pp. 178–200.

ground and die, it remains alone. But if it die, it brings forth much fruit."

Then, so that His listeners would understand that this applied not only to Himself but to everyone, He added: "He who loves his life, loses it, and he who hates his life in this world, keeps it unto life everlasting."

Therefore, in order to live, man has to die; he has to pass through death to life. These were hard words, and the disciples had already heard their Master say them more than once.[14] Yet they pointed out the only path for the true follower of Christ. He was repeating them again on this occasion, but now He concluded by showing clearly the glory reserved for those who are faithful in His service: "If anyone serve me, let him follow me; and where I am there also shall my servant be. If anyone serve me, my Father will honor him."

The road may be arduous, but it leads to glory, to the joy of being with Christ and honored by the Father.

Our Lord's fast-approaching death now rose before His eyes in all the horror of its sufferings and humiliations. Although He was God, He was also true man, and His heart contracted at the sight. As He stood speaking in the Temple, He had a sudden foretaste of the agony He would endure in Gethsemani: "Now my soul is troubled. And what shall I say? Father, save me from this hour!"

Later, in Gethsemani, He was to utter a very similar cry: "Let this cup pass away from me." But here, as in the garden ("Yet not as I will, but as thou willest"), He immediately added His complete acceptance of His Father's will: "No, this is why I came to this hour," —that is, to meet death. "Father, glorify thy name!"; obtain through My death the glory that is Thy due!

The anguish that Jesus felt here was a forerunner of the agonies of the Passion.

Then a voice from heaven was heard saying: "I have both glorified it [i.e., My name], and I will glorify it again!"

The crowds were troubled and puzzled by the sound, some think-

---

[14] Matthew 16:25; Mark 8:35; Luke 9:23 f.; cf. Matthew 10:39, and Luke 17:33.
This sentence from St. John is very similar to the words of our Lord reported by the Synoptic writers: "For what does it profit a man, if he gain the whole world, but suffer the loss of his own soul? Or what will a man give in exchange for his soul?" (Matt. 16:26; Mark 8:36; Luke 9:25). See above, p. 441, note 16, for the decree of the Biblical Commission concerning the true interpretation of this passage.

ing that it was thunder, while others believed that it was the voice of an angel. Calming their fears, Jesus said: "Not for me did this voice come, but for you."

Our Lord Himself had no need of this assurance by the Father. Then, looking into the future, He described how, by His own death, He would destroy death on men's behalf [15] and call them to life; how the prince of the world would be conquered and his empire destroyed; how from the ends of the earth, generation after generation would flee to the summit of Calvary to take refuge in the shadow of the cross. And as He spoke, He heard the far-off sound of the millions of voices which, down through the centuries, would sing victoriously: "*O Crux, ave spes unica:* Hail, O Cross, our only hope!"

Foreseeing all this, He cried out in stirring tones: "Now is the judgment of the world; now will the prince of the world be cast out. And I, if I be lifted up from the earth, will draw all things to myself."

The Jews were aware that Jesus called Himself "the Son of Man" and that He was speaking of His own death. But they also knew from the writings of their prophets that once the Messias came He would remain forever. Therefore our Lord's words seemed mysterious to them. They could not see the connection between the glorious Messias and the Son of Man who would suffer death. Hence they were puzzled and asked: [16] "We have heard from the Law that the Christ abides forever. And how canst thou say, 'The Son of Man must be lifted up'? Who is this Son of Man?"

Jesus did not deem it opportune to answer their questions, which were inspired by ignorance rather than by bad faith. Instead, He contented Himself with exhorting them to take advantage of the light, which was none other than Himself, for the short time He would remain among them. By following this light and acting according to it, they would come to be "sons of light" (John 12:36): "While you have the light, believe in the light, that you may become sons of light."

With this exhortation He closed His discourse: "These things Jesus spoke, and he went away and hid himself from them."

---

[15] "O death, I will be thy death; O hell, I will be thy bite" (Osee 13:14).

[16] Maldonatus (*in loc.*) was of the opinion that "after the phrase 'And I, if I be lifted up from the earth, will draw all things to myself,' Jesus added the words which He had already said in John 3:14, 'And as Moses lifted up the serpent in the desert, even so must the Son of Man be lifted up.'" That is possibly true, but we see no need to have recourse to such an hypothesis.

The Incredulity of the Jews [17]

Our Lord's mission was drawing to a close. Throughout His public ministry, He had been the Light sent by the Father to enlighten men and dissipate the shadows of death in which they lay. Therefore, as we come to speak about the end of His life, we feel compelled to ask what had been the effect of the light He had shed on men. Had they allowed themselves to be illumined by it?

St. John sadly provides the answer: "Now though he had worked so many signs in their presence, they did not believe in him" (12:37). Of course, even among the Jewish leaders themselves, there were exceptions to this general statement; for example, Nicodemus, Joseph of Arimathea, and others. But even these upright men had not had the courage to confess their faith openly: "because of the Pharisees they did not acknowledge it, lest they should be put out of the synagogue. For they loved the glory of men more than the glory of God" (v. 42 f.).

The whole history, even the very existence, of the Jewish people was pointed towards the Messias; the nation concentrated all its hopes and longings on Him; and yet, when at length the ardently-desired and ever-invoked Messias did come, the Jews rejected and refused to acknowledge Him. Century upon century was to pass after His coming and still this stiff-necked, rebellious people would continue to cry out: "We do not wish this man to be king over us."

This is truly a strange phenomenon; yet, on the whole, it is not difficult to guess at some of the causes leading up to it. The proud doctors of the Law, respected and regarded as teachers by the people, could not bring themselves to bow before a young man who had never studied in their schools and who came from the insignificant, despised little village of Nazareth in the uncultured province of Galilee. And it was this pride of theirs that blinded their eyes to the light. Imprisoned as they were in an intricate, stifling system of external observances, the Pharisees could not appreciate the young Rabbi's teaching on purity of heart and the worship of God "in spirit and in truth." But even more than all this, the difference between our Lord's concept of the Messias and that held by the Jews opened a wide gulf between Him and them. How could they accept the humble Artisan

[17] Cf. A. Charue, *L'incrédulité des Juifs dans le Nouveau Testament* (Gembloux, 1929).

from Nazareth, with His purely spiritual doctrine, as the national hero, the glorious conqueror who was to break the foreign yoke and regain for his people the primacy over all other nations? It must be confessed that although these prejudices, passions and false ideas raised lofty barriers against the new Messianic teaching, they were apparently justified to some extent by the descriptions left by the ancient prophets. But the Jews were not relieved of responsibility on that account. Our Lord's miracles were so plain to be seen, His teaching so clear, His reasoning so convincing, and His method of exposition so persuasive, that no soul of good will could fail to be moved to acknowledge His divine mission.

Such was the innate strength of our Lord's testimony to Himself that St. John (12:38), leaving aside the immediate and obvious reasons for the Jews' blindness and hardness of heart, goes seeking for another more hidden and more universal reason, and finds it in the prophecy of Isaias: "Lord, who has believed our report, and to whom has the arm of the Lord been revealed?" Therefore, we should not be surprised, much less scandalized, by the Jews' persistence in their unbelief, for it was foretold in the Old Testament and was destined to come about. The prophet Isaias went even further and pointed out the reason why the Chosen People did not accept the Messianic message (John 12:39): "This is why they could not believe, because Isaias said again, 'He has blinded their eyes, and hardened their hearts; lest they see with their eyes, and understand with their mind, and be converted, and I heal them.' " These are harsh words, and seem, at first glance, to represent God as being the positive cause of the Jews' obstinacy. But, as we have pointed out before, in accordance with Semitic ideas and the genius of the Hebrew tongue, the words simply mean that God *permitted* the obstinacy of the Jews: that is to say, for just reasons, perhaps in punishment for past infidelities, He refused to grant them those graces without which it was extremely difficult for them to receive our Lord's message humbly and obediently. That is why St. John says that "they *could not* believe."

What object did God have in permitting this to come to pass? In other words, what part did the defection of Israel play in the divine plans, in the designs of Providence? The evangelist does not answer this question for us, but St. Paul does, in his Epistle to the Romans. God, foreseeing in His infinite wisdom the resistance of the people to whom He had chosen to impart the Messianic message, brought this same resistance within the ambit of His plans for the redemption of the world, making it work towards the greater good of the Gentile nations. The Apostle expresses this doctrine vigorously: "By their offense salvation has come to the Gentiles, that they may be jealous of them. . . . Their offense is the riches of the world, and their decline the riches of the Gentiles. . . . The rejection of them is the reconciliation of the world. . . ." (Rom. 11:11, 12, 15). Thus in the plan of Divine Providence, the defection of Israel redounded to the benefit of the Gentile world. And in its turn, this advantage of the Gentiles will one day contribute to the conversion of the Jews: "Now if their offense is the riches of the world . . . how much more their full number!" (Rom. 11:12). That is the final solution of the formidable problem presented by the spectacle of a people who rejected and cursed the Messias for whom they had longed with all their strength for so many centuries.

It would take too long to describe all the shades of opinion held by modern Jews regarding Messianism. We shall, therefore, confine ourselves to examining their views on the Person of Jesus. Joseph Klausner, professor of exegesis at the Hebrew University in Jerusalem, can be taken as a reliable exponent of liberal Jewish thought. He ends his book, *Jesus of Nazareth,* with a chapter entitled, "What is Jesus to the Jews?" in which he says:

> From the standpoint of general humanity he is, indeed, "a light to the Gentiles." . . . But from the *national Hebrew* standpoint it is more difficult to appraise the value of Jesus. . . . There was in him something out of which arose "non-Judaism." . . . To the Jewish nation he can be neither God nor the Son of God. . . . Neither can he, to the Jewish nation, be the Messiah: the kingdom of heaven (the "Days of the Messiah") is not yet come. . . . But Jesus is, for the Jewish nation, *a great teacher of morality and an artist in parable.* . . . In his ethical code there is a sublimity, distinctiveness and originality in form unparalleled in any other Hebrew ethical code. . . .[18]

Among present-day Jews in several countries, there seems to be a movement towards acknowledging Jesus as the Messias, but always apart from the Catholic Church.[19]

[18] Joseph Klausner, *Jesus of Nazareth,* trans. by H. Danby (New York: The Macmillan Company, 1926), pp. 413 *f.*
[19] *The Catholic Biblical Quarterly,* 14 (1952), 72.

Last Teachings of Our Lord

The Tuesday after the triumphal entry into Jerusalem was the last day on which the Light that came into the world to enlighten men was to shine in the Temple. But unfortunately, instead of taking advantage of these last rays as Jesus had advised them to do the day before, the Jews only closed their eyes and hardened their hearts the more.

This last day was one of intense activity. All the parties of any importance in Jerusalem gathered their forces to launch a final attack on the hated Prophet from Nazareth; and He who is so gentle with sinners and men of good will, flashed forth the thunderbolts of His holy anger against His malevolent and hypocritical enemies, unmasking them before the people without fear of their vengeance, which He knew would encompass His death.

The Efficacy of Faith
(Matt. 21:20–22; Mark 11:20–26)

On Tuesday morning Jesus returned from Bethany to Jerusalem by the same route as the day before. As they passed the fig tree which He had cursed the previous day, the disciples marvelled at seeing it withered to the roots, and Peter exclaimed: "Rabbi, behold, the fig tree that thou didst curse is withered up."

St. Matthew's account gives the impression that the withering of the tree and the Apostles' amazement occurred immediately after the curse was pronounced. But as we have said, the first evangelist departs more than once from the proper chronological order and concentrates on the substance of an event or discourse without regard for circumstances of time and place.

Jesus did not reply directly to Peter's remark. Instead, using the incident of the fig tree as a starting point, He spoke in praise of faith, and stressed its infallible efficacy. It is most likely that, to illustrate His point, He gestured towards Mount Olivet, at the foot of which they were standing, as He said to the disciples: "Have faith in God. Amen I say to you, if you have faith and do not waver, not only will you do what I have done to the fig tree, but even if you shall say to this mountain, 'Arise, and hurl thyself into the sea,' it shall be done. Therefore I say to you, all things whatever you ask for in prayer, believe that you shall receive, and they shall come to you. And when you stand up to pray, forgive whatever you have against anyone, that your Father in heaven may also forgive you your offenses."

These last words are an echo of the Our Father. In order that faith may be efficacious it must be accompanied by love, by charity, which is shown especially in the forgiveness of injuries.

The Baptism of John
(Matt. 21:23–27; Mark 11:27–33; Luke 20:1–8)

When Jesus arrived at the Temple, He probably found people waiting there for Him, for St. Luke (21:38) tells us that "all the people came to him early in the morning in the temple, to hear him."

He was teaching in one of the porches, walking to and fro (cf. Mark 11:27), surrounded by the crowd which had gathered about Him the moment they espied Him, when a group of chief priests, Scribes and elders advanced resolutely and challenged Him: "By what authority dost thou these things? . . . Who gave thee this authority to do these things?"

They were referring to the expulsion of the profaners from the Temple on the previous day.[20] The crowd waited in suspense for His reply. The chiefs of the Temple were confident of victory because they knew that they alone could give such authority. But their attack did not disconcert Jesus, who said to them calmly, almost indifferently: "I also will ask you one question, and answer me; then I will tell you by what authority I do these things. Was the baptism of John from heaven or from men? Answer me."

In silence He awaited their reply while the bystanders looked expectantly from Him to His adversaries and back again, perhaps showing that they were on His side. The priests and Scribes were taken aback at His question, and found themselves on the horns of a dilemma. "They began to argue among themselves, saying, 'if we say, 'From heaven,' he will say, 'Why then did you not believe him?' But if we say, 'From men'—they feared the people; for all regarded John as really a prophet." Unable to think of anything better to say, they answered lamely: "We do not know."

---

[20] Some authors take these words to refer to our Lord's teaching in the Temple, but we regard this interpretation as less probable than the one we have given, for Jesus had often taught publicly there, and yet it had not occurred to His enemies to take Him to task for doing so.

Firmly Christ cut short the discussion: "Neither do I tell you by what authority I do these things."

We can readily imagine the confusion of the Sanhedrists, compelled to accept this devastating retort and to bear without a murmur the ill-concealed derision of the crowd.

The Parables of Reprobation

But even then our Lord did not allow His defeated enemies to depart without a stern warning, which He cast in the form of three parables that have most fittingly come to be called "the parables of reprobation" since they refer to the lot of the Jewish people, who, by their obstinate resistance to the light and the divine call, put themselves on a lower level than the Gentiles whom they so despised.

THE TWO SONS
(Matt. 21:28–32)

"A man had two sons; and he came to the first and said, 'Son, go and work today in my vineyard.' But he answered and said, 'I will not'; but afterwards he regretted it and went. And he came to the other and spoke in the same manner. And this one answered, 'I go, sir'; but he did not go. Which of the two did the father's will?"

The answer was not difficult, and the chief priests and elders replied unhesitatingly: "The first."

Applying the parable, Jesus continued: "Amen I say to you, the publicans and harlots are entering the kingdom of God before you. For John came to you in the way of justice, and you did not believe him. But the publicans and the harlots believed him; whereas you, seeing it, did not even repent afterwards, that you might believe him."

The Sanhedrists could say nothing to defend themselves, for they knew only too well that they had not accepted John the Baptist's testimony, while many poor sinners had been converted by his preaching and had repented of their sins.

THE VINE-DRESSERS
(Matt. 21:33–46; Mark 12:1–12; Luke 20:9–19)

As if He wished to give His adversaries no respite, Jesus immediately related another parable, drawn this time from the agricultural customs of Palestine: "There was a man, a householder, who planted a vineyard, and put a hedge about it, and dug a wine vat in it, and built a tower; then he let it out to vine-dressers, and went abroad. But when the fruit season drew near, he sent his servants to the vine-dressers to receive his fruits. And the vine-dressers seized his servants, and beat one, killed another, and stoned another. Again he sent another party of servants more numerous than the first; and they did the same to these. Finally he sent his son to them, saying, 'They will respect my son.'

"But the vine-dressers, on seeing the son, said among themselves, 'This is the heir; come, let us kill him, and we shall have his inheritance.' So they seized him, cast him out of the vineyard, and killed him."

The vine-dressers' crime was an appalling one, and Jesus, sure of His listeners' answer, put the case to them: "When, therefore, the owner of the vineyard comes, what will he do to those vine-dressers?"

Unhesitatingly they answered: "He will utterly destroy those evil men, and will let out the vineyard to other vine-dressers, who will render to him the fruits in their seasons."

No other verdict was possible, but some of His listeners, moved by misguided compassion, or perhaps because they saw the implications of the parable, cried out: "By no means."

But Jesus, transfixing them with a piercing glance, said to them: "What then is this that is written, 'The stone which the builders rejected, has become the corner stone'?"

The quotation is from Psalm 117:22. The rejected stone is the murdered Son, who shall come to be the Cornerstone, the Foundation of the society which is to be formed of the new vine-dressers to whom the vineyard shall be given. Our Lord's quotation from the psalm was an apt one, prompted as it was by the reaction of those listeners who had exclaimed: "By no means." Appropriate too were His next words: "Therefore I say to you, that the kingdom of God will be taken away from you and will be given to a people yielding its fruits."

It is only just that those who reject the Stone, i.e., the Son, should be rejected in their turn, and that their place should be taken by those who form part of the building which has the Son as its Cornerstone. Then, to show the strength and sovereign power of that Son whom the vine-dressers killed, our Lord continued the allegory, concluding with the terrible words: "And he who falls on this stone will be

Sira Photo

Watch-tower of a type common in Palestine, used to guard the vineyards and fields. This one stands in the neighborhood of Ephrem.

broken to pieces; but upon whomever it falls, it will grind him to powder." [21]

The Sanhedrists knew full well that in speaking about the vine-dressers and the builders who rejected the cornerstone, Jesus was referring to them. His allusion was clear, for the parable of the vine-dressers was a faithful picture of the history of the Israelites and of the unhappy fate which awaited them because of their resistance to grace and their perverse obstinacy. No wonder, then, that they would have liked to seize Him forthwith and place Him under arrest; but they feared the people, who made no secret of their esteem for Him

---

[21] As is obvious, we need not hold, as Buzy does (*S. Matt.*, p. 287), that verse 43 is completely separate from verses 42 and 44, and that it ought to follow immediately upon verse 41.

and who regarded Him as a true Prophet. Therefore they thought it more expedient to withdraw for the moment, and so, "leaving him, they went their way" (Mark 12:12).

THE MARRIAGE FEAST
(Matt. 22:1–14)

The third parable which our Lord related also concerned the rejection of the Jews: "The kingdom of heaven is like a king who made a marriage feast for his son. And he sent his servants to call in those invited to the marriage feast, but they would not come. Again he sent out other servants, saying, 'Tell those who are invited, Behold, I have prepared my dinner; my oxen and fatlings are killed, and everything is ready; come to the marriage feast.' But they made light of it, and went off, one to his farm, and another to his business; and the rest laid hold of his servants, treated them shamefully, and killed them.

"But when the king heard of it, he was angry; and he sent his armies, destroyed those murderers, and burnt their city. Then he said to his servants, 'The marriage feast indeed is ready, but those who were invited were not worthy; go therefore to the crossroads, and invite to the marriage feast whomever you shall find.' And his servants went out into the roads, and gathered all whom they found, both good and bad; and the marriage feast was filled with guests.

"Now the king went in to see the guests, and he saw there a man who had not on a wedding garment. And he said to him, 'Friend, how didst thou come in here without a wedding garment?' But he was speechless. Then the king said to the attendants, 'Bind his hands and feet and cast him forth into the darkness outside, where there will be the weeping, and the gnashing of teeth.' For many are called, but few are chosen."

The meaning of the parable is clear. The Jews had refused the invitation, and had even killed many messengers sent by the great king, God, with the result that the Gentiles were invited and admitted to the feast in their place. But among the Gentiles, too, there was one who was blameworthy, because he had not presented himself with the proper dispositions. Thus the parable of the wedding feast is a perfect unit and is basically analogous to that of the vine-dressers.

There are some authors who deny the unity of this narrative and hold that it is really a combination of three parables that were originally distinct from each other but later amalgamated, either by oral tradition or by the evangelist himself. Buzy, among others, accepts and defends this theory, and divides the parable as follows: (1) the wedding feast, or the unwilling guests—verses 2–5, 8–10; (2) the murderous guests—verses 6–7; (3) the wedding garment—verses 11–13. He holds that verse 14: "For many are called, but few are chosen," is an appendix originally unconnected with any of the three sections.[22] Thus the parable of the wedding feast is composed of four elements, originally independent of each other, but later simply placed one after the other to form the narrative as we know it.

On the supposition that all these elements are authentic, that is, that the evangelist reports them as they came from our Lord Himself, changing only the chronological and topographical context, the evolution of the parable is perfectly compatible with inspiration. As we have seen, the evangelists, St. Matthew in particular, do not always place the sayings and doings of our Lord in their proper context of time and place. But if we are to regard the proposed amalgamation of elements as scientifically well-founded, we shall need to have better evidence than the mere probability that it happened as a literary process. The arguments taken from the lack of cohesion in the parable do not seem sufficient;[23] nor do we think it probable that the evangelist or the ancient catechists practiced such complicated manipulations of their basic material.

Certainly it is odd that the punishing of the first guests should be recounted before we are told of the second group's being invited. However, we should not forget that the very nature of parables allows the insertion of unlikely details, provided that they help to emphasize the doctrine that is being taught.

The mention of the murderous guests in verses 6 and 7, far from impeding the development of the parable, forms, in its context, a perfectly harmonious part of the whole, since it shows the guests' varying degrees of guilt, ranging all the way from mere discourtesy to

---

[22] *Les Paraboles*, pp. 329–344; *RB* (1932), pp. 30–49, "Y a-t-il fusion de paraboles évangéliques?": "Constatons, pour finir, que ce texte de Saint Matthieu nous offre le cas unique de trois paraboles groupées en une seule, dont chacune conserve sa physionomie particulière: *le festin de noces ou les invités recalcitrants, les invités homicides et la robe nuptiale*" (p. 43).

[23] This is not the place to enumerate and refute these arguments. They are readily available in the commentaries and in the special works on the parables.

cruelty and murder. Nor is there any discordant note in the king's entering the banquet hall after the guests had assembled and punishing the one who had had the insolence to attend in unsuitable garments (vv. 11–13). The long-winded discussions as to whether this particular guest had or had not to go without a wedding garment and the speculations as to how he could have procured one, would be perfectly in order if it were a question of an historical narrative, but there is no reason to introduce them when dealing with a parable. The same applies to other details which are really more or less unlikely but which have no importance in this literary form.

The last sentence of the parable, "For many are called, but few are chosen," does present some difficulty, and it has been interpreted in many different ways. If our Lord had only the Jews in mind, then those who responded to the divine invitation were much less in number than those who refused it. But if His words were general in application, we must take them as referring to the whole parable, and not only to the incident of the wedding garment. In that case, those who are "called" are all those "who were invited"; those who are "chosen" are those who accepted the invitation. However, there is no question here of being chosen for eternal happiness,[24] but rather of being selected for the kingdom of God on earth. Actually, those who, up to the present, have entered this kingdom, are in the minority. Perhaps "few" can be interpreted in the sense of "not all" (since many do not respond); or the whole sentence can be understood as a kind of proverb which is applied to the contents of the parable in a general way.[25]

This parable of the king's wedding feast is strikingly similar to that of the great supper in Luke 14:15–24, not only in basic content but also in form. Therefore it is only natural that the question of their identity with each other should have been raised. Numerous authors have definitely decided in favor of their identity,[26] but we take a more

---

[24] We do not think that Buzy's categorical assertion is justified: *"élus, choisis,* sans doute *sauvés"* (*Les Paraboles,* p. 342; *S. Matt.,* p. 296). As Knabenbauer correctly observes: "Vocati itaque ii sunt ad quos invitandos servi iterum mittuntur; electi autem qui invitationi obsequuntur et gratia Dei tracti et adiuti revera Ecclesiae nomen dant fidem suscipiunt" (*In Matt.,* II, 253).

[25] Lagrange says that: "On ne peut, sans violence, l'appliquer seulement à la première partie de la parabole. Il résume donc toute la situation" (*Év. selon S. Matt.,* p. 425). But it sums up the whole situation only vaguely, and therefore it may properly be regarded as referring solely to the wedding feast.

[26] Cf. Buzy, *Les Paraboles,* pp. 322–328; *S. Matt.,* pp. 292 f. As against the identity, see Bover, *Est. Bibl.* (1929), pp. 8–27. For the names of some of the

reserved view since we do not believe that such a conclusion is scientifically justified. We say "scientifically" because here we are concerned solely with strict literary criticism.

Each of the two parables fits perfectly into the historical context in which it appears. In Luke (14:15–24) the parable is occasioned by the exclamation of one of our Lord's fellow guests: "Blessed is he who shall feast in the kingdom of God" (v. 15), and it is therefore in full harmony with the context. In Matthew (22:1–14), it follows immediately upon that of the vine-dressers, and contains the same doctrine as the latter in a very similar form.[27] Therefore, it, too, fits perfectly into its context. And it must be noted that the circumstances of time and place in which each parable was narrated are altogether different.

Now, if on two different occasions our Lord thought it necessary to insist on the same doctrine (the resistance of the Jews or of men in general to the invitation to enter the kingdom of God), need we be surprised if He used the same image on both occasions? Do we not find preachers often doing the same thing? In brief, we do not absolutely deny that the two parables are the same, but we do assert that, at the present stage of our knowledge, there is not a sufficiently solid scientific basis for maintaining their identity.

The Pharisees Try to Entrap Jesus

Obviously, the proud Sanhedrists could not resign themselves to their humiliating defeat, which had been rendered all the more galling because they had suffered it in the presence of the people. They thirsted for revenge, but since hitherto their direct attacks had been turned back on themselves, they resorted to more devious methods.

TRIBUTE TO CAESAR

(Matt. 22:15–22; Mark 12:13–17; Luke 20:20–26)

It is not surprising to find that the Jews earnestly discussed the question of whether or not it was lawful to pay tribute to the Romans.

---

authors who uphold one or the other opinion, see Simón-Dorado, *Praelectiones Biblicae, Nov. Test.* I pp. 825 f.

[27] Knabenbauer: "Haec parabola est quaedam continuatio doctrinae in antecedenti traditae." Lagrange: "Cette parabole vient si bien après les autres qu'on ne s'étonne pas qu'elle leur soit jointe mais plutôt qu'elle en soit separée par 21, 45 s."

The Chosen Race were profoundly theocratic, and submitting to tribute seemed to them like an acknowledgment of Caesar's authority, with corresponding prejudice to God's sovereignty. In fact, Judas the Gaulanite openly declared that paying tribute was a kind of slavery —a recognition that the Romans, and not God, were lords over the Jews.[28]

The Pharisees therefore resolved to confront Jesus with this thorny problem, for they were confident that, no matter how He answered, they would catch Him in His words. If He denied the legality of the tribute, they would denounce Him to the Roman authorities as an enemy of the Empire. If, on the other hand, He maintained that the tribute was lawful, they would accuse Him of denying God's sovereignty, and would thereby arouse the people's anger against Him. The trap was well laid, and in imagination the wily Sanhedrists were already savoring the fruits of victory.

There is no doubt that the Pharisees were the principal instigators of the plots against Jesus, but because they did not want to show their hand, they employed the Herodians and some of their own disciples as instruments. As we have already seen, these Herodians were not a religious sect but rather a political party which favored the dynasty of the Herods, and although they and the Pharisees were traditional enemies, they had long since joined forces with them against Christ (cf. Mark 3:6).

The Pharisees therefore gave these intermediaries of theirs detailed instructions as to how they should approach Jesus, and then withdrew to await the outcome. With every appearance of humility and with protestations of esteem and respect, the Herodians and the disciples of the Pharisees came to our Lord and said to Him:

"Master, we know that thou art truthful, and that thou teachest the way of God in truth, and that thou carest naught for any man; for thou dost not regard the person of men."

Their motive in using this approach was to ingratiate themselves with Him and to give an ostensible reason for consulting Him. Then, with simulated innocence, they hurled their barbed question: "Is it lawful to give tribute to Caesar or not?" [29]

---

28 *Wars* ii. 8. 1; *Ant.* xviii. 1. 1.

29 The word "tribute" here is a generic term embracing all the various classes of tribute, while the expression "the coin of the tribute" seems to refer to the poll tax. The latter was a personal tax which everyone, slaves included, between the ages of fourteen and sixty-five for males, and twelve and sixty-five for fe-

Jesus could read their hearts, but even if He had not been God, their trap was so obvious that He would have guessed their intentions. Surveying them sternly, He demanded: "Why do you test me, you hypocrites? Show me the coin of the tribute."

When they saw that He was not going to refuse to answer them, they were inwardly jubilant, no doubt thinking to themselves: "He has fallen into the trap!" With suspicious alacrity, they gave Him a denarius. Taking it in His hand, He asked them: "Whose are this image and the inscription?"

Without suspecting where the question was leading, they replied: "Caesar's."

Then, in a tone of authority, He commanded: "Render, therefore, to Caesar the things that are Caesar's, and to God the things that are God's."

The Herodians were dumbfounded, for the prey which they had thought was securely in their grasp had sprung the trap and eluded them. And the Pharisees, who were watching near at hand, had no choice but to withdraw in confusion.

In His reply to His enemies' question, Jesus marked out the bounds of the two powers, civil and religious. Each has its own proper sphere of action, and must not be confused with the other. This is the principle that should guide true, Christian politics.

THE RESURRECTION OF THE BODY
(Matt. 22:23–33; Mark 12:18–27; Luke 20:27–39)

Just as they had incited the Herodians to waylay our Lord, the Pharisees very probably urged the Sadducees also to spread a net to catch Him.

These Sadducees were a politico-religious party, representative of the aristocracy, and holding themselves aloof from the common people, whereas the Pharisees were, as we would put it, more democratic, and enjoyed greater popularity. In political affairs, the Sadducees were conciliatory and cooperated fully with the Roman

---

males, had to pay to Caesar (cf. Schürer, I, 513). Our Lord probably asked for a denarius, because the silver denarius, the Roman monetary unit, always bore the image of the Emperor and the appropriate inscription. The image on the coin which the Herodians showed Jesus was that of Tiberius, or perhaps Augustus, his successor. Our Lord may also have asked for a denarius because it was the coin most commonly used at the time.

authorities. In religious matters, however, they flaunted their scepticism, rejected tradition, denied the immortality of the soul and hence did not believe in the resurrection of the body.[30] They chose this latter doctrine as the subject of their debate with Jesus, not so much in order to find a pretext for accusing Him as to place Him in a quandary and hold Him up to ridicule before the people.

The Jews had a law, the Levirate law (cf. Deut. 25:5 *ff*.), which decreed that when a married man died without having a son, his brother was bound to marry his widow. It was upon this ordinance that the Sadducees based the case which they pretended to present to Jesus for solution: "Master, Moses said, 'If a man die without having a son, his brother shall marry the widow and raise up issue to his brother.' Now there were among us seven brothers. And the first, after having married a wife, died, and having no issue, left his wife to his brother. In like manner the second, and the third down to the seventh. And last of all the woman also died. At the resurrection, therefore, of which of the seven will she be the wife? For they all had her."

With majestic dignity, Jesus replied: "You err because you know neither the Scriptures nor the power of God. For at the resurrection they will neither marry nor be given in marriage, but will be as angels of God in heaven."

Thus He showed that there was actually no problem at all. However, He was not content simply to silence them, but went on to refute their error directly: "But as to the resurrection of the dead, have you not read what was spoken to you by God, saying, 'I am the God of Abraham, and the God of Isaac, and the God of Jacob'? He is not the God of the dead, but of the living. You are therefore entirely wrong."

By saying that the patriarchs continued to live on beyond the grave, our Lord affirmed the immortality of the soul. In addition, He implicitly confirmed belief in the resurrection of the body. In point of fact, it is only reasonable to expect that those who have been friends of God in this world shall be restored to full life by having their souls reunited with their glorified bodies, for God owes it to Himself to reward His friends with a life of happiness which the two constituent elements of man, his body and his soul, can enjoy.

[30] Cf. *Ant.* xviii. 1. 4.

There were several Scribes in the group as well, and although they were no friends of our Lord's, they believed in the resurrection of the body, and were happy to see their adversaries refuted. Therefore they exclaimed aloud: "Master, thou hast done well."

And the people standing around echoed their enthusiasm at Jesus' wise reply.

THE GREATEST COMMANDMENT
(Matt. 22:34–40; Mark 12:28–34)

When Christ had silenced the Sadducees, the Pharisees, who had hitherto kept in the background, directing operations from behind the scenes, once more openly entered the lists.

In the ancient Synagogue there were 613 precepts, 248 of which were positive, and the remaining 365 negative. These precepts were also divided into two main classes, according as they were difficult or easy. The difficult precepts later came to be called the principal or great ones, and the others were known as secondary or minor. As one would expect, the rabbis held interminable discussions as to which precepts were principal ones and which were secondary. And not only that, but they graded the principal precepts in order of importance, and, of course, they could not agree as to which ones should be given priority over the others, or which single precept should be regarded as the most important of all.[31]

Now, the Pharisees decided to delegate one of their number, a man well versed in the Law and, consequently, very interested in the matter, to place before Jesus one of the disputed points regarding the precepts, namely, the question as to which of the commandments of the Law ought to be regarded as the first in importance. Not that they wanted to be instructed and enlightened by the Prophet of Nazareth, whom they hated. Their idea was to test Him, put Him in a difficult position, and thereby lower Him in the people's estimation. But it happened that the Scribe selected to propose the question was one of those who had witnessed the discussion between Jesus and the Sadducees; perhaps he had even been among those who, in a moment of enthusiasm, had applauded His reply on that occasion. Therefore, in his bearing he showed none of the malice which his fellows nursed in their hearts, but was, instead, truly deferential and respectful. Ap-

[31] Cf. Str.-Bill., I, 900–905.

proaching Jesus, he inquired: "Master, which is the great commandment in the Law?"

Quoting Deuteronomy 6:5, our Lord replied: "Thou shalt love
the Lord thy God with thy whole heart, and with thy whole soul, and
with thy whole mind."

These are among the first words of the *Shema'*, the prayer which
every Jew had to say twice a day.[32] Then quoting Leviticus 19:18,
He continued: "And the second is like it, 'Thou shalt love thy neighbor as thyself.' There is no other commandment greater than these."

The Scribe was completely satisfied and proclaimed his approval
aloud, as if to defend our Lord from further annoyance: "Well
answered, Master," he said. Then he went on to repeat the two great
commandments, adding that they were greater than all holocausts
and sacrifices. The Scribe's sincerity won for him Christ's praise and
the consoling declaration: "Thou art not far from the kingdom of
God."

One after the other, all the parties—Herodians, Sadducees, and
Pharisees—had crossed swords with Jesus, trying to force Him into
an untenable position and discredit Him before the people. But He
routed them all, so that from then on, no one dared to ask Him
malicious questions (cf. Mark 12:34).

The Messias, the Son of David

(Matt. 22:41–46; Mark 12:35–37; Luke 20:41–44)

Now that the Pharisees no longer ventured to interrogate Him,
Jesus took the offensive, and inquired of them: "What do you think
of the Christ? Whose son is he?"

The answer was easy: everyone knew that the prophets had foretold that the Messias would be a descendant of the house of David.
Therefore they replied unhesitatingly: "David's."

Then Jesus, quoting from Psalm 109, asked them: "How then
does David in the Spirit call him Lord, saying,

    'The Lord said to my Lord:
    Sit thou at my right hand,
        till I make thy enemies
           the footstool of thy feet'?

If David, therefore, calls him 'Lord,' how is he his son?"

[32] See above p. 501, n. 19.

The whole of Jewish tradition definitely held that it was David who was speaking in the psalm, and that the psalm itself was truly Messianic. Granting these two points, Christ's objection was apparently unanswerable, for if the Messias was David's son, He would have to be regarded as inferior to His father, and therefore it was inconceivable that the father would have called the son his Lord.

The key to the enigma lay in the fact that the Messias was something more than the son of David, that He belonged to a higher sphere than His earthly ancestor. As man, the Messias was David's son, but as God, He was his Lord. Jesus did not wish to reveal the solution to the Pharisees at that time, but left them to solve the problem for themselves. They, however, not knowing what to reply, were reduced to a humiliating silence, while the great crowd that had been following the discussions with growing curiosity, revelled in our Lord's arguments and victories.

Denunciation of the Scribes and Pharisees
(Matt. 23:1-19; Mark 12:38-40; Luke 20:45-47)

Confounded and humiliated, the enemies of Jesus—Sadducees, Scribes and Pharisees—withdrew,[33] once again resolved to avenge their defeat by resorting to violence, while the crowd, which was growing larger every moment, remained grouped about Jesus and the Apostles.

As our Lord was acutely aware, the eve of His death had arrived. He saw, down to the last evil detail, all the malice and hypocrisy of the unworthy teachers of Israel. In this His last hour, He wished to warn His listeners, and, through them, the whole Chosen Race, against the bad example they had been given, often under the cloak of religion, by those who should have been a light in Israel. In order that His words might sink more deeply into the hearts of those who heard them, He, the meek and humble Lamb of God, launched thundering anathemas against the perfidious and hypocritical doctors of the Law.

First, however, so that He would not seem to be inciting His

[33] Prat (*Jesus Christ,* II, 220) presupposes that the Pharisees were present during our Lord's condemnation of them. But with Lagrange (*The Gospel of Jesus Christ,* II, 149) and Willam (*Das Leben Jesu* [Freiburg i. B., 1933], p. 388), we believe that Matthew 23:1 indicates instead that they had left, as would seem most natural in the context.

audience to disobey and contemn religious authority, He drew a distinction between doctrine and conduct: "The Scribes and the Pharisees have sat on the chair of Moses. All things, therefore, that they command you, observe and do. But do not act according to their works; for they talk but do nothing."

Then He went on to unmask their vanity, hypocrisy, pride and ambition, pointing out that they did all their good works to be seen by men, that they widened their phylacteries and enlarged their tassels, that they sought the first places at banquets and in the synagogues, and loved to be honored by being called "Rabbi."

Next, He exhorted His listeners to practice humility: "He who is greatest among you shall be your servant."

And He concluded His warning and advice to the people by saying: "Whoever exalts himself shall be humbled, and whoever humbles himself shall be exalted."

As if the thought of sincere, self-effacing humility summoned up before His mind the contrasting image of the Pharisees' diabolical, scheming pride, Jesus launched against them His terrible "Woes!": "But woe to you, Scribes and Pharisees, hypocrites! because you shut the kingdom of heaven against men. For you yourselves do not go in, nor do you allow those going in to enter.

"Woe to you, Scribes and Pharisees, hypocrites! because you devour the houses of widows, praying long prayers. For this you shall receive a greater judgment.

"Woe to you, Scribes and Pharisees, hypocrites! because you traverse sea and land to make one convert; and when he has become one, you make him twofold more a son of hell than yourselves.

"Woe to you, blind guides, who say, 'Whoever swears by the temple, it is nothing; but whoever swears by the gold of the temple, he is bound.'

"Woe to you, Scribes and Pharisees, hypocrites! because you pay tithes on mint and anise and cummin, and have left undone the weightier matters of the Law, right judgment and mercy and faith. These things you ought to have done, while not leaving the others undone. Blind guides, who strain out the gnat but swallow the camel!

"Woe to you, Scribes and Pharisees, hypocrites! because you clean the outside of the cup and the dish, but within they are full of robbery and uncleanness. Thou blind Pharisee! clean first the inside of the cup and of the dish, that the outside too may be clean.

"Woe to you, Scribes and Pharisees, hypocrites! because you are like whited sepulchres, which outwardly appear to men beautiful, but within are full of dead men's bones and of all uncleanness. So you also outwardly appear just to men, but within you are full of hypocrisy and iniquity.

"Woe to you, Scribes and Pharisees, hypocrites! you who build the sepulchres of the prophets, and adorn the tombs of the just, and say, 'If we had lived in the days of our fathers, we would not have been their accomplices in the blood of the prophets.' Thus you are witnesses against yourselves that you are the sons of those who killed the prophets."

Having pronounced these scathing indictments of His inveterate enemies, Jesus paused as if to catch His breath before continuing in a tone of biting irony: "Fill up, then, the measure of your fathers. Serpents, brood of vipers, how are you to escape the judgment of hell? Therefore, behold, I send you prophets, and wise men, and scribes; and some of them you will put to death, and crucify, and some you will scourge in your synagogues, and persecute from town to town; that upon you may come all the just blood that has been shed on the earth, from the blood of Abel the just unto the blood of Zacharias [34] the son of Barachias, whom you killed between the temple and the altar. Amen I say to you, all these things will come upon this generation." [35]

The vision of the catastrophe that was to come upon the Jewish people brought back to our Lord all He had done to avert the disaster. In tones of infinite tenderness and heartbroken sorrow, He took a sad farewell of the city which He had loved so much, the city which was going to crucify Him: [36] "Jesusalem, Jerusalem! thou who killest the prophets, and stonest those who are sent to thee! How often would I have gathered thy children together, as a hen gathers her young under her wings, but thou wouldst not! Behold, your house is left to you desolate. For I say to you, you shall not see me henceforth

---

[34] This is not Zacharias the son of Barachias mentioned in Zacharias 1:1, but Zacharias the son of Joiada (2 Par. 24:20–22). Joiada may also have been known as Barachias, as some authors believe, or the primitive Gospel text may have had Joiada, and some copyist changed it to Barachias. St. Jerome says that in the Gospel of the Nazarenes the reading given was "son of Joiada."

[35] See below, pp. 610 ff.

[36] This apostrophe is found also in Luke 13:34 f. See, our remarks above, p. 518, n. 10.

until you shall say, 'Blessed is he who comes in the name of the Lord!' " [37]

As He spoke, our Lord must have visualized the Holy City being reduced to rubble by the Roman catapults, the destruction of the Temple, and the homeless wandering of the nation that had once been God's Chosen People but who were to become outcasts, bearing on their foreheads the mark of the divine malediction. Yet, across the centuries, He also saw these errant sons returning to the bosom of their Father, and He heard the cry, "Blessed is he who comes in the name of the Lord," coming from the lips of those who, in a moment of madness, had rejected Him.

Some modern authors have set themselves up as zealous defenders of the Pharisees, and hold that our Lord's indictment of the party was unjust, or that it was due to the evangelists' prejudice.[38]

Certainly no one will claim that the evangelist has reproduced our Lord's indictment word for word, but the fact that the three Synoptic authors paint practically the same picture—although Matthew does so with firmer strokes and more vivid colors than the others—is a strong guarantee of its historical veracity.

Then, too, Christ's outspoken, unambiguous condemnation, which at first sight appears at variance with His usual gentle kindness, fits in perfectly with the general atmosphere of the Gospel narrative. We can truly say that, from the very beginning, His preaching and actions were in violent contrast with those of the Pharisees. They attributed supreme importance to the minute practices handed down from the ancients; they set great store by external legal purity; with haughty disdain, they kept aloof from sinners. Jesus, on the contrary, insisted above all on the great moral virtues; He emphasized purity of heart, spoke with and treated sinners kindly and showed Himself especially merciful to them. The Pharisees were supremely satisfied with themselves and despised others; they made a parade of their

---

[37] The quotation is from Psalm 117:26. "You shall not see me, etc." is usually taken to mean that the Jews will not know Jesus as He really is until they say: "Blessed is he, etc."; or else, and perhaps with greater probability, it is interpreted as a prophecy of the conversion of the Jews at the end of time, foretold also by St. Paul in Romans 11:25 ff.

[38] "It seems to me, however, that the entire chapter 23 of Matthew does not belong to the original Matthew (certainly not to the Logia) and was interpolated later, and hence the words 'Pharisees, hypocrites!' never came from the mouth of Jesus" (S. Zeitlin, The Pharisees and the Gospels [New York: Harper & Bros., 1938], p. 269). See also Zeitlin, Who Crucified Jesus? (New York: Harper & Bros., 1947), pp. 128–143; J. Klausner, op. cit., pp. 273–291.

religion, and avidly sought the respect and esteem of the people. Therefore it was only to be expected that they would not look with favor on the young Rabbi's growing popularity, and would do everything in their power to discredit Him and undermine His authority. Their envy and anger even drove them to the insane extreme of attributing His miracles to Beelzebub, the prince of devils.

This is not an exaggerated description of the Pharisees, for it is composed from numberless particular episodes whose historical character is unassailable, and therefore it corresponds with reality.

What attitude was Jesus to adopt when He was confronted with men of this type? Any attempt to win them by reasoning or persuasion was foredoomed to failure, for their pride and ingrained prejudices were an unsurmountable barrier. On the other hand, their grave and sober bearing, their show of deep piety, and their meticulous observance of even the smallest external practice impressed the people and won their respect and esteem. And they did not hesitate to use this high repute to weaken our Lord's influence and to prevent His hearers from accepting and following His teaching.

Under such conditions, there was only one way for Jesus to deal with His enemies, and that was to show them up to the crowd for what they were; He had to unmask them, not out of revenge, but rather for the good of the people. Nor was His action a revolt against duly constituted religious authority, for He expressly urged His listeners to obey the Scribes and Pharisees as successors of Moses: "The Scribes and Pharisees have sat on the chair of Moses. All things, therefore, that they command you, observe and do. But do not act according to their works" (Matt. 23:2 f.). They were to obey their teachers when they legitimately interpreted the Law, but were not to imitate their conduct. Thus He safeguarded the principle of authority while averting the evil consequences of bad example.[39]

The Widow's Mite
(Mark 12:41–44; Luke 21:1–4)

Our Lord's exhausting and strife-filled day in the porches of the Temple came to a close with a peaceful and touchingly devout scene within the sacred precincts.

---

[39] Cf. J. van der Ploeg, "Jésus et les Pharisiens," in *Mémorial Lagrange* (Paris, 1940), pp. 279–293.

The Court of the Women was a large square, measuring almost sixty-five yards each way. Along the north, south and east sides, and supported by columns, ran the galleries from which the women assisted at the religious functions. On the west side, a stairway of fifteen steps led up to the Court of Israel, the two courts being separated from each other by a balustrade. At the foot of the stairway, to one side, lay the *gazophylacium* or Treasury, the hall where the faithful deposited their offerings in one or the other of twelve receptacles, which were called trumpets or horns (*shofarot*) because of their shape. An inscription on each receptacle indicated the special purpose of the donation deposited therein: six of them were reserved for *voluntary* offerings.

Jesus and His Apostles retired to the Court of the Women, perhaps to rest on the stone benches along the wall, or on the stairway itself. At any rate, from where they sat they could see the faithful placing their offerings in the Treasury. It was not difficult to know, even from a distance, the alms each person gave, since the priests were there receiving the money, making sure that each one's offering was proportionate to the purpose for which it was intended, and frequently calling aloud the amount that was given,[40] for rich donors wanted everyone to hear what they contributed.

It happened that among the people who were donating appreciable sums, smugly receiving the not wholly disinterested congratulations of the priests and listening with great satisfaction as their offerings were proclaimed for all to hear, there was a poor widow who timidly approached and placed in the priest's hand "two mites, which make a quadrans," roughly equivalent to half a cent in our money.[41] It is not unlikely that when the priest saw the microscopic sum the widow had offered, he showed the coins to the bystanders, gave the poor woman a contemptuous look and acknowledged her gift with some sneering remark. We do know that, on one occasion, when a woman came with a handful of flour as an offering for the sacrifice, the priest said irritably to those who stood near: "Look at what this one has brought! How are we going to find enough here to

[40] Cf. Str.-Bill. II, 43 *f.*

[41] The Greek text says that she gave two *lepta,* the *lepton* being a Greek coin corresponding to half a Roman *quadrans,* four of which made an *as,* which in turn was worth one-sixteenth of a silver denarius. (As we have noted before, the denarius was approximately equivalent to 35 cents. Thus 2 *lepta* = 1 *quadrans* = ¼ *as* = $\frac{1}{64}$ denarius = approximately ½ cent in our money. —Translator.)

divide into two parts, one for eating and the other for the offering?" [42]
Something of this sort may have happened to the humble widow. Our
Lord, seeing the incident, made use of it to give His Apostles, and us,
a beautiful lesson: "Amen I say to you, this poor widow has put in
more than all those who have been putting money into the treasury.
For they all have put in out of their abundance; but she out of her
want has put in all that she had—all that she had to live on."

God regards the sacrifice involved and the spirit in which it is
made rather than the amount of the gift.

[42] Str.-Bill., II, 46.

25. The Great Eschatological Discourse[1]

(Matt. 24; Mark 13; Luke 21:5-36)

On this occasion, our Lord did not bring the day's activities to a close within the precincts of the Temple, as He had done on the previous two days. Instead, from Mount Olivet, on the way to Bethany, He opened up to His disciples the vast horizons of the future down to the end of time.

Night was drawing on, and Jesus, accompanied by His disciples, left the city to return to Bethany. As they walked along, the disciples were probably speaking among themselves about the magnificence of the Temple and the munificent gifts which they had just seen being presented there. After crossing the Brook Cedron and beginning the ascent of Mount Olivet, no doubt they paused a moment to look back at the Temple's majestic bulk. Turning to Jesus, one of them exclaimed: "Master, look, what wonderful stones and buildings!"

The rest of the group doubtless echoed their companion's sentiments. But their Divine Master did not

[1] F. Segarra, "Algunas observaciones sobre los textos escatológicos de Nuestro Señor," in *Gregorianum,* 19 (1938), 48-87, 304-475, 543-572; A. Vaccari, "Il discorso escatologico nei Vangeli," in *La Scuola Cattolica,* 68 (1940), 5-22; A. C. Cotter, "The Eschatological Discourse," in *Catholic Biblical Quarterly,* 1 (1939), 125-132, 204-213; Lagrange, "L'Avènement du Fils de l'Homme," in *RB* (1906), pp. 382-411, 561-574; A. Feuillet, "Le discours de Jésus sur la ruine du temple d'après Marc XIII et Luc XXI," in *RB* (1948), pp. 481-502; (1949), pp. 61-92; and "La synthèse eschatologique de Saint Matthieu," in *RB* (1950), pp. 62-91.

share their enthusiasm. Gravely He replied: "Dost thou see all these great buildings? There will not be left one stone upon another that will not be thrown down."

His solemn prediction must have struck the Apostles dumb with horrified amazement. The wonder of the world, reduced to ruins! The magnificent Temple of the God of Hosts, turned into a heap of rubble! As they continued on up the slope, the Apostles were sunk in thoughtful silence, for their Master's words had been quite clear, leaving no room for doubt. The Temple was doomed. But He had not told them when the disaster was to occur.

When they had recovered from the initial shock of the prophecy, they gathered into little groups as they went, and discussed their Master's words, while He walked out in front, alone, as if rapt in deep thought. Reaching a point on the hill opposite the Temple, He sat down and gazed across at the imposing structure outlined by the last rays of the setting sun. Peter, James, John and Andrew, who formed one of the small groups of disciples, approached Him, and it was probably Peter who, acting as spokesman for the group, asked Him privately: "Tell us, when are these things to happen, and what will be the sign when all these things will begin to come to pass?"

Meanwhile the rest of the disciples had arrived, and stood about their Master, waiting for Him to speak.

Our Lord's lengthy reply to Peter's question is usually called the *eschatological discourse,* because it deals with the end of time, or the *Synoptic Apocalypse,* since it is a revelation or *apocalypse* and is recorded in the three Synoptic Gospels. In it Jesus described not only the destruction of Jerusalem but also the trials through which His disciples would have to pass, and, finally, His second coming at the end of time. We can say, therefore, that He took in the course of the centuries at a glance and traced the future history of the kingdom which He had come to establish, down to His second coming and the end of the world. In this breath-taking summary of events, the destruction of Jerusalem was simply one of many episodes, but since it was a figure of the final catastrophe that would come upon the whole world, it stood out in high relief and received particular emphasis. The combination of two similar disasters necessarily renders the discourse somewhat obscure, particularly because the two events, although separated from each other by many centuries, are projected on the same plane, without regard for perspective. The obscurity is deepened still further by the enigmatic phraseology customary in prophecies, especially in those which take an apocalyptic form.

From ancient Christian times, very divergent opinions have been held on the theme and the division into parts of the eschatological discourse.[2] Several of the Fathers, including St. Hilary and St. Gregory the Great, believed that it dealt solely with the end of the world. But today the great majority of exegetes acknowledge that our Lord was speaking of two catastrophes, and they usually hold that the discourse is divided into two parts, the first referring to the destruction of Jerusalem, and the second to the end of the world.[3]

It is our opinion that, in the three Synoptic Gospels, the great discourse unfolds in *three* stages (Matt. 24:4–14, 15–20, 21–51; Mark 13:5–13, 14–18, 19–37; Luke 21:8–19, 20–24, 25–36), with eschatological elements in the first and third stages, and none in the second. Instead, the second stage refers to the destruction of Jerusalem, as is clearly apparent in Luke 21:20: "And when you see *Jerusalem* being surrounded by an army . . ." which is certainly paralleled by Matthew 24:15 and Mark 13:14 ("Therefore when you see the abomination of desolation. . . ."), as authors generally agree. This section of Luke closes with verse 24, but the dividing line between the second and third stages is not so clearly marked in Matthew and Mark. The solution to the difficulty depends on the meaning of the expression

---

[2] Cf. Buzy, *S. Matt.*, p. 312.

[3] Some authors have thought that, on this occasion, Jesus was speaking solely and exclusively about the destruction of Jerusalem, not because they saw no eschatological references in the actual text, but because they held that everything pertaining to the end of the world and the second coming was spoken by Jesus in other circumstances of time and place; see, for example, Luke 17, where specifically eschatological elements appear. This was the opinion favored by Le Camus, Cellini and others. In his commentary on St. Luke (1927, pp. 536 *f.*), Lagrange was inclined to this view, but later he seemed to change his mind in *The Gospel of Jesus Christ*, II, 172 *ff*.

This dissection of the discourse is not sufficiently justified, for there are clear eschatological references in all three Synoptic Gospels. In St. Matthew (24:3), the Apostles explicitly inquire: "Tell us, when are these things to happen, and what will be the sign *of thy coming* and *of the end of the world?*" It is to be presupposed that our Lord wished to reply to this double question. It is true that in Mark 13:4 and Luke 27:7, the question refers only to the destruction of Jerusalem, but this omission does not invalidate St. Matthew's text unless we say that the evangelist added the part about the second coming on his own account, to justify his recording here some of Christ's words which were spoken in different circumstances. However, such a procedure on St. Matthew's part is inadmissible. Cf. Vaccari, *loc. cit.*, pp. 12 *f.*; Lebreton, *Life and Teachings of Jesus Christ*, II, 197; Segarra, *loc. cit.*, pp. 350 *f*. The non-eschatological interpretation of the great discourse has more recently been upheld by F. Spadafora, *Gesù e la fine di Gerusalemme* (Rovigo, 1950).

"[great] tribulation" in Matthew 24:21 and Mark 13:19, a point which we shall discuss later.

We must proceed with greater reserve when forming a judgment on the initial stage in each Gospel. At first glance, this section seems to be concerned with the events leading up to the great catastrophe that was to come upon the Holy City; and, in fact, quite a few authors interpret it thus, and divide the whole discourse into two parts only. However, we would be very hesitant to make such an assertion. In Matthew 24:14 we read: "and then will come the *end* [τὸ τέλος]," a word which, in our opinion, must be understood in an eschatological sense, i.e., as referring to the end of the world, because our Lord had just been speaking about the Gospel's being "preached in the whole world," a goal which could scarcely have been attained before the destruction of Jerusalem.[4]

The same expression, τὸ τέλος, of Mark 13:7 and Luke 21:9 should be similarly understood, an interpretation which corresponds perfectly with the universal character of the word, for our Lord spoke simply of *"the* end," and not the end of a city or a particular district. In Luke 21:8, after the words "saying, 'I am he,' " which are found also in Matthew 24:5 and Mark 13:6, we read: "and, 'The time is at hand,' " an expression which, particularly when compared with Daniel 7:22, indicates the last days, that is, the appearance of the glorious kingdom. Therefore, it seems logical to us to conclude that, since the first part of the discourse contains such markedly eschatological references, it looks beyond the destruction of Jerusalem.

Nor is this a strained interpretation, for although Jesus had spoken only of the Temple, or the city, the disciples' question, as found in St. Matthew (24:3), probed much further into the future: "When are these things to happen, and what will be the sign *of thy coming* and *of the end of the world?"* They were primarily interested in these two points, and it was to this part of their inquiry that Jesus replied first. Consequently, as He spoke to His disciples, His eyes were fixed on the end of time and His second coming in glory and majesty. It is, therefore, this solemn advent, with all the signs announcing its approach, that forms the principal theme of the great discourse, while the destruc-

---

[4] Pirot (*S. Marc,* p. 559) makes great efforts to prove that our Lord's words concerning the world-wide spread of the Gospel were borne out before A.D. 70; and Lagrange seems to defend the same view (*Év. selon S. Marc,* p. 328). With Buzy, Knabenbauer and others, we believe that such an interpretation is extremely strained and against the obvious, natural meaning of the text.

tion of the Temple and the city, calamitous though it was, constituted only a secondary subject in comparison with the consummation of the whole world.

After the reference to the fall of Jerusalem the horizons of the discourse broaden, and the great tribulation appears in all its terror—the violent convulsion of the elements as a sign that the Son of Man is coming in glory and majesty. Everything in the third and last part of the discourse moves within the sphere of eschatology and culminates in the second coming, which is heralded by cosmic upheavals and celestial turmoil.

Authors are not agreed on the interpretation of the "great tribulation" (Matt. 24:21; Mark 13:19) in this awe-inspiring description. There are some who see in it nothing more than the calamities that fell upon Jerusalem. But with Knabenbauer, Lagrange [5] and Buzy, we hold that the expression should be understood in an eschatological sense. There can be no doubt that our Lord was referring, not to the destruction of Jerusalem, but to the final conflagration at the end of time when He spoke of "great tribulation, such as has not been from the beginning of the world until now, nor will be" (Matt. 24:21; Mark 13:19), in which all men would perish if God did not shorten the time for the sake of the elect (Matt. 24:22; Mark 13:20). It is this cataclysm which will be followed immediately by the great cosmic movements announcing the appearance of the Son of Man (Matt. 24:29 f.) and by the wonders and great signs worked by "false christs and false prophets . . . so as to lead astray, if possible, even the elect" (Matt. 24:24). This last prediction is clearly a reference to the era of Antichrist. Therefore, no matter how numerous and terrible the calamities that were to accompany the destruction of Jerusalem, they cannot fit our Lord's markedly eschatological description. Hence the third part of the discourse opens with verse 21 in St. Matthew and verse 19 in St. Mark.[6]

Our exegesis removes the difficulty which could arise from St. Matthew's words: "Immediately, after the tribulation of those days . . . (v. 29), with which the evangelist begins his description of

---

[5] *The Gospel of Jesus Christ*, II, 179 ff.

[6] One could object to this interpretation or division of the sections on the score that the particle γάρ: "For. . . ." (Matt. 24:21; Mark 13:19) seems to link these verses to what goes before, i.e., the destruction of Jerusalem. But, as Lagrange observes (*Év. selon S. Matt.*, p. 463) and Buzy agrees, here the particle is "une liaison de pure forme, sans portée pour les idées."

the second coming and the cosmic upheavals that herald it. "The tribulation of those days" is not the destruction of Jerusalem, but the appearance of Antichrist, which is to be followed *immediately* by the "great tribulation," that is, the great eschatological catastrophe.[7]

Obviously, we must acknowledge that none of the three evangelists has transmitted the discourse in the exact form in which our Lord spoke it, and that they all drew upon oral tradition which, of course, was not perfectly uniform in the way it described identical events, and much less so in its manner of recording the spoken word. If this holds good as regards discourses in general, it is even more true of the eschatological discourse, wherein are described two episodes, which, though very different from each other, yet possess many points of similarity. It is not surprising, therefore, to find that the accounts left by the three evangelists are not complete parallels. Nevertheless, although they may differ in details, the three accounts agree admirably with each other in content and development of ideas. At the beginning of each we find various warnings containing, as we have seen, some eschatological elements; next, each has a section referring to the destruction of Jerusalem, and all three close with the second coming of Christ and the events leading up to it. Therefore it is not rash to assert, or at least to regard it as probable, that our Lord followed this general sequence in His reply to His Apostles.

The literary form is practically identical in Matthew and Mark, but differs a little in Luke, who departs from the other Synoptic writers on two points. The third evangelist supplies a more detailed, concrete and vivid description of the destruction of Jerusalem—"And when you see Jerusalem being surrounded by an army. . . ." (v. 20); "And they will fall by the edge of the sword, and will be led away as captives to all the nations. And Jerusalem will be trodden down by the Gentiles. . . ." (v. 24)—touches of realism which do not appear in Matthew or Mark. In addition, while the division between the second and third sections is vague and indecisive in the first two Gospels, it stands out clearly in Luke's account, in which celestial disturbances

---

[7] If the "great tribulation" is to be understood as referring to the destruction of the Holy City, then our Lord seems to have asserted that His second coming would follow immediately upon the fall of Jerusalem. But clearly, that did not happen. To obviate this difficulty, the word εὐθέως ("immediately") is taken in the sense of "suddenly" or "unexpectedly," or it is regarded as the equivalent of the more general phrase in Mark 13:24, "in those days"; or, finally, it is explained by saying that "compared with eternity, all time is but a short moment" (cf. Knabenbauer, *In Matt.*, II, 343).

and the coming of the Son of Man (vv. 24–27) follow immediately upon the destruction of the city.

Which of these two forms is closer to the way in which our Lord actually delivered the discourse? It is hard to say. At all events, Luke seems to give the impression of having worked his material, an impression which is strengthened by what we know of his character. It is very likely that he was familiar with the texts of Matthew and Mark, and, without changing the sequence of thought, set out to present the various parts of the discourse in a clearer and more orderly form for the benefit of his readers.

We shall never know the exact words in which our Lord made these revelations to His disciples. But it is completely arbitrary to maintain that the Synoptic Apocalypse is simply a blending of two distinct discourses, one concerning the destruction of Jerusalem and the other the end of the world and the second coming of Christ.[8]

Of the three accounts, we prefer St. Luke's because, as we have said, it throws the three sections of the discourse into greater relief and distinguishes more clearly between them: "Take care not to be led astray. For many will come in my name, saying, 'I am he,'[9] and, 'The time is at hand.' Do not, therefore, go after them. But when you hear of wars and insurrections, do not be terrified; these things must first come to pass, but the end[10] will not be at once." Then he said to them, "Nation will rise against nation, and kingdom against kingdom; and there will be great earthquakes in various places, and pestilences and famines, and there will be terrors and great signs from heaven.

"But before all these things they will arrest you and persecute you, delivering you up to the synagogues and prisons, dragging you before kings and governors for my name's sake. It shall lead to your bearing witness. Resolve therefore in your hearts not to meditate beforehand how you are to make your defense. For I myself will give you utterance and wisdom, which all your adversaries will not be able to resist or gainsay. But you will be delivered up by your parents and brothers and relatives and friends; and some of you they will put to death. And you will be hated by all for my name's sake; yet not a hair of your head shall perish. By your patience you will win your souls."

It may seem surprising that in all three Synoptic accounts, our Lord did not immediately answer His disciples' question, but began

[8] Cf. Lagrange, *Év. selon S. Matt.*, p. 456.
[9] That is, the Messias. Cf. Matt. 24:5: "I am the Christ."
[10] Or "consummatio saeculi."

instead by warning them against the deception into which they could fall. However, if we consider the matter more closely, we shall see that His procedure was in full harmony with His state of mind at the time, and that the observation which He made elsewhere (Luke 6:45), applies very aptly here: "Out of the abundance of the heart the mouth speaks."

He had foretold the destruction of the Temple, but His glance penetrated much further into the future, and the majestic panorama of the history of His kingdom unfolded before His eyes. He saw the resistance with which it would meet, the misunderstandings, the attacks, the persecutions that lay in store for it; He knew the malicious cunning of His enemies and the weakness of His friends. He was aware of all these things, and therefore the first words He spoke were a cry of warning so that persecution, open or concealed, would not take His Apostles unawares. In addition, the fact that He, their Master, had foreseen and predicted everything that the future held in store would give them an added motive for confidence in the dark hours that lay ahead.

Everyone knows how our Lord's prophecies have been borne out to the letter, both during the centuries that have passed since He made them and in our own day. Persecution, either open or disguised, has relentlessly dogged the footsteps of the children of the kingdom; but, trusting in their Captain's word and supported by His strength, the Christians of every age have stood firm and constant in the face of the severest trials, testifying to their faith and emerging triumphant. The history of the Church has been the story of the eternal battle between good and evil, between the free sons of God and the slaves of sin, between light and darkness.

Having given His disciples a fatherly warning and shown them the trials and consolations that lay before them, our Lord went on to describe the fate of Jerusalem: "And when you see Jerusalem being surrounded by an army, then know that her desolation is at hand. Then let those who are in Judea flee to the mountains; and let those who are in her midst go out, and let those who are in the country not enter her. For these are days of vengeance, that all things that are written may be fulfilled. But woe to those who are with child, or have infants at the breast in those days! For there will be great distress over the land, and wrath upon its people. And they will fall by the edge of the sword, and will be led away as captives to all the nations. And

Jerusalem will be trodden down by the Gentiles, until the times of the nations be fulfilled." [11]

The Roman legions' tightening the band of steel about Jerusalem would be a clear omen of the city's approaching destruction. In Matthew 24:15 and Mark 13:14, another sign is given: "the abomination of desolation . . . standing in the holy place," as already prophesied by Daniel (9:27). This prophecy, which Jesus here confirmed, was fulfilled in the year 68, when the barbarous Zealots, under their leader John of Giscala, turned the Temple into a lake of blood, and, as Josephus says,[12] heaped up corpses until the number of victims reached not less than 8,500. Acting on our Lord's advice, the Christians of Jerusalem, led by their bishop St. Simeon, successor to St. James the Less, left the capital and retired to Pella, one of the cities of the Decapolis on the other side of the Jordan, across from Scythopolis. The punishment of Jerusalem, as foretold by Jesus, was carried out in every terrible detail. According to Josephus, 1,100,000 Jews perished during the siege of the city, 97,000 were carried away as captives, and 11,000 died of hunger. Jerusalem was indeed "trodden down," and from that time onward it remained under the foreign yoke, and a new era began, during which "the nations" held the Holy City of the Jews.

The destruction of Jerusalem was, in a sense, an image of the end of the world, and therefore it was logical for our Lord to pass from one idea to the other: "And there will be signs in the sun and moon and stars, and upon the earth distress of nations bewildered by the roaring of sea and waves; men fainting for fear and for expectation of the things that are coming on the world; for the powers of heaven will be

[11] This last sentence is very obscure. More than a few authors interpret it in the sense that the times of the nations will be fulfilled when the Gospel has been preached to them and has borne fruit among them. Such an interpretation is in harmony with Matthew 24:14: "And this gospel of the kingdom shall be preached in the whole world, for a witness to all nations; and then will come the end." St. Paul expressed an analogous idea in the difficult passage in his Epistle to the Romans (11:25 ff.), where he speaks of the blindness of Israel and the *full number of the Gentiles*. According to other authors, the sentence means that the times of the nations will be fulfilled when they cease to exist, i.e., at the end of the world. Still others hold that the words refer to the time when it will be the nations' turn to be chastised by God. But, in our opinion, "the times of the nations" should be understood as the period given or assigned to them by God for the punishment of the Jewish people's infidelity. Just as at another period of history, He chose the king of Assyria as "the rod and staff of [His] anger" (Isai. 10:5) to punish Israel, so also He wished to make use of the nations as an instrument of His wrath, allowing them to keep the Holy City of Jerusalem in subjection for a predetermined period of time.

[12] *Wars* iv. 5. 1.

shaken. And then they will see the Son of Man coming upon a cloud with great power and majesty. But when these things begin to come to pass, look up, and lift up your heads, because your redemption is at hand."

And He told them a short parable: "Behold the fig tree, and all the trees. When they now put forth their buds, you know that summer is near. Even so, when you see these things coming to pass, know that the kingdom of God is near."

To bring out more clearly the inevitability of the occurrences which He had foretold, Jesus added in a tone of special gravity and solemnity: "Amen I say to you, this generation will not pass away till all these things have been accomplished. Heaven and earth will pass away, but my words will not pass away."

An extremely delicate problem is posed by this emphatic assertion, which must have made a vivid impression on the hearers, and which all three evangelists have recorded for us (Matt. 24:34; Mark 13:30; Luke 21:32). A good number of non-Catholic authors have taken it as a clear proof that Christ was mistaken about the date of the end of the world.[13] According to their argument, He formally stated that the end of the world would come before the death of His contemporaries. But every one of those alive at the time died in due course, and still the world continued to exist as before. Hence, they conclude, Jesus was mistaken in His prediction.

The whole difficulty hinges on the interpretation of two expressions: (1) does "all these things" mean the destruction of Jerusalem or the end of the world? (2) what is the precise meaning of "this generation"? If "all these things" refers to the end of the world, and "this generation" means our Lord's contemporaries, then He *was* mistaken. But there are other ways of interpreting the text.

Some authors believe that the passage really deals both with the fall of Jerusalem and the end of the world, and that the word "generation" does not mean our Lord's contemporaries, but the Jewish *race* or *nation* in general, which will not disappear before the end of the world. Hence He was *not* mistaken in His prophecy.[14]

---

13 There would be no point in listing the proponents of this theory. See Lagrange, *The Gospel of Jesus Christ*, II, 182 *ff.* Cf. Karl Weiss, *Exegetisches zur Irrtumlosigkeit u. Eschatologie Jesu Christi* (*Neutest. Abhand:* Münster i. W., 1916), pp. 69–148.

14 This in the interpretation favored by Prat (*Jesus Christ*, II, 245), Knabenbauer (*op. cit.*, II, 349 *f.*: "Annuntiat itaque Christus iudaicam stirpem non esse exstinguendam usque ad adventum Christi"), and others.

It is certain that both profane and sacred authors have used the word "generation" to signify "race," "nation," or "people," and that in itself the term does not express a time relationship.[15] But in the present passage, the immediate context seems to give it a temporal tinge. In each of the three Synoptic Gospels, our Lord's statement concerning the fulfillment of "all these things" comes directly after His parable of the fig tree, which contains several very definite references to time: "When its branch is now tender . . . you know that summer is near. Even so, when you see all these things, know that it is near, even at the door" (Matt. 24:32 f.). Now, since He adds, "Amen I say to you, this generation will not pass away," immediately after those references, the context seems to demand that we interpret the word "generation" in a temporal sense, too. Again, it can be said that in many, even in the majority of cases when He spoke of "this generation," He was referring to the generation then alive, i.e., His contemporaries: for example, in Matthew 11:16 ("To what shall I liken this generation?"), Luke 11:19 ff. ("This generation is an evil generation . . . the men of this generation. . . ."); cf. Matthew 12:39; 17:17; Mark 8:12, 38; 9:19; Luke 7:31; 17:25.

But what of the expression "all these things"? Coming as it does after the twofold prophecy about Jerusalem and the second coming, it apparently refers to both events, that is, to all the things that had just been mentioned. However, although this interpretation is the obvious one, a careful scrutiny of the text will show that it is by no means inescapable. In reality, the words "all these things" are so vague and undefined that our Lord could have meant them to refer, not to all, but only to some of the things which He had mentioned, namely, to the circumstances of the destruction of Jerusalem. This interpretation is supported by a collation of the present passage with the sentence immediately following it: "But of that day and hour no one knows, not even the angels of heaven, but the Father only" (Matt. 24:36). The word δέ ("autem"), which we translate as "but," contrasts what follows with what goes before. Thus Jesus, answering the Apostles' question about the destruction of Jerusalem, predicted that that event would occur before the present generation passed (Luke 21:32; Matt. 24:34); and then, replying to the other part of the

15 Cf. Prat, *Rech. de Sc. Rel.,* 17 (1927), 316–324; L. de Grandmaison, *Jesus Christ,* III, 251 ff. Fr. Segarra (*loc. cit.,* pp. 48–87), after a close study of tradition, concludes that the Fathers understood the word "generation" (γενεά) in the sense of "race," "people," "nation."

inquiry, He said that no one except the Father knew when the end of the world would come. It should be noted that the expression "that day" (ἡμέρας ἐκείνης)—the day of God, the day of judgment—makes our Lord's replies perfect parallels to the Apostles' questions.

It would be rash to claim that our explanation has lifted all the veils from the great eschatological discourse. But we do assert that there is absolutely no reason for saying, as the so-called eschatologists do, that Christ proclaimed that His glorious coming and the end of the world would coincide with the destruction of Jerusalem. It is not only possible but even probable that the Apostles interpreted their Master's words in this way. Their question, as formulated by St. Matthew (24:3), seems to indicate that they did. But, as we know, even after three years of close association with Jesus, they still entertained some false ideas. Why did our Lord not express Himself more clearly on this occasion by throwing into sharp relief the great time-gap between the two catastrophes? The answer remains God's secret. Again, the first generation of Christians certainly lived in expectation of the second coming of Christ, yet it is no less certain that both St. Paul (2 Thess. 2:1 ff.) and St. Peter (2 Pet. 3:1 ff.) openly and resolutely combatted this misconception entertained by their contemporaries.

St. Matthew and St. Mark record several other signs of the approach of our Lord's second coming. False Christs and pseudoprophets will arise, and some of the people will say, "Behold, here is Christ," while others will say, "No, there he is," or "Behold, he is in the desert," or "Behold, he is in the inner chambers." Even before the fall of Jerusalem, several impostors claimed to be the Messias—Theodas (cf. Acts 5:36), Judas the Galilean (cf. Acts 5:37), and a certain Egyptian (cf. Acts 21:38). But false claimants such as these will be more numerous at the end of the world, and God will permit them to work wonders, no doubt through the power and instrumentality of Satan, whose ministers they will be, as St. Paul tells us (2 Cor. 11:15).

The scene that will be enacted at the second coming, as described by St. Matthew (24:30 f.), will indeed be an awe-inspiring one. After the celestial upheavals, there will appear in the sky the sign of the Son of Man, the sign of the cross (as many Fathers interpret the phrase), which will not be a battle-standard, as some authors, e.g., Lagrange, believe, but an emblem of glory and victory. On beholding the sign of power and majesty, all the tribes of the earth will lament the fact that they rejected it in the past. Then, with a trumpet-call, the angels will summon the elect from the four corners of the earth to gather around the Son of Man and form a glorious crown for Him who was once humbled and despised.

Matthew (24:29) and Mark (13:24 f.) give us a description of the heavenly upheaval which will precede the second coming: "The sun will be darkened, and the moon will not give her light, and the stars will fall from heaven, and the powers of heaven will be shaken." In order to evaluate properly the scope and meaning of the terms used by the evangelists, we must turn to the Old Testament and examine the images which the prophets were accustomed to employ in describing great calamities which were to occur in the more or less distant future. For example, in foretelling the destruction of Babylon, Isaias portrayed the day of the Lord thus: "The stars of heaven and their constellations shall not display their light: the sun shall be darkened in his rising, and the moon shall not shine with her light" (14:10). Ezechiel, when speaking to Egypt in the name of God, declared: "And I will cover the heavens when thou shalt be put out, and I will make the stars thereof dark. I will cover the sun with a cloud and the moon shall not give her light" (32:7); and Joel, describing the day of the Lord, said: "The earth hath trembled, the heavens are moved: the sun and moon are darkened and the stars have withdrawn their shining" (2:10).

Did these prophets believe and wish to assert that the very heavens would be in turmoil when their fearful prophecies came to pass? Apparently not, for they seem to be using here a kind of stereotyped formula, an oriental way of describing the terrible destruction which the Lord Yahweh would bring on the peoples in question. And in like manner, when our Lord came to depict the end of the world, He appears to have employed the same formula in the same sense.[16]

As regards the time of the second coming of the Son of Man, that is a secret reserved to the Father alone and unknown to men, angels, and apparently even to the very Son Himself: "But of that day or hour no one knows, neither the angels in heaven, nor the Son, but the Father only" (Mark 13:32; Matt. 24:36).

It seems extraordinary that the evangelist should include the Son among those who do not know the secret of "that day or hour." Some of the Fathers hold that, as Man, the Son did not know the secret, but that as God He did. However, this is not an adequate explanation of

[16] That is how Lebreton, Lagrange, Buzy, Pirot, Benoit, Huby and others interpret the passages.

the difficulty. Even as Man, our Lord possessed the Beatific Vision and had infused as well as experimental knowledge, and therefore as Man He knew perfectly well when the second coming would occur. Hence the sentence just quoted must be understood in the sense that Christ, as the Father's Legate, was not commissioned to reveal to men the time of His second coming, and that therefore, in practice, it was as if He did not know the truth in question; that is, His knowledge of it was not *communicable* knowledge. This is St. Augustine's solution.[17]

Although the time of the second coming is uncertain, its manner is not. The Son of Man will appear like a flash of lightning: "as lightning comes forth from the east and shines even to the west, so also will the coming of the Son of Man be" (Matt. 24:27); and just as the Flood caught men unawares, "eating and drinking, marrying and giving in marriage," so also will the Son of Man come at the time He is least expected (Matt. 24:37–39).

In this fashion, our Lord exhorts us ever to watch and pray, so that, even though He comes unexpectedly, He will not find us unprepared for the last day: "Therefore you must also be ready, because at an hour that you do not expect, the Son of Man will come" (Matt. 24:44).

Three Parables

In order to impress deeply upon the Apostles and the Christians of all time the supreme importance of being prepared for His second coming, our Lord narrated, not one, but three parables, each containing the same central idea.

THE FAITHFUL AND UNFAITHFUL SERVANTS
(Matt. 24:45–51; Mark 13:34–47)

In this parable, Jesus drew a sharp contrast between the conduct of the two servants, between the loyalty of the one and the unfaithfulness of the other. The wicked servant, seeing that his absent master was long in returning home, concluded that he would either never come back at all, or would do so only after a very lengthy period. Then, since there was no one to check him, he began to lord it over his fellow servants, wounding some and maltreating others. Not only that, but

---

[17] "Filium hominis dixit nescire illum diem quia in magisterio eius non erat ut per eum sciretur a nobis" (*In Psal. 36: PL* 36, 355; cf. K. Weiss, *op. cit.,* pp. 45–51).

he gave himself up to feasting and roistering with drunkards. His master, however, did return when least expected, caught the wicked servant red-handed, and punished him as he deserved. The moral of the parable is plain: although our Lord may be late in coming, we should not be presumptuous but should always be prepared, for He can come at the most unexpected moment.

THE TEN VIRGINS

(Matt. 25:1–13)

The parable of the ten virgins is based on the customs of the day, and is both more complete and much more picturesque than the one about the two servants. The climax of this parable comes when the bridegroom arrives at his bride's house just when the foolish virgins have gone to buy oil for their lamps.

Among present-day Arabs in Palestine, it is not customary for the bridegroom to go seeking the bride.[18] Instead, she sets out from her parents' home accompanied by her women friends, and, in small towns, by all the young people of the neighborhood, the youths going before her and the girls falling in behind. All sing a refrain, keeping time by beating small drums and clapping their hands, as they make their way on foot or on horseback to the house of the groom, who is waiting there to receive his bride. When the bridegroom lives in another town, the bride's friends put colorful trappings and harness on a camel, and place a small platform on the animal's back. Over the platform they raise a tent, in which the bride reclines on richly decorated cushions. Sometimes she is accompanied by several maidens who serve as her ladies-in-waiting. The bridal procession is usually very colorful and picturesque, and we had the good fortune to witness one on the plain of Esdrelon. The cortège was headed by a group of men mounted on spirited camels; next came six or seven other camels, one behind the other, each led by a man on foot and carrying a platform covered with a mattress upon which three, four or even five women were placidly sitting. The last camel was distinguished from the others by the richness of its trappings, and it bore on its back a magnificent tent in

---

[18] This is the custom, however, among certain tribes of Bedouins. The women set up a tent at the edge of the encampment and accompany the bride thither. As night closes in, the bridegroom goes to seek her and leads her with great ceremony to his own tent. Cf. Jaussen and Savignac, "Coutumes des Fuqarà" (Suppl. to Vol. II of *Mission archéologique en Arabie* [Paris, 1914]), p. 21.

Jewish lamps and vessels.

which we could see the bride, accompanied by several maidens of her own age. The rest of the procession was formed of men, women and children on foot or on donkeys, all singing and clapping their hands in celebration of the happy event.

But this was not the procedure among the ancient Jews. Instead, the bridegroom, accompanied by his *paranymph* and other friends, went to seek his bride, who awaited him, surrounded by her companions. When he arrived, she joined him, and together, escorted by their combined retinues, they returned to his house, where the nuptial feast was held. The procession to the bridegroom's house was a solemn one. The bride, wearing a crown on her head, was carried in a litter, around which the groom and his friends formed a guard of honor. As they walked, the company sang songs in praise of the young couple, and if darkness had fallen, they carried torches or lamps to light their way.[19]

In view of these customs, the circumstances of the parable are easily understood. The virgins, that is, the young women, went to their friend's house to act as her bridesmaids. The fact that the parable gives their number as ten has no particular significance. They knew that night would have fallen before the bridal procession began, and therefore each of them brought a lamp. Five of them, or simply several of them, realized that the bridegroom might be very late in coming, and

[19] For these and many other details see Str.-Bill., I, 500–517, 969; S. Krauss, *Talmudische Archäologie* (Leipzig, 1911), II, 34–43, Musil (*Arabia Petraea*, III, 195) says that in one place east of the Jordan, if the wedding is at night, the bride's attendants carry oil lamps, as did the virgins in the parable.

so provided themselves with a plentiful supply of oil, either by bringing larger lamps than usual or by carrying extra fuel in small pitchers,
thereby showing their prudence and foresight.

As it turned out, they had to wait such a long time for the groom
that sleep overcame them. Finally, at midnight, they were awakened
by the cry: "Behold, the bridegroom is coming, go forth to meet him!"
Excitedly they sprang up, but when they reached for their lamps they
saw that the flames were flickering low for want of fuel. The five
prudent virgins were not troubled, for they had more oil. For a
moment the others were at a loss what to do, but they soon sought the
nearest remedy for their thoughtlessness by asking their companions to
give them some of their extra supply. The prudent virgins, however,
refused, pointing out sensibly: "Lest there may not be enough for us
and for you, go rather to those who sell, and buy for yourselves."

The foolish virgins had no other choice but to hasten off in search
of oil. But since it was midnight, they found that the oil merchant had
retired, so that they had to awaken him. Yawning and grumbling to
himself, the merchant took his time about opening his shop and getting
them the oil, with the result that although they ran back as fast as they
could, they found that the bridegroom had entered the house while
they were away, and that the door was shut against them. They
knocked as loudly as they were able, hoping that someone would come
and let them in. Their hopes were vain, for although the bridegroom
heard them, he did not open the door, but only called out sharply: "I
do not know you."

Our Lord ended the parable by pointing out the moral it contained: "Watch, therefore, for you know neither the day nor the hour."

THE TALENTS
(Matt. 25:14–30)

The third parable which Jesus narrated was that of the talents.[20]

---

[20] There is an obvious similarity between this parable and the one concerning the
gold pieces (Luke 19:12–26). The theme is identical in both cases—the re-
warding of those who traded with the money they received, and the punishment of those who let the money entrusted to them lie idle. It is no wonder,
therefore, that some of the Fathers, such as St. Ambrose and St. Jerome, believed that the two narratives were the same parable presented in different
forms, and that Maldonatus and some modern authors, among them Lagrange,
Buzy and Pirot, agree. But since, on the other hand, there are many notable
differences between the two stories (ten servants; three servants; one gold piece
to each of the ten; five, two and one talent respectively to the three servants;

He told it immediately after the preceding one, as if the two formed a unit, no doubt because both had the same central idea and contained the same lesson, namely, that everyone should always be ready and prepared for the second coming of Christ. Nevertheless, each parable views the matter from a different angle: that of the ten virgins stresses the vigilance which we should exercise so that the second coming may not find us unprepared, while the episode of the talents refers directly to the care with which we should fit ourselves for it: "For it is like a man going abroad, who called his servants and handed over his goods to them. And to one he gave five talents, to another two, and to another one, to each according to his particular ability, and then he went on his journey. And he who had received the five talents went and traded with them, and gained five more. In like manner, he who had received the two gained two more. But he who had received the one went away and dug in the earth and hid his master's money.

"Then after a long time the master of those servants came and settled accounts with them. And he who had received the five talents came and brought five other talents, saying, 'Master, thou didst hand over to me five talents; behold, I have gained five others in addition.' His master said to him, 'Well done, good and faithful servant; because thou hast been faithful over a few things, I will set thee over many; enter into the joy of thy master.'

"And he also who had received the two talents came and said, 'Master, thou didst hand over to me two talents; behold, I have gained two more.' His master said to him, 'Well done, good and faithful servant; because thou hast been faithful over a few things, I will set thee over many; enter into the joy of thy master.'

"But he who had received the one talent came and said, 'Master, I know that thou art a stern man; thou reapest where thou hast not sowed and gatherest where thou hast not winnowed; and as I was afraid, I went away and hid thy talent in the earth; behold, thou hast

narrated in Jericho to the crowd; on Mount Olivet to the disciples alone, etc.), other Fathers, such as St. John Chrysostom, and many exegetes, ancient as well as modern, hold that there are two distinct parables (Cornelius a Lapide, Knabenbauer, Schanz, Fillion, Dausch, Gomá, Simón-Dorado, Plummer; Zahn is undecided). As Plummer, a Protestant, says: "It is more likely that Jesus should utter somewhat similar parables on different occasions than that Mt. and Lk. should have made very serious confusion as to the details of the parable as well as regards the time and place of its delivery" (*A Critical and Exegetical Commentary on the Gospel According to St. Luke*, p. 437). For our part, without trying to minimize the force of the arguments for the identification of the two, we regard the distinction between them as more probable.

what is thine.' But his master answered and said to him, 'Wicked and slothful servant! thou didst know that I reap where I do not sow, and gather where I have not winnowed? Thou shouldst therefore have entrusted my money to bankers, and on my return I should have got back my own with interest. Take away therefore the talent from him, and give it to him who has the ten talents. For to everyone who has shall be given, and he shall have abundance; but from him who does not have, even that which he seems to have shall be taken away. But as for the unprofitable servant, cast him forth into the darkness outside, where there will be the weeping, and the gnashing of teeth.' "

The sum which the first servant received was a very large one, a talent of silver being worth about $2,100 in our money, so that he was entrusted with the equivalent of $10,500. Each of the other two servants also received a considerable sum, approximately $4,200 and $2,100 respectively. The different capabilities of each servant were the reason for such an unequal distribution. It is not certain that Jesus wished to give this inequality any particular significance. Most probably He merely meant it to show that the master knew his servants' abilities and that, like a prudent man, he allotted to each one a sum proportionate to his business acumen. This is the view favored by Maldonatus.[21] The doctrinal point of the parable is that every man, while he is on earth, must work with the natural and supernatural gifts, great and small, which God has given him, thus preparing to render a good account of himself when, at the end of time, the Son of Man will come to reward or punish each one according to his merits.

We should note that the master does not reserve for himself the talent taken from the slothful servant, but gives it to the good servant who already has ten. Thus the punishment of the one becomes the gain of the other. The conclusion of the parable: "For to everyone who has shall be given, and he shall have abundance; but from him who does not have [i.e., who has little], even that which he seems to have shall be taken away," is a kind of maxim or aphorism found also in Matthew 13:12; cf. Luke 19:24–26. It is, in simple form, what spiritual authors tell us about the economy of grace. Correspondence with one grace gains another for us, while, on the contrary, resistance or neglect may cause us to lose the graces we already possess.

[21] ". . . Sed quod id homines facere soleant et voluit Christus in parabolis vero similia et fieri solita narrare, etiamsi nihil ad finem parabolae pertinerent" (*in loc.*).

The Final Judgment
(Matt. 25:31–46)

In describing the final judgment, our Lord painted a majestic portrait in which He depicted Himself, the Son of Man, seated on a royal throne, surrounded by choirs of angels and judging all the nations of the earth. His word-picture was a fitting conclusion to the parables which so strongly inculcated the need for vigilance: "But when the Son of Man shall come in his majesty, and all the angels with him, then he will sit on the throne of his glory; and before him will be gathered all the nations, and he will separate them one from another, as the shepherd separates the sheep from the goats; and he will set the sheep on his right hand, but the goats on the left.

"Then the king will say to those on his right hand, 'Come, blessed of my Father, take possession of the kingdom prepared for you from the foundation of the world; for I was hungry and you gave me to eat; I was thirsty and you gave me to drink; I was a stranger and you took me in; naked and you covered me; sick and you visited me; I was in prison and you came to me.'

"Then the just will answer him, saying, 'Lord, when did we see thee hungry, and feed thee; or thirsty, and give thee drink? And when did we see thee a stranger, and take thee in; or naked, and clothe thee? Or when did we see thee sick, or in prison, and come to thee?'

"And answering the king will say to them, 'Amen I say to you, as long as you did it for one of these, the least of my brethren, you did it for me.'

"Then he will say to those on his left hand, 'Depart from me, accursed ones, into the everlasting fire which was prepared for the devil and his angels. For I was hungry, and you did not give me to eat; I was thirsty and you gave me no drink; I was a stranger and you did not take me in; naked, and you did not clothe me; sick, and in prison, and you did not visit me.'

"Then they also will answer and say, 'Lord, when did we see thee hungry, or thirsty, or a stranger, or naked, or sick, or in prison, and did not minister to thee?'

"Then he will answer them, saying, 'Amen I say to you, as long as you did not do it for one of these least ones, you did not do it for me.'

"And these will go into everlasting punishment, but the just into everlasting life."

We should like to comment on two points only: first, the great prominence given to the works of mercy, the fruit of charity, that virtue which our Lord stressed so insistently and which He pointed out as the distinctive mark of His disciples; and second, the twofold aspect of the judgment, terrible for the disloyal, lazy servants who despised the warnings of their Master, who shall come as a just Judge to condemn them, and consoling for the faithful servants who shall hear their Lord speak the joyful words: "Come, blessed of my Father, take possession of the kingdom prepared for you from the foundation of the world."

The Betrayal by Judas

(Matt. 26:3–5, 14–16; Mark 14:1–2, 1–11; Luke 22:1–6)

The great renown which Jesus had won by raising Lazarus, combined with His triumphal entry into Jerusalem and the biting invectives which He had hurled against the Scribes and Pharisees, fanned the Sanhedrists' anger to such heat that they decided to rid themselves of Him quickly and forever. To concoct a scheme for attaining this objective, they held a meeting, not a formal and solemn conclave in the great hall at the side of the Temple, but a secret gathering in the house of Caiphas the high priest, which was attended by the representatives of all three authorities—chief priests, Scribes, and elders or noted personages. The Passover was now only two days away: "It was two days before the Passover and the feast of the Unleavened Bread" (Mark 14:1; cf. Matt. 28:2).

All present at the meeting were agreed that Jesus must be put to death, and that He should not be arrested publicly, but should rather be seized by stealth for fear of the people. It is probable, however, that there were many different opinions as to the best moment for apprehending Him. Doubtless some clamored for immediate action, so that everything would be completed in time to enable them to celebrate the Passover in peace and triumph. But others believed that it would not be easy to arrest, try, condemn and execute Jesus so quickly, and therefore they advised deferring the whole scheme until after the feast, when all the pilgrims would have left the city, thus lessening the danger of a riot if anything went wrong. In the meantime, they could keep a close watch on the Galilean Prophet so that He would not escape.

This seemed to be the procedure most likely to be adopted when a new, unexpected factor came to light. Judas Iscariot, one of the Twelve, found out about the meeting of the Sanhedrists and, knowing the reason for it, presented himself before the assembly with the brazen offer: "What are you willing to give me, and I will deliver him to you?"

Here was an undreamed-of opportunity, one that they could not afford to miss! All they had to do was make an offer. The traitor was not even exacting in his terms, but was content to take whatever they wished to give him, since it would all be clear profit. They decided on thirty pieces of silver, the price of a slave (Exod. 21:32)! [22]

Satan himself had urged the traitor on to commit his horrendous crime; as St. Luke tells us (22:3 *f.*): "Satan entered into Judas, surnamed Iscariot, one of the Twelve. And he went away and discussed with the chief priests and the captains, how he might betray him to them."

But this was not the first time that the devil had taken possession of Judas' soul. The traitor had continued to live in close association with Jesus, but for a long time past, his thoughts and his heart had been very far from his Divine Master.

When our Lord had promised the Eucharist at Capharnaum and had told His disciples that they would eat His flesh and drink His blood, many of them had been so scandalized that they would no longer walk with Him; but Peter, in the name of the Apostles, had protested stoutly that they would always remain faithful to Him. To this declaration of loyalty, Jesus had replied: "Have I not chosen you, the Twelve?" as if to say: "I am well aware of your faith and your good will, which are the fruit of my choosing you." But He added sorrowfully: "Yet one of you is a devil."

Jesus was here referring to Judas, as St. John tells us explicitly: "Now he was speaking of Judas Iscariot, the son of Simon; for he it was, though one of the Twelve, who was to betray him" (John 6:72).

One of the vices which the devil had planted in the traitor's heart was the consuming avarice which led him to steal from the common fund. Indeed St. John (12:6) bluntly calls him a thief: "He was a thief, and holding the purse, used to take what was put into it." Perhaps he was also consumed with envy and despair at seeing other Apostles preferred to him. No doubt these unworthy sentiments had

[22] Approximately $42.00 in our money (Translator).

caused him to draw away little by little from Jesus until finally he came to regard his Master with actual antipathy and hostility. It is also possible that he had at first looked for the founding of a temporal kingdom in which he would hold a distinguished post; but when he realized that his hopes of worldly success were vain, he turned his back contemptuously on his Divine Master. The other Apostles also had looked forward to a glorious Messianic kingdom, but their humility and love for Jesus kept them faithful to Him, whereas Judas, lacking these virtues, turned traitor.

Some authors have tried to make Judas out to be a man of noble character, intelligent and well-educated, in contrast to the other Apostles, who were uncultured and ignorant. These writers say that his handing Jesus over to the Jews was inspired by a worthy motive, and that in so doing he only wished to have our Lord show His divine power over the enemies who were harassing Him.[23] Klausner regards Judas' action as simply "the performance of a religious duty," a proof of his loyalty to legitimate authority, for since Jesus was "a beguiler and one who led astray," He had to be removed.[24] We need not pause to explode such myths, for they are in evident opposition to the clear and repeated declarations of the evangelists and of Christ Himself.

It has also been advocated that Judas' act of flinging down the thirty pieces of silver in the Temple was a sign of the "great love" which the traitor still felt for Jesus in the depths of his heart. But such a theory is based on a psychological impossibility. Actually there is a perfectly logical explanation of Judas' conduct after the betrayal. Despite his feelings of antipathy, perhaps even of hatred, he knew that Jesus was innocent, and when he saw Him condemned ("Then Judas, who betrayed him, when he saw that he was condemned, repented"; Matt. 27:3), he realized the true enormity of his crime. In a vain endeavor to throw off the weight of his guilt, he flung from him the price of his iniquity. There is no question of love here, but only of shame and despair.

From the moment he made the compact with the chief priests, Judas "was watching for an opportunity to betray [Jesus] without a disturbance" (Luke 22:6). The opportunity he sought was not long in coming; in fact, to his own undoing, he found it the very day after the secret meeting of the Jewish leaders at which he had appeared.

[23] Cf. Cheyne-Black, *Encyclopaedia Biblica* (London, 1899–1903), II, 26–27.
[24] *Jesus of Nazareth*, pp. 325–329.

26. The Last Supper: Agony in the Garden

In beginning to speak of the Passion, we are entering what can be called the sanctuary of Christ's life. His whole sojourn on earth is shrouded in the mystery of the hypostatic union, but no part of it is veiled so deeply as that ever-memorable day on which He, the Word of God, the Son of the Eternal Father, appeared before the world "despised and the most abject of men, a man of sorrows" (Isai. 53:3), nailed to the cross like a criminal. So majestic, so sacred, so divinely tragic are these scenes, that the soul feels itself moved to contemplate them in loving silence rather than to describe them in the halting words of human language.

Preparations for the Last Supper

Peace reigned in the little house at Bethany, but joy was absent as dawn ushered in that Thursday which future generations were to call holy. Sorrow and a vague foreboding weighed heavily upon Jesus' loyal friends, for on the preceding Monday and Tuesday He had come to dangerously close grips with His enemies. It was evident that the prolonged battle had now reached its inevitable crisis, and that the issue was soon to be decided.

Since the Paschal supper was to be eaten that Thursday evening, the disciples asked Jesus: "Where dost thou want us to prepare for thee to eat the passover?"

He replied by selecting two of their number, Peter

624

and John, and instructing them: "Go into the city, and there will meet you a man carrying a pitcher of water; follow him. And wherever he enters, say to the master of the house, 'The Master says, "Where is my guest chamber, that I may eat the passover there with my disciples?" ' And he will show you a large upper room furnished; there make ready for us."

Although Judas, as treasurer of the group, was the most obvious choice for this assignment, our Lord did not send him, but selected instead His beloved disciple and His future Vicar on earth. No doubt the traitor was busily engaged in making his own evil arrangements.

When they set off to execute their commission, the two Apostles probably ascended Mount Olivet, and, following the path which now skirts the Carmelite convent, went down along the southernmost of the three roads to the Valley of the Cedron. From there they could have entered the city through the Gate of the Fountain, near the pool of Siloe, and climbed the stairway, the remains of which are still to be seen near the Church of St. Peter *in Gallicantu*. Or they might have taken the northernmost road, the one nearest the walls of the Temple, which led to the hill of Ophel. From there they could have crossed the Tyropoeon Valley, and entered the section of Jerusalem which Josephus calls the "Upper Market." [1] At any rate, once in the city, they met the man carrying a pitcher of water, which he had probably drawn from the pool of Siloe, and everything else followed just as their Lord had foretold. The householder to whom the Apostles brought their message must have been well known to Jesus. Most likely he was a rich man or at least a personage of some standing in the community, and he may have been one of those disciples who, like Nicodemus, admired Christ and followed Him more or less secretly. There is some reason to believe that he was the father of young John Mark.

Meanwhile, in Bethany, the moment of farewell had come. The Apostles were there, waiting uneasily to accompany their Master into the uncertain, dangerous future. Doubtless our Lady was present, too. Had her Son revealed to her the great mystery, the tragic outcome of that day and the eventual glorious triumph? Whether or not He had done so, it was now, more than ever before, that she felt her soul transfixed by the sword foretold by Simeon; but the depth of her sorrow was matched by the firmness of her faith and the magnanimity of her resignation. There, too, was Mary, the gentle, recollected, con-

[1] *Wars* v. 4. 1.

templative Mary of Bethany, regarding her Master in loving, grieving silence. Beside her stood the other Mary, Mary Magdalene, who had accompanied and tirelessly served Jesus during His missionary journeys, and who was soon to run swiftly to the sepulchre in search of Him whom she loved so ardently. Present also to say farewell to their Divine Guest were the solicitous Martha and her brother Lazarus. Jesus took His leave of these faithful friends and, accompanied by His Apostles, made His way to Jerusalem, ascended Mount Sion, and entered the house which had been prepared for the celebration of the Paschal supper.

THE SITE OF THE CENACLE

Today the Cenacle is venerated on Mount Sion, in the southwest of Jerusalem, a site which is justified by an ancient tradition going back to the first centuries of the Christian era. From St. Epiphanius (A.D. 392) we know that at the time of the Emperor Hadrian's journey in Palestine (during the years 130–131), there was on the hill a small church which was regarded as the scene of the Holy Spirit's descent upon the Apostles.[2] In the fourth century, the place where the descent of the Holy Spirit occurred was identified with the room in which the Last Supper was eaten, as is clear from the *Didascalia Addai,* in which we read: "From there [Mount Olivet] they ascended to the upper room, where our Lord had eaten the Passover with them. . . . Just as in this upper room the mystery of the Body and Blood of our Lord was instituted in order to rule over the world, so also the doctrine of His preaching began in this place to reign over the world."[3] The identification occurs also in Hesychius Presbyter (A.D. 440), where he is drawing a parallel between Bethlehem and Sion: "Thou [Bethlehem] drawest milk from virginal breasts, while the latter [Sion] draws the *Spirit* from the bosom of the Father. Thou hast baked bread, but Sion has spread a supper [$\delta\epsilon\hat{\iota}\pi\nu o\nu$]."[4] From then on, the tradition con-

---

[2] "Hadrian . . . went to the celebrated and noble city of Jerusalem. . . . He found it razed to the ground, the Temple of God destroyed and trodden underfoot, except for a few houses and a small church of God [$\kappa\alpha\grave{\iota}\ \tau\hat{\eta}s\ \tauo\hat{v}\ \Theta\epsilon o\hat{v}$ $'E\kappa\kappa\lambda\eta\sigma\acute{\iota}\alpha s\ \mu\iota\kappa\rho\hat{\alpha}s\ o\mathring{v}\sigma\eta s$]." The saint goes on to say that this church was on the spot where the Apostles, upon returning from Mount Olivet after the Ascension, went up to the Cenacle, or the upper room ($\epsilon\mathring{\iota}s\ \tau\grave{o}\ \mathring{v}\pi\epsilon\rho\hat{\wp}o\nu$). (*Liber de mensuris et ponderibus,* XIV: PG 43, 260.)

[3] Nau, *La Didascalie des douze Apôtres* (Paris, 1912), p. 223; cf. Baldi, *Enchiridion,* p. 606.

[4] *Quaestiones: In Jacobum fratrem Domini: PG* 93, 1480.

The Cenacle.

tinues without variation,[5] and must be accepted as trustworthy because the place in question was well known, and also because a community of Christians, ruled by their own bishop, had resided constantly in Jerusalem, except for the short interval in the year 70 when they withdrew to Pella.

We cannot be as certain that the house of Mary, the mother of John Mark (Acts 12:12), was the scene of the Last Supper, and that here, too, occurred the happy death of the Blessed Virgin, two matters about which there is a great variety of opinion. As regards the first possibility, we know that it has a fairly ancient tradition to support it. About the year 530, Theodosius wrote explicitly: "It was the house of St. Mark the Evangelist." [6] And his grounds for saying so must have been a tradition already established, perhaps long before the date at which he wrote. The same identification apparently derives some support from the Acts of the Apostles, 12:11–17. When St. Peter was freed from prison by the angel, "he went to the house of Mary, the mother of John who was surnamed Mark, where many had gathered

---

[5] It is true that there were passing variations, but since these were unimportant and were begotten of erroneous exegesis, they do not merit attention.

[6] "Ipsa fuit domus sancti Marci evangelistae" (*De situ Terrae Sanctae,* in Geyer, *Itinera,* p. 141).

Basilica of the Dormition, built partly on the site of Sancta Sion
or the Church of the Cenacle.

together and were praying." Yet he did not stay there, but "departed, and went to another place." This passage gives the impression that John Mark's house was the center where the faithful met to pray, and that St. Peter did not wish to stop long there because it was well known as a gathering point for the followers of Christ and was consequently too dangerous a spot in which to shelter.

Today a magnificent basilica stands near the Cenacle and partly on the site once occupied by the Church of Sancta Sion. In memory of the death of our Lady, it is called the Basilica of the Dormition, a title which is based on the supposition that the Mother of God lived in the Cenacle and died there. However, some authors hold that our Lady died at Ephesus. Neither opinion can claim more than a degree of probability, yet we believe that ecclesiastical tradition favors Jerusalem.

The Church of Sancta Sion, which was described by the pilgrim Etheria (A.D. 385), was burned down by the Persians in 614, rebuilt by St. Modestus, Patriarch of Jerusalem, and again reconstructed by the Crusaders, only to fall into ruins at the beginning of the fourteenth century. The Franciscans built it up again and occupied it until June, 1551, when the Moslems, under the pretext that it contained the tomb of David, drove them out of it. Today the chapel of this Franciscan

reconstruction still stands but is now a mosque whose Moslem occupants point it out as the Cenacle.[7]

THE MANNER OF CELEBRATING THE PASSOVER

In Exodus 12:8–12, the manner of celebrating the Passover is
prescribed in the following terms: "And they shall eat the flesh [of the
sacrificed lamb] that night [the night of the 14th of Nisan] roasted at
the fire: and unleavened bread with wild lettuce. You shall not eat
thereof any thing raw, nor boiled in water, but only roasted at the
fire. You shall eat the head with the feet and entrails thereof. Neither
shall there remain any thing of it until morning. If there be any thing
left, you shall burn it with fire. And thus you shall eat it: You shall
gird your reins, and you shall have shoes on your feet, holding staves
in your hands, and you shall eat in haste; for it is the Phase (that is the
Passage) of the Lord."

As the centuries went by, these ceremonies were modified, some
being dropped and new ones added. Thus in the New Testament times,
the participants did not stand but sat, or rather reclined in the Roman
manner, as the Gospel phrase indicates (ἀνέκειτο; ἀνέπεσεν: "he reclined"; Matt. 26:20; Luke 22:14). The purpose of the change was
to show that the Jews were no longer slaves, as in Egypt, but were now
their own masters. In our Lord's day, the ritual was as follows: during
the Paschal supper four cups of wine had to be circulated, even in the
poorest households.[8] These cups played a very important part in the
ceremony, and all the other details revolved around them. When the
first cup was filled, it and the supper were blessed. Then the bitter
herbs, the unleavened bread, and the sauce or *haroseth* were distributed. Next came the second cup, after which the father of the
family explained the signifiance of the ceremony, and all recited the
first part of the *Hallel* (Ps. 113–118; Vulgate Ps. 112–117). The third
cup was then filled and a blessing was pronounced over the supper.

---

[7] For further details see the learned article by Fr. Power in *Dict. de la Bible*,
Suppl. I, cols. 1064–1084, and *Jérusalem Nouvelle* by Frs. Vincent and Abel,
pp. 421–481, in which there is a very detailed discussion of points that are still
doubtful, such as the exact structure of the Church of Sancta Sion and its precise relationship with the Upper Room, i.e., with the Cenacle properly so called.
  In the Jewish-Arab war (1948), the Cenacle passed into the hands of the Jews,
and they converted the lower part into a synagogue.
[8] *Mishnah, Pesahim* 10:1; but see above, p. 248, n. 8.

Finally the fourth and last cup was circulated, and the ritual closed with the recitation of the rest of the *Hallel*.[9]

THE DATE OF THE LAST SUPPER

We know from the Gospels that the Last Supper was celebrated on a Thursday, that our Lord was crucified on a Friday, and that He rose from the dead the following Sunday. But it is not so easy to determine the *dates* of these events.

According to Exodus 2:6–10, the lamb had to be sacrificed and eaten on the 14th of Nisan. The next day, the 15th, was "the solemnity of the unleavened bread" (Lev. 23:6), and it began the series of seven days which extended to the 21st inclusive (Lev. 23:7–8; Exod. 12:18). But since unleavened bread had to be eaten with the lamb on the 14th (Exod. 12:18), this day was usually called the first day of the unleavened bread.[10]

We learn from the three Synoptic Gospels that Jesus celebrated the Passover, that is, He ate the Paschal lamb, on the 14th: "On the first day of the Unleavened Bread, when it was customary for them to sacrifice the passover. . . ." (Mark 14:12). Obviously, the first day of the unleavened bread could not have been the 13th, but must have been the 14th, the day on which the lamb was sacrificed, and which was therefore called "the phase [or Passover] of the Lord" (Lev. 23:5). St. Luke (22:7) tells us that "the day of the Unleavened Bread came, on which the passover had to be sacrificed." St. Matthew (26:17) is less explicit ("On the first day of the Unleavened Bread"), but there is no doubt that he wishes to specify the same day as the other two Synoptic authors.

St. John, on the contrary, seems to say that Jesus celebrated the Passover on the 13th and died on the 14th. As a matter of fact, he says that Christ was tried and crucified on "the Preparation Day of the Passover" (19:14; cf. v. 31), which was the vigil of the great feast, i.e., the 14th. In addition, he calls the Sabbath that came immediately after Jesus' death "a *solemn* day" (19:31); and so far as we can guess, he does so because that year, the feast of the Passover, the 15th of Nisan, came on a Sabbath. Consequently, our Lord would seem to have died on the 14th. Then, too, St. John tells us indirectly that on

---

[9] Cf. above, pp. 247 *f*. A description of the Passover as it is celebrated today is given on pp. 248 *ff*.
[10] Cf. *Wars* v. 3. 1.

the day of Christ's death, the Jews had not yet eaten the Passover: "They themselves did not enter the praetorium, that they might not be defiled, but might eat the passover" (18:28). Finally, there is an extrinsic reason for saying that our Lord died on the 14th: it is most unlikely that the Jews would have crucified Him on the very day of the Passover, or that they would have broken the solemn law of the Sabbath rest.

We know that there is no real contradiction between St. John and the Synoptic Gospels, not only because of divine inspiration, but also because it is inconceivable that any of the evangelists would have erred in reporting so vital and so obvious a fact as the Crucifixion. Even so it is not easy to harmonize the two accounts.

It seems less difficult to reconcile St. John's narrative with that of the Synoptic authors, than vice versa. In fact, it is possible to give a more or less satisfactory answer to many of the difficulties arising out of the difference between the fourth Gospel and the other three. Thus the "Preparation Day of the Passover" was not the vigil of the Passover (i.e., the 14th) but the Passover itself, Friday the 15th. John calls it "the Preparation Day" because it prepared for the next day, the Sabbath (in that sense every Friday was a "preparation"), and he adds "*of* the Passover" because it coincided with the feast. He calls the Sabbath "a *solemn* day," not because it was the feast of the Passover (i.e., the 15th), but because it fell within the Paschal period. In speaking about the Passover which the Jews wished to eat (18:28), he was not referring to the Paschal lamb, but to the special sacrifices which were offered on the day of the Passover. Finally, once the Jews had Jesus in their power, they would have wanted to kill Him as quickly as possible, and would not have let the Sabbath rest or the feast interfere with their plans, especially since certain urgent cases dispensed from the law of rest.[11]

However, as we pointed out above, these solutions are far from being fully satisfactory. In its obvious and natural sense, "the Preparation Day of the Passover" was the vigil of the feast, i.e., the 14th, on which preparations were made for the celebration of the Passover. To say that it was Friday, the 15th, and to hold that it was called "the Preparation Day *of the Passover*" because it coincided with the feast,

---

[11] This interpretation of St. John's narrative has recently been proposed and skillfully defended by W. B. Robinson, "The Date and Significance of the Last Supper," in *The Evangelical Quarterly*, 23 (1951), 126–133. There is a brief summary of his arguments in *Verb. Dom.*, 31 (1953), 111–112.

certainly seems to do violence to the text. However, it is quite possible that the Sabbath was called "a *solemn* day" simply because it fell within the Paschal period. The solution to the argument about the breaking of the Sabbath rest may be somewhat strained, yet it still has some value. But the proposed interpretation of the phrase, "that they [i.e., the Jews] might eat the passover" (John 18:28), appears unacceptable, since "to eat the passover" can mean only one thing, i.e., to eat the Paschal lamb. Making it refer to the other sacrifices that were offered during the Paschal period is little more than a subterfuge.

We would have a very simple solution to the problem if the Friday on which our Lord died was regarded by some of the Jews as the 14th and by others as the 15th. Thus we could say that St. John had followed the former reckoning and the Synoptic writers the latter. Then the two accounts would harmonize perfectly. Actually, such a solution has been proposed, not only in our own day, but as far back as Petavius (Denis Petau, died 1652).

Is this answer a mere ruse, or are there sufficient reasons for affirming the existence of the suggested double computation of dates? We must confess that there is no proof that such a twofold reckoning really did take place in the year of our Lord's death. But we know that there were arguments and differences of opinion between the Sadducees and the Pharisees of that period regarding the dates of the feasts, and hence we can reasonably conclude that it was possible and even probable that the proposed double computation of the date of the Passover did occur in the year of the Crucifixion.

It is a fact that, although the Law explicitly specified definite dates for certain feasts and ceremonies, the Jews did not always obey if they thought they had a plausible reason for introducing some change. Thus, for example, the pious king Ezechias did not scruple to order the Passover to be celebrated in the second month when circumstances had prevented its being held during the first month, that is, on the 15th of Nisan. Then too, rabbinical literature makes it abundantly clear that a number of laws were interpreted differently by various schools. A typical example of this divergence of opinion was the dispute concerning the date of Pentecost, a feast which the Law commanded to be celebrated fifty days after the offering of the sheaf of corn during the Paschal octave. The Sadducees, including most of the priests and the powerful family of Boethus, maintained that Pentecost had to be celebrated on the day after the Sabbath (i.e., on Sunday), and that therefore the sheaf had to be offered on the Sunday during the octave of the Passover. But the Pharisees held that Pentecost could be celebrated on any day of the week, and therefore they always offered the sheaf on the day after the Passover, that is, on the 16th of Nisan.

Because of their views on the matter, the Sadducees used to postpone the first of Nisan by one day in a year when the Passover was due to fall on a Friday, and anticipate it by one day when the Passover was due to come on a Sunday. Thus in those years, they would sacrifice the lamb on a Friday, celebrate the Passover on a Saturday, and offer the sheaf on a Sunday.

Now, if we suppose that, in the year of our Lord's death, the Passover was due to fall on a Friday, the Sadducees would have eaten the Paschal lamb on Friday, which they would reckon as the 14th, and would have celebrated the Passover on Saturday, their 15th; while the Pharisees, who would not have changed the dates, would have eaten the Paschal lamb on Thursday, the actual 14th, and celebrated the Passover on Friday, the actual 15th. This would provide a satisfactory answer to the difference between the Synoptic writers and St. John, on the hypothesis that the former followed the Pharisees' computation, and the latter that of the Sadducees. Thus the same day, Friday, would have been the 15th for the Pharisees and the 14th for the Sadducees, and the two accounts are therefore in perfect harmony.

This theory is confirmed by the fact that it does away with the necessity of invoking dispensations from the law of Sabbath rest to explain certain passages in the Synoptic Gospels. We know that all work was forbidden on the first day of the Passover: "The first month [Nisan], the fourteenth day of the month at evening, is the phase of the Lord. And the fifteenth day of the same month is the solemnity of the unleavened bread of the Lord. . . . The first day [i.e., the 15th] shall be most solemn unto you and holy: *you shall do no servile work therein*" (Lev. 23:5–7; cf. Exod. 12:16). But from Mark 15:46 we learn that on the day of our Lord's death Joseph of Arimathea bought a linen cloth, and from Luke 23:56, that the holy women prepared spices and ointment. In Mark 14:43–47, we are told that a great crowd came out with swords and clubs to seize Jesus, and we also know that the chief priests had decided not to arrest Him on the feast for fear of a riot among the people (Matt. 26:5; Mark 14:2). Hence the day on which our Lord was arrested and crucified could not have been the first day of the Passover, which was a day of rest. As we have suggested before, we can explain plausibly enough how all these activities could have occurred on a day of rest. But the hypothesis of a double computation of dates solves the problem at least satisfactorily, for the difficulty is removed if we presuppose that the people who engaged in these activities did not celebrate the Passover on Friday, the day of Christ's death, but followed the Sadducees' reckoning and held the feast on Saturday.

Some may object that all mention of a double computation of dates is mere theorizing. Furthermore, is it likely that St. John, who must have been very familiar with the Synoptic accounts, would have used a different system of reckoning dates in his Gospel? And why would he have followed the Sadducees' method when, so far as we can gather, the great mass of the people used the Pharisees' computation?

Indeed it is not easy to give a satisfactory explanation for St. John's preference. Yet it would be imprudent to deny that he could have had good reasons about which we know nothing. We must admit that the difference in reckoning dates is only a theory; but it is a plausible theory based on proven historical facts, and therefore possessing a strong probability. And if it enables us to solve easily and satisfactorily a problem that otherwise seems insoluble, we are fully justified in accepting it as the key to the solution.

In order to show that it was possible and even probable that at times not all the Jews celebrated the Passover on the same day, authors often point to the primitive method by which the beginning of the month was fixed, namely, the observation of the new moon. Thus it could happen that the new moon would be seen in one place sooner than in another, and that therefore the month of Nisan could begin a day earlier in one locality than it did elsewhere. But even if a divergence did sometimes occur in this manner, it is scarcely possible in the case under discussion, for it is hard to see how the people of one district, namely, Jerusalem, could ever have differed so much among themselves concerning the occurrence of the new moon, the beginning of the month, and consequently, the celebration of the Passover.[12]

Great interest has been awakened by a new theory suggesting that our Lord celebrated the Last Supper on Tuesday of Holy Week, and that He appeared before the various tribunals on Wednesday, Thursday and the morning of Friday, the day on which He died.[13]

---

[12] In Str.-Bill., II, 812–853, there is a lengthy and erudite dissertation on the day of our Lord's death (*Der Todestag Jesu*), which contains many further details.

[13] See A. Jaubert, "La date de la dernière Cène," in *Revue de l'histoire des*

If we are to understand this theory, we must bear in mind that the ancient priestly calendar in Israel was based on the solar year. In the *Book of Jubilees,* dating from the second half of the second century B.C., and in the more ancient *Book of Henoch (Ethiopic),* which it quotes, the old solar calendar is employed and defended against the lunar calendar, which was introduced into Palestine when the country passed from the dominion of the Pharaohs to that of the Seleucids, who followed the latter calendar.

According to the ancient priestly calendar, the year always began on the fourth day of the week, i.e., our Wednesday,[14] and since the ecclesiastical year started with the month of Nisan, the first of that month always fell on Wednesday. Therefore the 15th of Nisan would also be a Wednesday, and hence the Paschal lamb would be eaten on Tuesday the 14th, in which case our Lord celebrated the Last Supper on a Tuesday. This reckoning is not at all improbable, for it could have happened that Jesus followed the ancient priestly calendar in celebrating the Passover, as His contemporaries, the ascetics of Qumran, appear to have done.[15]

In itself this is no more than a plausible theory, yet we find it confirmed by very trustworthy evidence. Thus in the *Didascalia Apostolorum,* a document dating from the second century or the beginning of the third, we read:

This [the coming of Judas] took place on Wednesday. After eating the Passover on Tuesday evening, we went to the Mount of Olives. . . . "On Tuesday evening I ate My Passover with you and during the night they seized Me." . . . On the following day, which was Wednesday, He was held in the house of the high priest, Caiphas. On the same day the leaders of the people met in council to judge Him. On the following day, which was Thursday, they brought Him to the governor, Pilate; and He was held by Pilate throughout Thursday night. On Friday morning they brought forward many accusations before Pilate . . .; and they crucified Him on the same day, Friday." [16]

St. Epiphanius writes: "A fast is observed on Wednesdays and

religions, 145 (1954), 140–173; cf. *Biblica,* 36 (1955), 403–413; *La Maison-Dieu,* 43 (1955), 165–167; *Apostolado Sacerdotal* (1955), pp. 311–313; *RB* (1952), pp. 200 *f.*

[14] Cf. *RB* (1952), p. 200; *Biblica,* 36 (1955), 403.

[15] Among the manuscripts discovered at Qumran was part of the *Book of Jubilees,* which, as we have said, employed and defended the solar calendar on which the ancient priestly one was based.

[16] Ed. Funck (Paderborn, 1905), V, 14, 4, 5, 20, pp. 272–280.

Fridays because our Lord was taken prisoner at the beginning of Wednesday and was crucified on Friday." [17]

Another witness is St. Victorinus, who tells us that "Jesus Christ . . . was seized by the impious on the fourth day." [18]

The material which we have just summarized is indeed impressive. But does it offer a definitive solution to the problem? The testimony of the *Didascalia Apostolorum* is unequivocal; its terms are clear and precise, and it is confirmed by the short historical notes written by St. Epiphanius and St. Victorinus. Hence it would be arbitrary and unjust to refuse even to consider the theory that our Lord celebrated the Passover according to the ancient priestly calendar. In addition, it is hard to see how all the events of the trial, especially the appearances before the various tribunals, can be fitted into the space of one night and one morning. However, we must acknowledge that the theory presents its own difficulties.

There is no doubt that each of the four Gospels gives the impression that the trial began and ended between Thursday night and Friday noon. Some may perhaps say that the evangelists concerned themselves with the events alone, and paid no attention to chronological sequence. But this does not seem to have been the case, because the Gospels provide several specific chronological references. Thus, when Judas left the Cenacle, "it was night" (John 13:30); the Sanhedrin met "when morning came" (Matt. 27:1); "as soon as it was morning" (Mark 15:1); "as soon as day broke" (Luke 22:66); "It was now about the sixth hour, and there was darkness over the whole land until the ninth hour" (Luke 23:44); "On the first day of the week, Mary Magdalene came to the tomb, while it was still dark" (John 20:1). We agree that these details do not refer strictly to the succession of events, but when we consider that the evangelists took pains to record them carefully, it is difficult to explain why the Gospels fail to cast any light on the events of Wednesday and Thursday of Holy Week.

It should also be noted that neither in Josephus, nor in Philo, nor in the immense volume of rabbinical literature do we find the slightest hint that a part of the people, or any particular sect, celebrated the Passover according to the ancient priestly calendar. The ascetics of Qumran certainly had the *Book of Jubilees*, but we cannot conclude

---

[17] *Epiphanius de Fide,* ed. Holl (Leipzig, 1933), p. 522: *PG* 42, 825.
[18] *De fabrica mundi: PL* 5, 304. "Homo Christus Jesus . . . tetrade ab impiis comprehensus est."

therefrom that they celebrated the Passover according to the calendar defended in that book.

We must grant that a little more than twelve hours seems a very short period for the unfolding of the events of the Passion. Nevertheless, if we take into account the urgency of the case and the Jews' anxiety to execute our Lord before celebrating the Passover, we shall perhaps not find it so difficult to understand how the whole Passion could have been fitted into such narrow limits. The sequence of events would then have been somewhat as follows: the Sanhedrin convened on Thursday night and in the small hours of Friday morning; our Lord was brought before Pilate, who sent Him to Herod; Herod sent Him back to Pilate, who ordered Him to be scourged, then presented Him to the people and, finally, condemned Him. The Sanhedrin's trial was a summary one, and it could be said that Pilate did not even institute proceedings against Jesus. He heard no depositions of witnesses, but, violently urged on by the Jews and intimidated by their threats, merely pronounced sentence. If, then, we take these circumstances into consideration, we can see how the whole Passion could have occurred in a relatively short space of time.

But how are we to explain the definite statements of the *Didascalia Apostolorum*, St. Epiphanius and St. Victorinus? We must admit that we can see no wholly satisfactory solution to this difficulty. Perhaps it would not be rash to suppose that the *Didascalia* reflects a merely regional tradition whose origin we cannot even trace; and the same may hold good for St. Epiphanius and St. Victorinus. Be that as it may, it is certain that, while this documentary evidence is worthy of being taken into consideration, we must not forget the difficulties which we have briefly pointed out. Therefore, since it would be premature to form a definite judgment on the implications of this evidence, it is wisest to maintain a prudent reserve in regard to the solution of the problem.

The Last Supper

"And when the hour had come, he reclined at table and the twelve apostles with him. And he said to them: 'I have greatly desired to eat this passover with you before I suffer; for I say to you that I will eat of it no more, until it has been fulfilled in the kingdom of God' " (Luke 22: 15–16).

How touching are our Lord's opening words! He had ardently longed to celebrate the Last Supper, because He was going to leave us the most precious pledge of His love, the most holy sacrament of the Eucharist; because, after it, He was going to accomplish the redemption of men, for which He had come into the world; and because He would celebrate no other supper until He sat at the eternal, divine banquet in heaven.[19]

While Jesus was thus revealing to the Apostles His love and sorrow, a dispute arose among them as to which of their number was the greatest. The argument was probably caused by the order of precedence in which they were reclining at table.

As we have already pointed out, in our Lord's day the participants in the Paschal supper did not follow the prescriptions laid down in Exodus 12:11, that is, they no longer ate standing, with staves in their hands. Instead, they followed the custom in use among the Greeks, Romans and other peoples, which had been adopted in everyday life by the Jews as well. On three sides of a table, which was ordinarily rectangular in shape, they placed wide couch-like benches, upon which the guests half-reclined, with cushions under their left arms, their right hands remaining free for eating. The fourth side of the table was left unoccupied to allow the servants to pass in and out. In reality, the whole arrangement was simply the *triclinium* of the Romans. Dishes of food were placed on the table and several guests helped themselves from each dish.

The places at the head of the table were, of course, the seats of honor. Although we are not told the order in which the Apostles were seated at the Last Supper, we can deduce it, in part at least and with some degree of probability, from the Gospel narrative.[20] Our Lord certainly occupied the central position (1) at the head of the table, with Peter, perhaps, at the left (2), and John at the right (3). The traitor, Judas, was in the first place on the right-hand side of the table (X). This seating arrangement would explain how Jesus was able to

[19] Christ announced that He would not eat the Passover again on earth, thereby clearly foretelling His death. But He also said that He would celebrate it in heaven, where it would appear in its plenitude and perfect reality. The kingdom of God as mentioned here in Luke 22:16, 18; Matthew 26:29 and Mark 14:25, is not the kingdom of God on earth after the Resurrection (Lagrange), but the eternal kingdom of God in heaven (Buzy, Pirot, Knabenbauer).

[20] See diagram, p. 639. We describe the positions of the diners as viewed by an observer standing at the top of the hall and looking down over our Lord's couch.

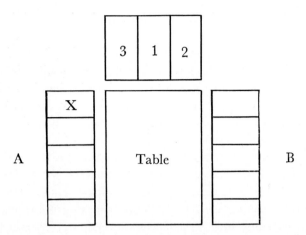

reach over and give a piece of bread to Judas, how Peter was able to speak to John and how the beloved disciple leaned upon Jesus' breast. Since the diners reclined on their left sides, with their heads next to the table, those who were at the left-hand side of the hall (B) faced up towards the places of honor, while those at the right (A) faced down the room.

Our Lord cut short the Apostles' argument about precedence by admonishing them gravely: "The kings of the Gentiles lord it over them, and they who exercise authority over them are called Bene-factors. But not so with you. On the contrary, let him who is greatest among you become as the youngest, and him who is the chief as the servant. For which is the greater, he who reclines at table, or he who serves? Is it not he who reclines? But I am in your midst as he who serves" (Luke 22:25–27).

Jesus Washes the Apostles' Feet
(John 13:1–17)

Jesus did not simply tell the Apostles how they should act towards one another; He showed them by His own example the manner in which they should serve their brethren. Several of the Fathers see in His actions here a secondary lesson, namely, the great purity with which we should approach the sacrament of the Eucharist.

Before describing the washing of feet, St. John inserts a short but significant prelude (13:1–5): "Before the feast of the Passover, Jesus, knowing that the hour had come for him to pass out of this world to the Father, having loved his own who were in the world, loved them to the end." [21]

"And during the supper, the devil having already put it into the heart of Judas Iscariot, the son of Simon, to betray him, Jesus, knowing that the Father had given all things into his hands, and that he had come forth from God and was going to God, rose from the supper and laid aside his garments, and taking a towel girded himself. Then he poured water into the basin. . . ."

As Christ made His preparations, the Apostles watched Him in respectful silence, not knowing what He intended to do. He did not leave them long in doubt, for, approaching Peter, He knelt before him and began to wash his feet. The Apostle, aghast at the thought of his Master's performing such a menial task, exclaimed: "Lord, dost thou wash my feet?"

Quietly Jesus replied: "What I do thou knowest not now; but thou shalt know hereafter." [22]

"Thou shalt never wash my feet!"

"If I do not wash thee, thou shalt have no part with me."

Peter's unwillingness, begotten of humility, vanished before this threat of losing his beloved Master's friendship, and, impulsive as ever, he hastened to assure Jesus: "Lord, not my feet only, but also my hands and my head!"

Christ's reply was enigmatic: "He who has bathed needs only to wash, and he is clean all over. And you are clean, but not all." [23]

The last words, "but not all," were a delicate allusion to Judas; they were the call of the Good Shepherd to the straying sheep. But the traitor was so set on carrying out his diabolical scheme that neither the touch of Christ's divine hands nor the humble service which his Lord rendered him could soften his stony heart.

Donning His outer garment once more and resuming His place at the table, Jesus addressed His Apostles: "Do you know what I have done to you? You call me Master and Lord, and you say well, for so I am. If, therefore, I the Lord and Master have washed your feet, you also ought to wash the feet of one another. For I have given you an

---

[21] Not in a temporal ("up to the last moment") but in an intensive sense ("to the very extreme of love"). He had always loved them, but He loved them now more than ever before.

[22] "Hereafter" does not refer, as some would have it, to the enlightenment which the Apostles were to receive later from the Holy Spirit, but to the explanation which Jesus Himself gave them in verses 13 ff.

[23] Here our Lord made a transition from bodily to spiritual cleanliness.

example, that as I have done to you, so you also should do. Amen, amen, I say to you, no servant is greater than his master, nor is one who is sent greater than he who sent him. If you know these things, blessed shall you be if you do them. I do not speak of you all.[24] I know whom I have chosen; but that the Scripture may be fulfilled,[25] 'He who eats bread with me has lifted up his heel against me.' [26] I tell you now before it [the betrayal] comes to pass, that when it has come to pass you may believe that I am he [the Messias, God's Envoy]. Amen, amen, I say to you, he who receives anyone I send, receives me; and he who receives me, receives him who sent me." [27]

The Traitor
(John 13:21–32)

Now, more keenly than ever before, our Lord felt the treachery of Judas, that thorn which He had carried in His heart for so long. So great indeed was His pain that "he was troubled in spirit and said solemnly, 'Amen, amen, I say to you, one of you will betray me.' "

His quiet, sorrowful statement raised a veritable storm in the breasts of the Apostles. Deeply perturbed, they looked at each other, not knowing to whom He was referring. They were horrified at the very thought of such a crime, and, as if doubting even themselves and the testimony of their own consciences, they asked fearfully: "Is it I, Lord?"

But Jesus only reiterated and amplified His original words: "He who dips his hand into the dish with me, he will betray me. The Son of Man indeed goes his way, as it is written of him; but woe to that man by whom the Son of Man is betrayed! It were better for that man if he had not been born."

Judas, compelled to follow the others' example if he did not wish to show his hand, also asked: "Is it I, Rabbi?"

"Thou hast said it."

[24] That is, not all of them were to be blessed. Jesus knew that Judas had already undertaken to betray Him, and that he would carry out his plans.

[25] By carrying out his evil but perfectly free decision, the traitor would bring to pass the words of Sacred Scripture.

[26] Ps. 40:10.

[27] The meaning of this last sentence is perfectly clear, but not so its connection with what went before. Some authors suspect that the evangelist omitted part of our Lord's discourse, whence the lack of coherence. At all events, these words were very consoling for the Apostles, as they are for all those who can legitimately claim to be God's envoys.

The traitor knew that his plot was discovered, but even then he did not repent. However, our Lord's reply to his question at first went unnoticed by the other Apostles, who were still dazed by Jesus' words. After the initial shock had worn off, Peter could not rest until he found who was threatening his beloved Master's safety. He could have asked Jesus directly, since he was beside Him, but he did not dare. Raising himself up a little off the couch upon which he was reclining, he spoke over our Lord's shoulder to John, gesturing to him to ask the Master: [28] "Who is it of whom he speaks?"

John, leaning close to Jesus and resting his head on his Lord's breast, asked in a low voice: "Lord, who is it?"

In the same low tone, Christ replied: "It is he for whom I shall dip the bread, and give it to him."

Suiting the action to the word, He moistened a piece of bread and gave it to Judas. Among orientals, such a gesture was, and still is, a mark of special esteem. In this instance it was another appeal to Judas to repent. But the traitor refused to listen, and that is why the evangelist tells us that "after the morsel, Satan entered into him." [29]

Seeing that His appeal had failed, Jesus said to His betrayer: "What thou dost, do quickly."

"But none of those at the table understood why he said this to him. For some thought that because Judas held the purse, Jesus had said to him, 'Buy the things we need for the feast'; or that he should give something to the poor. When, therefore, he had received the morsel, he went out quickly. Now it was night."

Dark indeed was the night that veiled the traitor's furtive, sacrilegious preparations, but darker still were the shadows that reigned within his evil heart.

From ancient Christian times, authors have been arguing as to whether or not Judas received Holy Communion. According to the sequence of events which we have been following, he did not do so, for he had left the Cenacle before the institution of the Eucharist. Several of the Fathers and quite a few ecclesiastical writers hold that he did not receive Communion,[30] while others prefer the opposite interpretation. The only argument in favor of Judas' Communion is the text

---

[28] See above, pp. 638 f. for a description of the Apostles' position at the table.

[29] Satan was already in him (cf. v. 2), but with his obstinate resistance to this new proof of Jesus' love for him, the devil's power over him was strengthened still further.

[30] Cf. Knabenbauer, *In Matt.* 26:26–28.

from St. Luke (22:20–21) which reads: "This cup is the new covenant in my blood, which shall be shed for you. But behold, the hand of him who betrays me is with me on the table." Plainly, our Lord was speaking here of the Eucharist and the traitor, who, consequently, was present at the institution of the Blessed Sacrament. But we should note that the other Synoptic authors (Matt. 26:21–29 and Mark 14:18–25) place the denunciation of Judas before the institution of the Eucharist, and that both of these evangelists set themselves to narrate the denunciation clearly and in detail, while St. Luke (22:1) touches on it only indirectly and briefly. That being so, we are justified in preferring the sequence followed by Matthew and Mark, and in holding that St. Luke's observation is not in its proper chronological place, a state of affairs which is not rare in the Gospels. Hence, although we cannot be absolutely sure on the point, we may say that it is at least much more probable that Judas did not partake of the Eucharist.

When the traitor had departed, Jesus appeared as if He had been relieved of a great burden. Contemplating in spirit the wondrous effects of His Passion, He began to speak of the glory which the Son of Man was to receive and which was to redound to the Father's honor, since in the Passion of the Son the justice, goodness and mercy of the Father were to shine forth.

"When, therefore, he [Judas] had gone out, Jesus said: 'Now is the Son of Man glorified, and God is glorified in him. If God is glorified in him, God will also glorify him in himself,[31] and will glorify him at once." [32]

Institution of the Eucharist

(Matt. 26:26–29; Mark 14:22–24; Luke 22:19–20; 1 Cor. 11:23–25)

A little less than a year had passed since Jesus had delivered the discourse on the Bread of Life in the synagogue at Capharnaum. On that occasion, when He told His listeners that they would have to eat His flesh and drink His blood if they wished to live, many of them had protested violently, and many of His disciples had left Him. In the interval, our Lord does not seem to have referred to what He had said at Capharnaum, yet the Apostles must have remembered His words.

---

[31] That is, in God, in the Father, who was to make the humanity of Christ partake in His own glory (cf. John 17:5). Such, at least, is the more probable interpretation. This meaning holds good whether we read ἐν ἑαυτῷ, or ἐν αὐτῷ.

[32] At the Resurrection, without waiting for the supreme glorification in heaven.

And now the time had come to fulfill in the Cenacle the promise He had made in the synagogue and to show the Apostles the meaning of His mysterious announcement that they were to eat His flesh and drink His blood.

"And while they were at supper, Jesus took bread, and blessed and broke, and gave it to his disciples, and said, 'Take and eat; this is my body.' And taking a cup, he gave thanks and gave it to them, saying, 'All of you drink of this, for this is my blood of the new covenant, which is being shed for many unto the forgiveness of sins. But I say to you, I will not drink henceforth of this fruit of the vine,[33] until that day when I shall drink it new with you in the kingdom of my Father.' "[34]

In this passage we find expressed:

(1) Transubstantiation ("This is my body. . . . This is my blood"): "That which before was bread is now my Body; that which before was wine is now my Blood." Impanation, that is, the presence of Christ *in the bread,* is therefore excluded.

(2) The Redemption—the death of Christ and its sacrificial character: "This is my blood . . . which is being shed for many unto the forgiveness of sins."

(3) The conferring of the sacrament of Orders on the Apostles: "Do this in remembrance of me." Christ here gave the Apostles the power to do what He had just done, that is, He conferred on them the sacrament of Orders. These words are found only in St. Luke and St. Paul; they do not appear in either St. Matthew or St. Mark. But this is not sufficient reason for excluding them from the Gospel text, as some have claimed. One evangelist frequently omits what another includes.

Protestants in general deny that our Lord intended to change bread into His Body and wine into His Blood, and they maintain that He meant only to hold up the bread and wine as *symbols* of His Body and Blood. Thus, they say, when He pronounced the words "This is my body. . . . This is my blood," He simply meant "This bread *represents* my body. . . . This wine *represents* my blood." But a very little

---

[33] Jesus was not referring to the consecrated wine, i.e., His Blood, but to the ordinary wine that was being drunk at the supper.

[34] This is not the period between the Resurrection and the Ascension, i.e., the forty days during which Christ remained on earth, but rather His Father's kingdom in heaven. Here He was foretelling His death, and saying that the day would come when He would rejoice with them at a banquet in heaven.

reflection will show that such an interpretation does not correspond to the obvious meaning of the two declarations. Our Lord said categorically: "This is my body," thereby clearly establishing an equation of identity between the subject and the predicate of His statement: the bread is the body, i.e., that which Christ holds in His hands was bread, but is now His Body. Every other interpretation does violence to the text. Furthermore, the whole primitive Church understood Christ's words to mean true transubstantiation. St. Paul is the authentic representative of this belief in his time, and the generations that came after him agreed with him.

Even the rationalists acknowledge that the Protestant interpretation is false, but since they do not want to admit the miracle either, they try to prove that the incident at the Supper never happened at all. With a great display of learning, they declare that the references to the Eucharist in the Synoptic Gospels, and even in St. Paul, are later interpolations not found in the primitive texts. It would be beside the point here to follow the process by which they arrive at such a radical conclusion: we leave that to specialized works on the subject. Suffice it to say that, on close examination, the reasons which they advance under the impressive title of "textual criticism," inevitably give the impression that their whole tissue of observations and so-called critical considerations is intended to prove, by hook or by crook, that Christ did not change bread and wine into His Body and Blood.

The Discourse After the Last Supper
(John 13:33—17:26)

Our Lord's words to the Apostles after the Last Supper are not so much a discourse as an outpouring of the emotions which filled His heart on that memorable night. He spoke as a father saying farewell to his sons and earnestly warning and counselling them; as a teacher giving his pupils a last, vital lesson; as a friend, deeply grieved because the hour of separation had come. He poured out His soul to His Apostles, and to His Father whom He loved so much and to whom He was soon to return. How then can we expect to find the logical order of an academic discourse in this torrent of ideas and sentiments that came from both heart and mind, these currents that cross and mingle, advance and recede? Yet the heart, too, has its own logic which is not the same as that of the intellect. Therefore it is difficult to outline a concise plan of these chapters of St. John. However, we can divide them, although only rather generally, into three parts: chapters 13–14—warnings, and dialogue with the Apostles; chapters 15–16—allegory of the vine and the branches; persecutions: chapter 17—the priestly prayer of Christ.

OUR LORD'S WARNINGS: THE COMMANDMENT OF LOVE

"Little children, yet a little while I am with you. You will seek me, and, as I said to the Jews, 'Where I go you cannot come,' [35] so to you also I say it now. A new commandment I give you; that you love one another: that as I have loved you, you also love one another. By this will all men know that you are my disciples, if you have love for one another."

The precept of brotherly love was not unknown among the Jews. In Leviticus 19:18 they were commanded: "Seek not revenge, nor be mindful of the injury of thy citizens. Thou shalt love thy friend as thyself." Therefore the commandment of charity existed under the Old Law. But it is not clear whether this charity was restricted to the Jews' fellow countrymen, as seems to be indicated by the parallelism between the first and second parts of the verse just quoted, and to the foreigners who lived among them, or whether it extended to all men in general. At any rate, in our Lord's time the doctrine of "Thou shalt love thy neighbor and shalt hate they enemy" was common. Against this maxim He had stated His own teaching: "But I say to you, love your enemies" (Matt. 5:43 *f.*). Hence the commandment which He gave had every right to be called new; first, because it plainly included all men, without distinction of race, and was universal in the widest sense of the word; and secondly, because it embraced even one's enemies. It was a new commandment for a third reason also: the Old Law said, "Thou shalt love thy friend as *thyself*," while Jesus bade His disciples, *"as I have loved you,* you also love one another." His love for us is to be the rule and standard of our love for our brethren, a love that looks for no reward, that is generous and efficacious, showing itself in deeds. Jesus so esteemed this commandment and attributed so much importance to it that He called it *His* commandment: "This is my commandment" (John 15:12), and He wished its observance to be the distinctive mark

---

[35] Cf. John 7:34; very soon Jesus was to go to the Father, whither the Apostles could not yet follow Him.

of His disciples, who were to be signed with the seal of love. Thus Christianity can truly be called the religion of love.

PETER'S RASH PROMISE

(John 13:36–38; Luke 22:31–38)

When Peter heard Jesus say: "Where I go, you cannot come," he was afraid that he was going to be separated from his beloved Master, and therefore asked anxiously: "Lord, where art thou going?"

"Where I am going thou canst not follow me now, but thou shalt follow later."

Peter could not resign himself to waiting but wanted to go at once with Jesus, even though doing so meant running the risk of death: "Why can I not follow thee now? I will lay down my life for thee."

Since Peter persisted in his request, Jesus unfolded before his eyes the dark events of the future. Sadly He made the awful prediction: "Wilt thou lay down thy life for me? Amen, amen, I say to thee, the cock will not crow before thou dost deny me thrice." And He added: "Simon, Simon, behold, Satan has desired to have you, that he may sift you as wheat. But I have prayed for thee, that thy faith may not fail; and do thou, when once thou hast turned again,[36] strengthen thy brethren." [37]

But Peter was so sure of himself that he protested vehemently: "Lord, with thee I am ready to go both to prison and to death!"

Jesus did not argue with His Apostle, but simply confirmed what He had already said: "I tell thee, Peter, a cock will not crow this day, until thou hast thrice denied that thou knowest me." Then leaving aside the painful subject, He asked the Apostles: "When I sent you forth without purse or wallet or sandals, did you lack anything?"

When they replied, "Nothing," he went on:

"But now, let him who has a purse take it, and likewise a wallet; and let him who has no sword sell his tunic and buy one.[38] For I say

---

[36] Some authors take this to refer to Peter's perfect conversion under the influence of the Holy Spirit on Pentecost day; but the majority of exegetes interpret it as meaning his conversion after his denials of Christ, which is the more probable explanation.

[37] In Peter's being instructed to strengthen his brethren there is an allusion to his primacy, not as a private individual, but as the future Vicar of Christ, whose legitimate successors are the Roman Pontiffs.

[38] It is probable that this sentence should be taken in an allegorical sense. Christ meant that the persecution that was coming would be so violent that it was

to you that this which is written must yet be fulfilled in me, 'And he was reckoned among the wicked.' [39] For that which concerns me is at its end."

The Apostles, eager to please Him, said: "Lord, behold, here are two swords."

To which He replied: "Enough." [40]

WORDS OF CONSOLATION

(John 14:1–24)

Christ's somber prophecy of Peter's denial, which He spoke so firmly and clearly, undoubtedly made a deep and painful impression on the other Apostles. If Peter, to whom Jesus had given such pre-eminence among them, was going to fall, how could they be sure that they would remain faithful? Our Lord, therefore, wished to calm their fears and strengthen them to bear the trials that were to come upon them.

He told them that He was leaving to prepare a place for them in heaven, and that He would come one day to take them to Himself. He assured them that they would perform great wonders, greater even than those He had done, and that whatever they asked the Father in His name would be given to them. And He promised them the Holy Spirit, the Consoler, the Spirit of Truth, who would comfort and enlighten them.

His words were those of a loving father doing his utmost to console and encourage his sons from whom he was soon to depart. We, too, can find comfort in our Lord's farewell to His Apostles, for what He said to them was addressed also to all who, through the ages, would believe in Him.

"Let not your heart be troubled. You believe in God, believe also in me. In my Father's house there are many mansions. Were it not so, I should have told you, because I go to prepare a place for you. And if I go and prepare a place for you, I am coming again, and I will take you to myself; that where I am, there you also may be. And where I go you know, and the way you know."

---

necessary for them to take every precaution and even, humanly speaking, to provide themselves with arms for defense.

[39] Isaias 53:12.

[40] Jesus meant that He was not speaking of material weapons.

Ingenuously, Thomas objected: "Lord, we do not know where thou art going, and how can we know the way?"

Jesus answered him indirectly by declaring majestically: "I am the way, and the truth, and the life. No one comes to the Father but through me. If you had known me, you would also have known my Father. And henceforth you do know him, and you have seen him."

Christ is the *way:* it is only through Him that we can reach the Father, as He Himself said; it is only through Him that we can go from sin to the state of grace and obtain eternal happiness; He alone is the Model whom we should strive to imitate. He is the *truth:* He is the very Word of God, infinite truth; He teaches us truth and at the same time gives us light to understand it. He is the *life:* He possesses in Himself infinite life; He is the beginning, the wellspring and the origin of our supernatural life.

When our Lord had finished speaking, Philip asked of Him: "Lord, show us the Father and it is enough for us."

The Apostle's question earned him a mild, but well-deserved reproof: "Have I been so long a time with you, and you have not known me? Philip, he who sees me sees also the Father. How canst thou say, 'Show us the Father'? Dost thou not believe that I am in the Father and the Father in me? The words that I speak to you I speak not on my own authority. But the Father dwelling in me, it is he who does the works. Do you believe that I am in the Father and the Father in me? Otherwise believe because of the works themselves."

The Apostles had been very slow in comprehending their Master's teachings. By this time, after several years of instruction and close association with Him, they should have been well aware of His relationship with the Father. Hence the note of sad wonder in His reproach. Yet He explained with loving patience the perfect unity that existed between God the Father and Him, the Son, One being in the Other, and Both having the same divine nature. Consequently, the words which He spoke and the works that He did, were the words and works of the Father. As a proof and guarantee of this truth, He appealed to His own works which the Apostles themselves had witnessed: "Amen, amen, I say to you, he who believes in me, the works that I do he also shall do, and greater than these he shall do, because I am going to the Father. And whatever you ask in my name, that I will do, in order that the Father may be glorified in the Son. If you ask me anything in my name, I will do it."

His reference to His works led Him on, as it were, to speak of those which they, the Apostles, would do one day. In order to give them confidence in facing the future without Him, He told them that their deeds would be even greater than His own, not in the sense that they would perform more stupendous miracles than He, but that they would gather more abundant spiritual fruit and would extend the kingdom of God more rapidly than He had done. They would be able to do all this precisely because He had left them and ascended to the Father, for He would assist them from heaven and would make their ministry fruitful. And since they would have to pray in order to receive these graces, He promised that whatever they asked in His name, that is, in union with Him and through His intercession, He Himself would grant to them. In this way, with the expansion of the kingdom of Christ by virtue of the graces which He gave, everything would contribute to the glory of the Father, which would at the same time be the glory of the Son: "If you love me, keep my commandments. And I will ask the Father and he will give you another Advocate to dwell with you forever, the Spirit of truth whom the world cannot receive, because it neither sees him nor knows him. But you shall know him, because he will dwell with you, and be in you.

"I will not leave you orphans; I will come to you. Yet a little while and the world no longer sees me. But you see me,[41] for I live and you shall live. In that day you will know that I am in my Father, and you in me, and I in you. He who has my commandments and keeps them, he it is who loves me. But he who loves me will be loved by my Father, and I will love him and manifest myself to him."

He would have to absent Himself in order to go to the Father, but He would not leave them unbefriended. He would send them the Consoler, the Advocate, the Defender, the Spirit of Truth, whom they already knew and who dwelt in them, but who would then be communicated to them in greater measure. And not only that, but He Himself would return and appear to them in triumph after His Resurrection. These appearances were to be the beginning of a new life which would be intensified with the coming of the Holy Spirit, and which would continue ever more vigorous and powerful, not only in them but in all who kept His commandments.

Then Jude ("Judas, not the Iscariot") asked Him: "Lord, how is it that thou art about to manifest thyself to us, and not to the world?"

---

[41] They would know Jesus better after the Resurrection. It is to this period of time that the following words, "In that day," refer.

In answer, Jesus said: [42] "If anyone love me, he will keep my word, and my Father will love him, and we will come to him and make our abode with him. He who does not love me does not keep my words. And the word that you have heard is not mine, but the Father's who sent me."

The touchstone of love is the observance of the commandments. He who fulfills the divine will is loved by the Father, and the three Divine Persons will come down to him and take up Their abode in him, so that his soul will be truly a temple of the Holy Trinity.

THE GIFT OF PEACE

(John 14:25–31)

"These things I have spoken to you while yet dwelling with you. But the Advocate, the Holy Spirit, whom the Father will send in my name, he will teach you all things, and bring to your mind whatever I have said to you.

"Peace I leave with you, my peace I give to you; not as the world gives do I give to you. Do not let your heart be troubled, or be afraid. You have heard me say to you, 'I go away and I am coming to you.' [43] If you loved me, you would indeed rejoice that I am going to the Father, for the Father is greater than I. And now I have told you before it comes to pass, that when it has come to pass you may believe. I will no longer speak much with you, for the prince of the world is coming, and in me he has nothing. But he comes that the world may know that I love the Father, and that I do as the Father has commanded me. Arise, let us go from here."

The Holy Spirit would assume the role of Teacher of the Apostles. He would make clear to them the truths they had heard from Jesus but had not understood. He would reveal to them the meaning of the Scriptures, would guide them along the path which they should follow, and would be their consolation in sorrows and their strength in adversity. Besides the promise of the Holy Spirit's coming, Jesus gave peace to His Apostles. His words were not a mere formula of farewell,

---

[42] His reply was an indirect one. He would not manifest Himself to the world because it did not fulfill the indispensable condition of loving Him and keeping His word.

[43] This may refer to His return (cf. vv. 3, 18), either after the Resurrection or when He would come to take the Apostles with Him to the place in which He was.

but the pledge of a precious gift which they would bear in their hearts and which would render them serene in the midst of the storms which the world would raise against them.

The command, "Arise, let us go from here," seems so categorical that many authors (e.g., Patrizi, Fillion, Westcott, and others) believe that Christ and His Apostles left the Cenacle at this point and that therefore the discourses that follow (chapters 15–17) were spoken on the road to Gethsemani. However, it is not easy to see how our Lord could have conveniently spoken at such length to the Apostles as the company made its way through the narrow, winding streets of Jerusalem. Some writers overcome this difficulty by supposing that the group stopped at a quiet, open place, or that our Lord did not speak until they were outside the walls of the city and were approaching Gethsemani. These theories are certainly possible, but they still seem somewhat arbitrary. There is, moreover, a very solid reason for rejecting them, for in John 18:1, we read: "After saying these things, Jesus went forth with his disciples beyond the torrent of Cedron," and the whole context makes it plain that the words "went forth" refer, not to the city, as some believe, but to the Cenacle. For the rest, it would have been very natural, especially in view of the circumstances, for our Lord to have prolonged His conversation with His Apostles even after He had said, "Arise, let us go from here." He had so many things to say before He was taken from them! As Knabenbauer correctly remarks: "We often say, 'Let us go,' and yet we do not go immediately but tarry a little longer"; and Cornelius a Lapide holds much the same opinion.[44] Such a course of action is so likely that it is strange that anyone should even ask: "If He did not leave, why did He give the sign for departure?" There are many other authors who hold that Christ did not go forth from the Cenacle immediately after giving the command (e.g., Maldonatus, Calmes, Tillmann, B. Weiss, Gomá and Vilariño).

Another, graver problem arises here in connection with chapters 15 and 16, namely, is this section a part of the original Gospel of St. John? Was it really spoken by Jesus, inside or outside the Cenacle, on the night of the Last Supper?

Lepin,[45] Durand,[46] Lebreton [47] and others believe that when St.

---

[44] "Sicut solent valedicentes amici qui aegre ab amicis avelluntur sermonem abruptum resumere, sic Christus stando novum sermonem resumpsit" (in loc.).
[45] La valeur historique du Quatrième Évangile (Paris, 1910), II, 101.
[46] Év. selon S. Jean (Paris, 1927), pp. 409–411.
[47] Life and Teachings of Jesus Christ, II, 268, n. 1.

John had completed the first draft of his Gospel and was thinking back over the events of the Last Supper, he remembered other sayings of Jesus which he then wrote down and inserted into the already-existing manuscript, thus forming chapters 15 and 16 of his Gospel as we know it.

Did our Lord say everything contained in these chapters on the night of the Last Supper? Lagrange suspects that the chapters in question do not form a compact unit, but are composed of parts of discourses delivered at different times and in different places. He says that the material is made up of three sections, each with its own theme: (1) 15:1–17; (2) 15:18–16:4a; (3) 16:4b–33. The first would fit very well after the choice of the disciples-Apostles, and before their first mission (Matt. 10); the second corresponds to the Synoptic authors' eschatological discourse; and the third is a completion of St. John's chapter 14.

Lagrange's theory differs considerably from that of Lepin and Durand, who take it for granted that the whole discourse was pronounced by Jesus on the night of the Supper, although it was not included in the first draft of the Gospel. Lagrange, on the contrary, is inclined to believe that the first two parts were spoken in very different times and places.

The doctrine of divine inspiration offers no serious objection to St. John's having inserted the two chapters after the original whole was completed. In fact, authors generally admit that this is what happened in the case of his last chapter (21). In addition, this hypothesis has the undoubted advantage of removing the difficulty raised by the last sentences of chapter 14: "I will no longer speak much with you. . . . Arise, let us go from here." However, we do not think that this is sufficient reason for regarding the theory of a later addition as well-founded. As we have already said, in everyday life we often find that a conversation which has apparently come to an end starts up afresh and continues as if never interrupted.

The repetition of certain ideas, the similarities between this and other passages occurring in different circumstances of time and place, the lack of firm cohesion between the various sections of the passage—none of these affects the likelihood of its having been spoken in the Cenacle after the Last Supper.

As Tillmann observes, in this discourse, which sprang directly from the heart, we need not look for a rigid marshalling of ideas and an uninterrupted process of reasoning.[48] The truth of this remark is clear when we remember what happens in similar circumstances in everyday life. Such discourses as our Lord's are not to be judged solely by the standards of logic but also, and more particularly, by those of psychology.

Equally unsatisfactory is the theory of a change in the order of chapters. No one will deny the possibility of such transpositions, but they must be supported by very solid reasons before we can accept them.[49]

Fr. Gächter introduced a new element into the solution of the problem by dividing the controverted chapters into strophes, but his theory has not found great favor among exegetes.[50]

Therefore, when all is said and done, we still maintain that the discourse in chapters 15 and 16 of St. John was delivered by our Lord in the circumstances indicated by the evangelist.

THE MYSTICAL VINE

(John 15:1–11)

In order to bring home to the Apostles and to Christians of all times their intimate union with Him, Jesus made use of a beautiful allegory, that of the vine and its branches. The vine was very common in Israel and it appeared in the proverbial phrase, expressive of widespread peace, which depicted each man as resting "under his vine and under his fig tree, from Dan to Bersabee" (3 Kings 4:25). In Scripture, too, the vineyard was used as a figure of the people of Israel: Isaias, in his beautiful parable of the loved one and the vineyard, says: "I will sing to my beloved the canticle of my cousin concerning his vineyard. My beloved had a vineyard on a hill in a fruitful place. And he fenced it in, and picked the stones out of it, and planted it with the choicest vines, and built a tower in the midst thereof, and set up a wine-press therein. And he looked that it should bring forth grapes: and it brought forth wild grapes" (Isai. 5:1–2).

In our Lord's allegory-parable, the vine is Christ Himself; we are

---

[48] *Das Johannesevangelium* (Bonn, 1922), p. 288.

[49] Fr. Brinkmann has made a close study of the manner in which an alteration in the order of the various parts of the text could have been introduced into the codices (*Gregorianum*, 20 [1939], 55–82, 563–569; 22 [1941], 503–505. See also *Verb. Dom.*, 19 [1939]).

[50] "Der formale Aufbau der Abschiedsrede Jesu," in *Zeit. f. kath. Theol.*, 58 (1934), 155–207; in particular, pp. 203 *ff.*

the branches and the Father is the vine-dresser. The branch receives everything from the trunk, and once severed therefrom it dies and is good only for burning. Christ, the Head of the Mystical Body, communicates His own life to His members, the faithful; therefore those who are cut off from Him, die and are destined for the eternal fire. Without Christ we can do nothing; but with Him, united to Him, we can do all things, as St. Paul assures us: "I can do all things in him who strengthens me" (Phil. 4:13).

"I am the true vine, and my Father is the vine-dresser. Every branch in me that bears no fruit he will take away; and every branch that bears fruit he will cleanse, that it may bear more fruit. You are already clean because of the word that I have spoken to you. Abide in me, and I in you. As the branch cannot bear fruit of itself unless it remain on the vine, so neither can you unless you abide in me. I am the vine, you are the branches. He who abides in me, and I in him, he bears much fruit; for without me you can do nothing. If anyone does not abide in me, he shall be cast outside as the branch and wither; and they shall gather them up and cast them into the fire, and they shall burn. . . . If you keep my commandments you will abide in my love, as I also have kept my Father's commandments, and abide in his love. These things I have spoken to you that my joy may be in you, and that your joy may be made full."

The observance of the Commandments is the indispensable condition for persevering in the love of Christ, and for remaining united to Him as the branch is to the vine. Elsewhere He had taught the same thing in other words: "Not everyone who says to me, 'Lord, Lord,' shall enter the kingdom of heaven; but he who does the will of my Father in heaven shall enter the kingdom of heaven." The mere fact that a man has prophesied, cast out devils or worked miracles will not profit him if he has not kept the Commandments. And, while all of God's precepts must be observed, there is one to which Jesus attributed special importance and about which He now spoke to His Apostles.

THE PRECEPT OF FRATERNAL CHARITY
(John 15:12–17)

"This is my commandment, that you love one another as I have loved you. Greater love than this no one has, that one lay down his life for his friends. You are my friends if you do the things I command you. No longer do I call you servants, because the servant does not know what his master does. But I have called you friends, because all things that I have heard from my Father I have made known to you. . . . These things I command you, that you may love one another."

All the Commandments were Christ's, but by calling one of them "*my* commandment," He wished to make us understand His great esteem for it and the importance He attached to it. The love which He desires men to have for each other is but a pale reflection of that which He Himself has shown for us. So personal and so profound is this love of His that He did not hesitate to call us by the tender name of "friends" and to allow us to share in the very secrets of His Father.

But unfortunately this brotherly love was not to reign always among men, for the spirit of the world was destined to rear itself up against the spirit of Christ. Therefore He foretold to the Apostles the persecutions which they would have to face, so that when the time of trial did come they would remember that their Master had forewarned them, and the knowledge would give them new courage to fight on valiantly until they emerged triumphant.

THE WORLD'S HATRED FOR THE DISCIPLES OF CHRIST
(John 15:18—16:4)

"If the world hates you, know that it has hated me before you. If you were of the world, the world would love what is its own. But because you are not of the world, but I have chosen you out of the world, therefore the world hates you. Remember the word that I have spoken to you: No servant is greater than his master.[51] If they have persecuted me, they will persecute you also; if they have kept my word, they will keep yours also. . . .

"These things I have spoken to you that you may not be scandalized. They will expel you from the synagogues. Yes, the hour is coming for everyone who kills you to think that he is offering worship to God. And these things they will do because they have not known the Father nor me. But these things I have spoken to you, that when the time for them has come you may remember that I told you."

The highest honor and the greatest glory we can receive is to be allowed to suffer persecution for Christ. If the world persecutes us, it is

[51] Cf. John 13:16.

because we do not belong to it but to Christ. And woe to us if the world regards us as its own!

Because the Apostles needed enlightenment of mind and strength of will to triumph over the violence and cunning of the enemy, Jesus promised them that the Holy Spirit would come to give them light and strength and to be their Advocate, Defender and Consoler.

THE WORK OF THE HOLY SPIRIT

(John 16:4–15)

"These things, however, I did not tell you from the beginning, because I was with you.

"And now I am going to him who sent me, and no one of you asks me, 'Where art thou going?' [52] But because I have spoken to you these things, sorrow has filled your heart. But I speak the truth to you; it is expedient for you that I depart. For if I do not go, the Advocate will not come to you; but if I go, I will send him to you. And when he has come he will convict the world of sin, and of justice, and of judgment: of sin, because they do not believe in me; of justice, because I go to the Father, and you will see me no more; and of judgment, because the prince of this world has already been judged.

"Many things yet I have to say to you, but you cannot bear them now. But when he, the Spirit of truth, has come, he will teach you all the truth. For he will not speak on his own authority, but whatever he will hear he will speak, and the things that are to come he will declare to you. He will glorify me, because he will receive of what is mine and declare it to you. All things that the Father has are mine. That is why I have said that he will receive of what is mine, and will declare it to you."

In the sentence, "And when he has come he will convict the world of sin, and of justice, and of judgment . . . ," "sin" refers to men, "justice" to our Lord, and "judgment" to Satan. The sense is that the

---

[52] This statement of our Lord's, containing as it does an air of reproach, is indeed surprising in view of the fact that, in 13:36, Peter had explicitly inquired: "Lord, where art thou going?" Again, in 14:5, Thomas had remarked: "Lord, we do not know where thou art going, and how can we know the way?" Some exegetes regard this inconsistency as evidence of different authorship. The true solution, however, is much simpler. The Semitic style of expression often disregards certain nuances of meaning. Thus in the passage under consideration our Lord's words actually meant: "No one of you asks me *any more*. . . ," or "*No longer* does one of you ask me. . . ." Cf. Joüon, *Rev. Sc. Rel.*, 18 (1928), pp. 500 *f*.

Holy Spirit will condemn men for not having believed in the Messias; He will make manifest the justice of Christ, that is, His veracity, the truth of His doctrine and consequently His perfect right to credence; and finally, the Holy Spirit will pronounce sentence on the devil, who has already been judged and defeated by the very death of the Saviour.

The same Spirit was to be for the Apostles a Teacher of truth who would enlighten their minds. He would speak that which He had heard from the Son, who would send Him; He would announce to them that which He had received from the Son, from whom He proceeds. Thus our Lord here indicated that the Holy Spirit proceeds in the same way from the Word as from the Father.

FROM PRESENT SORROW TO FUTURE JOY
(John 16:16–33)

When the moment of departure arrived, the Divine Master announced it in enigmatic words: "A little while and you shall see me no longer; and again a little while and you shall see me. . . ."

He was speaking of His death and Resurrection, not of His second coming at the end of time. In a short while, no more than a day, He was to be taken from them by death; and after another short while, He was to allow them to see Him risen from the tomb. He would then speak again with them in visible form and would afterwards remain with them in invisible form, never to be separated from them again.

But the Apostles did not understand Him. He had said that He was going to the Father; how then would they see Him again after His departure? And was He not to found a kingdom on earth? How could He go away, leaving their ardent hopes unfulfilled?

Bewildered by His words, they asked each other in low voices: "What is this he says to us, 'A little while and you shall not see me, and again a little while and you shall see me'; and, 'I go to the Father'?. . . . What is this 'little while' of which he speaks? We do not know what he is saying."

Seeing that they wished to question Him, Jesus forestalled them, not, however, by replying to their unspoken query, but by unfolding before their eyes the panorama of the future with its alternating sorrow and joy, humiliations and victories: "You inquire about this among yourselves because I said, 'A little while and you shall not see me, and again a little while and you shall see me.' Amen, amen, I say to you, that you shall weep and lament, but the world shall rejoice; and you shall be sorrowful, but your sorrow shall be turned into joy. . . . You . . . have sorrow now; but I will see you again, and your heart shall rejoice, and your joy no one shall take from you. . . . In the world you will have affliction. But take courage, I have overcome the world."

How heartening is Christ's victory! Since the world has been subjugated by Him, it has already lost much of its strength and will therefore be the more easily conquered. When we are united to Him, we partake in His strength and fight with His weapons. Our victory, then, is secure: "Thanks be to God who has given us the victory through our Lord Jesus Christ" (1 Cor. 15:57). And St. John tells us why we shall conquer the world: "You are of God, dear children, and have overcome him, because greater is he who is in you than he who is in the world" (1 John 4:4). Christ is in us and fights for us, and so we need not fear the world. We may fall in the fray, but the final victory will be ours, or rather, Christ's.

In his Apocalypse, St. John sets down the heavenly hymn celebrating the victory of the good angels over the bad and of just men over the devil and his followers: "And I heard a loud voice in heaven saying, 'Now has come the salvation, and the power and the kingdom of our God, and the authority of his Christ; for the accuser of our brethren has been cast down. . . . And they overcame him through the blood of the Lamb. . . .'" (Apoc. 12:10 f.)

THE PRIESTLY PRAYER OF CHRIST

(John 17)

Hitherto our Lord had been addressing His Apostles, instructing, consoling and encouraging them. But now, when He was about to begin His offering of the supreme sacrifice, He turned His eyes towards His Father, and from the depths of His heart, poured forth what has come to be known as His "priestly prayer" because in it He spoke both as High Priest and as Victim, offering Himself in sacrifice for the glory of the Father and the redemption of mankind. His sublime words were the expression of the thoughts and feelings that filled His breast to overflowing—love and reverence for the Father, tender affection for the Apostles and for all men.

First He asked the Father to glorify Him in heaven as He had already glorified Him on earth (vv. 1–5). Then He prayed for the Apostles, that they might be protected and guarded from all evil, that they might be established and confirmed in the truth (vv. 6–19). Finally, He prayed for the Church, that is, for all those who would believe in Him, asking the Father to keep them always closely united to each other and to make them partakers one day in the glory of Christ (vv. 20–26).

Raising His eyes to heaven, He exclaimed: "Father, the hour has come! Glorify thy Son, that thy Son may glorify thee, even as thou has given him power over all flesh, in order that to all thou hast given him he may give everlasting life. Now this is everlasting life, that they may know thee, the only true God, and him whom thou hast sent, Jesus Christ. I have glorified thee on earth; I have accomplished the work that thou hast given me to do. And now do thou, Father, glorify me with thyself, with the glory that I had with thee before the world existed."

Here Jesus used two terms which are in a certain sense correlative, the glory of the Son and the glory of the Father. He asked the Father to glorify Him in the Resurrection and the Ascension so that men would see and extol the Father's omnipotence in these two great miracles (v. 1). The Son had already glorified the Father by revealing Him to men through His preaching, His miracles and His faithful fulfillment of God's will. As a reward for His work, Jesus now asked that the glory which He had from all eternity, that is, the glory of the Word, might be extended to the Incarnate Word, Christ, the God-Man (v. 2 f.).

The hour had come! More than once (cf. John 7:30; 8:20) the Jews had wished to seize Christ and put Him to death, but "his hour had not yet come." Now, finally, it had arrived, His hour of battle and triumph, the hour He had feared and desired, and for which He had come into the world (John 12:27).

"I have manifested thy name to the men whom thou hast given me out of the world. They are thine, and thou hast given them to me, and they have kept thy word. Now they have learnt that whatever thou hast given me is from thee; because the words that thou hast given me I have given to them. And they have received them, and have known of a truth that I came forth from thee, and they have believed that thou didst send me.

"I pray for them; not for the world do I pray, but for those whom thou hast given me, because they are thine. . . . Holy Father, keep in thy name those whom thou hast given me, that they may be one even as we are. . . . I have given them thy word; and the world has hated them, because they are not of the world, even as I am not of the world. I do not pray that thou take them out of the world, but that thou keep them from evil. . . . Sanctify them in the truth. Thy word is truth. Even as thou hast sent me into the world, so I also have sent them into the world. And for them I sanctify myself, that they also may be sanctified in truth."

Our Lord asked two things of His father for the Apostles; that He would "keep [them] in [His] name," and "sanctify them in the truth." By "name" He meant the doctrine which His Father had entrusted to Him for revelation to men. Therefore He asked that the Apostles might remain always faithful to this doctrine, that they might retain it pure and free from all error, and that it might become the principle of an intimate fraternal unity among them.

By praying that they might be sanctified in the truth, our Lord did not ask specifically to have sanctifying grace bestowed on them. Rather, according to the sense of the Hebrew word *qadash,* He wished them to be separated from the common run of men and consecrated to the service of the truth, that is, to the preaching of the true doctrine, the Gospel. He prayed that they might be trained and prepared to exercise their exalted ministry worthily and fittingly.

When He said that He sanctified Himself for them (v. 19), He meant that He consecrated Himself, offering Himself in sacrifice to the Father, so that the Apostles might in turn be sanctified in the truth.

Having prayed for the Apostles, Jesus turned His gaze down the course of the centuries and with infinite tenderness besought His Father: "Yet not for these only do I pray, but for those also who through their word are to believe in me, that all may be one, even as thou, Father, in me and I in thee; that they also may be one in us, that the world may believe that thou hast sent me. And the glory that thou hast given me, I have given to them, that they may be one, even as we are one: I in them and thou in me; that they may be perfected in unity. . . ."

The intimate union of the faithful among themselves and with God could not be expressed more clearly, more tenderly or more forcefully. It is a union modelled on that which exists between the Three Divine Persons. And this union of the faithful is to be fulfilled in God ("in us": v. 21). Since Christ is in the faithful (Eph. 3:17) and the Father is in Christ ("I in them and thou in me": v. 23), then the faithful are united to the Father. Christ is the point of union in which the Father and the faithful meet and join. Truly the faithful are "perfected in unity." Their charity is perfect because it is founded upon and rooted in God: their minds and wills are one because they are wholly possessed by Him. This is, as it were, the divinization of the faithful ("partakers of the divine nature"; 2 Peter 1:4) in Jesus Christ, in the bosom of the Holy Trinity.

This intimate divine union will be a light shining in the world, and the world will acknowledge Him who is the principle and origin of this light, and will believe that Christ is the Father's Envoy, the true Messias.

Our Lord closed His prayer with the tender words: "Father, I will that where I am, they also whom thou hast given me may be with me; in order that they may behold my glory, which thou hast given me, because thou hast loved me before the creation of the world. Just Father, the world has not known thee, but I have known thee, and these have known that thou hast sent me. And I have made known to them thy name, and will make it known, in order that the love with which thou hast loved me may be in them, and I in them."

How generous, how divinely liberal is Jesus to the faithful! He gives them the glory which the Father bestowed on Him. He gives them not only immortality and the gift of miracles but also divine sonship insofar as men are capable of it ("But to as many as received him he gave the power of becoming sons of God": John 1:12). He wills that they may one day be where He is, in heaven, and that they may contemplate His glory, not only the glory of His holy Humanity but also that glory which He received from the Father by eternal generation before the world existed.

Our Lord closed this sublime and touching prayer by asking His Father to love the faithful with the same love He had shown to Him, His Son, and that He, Christ, might remain always in them so that the Father might embrace them and Him in His love.

The Agony in the Garden
(Matt. 26:36–56; Mark 14:32–50; Luke 22:40–53; John 18:1–11)

It was about ten o'clock when, having brought the Supper to a close and intoned the final hymn,[53] our Lord left the Cenacle with His Apostles to go to Mount Olivet.

There were three possible routes from the Cenacle to Gethsemani: the northern one, which went through the courts of the Temple, entering by one of the gates on the south side, e.g., the Huldah Gate, and coming out on the east side; the southern route, which went down the stairway leading to the pool of Siloe and then ascended the Valley of the Cedron (the stairway can still be seen near the Church of St. Peter *in Gallicantu*); and finally, the middle route, which wound through the twisting streets on the hill of Ophel, not far from and parallel to the present-day wall about the Temple precincts. Our Lord probably did not wish to pass through the Temple, since it was crowded on account of the feast. Instead, He very likely chose to descend the steps to the pool of Siloe, leaving the city through the Gate of the Fountain and crossing the Brook of Cedron [54] by one of the small bridges that spanned it, perhaps at the spot where a bridge still stands, near the so-called Tomb of Absalom, a monument which may have been a mute witness of the sad company's passing.

The full moon shone brightly, its cold beams lighting up the gloomy valley but leaving untouched the darkness that cast its shadows over the Apostles' hearts as they walked along in silence, torn by doubt and anxiety, full of sad thoughts, and not knowing where the night's events were going to end.

Breaking the melancholy silence, Jesus declared to them: "You will all be scandalized this night; for it is written, 'I will smite the shepherd, and the sheep will be scattered.' But after I have risen, I will go before you into Galilee."

All except Peter received His sorrowful prediction without a word. Unable to conceive how such cowardice could be possible, the fiery Apostle burst out: "Even though all shall be scandalized, yet not I."

He was far from suspecting that his vehement protest would very soon change to a wretched betrayal.

"Amen, I say to thee," replied Jesus, "today, this very night, before a cock crows twice, thou wilt deny me thrice." [55]

---

[53] The second part of the *Hallel,* Psalms 113–118 (Vulgate Ps. 112–117). The word *Hallel* is an abbreviation of *Halleluyah,* "Praise be to Yahweh!"

[54] The name comes from the Hebrew *qadar* = "to be dark or muddy" (cf. 2 Kings 15:23; *Ant.* viii. 1. 5).

[55] See below, p. 695, for comment on the number of times Peter denied our Lord.

Front view of the Basilica of Gethsemani.

But Peter only protested the more: "Even if I should have to die with thee, I will not deny thee!"

Jesus made no response, and the other Apostles added their promises of loyalty to Peter's.

After following the bank of the Brook of Cedron for a short distance, the group finally reached Gethsemani (*gat shemen*=oil-press), at the foot of Mount Olivet. As its name indicates, Gethsemani was a farmhouse or country-house where there was a press for extracting the oil from the olives that grew on the mount. The house probably belonged to one of Jesus' friends or acquaintances, perhaps John Mark's father, for the evangelists note (John 18:2; Luke 22:39) that it was His custom to go there to pray. No doubt the traitor had accompanied Him there on more than one occasion.

In the time of the Emperor Theodosius (A.D. 379–393), a church was built here, and according to the Spanish pilgrim Etheria, it was a beautiful edifice. Later, it was destroyed by the Persians and rebuilt by the Crusaders only to fall into ruins and disappear. The site was discovered in 1920 by the Franciscans, who built the present magnificent basilica, before the altar of which the Stone of the Agony can be seen.[56] Alongside the basilica there are eight very ancient olive trees which may be a thousand years old. It is inconceivable, however, that they could be the same trees that grew there in our Lord's day. Apart from any other reason, all the trees around the city were cut down during the siege of Jerusalem by Titus, and it is not likely that a grove so near at hand would have been spared. They could, of course, be the descendants of the olive trees that witnessed the tragic scene at Gethsemani, and hence they are worthy of veneration.

When they arrived at the garden, Jesus told eight of the eleven Apostles to remain at the entrance, warning them to pray that they might not fall into temptation. Then taking Peter, James and John with Him, He went among the trees. Once alone with His three especially beloved Apostles, He allowed them to glimpse the tempest that raged within His heart. So burdened was He by sadness, so oppressed by fear, that a moan of anguish escaped His lips: "My soul is sad, even unto death."

Then, as if cutting the last tie that bound Him to earth and renouncing the only solace that remained to Him, He tore Himself from the company of His friends. After charging the three Apostles to pray and watch with Him, He went a stone's throw, about forty or fifty paces, deeper into the grove.

There alone, in the deep silence of the night and in the presence of His Father, He fell on His knees and, with His forehead pressed to the ground, cried out in torment: "Father, if it is possible, let this cup pass away from me; yet not as I will, but as thou willest."

Even in the grip of His crushing agony, the Good Shepherd, ever solicitous for His sheep, interrupted His prayer to assure Himself that all was well with His disciples. But how pained He must have been to find them deep in slumber: "Simon, dost thou sleep?" He asked sadly. "Could you not, then, watch one hour with me? Watch and pray, that you may not enter into temptation. The spirit indeed is willing, but the flesh is weak."

Turning away once more, He repeated His prayer with redoubled fervor: "My Father, if this cup cannot pass away unless I drink it, thy will be done."

Again He came back to His Apostles, only to find them sleeping as

---

[56] For several centuries, the nearby Cave of the Agony was regarded as the scene of the mystery. Cf. G. Orfali, *Gethsémani, ou notice sur l'Église de l'agonie ou de la prière, d'après les fouilles récentes* (Paris, 1924).

before. Their eyes had once more grown heavy, and, ashamed of themselves for giving in to their fatigue, they did not know what to say to Him.

For the third time Jesus returned to pray. His soul was so beset by anguish, and His heart so torn with conflicting emotions that He broke out in a sweat of blood, which forced its way through all the pores of His skin, soaking His garments and running in streams down His body onto the ground.

What a fearful spectacle! The God of Heaven reduced to a worm of earth! Omnipotence become weak, the Glory of the angels become an object of opprobrium to men, He who was Heaven's Joy plunged in deepest sorrow and bitterest desolation! Only divine love could work such a strange miracle, and only an awed, respectful silence can adequately venerate it.

This is indeed an unfathomable mystery! Jesus begging His Father not to make Him drink the bitter chalice! He who from the first instant of His earthly existence had so generously offered Himself: "Behold I come . . . to do thy will, O God" (Heb. 10:7); He who had longed so ardently for the moment of His Passion; He who had known that He would have to wash away the sins of the world with His Blood, and that the redemption of mankind had to be accomplished by His death, now seemed to draw back and refuse the chalice which His Father was offering Him. Terrible must have been the agony and inconceivable the torment which brought Jesus to such a pass! His cup of bitterness was not so much the grievous consequences which His murder would have for the Jewish people, nor the persecutions that the faithful would suffer for His sake down the centuries. Instead, His pain and grief were caused by the thought of the torture and humiliations which He was about to suffer, by the blindness of the Jews, the ingratitude of so many of those whom He wished to redeem and who would spurn His Blood beneath their feet, making His Passion vain for them. The vision of all this rose before His eyes and filled Him with soul-crushing fear and heart-rending sorrow.

But how could such feelings find a place in Christ's soul if from the first moment of His life He enjoyed the Beatific Vision, which was never interrupted, even during His Passion? From our own experience we are aware that we can feel both pain and joy at the same time. But the joy that comes from the vision of God face to face so penetrates and enfolds the soul that it necessarily excludes even the smallest shadow of sorrow. We simply do not know how Jesus could suffer the Agony while enjoying the Beatific Vision: it is a great mystery which we are not given to understand. With His infinite power, God must have nullified the influence which the Vision normally exercised on our Lord's soul, so that although the Vision itself was not interrupted, its effects were temporarily suspended.

Was it possible for Christ to desire something that was contrary to the Father's will? By no means. His wish to avoid drinking the chalice was a conditional one: "If it is possible . . .," that is, if it was not contrary to God's will or plans, a thought which He expressed even more explicitly by adding: "yet not my will but thine be done." His wish was an inefficacious one, or as St. Thomas calls it, a *natural* as opposed to a *reasoned* wish.[57]

The Father did not abandon His Son in His hour of agony but sent an angel, not to withdraw the chalice, but to encourage and strengthen Him to drink it to the dregs.

What a stupendous example of humility our Lord gave us here! He, the King of Angels, allowed Himself to be consoled and heartened by one of His creatures. Some copyists thought such condescension unfitting on Christ's part, and they eliminated this incident and the account of the bloody sweat (Luke 22:43 f.), with the result that these episodes are lacking in several codices. But such an omission is no reason for doubting the authenticity of the events as recorded in other manuscripts.

Strengthened and encouraged by the angel's visit, Jesus rose from prayer, and returning to His Apostles, said to them: "Sleep on now, and take your rest! Behold, the hour is at hand when the Son of Man will be betrayed into the hands of sinners. Rise, let us go. Behold, he who betrays me is at hand."

In the meantime, the chief priests and elders had been laying their plans in Jerusalem. They remembered Jesus' recent triumphal entry into the city, and they were well aware that among the crowds present for the feast there were many Galileans who admired and supported the Prophet of Nazareth. Therefore, having good reason to

---

[57] "Christus pro se oravit dupliciter: uno modo exprimendo affectum sensualitatis, vel etiam voluntatis *simplicis,* quae consideratur ut *natura;* sicuti cum oravit a se calicem passionis transferri; alio modo exprimendo affectum voluntatis *deliberatae,* quae consideratur ut *ratio;* sicuti cum petiit gloriam resurrectionis" (III, q. 21, a. 3). The "voluntas *simplex*" is the "voluntas *naturalis*"; and the voluntas *deliberata*" is the "voluntas *rationis.*"

fear that a riot would ensue when they tried to arrest Him, they asked
Pilate for a detachment of Roman soldiers to intervene if necessary and
restrain the mob. Thus it came about that the chief priests' guards,[58]
armed with swords and clubs, and carrying lanterns, were accompanied
by a cohort (σπεῖρα) led by a tribune (χιλίαρχος; John 18:3, 12). It is
hard to say how many soldiers were there, for although a cohort was
the tenth part of a legion, which usually (but not always) numbered
4,200 men, the word was often used in a vague sense and sometimes
came to mean the equivalent of a *manipulum,* which was composed of
from 120 to 200 soldiers.

Since many, perhaps even the majority, of those who came to
arrest Jesus did not know Him by sight, Judas had to single Him out
for them, and he did so with a kiss. Christ did not refuse to accept
the traitorous embrace, but made it an occasion for appealing for the
last time to the perfidious Apostle, whom He called by the sweet name
of friend: "Friend, dost thou betray the Son of Man with a kiss?"

No sooner had Judas given the signal agreed upon, the kiss of
betrayal, than the wolves made as if to leap at their Prey. But Jesus
stopped them with a gesture, for He wished to make it plain that He
was going to His death of His own free will and under no compulsion.

"Whom do you seek?" He asked calmly.

"Jesus of Nazareth!" they snarled.

"I am he."

This simple reply, these three short words, felled them to the
ground as if they had been struck by lightning: brute force was vanquished by moral strength.

"He asked them again, 'Whom do you seek?'

"And they said, 'Jesus of Nazareth.'

"Jesus answered, 'I have told you that I am he. If, therefore, you
seek me, let these go their way.' "

The disciples, seeing that their Master's foes were about to seize
Him, asked Him excitedly: "Lord, shall we strike with the sword?"

Peter, carried away by his impetuous nature and by his great love
for Jesus, did not wait for an answer but straightway attacked the
nearest enemy, who happened to be Malchus, a servant of the chief
priests, cutting off his ear. How little did the fiery Apostle understand
the plans and designs of God!

[58] Besides the chief priests and elders, St. Luke (22:4, 52) mentions "the captains [στρατηγοί] of the temple." These were the priests who directed the Levites
charged with keeping order in the Temple precincts, Cf. Acts 4:1; 5:24–26.

"Put back thy sword into its place," Jesus commanded him, "for all those who take the sword will perish by the sword. Or dost thou suppose that I cannot entreat my Father, and he will even now furnish me with more than twelve legions of angels? How then are the Scriptures to be fulfilled, that thus it must happen?"

Having said this, He touched Malchus' ear and healed him.

Then, turning to the priests and magistrates and the rabble that had come with them, He upbraided them severely: "As against a robber you have come out, with swords and clubs, to seize me. I sat daily with you in the temple teaching, and you did not lay hands on me. But this is your hour, and the power of darkness."

Time and time again His enemies had longed to seize Him, but God had restrained them. Now the Lord let them have a free hand, and they used their liberty to satisfy their hatred and desire for revenge, not knowing that they were thereby fulfilling the ancient prophecies and carrying out the eternal plans of the Most High. Satan's hour had come. Some authors take the word "darkness" as referring to the night, but that is not what is meant. "The power of darkness" is the power of Satan himself who had taken possession of Judas, was urging on the chief priests and elders, and would not relax his efforts until he saw the Son of Man hanging upon the cross.

When God's restraining hand was lifted, and only then, the bloodthirsty butchers flung themselves on the innocent Lamb, who meekly allowed Himself to be seized and bound like a victim being led to the slaughter.

Seeing their Master in the hands of His mortal enemies, the Apostles were terrified and thrown into utter confusion, for despite His repeated and unmistakable predictions, they still understood nothing of the mystery of the cross. They had often seen incontrovertible proofs of their Master's power; in fact, just a few moments before, they had witnessed the majesty and irresistible force of His words, and they fully expected the whole incident to end in His vanquishing His foes. But when they saw Him roughly seized and bound like a criminal, they were so overcome with terror that, forgetful of their protestations of loyalty, they fled headlong from the garden, leaving their Master alone in the hands of His executioners.

27. Trial and

Condemnation

(Matt. 26:57—27:31; Mark 14:53—15:19;
Luke 22:54—23:25; John 18:13—19:16)

When Jesus was seized and securely bound, the motley crowd set out along the rocky banks of the Cedron. At this point, St. Mark relates an interesting episode:
"And a certain young man was following him, having a linen cloth wrapped about his naked body, and they seized him. But leaving the linen cloth behind, he fled away from them naked."

A good number of authors believe that this young man was none other than Mark himself, who is the only evangelist to record the incident (14:51 *f.*). As we have already pointed out, some commentators hold that the garden and house at Gethsemani belonged to Mark's family, and it is possible that he was sleeping there that night and, awakened by the noise of the crowd, ran out to see what was happening.

Crossing the Cedron, the jubilant mob ascended the hill of Ophel and made their way through the lower city, which covered the top and sides of Mount Sion, where stood the palaces of Annas and Caiphas.

The Palaces of Annas and Caiphas

Authors are unanimous in placing the palaces of Annas and Caiphas on Mount Sion, that is, on the hill in the southwest part of the city; but opinions are divided when it comes to selecting the precise location of the buildings. Some say that Caiphas' palace stood on the site of the Armenian sanctuary near the Cenacle, between the latter and the so-called Gate of David, while others identify it with the notable ruins discovered on the property of the Assumptionist Fathers, a little farther to the east, on the slope of the mount.[1]

The little Church of the Angels, which stands within the precincts of the large Armenian monastery of St. James the Greater and which serves the convent of Deir ez-Zeituneh, is today pointed out as the site of Annas' house. The tradition supporting this identification is of very little value, for it goes back only to the fifteenth century. The first person to mention the Church of the Angels in this connection seems to have been Felix Fabri (1483).[2] It is perhaps more probable that the two palaces stood side by side. At any rate, all the ancient pilgrims locate them both on Mount Sion.

The Praetorium

For many centuries Pilate's praetorium was thought to have been the Fortress Antonia, built by Hyrcanus at the northwest corner of the Temple and restored by Herod the Great.[3] In fact, every Friday the Way of the Cross begins at this point. Yet some very noteworthy authors prefer to locate the praetorium in the palace which Herod the Great himself had built near the present Jaffa Gate.[4] There is no doubt that this palace was the ordinary residence of the Roman procurators when they came from Caesarea to Jerusalem, and we know that one of these officials, Gessius Florus, pronounced sentence, that is, set up his praetorium there.[5]

---

[1] This identification has been the subject of lively discussions, and it must be admitted that no definitive solution has yet been reached. In favor of the Assumptionist Fathers' site, see Marchet, *Le véritable emplacement du palais de Caïphe et léglise Saint-Pierre à Jérusalem* (Paris, 1927); Power, *Biblica*, 9 (1928), pp. 167–186; 10 (1929), pp. 275–303, 394–416. In favor of the Armenian sanctuary, see Vincent, *RB* (1929), pp. 155–159.

[2] Cf. Baldi, *Enchiridion*, p. 730.

[3] *Ant.* xviii. 4. 3.

[4] Cf. *Wars* v. 4. 3–4.

[5] *Wars* ii. 14. 8. There is not the slightest evidence that the procurators took up residence in the Fortress Antonia when they came to Jerusalem. Several passages from Josephus are usually brought forward to prove that they did so: (1) *Ant.* xx. 1. 1; xv. 11. 4; but the only deduction to be made from these references is that there was a Roman garrison in the Fortress, whose leader was a kind of representative of the procurator; (2) *Ant.* xx. 5. 3; *Wars* ii. 12. 1: on the basis of these passages it has been asserted that "Ventidius Cumanus (45–52) inter

The First Station of the Cross, in the courtyard of the Fortress Antonia.

It is true that when a disturbance did occur, it was usually in the outer court of the Temple, a fact which is used to support the identification of the praetorium with the Fortress Antonia. For, say the proponents of the theory, the procurator would very likely have taken up his residence in the Fortress because it overlooked the outer court and was an excellent vantage point from which the soldiers could watch the movements of the crowds and swoop down on them at the first sign of trouble.

The point is well taken; but the procurator could easily have in-

festa paschalia rebellionem in templo ortam vi militari repressit, et in Antonia praesens supponitur" (Baldi, *Enchiridion,* p. 742). But we believe that a close reading of the whole of Josephus' narrative gives the impression that the procurator was not present. Considering the wealth of detail supplied by the historian, and the fact that Cumanus loomed so large in the episode, it is difficult to see why Josephus would not have mentioned his presence if he had been there in person. Moreover, the narrative deals expressly with a disturbance during the days of the Passover festivity.

stalled his lieutenant in the Fortress, as he actually did,[6] while he himself remained in the palace-fortress of Herod the Great, which stood on
higher ground than the Fortress Antonia, and from which he could
watch the whole city. This would seem the most natural arrangement
in the circumstances.

As regards the elevation of the praetorium, St. John notes (19:13)
that the place where Pilate sat "on the judgment seat" (ἐπὶ βήματος)
was called *Lithostrotos* ("a stone pavement") in Greek and *Gabbatha*
("an elevated place") in Hebrew (Aramaic). If the latter word must
be taken to refer to the hill upon which the praetorium was built (a
very doubtful reference), then the description suits the palace of
Herod the Great, on the summit of the city's western hill, better than
it does the Fortress Antonia, which stood at the *foot* of Mount Bezetha,
on the same level as the outer court of the Temple.[7]

After reviewing the tradition on the point, Fillion seems to decide
in favor of the Fortress Antonia: "Where was that residence [i.e.,
Pilate's] in the year of the Saviour's Passion? It is difficult to answer
this question, which is of no small interest to Christian piety. The
Evangelists do not furnish any exact indication as to what part of the
city was occupied by the praetorium. . . . Tradition, usually so valuable
a source of information in such cases, rather adds to the difficulty in
the present instance, for it changed in the course of time. In the year
333, it placed the praetorium in the Tyropoean valley; at the time of
the Crusades, not far from the Cenacle; only in the fourteenth century
did it fix it in the Antonia citadel, located at the northwest corner of
the Temple. . . ."[8] However, the last-named tradition actually goes
back further than the fourteenth century. The first writer to mention

---

[6] Cf. *Ant.* xviii. 4. 3.

[7] Fr. Ricciotti's observation could be misleading: ". . . It [the Antonia] was truly
situated on a 'height,' that of Bezatha [*sic*], which Josephus calls the 'highest of
all' the hills of Jerusalem. . . ." (*The Life of Christ*, p. 611). Josephus certainly
does say that Mount Bezetha was the highest hill in Jerusalem (*Wars* v. 5. 8);
but the Fortress Antonia was built, not on the summit, but at the *foot* of Mount
Bezetha. As Fr. Benoit very correctly observes: "On notera que l'Antonia est
construite en contrebas de cette coline [Bezetha], dont elle est séparée par un
large fossé" (*RB* [1952], p. 549). Then, too, Fr. Ricciotti's statement about the
pavement does not seem sufficiently well founded: "It can be considered practically certain . . . that this recently discovered pavement [on the side of the
Fortress Antonia] is the *Lithostrotos* of the Evangelist" (*op. cit.*, p. 612). Many
places in Jerusalem were paved with large slabs of stone, and no doubt this
type of pavement was to be found also in Herod's great palace-fortress.

[8] *The Life of Christ*, trans. by Newton Thompson (St. Louis: B. Herder Book
Company, 1927), III, 482-3.

the Fortress Antonia as the site of our Lord's trial before Pilate was Theodoric in the year 1172, that is, towards the end of the twelfth century.[9]

In a very learned article, Fr. Benoit has brought forward cogent arguments for the localization of the praetorium in the palace of Herod the Great.[10] In regard to the *Lithostrotos,* he says that "at this period pavements made of great slabs of stone were common in the Graeco-Roman world . . . and it is difficult to see why . . . Herod would not have paved the principal streets of the city, and particularly the main squares, such as the one which must have opened in front of the royal palace."

Fr. Benoit's article was preceded by another written by Fr. Vincent,[11] who holds the contrary opinion, i.e., that the praetorium was set up in the Fortress Antonia. Fr. Vincent's main argument is that the various episodes of the Passion fit very well into the background of the Antonia. But there are two objections to this reasoning: first, does the accepted reconstruction of the fortress correspond perfectly with the original?; and second, even with Josephus' description,[12] do we know enough about the details of the palace of Herod the Great to assert that the Gospel narrative is less adaptable to it than to the Fortress Antonia? Fr. Benoit believes that certain episodes are more easily explained against the background of Herod's palace than against that of the Antonia.

Not even the slightest trace remains of the palace in which Herod Antipas received and mocked our Saviour; however, the common opinion is that it was the ancient palace of the Machabees or the Hasmoneans, which was situated on a height opposite the outer court of the Temple and probably beside the more easterly of the two synagogues of the Askenazim.[13]

If, in view of the traditional starting point of the Stations of the Cross, we accept the theory that the Fortress Antonia was the location of the praetorium, we can easily trace our Lord's steps during the course of His Passion:

(1) From Gethsemani to the palaces of Annas and Caiphas, along the route we have indicated;

[9] Cf. Baldi, *Enchiridion,* no. 924; see *ibid.,* nos. 906–929, for the variations of the tradition.
[10] *RB* (1952), pp. 531–550.
[11] *RB* (1952), pp. 513–530.
[12] *Wars* v. 4. 4; *Ant.* xv. 9. 3.   [13] *Ant.* xx. 8. 11.

(2) From Caiphas' palace to the praetorium, across the city from southwest to northeast;

(3) From the praetorium to Herod Antipas, ascending in a southerly direction to the heart of the city;

(4) From Herod back to Pilate;

(5) From the praetorium to Calvary, ascending Mount Gareb in a westerly direction.[14]

The Sanhedrin

The Sanhedrin (=assembly) was the supreme tribunal of the Jews, and was composed of seventy-one members, including the president, who was the high priest. The number seems to have been inspired by Exodus 24:1, 9, which tells how seventy elders of Israel went up the mountain with Moses. The members of the Sanhedrin were divided into three categories: *chief priests,* or heads of the great priestly families; *Scribes,* or doctors of the Law; and *elders,* or distinguished laymen. Besides the Great Sanhedrin of Jerusalem there were lesser sanhedrins in many cities; Josephus refers, for example, to those of Gadara, Amathus, Jericho and Sephoris.[15] Even in the capital itself there were several of these lesser tribunals.[16] The word *synedrion* occurs first in Josephus.[17] The same historian uses the word βουλή for the place in which the Sanhedrin met, which was very close to the Xystos, mentioned in the same passage.[18] In the *Mishnah* the meeting place is called the "Chamber of Hewn Stone" (*lishkath ha-gazith*).[19] According to Josephus, this chamber stood a little to the east of the Xystos, adjacent to the western cloister of the Temple.[20] There is a traditional belief that forty years before the destruction of the Temple, the Sanhedrin was transferred to a place called the *hanôth,* which is commonly translated as the "shops," but whose location is not known. Some think that the term refers to the magnificent porches about the Temple,

---

[14] Our Lord probably left the city through the Gate of Ephraim, which could well be the one whose ruins are venerated today in the Russian Hospice, near the Holy Sepulchre, on the basis of the theory that these ruins formed part of the second wall of the city, as some noteworthy authors believe solidly probable.

[15] *Ant.* xiv. 5. 4.

[16] Cf. Schürer, II, 236.

[17] *Ant.* xiv. 9. 3–4.

[18] *Wars* v. 4. 2.

[19] *Middoth* 5:4.

[20] *Wars* v. 4. 2; cf. *ibid.,* ii. 16. 3, where he also mentions the Xystos as being beside the palace of the Hasmoneans.

while others hold that the place designated was outside the city. Schürer is of the opinion that the transferral is not historical.[21] When the Temple was destroyed in A.D. 70, the Sanhedrin, which by that time had undergone considerable modification, left Jerusalem and went to Jamnia, present-day Yebna, near the coast, between Jaffa and Eshdud.

The powers of the Sanhedrin varied according to the caprices of the Roman governors. As is evident from an incident related by Josephus, it could pronounce and execute sentence of death in the time of Hyrcanus II.[22] The historian tells us that Herod the Great, while governor of Galilee, had had a certain Ezechias killed. The dead man's friends went to Hyrcanus to protest, asserting that *no one could be executed without the authorization and sentence of the Sanhedrin.* And Hyrcanus ordered Herod to appear before the Sanhedrin to account for his action.

When Herod himself ascended the throne, not only did he greatly curb the activity of the Sanhedrin, but he kept the tribunal very much in the background during his entire reign. When the Roman procurators were in power, the *jus gladii* was reserved to them. Josephus tells us that the first procurator, Coponius, "received from Caesar the power of [life and] death," [23] a phrase which should apparently be understood in the sense that this power was reserved exclusively to the procurator. And it was a written tradition among the Jews that "forty years before the destruction of the Temple the right to condemn to capital punishment was taken from the Israelites." [24] The Jewish leaders acknowledged as much when they said to Pilate: "It is not lawful for us to put anyone to death" (John 18:31). Some authors interpret this to mean that the Jews could not condemn anyone to be *crucified,* but that they could, nevertheless, sentence a criminal to be stoned. However, the Jews' assertion is so categorical that it seems to exclude every form of execution, and it is all the more definitive in view of what we have just said.[25]

---

[21] II, 265.

[22] *Ant.* xiv. 9. 3–4.

[23] *Wars* ii. 8. 1.

[24] See this passage and a discussion of it in Schürer, II, 261, n. 79, and Str.-Bill., I, 1027.

[25] Regarding this power of the Sanhedrin, see the very learned article by Holzmeister, "Zur Frage der Blutgerichtsbarkeit des Synedriums," in *Biblica,* 19 (1938), 43–59, 151–174. Professor J. Jeremias, in an article entitled "Zur Geschichtlichkeit des Verhoers vor d. Hohen Rat," in *Zeit. f. d. neutestament. Wissenschaft* (1950–51), 145–150, deals with this question of the *jus gladii* and

Several incidents are usually quoted to prove that the Sanhedrin had the *jus gladii* in our Lord's day, for example, the Acts of the Apostles (7:8–59) tells us that Stephen was brought before the Sanhedrin, that he spoke in his own defense and that as a result of his speech he was dragged outside the city and stoned as a blasphemer. But this incident, instead of being the execution of a formal sentence passed by the tribunal, was simply a minor riot or, as we would call it today, a lynching.

We also know that the high priest, Annas, son of the Annas mentioned in the Gospel, had St. James the Less stoned; therefore, some authors conclude, he had the power to pass sentence of death. But Josephus notes that Annas' procedure was unlawful.[26] The high priest took advantage of the interregnum between the departure of the procurator Festus and the arrival of his successor Albinus to rid himself of the Apostle. When Albinus took over the reins of government, he condemned Annas' conduct and declared that he had exceeded his powers, and King Agrippa II punished the high priest by removing him from the office which he had held for only three months.

The origin of the Sanhedrin is rather obscure. We know that in Moses' time mention was made of "the ancients of Israel" (Exod. 3:16, 18). In Deuteronomy 27:1, we are told that "Moses with the ancients of Israel commanded the people. . . ." And in Numbers 11:16 *f.* we read that God commanded Moses to gather together "seventy men of the ancients of Israel" to help him in governing the people. Centuries later we find Esdras acting on the advice of the

brings forward two new arguments in favor of the negative thesis: (1) the episode of the adulteress (John 8:3 *ff.*). He says that the incident is made clearer and more forceful if it is granted that the tribunal had condemned the woman but could not carry out the sentence. The Pharisees' question did not refer to the interpretation of the Law, which was obvious, but to its application. If Jesus had answered in the affirmative, He would have set Himself up against the Roman authorities, who had deprived the Jews of the *jus gladii;* and if He had answered in the negative, He would have gone against the Law itself. However, we believe that there is no reason to suppose that the woman had already been condemned by the tribunal; instead, she was probably brought directly to Jesus so that He might judge the case. See above, pp. 467 *f.*

(2) In a rabbinical document, *Megillath Ta'anith* ("Scroll of Fasting") 6, which enumerates the feast days on which fasting was not permitted, we read: "On the 17th day of 'Elul [August-September], the Romans left Jerusalem"; and "on the 22nd day of this month *we again began to condemn malefactors to death.*" This seems to indicate that during the Roman domination the Jews did not possess the power of pronouncing a capital sentence. Cf. *Verb. Dom.*, 31 (1953), 109.

[26] *Ant.* xx. 9. 1.

princes and ancients in giving a command to the people (1 Esdras 10:8). From Deuteronomy 21:1–9, 18–21, we know that the assembly of the ancients had the right to pass the death sentence, as is evident also from the incident of Susanna and the two ancients (Dan. 13) during the Babylonian Captivity.

However, a formally constituted assembly, such as the Sanhedrin was in the time of Christ, seems to date back only to the Hellenic period, although it is possible that there had been a similar tribunal under the Persian domination. In 1 Machabees 14:28 we read about "a great assembly [συναγωγή] of the priests . . . and the princes of the nation and the ancients of the country"; and in 1 Machabees 12:6 there is mention of the senate (γερουσία) of the nation. Josephus refers to the senate for the first time in his *Antiquities of the Jews,* xii. 3. 4, where he reproduces a letter from Antiochus III to Ptolemy IV; but, as we have already pointed out, he uses the word *synedrion* only when speaking of the time when Herod was governor of Galilee.[27]

During the Hasmonean regime, the senate was undoubtedly a politico-religious assembly. It lost this dual character under the rule of the family of Herod, but regained it to some extent during the administration of the Roman procurators, for Josephus says that after the death of Herod and his son Archelaus, "the government became an aristocracy, and the high priests received authority over the nation."[28] At any rate, all the New Testament cases in which the Sanhedrin intervened were matters of religion: in Matthew 26:65, the high priest declared that Jesus was a blasphemer; in Acts 4:1 *ff.* the Sanhedrin questioned Peter and John about their preaching; in 5:17 *ff.* they imprisoned the Apostles on account of their doctrine; and in 22:30—23:1 *ff.* they accused St. Paul of breaking the Law. And this jurisdiction over religious matters was not limited to Judea and Samaria, but extended to all Jews, as is evident from the message which they sent to John the Baptist when he was baptizing on the other side of the Jordan, in Perea, which was ruled by Antipas (cf. John 1:19 *ff.*), and also from the permission which they gave Saul to go to Damascus and bring back to Jerusalem the Christian Jews he found there (cf. Acts 9:2; 22:5; 26:12).[29] Therefore it is not correct to say, as some do, that while Jesus was in Galilee He was not under the juris-

[27] *Ant.* xiv. 9. 3–4.
[28] *Ant.* xx. 10.
[29] Cf. Felten, *Neutestamentliche Zeitgeschichte* (Regensburg, 1925), I, 320.

diction of the Sanhedrin, although it is true that while He was in a district far removed from Jerusalem He was of course less exposed to the tribunal's machinations and enmity than if He had been in the capital itself.[30]

Annas (*Hanan*=merciful), son of Seth, was high priest for nine years, from A.D. 6 to 15. No less than seven members of his family held the office; five sons, namely, Eleazar, Jonathan, Theophilus, Matthias, and Annas the younger; his grandson, the son of Theophilus; and his son-in-law, Caiphas. It is not surprising, therefore, that he wielded great influence. Josephus says that the people considered him happy and fortunate; [31] but his reputation did not match his supposed happiness, for he was known to be grasping and overbearing, vices which were common to other great priestly families such as those of Boethus, Phabi and Camithus, as well as that of Annas. Of these priests Josephus tells us that they stirred up riots in the city, and that their avarice and arrogance reached such extremes that they sent their servants to the threshing floors to exact on their account the tithes which were due to the ordinary priests, leaving the latter to die of hunger.[32] And it was commonly said that they bought the dignity of the high priesthood for gold and added to their wealth by evil means.[33]

Caiphas, or rather Joseph Caiphas, the son-in-law of Annas, held the office of high priest for eighteen years, whereas his two immediate predecessors, Eleazar, son of Annas, and Simon, son of Camithus, had retained that dignity for only a year. He was nominated in A.D. 18 by the proconsul Vitellius, who selected his (Caiphas') brother-in-law Jonathan, son of Annas, to succeed him. Jonathan remained in office only a year.[34] We know little about Caiphas' life, but from his conduct in our Lord's trial we can gather that he was both violent and unscrupulous. And it would not be rash to suspect that he attained and kept his high office by shameless bribery, fawning flattery and base compromise.

Pontius Pilate, the fifth Roman procurator of Judea and the immediate successor of Valerius Gratus, held his office for the relatively

---

[30] Regarding the nature and history of the Sanhedrin see Schürer, II, 237–267; Holzmeister, *Historia aetatis Novi Testamenti* (Romae, 1938), pp. 208–222; Felten, *op. cit.,* I, 312–328.

[31] *Ant.* xx. 9. 1.

[32] *Ant.* xx. 8. 8.

[33] Str.-Bill., II, 569.

[34] *Ant.* xviii. 2. 2; 4. 3.

long period of ten years, from his nomination by Tiberius in 26 until his removal in 36 by Caligula, Tiberius' successor.

If we had no other documents to draw on except the Gospel narrative of the Passion, we should put Pilate down as a weakling, an opportunist who sacrificed justice to self-interest. But we do have other sources of information concerning his character. Thus Philo tells us that King Agrippa I, in his legation to Caligula, accused Pilate of "vexations, robbery, injustices, outrages," of having citizens put to death without any trial, and of being cruel and irascible.[35]

Although it is quite possible that this account of Pilate's character is an exaggerated one, it is confirmed to a certain extent by several incidents recorded by Josephus. The historian relates how the procurator had his soldiers bring their standards, which bore Caesar's image, into Jerusalem, a course of conduct which his predecessors had avoided out of respect for the laws of the Jews: "Pilate was the first who introduced these images into Jerusalem. He did so unknown to the people, for he acted at night." The sacrilege started a riot in the city and a delegation was sent to Caesarea, where Pilate resided. The procurator was at first unrelenting and arrogant, but when he saw that the Jews were ready to suffer death rather than permit such an insult to their religion, he had to capitulate.[36] On another occasion, he procured some golden shields dedicated to Tiberius, without images but bearing certain inscriptions, and had them hung in the palace of Herod the Great, where he lived while in Jerusalem. Once more the people were outraged, and although they begged the procurator to remove the shields, "he answered their appeal with an angry negative, for he was a man of harsh and stubborn character." But once again he had to suffer the humiliation of being forced to yield, for the Jews went to Tiberius, who wrote ordering him to remove the offending shields immediately.[37] At another time, he undertook the laudable task of constructing or restoring an aqueduct to carry water to Jerusalem. But he vitiated his good action by taking money from the Temple treasury to finance the scheme. Such a sacrilege wounded the people's feelings deeply and caused a riot in which thousands of citizens took part, some of them hurling abuse at the procurator. Pilate had some of his soldiers dressed like Jews mingle with the crowd, and on a prearranged

---

[35] *Legatio ad Gaium* § 38.1. 299 *ff.*, in *Philonis Alexandrini Opera quae supersunt* (Berolini, 1915), VI, 175.

[36] *Ant.* xviii. 3. 1; *Wars* ii. 9. 2–3.

[37] Philo, *loc. cit.*

signal from him, they laid about them with cudgels, killing many of the mob and wounding others.[38] Finally, he committed another act of cruelty, one which was the immediate cause of his downfall. In A.D. 35, a certain adventurer persuaded the Samaritans that Moses' sacred vessels were hidden on Mount Garizim, their holy mountain, and promised that he would show them where they lay. As a result, a great number of Samaritans gathered to ascend the mountain and take possession of the treasure. But Pilate, fearing a disturbance, forestalled them by stationing cavalry and infantry on the road to Mount Garizim, and when the crowd found their way barred, there ensued a pitched battle in which many Samaritans were killed and others taken captive, while the more fortunate escaped. Ruthlessly, the procurator executed those of the leaders whom he had captured. When the Samaritans appealed to Vitellius, the proconsul of Syria, he commanded Pilate to go to Rome and defend himself before the Emperor. But the Emperor died before the procurator reached the capital.[39]

Such episodes as these are what one would expect during the administration of a man who, as St. Luke tells us (13:1), slaughtered a group of Galileans while they were offering sacrifice.[40]

It is therefore evident that the procurator who passed sentence on Jesus was not only a weakling and an opportunist but also a harsh, cruel, arrogant soldier, totally lacking in diplomacy, who took no account of the laws and legitimate customs of his subjects, but callously wounded their patriotic and religious sensibilities, provoking vehement protests and bloody riots which could easily have been avoided.

Of Pilate's life after his condemnation of Jesus we know nothing. Many different legends have been woven about him, e.g., that he committed suicide, or that he was sentenced to death by Nero, or that he was exiled to Vienne in Gaul. It does seem very probable, however, that he died a violent death.[41]

Before Annas and Caiphas

Annas, father-in-law of the reigning high priest, Caiphas, was the moving spirit behind everything that went on in Jerusalem at that time. He himself had been high priest for nine years, and by bribery

[38] *Ant.* xviii. 3. 2; *Wars* ii. 9. 4.
[39] *Ant.* xviii. 4. 1–2.
[40] Cf. Schürer, I, 488–492.
[41] See Schürer, I, 492 *f.*, where a copious bibliography will be found.

and cunning had succeeded in keeping the office in his family for half a century. He was universally hated, but he was also feared and outwardly respected, for all felt the force of his malevolent influence. It was before this man, in whom wealth and avarice, arrogance and servility formed a repugnant combination, that Jesus was led to be tried.

In his eagerness to be present when the despised Prophet arrived, the old pontiff shrugged off the fatigue which weighed upon him owing to his advanced age and the lateness of the hour. When the Prisoner finally came, he received Him with lofty contempt and the ill-concealed joy of satisfied pride. Immediately, he set about questioning Jesus concerning His disciples and doctrine, confident that the Prisoner would welcome the opportunity to defend Himself before such a great dignitary as he; or he may have hoped to obtain a confession which he could use in his criminal plans.

But Jesus did not satisfy Annas' desire. Instead, He declared: "I have spoken openly to the world; I have always taught in the synagogue and in the temple, where all the Jews gather, and in secret I have said nothing. Why dost thou question me? Question those who have heard what I spoke to them; behold, these know what I have said."

Our Lord's answer was a model of prudence, even apart from the fact that a person's own testimony concerning himself was not regarded as valid in court, for, as the *Mishnah* says: "None may be believed when he testifies of himself." [42]

So dignified and pertinent an answer disconcerted the haughty priest, leaving him undecided as to what he should do next, for although Christ's calm words wounded his pride, they were too full of wisdom to allow of punishment. However, one of the attendants relieved Annas of the need to reply by striking Jesus across the face and demanding: "Is that the way thou dost answer the high priest?" The cruel blow aroused a murmur of approval in the assembly, while Annas looked on complacently. Christ's only reaction to the attack was to say quietly: "If I have spoken ill, bear witness to the evil; but if well, why dost thou strike me?"

But His words were drowned by the jeering laughter of His enemies: the voice of truth and justice went unheard amid the applause given to violence and iniquity.

[42] *Ketuboth* 2:9.

Annas had been avenged by his underling, but the humiliation still rankled. Yet the Prisoner's bearing was so noble, His voice so firm and His dignity so unassailable that even the proud old high priest did not dare to question Him further. Rather, he judged it more prudent to bring the session to a close and send the Prisoner, bound as He was, to his son-in-law Caiphas, the reigning pontiff.

St. John is the only one who tells us that Jesus was led first, not to the high priest, but to Annas (18:13). But that is no reason for doubting the fact, particularly since, of all the Apostles, John was the one who kept closest to Jesus during His Passion. Caiphas might have arranged matters thus as a mark of deference to his father-in-law, who still wielded great authority. The old man had been high priest from A.D. 6 to 15, and in the Acts of the Apostles (4:6) he is named first, even before Caiphas himself. Then too, as father-in-law of Caiphas, who reigned for eighteen years (18–36), he undoubtedly had great influence in the city.

Our Lord, then, was brought first to Annas' house. But did the interrogation of Jesus and Peter's denials take place there or in the palace of Caiphas?

St. John's narrative (18:13–27) does present some knotty problems. First of all, it seems to contradict the Synoptic writers' versions by apparently placing Peter's denials in Annas' house, whereas the other evangelists locate them in the palace of Caiphas. Then there is another and perhaps graver difficulty which Fr. Murillo expresses as follows: "In verse 13b St. John names Caiphas and calls him the high priest of that year, and from then on he introduces no one else to whom this title could be applied. Therefore the obvious inference is that the high priest to whom the evangelist refers in the subsequent verses is none other than Caiphas." [43] But if the interrogation took place in the palace of Caiphas, then both these difficulties vanish, the Synoptic Gospels and St. John's account are brought into perfect harmony with each other, and the title of high priest is applied to Caiphas alone.

Therefore a number of exegetes, both ancient and modern (e.g., Salmerón, Cornelius a Lapide, Lebreton, Lagrange and Fillion), have been inclined to place the interrogation of Jesus and Peter's denials in the palace of Caiphas and not in Annas' house. In this case Annas, content with the deference shown him by his son-in-law, probably did

[43] *Evangelio de San Juan,* p. 497.

not even question the Prisoner but sent Him immediately to Caiphas. On the basis of this hypothesis the narrative flows smoothly along. But the text itself presents an obstacle to such an explanation, for in verse 24 we read that "Annas sent him [Jesus] bound to Caiphas, the high priest." Hence everything that went before took place in Annas' house. Some authors answer this objection by translating the verb used, not by "he sent," but by "he had sent," a reading which is justly rejected by many modern writers who solve the problem by placing verse 24 between verses 13 and 14. There is some textual evidence to support this arrangement, for in the Sinaitic Syriac version and in St. Cyril of Jerusalem the verse in question comes immediately after our verse 13.

There is no doubt that the transposition of verse 24 is a very tempting solution to the difficulties we have mentioned. Yet we do not believe that the suggested change, attractive though it is, has any solid backing. From the point of view of external literary criticism, the transposition does not even merit discussion, as Lagrange correctly observes.[44] What probative power can a single version (apparently a doctored one at that) and a single Father have in the face of the great mass of manuscripts, versions and ecclesiastical writers? But what of internal criticism? In our opinion, it, too, favors the usual arrangement of the text, for if verse 24 did originally follow verse 13, no copyist or exegete would have even thought of removing it, since it would have fitted very well where it was and the narrative would have offered no difficulty. On the other hand, the transposition of verse 24 to follow verse 13 could have been made for the very reasons that move many present-day commentators to favor it. And it is hard to imagine how a merely fortuitous or involuntary displacement of the verse could have occurred.[45]

But if the transposition cannot be upheld, how are we to solve the two difficulties presented above? According to St. John's account, Peter's first denial probably took place on his entry into Annas' house or soon afterwards, the second denial occurred in the same place as the first, as can be seen from John 18:25 collated with verse 18, as did the third also.

Neither tradition nor archaeology tells us anything about Annas' house. Very possibly it was next to that of his son-in-law, and on the

---

[44] "Si cette question textuelle devait être tranchée d'après les autorités diplomatiques, il n'y aurait aucun doute" (Év. selon S. Jean, p. 459).

[45] In this regard, see Fr. Benoit's acute observations in his article "Jésus devant le Sanhedrin," in Angelicum, 20 (1948), 151 ff.

basis of that hypothesis, it is easy to explain why St. John locates the denials in Annas' house while the Synoptic writers place them in the palace of Caiphas. However, if the future brings to light evidence to prove that the two houses were situated at a distance from each other, then the problem will have to be re-examined.

The other difficulty, which Lagrange considers the principal one,[46] does not arise merely from the fact that the title of high priest is conferred on Annas. As evidence of this, it is enough to recall St. Luke's words (3:2), "during the high priesthood of Annas and Caiphas." Then, too, the Acts of the Apostles calls Annas the high priest (4:6); and we know from Josephus that those who had been invested with the office retained the title even after they had ceased to reign, for the historian speaks of "high priests" in the plural.[47] Therefore there was nothing unusual in St. John's calling Annas the high priest although Caiphas held the office at the time. Instead, the difficulty arises from the fact that in the same passage (18:13–24), St. John applies the title "high priest" first to one and then to the other, thus causing some confusion. But, as Lagrange aptly observes, the evangelist was perhaps relying upon the common sense of his readers to untangle the references.[48] In reality, there was no confusion for St. John's contemporaries, since they knew very well that Annas was commonly given the title of high priest. Thus, when in John 18:13 they were informed that Jesus was brought to Annas, and were then told of His being questioned by the high priest, they knew that the latter term referred to Annas. Therefore, for a correct understanding of the passage we must take account of the historical background of the fourth Gospel.

In addition, there is a psychological reason why Annas would have interrogated Jesus. In view of the old priest's authority, pride and natural curiosity, it is very unlikely that, when he had before him the Prisoner with whom he had been so preoccupied, he would have sent Him immediately to Caiphas without speaking to or questioning Him. We believe that even if we had not St. John's account we would have noticed the psychological unlikelihood of such a sequence of events.

Because Christ's appearance before Annas was not a trial properly so called, the old high priest merely questioned Him generally about His disciples and doctrine. The interrogation was, of course, perfectly superfluous because everyone knew the Prisoner's doctrine, preached as

---

[46] *Op. cit.,* p. 461.
[47] *Life* 38.
[48] *Op. cit.,* p. 461.

it had been openly in broad daylight. When Jesus pointed this out to Annas, the high priest must have felt the force of his Prisoner's answer, for apparently he did not insist on continuing the interrogation but judged it more prudent to bring the session to a close and leave the whole matter in the hands of his son-in-law.

Jesus, therefore, was led to the palace of Caiphas to be confronted by the members of the Sanhedrin, some of whom had been waiting there since the early hours of the evening, while others had come with the Prisoner or had been summoned by Caiphas. Although they were resolved to pass sentence of death on our Lord, these grave doctors of the Law did not wish to condemn Him without at least the semblance of a trial because they wanted their verdict to seem inspired solely by zeal for the glory of God and not by personal hatred.

They had sought for witnesses to testify against Him and had found more than enough—at a price. Many came forward to accuse the Prisoner, but their evidence was contradictory, and despite bribery, promises and threats, truth proved more powerful than malice. When the unjust judges saw that their efforts had been fruitless, they looked at each other in desperation and began to ply Jesus with crafty questions. But He remained silent. Finally, two witnesses were produced whose evidence seemed as if it were going to be decisive: "We ourselves have heard him say, 'I will destroy this temple built by hands, and after three days I will build another, not built by hands.' "

But St. Mark goes on to say that "even then their evidence did not agree" (14:59).

Caiphas, exasperated at seeing his plans being frustrated and forgetful of his dignity, turned furiously on the Prisoner and shouted: "Dost thou make no answer to the things that these men prefer against thee?"

Jesus met the angry outburst with silence. All around Him the Sanhedrists surged like a stormy sea, the waves of their indignation and anger dashing against Him. But He stood firm as a rock, dominating them by the eloquence of His silence. Though balked for the moment, Caiphas did not relinquish his purpose. With sacrilegious lips he invoked the name of God to wring from the Prisoner His own death sentence: "I adjure thee by the living God that thou tell us whether thou art the Christ, the Son of God."

Jesus well knew the perfidy and bad faith hidden in this demand.

He knew, too, that Caiphas had no right to an answer. But still He replied, for He wished to bear clear and incontrovertible witness to His identity before the high priest and in the presence of the supreme tribunal of the Jews: "Thou hast said it. I am. Nevertheless, I say to you, hereafter you shall see the Son of Man sitting at the right hand of the Power and coming upon the clouds of heaven."

This solemn declaration was to ring in the hearts of countless generations, who would adore the despised, fettered Prisoner as the Messias, the immortal King of Ages, the Son of God.

Caiphas must have understood the title "Son of God" in the sense of natural divine filiation and not simply as a synonym for the Messias. It is not possible that he was ignorant of the repeated declarations for which the Jews had deemed Jesus deserving of death: "This . . . is why the Jews were seeking . . . to put him to death; because he was . . . calling God his own Father, making himself equal to God" (John 5:18); "Not for a good work do we stone thee, but for blasphemy, and because thou, being a man, makest thyself God" (John 10:33). Hence there can scarcely be any doubt as to what Caiphas meant. Consequently, by His definitive answer "I am," Jesus made a formal and unequivocal declaration of His divinity, and He further confirmed what He said by referring to Psalm 109:1 and to the magnificent description of the future Messias written by the prophet Daniel (7:13).

But to the willfully obtuse minds of His hearers His words sounded like blasphemy. "He has blasphemed!" shouted the high priest, tearing his garments, "what further need have we of witnesses? Behold, now you have heard the blasphemy. What do you think?"

With one voice the Sanhedrists pronounced their sentence: "He is liable to death."

Their indignation at the supposed blasphemy served as a convenient mask for their unholy joy at having found a way to condemn their Prisoner to death without need for witnesses. It was specifically laid down in Leviticus 24:16 that "he that blasphemeth the name of the Lord, dying let him die." And what blasphemy was greater than to make oneself equal to God?

Caiphas had apparently triumphed, but only apparently, for the real victor was the Prisoner. Jesus had willed to go to His death, but not on a political charge. He had willed to put the seal of His Blood on His declaration that He was the Son of God. And He was to do so, for He was condemned for having proclaimed Himself the Son of God.[49]

The vociferous condemnation was followed by a rain of insults and blows. St. Luke seems to record that it was the guards who heaped these indignities on Jesus: "And the men who had him in custody began to mock him and beat him" (22:63), but St. Matthew (26:66–67) gives the impression that the Sanhedrists also took part in torturing the Prisoner, as does St. Mark when he distinguishes between "the attendants [who] struck him with blows of their hands" and "some [who] began to spit on him. . . ." (14:65). Therefore it is very probable that they all laid their sacrilegious hands on our Lord, striking Him, spitting in His face, blindfolding Him and asking with brutal sarcasm: "Prophesy to us, O Christ! who is it that struck thee?"

At this point there arises a problem which has been widely discussed but has not yet been definitely solved. Was our Lord's trial conducted according to all the prescriptions of Hebrew jurisprudence? Was it a legal trial? [50]

It is well established that a trial in the strict sense took place, not, however, in Annas' house but before Caiphas.[51] The whole Sanhedrin came together, witnesses were called, and in the end "they all condemned him as liable to death" (Mark 14:64). The same conclusion

---

[49] Jewish writers (e.g., Zeitlin, Klausner) try to prove that it was an exclusively political motive which caused the leaders of Israel to hand Jesus over to the Roman procurator; the Jews feared that if they did not do so they would be regarded as accessories to the treason against Rome which Jesus had committed by proclaiming that He was the king of the Jews (S. Zeitlin, *Who Crucified Jesus?* [New York: Harper & Brothers, 1942], pp. 167–172; J. Klausner, *Jesus of Nazareth*, pp. 345–348). This is not merely closing one's eyes to the facts; it is a downright distortion of history. The whole narrative, with all its details, protests against such an interpretation.

[50] J. Blinzler gives a short but clear and concise exposition of the problem in his article "Geschichtlichkeit und Legalität des jüdischen Prozesses gegen Jesus," in *Stimmen der Zeit* (February, 1951), pp. 345–357. He deals more extensively with the subject in his book *Der Prozess Jesu* (Stuttgart, 1951). See also J. Imbert, *Est-ce Pilate qui a condamné Notre Seigneur Jésus-Christ?* (Paris, 1947); K. L. Schmidt, "Der Todesprozess des Messias Jesu," in *Judaica* (1945), pp. 1–40. The Jewish point of view is clearly expressed in J. Klausner, *op. cit.*, pp. 339–348 and in S. Zeitlin, *op. cit.*, pp. 161–179.

[51] The Anglican clergyman, H. Danby, denies or at least doubts that there was a real trial: see his article, "The Bearing of the Rabbinical Criminal Code on the Jewish Trial Narratives in the Gospels," in *The Journal of Theological Studies*, 21 (1919), 51–76. According to him, there was no formal trial but only a "preliminary investigation" before the real trial, which was reserved to the Roman governor (pp. 56 *ff.*). But his arguments are far from convincing. Klausner is of the same opinion as Danby ("A preliminary judicial investigation": *op. cit.*, p. 334). For the names of other authors who defend the same thesis, see Blinzler, *loc. cit.*, p. 346.

can be drawn from the behavior of the Jews when they went before Pilate. When the procurator asked what charges they wished to bring against the Prisoner, they answered resentfully: "If he were not a criminal we should not have handed him over to thee" (John 18: 29 f.). They wanted Pilate to condemn Jesus to death without any further investigation and solely on the basis of the sentence they had passed on Him.

The evidence of these facts is such that those who deny that a religious trial took place are forced to thrust aside the Gospel narrative, whose historical character they audaciously reject.[52]

The Sanhedrin, then, tried Jesus and passed sentence upon Him. But in doing so did they observe the legal formalities? We shall find the answer by comparing the procedure followed by the Sanhedrin with the rules laid down by jurisprudence and formulated in the treatise *Sanhedrin* in the *Mishnah*.[53] According to the *Mishnah*, "In capital cases they hold the trial during the daytime and the verdict also must be reached during the daytime."

"In non-capital cases the verdict, whether of acquittal or of conviction, may be reached the same day; in capital cases a verdict of acquittal may be reached on the same day, but a verdict of conviction not until the following day. Therefore trials may not be held on the eve of a Sabbath or on the eve of a Festival-day."

"The blasphemer is not culpable unless he has pronounced the Name itself [of Yahweh]."

"How did they admonish the witnesses in capital cases? They brought them in and admonished them, [saying,] '. . . Know ye . . . that capital cases are not as non-capital cases: . . . in capital cases the witness is answerable for the blood of him [that is wrongfully condemned] and the blood of his posterity [that should have been born to him] to the end of the world.' " Then follow numerous warnings to assure that they tell only the truth.

Obviously, these prescriptions were not observed in our Lord's trial, which was on a capital charge. He was tried and sentenced to death at night, and the execution of the sentence was carried out on the same day as the condemnation. We know definitely that Jesus died on a Friday; therefore, the trial was illegally held on the eve of the Sabbath. He had not pronounced the sacred name of Yahweh: the witnesses had not been warned to tell the truth; indeed, the whole

---

[52] Cf. Blinzler, *loc. cit.*   [53] *Mishnah, Sanhedrin* 4:1; 7:5; 4:5.

context leads one to the conclusion that, on the contrary, they had been induced to give false testimony against the Prisoner.

Consequently there is not the slightest doubt that the Sanhedrin, in their anxiety to finish the trial and execution before the Passover, had brushed aside all the legal formalities, perhaps on the pretext that pressure of time dispensed them therefrom. Hence our Lord's trial was absolutely illegal. Even Klausner recognizes this fact:

> It is true that, if we compare the judicial procedure detailed in the *Mishna* and *Tosefta* of the *Tractate Sanhedrin*, with what we learn, particularly in Mark and Matthew, of the trial of Jesus, we are bound to conclude that the Sanhedrin broke every prescribed law of procedure.[54]

Zeitlin tries to exonerate the Jews by drawing a distinction between a religious Sanhedrin and a political one,[55] the latter not being obliged to observe the legal prescriptions. It was this political Sanhedrin, he maintains, and not the religious one, that tried the cause of Jesus:

> In establishing that the Sanhedrin which was assembled in the house of Caiphas was not a religious Sanhedrin but was a political Sanhedrin, we remove automatically all the apparent discrepancies and illegalities in connection with the trial of Jesus.[56]

Zeitlin piles assertion upon assertion, but produces no proof that such a twofold Sanhedrin existed. For the rest, all the circumstances clearly point to a religious trial and to the fact that when the Jews accused Jesus before Pilate of political crimes, they did so because they realized that the procurator would pay slight attention to merely religious matters.

But were the prescriptions set down in the *Mishnah* in force in our Lord's time? If they were not, then our whole argument is invalidated.

The *Mishnah* was the result of rabbinical literary activity which had been going on for several centuries and which was brought to a close towards the end of the second century A.D. by Rabbi Judah ha-Nasi (or the Patriarch). Now, a number of authors believe that the catastrophe of A.D. 70 had a profound effect on the institutions of the Jewish community and that, due to the influence of the Sadducees, who were in the majority in the Sanhedrin, the Hebrew penal code in

[54] *Op. cit.*, p. 333.
[55] *Op. cit.*, pp. 68–83.
[56] *Ibid.*, p. 165.

our Lord's time was much more severe than it became after the destruction of Jerusalem as a result of the milder spirit of the Pharisees.[57] If this is so, then it would be an anachronism to say that in the first decades of our era certain laws were in force which were not introduced into Hebrew jurisprudence until after the destruction of Jerusalem in A.D. 70.

Of course, such an evolution is possible; but we do not think that the arguments for it are convincing.[58] Yet the possibility, or the faint probability even, that such a change did occur makes it advisable for us not to regard the judicial norms found in the *Mishnah* as proof positive that our Lord's trial was illegal.

But we can affirm that there was a double trial in the sense that Jesus was brought before both religious and civil judges and was interrogated by them. However, in regard to the process that took place in Pilate's court the term "trial" can scarcely be used in its strict sense since the procurator confined himself to stating that the accusations against the Prisoner were inadequate. Nor did he act as a true judge when condemning our Lord to death: instead, he gave in to the clamorous demands of the Jews because he was afraid to do otherwise.

We must add that the religious trial was undeniably lacking in good faith, since vindictiveness played a predominant and even decisive part in it, a circumstance which was much more reprehensible than the mere omission of certain legal formalities.

When the Sanhedrists heard Jesus say that He was the Messias, the Son of God, it is possible that they thought He had blasphemed. But such a conclusion, such willful ignorance on their part, would have been gravely culpable because they had deliberately closed their eyes to the light. Their bad faith and malevolence showed up unmistakably

---

[57] Josephus says that the Sadducees were "harsher and more cruel than the other Jews." No doubt by "the other Jews" he meant the Pharisees (*Ant.* xx. 9. 1). Cf. Blinzler, *loc. cit.,* pp. 353 *f.*

[58] In the *Mishnah, Sanhedrin* 7:2, we read: "Rabbi Eliezer ben Zadok said: 'It happened once that a priest's daughter committed adultery and they encompassed her with bundles of branches and burnt her . . . because the court [which was made up of Sadducees] at that time had not right knowledge.'" Therefore a change had taken place. In fact, again according to the *Mishnah* (*ibid.*), the new method of burning a criminal was to place a lighted wick or molten lead in the victim's mouth and so burn his entrails.

This case proves that a change had occurred in one particular point, but we maintain that we would not be justified in making a generalization on so flimsy a basis, as do Klausner (*op. cit.,* p. 343), Blinzler (*loc. cit.,* p. 354) and Danby (*loc. cit.,* pp. 64 *ff.*).

when they appeared before Pilate. They had condemned Jesus for claiming to be the Son of God and for that alone. But knowing that such a charge would not make the slightest impression on the procurator, they changed their tactics and charged their Prisoner with three civil crimes of which, as they well knew, He was innocent. They were perfectly aware that He had never proclaimed Himself king, that He had never stirred up the people against the Romans and that, far from having advised them to refuse tribute to Caesar (cf. Luke 23:2), He had expressly counselled: "Render . . . to Caesar the things that are Caesar's and to God the things that are God's."

Therefore, when accusing Jesus before Pilate, the Sanhedrists were not motivated by sincere convictions but by the accumulated rancor, envy and hatred of two years and more. His death was an act of pure revenge, a murder flimsily disguised by legal formalities.

Peter's Denials

Though the iniquity of His judges grieved Jesus deeply, His loving heart was wounded even more sharply by the defection of one of His most intimate friends.

While insults and blows were being rained on the uncomplaining Lamb of God, one of His best-loved disciples, Simon Peter, upon whom He had bestowed special marks of distinction, was shamefully denying Him in the courtyard of the very palace in which He was being mocked and buffeted. The Apostle had fled from the garden after our Lord had been arrested, but when his first panic had died down, his great love for his Master had overcome his fear to some extent and he had plucked up enough courage to follow the Prisoner at a distance.

When he arrived at the palace of the high priest, he was at first denied admittance but was finally allowed to enter when one of Jesus' disciples, who was known to the servants, spoke to the portress on his behalf. The common belief is that this disciple was none other than St. John himself, since he alone mentions this detail (John 18:15–16).

Little did Peter suspect the abyss into which he was about to plunge. Just as he was entering the courtyard, the portress looked closely at him, apparently searching her memory in an effort to recall where she had seen him before: "Art thou also one of this man's disciples?" she asked.

Surprised and uneasy, Peter replied quickly, scarcely realizing what he was saying: "I am not."

With that, he hurried on into the courtyard, where he found a crowd of attendants of the Sanhedrin and servants of the high priest grouped around a fire warming themselves and airing their views on Jesus' arrest. Deciding that here was a good chance to find out what was happening to his Master, Peter joined them. But he was not long there when the same importunate maid-servant approached him and, after staring at him fixedly for a while, said to the bystanders: "This man also was with Jesus the Galilean."

Vehemently, Peter denied all acquaintance with Jesus: "I do not know what thou art saying. I do not know this man."

He spoke so decisively that the servants did not pursue the subject; yet some of them kept glancing inquisitively at him. Aware that he was being watched, Peter thought that it would be safer to get away from the palace altogether. With this object in mind, he withdrew from the group about the fire and was making his way through the vestibule to the main gate when the cock crowed for the first time. Just as he was about to pass through the gate, the persistent maid-servant confronted him again and, convinced that she was right, exclaimed to the people standing around: "Surely, this is one of them!"

Another maid-servant chimed in with: "This man also was with Jesus of Nazareth."

At this, one of the bystanders confronted Peter with the accusation: "Certainly, thou art one of them!"

"No," stammered the flustered Apostle, adding with an oath that he did not know Jesus.

Seeing that his line of retreat was cut off by the group of inquisitive servants, Peter turned back to the courtyard in the hope of concealing himself in the crowd there. But his encounter at the gate had not gone unnoticed, and when he reappeared in the courtyard, the same question was again flung at him: "Art thou also one of his disciples?"

Without hesitation, he uttered a flat denial: "I am not."

For about an hour after that, the Apostle was left unmolested, and drawn by his desire to hear what was being said about his Master, he gave up the idea of leaving the palace. But just when he thought he had seen the end of the embarrassing questions, he was accosted by a relative of the man whose ear he had cut off in the garden. Looking at him searchingly, the stranger asked: "Did I not see thee in the garden with him?"

Again Peter denied the allegation, but some of the bystanders, drawing near, insisted: "Surely thou art one of them, for thou also art a Galilean, for even thy speech betrays thee." [59]

Terrified of being associated with Jesus, Peter "began to curse and to swear that he did not know the man." At that moment, our Lord was being led from the hall in which He had appeared before Caiphas, and as He crossed the courtyard, He turned and looked at Peter. The merciful eyes of the Master met the shamed gaze of the disciple: the cock crowed once more, and Peter "went out and wept bitterly."

On the slope of Mount Sion, a short distance from Caiphas' palace, there is a cave which is venerated as the place where Peter wept. Tradition says that, during the rest of his life, the Apostle wept whenever he heard a cock crow and that his tears formed two furrows down his cheeks. He had sinned, but he had repented bitterly, and God had pardoned him.

The four evangelists' accounts leave the reader uncertain as to the order in which the denials occurred, their number and the exact location in which each took place. But we need not be surprised at that, for the Gospels did not aim at providing a complete narrative. One evangelist selected certain details, another chose to record other circumstances, and since Peter was questioned by several different persons and in several different places, it is no wonder that, when we come to reconstruct the whole episode, we are unable to allot to each element the precise position it should occupy and to link the events together in such a way as to form a complete, orderly unit.

If we are to reconstruct the incidents, it would be best to begin by specifying the various parts of the high priest's palace mentioned in the Gospels. They are: the *gateway* of the palace ($\pi\nu\lambda\acute{\omega}\nu$; Matt. 26:71); the *wicket* (($\theta\acute{\nu}\rho\alpha$; John 18:16) or small door cut in the principal gate, such as can still be seen in ancient castles and old walled estates; next came the *vestibule* ($\pi\rho o\alpha\acute{\nu}\lambda\iota o\nu$; Mark 14:68) or forecourt, from which one passed to the *courtyard* proper ($\alpha\grave{\nu}\lambda\acute{\eta}$; Matt. 26:29; Mark 14:66), which was open to the sky. All of these places were, of course, at

---

[59] This episode is reminiscent of that of the Ephraimites (Judges 12:6), who, being unable to pronounce the sound "sh," used to say "sibboleth" instead of "shibboleth." Regarding the linguistic peculiarities of the Galileans, see Str.-Bill., I, 157. The people of Beisan, Beit-Haifa and Tibon pronounced the letters *aleph* and *ayin* alike.

ground level, whereas Jesus was brought to the second floor of the palace, where meetings were usually held.

If we keep these details in mind we shall find it less difficult to follow Peter in the sad course of his denials. But, needless to say, our reconstruction of the succession of events is purely hypothetical.

Peter was standing outside at the gate (θύρα) when the other disciple interceded with the portress for him. She allowed him to enter, but when he had just crossed the threshold, or perhaps shortly afterwards, she asked him the question: "Art thou also one of this man's disciples?" To which he answered: "I am not."

The Apostle then went on into the courtyard (αὐλή) and remained there (κάτω; Mark 14:66), i.e., he was on the ground level as opposed to the second floor. He was outside (ἔξω; Matt. 26:69), that is, in the open air and not in one of the inner rooms. It was here that he denied his Master several times.

In order, perhaps, to escape being questioned, he went from the courtyard towards the vestibule (προαύλιον) Mark 14:68) or towards the gateway (πυλών; Matt. 26:71), which is the same thing, but did not leave the precincts of the palace. Here again he was beset by questioners.

Seeking refuge once more from his inquisitors, he returned to the courtyard and joined in the conversation of the group around the fire, perhaps with the idea of hiding his real purpose in being present in the palace. Here again he denied Christ, reinforcing his denials with an oath.

While Peter was near the fire, Jesus passed on His way from the chamber on the second floor to a room on ground level where He spent the rest of the night. As He went by, He looked at Peter.

St. John seems to locate the denials in Annas' house: see John 18:24 and context, as well as our remarks on verse 24.[60] The other evangelists do not mention Annas in this connection.

From the foregoing, it is obvious that Peter denied Christ more than three times. All told, he may have uttered six, seven, or perhaps even as many as eight denials. However, commentators usually divide them into *three* groups.

The fact that there are differences in the evangelists' accounts does not invalidate the historical character of the Gospel narratives but rather confirms it.

[60] See above, pp. 683 *ff.*

The Fate of Judas
(Matt. 27:3–10; Acts 1:18–19)

When Judas heard that Jesus had been condemned, he realized the true enormity of his crime. But, lacking faith in God's mercy, he did not weep tears of loving repentance as Peter did. The thirty coins which he had received so greedily now became an insupportable weight, so that he felt compelled to rid himself of them and retract the sacrilegious contract he had made. With this purpose in mind he hastened, not to Caiphas' palace, as some authors believe, but to the Temple itself. To the chief priests whom he found there he cried: "I have sinned in betraying innocent blood."

Derisively they answered: "What is that to us? See to it thyself."

For a moment, their callous indifference left the wretched traitor at a loss as to what he should do. Then, coming to a swift decision, he flung the pieces of silver on the floor before them and ran out of the Temple.

Where did he run to? On the outskirts of Jerusalem, almost at the bottom of the gloomy Valley of Ben-Hinnom, pilgrims are still shown the spot where the body of a man had been found, disemboweled and with the face horribly contorted. Judas, upon leaving the Temple, had hanged himself.

This tragic end was but the final step in a series of infidelities. The traitor had regretted his treachery, but his was not the sorrow of a penitent. He saw the gravity of his sin, but lacked the humility to throw himself at the feet of the One against whom he had sinned. Although he wept, his tears were not those of humble repentance but of proud despair. The name Haceldama, in Hebrew *haqel dema* ("field of blood"), recalls both the horrifying death of Judas and the cold hypocrisy of his accomplices, the priests, who gathered up the thirty coins and, deciding that it was not lawful to put them back in the Temple treasury because they were blood money, used them to buy a field to serve as a burial place for strangers. Yet perhaps their action was a disposition of Providence to insure that the place stained by the blood of the unfaithful Apostle should be forever a fear-inspiring reminder of his terrible end.

We read about the death of Judas both in St. Matthew (27:5 *ff.*) and in the Acts of the Apostles (1:18 *f.*); but the collation of the two passages offers some difficulty. St. Matthew says simply that "he hanged himself" (v. 5); but the Acts tell us that "falling headlong, he burst asunder in the midst and all his bowels gushed out." However, there is no contradiction involved: it could have happened that, when the unhappy traitor had hanged himself, the rope or the branch from which he was suspended broke and he plunged from a height onto a rock, upon which he was disemboweled by the impact of his fall.

But it is not so easy to reconcile the references in the two passages to the place name "Haceldama, that is, the Field of Blood." According to St. Matthew (v. 7), it was the chief priests who bought the field, which came to be known as "the Field of Blood" because it had been purchased with the money paid for the blood of Christ. But the Acts (v. 18 f.) tell us that it was Judas who bought a field with "the price of his iniquity," and that this field was given its name because it was stained with his blood. How are we to harmonize the two accounts? If Judas bought a field with the money which he received from the Jews, how was it possible for the chief priests also to buy one with the same coins?

The usual explanation is that the actual purchasers were the chief priests, who used for this purpose the thirty coins which Judas had flung down in the Temple. But since this money was regarded as still belonging to the traitor, St. Peter was able to say in the Acts that Judas had bought that which, in reality, the priests had purchased with his money.[61]

If that is so, and if there is question of only one field, then we must say that the field in which Judas hanged himself was the same one which the Jews bought later. This seems to follow clearly from the account in the Acts of the Apostles. In fact, in verse 18, we are told that the traitor bought a field (which, according to what we have said above, was in reality the one that the Jews bought with his money); and in verse 19 we read that the field was called "the Field of Blood" because it was stained with Judas' blood.

The fact that in St. Matthew the field received its name from the blood of Christ and in the Acts from the traitor's blood is no argument against inspiration, since the sacred authors are only pointing out the two different and equally valid derivations of the one popular name given to the field.

Another difficulty concerning the field arises out of the quotation

---

61 "Alii quidem agrum emerunt, ipse vero quoque utpote qui pretium agri solvit" (Michael Glyca: PG 158, 904).

from Jeremias which we find in Matthew 27:9*f.*; "Then was fulfilled what was spoken through Jeremias the prophet, saying, 'And they took the thirty pieces of silver, the price of him who was priced, upon whom the children of Israel set a price, and they gave them for the potter's field, as the Lord directed me.' " These words undoubtedly refer to Jeremias 32:6–7; however, the thirty pieces of silver are not mentioned in this passage but in Zacharias 11:12 *f*. Many authors have solved the difficulty by saying that the evangelist wrote "Jeremias" instead of "Zacharias," or that the original text had only the word "prophet" and that some ignorant copyist inserted the name Jeremias. But we can give a sufficiently satisfactory explanation of the text as it stands. The evangelist combined two passages, one from Jeremias and the other from Zacharias, but gave only the name of the former. Jeremias speaks of a field which God commanded him to buy, while Zacharias is speaking of the miserly wages which the people gave him, Yahweh's representative, as the pastor of Israel, and which God, dissatisfied, ordered him to throw to the potter. The points of similarity between the two Old Testament passages and the Gospel narrative are obvious. The chief priests, as representatives of Israel, gave thirty pieces of silver for Jesus; the coins were thrown down in the Temple and were used to buy a potter's field. Thus in the combination of the two prophetic passages we find all, or almost all, the elements of the Gospel account.

In later centuries many legends were woven around the death of the unfaithful Apostle, but it would be a waste of time to dwell on them. However, by way of example, we shall relate two of them. Judas did not die right away but, having fallen from the tree, lived on for some time in a secret place. Later, grossly swollen, he threw himself from a height, his belly burst open and his entrails gushed out.[62] Or again, having survived his attempted suicide. Judas was constantly exhorted by the other Apostles to do penance, but without result. Immediately after our Lord's Ascension, he swelled up so much that he burst asunder and died.[63]

Jesus Before Pilate
(Matt. 27:11–25; Mark 15:1–15; Luke 23:2–25; John 18:28—19:16)

On Friday morning a strange atmosphere of tension reigned in

[62] Cf. Euthymius Zigabenus: *PG* 129, 705.   [63] Cf. Cedrenus: *PG* 121, 384.

Jerusalem. The news of the arrest of the young Prophet of Nazareth had spread through the city like wildfire, saddening some and causing others to rejoice with unholy glee. Speculation was rife and the air was alive with questions: "Is it true that they have seized Jesus the Galilean? Where is He? Have they tried Him? Are they going to kill Him?" The answers were not long in coming.

"As soon as day broke [on Friday], the elders of the people and the chief priests and Scribes gathered together; and they led him away into their Sanhedrin, saying, 'If thou art the Christ, tell us.' And he said to them, 'If I tell you, you will not believe me; and if I question you, you will not answer me, or let me go. But henceforth, the Son of Man will be seated at the right hand of the power of God.'

"And they all said, 'Art thou, then, the Son of God?' He answered, 'You yourselves say that I am.' And they said, 'What further need have we of witness? For we have heard it ourselves from his own mouth.' And the whole assemblage rose, and took him before Pilate."

This assembly was not the same one which had been convened the night before. St. Luke explicitly says that the elders, the chief priests and the Scribes "gathered together" (22:66), and St. Mark adds "and the whole Sanhedrin" (15:1). But why had they met again when they had already declared Jesus deserving of death? Were they trying to legalize their actions of the night before by holding a daylight session, since a trial held at night was not a true, legal trial? It is possible that they were; yet when we consider the Jewish leader's state of mind and the urgency of the case, it is scarcely credible that they would have bothered to observe the niceties of legal procedure.[64] It is more likely that they met to confirm their verdict and to draw up the charges which they were going to make against the Prisoner in Pilate's court.

At this second convocation of the Sanhedrin our Lord repeated His majestic declaration of the night before, and the Sanhedrists reiterated their sentence of death against Him. The similarity between the two occasions has led some authors to believe that there was really only one assembly. But the fact remains that both St. Luke (22:66) and St. Mark (15:1) expressly say that early in the morning the chief priests held a consultation with the elders and the Scribes, while St. Matthew, who has already minutely described the night assembly, seems to imply the same (27:1). Actually, it would be in character for the Jews to

[64] Furthermore, we must bear in mind the observations made above (pp. 689 ff.) concerning these formalities.

desire to have Jesus repeat in full session the declaration which had scandalized them so much the night before and for which they had condemned Him to death.[65]

On that same morning a motley, jostling crowd issued from the palace of the high priest and made its way to the praetorium, the residence of the Roman procurator. In the throng the most prominent members of the capital's society rubbed shoulders with the humblest citizens. Stately priests, venerable elders and learned doctors of the Law mingled with the servants and attendants of the Sanhedrin. And in the middle of the ill-assorted multitude walked Jesus of Nazareth. The great Prophet who had entered the Holy City only a few days before amid enthusiastic acclamation was now being led to His death, bound like a criminal.

From all parts of the city people flocked to see with their own eyes a sight which they could scarcely bring themselves to imagine. Never before had the towering Herodian fortress witnessed such crowds and such excitement.

At what time did the priests and elders bring their Prisoner to the praetorium? According to St. John (18:28), they did so at daybreak ($\mathring{\eta}\nu$ δὲ πρωί). But evidently this expression should be taken in a rather wide sense, because St. Mark (15:1) uses it to indicate the time of the second meeting of the Sanhedrin.

At any rate, although the hour was an untimely one for ordinary interviews, the procurator was waiting for the Prisoner, of whose coming he had doubtless been forewarned. When Jesus was brought into the praetorium, Pilate looked searchingly at Him, but being unable to see any traces of criminality in the bruised, spittle-stained face, he was reluctant to confirm the Sanhedrin's sentence of death without making a preliminary examination. He was not going to bow to the Jewish leaders' wishes as readily as they expected.

The proud Sanhedrists imagined that, once Jesus had been condemned by the supreme Jewish tribunal, the procurator would not hesitate to endorse the verdict. But Pilate thought otherwise, for, after all, was he not Rome's representative? Then, too, he was no doubt

---

[65] Regarding the question of the two meetings of the Sanhedrin (one at night and the second on the following morning), see Fr. Benoit, "Jésus devant le Sanhédrin," in *Angelicum,* 20 (1943), 143–151, 157–164. We do not think that his solution of a "dédoublement littéraire" (pp. 157, 164) rests on solid foundations. His assertion that "il devient pratiquement certain qu'il n'y eut qu'une seule séance du Sanhédrin, au matin" (p. 157) goes further than scientific rigor permits.

aware of the real reason for Jesus' trial. He had, therefore, to find out exactly what accusations were being brought against the Prisoner so that he might assess His guilt or innocence. Since the sanctimonious accusers did not wish to contaminate themselves by entering the house of a Gentile, Pilate condescended to humor them by appearing outside on the balcony, from which he interrogated them: "What accusation do you bring against this man?"

The question angered the Jews, for they regarded it as an intolerable insult. Would they, the respected teachers of Israel, have brought the Prisoner here without very good reason? Refusing to make a specific accusation, they replied curtly: "If he were not a criminal we should not have handed him over to thee."

Their words clearly demonstrated their bad faith. They had condemned Jesus for having said He was the Son of God, that is, for a purely religious crime, and now they gave Pilate to understand that their Prisoner was a common malefactor.

The procurator, stung by their haughty answer, cut short the interview by saying ironically: "Take him yourselves, and judge him according to your law."

He was well aware that they were not authorized to carry out a death sentence, as they themselves were now forced to admit:

"It is not lawful for us to put anyone to death." [66]

St. John sees here the fulfillment of a prophecy made by Jesus Himself: "And as Moses lifted up the serpent in the desert, even so must the Son of Man be lifted up. . . . And I, if I be lifted up from the earth, will draw all things to myself" (John 3:14; 12:32 *f.*). If the Jews had had the right to put their Prisoner to death they would have stoned Him, but condemnation by the Roman procurator meant crucifixion, the form of death predicted by Jesus for Himself.

When the Jews saw that Pilate was not going to ratify their sentence without a preliminary hearing, they began to formulate their charges: "We have found this man perverting our nation, and forbidding the payment of taxes to Caesar, and saying that he is Christ a king."

The last accusation must have sounded extraordinary to Pilate. That Man a king? Where was His court? Where was His army? The procurator showed his amazement at the charge by going back inside

[66] See our remarks above (pp. 676 *ff.*) on the *jus gladii.*

the praetorium and questioning Jesus: "Art thou the king of the Jews?"

Looking at Pilate with eyes that saw into the depths of his heart, our Lord did not answer like a criminal, but asked majestically: "Dost thou say this of thyself, or have others told thee of me?" This was a delicate warning to the procurator not to act on the Jews' accusations and thus incur the responsibility of imposing an unjust sentence.[67]

Pilate, resenting the question, retorted irritably: "Am I a Jew? Thy own people and the chief priests have delivered thee to me. What hast thou done?"

Jesus, perceiving in the procurator a glimmer of good will, wished to enlighten him on the nature of His kingdom: "My kingdom is not of this world. If my kingdom were of this world, my followers would have fought that I might not be delivered to the Jews. But, as it is, my kingdom is not from here."

"Thou art then a king?" asked Pilate quickly.

"Thou sayest it; I am a king. This is why I was born, and why I have come into the world, to bear witness to the truth. Everyone who is of the truth hears my voice."

"What is truth?" inquired Pilate ironically.

Here was a meeting of the Champion of truth with the professed skeptic; of the Master who came to teach the truth with the superficial cynic who was not concerned with it; of the strong Man, firm in His convictions, faithful to His principles, with the weak, vacillating opportunist blown about by every wind of opinion. We shall see how Pilate, despite the fact that he was not ill-disposed towards Jesus, gave in to the Jews little by little until, in the end, he passed sentence of death on a Man whom he knew in his heart to be innocent.

When the procurator asked, "What is truth?" he was not looking for an answer. His query was half incredulous, half mocking and designed to cut short a discussion of matters which he neither understood nor cared about. Convinced that there was nothing to fear from

[67] Several authors see in our Lord's counter-question a very different meaning (Lagrange, Braun, M. Sales). According to them, Jesus was asking Pilate to indicate whether he was referring to political or religious kingship. If it was the former, our Lord would have replied, "No"; if the latter, "Yes." While we do not deny that this explanation has some probability, we believe that Pilate's question was, in itself, clear enough. And actually, our Lord went on to answer it: "My kingdom is not of this world . . ." thereby stating two things at once, namely, that He was truly a king and that the procurator had nothing to fear from His kingship.

have been overlooked by the hill, a grave disadvantage which the builders would certainly have avoided. In answer we say that the hill was only twelve or fifteen feet in height and that the wall could easily have been built high enough to dominate it. Moreover, it is not improbable that the wall was defended at that point by a ditch which ran between it and the hill.[33] Finally, it is possible that, as Schick suggests, there was a fortress at this point destined precisely for the strengthening of the weak spot in the city's defenses.[34]

Therefore topography does not oppose and archaeology even supports the theory that the site now occupied by the Basilica of the Holy Sepulchre was outside the city at the time of Christ.

At first the hill of Calvary was enclosed within the Basilica of Constantine, not roofed over, however, but left open to the sky and surmounted by a huge cross of silver. Later a chapel was built on it and it was incorporated into the present church, built by the Crusaders.

The Cross [35]—Originally the Latin word "crux" meant torture" but it later came to be applied to the cross as the most painful instrument of execution. From ancient times the cross was known in two forms, simple and composite. The *simple* cross was merely a stake or post to which the criminal was tied and left to die of hunger and thirst or to be devoured by wild animals. Sometimes the condemned man was impaled upon the stake.[36] The *composite* cross was of various kinds: (1) *crux decussata*, commonly called St. Andrew's Cross, which was shaped like an X.[37] (2) The *crux commissa* or *patibulata* [38] is the one

---

[33] Cf. Vincent, *RB* (1902), p. 54; Schick, *loc. cit.*, p. 264.

[34] *Loc. cit.*, p. 268.

[35] See Holzmeister, *Crux Domini atque crucifixio, quomodo ex archaeologia romana illustrentur* (Romae, 1934), taken from *Verb. Dom.*, 14 (1934); Gómez-Pallette, "Cruz y crucifixión," in *Est. Ecles.*, 20 (1946), 535–544; 21 (1947), 85–109. In these two highly-recommended studies the reader will find references taken from the Fathers and from profane writers, which we omit for the sake of brevity.

[36] ". . . Alii per obscoena stipitem egerunt. . . ." (Seneca *Consol. ad Marciam* 20).

[37] No doubt it is to this cross that St. Jerome was referring when he wrote: "sed in mysterio crucis decussatis manibus, qui stabat ad sinistram Jacob, dextrae manus eius accepit benedictionem . . ." (*Comm. in Jer.*, c. 31: *PL* 24, 875). Of this cross, Holzmeister says: "Tale monstrum nunquam revera adhibitum est, nam primum documentum quod eius mentionem facit, est saeculi X, prima vero imago saeculi XIV"; and he quotes Künstle, *Ikonographie der christl. Kunst*, II, *Ikonographie der Heiligen* (Freiburg, 1928), pp. 58–60. As against this assertion, there is a text in Josephus which says that during the siege of Jerusalem the Roman soldiers seized those who came out foraging for food and crucified them, "some in one way and others in another: ἄλλον ἄλλῳ σχήματι" (*Wars* v. 11. 1). But σχῆμα does not necessarily refer to the shape of the cross,

shaped like a capital T: it is usually called St. Anthony's Cross.[39] (3) The crux *immissa* or *capitata* was similar in shape to the *crux commissa* except that the vertical bar extended a little above the crossbar in this fashion: ✝. This, of course, is the Latin cross. (4) The *crux quadrata* also consisted of two bars crossed at right angles, but the four arms were of equal length, like this: +. This is called the Greek cross. We shall not concern ourselves with the *crux gammata* and *crux ansata*, since they are of no interest to us here.

Which of these forms did our Lord's cross take? Authors are not agreed on the point, some being inclined to favor the *crux commissa* (T), others the *crux immissa*, or Latin cross (✝). The latter seems the more probable one for two reasons: first Pilate's inscription, "Jesus of Nazareth, the King of the Jews," could very conveniently have been placed on the extension of the vertical beam; second, the similes which quite a few of the Fathers and ecclesiastical writers use (e.g., the mast of a ship) clearly show that they had this form of cross in mind.[40]

since the victims could have been made to assume various positions on crosses that were all made in the usual form. Some would have been crucified head upwards, others head downwards, and still others nailed by one hand and one foot only. This is all the more probable because Josephus goes on to say that the soldiers varied the usual procedure "by way of jest." Furthermore, if the *crux decussata* had been used for executions, it is very strange that no mention was made of it until the tenth century. See G. Ricciotti, *The Life of Christ*, p. 627, n. 15.

[38] It got this second name from the fact that the horizontal beam was originally the crossbar used for making a door secure. When this crossbar was removed, the door could be opened, whence came the name *patibulum*, from the verb *pateo*, "to lie open" ("quod hoc ligno remoto valvae *pateant*." Cf. Forcellini, *Totius Latinitatis Lexicon* [Prati, 1868], under "*patibulum*"). This bar was placed on the condemned man's shoulders and neck, his arms were tied to it, and he was led to the place of execution ("*patibulum* ferat per urbem, deinde affigatur cruci": *Ibid.*).

[39] It was so called because St. Anthony the Hermit is supposed to have worn on his cloak a cross in the form of the letter *tau*. Cf. *Dict. d'Arch. Chrét.*, III, col. 3061, n. 10.

[40] It is interesting to note how the well-known satirical cross of the Palatine is used as an argument for both forms. Prat wrote: "The satirical cross of the Palatine has . . . the form of a Latin cross" (*Jesus Christ*, II, 506), while Fr. Gómez-Pallette asserts: "In the case under discussion [i.e., the satirical sketch in the Palatine] the cross depicted is undeniably the *crux commissa*," that is, "in the shape of the letter *tau*" (*Est. Ecles.* [1947], p. 92).

Perhaps the wide divergence of opinion expressed by these two authors is due to the fact that each had a different reproduction of the sketch before him as he wrote. The drawing is reproduced in *Dict. d'Arch. Chrét.* (III, cols. 3051–2), *Dict. des Ant. Gr. et Rom.* (ed. Daremberg et Saglio, II, 1575), and *Lexicon für Theologie und Kirche* (II, cols. 913–914). All three of these illustrations show that there is something projecting above the horizontal bar or *patibulum*, but whereas the projection appears quite clearly in the illustrations

Apparently the cross did not have a small projection upon which the victim's feet could rest. Such a support would not have been sufficient to prevent the weight of the body from tearing the hands from the nails. Instead, about halfway up the front of the vertical beam, there was a stout peg which served as a kind of seat for the condemned man. Hence the Latin phrase *"cruci inequitare:* to ride on the cross." St. Justin tells us explicitly:

[The cross] is a vertical stake whose top projects like a horn when another stake is fitted to it. . . . Halfway down [the vertical beam]

in the *Dict. des Ant. Gr. et Rom.* and the *Lexicon für Theologie und Kirche,* it is blurred in the *Dict. d'Arch. Chrét.*

At all events, today the more generally accepted conclusion is that the cross represented in the Palatine drawing is the Latin cross. C. M. Kaufmann (*Handbuch der Christlichen Archäologie* [Paderborn, 1922], p. 358) writes: "The end of the long beam projects above the head. The drawing itself leaves no doubt that the satirical artist wished to depict a *crux immissa,* such as is in use today. There is no question of a cross in the form of *tau,* as Garrucci, Kraus and others believed." And Victor Schultze, in the *Realencyklopädie für protest. Theol. und Kirche* (XI, 91), says: "The satirical crucifix of the Palatine, which dates back to the beginning of the third century, represents the cross as possessing four arms ['das vierarmige Kreuz']."

We have had an opportunity to see the original sketch, and we have not the slightest doubt that it depicts the *crux commissa* (T), not the *immissa* or Latin cross (†). The drawing is a rear view of a crucified figure and therefore the lines of the cross are perfectly distinguishable.

In the sketch, a vertical line extends above the horizontal bar of the cross, thus giving rise to the Latin cross theory. However, this line does not form part of the cross itself, for it is not a continuation of the vertical beam but begins a little to the left of it, and actually represents the support for the tablet bearing the inscription, which is depicted as a sort of plaque fixed at the top of the vertical line. See drawing in *Catholic Encyclopedia* (New York: Gilmary Society), I, 793.

This explanation was the one given by Fr. Garrucci, who, in 1856, discovered the drawing within the precincts of the Palatine in Rome, in the place now called the *Pedagogium.* He supplied a very accurate reproduction of the drawing in his great work, *Storia dell'arte cristiana* (Prato, 1880), VI, tavola 483, with a short interpretation on pp. 135 *f.,* and a much longer one in *Civiltà Cattolica,* IV (1856), 531–540.

Some authors hold that the sketch is not a blasphemous, satirical representation of Christ crucified, but simply a pagan charm to ward off evil: "Le personage qui est pendu à la croix serait le diable à tête d'âne, tandis que le Θεός, qu'implore selon l'inscription Alexamenos, serait le dieu qui a été vaincu par le diable. Et le dessin serait destiné à exorciser le dieu mauvais en lui présentant son impuissance." This is the interpretation given by L. Vischer in *Revue de l'histoire des Religions,* CXXXIX (1951), 29 *f.* and, before him, proposed by Städler in *Bulletino della Commissione Archeologica di Roma, LXIII* (Roma, 1935), 87–102.

This explanation seems very far-fetched. The interpretation which Fr. Garrucci suggested from the start and which was then generally accepted, still remains the most probable one.

there is a protuberance which [also] looks like a horn and which is meant to serve as a seat for the one who is being crucified.[41]

It is interesting to note that St. Justin is speaking here of the *crux immissa* or Latin cross, with the vertical beam projecting above the horizontal one.

The Nails—We can say with certainty that four nails and not three were used in our Lord's crucifixion, for the feet were nailed separately and not one on top of the other. By way of confirmation, we can add that four nails are used in the aforementioned satirical drawing found on the Palatine, which, as we have said, probably dates back to the first half of the third century.

There are two completely different conceptions of the manner in which our Lord carried the cross to Calvary and was nailed on it there. The more common and, to some extent, the traditional one is that He was made to carry the complete cross, that is, the vertical beam with the horizontal bar already attached, the whole taking the shape of the Latin cross. When He arrived at Calvary, the cross was placed flat on the ground, He was stretched on it and nailed to it, and only then was it raised aloft. Or else the cross was first placed upright in the ground and He was lifted up and nailed to it. According to the second opinion, our Lord was burdened only with the horizontal bar, which was placed on His neck and shoulders and to which His arms were then tied. When He reached Calvary, the vertical beam was already standing, waiting to receive Him. His hands were nailed to the cross-bar, and He was lifted up with it to the point where it was to be fixed to the vertical beam. Finally His feet were nailed to the upright of the cross.

Which of the two conceptions is the more likely one? The second agrees better with the descriptions found in the Greek and Latin classics, and therefore should be considered the more probable.[42] In favor of the first method, there is certainly a centuries-old tradition, which, however, has a limited value because it dates back only to the sixth or seventh century.

Was our Lord crucified completely naked? We have no documents concerning the Jewish customs on this point in the case of crucifixion. But we do know what the usual practice was in executions by stoning.

[41] *Dial. cum Tryph.* 91. 12: *PG* 6, 693.
[42] "Patibulo suffixus in crucem tollitur"; "in crucem agere, tollere"; "in crucem agi, tolli, elevari." But see below, p. 730, n. 46 in favor of the whole cross.

The *Mishnah* prescribes that men condemned to die by stoning were to "be kept covered in front and a woman both in front and behind." [43] However, the *Mishnah* also tells us that "the Sages say: 'A man is stoned naked but a woman is not stoned naked.' " We know that, with the introduction of pagan athletic contests, the Jews had become accustomed to nudity, for some of them had the foreskin restored artificially in order to conceal the fact that they had been circumcised (cf. 1 Mach. 1:16). The Romans definitely stripped their victims of all garments, leaving them entirely naked. Hence, if we are to judge by the Roman practice, our Divine Redeemer was crucified in this manner. However, it is not unlikely that devout bystanders had procured a loincloth for Jesus and that the soldiers allowed Him to wear it at His execution.

The Time of the Crucifixion—On this point there seems to be a certain divergence between St. Mark (15:25) and St. John (19:14–16). St. Mark says: "Now it was the *third* hour and they crucified him," whereas, according to St. John, "it was . . . about the *sixth* hour" when Pilate "handed him over to them to be crucified."

An easy way to account for the difference would be to blame it on a copyist of Mark's Gospel, as some authors do, following St. Jerome, who held that some copyists mistook the Greek letter *digamma* (F, which stood for "six") for the letter *gamma* (Γ, which represented "three").[44] Such an error could have occurred, and therefore this solution, besides being very convenient, has a degree of probability, which, however, is very slight due to the fact that the immense majority of manuscripts contain the above-mentioned numerical difference. Consequently, we must look for another explanation: and we find one in the evangelists' different methods of computing time. St. Mark follows the division of the day into four sections—the first hour (from 6:00 A.M. to 9:00 A.M.), the third (from 9:00 A.M. to noon), the sixth from noon to 3:00 P.M.), and the ninth (from 3:00 P.M. to 6:00 P.M.). But St. John reckons time according to the division of the day into twelve hours, as he does in other passages too (e.g., in 1:40; 4:6; 4:52); he alone among the evangelists uses this method. Thus St. John's "*sixth* hour" (i.e., 11:00 A.M to noon, exactly as in 4:6), coincides partly with St. Mark's "*third* hour," which covers the period

---

[43] *Sanhedrin* 6:3.
[44] "Error scriptorum fuit, et in Marco hora sexta scriptum fuit; sed multi episemum [i.e., the *digamma*] graecum putaverunt esse *gamma*" (*Breviarium in Ps. 77: PL* 25, 1046).

from 9:00 A.M. to noon. St. John is more exact than St. Mark, but there is no contradiction between them.

The Way of the Cross—When sentence had been passed, execution followed almost immediately. The cross was placed on our Divine Saviour's shoulders and He began the gruelling journey to Calvary. With what sentiments of love for men, of perfect, humble submission to His Eternal Father, must Jesus have embraced the rough cross that was to be the instrument of His most painful death!

Accompanied by a band of soldiers, the centurion who was charged with carrying out the sentence went in front to clear the way. Next came the herald, proclaiming the reason for the execution. Then came our Lord, burdened with the heavy cross, surrounded by more soldiers and, as an added insult, with two common criminals as companions. Bringing up the rear was a large crowd, eager to witness the bloody spectacle of the crucifixion.[45]

Jesus, worn out by all He had suffered, began to falter and stagger under the weight of the cross. As they were passing through the city gate, the soldiers, fearing that their Prisoner would die on the way and thus escape execution, compelled one of the bystanders, a man named Simon of Cyrene, to take the cross and carry it after Jesus. Unwillingly at first, Simon undertook the distasteful task, but it is very likely that contact with the sacred wood of the cross enlightened his mind and moved his heart so that he came to bear with loving respect the burden which he had received with repugnance and aversion. His name and the names of his two sons, Alexander and Rufus, have been immortalized in the Gospel.[46]

---

[45] If the praetorium was in the Fortress Antonia, then our Lord went to Calvary by practically the same path as that which is followed today in the Way of the Cross. Of course, the modern route diverges slightly from the original Via Dolorosa, partly because of the layout of the streets and buildings. Then, too, as is well known, the various Stations are of comparatively recent date.

[46] The incident is mentioned by the three Synoptic writers (Matt. 27:32; Mark 15:21; Luke 23:26), and their mode of expression indicates that Simon carried the cross *for* and not *with* Jesus. That is how St. Jerome interprets the matter (cf. Knabenbauer), as does Suárez, who writes: ". . . Quod duobus modis intelligi potest. Primo, ut non fuerit Christo crux sublata, sed Simon conductus fuerit, ut simul cum Christo illam portaret. . . . Alio vero modo exponi possunt illa verba Lucae . . . id est, quod Christus anteiret, sequeretur autem Simon portans crucem. Et hoc significant magis verba Evangelistarum. . . ; atque est communior Patrum expositio" (*In 3 p., q. 46, disp. 36, sect. 2, no. 2: Opera* [Ed. Vivès], XIX, 563). This is also the opinion held by Knabenbauer, Lagrange, Fillion, Simón-Dorado, Gomá, Vilariño and others. As we have already seen, it is not possible to say with certainty whether our Lord bore the whole cross (cf. John 19:17), or only the horizontal beam

While the mass of the spectators hurled insults and blasphemies at Jesus, there were some good women who had the courage to express their compassion for the Divine Victim by weeping unashamedly and bewailing aloud His cruel fate. Forgetful of His own sufferings and thinking only of the calamities which were to come upon these women, Jesus turned to them and said: "Daughters of Jerusalem, do not weep for me, but weep for yourselves and for your children. For behold, days are coming in which men will say, 'Blessed are the barren, and the wombs that never bore, and breasts that never nursed.' Then they will begin to say to the mountains, 'Fall upon us,' and to the hills, 'Cover us!' For if in the case of green wood they do these things, what is to happen in the case of the dry?"

Passing through the gate, probably that of Ephraim, the cortège came in sight of the hill which stood exactly opposite Mount Moria and upon which the new Isaac was to be sacrificed. As we have already said, Calvary was a hillock or mound about fifteen feet in height standing very near the city walls, on the slope of Mount Gareb. Slowly, painfully, His ebbing strength almost exhausted, Jesus made His way to this insignificant, perhaps even abominated, hill which He was to hallow for all time by shedding upon it His precious blood.

The Jews had the merciful custom of giving a condemned man a cup of wine, perfumed with a grain of incense, to help dull his sensibility to pain. Apparently the practice was based on a passage from the Book of Proverbs: "Give strong drink to the man who is about to die" (31:6). This solace was now offered to Jesus, perhaps by some of the compassionate women of Jerusalem or by some of those who had accompanied Him during His public life. To show His gratitude He tasted the wine but did not drink it, for He wished to drain the chalice of suffering to the dregs.

Stripping their Victim of His clothing, the executioners divided it among them. But when they came to His seamless tunic, which perhaps had been woven by the Blessed Virgin's own hands, they cast lots

---

known as the *patibulum*. The latter seems to have been the practice in Rome, but it may well have happened that in Jerusalem the complete cross was placed on our Lord's shoulders. In 19:17, St. John certainly uses the same term as in 19:25 and 31, where he is definitely referring to the completed cross. See above p. 728.

No doubt the soldiers came upon Simon as they were leaving the city, for St. Matthew's expression (27:32, "as they went out") apparently cannot refer to their emerging from the praetorium. This is how Knabenbauer, Lagrange and others understand the phrase.

for it because they did not wish to tear it. Thus the Lord of the universe was despoiled of everything, even His very garments.

Then came the awful moment of crucifixion. The immaculate Lamb of God was stretched upon the altar of the cross, and the hammer-blows echoed down the hillside as the four great nails were driven through the tender flesh of the Divine Victim's hands and feet, pinioning Him to the rough wood. The cross was then raised upright [47] and our Lord's sacred body was suspended between heaven and earth, supported by the wooden peg set into the middle of the vertical beam to prevent the victim's weight from tearing his hands and feet from the nails. Above His head was placed a wooden tablet with the inscription: "Jesus of Nazareth, the King of the Jews," written in three languages, Hebrew, Greek and Latin.

But the wording of the inscription angered the Jews; only a few hours before, they had proclaimed that they acknowledged no king but Caesar. Hastening back to Pilate, they protested: "Do not write, 'The King of the Jews,' but, 'He said, I am the King of the Jews.'"

But the procurator, exasperated and only too glad to have an opportunity of humiliating them, curtly replied: "What I have written, I have written."

The Seven Last Words

The cross was not only the altar upon which Jesus sacrificed Himself, it was also a pulpit from which He preached His last words, those seven precious jewels which His children lovingly gathered up and passed on from generation to generation.

Christ's enemies had conquered. Circling about the cross, they gloated over their triumph and baited their Victim even while He was suffering His death-agony: "Aha, thou who destroyest the temple, and in three days buildest it up again, save thyself! If thou art the Son of God, come down from the cross!"

Others, adding blasphemy to their mockery, jested among themselves: "He saved others, himself he cannot save! If he is the King of Israel, let him come down now from the cross, and we will believe him. He trusted in God; let him deliver him now, if he wants him; for he said, 'I am the Son of God.'"

While the Sanhedrists were shouting these insults and blasphemies,

[47] See above, p. 728.

which the crowd re-echoed like a chorus, our Lord broke His long silence to address a tender appeal to His Eternal Father: "Father, forgive them, for they do not know what they are doing."

The Jews had certainly sinned and therefore Jesus prayed that they might be pardoned; but they were also ignorant, not knowing that they were killing the King of Glory, for as St. Paul says: ". . . had they known it, they would never have crucified the Lord of glory" (1 Cor. 2:8), and as St. Peter before him had declared: "And now, brethren, I know that you acted in ignorance, as did also your rulers" (Acts 3:17). It is true that their ignorance was culpable and did not exempt them from responsibility. Yet it did lessen the gravity of their sin, and it was this extenuating circumstance that the Divine Victim pointed out in His appeal to the Father, thereby giving us an heroic example of forgiveness of enemies.

Some authors, such as Edersheim, Fillion and Ricciotti, suggest that our Lord may have said the first of these words while He was being nailed to the cross. If that was so, then He was referring, at least directly and primarily, to the Roman soldiers. But we hold that no conclusion can be drawn from Luke's passage, the only place in the Gospels in which the prayer is recorded. With Lagrange, we are more inclined to think that our Lord spoke these words after He had been lifted up on high between the two thieves, and that He was referring both to the part the Jews had played in His crucifixion and to the mockery and insults which were being hurled at Him.

We must note that these words are missing from a good number of codices. It may have happened that the phrase "for they do not know what they are doing" struck some copyist as exaggerated and spurious, with the result that he suppressed it.

Our Lord's first word from the cross was a prayer for His enemies in which He sought blessings for them in return for their curses, and expressed His love in return for their hatred. His second word, too, was one of pardon. Of the two criminals who had been crucified with Him, one lent his voice to the infernal chorus chanted by the Scribes and Pharisees. In impotent despair he snarled: "If thou art the Christ, save thyself and us!"

The other criminal's attitude was in direct contrast to his companion's, for in spite of his evil life he still retained some spark of virtue and nobility, as sometimes happens in even the greatest malefactors. Our Lord's whole bearing, His silence, meekness and patience in suffering, must have made a deep impression on the second thief. No doubt he knew that his Fellow-Victim was the Prophet of Nazareth who had had the reputation of being a miracle-worker and who had been acclaimed as the promised Messias by the crowds only a few days before. Moved, therefore, by a sense of justice, he upbraided his companion for speaking as he did to Jesus: "Dost thou not even fear God, seeing that thou art under the same sentence? And we indeed justly, for we are receiving what our deeds deserved; but this man has done nothing wrong."

With these words a despicable criminal became a glorious panegyrist of the Saviour. At the very moment when the chief priests and Scribes, the aristocrats and the rabble, were insulting Jesus, calling Him a deceiver, an impostor and an evildoer, the good thief valiantly proclaimed His innocence. He went even further, for, enlightened and inspired by grace, he acknowledged our Lord as the true Messias, the longed-for Monarch of God's kingdom. In words that revealed his faith in the resurrection of the body, he requested humbly yet confidently of Jesus: "Lord, remember me when thou comest into thy kingdom."

His courage and faith were rewarded by the wonderful promise: "Amen I say to thee, this day thou shalt be with me in paradise."

On that same day, he was to rejoice with Christ in "paradise," a word which here signifies the Limbo of the patriarchs, to which Christ's soul was to descend, making it a true heaven by His presence.

That is the way St. Luke narrates the episode (23:39 ff.). The other two Synoptic authors simply say that those who were crucified with Christ reproached Him also (Matt. 27:44; Mark 15:32). No doubt the evangelists are here using the categorical plural, and are merely recording that insults were being hurled at Jesus from among the group of Scribes and Pharisees and from among the thieves, no distinction being made between individual members of either category. We can also say, as do a number of authors, that at first both criminals abused Jesus, but that later one of them was touched by grace and became His ardent defender. This is certainly a plausible explanation and one which harmonizes the two apparently contradictory versions. Even so, we regard the first explanation which we have given as the more probable one.[48]

[48] Many legends grew up around the figures of the two thieves. The names by which they are most commonly designated are Dismas, the good thief, and Gestas, the bad. In the apocryphal Arabian *Gospel of the Infancy*, they are called Titus and Dumachus respectively, and are depicted as bandit chiefs

During her Son's prolonged agony, the Blessed Virgin stood at the foot of the cross, accompanied by the holy women and St. John. Heartbroken, but with heroic constancy in her august office of coredemptrix of the human race, our Lady offered the sacrifice of her Divine Son to the Eternal Father.

Darkness had now fallen over the earth, and a deathlike silence reigned on Calvary. Speaking from the cross for a third time, Jesus addressed His holy Mother: "Now there were standing by the cross of Jesus his mother and his mother's sister,[49] Mary of Cleophas, and Mary Magdalene. When Jesus, therefore, saw his mother and the disciple standing by, whom he loved, he said to his mother, 'Woman, behold thy son.' Then he said to the disciple, 'Behold thy mother.' "

Our Lord's words show His tender filial love for His holy Mother, for even in the midst of unspeakable torments of body and soul He was concerned with providing her with someone who would aid and console her in her loneliness and surround her with the loving care of a devoted son. His choice of John as His Mother's protector was also a sign of His predilection for the Apostle, for He thereby gave him the high privilege of being a son to the Mother of God. That is how St. John understood His Divine Master's words, as he himself tells us: "And from that hour the disciple took her as his own" (John 19:27).

From at least as early as the twelfth century,[50] Christian piety has seen in the third word from the cross a universality and spiritual meaning that is very consoling to the faithful. Our Lord's words were not addressed exclusively to St. John, but to all humanity as well, and that in no accommodated or consequent sense but in their full and literal meaning (*sensus plenior*). Such an assertion may not be susceptible

---

whom the Holy Family met in the desert on their flight into Egypt. Titus defended the travellers against his companion's rapacity, and Jesus predicted that within thirty years both of them would be crucified with Him, Titus on His right and Dumachus on His left, and that Titus would precede Him into Paradise.

[49] It is a debated point whether this sister of our Lady was Mary of Cleophas, in which case only three women are mentioned here, or whether "his mother's sister" and "Mary of Cleophas" were two distinct persons. It is not possible to give a certain and wholly satisfactory answer to the problem. We regard the second interpretation as the more probable one, and hold that the unnamed sister of our Lady was Salome, the mother of James and John, whom the fourth evangelist modestly refrained from naming in his narrative. See above, pp. 241 *f.*

[50] Cf. C. A. Kneller, "Joh. 19:26–27 bei den Kirchenvätern," in *Zeit f. kath. Theol.*, 40 (1916), 597–612; V. Laridon, *Collationes Brugenses*, 46 (1950), 177–180.

of overwhelming proof, yet it rests on a solid foundation and should be regarded as at least highly probable.[51] In view of the solemn circumstances in which our Lord spoke, it does not seem that His intention was to refer exclusively to St. John's taking care of His holy Mother. Furthermore, there was no danger that our Lady would be abandoned by her own relatives, among whom was her sister, who was either St. John's mother Salome, or else Mary the mother of James the Less and Joseph. From the height of the cross, our Lord's gaze extended to all humanity, and in that supreme moment He wished to strengthen the link of maternal and filial love between His own Mother and mankind. And just as in the Garden of Eden God had made Eve the mother of all the living, so on Calvary the Son of God made the second Eve the mother of all the redeemed. This was, as it were, man's third title to the spiritual maternity of Mary, which had begun at the Incarnation when she became Mother of God and which was completed at the foot of the cross when she became coredemptrix in union with her Divine Son.

Although, as we have said, this interpretation is not completely certain, it is at least solidly probable and is fully confirmed by numerous ecclesiastical documents, one of which is the Encyclical *Rerum Ecclesiae* of Pius XI, in which His Holiness said that on Calvary the most holy Queen of the Apostles had all men entrusted to her maternal heart.[52]

Thus St. John represented all men and therefore, from the cross, our Lord says to each of us: "Behold thy mother" and gives us over to the care of Mary's tender heart.

The physical pain which Christ suffered on the cross was great, but immeasurably greater were His spiritual torments. The sorrow, desolation and abandonment of Gethsemani now reached their climax

---

[51] Several interesting and mutually complementary articles have been written in favor of this interpretation: J. M. Bover, "La maternidad de María expresada por el Redentor en la cruz," in *Est. Bibl.* (1941), pp. 627–646; P. Gächter, "Die geistige Mutterschaft Marias, Ein Beitrag zur Erklärung von Jo. 19:26 s." in *Zeit f. kath. Theol.*, 47 (1923), 391–429; and in his book *Maria im Erdenleben* (Innsbruck, 1953), pp. 201–226; J. Leal, "Beata Virgo omnium spiritualis Mater ex Jn. 19:26–27," in *Verb. Dom.*, 27 (1949), 65–73; "Sentido literal mariológico de Jo. 19:26–27," in *Est. Bibl.* (1952), 303–319; V. Laridon, *loc. cit.*, pp. 205–208.

[52] "Sanctissima regina Apostolorum Maria, cum homines universos in Calvaria habuerit materno animo suo commendatos. . . ." (*Acta Apost. Sedis,* 18 [1926], 83).

and drew from the Divine Victim a cry of anguish which rang out through the silent darkness of Calvary:

"Eli, Eli, lamma sabacthani? . . .

"My God, my God, why hast thou forsaken me?"

This was the cry which the prophet David placed on the lips of the Messias (Ps. 21, Hebrew Ps. 22):

"O God, my God . . .: why hast thou forsaken me? . . .

O my God, I cry by day, and thou dost not answer:

and I cry by night without finding rest. . . .

All they that see me make a mockery of me;

Opening their mouths, they shake their heads and say

'He hoped in Yahweh, let him free him.

Since he loves him, let him save him. . . .' "

These words of Christ on the cross were not a cry of despair, nor can they be properly called a complaint. Jesus knew that His Father had not abandoned Him, that He loved Him as much in the shadows of Calvary as in the glory of Mount Thabor when He had proclaimed: "This is my beloved Son, in whom I am well pleased." Our Lord's cry was indeed one of deep pain, but of pain that was borne lovingly and willingly. In a mysterious way which we have not been allowed to penetrate, the Father suspended the beatific influence of the Divinity on the Humanity of Christ, so that His soul was allowed to experience such sorrow, anguish and loneliness that He felt as if He had been abandoned. And although Jesus freely accepted and willed this psychological state, it still wrung from His lips a cry in the form of a lament which revealed the depth of His agony.[53]

Not understanding Jesus' cry or else intending to mock Him, some of those who were present exclaimed: "This man is calling Elias."

And others replied scornfully: "Wait, let us see whether Elias is coming to save him."

As a result of the ill-treatment of the night before, His loss of blood at the scourging and crowning with thorns, His exhausting journey to Calvary, and, above all, His crucifixion, Jesus was burning with thirst, a thirst which, though it had come to be one of His severest torments, He bore patiently for the redemption of men. Yet because this pain was the subject of a prophecy (Ps. 68:22; 21:16), He exclaimed aloud: "I thirst."

[53] See W. J. Kenneally's short article, "Eli, Eli, lamma sabacthani?" in *Cath. Bibl. Quarterly,* 8 (1946), 124–134.

Near at hand there was a vessel containing vinegar, or rather a mixture of water and vinegar called *posca,* which was supplied to the Roman soldiers and which was also used by the Jews, for we read in the Book of Ruth (2:14) that the reapers of Booz drank it. One of the soldiers took a sponge dipped in this liquid, stuck it on the end of a reed and held it to Christ's lips. But He barely tasted it.

Then, knowing that He had finished the great work which His Father had given Him to do, that all the prophecies had been fulfilled, and that the redemption of the world had been accomplished, Jesus exclaimed: "It is consummated!"

These three words summarize a lifetime of battle, of sacrifice, of faithful, persevering submission to the will of the Father. The Divine Warrior, victorious a thousand times over, was at last able to lay down His arms and rest. Nothing more remained to be done. *Consummatum est!*

The supreme moment, then, had arrived. He who had come from the Father was about to return to Him, and death was going to claim as its prey the God-Man, who was not subject to death. The Author of life was going to die, but in His very dying He would triumph over death: "Father, into thy hands I commend my spirit."

And bowing His head, He died.

In profound, reverent silence, let us contemplate the Son of God nailed to a cross like a common criminal. Yet He who was mockingly called the King of the Jews was to change the disgraceful gibbet into a throne of glory from which He would extend His dominion over the whole world. And millions of hearts were to turn to Calvary in humble and devout adoration of the Divine Victim hanging pale and lifeless on the harsh wood.

The Author of nature was dead, and nature proclaimed its sorrow. The earth trembled, rocks were split asunder, tombs were opened, and the veil of the Temple was rent from top to bottom.[54] The evangelists,

---

[54] There were two veils in the Sanctuary of the Temple, one before the Holy Place, which contained the altar of incense, the loaves of proposition and the seven-branched candlestick; and the other before the Holy of Holies, which was reserved for the Ark of the Covenant (cf. *Wars* v. 5. 4–5). We do not know to which of these veils the evangelists were referring, and the context gives us no clue. A certain number of authors say that only the veil before the Holy Place was torn, and others think that both were rent, but the great majority of the Fathers and recent writers believe that the evangelists were speaking of the veil hanging before the Holy of Holies. We, too, think that this last opinion is much the more probable one. The rending of the veil symbolized the abrogation of the Old Law, in which the Ark of the Covenant occupied

anticipating later events, add that many of the dead arose, no doubt at the Resurrection of Christ; and at His Ascension they accompanied Him to heaven.

When the centurion saw the prodigies of nature which followed Christ's death, he was moved to exclaim: "Truly this was a just man. . . . Truly he was the Son of God."

Overcome with fear, those who had been present on Calvary descended the hill, striking their breasts and acknowledging that the crucified Victim had indeed been "a just man," the Son of God. The Redeemer's Blood was beginning to bear fruit.

But the sacrificed Lamb of God had not yet shed all His blood, and He wished to give us the last drops that still remained in His heart (John 19:31–34): "The Jews therefore, since it was the Preparation Day, in order that the bodies might not remain upon the cross on the Sabbath (for that Sabbath was a solemn day), besought Pilate that their legs might be broken, and that they might be taken away. The soldiers therefore came and broke the legs of the first, and of the other, who had been crucified with him. But when they came to Jesus, and saw that he was already dead, they did not break his legs; but one of the soldiers opened his side with a lance, and immediately there came out blood and water." [55]

St. John perceived such a depth of mystery in the lance-thrust and in the fact that none of our Lord's bones was broken that he added solemnly (19:35–37): "And he who saw it has borne witness, and his witness is true; and he knows that he tells the truth, that you also may believe. For these things came to pass that the Scripture might be fulfilled, 'Not a bone of him shall you break.' [56] And again another Scripture says, 'They shall look upon him whom they have pierced.' " [57]

St. Augustine's commentary on the passage is well known: "The evangelist here used a carefully chosen word, for he did not say that one of the soldiers wounded or struck Christ's side or anything like that, but that he *opened* His side, as if to indicate that a door of life

a pre-eminent place. Hence it is logical to suppose that the veil which hung before the repository of the Ark was the one that was torn. The Ark itself had disappeared in the destruction of Jerusalem in 587 B.C., but the Holy of Holies remained unchanged. Actually there were two veils or curtains hanging in front of the Holy of Holies, one being suspended a cubit (about eighteen inches) from the other. Cf. the *Mishnah, Yoma* 5:1.

[55] See Fr. Vaccari's interesting note on the reading "exivit *aqua et sanguis*" in *Verb. Dom.,* 17 (1937), 193–198.

[56] Exodus 12:46.

[57] Zacharias 12:10.

was made therein from which the sacraments of the Church flowed, those sacraments without which no one can enter into true life." [58] St. John Chrysostom is even more explicit when he says that the two streams (of blood and water) did not flow without reason and by chance, but because the Church is formed from them both, as is known to the faithful, who are reborn through water and fed by the Body and Blood.[59] That is, the water represents baptism, and the blood the Eucharist. And it is the common opinion of the Fathers that, just as Eve was formed of Adam's rib while he slept, so too the second Adam fell asleep upon the cross in order that the Church might come forth from His side.[60]

The evangelist does not tell us whether it was Christ's right or left side that was opened by the lance. Some authors think that, since the soldier probably held the lance in his right hand, he thrust it into our Lord's left side. But it would be rash to make any definite statement on the matter.

As regards the flow of blood and water from the wound, some writers suggest that it could have been a completely natural occurrence. Thus if the heart had previously been ruptured, there would have been an internal hemorrhage, and the blood, collecting in the pericardium, would have separated into a watery liquid called serum and a viscid mass of red globules, both of which would have flowed out when the pericardium was pierced by the lance. At all events, in the designs of God the phenomenon was clothed with a mysterious symbolism.

St. Mark (15:44) notes that Pilate was surprised when he heard that Jesus had died so soon. This reaction of the procurator's seems to justify the opinion that our Lord did not die as a result of the crucifixion, but by a sovereign act of His will.

In reality it was by no means uncommon for victims of crucifixion to remain alive on the cross for two days or even longer. For the rest, there is a certain fitness in the idea that Jesus, the Giver of life, did not cease to live as a result of a natural law but rather by an act of His will. However, in view of the atrocious torments that preceded the actual crucifixion, it would not be surprising if our Lord, no matter how robust His constitution, had succumbed after hanging for three long hours on the cross. Nor should it be forgotten that although His

---

[58] *Tract. 120 in Ioan.*, 2: *PL* 35, 1953.
[59] *In Ioan.* hom. 85. 3: *PG* 59, 463.
[60] See S. Tromp, "De Nativitate Ecclesiae ex Corde Jesu in cruce," in *Gregorianum,* 13 (1932), 489–527.

unspeakable anguish of soul cannot be regarded as the cause of His death, yet it must have hastened the end.[61]

The Burial

Among the secret disciples of Christ there was an important personage named Joseph of Arimathea, who had received his name from his native city, the ancient Rama or Ramathaim-Sophim, birthplace of Samuel the prophet,[62] which was probably present-day Rentis, a town that lies a short distance southeast of Ras el-'Ain, and not Ramleh, near Jaffa, as some authors think. In a few short phrases the evangelists depict Joseph's noble character: "a councillor, a good and just man . . . of high rank, who likewise was looking for the kingdom of God . . . a disciple of Jesus." It is true that hitherto he had not openly followed Christ, for fear of the Jews. But now, casting all timidity aside, he went boldly to Pilate and asked him for the body of Jesus (Mark 15:43). In the existing circumstances his action was nothing less than heroic, not because he might have been rebuffed by the procurator, whose favorable dispositions towards the Victim were known, but because he was exposing himself to the anger of his colleagues, the Sanhedrists, and was braving the fury of the whole Jewish people.

Once Pilate had learned from the centurion that Jesus was dead, he made no difficulty about granting the permission requested, and Joseph set about arranging for the burial of the sacred body. In his task of love, he was assisted by another secret disciple, Nicodemus, who had come to Jesus by night, and who, as St. John carefully notes (19:39), now brought with him "a mixture of myrrh and aloes, in weight about a hundred pounds," that is, about seventy pounds in our system of weights—a princely gift and a clear indication of his love for the dead Master.

Fortunately, Joseph of Arimathea owned a new sepulchre in which no one had been buried, cut out of the rock close at hand. It was usual for prominent families to have their own special tombs, which in many cases were located on their estates.

---

[61] Regarding death by crucifixion from the medical point of view, see Engelbert Sons, "Die Todesursache bei der Kreuzigung," in *Stimmen der Zeit,* 146 (1950), 60–64; Pierre Barbet, *A Doctor at Calvary: The Passion of Our Lord Jesus Christ as Described by a Surgeon,* trans. by the Earl of Wicklow (New York: P. J. Kenedy & Sons, 1954).

[62] 1 Kings 1:1; concerning this city see *Biblica,* 12 (1931), 119–123.

Sira Photo

*The sepulchre of the family of Herod. At right center is the stone
disk used for closing the tomb.*

Jewish tombs took several forms: *well tombs* were of some depth,
were reached by descending a number of steps, and were closed by a
horizontal slab of stone: Lazarus' tomb at Bethany was of this type;

Sira Photo

An ancient Jewish tomb. The large stone disk which is clearly visible at the left can be rolled forward to seal the entrance. Our Lord's sepulchre was closed in this manner.

chamber tombs, whose entrances stood at ground level, for example, the family vault of Queen Helena of Adiabene, in Jerusalem, called the Tomb of the Kings. Some of these chamber tombs had a simple stone bench running along three of the four sides, while others had one or two benches, surmounted by *arcosolia* or arched depressions, cut out of the walls. The third type, the *kokim* or *oven tombs,* were simply horizontal cavities cut into the rock to receive the individual corpses: this kind of tomb was very common and many examples of it can still be seen in the vicinity of Jerusalem.

The tombs were closed in a great variety of ways. The simplest method of sealing off *chamber* and *oven tombs* consisted in placing a slab of stone over the tomb-mouth and keeping it in position by rolling a more or less round boulder against it. Examples of this method can be seen in the excavations of the ancient city of Bethsames in the Wadi es-Surar. As we have said, the subterranean or *well tombs* were closed with a horizontal flagstone. The most characteristic device for covering the entrance to *chamber tombs* was a great stone disk, somewhat like a millstone, which rested on an inclined plane in such a way that it

would roll down by its own weight and seal off the entrance. When
the disk was rolled back to allow access to the sepulchre, it ran into a
slot cut out of the wall at one side of the doorway. Stones of this type
can still be seen today in the aforementioned Tomb of the Kings, in
Herod's family sepulchre, which is also situated in Jerusalem, on the
hill of Nikefurieh, opposite the Pontifical Biblical Institute, and in two
tombs in Abughosh, about ten miles west of the Holy City.

In a number of cases there was a vestibule leading into the burial
chamber proper; and some sepulchres were veritable cemeteries in
themselves, e.g., the so-called Tomb of the Prophets on Mount Olivet.

We shall pass over other details of lesser importance that can be
seen in the numerous ancient tombs which have been preserved, some
of them almost intact, down to our own times. Among the latter, the
one that holds the greatest interest for us is that known by the name
of Joseph of Arimathea, and situated beneath the Basilica of the Holy
Sepulchre, beside the chapel of the Syrians.

Joseph of Arimathea's tomb was a chamber dug out of the rock
about fifty feet northwest of Calvary. Access to it was gained through
a vestibule,[63] at the inner end of which stood the round stone for sealing off the low, narrow entrance to the burial vault proper. The vault
itself contained a bench cut out of the rock, destined to receive the
corpse. We do not know if there was an *arcosolium* or arched cavity
over the bench, nor if the bench itself was quite flat or, instead, slightly
concave.

St. John's description (20:12), ". . . two angels in white sitting,
one at the head and one at the feet, where the body of Jesus had been
laid. . . ." is not sufficiently explicit to warrant the conclusion that on
one end of the bench there was a small protuberance on which the
head of the corpse rested, as on a pillow. Nevertheless, the bench
probably had such a stone pillow, since examples of a similar arrangement are still to be seen in a number of tombs.

"Now when it was evening . . . there came Joseph of Arimathea.
. . . And Joseph brought a linen cloth. . . . And there came also
Nicodemus (who at first had come to Jesus by night), bringing a mixture of myrrh and aloes, in weight about a hundred pounds. They
therefore took the body of Jesus and wrapped it in linen cloths with the
spices, after the Jewish manner of preparing for burial."

[63] Very probably the entrance to the vestibule was left open, without a door. According to the testimony of St. Cyril of Jerusalem (*PG* 33, 354), the vestibule
was destroyed when the Basilica of Constantine was being built.

Interior of the Holy Sepulchre.

The evangelists also note that "the women who had come with him from Galilee . . . Mary Magdalene and Mary the mother of Joseph . . . were there, sitting opposite the sepulchre . . . looking on, and [they] saw where . . . and how his body was laid."

The three Synoptic writers and St. John give quite distinct, but by no means contradictory, accounts of our Lord's burial (Matt. 27:57–66; Mark 15:42–47; Luke 23:50–56; John 19:31–42). The first three Gospels tell us simply that Jesus' body was wrapped in a linen cloth, which Matthew expressly describes as clean, or rather, spotlessly white (27:59). But St. John is more explicit and supplies several interesting details: they wrapped Christ's body "in linen cloths with the spices," which were "a mixture of myrrh and aloes, in weight about a hundred pounds," and there was a "handkerchief . . . about his head" (20:7). Therefore three objects are mentioned in the Gospels: σινδών (sindo, a linen sheet), ὀθόνια (lintea, linteamina, linen cloths), and σουδάριον (sudarium, a handkerchief), as well as the mixture of myrrh and aloes (John 19:39).[64]

These facts allow us to reconstruct, although not with complete certainty, the procedure followed by Joseph of Arimathea and Nicodemus in preparing our Lord's body for burial. There were two ways, slightly different from each other, in which they could have performed their sorrowful task. The first method was to bind the limbs of the corpse with bandages upon which the mixture of myrrh and aloes had been spread, then the whole body was wrapped in a sheet, the head being left exposed and later covered with a smaller piece of cloth called the sudarium or handkerchief.[65] The second method consisted in first wrapping the body in the sheet along with the spices, and then binding the bandages around it, as seems to have been done with Lazarus, who "came forth [from the tomb] bound feet and hands with bandages" (John 11:44), which, no doubt, had been wound around the sheet covering his body. If this was the method used in our Lord's case, then the sheet was in immediate contact with his sacred body.

It may seem surprising that St. John does not mention the linen sheet, but a little reflection will show the reason for the omission. The author of the fourth Gospel simply wished to fill out the Synoptic writers' narrative, and since all three of his predecessors had written about the sheet, there was no need for him to refer to it, particularly since it was commonly used in burials and could, therefore, be taken

---

[64] There is some discussion as to whether the "aloes" used were the medicinal variety or rather the aromatic aloes derived from the tree *Aquilaria agallocha*. Cf. Braun in *Nouv. Rev. Théol.* 66 (1939), 1026, in favor of the latter, which seems to be the more likely substance for the purpose.

[65] This is the view favored by Fillion, *The Life of Christ*, III, 560; Ricciotti, *op. cit.*, p. 644, cf. p. 502; Vilariño, *Vida de N.S. Jesucristo* (Bilbao, 1941), p. 658; Prat, *Jesus Christ*, II, 404.

for granted. Consequently, instead of being a cause for comment, St. John's silence is only to be expected.

This solution of the apparent discrepancy between the first three Gospels and St. John's is certainly satisfactory.[66] But there is another and still more acceptable explanation based on the philology of the word ὀθόνια. This word does not mean specifically either "sheet" or "bands," but has a wider and less concrete significance, and simply denotes "linens," or *linteamina,* as St. Jerome translates it. Therefore it includes both sheets and bands, so that St. John's phrase, "they . . . wrapped it [the body] in linen cloths [*othoniois*]," can, and probably should, be taken as meaning both the sheet and the bandages.[67]

None of the four evangelists tells us whether or not the sacred body was bathed before being wrapped in the shroud. It was certainly customary to wash a corpse before burial, as can be seen from the case of Tabitha (Acts 9:37) and the text of the *Mishnah,* which speaks of washing the dead person.[68] Hence our Lord's body was undoubtedly washed before being placed in the tomb.[69] Nor is it likely

---

[66] The same cannot be said of those theories which try to harmonize the Synoptic Gospels with St. John's by presupposing that all four accounts are dealing with one and the same object, viz., the linen sheet, which is represented as whole and entire by the Synoptic writers and as cut into strips or bands by St. John. In our opinion, such an explanation is most improbable and does not merit refutation. See J. Blinzler, *Das Turiner Grablinnen und die Wissenschaft* (Passoviae, 1952), pp. 22 and 47, n. 63.

[67] This meaning of the word is clearly seen in a papyrus of the early fourth century (320) found in Hermopolis, present-day Asmunein, in Upper Egypt, and published by the John Rylands Library, Manchester, 1952, Vol. IV, 117 *f.* The papyrus was part of the archives of a Roman administrative official named Theophanes. While on a journey from Egypt to Antioch, Theophanes noted in his diary the items of his baggage, including his personal linen. On line 9, col. 1, he wrote the title "Note on the *othonion* [ὀθονίων]," and underneath it, on line 13, apparently as forming part of the *othonia,* he listed a *phakiarion* (φακιάριον) i.e., a cloth used on the face, equivalent to a *sudarium* or handkerchief; and on line 17, he listed four *sindonia* (σινδόνια) or sheets. Hence the generic term *othonia* includes both sheets and handkerchiefs. Theophanes also mentions bandages (col. 2, line 41), but only under the general classification of *stromata.* It is probable that St. John wished to include them under the name *othonia,* although when referring to them specifically in 11:44, he calls them *keiriai.* Regarding Theophanes' diary, see A. Vaccari, *Secoli sul mondo* (Torino: Marietti, 1955), pp. 438–442; B. Ubach, *Miscellanea Biblica* (Montisserrati, 1953), pp. 375–386.

[68] *Shabbath* 23:5: "They may make ready [on the Sabbath] all that is needful for the dead, and anoint it and wash it. . . ." It was taken for granted that the body should be both washed and anointed, and the one seems to have been no less important than the other.

[69] This is the common opinion; e.g., among others, Lagrange says: "After the sacred body stained with the precious blood had been washed clean. . . ." (*The Gospel of Jesus Christ,* II, 278): and Prat remarks that "the body had to be

that lack of water would have prevented Joseph and Nicodemus from washing the sacred body in some fashion. The evangelist (John 19:41) notes that the tomb was in "a garden," and no matter in what sense this word is taken, there was very probably a well, reservoir or cistern in the place. And even if there was no water to be had on the spot, it would have been very easy for the disciples to get some from a house in the city, which was close at hand. Finally, since Nicodemus had come provided with the "hundred pounds" of spices, it is quite possible that he had also brought the water needed for bathing the body before the spices were applied.

Not all authors interpret St. John's words as we have just done. According to some, the ὀθόνια (*linteamina*) were small linen cloths which were placed at either side of Christ's face,[70] while the σουδάριον was either the linen sheet itself, as mentioned by the Synoptic writers,[71] or a strip of cloth which was passed under the chin and tied on top of the head to keep the mouth closed.[72] The *Mishnah* mentions the closing of the corpse's mouth.[73]

We have already spoken of the proper specific meaning of the word *othonia*. As regards the handkerchief (*sudarium*), it seems undeniable that St. John speaks of it as being distinct from the linen sheet. In referring to it after the Resurrection (20:7) and at the raising of Lazarus, he mentions it in connection with the head. In the case of Lazarus (11:44), he explicitly distinguishes it from the bandages and consequently from the linen sheet wrapped around the body; and he tells us that when Peter entered Christ's tomb (20:6 f.), he saw the ὀθόνια (*linteamina:* "linen cloths") *and* the σουδάριον (*sudarium:* "handkerchief"). Not only that, but Peter also "saw . . . [that] . . . the handkerchief which had been about his head, [was] not lying with the linen cloths, but [was] *folded in a place by itself."* [74] The Gospel text

carried into this vestibule to be washed, as was the custom. . . ." (*op. cit.,* II, 404).

[70] "Quanto al termine ὀθονίοις, si può intendere di alcune *fasce, pannolini,* che servirono per circundare sopra tutto i lati del Volto del Salvatore" (Scotti, *Scuola Cattolica,* 67 [1939], 231).

[71] ". . . come il σουδάριον non sia altra che la Sindone" (*ibid.,* pp. 235 f.).

[72] "Se il σουδάριον non e la Sindone, allora diviene semplicemente una fascia per legare la mandibola" (*ibid.,* p. 235).

[73] *Shabbath* 23:5.

[74] See Fr. Braun's philological study in *loc. cit.,* 900–935, 1025–1046, particularly 906 *ff.,* as well as his articles, "La sépulture de Jésus," in *RB* (1936), 34–52, 184–200, 346–363. Fr. E. A. Wuenschel presents a different interpretation in the *Cath. Bibl. Quarterly,* 7 (1945), 405–437; 8 (1946), 135–178.

gives the impression that the handkerchief was used to cover our Lord's head and face, as was the custom and as is clearly apparent in the description of the raising of Lazarus.[75] So far as we can see, there is no indication that it was employed to keep the jaws closed or that it was simply folded and placed beside Christ's head.

The Synoptic authors' extreme brevity seems to suggest that our Lord's burial on Friday afternoon was only a temporary interment, and that Joseph of Arimathea and Nicodemus, without any preparation, simply wrapped the sacred body in a sheet and placed it as it was in the tomb, leaving the customary rites to be performed later. Such a procedure would seem to have been advisable and even necessary because of the short time at their disposal.

But St. John corrects that impression, for his description makes it plain that all the customary rites were performed on that very Friday afternoon—the body was wrapped in the *othonia* with the spices, and the head was covered with the handkerchief, the special cloth reserved for that purpose. In a word, he includes all the usual appurtenances of a burial. It is true that he does not mention the washing of the body, but his silence does not authorize us to conclude that this part of the procedure was omitted.

However, we may ask if there was time for all this preparation. The chronological data supplied by Matthew (27:57) and Mark (15:42), "Now when it was evening . . .," and by Luke (23:54), ". . . the Sabbath was drawing on," certainly seem to imply that the time available was not sufficient for the performance of the usual burial practices. Yet if we examine the matter closely we shall see that the disciples had enough time to accomplish their task.

The Greek word ὀψία, "evening," can mean the period between 3:00 P.M. and 6:00 P.M., as Knabenbauer and Lagrange correctly point out,[76] and as can be seen in any Greek lexicon. In addition, if Good Friday fell on April 7th, as it very probably did, sunset was at 6:23 P.M. And two hours would have been more than enough for

[75] John 11:44; καὶ ἡ ὄψις αὐτοῦ σουδαρίῳ περιεδέδετο: et facies illius sudario erat ligata: "enveloppée d'un suaire" (Lagrange): "envuelta en un sudario" (Bover, Colunga). The rabbinical writings offer no positive proof that this custom was general in our Lord's day, but neither are there any grounds for asserting the contrary.

[76] "Tempus est pomeridianum ab hora nostra tertia usque ad sextam" (Knabenbauer, *In Matt., in loc.*); ". . . Il est très naturel que le temps entre trois et six ait été précisément employé par les démarches de Joseph, et c'est sans doute ce que pensait Marc" (Lagrange, *Év. selon St. Marc, in loc.*).

taking our Lord's body down from the cross, washing it at least sum-
marily, applying the spices, enfolding it in the shroud and placing it on
the bench in the tomb. Finally, we should bear in mind that the tomb
itself was close to Calvary, at a distance of only about fifty feet.[77]

Some may object that this burial was only temporary and incomplete because the holy women observed closely where the body
was being laid and prepared additional spices to anoint it again. We
answer that a large quantity of spices ("about a hundred pounds")
had already been used, and that there was no need for more. Then, too,
the women could have done nothing more than sprinkle the additional
spices on the shrouded body. Actually, their solicitude was inspired
solely by love for their Master, whom they wished to honor by lavishing
on His sacred body the aromatic substances which they had prepared
with their own hands.[78]

The Jews had not forgotten what Jesus had said about His Resurrection, and although they did not take His words as a true prophecy
or even dream that He could ever rise from the grave, they feared that
His disciples would give His promise the appearance of having been
fulfilled by stealing His body and spreading the rumor that He had
raised Himself from the dead. And the fraud seemed all the easier to
accomplish because the body had been buried in a sepulchre belonging
to one of His friends, who would be likely to be a party to His Apostles'
plotting and carrying out the deception.

This line of thought drove the Jewish leaders to take the obvious
and logical step of going to the procurator with a request that a guard
be placed over the tomb: "Sir, we have remembered how that deceiver
said, while he was yet alive, 'After three days I will rise again.' Give
orders, therefore, that the sepulchre be guarded until the third day, or
else his disciples may come and steal him away, and say to the people,

[77] At first glance the text from the *Mishnah* (*Shabbath* 23:5) which we quoted
above on p. 747, n. 68 may seem to have permitted the burial rites to be performed even on the Sabbath. However, it is clear from the context that the
permission applied only to the preparation of the corpse and not to its being
placed in the tomb.

[78] Some authors see in the holy women's going to the tomb a narrative parallel
to that of Joseph of Arimathea and Nicodemus, the two accounts being the
reflection of two distinct and independent traditions, one representing Joseph
as placing Jesus in the tomb, and the other the holy women as anointing His
sacred body. That is the opinion of Goguel, for example, in his book, *La foi
à la résurrection de Jésus dans le Christianisme primitif* (Paris, 1931) p. 131.
But there is not the least indication of the existence of a double tradition, or
rather of two such ways of narrating the same event, whereas our explanation
of the women's actions is in conformity with history and psychology.

'He has risen from the dead'; and the last imposture will be worse than the first."

Pilate must have thought their fears empty and ridiculous, but because it was such a small matter and because he did not wish to offend them now, having already sacrificed his conscience to placate them, he granted their request, but left them to see to the details: "You have a guard; go, guard it as well as you know how."

And he placed at their disposal some of the soldiers from the Roman garrison, as can be seen from Matthew 28:14: "So they went and made the sepulchre secure, sealing the stone, and setting the guard."

The practice of using a seal for security's sake was common among the Jews and in the Orient in general. Thus in Job 14:17 there is mention of sealing a bag, in Daniel 6:17 of sealing the stone at the mouth of the lion's den, and, again in Daniel (14:10, 13), of sealing a door.

Once again, the chief priests were the unwitting instruments of God. In the designs of Providence their very precautions were to make the great miracle of the Resurrection more evident and more incontrovertible still.

29. The Glorified Life

The Resurrection
(Matt. 28; Mark 16; Luke 24; John 20–21)

The triumph of the Sanhedrists was complete. The spurious Prophet of Nazareth was dead and buried, His handful of disciples scattered, and in a short time all that would remain of Him and His work would be a fast-fading memory. Not for years had the leaders of the Jews celebrated the Passover with such self-satisfaction and joy.

It was in this frame of mind that the chief priests, the Scribes and the Pharisees passed Friday night and the whole of the Sabbath. But at dawn on the third day, their peaceful sense of security and their self-congratulation were changed into bewildered agitation and frightened uncertainty: "Now late in the night of the Sabbath, as the first day of the week began to dawn . . . there was a great earthquake, for an angel of the Lord came down from heaven, and drawing near rolled back the stone, and sat upon it. His countenance was like lightning, and his raiment like snow. And for fear of him the guards were terrified, and became like dead men."

The guards had good cause to be terror-stricken. The tomb had been closed with a huge stone upon which a seal had been placed; within the burial chamber there had been a cold corpse; and all around silence and solitude had reigned since the eve of the Sabbath. But in the twinkling of an eye everything had changed! The very earth had shaken, and a shining supernatural being had appeared and rolled back the ponderous stone as if it had been a pebble. No wonder, then, that as soon as the guards recovered the power of their limbs they fled from that awesome place and ran to tell the chief priests who had posted them there.

What they had seen was Christ's triumph over death and the fulfillment of His prophecy: "For even as Jonas was in the belly of the fish three days and three nights, so will the Son of Man be three days and three nights in the heart of the earth" (Matt. 12:40).

Christ's soul was again united with His most holy body, imparting to it new qualities—impassibility, "brightness," "agility," and "subtility." And that body, which had been killed, wounded and disfigured, and had lain in the funereal darkness of the tomb, now rose resplendent and beautiful, retaining only the five wounds, shining like five suns, to be presented to the Father to plead for the very men who had inflicted them.

Thus was death conquered, the devil vanquished, and the world freed from its toils. The weeping on Calvary gave way to the thunderous acclamations of a host of souls who, released from the shadows of Limbo, formed an escort around the Conqueror of Death.

What was the attitude of the Sanhedrists when confronted with the news of the supernatural occurrences at the tomb? Instead of opening their eyes and recognizing so well-attested and obvious a miracle, they took refuge in evasion, bribery and lies. Hurriedly, the chief priests and elders assembled and agreed that the best thing they could do would be to pay the guards handsomely to say: "His disciples came by night and stole him while we were sleeping." St. Augustine's comment on their action is very apposite: "You bring forward witnesses who had been asleep! O wretched Synagogue, it was really you who were sleeping when you gave such advice!" [1]

---

[1] *Tract. super Psalmos,* in Ps. 63:7. An inscription published by Franz Cumont in the *Revue historique,* CLXIII (1930), 567–571, is of interest in connection with this supposed stealing of Christ's body by the Apostles. The inscription is a "rescript of Caesar" dealing with the violation of tombs, and the last lines read: "Let no one ever be permitted to transfer them [the bodies of the dead] from one place to another. On the contrary, I command that he who is condemned for violating a sepulchre shall suffer the death penalty."

The decree was first drawn up in Latin and then translated into Greek. The Greek translation, engraved on a marble slab, found its way into the former Froehner collection, in the inventory of which the following note appears: "A

The leaders of Israel have not lacked imitators in later centuries, particularly in modern times. Some of these latter-day disciples of the chief priests and elders have not been any more prudent or cautious than their teachers. In fact, to explain away the Resurrection, which they regard as impossible, some of them have evolved the hypothesis that it was the Jews themselves who stole our Lord's body by night and hid it in an unknown place, not because they feared that Jesus would come to life again, but to prevent the tomb from becoming a pilgrim's shrine for the admirers of the Nazarene.[2]

Klausner rightly regards this explanation as frivolous, yet the one which he himself gravely advances is no less arbitrary and opposed to all historical criticism:

We must assume that the owner of the tomb, Joseph of Arimathaea, thought it unfitting that one who had been crucified should remain in his own ancestral tomb. . . . [He], therefore, secretly removed the body at the close of Sabbath and buried it in an unknown grave.[!] [3]

Others maintain that our Lord did not really die at all, and that therefore He could not have risen from the dead. They say that when

marble slab sent from Nazareth in 1878." The lettering of the inscription seems to indicate that it dates from the beginning of the Christian era.

The inscription spontaneously recalls the passage from St. Matthew (28:12–15) which tells how the chief priests and the elders suggested to the soldiers that they tell the governor: "His disciples came by night and stole him while we were sleeping."

Did this rumor, which was spread abroad among the Jews (Matt. 28:15), occasion the Emperor's decree? Cumont believes that it very probably did; he says that Pilate no doubt informed the Emperor of the theft with which the Jews had charged the disciples of Christ, and asked for instructions as to how he should proceed in the matter. In answer to his inquiry, the Emperor issued the rescript.

The theory is certainly possible and, to a certain extent, even probable, but since many questions remain unanswered, scientific prudence demands that we proceed with great caution. Are we certain that the emperor who wrote the rescript was Tiberius and not one of his successors? Was the inscription actually set up in Nazareth? Would one single incident have been sufficient motive for an imperial decree? And if so, may not the incident have been a different one from that mentioned by St. Matthew? These are difficult questions to answer, and therefore the opinions on the relationship of the decree with the Gospel text remain mere probabilities.

A reproduction of the inscription and some observations on it can be found in *RB* (1930), pp. 567–571. An unfavorable verdict on the value of the inscription appears in an article by M. Goguel in *Rev. d'Hist. et de Phil. religieuses,* 10 (1930), 289–293, and in Ricciotti, *The Life of Christ,* pp. 654 *f.*

[2] Cf. Albert Reville, *Jésus de Nazareth* (Paris, 1906), II, 420 *f.*

[3] *Jesus of Nazareth,* p. 357.

He was taken down from the cross, He was in a cataleptic state from which the strong, sharp odor of the spices revived Him.[4]

Finally, others reject such theories as absurd and unworthy of any serious-minded person, and offer what they regard as a truly scientific explanation, founded on nothing less than the laws of human psychology. Their hypothesis can be called the theory of fantasy or hallucination. According to them, the Apostles, although they had no wish to deceive anyone, actually deceived themselves. When they had recovered from the shock of Christ's crucifixion and death, they began to recall His miracles, and their love and admiration for Him was so great that they could not bring themselves to believe He had died once and for all. In the end, their desire for His presence became so great and their inflamed imaginations pictured Him so vividly that they convinced themselves that He had risen from the dead. Above all, they were sure He had appeared to them, and consequently they had implicit faith in His Resurrection. This theory is upheld by Guignebert, whose basic thought is that faith in the Resurrection is founded on the apparitions, and that these apparitions were purely imaginary. The Apostles *sincerely believed* that they had seen Christ, whereas in reality they had not done so.[5]

[4] Cf. Friedrich Spitta, *Die Auferstehung Jesus* (Göttingen, 1918). On pp. 82 *f.*, this author presents the following description as being strictly scientific: no one visited the tomb on the Sabbath; at some time during the night of Saturday-Sunday the Resurrection (i.e., the disappearance of the body) occurred, and when Mary Magdalene went to the tomb she found it empty. It is impossible to say whether Jesus freed Himself from the shroud or whether someone helped Him, although the latter is the more probable explanation.

A similar theory is proposed by W. B. Primrose in his article, "A Surgeon Looks at the Crucifixion," in *The Hibbert Journal*, XLVII (1948–49), 382–388: "It is possible to suggest that Jesus may not have died on the cross although he suffered the experience of dying, his higher faculties disappearing as vitality gradually failed to support them." A short while later came the "revival"!

[5] Cf. C. Guignebert, *Jésus* (Paris, 1947), pp. 601–661: "Sous sa forme première la foi en la Résurrection est sortie d'une réaction, dans la conscience de Pierre et de ses compagnons, de leur confiance en Jésus, un moment déprimée par le coup inattendu de l'arrestation et du supplice du Maître. Cette réaction a été conditionnée par un certain milieu; c'est lui aussi qui a déterminé les conclusions qu'elle a fondées et en a assuré le succès" (p. 661). This author's denials are just as sweeping as his assertions: "L'histoire de la mise au tombeau et celle de la découverte du tombeau vide sont solidaires, la première prépare la seconde et n'est faite que pour elle. L'une et l'autre n'ont pu se constituer que loin de Jérusalem et hors du cercle des disciples directs, une quarantaine d'années, *au plus tôt,* après la mort de Jésus, c'est-à-dire, peu après la ruine de Jérusalem; en un temps où, pratiquement, il n'était plus guère possible à personne de tenter la moindre recherche sur place. La vérité est que nous ne savons pas et que, selon toute apparence, les disciples n'ont pas su plus que nous, où le corps de Jésus, descendu de la croix, probablement par les bourreaux, a été jeté; il y a

Although this hypothesis appears more scientific than the others, it really is no more true to history than they. The Apostles cherished no hope of Christ's Resurrection; they considered the holy women's reports mere nonsense, and it was only very reluctantly that they finally believed the incontrovertible evidence of the miracle. But according to the rationalists, these skeptical, incredulous and cowardly disciples worked themselves up into such a state of enthusiasm and courage that they believed their Master had come to life again. In fact, if the rationalists are right, so well did the Apostles deceive themselves that they went forth to the four corners of the earth to preach Christ's wholly imaginary Resurrection and to die for His unsubstantiated teaching! Obviously, such a theory is in complete conflict with the most fundamental laws of psychology.

In reality, the evidence for the Resurrection is so convincing that only those who are blindly prejudiced will reject it. The denials of hostile critics, their arbitrary manipulation of, and absolute contempt

chance pour que c'ait été au *pourrissoir* des suppliciés, plutôt que dans *un tombeau neuf"* (pp. 614 *f.*)

Such assertions do not defend, but rather offend, the canons of history.

Maurice Goguel is another proponent of the same theory and one of the authors who has written at great length on the problem of Christ's Resurrection. In his book *La foi à la résurrection de Jésus dans le Christianisme primitif* (Paris, 1931), pp. i–xi, 469, he has summarized his obviously rationalistic doctrine in the following words: "Au bout d'un temps qu'il est impossible d'évaluer, les disciples que la mort de Jésus avait abattus ont repris courage. Rentrés en Galilée et soustraits aux souvenirs directs qu'évoquaient les lieux qui avaient vu la défaite de leur Maître et l'effondrement de leurs espérances, ils ont revécu, là même où ils avaient commencé à les faire, les expériences spirituelles de leur vie commune avec lui. L'empreinte qu'il avait mis sur leur âme était trop profonde pour pouvoir être définitivement effacée. Ils on continué à rêver au moment glorieux de l'avènement du Messie. Les paroles de Jésus qui les avait avertis qu'avant de paraître glorieusement le Fils de l'homme devait beaucoup souffrir et être rejeté, sont revenues à leur mémoire et ont préparé la résurrection de leur foi. Insensiblement, ils en sont venus à ne plus voir dans la réalisation du Royaume de Dieu un rêve désormais irréalisable, mais une espérance, faible d'abord peut-être, mais qui est allée en prenant de plus en plus de consistance. Ils ont pris ainsi l'habitude de penser à Jésus, non plus comme à un mort, mais comme à un vivant, car, c'était avant la résurrection du dernier jour que le Messie devait paraître puisque c'était lui qui devait y présider. Ainsi s'est formée l'idée que, pour permettre à Jésus de réaliser son oeuvre messianique, Dieu lui avait accordé une revanche et que, comme il l'avait fait autrefois pour Hénoch, pour Moïse et pour Élie, il l'avait mystérieusement enlevé au ciel, le réservant ainsi pour un triomphe futur. C'est donc dans le coeur des disciples qui l'avaient aimé et qui avaient cru en lui que Jésus est d'abord ressuscité" (pp. 393 *f.*).

But plausible as Goguel's theory may seem, it is simply a chain of arbitrary assertions with no basis in history or psychology.

for, the Gospel texts,[6] and their forced and often grotesque explanations only serve to throw into sharper relief the authenticity of the miracle.

Therefore, with St. Paul we can triumphantly cry: "Christ has risen from the dead, the first fruits of those who have fallen asleep. For since by a man came death, by a man also comes resurrection from the dead. For as in Adam all die, so in Christ all will be made to live. . . . 'Death is swallowed up in victory! O death, where is thy victory? O death, where is thy sting?' " (1 Cor. 15:20–23, 54–55).

The Apparitions:

OUR LORD'S APPARITION TO HIS HOLY MOTHER

The Gospel tells us nothing of this apparition, but Christian tradition takes it for granted: the Doctors in general and the body of the faithful have always believed that after His Resurrection our Lord appeared first to His Mother. And indeed, was it not just that she who had shared most in His Passion should have been the first to participate in His glory? Would He who was so generous to Mary Magdalene have been less so to His own Mother? As Suárez says, we should believe without any shadow of doubt that after His Resurrection Christ appeared first to His Mother, for such is the almost unanimous opinion of all the faithful and the Doctors of the Church, as well as the teaching of every Catholic writer who dealt with the subject.[7] The same "Doctor Eximius" then goes on to quote some verses from the *Easter Hymn* of the fifth-century poet, Sedulius, in confirmation of his thesis.[8]

---

[6] Concerning this treatment and interpretation of the texts, see L. de Grandmaison, *Jesus Christ* III, 199 *ff.*, and F. M. Braun, *La sépulture de Jésus à propos de trois livres récents* (Paris, 1937).

[7] "Absque ulla dubitatione credendum est Christum post resurrectionem primum omnium matri suae apparuisse. Quae sententia ex ipsis terminis adeo est per se credibilis, ut fere sine controversia omnium fidelium et Doctorum animis insederit, atque ita docent omnes scriptores catholici qui hanc quaestionem attigerunt" (*In Part. III*, q. 55, d. 49, sect. 1, no. 2, [Ed. Vivès] XIX, 876). This apparition can be regarded as *private* and *filial*, as distinct from the ones that followed, which were public proofs of Christ's Resurrection. Cf. Simón-Dorado, *Praelectiones Biblicae, Nov. Test.* I, 1007.

[8]   "Discedat synagoga, suo fuscata colore,
Ecclesiam Christus pulchro sibi iunxit amore;
haec est conspicuo radians in honore Mariae,
quae cum clarifico semper sit nomine mater,
semper virgo manet. Huius se visibus adstans
luce palam Dominus prius obtulit, ut bona mater

Our Lord, then, did appear to His holy Mother. What joy she must have felt at embracing once more her Son, who, a short while before, had been placed lifeless and disfigured in her arms, but who now returned to her glorious and triumphant! "What a torrent of joy must have flooded the Mother's soul when the Risen Son offered to her kiss the wounds in His flesh, that flesh which she had conceived and borne in her own body!" [9]

APPARITION TO THE HOLY WOMEN

(Matt. 28:1–10; Mark 16:1–8; Luke 24:1–10; John 20:1–10)

The holy women spent the Sabbath in the repose demanded by the Law, waiting impatiently for the moment when they could hasten back to the sepulchre in which their beloved Master lay. Dawn had scarcely come [10] on the first day of the week, our Sunday, when Mary Magdalene, Joanna, Mary the mother of James, and other holy

> grandia divulgans miracula, quae fuit olim
> advenientis iter, haec sit redeuntis et index."
> (*Carmen Paschale: PL* 19, 742 *f.*)

[9] Rupertus, *De divinis officiis*, 1. 7. cap. 25: *PL* 170, 205 *f.*

See Fr. Holzmeister's brief but pithy article in *Verb. Dom.*, 22 (1942), 97–102, in which he studies the witness of tradition for and against our Lord's appearance to His Mother (Pars historica), and brings forward the intrinsic arguments in favor of that appearance (Pars critica). He does not go so far as to say that the appearance is certain, but he does regard it as very highly probable. It is interesting to find that St. Ephrem interprets our Lord's words to Mary Magdalene, "Do not touch me" (John 20:17), as being addressed to our Lady (cf. *ibid.*, 97 *f.*, and *Zeit f. kath. Theol.*, 46 [1922], 581).

[10] When St. Mark says "very early" and "when the sun had just risen" (16:2), he does not mean that they left the house very early in the morning and arrived at the tomb only after the sun had already come up. The journey was relatively short and would have taken only a quarter of an hour or even less. The evangelist's second chronological reference is intended to modify the first one, or rather to make it more precise. It was as if he said: "They set out very early, at sunrise," or "The first rays of the sun had scarcely begun to scatter the shades of night when they set out." If we understand Mark's account in this way, we can easily harmonize it with Matthew's (28:1) "as it began to dawn," with Luke's (24:1) "at early dawn," and with John's (20:1) "while it was still dark," because, when referring to the period just before sunrise, one can say with truth that it is not yet full day. For the rest, it would be ridiculous to claim that these chronological indications must be interpreted with mathematical rigor: instead, they should be taken in a broad and rather general sense.

As regards the actual day on which the events occurred, all four evangelists say that it was the first day of the week, i.e., the day after the Sabbath. It was therefore our Sunday. The phrase "Vespere autem sabbati" in the Latin version of St. Matthew's Gospel is obscure and inexact, and should be rendered, "When the Sabbath had passed."

women braved the wrath of the Jews and courageously set out for the tomb, laden with spices. It is not difficult to retrace, at least in general, the path they followed. Almost opposite the Citadel or Tower of David, and beside the Protestant Christ Church, there is a Moslem house inside which are preserved the ruins of an ancient church known to the pilgrims as the Church of the Three Marys. If the holy women left from the Cenacle, as is probable, this traditional site was on the route which they most likely followed to reach the tomb and which led out of the city through the Gennath Gate or the Gate of Ephraim.

As they were hurrying along, they suddenly remembered a difficulty which, in their desire to do honor to their Master's body, had not occurred to them before. They recalled that the tomb was closed with a large stone disk which they would not be able to roll back, and they realized that at such an early hour they would not be likely to find anyone in the lonely garden to help them. (They probably knew nothing about the guards who had been placed there by the Jewish leaders.) Nevertheless, they did not abandon their purpose, but continued on their way. And how great must their astonishment have been when, upon drawing near, they saw the stone rolled back and the tomb laid open! Mary Magdalene, impetuous and ardent, needed no more evidence to convince her that her Master's tomb had been rifled and His body stolen. The thought that He might have arisen never even entered her head! Without so much as pausing to glance inside the burial chamber, she fled back to the Cenacle and gasped out her news to Peter and John: "They have taken the Lord from the tomb, and we do not know where they have laid him."

Meanwhile, however, the other holy women had entered the sepulchre, where they were amazed to see a young man, clothed in a white robe and sitting at the right side of the tomb, who said to them: "You are looking for Jesus of Nazareth, who was crucified. He has risen, he is not here. Behold the place where they laid him. But go tell his disciples and Peter that he goes before you into Galilee; there you shall see him, as he told you."

Upon receiving the angel's message, the holy women, filled with fear yet joyful, fled from the tomb, but for the moment said nothing to anyone of what they had seen and heard. Later, however, when they had recovered from the shock of the vision, they delivered the message they had received (Matt. 28:8), but it was taken to be so much nonsense and no one believed them (Luke 24:11).

In the meantime, Peter and John had heard Mary Magdalene's strange tale, and had set out in haste for the tomb. Spurred on by the unlooked-for development, they both ran as fast as they could, but John, being younger and more agile, reached the sepulchre first. However, out of respect for Peter he did not enter, but, bending down to look inside, saw the linen cloths lying there.[11] When Peter came up, he did not hesitate but went straight in "and saw the linen cloths lying there, and the handkerchief which had been about his head, not lying with the linen cloths, but folded in a place by itself. Then the other disciple also went in, who had come first to the tomb."

Christ's body was certainly no longer in the tomb, but it was no less certain that it had not been stolen. No thief would have taken the time to remove the linen cloths, especially in view of the fact that the spices would have caused them to adhere to the corpse. Then, too, it would have been much easier to carry off the body just as it was, wrapped in its shroud. And it would have been an unusual thief who would have removed the handkerchief separately, folded it neatly and laid it aside by itself. Therefore when St. John saw the empty tomb and the linen cloths lying loose, he believed that his Master had risen: "And he saw and believed" (John 20:8). He himself tells us that he believed because of what he saw and not on account of the prophecies, "for as yet they did not understand the Scripture, that he must rise from the dead." Was Peter also convinced? It is probable that he was: the body was gone and there had been no robbery, hence the conclusion was inescapable. However, the Gospel does not explicitly state that Peter did believe, although St. Luke (24:12) tells us that "Peter . . . went away wondering to himself at what had come to pass," that is, turning over in his mind what he had just seen.

---

[11] John 20:5; κείμενα τὰ ὀθόνια. Many authors translate this phrase as "the linen cloths placed *on the ground*," or "lying *on the ground*," while others (e.g., Tillmann) say that the cloths were on the *bench* in the tomb. But the text does not specify where the cloths were. The evangelist's meaning is that they were no longer wrapped about Christ's body but were lying there empty. That is exactly what St. Luke says (24:12); τὰ ὀθόνια κείμενα μόνα; "linteamina *sola* posita"; "the linen cloths *lying by themselves*." Therefore we translate the phrases from John 20:5 and 7 as "lying there," or as "lying empty." It is true that Luke 24:12 is lacking in a certain number of codices, yet, with Knabenbauer, Lagrange, Marchal and others, we believe that it should be regarded as authentic.

APPARITION TO MARY MAGDALENE

(John 20:11–18)

The two Apostles returned to the Cenacle, but not so Mary Magdalene, who had followed them back to the tomb in the hope of finding out what had happened to her beloved Master. When her hopes were disappointed, she could not restrain her tears as she stood desolate beside the empty sepulchre. Still weeping, she entered the vestibule and stooped down to gaze once more at the place where Jesus' body had lain. But the burial chamber was not empty as she had expected it to be, for there were two angels in white sitting, one at the head and one at the feet, where the body of Christ had been laid. The heavenly visitors addressed her: "Woman, why art thou weeping?"

She replied, "Because they have taken away my Lord, and I do not know where they have laid him."

Her Lord did not leave her long in mourning, for He willed to reward her persevering love by allowing her to see Him. Perhaps because she was anxious and distraught, or because she heard a light footfall behind her, she looked around and saw a man standing there, who asked her: "Woman, why art thou weeping? Whom dost thou seek?"

Because the tomb stood in a garden, which perhaps belonged to Joseph of Arimathea, Mary Magdalene mistook the newcomer for the gardener and, absorbed as she was in the thought of Jesus and her desire to recover His body, she answered: "Sir, if thou hast removed him, tell me where thou hast laid him and I will take him away."

But how could she, a weak woman, have hoped to carry away the heavy body of her Master? Yet love knows no impossibility.

The Stranger did not answer her as she expected; instead, in the sweet tone of voice which she knew so well, He called her by name: "Mary!"

Immediately the cloud of sorrow was lifted from her soul, and with a heart bursting with joy, she fell at Christ's feet with the ecstatic cry: "*Rabboni*, Master!"

How truly does the author of the *Imitation* say: "If Jesus speaks but one word, we feel great consolation. . . . Happy hour, when Jesus calls us from tears to joy of spirit!" [12]

In her desire never to be separated from her Lord again, Mary clung to His feet, but He admonished her gently: "Cease touching me, for I have not yet ascended to my Father, but go to my brethren and say to them, 'I ascend to my Father and your Father, to my God and your God.'"

Christ did not forbid her to touch Him, for why would He have restrained her spontaneous gesture of devotion? Instead, He told her not to continue clasping His feet, to cease bestowing on Him this mark of affection; [13] first, because He had not yet ascended to the Father but was still on earth, and therefore she would have further opportunities of seeing Him and rejoicing in His presence; and second, because she was to carry a message immediately to the Apostles, telling them that their Master was going to ascend to the Father.

This message was indeed a strange one. The Ascension was not to take place for forty days more; why, then, was there such need for haste? Jesus knew that He was about to appear to the Apostles that very day: could He not have waited until then to tell them of this as yet far-off event?

The difficulty is a very real one, and perhaps cannot be solved satisfactorily.[14] The most likely explanation seems to be that this meeting with Mary Magdalene was our Lord's first public appearance after His Resurrection. It would seem appropriate, then, that His first message to His Apostles should have been the annunciation of His Resurrection, the fact that concerned them most at the time. Yet He did not speak of His Resurrection, but solely of His future Ascension. How, then, explain this apparent anomaly? We find the answer in verse 17 itself, where Jesus said to Mary Magdalene: "I have not yet *ascended* to my Father." By speaking of His Ascension, He was announcing, indirectly but clearly, His Resurrection, which had, of course, to come first.

[12] Bk. II, chap. 8.

[13] The text allows and even demands this interpretation. The aorist imperative is used to forbid the person addressed to begin an action, but the present imperative, as used in this text, presupposes that the action has already been started. Cf. Zorell, *N. T. Lexicon Graecum,* under ἅπτομαι; and Joüon, *Rech. de Sc. Rel.,* 18 (1928), 501.

[14] Wikenhauser calls this passage (John 20:17) a "crux interpretum."

In view of the difficulty of the passage, it would be remarkable if it had not given rise to many different interpretations. Of these we shall mention only the one favored by distinguished authors such as Lagrange,[15] Prat,[16] and Spicq.[17] According to this theory, the relationship between Jesus and His Apostles was not the same after the Resurrection as it had been before it. In the existing circumstances the familiarity which had obtained between the Master and His disciples and which had contained a human element was no longer fitting. Mary Magdalene was not aware of the change, and Jesus wished to point it out to her by commanding her to cease touching Him, and to tell the Apostles of the new relationship that must exist between Him and them.[18]

But in our opinion, this explanation does not fit in with our Lord's bearing towards His disciples as recorded in the Gospels. Could He have shown them more familiarity than He did when He ate in their presence in the Cenacle, or when, on the shores of the Lake of Gennesareth, He asked them if they had anything to eat, or when He made them sit down beside Him and lovingly served them Himself? These marks of condescension, given after the Resurrection, surely cannot be regarded as less loving than those they had received from Him during His mortal life.

Obeying her Master's command, Mary Magdalene ran to announce to the disciples that she had seen Him alive, and that He had given her a message for them. St. Mark (16:10 f.) has recorded for us the manner in which her news was received: "She went and took word to those who had been with him, as they were mourning and weeping. And they, hearing that he was alive and had been seen by her, did not believe it."

It is by no means improbable that by this time the other holy women had likely set out to return to the sepulchre, but while they were on the way, Jesus appeared to them and greeted them, saying "Hail!" Overcoming their initial amazement at seeing Him alive, and encouraged by His kind salutation, they approached Him, embraced His feet and worshipped Him.

---

[15] Év. selon S. Jean, in loc.

[16] Jesus Christ, II, 422 f.

[17] Rev. Sc. Phil. et Théol., 32 (1948), 226 f.

[18] As Lagrange says (loc. cit.): "Marie ne l'a pas compris, et il importe que les disciples en soient informés avant de le voir."

Thus the sequence of the apparitions to the holy women seems to have been as follows:

(1) The holy women went to the tomb.

(2) Mary Magdalene ran back to the Cenacle, while the others remained, saw the angels and received a message which at first they kept to themselves but later communicated to the Apostles.

(3) Meanwhile, Mary Magdalene hurried back to the tomb, following Peter and John.

(4) The two Apostles returned to the Cenacle, while Mary stayed at the tomb and saw Jesus.

(5) The other women were going back once more to the sepulchre when they, too, saw Jesus.

Some authors try to remove the apparent contradictions in the Gospel accounts by saying that the three passages, Matthew 28:9 f., Mark 16:9–11, and John 20:11–18 refer to one and the same apparition. Thus they hold that the apparition to the holy women narrated by Matthew is the same as that to Mary Magdalene, recorded by Mark and John. This is so, they say, because St. Matthew's plural, which he uses no less than nine times, is the *categorical* plural and refers only to Mary Magdalene. Hence Jesus did not appear to the holy *women*, but to Mary Magdalene alone; and this is the apparition to which the three evangelists are alluding.

However, viewing the matter from a critico-historical standpoint, we find it difficult to admit that Matthew 28:9 f. refers to Mary Magdalene and is parallel to Mark 16:9–11 and John 20:11–18. We do, of course, recognize that there is such a thing as a categorical plural, and that it can be legitimately employed, but we are of the opinion that its application here would be a very strained one and most unlikely. Our supposition that the holy women returned to the tomb a second time is perfectly acceptable from a psychological point of view and is, we believe, the most scientific and satisfactory solution of the problem.[19]

THE DISCIPLES FROM EMMAUS

(Luke 24:13–35)

It would be consoling if we were able to trace the route followed

---

[19] In favor of the proposed identification of apparitions, see J. Leal in *Est. Bibl.*, 7 (1948), 5–28, where many authors are cited, and in *Verb. Dom.*, 26 (1948), 207–212. J. Bover wrote against the theory in *Est. Bibl.*, 4 (1945), 5–13.

by the two disciples from Emmaus and their Companion right up to the breaking of bread. But unfortunately, no one has yet succeeded in locating with certainty the place which the Gospel calls Emmaus. No less than six sites have been proposed: (1) the Emmaus of 1 Machabees 4:3, a village whose name was changed to Nicopolis during the Roman epoch; the original name was later revived and is still perpetuated in modern 'Amwâs, a little town about 160 stadia or nineteen miles west of Jerusalem, near the Jaffa highway; (2) el-Qubeibeh, about sixty stadia or eight miles northwest of the Holy City; (3) Qoloniyeh, and (4) Abughosh, the first being situated thirty stadia,[20] about four miles, and the second about ten miles west of Jerusalem on the Jaffa road; (5) Khirbet el-Khamaseh, a short distance south of the ancient Roman road that ran from the region of Bethlehem to the Wadi es-Sant ("valley of the terebinth"); and finally (6) Artas or Ortas, a small village located a short distance south of Bethlehem. The last four places can be discarded immediately as being improbable, so that we are left with 'Amwâs and el-Qubeibeh.

In solving the problem we can draw on four sources of information—archaeology, history, philology, and tradition; and since no single one of these can supply a definitive answer, we must derive our solution from a combination of all four, a delicate task because it is not easy to estimate the exact value of each element.

In 'Amwâs there are still preserved the ruins of an ancient basilica which dates back to the third or the beginning of the fourth century, while there is a dispute as to whether the church at el-Qubeibeh, which was restored by the Franciscans, was built by the Crusaders or was already standing in the Byzantine period. Within the precincts of this latter church one can still see the remains of a house which is reputed to have belonged to Cleophas, one of the two disciples from Emmaus.[21] If we are to judge by the antiquity of the ruins, 'Amwâs certainly wins the palm; but although we must take this factor into account, we do not believe that it is a solid enough foundation upon which to base our final selection.

In fact, at first sight, the historical details contained in the Gospel account seem to militate strongly against 'Amwâs. One is inclined to question how the disciples could have walked to and from Jerusalem,

---

[20] Cf. *Wars* vii. 6. 6.

[21] Fr. Bagatti has published an interesting study of the ruins at el-Qubeibeh and the surrounding district, entitled *I monumenti di Emmaus el-Qubeibe e dei dintorni* (Gerusalemme, 1947).

*In the foreground, ruins of a church with three apses, a short distance from
'Amwâs. Some believe that the building dates back to the third century and
that it was partially reconstructed by the Crusaders.*

a round trip of some thirty-eight miles, in one day. Then, too, a short
distance from the village to which they were going, they said to their
unknown companion: "Stay with us, for it is getting towards evening,
and the day is now far spent" (Luke 24:29). Therefore it was apparently near sunset, and if the village was as much as nineteen miles
from Jerusalem they would not have had time to return to the Holy
City before dark after Christ had revealed Himself to them. A number of authors do not hesitate to regard this difficulty as grave enough
to rule out 'Amwâs entirely. However, a close inspection of the text
minimizes and may even remove the objection. The two indications
of time, "it is getting on towards evening" and "the day is now far
spent," may refer, not to sunset, but to some time after midday, 2:00
P.M., for example, an interpretation that is fully confirmed by the
episode of the Levite in Judges 19:1–15, in which the very same expression is used in this sense (v. 9). The two disciples must have left
Jerusalem before our Lord appeared to Mary Magdalene, for they
apparently had not heard of that event. They therefore probably set
out about 9:00 A.M. It may seem exaggerated to say that they could
have gone to 'Amwâs and returned again to Jerusalem all in the one
day; yet the present writer has known several persons who have more
than once made the journey on foot in that length of time.

In our opinion philology, or rather textual criticism, and tradition are the two most fruitful sources of information, and it is upon them that, in the last analysis, we must depend for the solution of the problem. As regards textual criticism, there are two disputed readings of the text: one says that the distance between Jerusalem and Emmaus was sixty stadia, and is found in the vast majority of the manuscripts; the other states that the distance was 160 stadia, but this appears in only a few manuscripts, namely, six uncial codices—among them the Codex Sinaiticus—and five minuscule codices.[22] The great preponderance of codices containing the number sixty appears to tip the balance in favor of this reading, thus excluding ʿAmwâs. Indeed, some authors regard this argument as so cogent that they consider it as final. Lagrange writes that, judging by the manuscripts, the question is settled and the correct reading must be "sixty stadia." [23] Yet it will not be a waste of time to pause for a moment to examine the matter more closely.

It is easy to imagine how a copyist, thinking that the disciples could scarcely have made two journeys of 160 stadia each, a total of thirty-eight miles, in one day, might have concluded that the figure was an error in transcription, and might have changed it to sixty, which was, in his opinion, a more reasonable number. He would have been all the more likely to do so if, as is quite possible, he interpreted *"advesperascit"* as meaning that the sun was about to set when the travellers approached the village. We have no positive proof that such a procedure did take place, but there is no improbability about it in view of the liberties customarily taken by these scribes, about whom St. Jerome speaks in such unflattering terms. On the other hand, the copyists may have changed sixty to 160. Fortunately, we have a positive indication of such a change. An annotation on Manuscripts 39 and 194 warns that: "one must read 160 because that is the reading of the exact texts, and the confirmation which Origen gives to the truth." [24] The annotator's warning is of great interest for our purpose because it shows that, at the time, there were manuscripts containing the

---

[22] Details of these codices can be found in Abel, *Emmaus, sa basilique et son histoire* (Paris, 1932), pp. 304 *f.*, and in Vaccari, "L'Emmaus di S. Luca: Punti sugli i," in *Antonianum,* 25 (1950), 493–500, *Verb. Dom.,* 17 (1937), 126–128, 189 *f.* See also Antonine de Guglielmo's article, "Emmaus," in *Cath. Bibl. Quart.,* 3 (1941), 293–301.

[23] "A juger d'après les manuscrits, la question est tranchée; il faut lire soixante stades" (*RB* [1896], p. 89).

[24] Cf. Abel, *op. cit.,* pp. 304 *f.;* Vaccari, *loc cit.,* p. 497.

reading "160," and that these were considered the best, at least by some. Then, too, an appeal is made to Origen's testimony and authority, a fact which, however, does not mean to say that Origen was the first to introduce the reading "160."

It is at this point that the fourth source mentioned above, viz., tradition, comes into play. As everyone admits, ancient tradition as represented by Origen, Eusebius, St. Jerome, Hesychius of Jerusalem, and others, is decidely in favor of 'Amwâs. It is not necessary to quote the texts here because they are quite clear, and no one disputes their authenticity and meaning.[25] What is called into question is their probative value, which some authors attack at its very source by maintaining that Origen's evidence is useless, and hence that the others are likewise of no value because they all drew upon him. If the wellspring is contaminated, the whole stream is poisoned.

Origen visited Palestine in 215, and openly declared himself in favor of Emmaus-Nicopolis, or 'Amwâs as it is called today. We know that he took great pains to collect the local traditions and that he made a close study of place names. Of course, we cannot have blind faith in his accuracy; yet his topographical findings do merit our attention and should be accepted as facts whenever no well-founded objections are raised against them. But cogent objections have been made against some of his topographical findings. He changed the "Bethania trans Jordanem" of John 1:28 into "Bethabara" because he found the latter name in that region but could unearth no trace of the former; and in similar fashion he changed "Gadareni" (or "Geraseni") to "Gergeseni" because there was no lake near Gadara (or Gerasa) into which the swine could have plunged.[26]

Yet, although Origen may have made mistakes in both these cases, his very method of approach shows his preoccupation with geography and his respect for tradition. And seeing that Emmaus is a site of such singular importance, it would not be arbitrary to say that he paid special attention to the problem of its identification. He

[25] They can be found in Abel, *op. cit.,* pp. 410 ff.; Baldi, *Enchiridion,* no. 980 *ff.;* cf. Prat, *Jesus Christ,* II, 533.

[26] Cf. Lagrange, "Origène, la critique textuelle et la tradition topographique," in *RB* (1895), pp. 501–524; (1896), pp. 87–92. For the texts from Origen, see *RB* (1895), p. 503 (Bethabara), and p. 514 (Gergeseni); Vaccari, *loc. cit.,* p. 498. Fr. Buzy wrote against Fr. Lagrange's articles in *Rech. de Sc. Rel.,* 5 (1914), 395–415: "Emmaüs et l'ancienne tradition locale."

certainly knew of the existence of Emmaus-Nicopolis, which, as we know, was situated 160 stadia from Jerusalem. But if all the codices had sixty stadia, then the most elementary prudence and the most rudimentary idea of textual criticism would have led him to inquire into the possible existence of another Emmaus at that distance from Jerusalem. Now, if, sixty stadia from the Holy City, as the texts indicated, there was a sanctuary which was popularly known as Emmaus, and which was commonly connected with the gospel episode, Origen could not possibly have been ignorant of it. And if he had known of such a sanctuary (e.g., modern el-Qubeibeh), it is morally impossible that he would have disregarded it and all the documentary evidence that went to support it, and arbitrarily have chosen Emmaus-Nicopolis (modern 'Amwâs) instead. Therefore we must conclude that in his day there already existed an ancient tradition which pointed to Nicopolis as the Emmaus of the Gospel even though it was 160 stadia from Jerusalem.

To sum up: we must acknowledge that whereas the arguments we have drawn from archaeology, history and philology are weak, tradition is decidedly in favor of Emmaus-Nicopolis. As late as 1336, Ludolph of Sudheim referred to the Emmaus of the Gospel as Nicopolis,[27] but the first testimony in favor of el-Qubeibeh quoted by Baldi goes back only as far as 1485.[28] That, in itself, would be sufficient motive to give the preference to Nicopolis, particularly when we consider that the objections raised against the tradition are far from convincing and that it has stood firm against the strong current of textual opposition.

For this reason some authors regard the identification of Emmaus with Nicopolis ('Amwâs) as morally certain.[29] We, however, refrain from subscribing to this opinion because of the great preponderance of textual evidence against it. On the other hand, since it is hard to account satisfactorily for the genesis of this textual tradition, it must be accepted with some reserve. Therefore, we shall content ourselves with saying that, as matters stand now, the identification of the

[27] "Non longe ibi est Emaus, ubi Dominus in fractione panis duobus discipulis apparuit, quae dicitur Nicopolis" (Baldi, *Enchiridion,* no. 1002).

[28] "Dalla predicta cita de Rama verso Hyerusalem quindece miglia, se trova lo Castello de Emaus su la strada maestra, el qual se chiama *Chubebe* in lingua moresca": P. Francesco Suriano (Baldi, *Enchiridion,* no. 1005). Baldi then goes on to say that all subsequent authors from the fifteenth to the eighteenth centuries hold the same view.

[29] Cf. A. Arce, O.F.M., "Emmaús y algunos textos desconocidos," in *Est. Bíbl.,* 13 (1954), 53–90.

Emmaus of the Gospel with Nicopolis ('Amwâs) should be regarded as the more probable of the two theories.

Despairing of ever seeing their Master's Resurrection, and convinced that everything was at an end, two of Jesus' disciples, one of whom was named Cleophas, decided to return to their village of Emmaus. Three roads, each of which later became a Roman highway, led to the village—the well-known Bethoron road, which was the most northerly; the one that passed through Beit Iksa, Biddu, el-Qubeibeh and Beit 'Anan; and finally, the most southerly of the three, which went by Qiryathiarim, present-day Abughosh.[30] This last route was the most likely one for them to have taken, and we shall go with them along it.

On leaving Jerusalem, they headed west along the ancient road which today descends in a straight line from the Jewish colony of Gabaat Saul, not far from Lifta, to the floor of the valley, near Motza and Qoloniyeh. From there they climbed the steep hill of Kastal and went down the other side to Qiryathiarim. As they walked, their conversation revolved about the events of the past few days, which filled their minds and hearts to the exclusion of all else.

Suddenly they thought they heard the sound of footsteps behind them, and being suspicious of strangers in the circumstances, they drew aside to allow the newcomer to pass. The lone traveller, however, did not go by but stopped, greeted them and showed signs of wishing to walk along with them. Doubtless they did not relish the prospect of having a stranger as a travelling companion; but they did not object, and the newcomer fell in beside them, asking as he did so: "What words are these that you are exchanging as you walk and are sad?"

Cleophas, who must have been the elder of the two disciples, answered in a tone of undisguised amazement: "Art thou the only stranger in Jerusalem who does not know the things that have happened there in these days?"

They were certainly far from recognizing their companion, who then went on to inquire ingenuously: "What things?"

The two disciples, each helping the other to fill out the story, began to tell him all that had happened: "Concerning Jesus of Nazareth, who was a prophet, mighty in work and word before God and all the people; and how our chief priests and rulers delivered him up to be

[30] Cf. Abel in *RB* (1925), pp. 350 *f.*: Dalman, *Sacred Sites and Ways,* pp. 221 *ff.*

sentenced to death, and crucified him. But we were hoping that it was he who should redeem Israel. Yes, and besides all this, today is the third day since these things came to pass."

"It is true," they added skeptically, "that certain women of our company, who were at the tomb before it was light, astounded us, and not finding his body, they came, saying that they had also seen a vision of angels, who said that he is alive. So some of our company went to the tomb, and found it even as the women had said."

"But," they concluded with an air of incredulity, "him they did not see."

Perhaps somewhat to their surprise, the stranger chided them for their lack of faith: " 'O foolish ones and slow of heart to believe in all that the prophets have spoken! Did not the Christ have to suffer these things before entering into his glory?'

"And beginning then with Moses and with all the Prophets, he interpreted to them in all the Scriptures the things referring to himself."

Conversing as they walked along, they approached Emmaus, the place to which the disciples were going, but when they reached the side road leading to the village, the stranger made as if to continue along the main highway. The disciples, however, had been so impressed and won by him that they urged him to remain with them: "Stay with us, for it is getting towards evening, and the day is now far spent."

Graciously, the unknown traveller acceded to their sincere invitation and accepted their hospitable offer. Hungry as they were from their five or six hours' journey on foot, the hosts did not delay in ushering their guest into the house and providing him and themselves with a well-earned meal.

"And it came to pass when he reclined at table with them, that he took the bread and blessed and broke and began handing it to them. And their eyes were opened, and they recognized him."

The stranger was none other than Jesus, their Master! The shock of recognition was so great that for a moment they could only stare at their Guest in amazement. Recovering themselves, they made to leap to their feet, but before they could do so, Jesus had vanished from their sight. No longer concerned with food, they immediately rose from the table and without losing a moment, set out to return to Jerusalem, exclaiming to each other: "Was not our heart burning within us while he was speaking on the road and explaining to us the Scriptures?"

Love lent wings to their feet as they rapidly retraced their steps to the capital. Upon arriving there, they went straight to the Cenacle, where they found the Apostles gathered together. And we can readily imagine with what excitement they related in detail all that had happened on their journey and how they had recognized Jesus in the breaking of the bread.[31] And they became even more enthusiastic when they in their turn heard that the Master had appeared to Peter also, so that, even before their arrival, all the disciples had become convinced that the Lord had truly arisen. But their ardor was dampened when, as St. Mark (16:13) seems to imply, they found that some of their audience doubted the truth of their story. Perhaps their very enthusiasm led some of their hearers to question the reality of the experience which they had narrated so excitedly.

FIRST APPARITION IN THE CENACLE
(Mark 16:14; Luke 24:36–42; John 20:19–23)

The two disciples were protesting that what they said was true and were still trying to convince the doubters by appealing to the fact that Peter also had seen the Lord, when suddenly Jesus appeared in the Cenacle, greeting them with the reassuring words: "Peace to you! It is I, do not be afraid."

But despite the gentle salutation, they were stricken with terror because they had barred the doors for fear of the Jews and knew that no man of flesh and blood could have entered so silently. They thought, therefore, that their Visitor was a ghost (cf. Luke 24:37).

Seeing that they were terrified by His coming, Jesus continued: "Why are you disturbed, and why do doubts arise in your hearts? See my hands and feet, that it is I myself. Feel me and see; for a spirit does not have flesh and bones, as you see I have."

Then with ineffable condescension, He showed them His hands and His feet. But how mysterious are the workings of the human

---

[31] Did our Lord *consecrate* the bread? Several of the Fathers and many exegetes, particularly those of the sixteenth and seventeenth centuries, believed that He did, their main reason being the phrase "in the breaking of the bread" (Luke 24:35), which in Acts 2:42 signifies the Eucharist. But there does not seem to be enough evidence to warrant such a conclusion, and therefore the majority of modern authors (e.g., Knabenbauer, Lagrange, Prat, Fillion, Gomá) favor the negative opinion.

mind! Even then they could not bring themselves to believe, or rather, they believed and disbelieved at the same time. A strange medley of feelings filled their hearts—overpowering joy at seeing their Master, and fear that the whole incident would turn out to be an hallucination; eagerness to believe that their vision was a reality, and unwillingness to allow themselves to be deceived by an illusion. In one short phrase St. Luke aptly describes their state of mind (24:41): "They still disbelieved and marvelled for joy."

Showing even greater condescension to their weakness, Jesus asked: "Have you anything here to eat?"

Timidly they offered Him a piece of broiled fish, which He took and ate before their very eyes, not because He had need of food, but solely to strengthen their faith.[32]

Then, having dispelled their doubts, Jesus said to them: "These are the words which I spoke to you while I was yet with you, that all things might be fulfilled that are written in the Law of Moses and the Prophets and the Psalms concerning me."

Repeating His salutation, He continued: " 'Peace be to you! As the Father has sent me, I also send you.'

"When he had said this, he breathed upon them, and said to them, 'Receive the Holy Spirit; whose sins you shall forgive, they are forgiven them; and whose sins you shall retain, they are retained.' "

SECOND APPARITION IN THE CENACLE
(John 20:24–29)

On the occasion of Christ's first appearance in the Cenacle, all the Apostles had been present with the exception of Thomas, who may have had a legitimate reason for his absence, or who may perhaps have been an individualist, more inclined to follow his own bent than to act as the other Apostles did. At any rate, his later attitude showed that he was both impulsive and stubborn, yet possessed of a noble generosity.

When Thomas rejoined his fellow-Apostles, they greeted him with the jubilant announcement: "We have seen the Lord!"

But instead of rejoicing with them and showing regret at not having been present, he expressed doubt as to the reality of the appari-

---

[32] The honeycomb and our Lord's sharing of the remains of His meal do not seem to have been mentioned in the original authentic text.

tion, and may perhaps even have mocked them for being so credulous.

Finally, when he saw that the others were adamant in their conviction that they had really seen Jesus, he brought the argument to a close with a formal declaration which seemed almost like a challenge to his Divine Master: "Unless I see in his hands the print of the nails, and put my finger into the place of the nails, and put my hand into his side, I will not believe."

Jesus took him at his word: "And after eight days, his disciples were again inside, and Thomas with them. Jesus came, the doors being closed, and stood in their midst, and said, 'Peace be to you!' Then he said to Thomas, 'Bring here thy finger, and see my hands; and bring here thy hand, and put it into my side; and be not unbelieving, but believing.'"

This loving invitation, which was at the same time a stern reproach, so overwhelmed the doubting Apostle that he sank to his knees before Jesus and stammered out: "My Lord and my God!"

Christ pardoned his incredulity, but did not spare him the reprimand he had deserved: "Because thou hast seen me, thou hast believed. Blessed are they who have not seen, and yet have believed."

APPARITION ON THE SHORE OF THE LAKE
(John 21:1–23)

This scene, enacted on the shore of the Lake of Gennesareth, is enchanting in form and supremely interesting in substance. In accordance with their Lord's command, the Apostles had returned to Galilee, most likely to Capharnaum, where they probably stayed at the house of Peter's mother-in-law or in the home of one of the other disciples. St. John, to whom we owe the narrative, gives us the names of those who were gathered there: Simon Peter; Thomas, also called Didymus; Nathanael, from Cana in Galilee; the sons of Zebedee, James the Greater and John himself; and finally, two others, who were disciples of Jesus and perhaps Apostles as well, whose names the evangelist does not mention.

One day, while they were waiting for their Lord to appear to them, Peter announced with his usual impetuous determination: "I am going fishing."

His six companions replied: "We also are going with thee."

Leaving the town, they went out to the anchorage and climbed aboard one, or perhaps two, of the boats in which they had so often fished before and which belonged to the families of the four great Apostles. It was probably sunset or perhaps even later still when they set sail, for that was the usual time for fishing on the lake, as we gather from St. Luke (5:5): "the whole night through we have toiled. . . ." Even today in Tiberias, one can still see the boats leaving the tiny port in the evening for their night's work.

But although the six fishermen spent the whole night casting their nets in various parts of the lake, they caught nothing. The weary, fruitless hours of darkness were coming to an end and day was breaking when they heard someone calling to them from the shore: "Young men, have you any fish?"

In no mood for conversation, they answered curtly: "No."

The stranger, however, was not put off by their manner, but told them: "Cast the net to the right of the boat and you will find them."

We do not know exactly where this episode occurred because the Gospel does not tell us, and it is not possible to draw any conclusions from the context. We can, however, gather that the vessel was near the shore since they were able to hear and speak to their interrogator. In addition, the evangelist explicitly says that when they had filled the net they were only about 200 cubits, roughly 100 yards, from land.

An ancient tradition locates the incident on the western shore of the lake near the beautiful little valley of et-Tabgha, which is, most likely, the site of the famous *Heptapegon* or "seven fountains" mentioned by many of the ancient pilgrims.[33] This valley or lowland is bounded on the north and south by two hills. The southern hill is called Tell el-Oreimeh, and its summit was probably the site of Gennesareth or Kinnereth, which gave its name to the plain so enthusiastically described by Josephus.[34] On the northern hill, now surmounted by a hospice or *pension* run by Franciscan Sisters, our Lord delivered His Sermon on the Mount, an event which is commemorated by a small basilica built on the hillside. A number of the ancient pilgrims locate the second multiplication of the loaves and fishes at the foot of this same hill.[35] In fact, one can still see here the ruins of a fourth-

---

[33] The Spanish pilgrim Etheria describes the place as follows: "Ibidem vero super mare est campus herbosus, habens foenum satis et arbores palmarum multas et iuxta eas septem fontes qui singuli infinitam aquam emittunt" (Geyer, *Itinera,* p. 113).

[34] *Wars* iii. 10. 8.

[35] But see above, p. 424.

The Church of the Mensa Christi.

century church, the apse of which contains a mosaic depicting a basket with five loaves and two fishes.

A short distance east of this site lie the ruins of another ancient church, discovered early in 1934 and since reconstructed by the Franciscan Fathers. The original building was rectangular in shape and relatively small. At one end, in front of the apse, there is a large block of stone set in the ground and extending from one side of the church to the other. The stone is uncut except for a shallow depression on the Gospel side which no doubt was made there to allow free access to the apse. The fact that the stone occupied the most prominent place in the building indicates the veneration in which it was held by the faithful. Indeed, everything points to its being the *Mensa* at which Christ sat with His disciples, as mentioned in the *Commemoratorium de Casis Dei,* a document of the early ninth century which also contains an official report from the Patriarchate of Jerusalem to Charlemagne concerning the state of the holy places.[36] And Etheria must

[36] "Item iuxta mare ecclesia quam vocant duodecim thronorum et ibi fuit Dominus cum discipulis suis: ibi est *mensa,* ubi cum illis sedit" (Tobler, *Descriptiones Terrae Sanctae ex saeculo VIII, IX, XII, et XV* [Leipzig, 1874], pp. 81 f., 366). The name *Mensa Christi* or *Tabula Christi,* which we find in

have been referring to this block of stone when she wrote: "Not far from there one can see the stone steps upon which the Lord stood." [37] In fact, on the south side of the little church and facing the sea, there are several steps cut into the rock, which, although worn by time and the elements, are still plainly visible, and which were once used to reach the basilica from the south.

Not only do we have this age-old, continuous tradition, but we also know that this part of the lake was a particularly good fishing ground, for, as Biever tells us, "the little bay of 'Ain et-Tabgha and the estuary of the Jordan are the two places which most abound in fish. It is in these two spots that the fishermen set up camp during the winter." [38] Therefore we do not hesitate to agree with Dalman when he says that there is a solid foundation for believing that our Lord's apparition to His Apostles took place at the *Heptapegon*.[39]

We know from the Gospel that the Apostles were told to cast the net to the right of the boat, a detail in which the Fathers and ecclesiastical writers discover a mystical significance and about which they write at great length. According to them, casting the net to the right means working with Christ and being sustained by Him: it is then that the haul is abundant because, while we toil outwardly with our hands, He acts interiorly with His grace. According to St. Augustine's interpretation, the fish at the right of the vessel represent the faithful who, on the day of judgment, will be at the right of the Supreme Judge.

Although the Apostles had probably already cast their net in that spot without result, they did as the stranger bade them. Their obedi-

many of the pilgrims' descriptions, creates a certain amount of confusion because some of them apply it to the stone on which Jesus placed the loaves and fishes, others to the one on which He sat to eat with His disciples after the Resurrection, and still others make it refer to the hill upon which He performed the miracle of the multiplication of the loaves and fishes.

[37] "Non longe autem inde cernuntur gradus lapidei, super quos Dominus stetit" (Geyer, *loc. cit.*).

[38] *Conférences de St. Étienne, 1910–1911* (Paris, 1911), p. 291. In his book, *Studies in Galilee* (Chicago: University of Chicago Press, 1909), p. 38, Ernest Masterman writes: "The bay at et Tabigah is, during the early months of spring (the Gospel incident took place in April), a wonderful place for fish; they swarm there, attracted by the copious hot springs which, loaded with vegetable débris, here pour their waters into the lake. For about three months— mid-January to mid-April—the fishermen make this their headquarters, erecting a few tents or reed huts on the shore. . . ."

[39] Cf. *op. cit.*, pp. 133 *ff*. Regarding the authenticity of this site, see the interesting book by R. P. Teófilo Antolín, O.F.M., *El Santuario de la Aparición del Señor y del Primado de San Pedro en el lago de Tiberíades* (Roma, 1938).

ence was richly rewarded, for their haul was so great that they were scarcely able to draw it aboard.

Love is not only a fire that burns, it is also a light that illuminates; and purity, which spiritualizes the body, also sharpens the soul's vision. Thus John, the beloved disciple, the virgin Apostle to whom Christ had entrusted His own Mother, saw that the stranger on the shore was none other than the Lord Himself. Turning to Peter, he cried: "It is the Lord!"

A word was enough for the chief Apostle. With his characteristic impetuosity which was at once the source of generous acts and of lamentable imprudences, he girt his tunic about him and plunged into the water, determined to be the first to greet the Master, and too impatient to wait until the boat could put in to land.[40]

What a contrast there was between John's serene intuition and Peter's eager haste! Both of them loved Jesus, yet how different were their reactions! But our Lord was pleased with each of them, for basically holiness is the same although it may be expressed in very diverse ways. Mary and Martha were sisters and both loved Jesus, but the one sat quietly at His feet while the other busied herself in preparing food for Him. There have always been and there will always be Marys and Marthas in the Church. By a happy combination of natural temperament and the gentle impulse of grace, there will be contemplative souls who spend their days in adoration at the foot of the altar and fiery apostles who roam the mountains and valleys in the conquest of the kingdom of God. There will be those who, like St. Jerome, do violent battle with heretics, as well as those who, like St. Francis de Sales, draw erring souls to the truth by their sweetness of character. And we shall always be charmed by the

[40] Peter had laid aside his tunic while he was working. Some authors believe that he simply tightened at the waist the garment which he already had on, a kind of sleeveless smock used by farm workers. But the word ἐπενδύτης, which St. John uses, definitely indicates an outer, superimposed or added garment, which was not worn next to the skin. Hence the Apostle did not draw in the garment which he was wearing but another one, which could not have been the cloak but must have been the tunic. This is the interpretation commonly given by exegetes (e.g., Tillmann, Knabenbauer, Gomá, Fillion). The adjective "naked" here means "half-clothed." Some authors maintain that there would have been nothing strange in Peter's being completely naked, because, they say, the fishermen on the Lake of Tiberias usually strip to the skin when working. But the present writer has often visited the lake and has observed the fishermen engaged in all types of fishing, yet not once has he seen any of them entirely unclothed.

spontaneous outbursts of love in souls like that of St. Francis of Assisi and led to wonder at the indomitable, reasoned will power of men like St. Ignatius Loyola.

When Peter finally gained the shore, he stood for a moment with the water streaming from him, as if he were afraid to approach his Master. But seeing that Jesus looked kindly at him, he plucked up courage and drew near. What did Simon Peter say to Jesus, and what did our Lord reply? Unfortunately, we do not know the intimate conversation that took place there on the lake shore, and it will forever remain a secret.

In a little while the others arrived, dragging the net in the water behind the boat, as the Greek text indicates. A touching surprise awaited them, for their Master had prepared a fire upon which He had placed a fish to broil, and beside the fire He had set out some bread. In His love for them as Father and Friend, He had provided a meal by His omnipotent power, for the Fathers say that the fish and bread were not products of nature but the result of a miracle.

However, before they ate, He wished them to realize the extent of the prodigy He had wrought when they had cast their net at His orders: "Bring here some of the fishes that you caught just now."

Always quick to do his Master's bidding, Peter jumped into the boat and dragged the net ashore. Spreading it out, the Apostles counted the fish caught in its meshes and found that there were 153, all of them large. Nor was that the only wonder, for although the haul had been so bountiful, the net had not torn under its weight.

Kindly, Jesus said to them: "Come and breakfast."

When they had seated themselves near the fire, with His own hands Christ distributed the bread and fish. A religious silence reigned over the group, for none of them dared ask Him, "Who art thou?" knowing that He was their Lord.

After the frugal meal, Jesus set about fulfilling the promise which He had made in Caesarea Philippi a year before. When, in the valley of the Jordan, Andrew had brought Peter to meet Him for the first time, He had addressed His new disciple in the mysterious words: "Thou art Simon, the son of John; thou shalt be called Cephas (which interpreted is Peter)," that is, Rock.

The change of name indicated that Christ had special plans for the Galilean fisherman, plans which had later become clear and

Sira Photo

Chapel of the "Primacy of Peter" and Lake of Gennesareth.

explicit on the occasion of Peter's confession, when our Lord had said to him: "Thou art Peter [i.e., Rock,] and upon this rock I will build my Church, and the gates of hell shall not prevail against it."

Thus did Christ promise to Peter the primacy over the other Apostles. As Peter himself no doubt realized, the honor was here only promised and not yet conferred. But since that fatal night in Caiphas' house, he must have thought more than once that his denials had rendered him forever unfit to receive such a dignity. How could Jesus choose as the foundation of His Church a coward who had trembled at the voice of a servant girl? How could He entrust His Apostles and His faithful followers to one who had so shamefully betrayed Him?

Yet Christ willed to carry out His promise, and was going to exact from Peter nothing more than three protestations of love to cancel out his denials.

And so, when they had eaten the meal, He turned to Peter, gestured towards the other disciples, and asked: "Simon, son of John, dost thou love me more than these do?"

The unexpected question threw Peter into confusion, and he did not know how to reply, since the phrase "more than these do" reminded him vividly of his former arrogance, which had been the prelude to such lamentable falls. At length, not daring to compare

Flock of sheep grazing near Jerusalem. The rectangular arch in the foreground gives access to the tomb of Herod's family. The tall building in the background is the Pontifical Biblical Institute.

himself with the others, he answered humbly: "Lord, thou knowest that I love thee."

"Feed my lambs."

Again Jesus questioned him: "Simon, son of John, dost thou love me?"

And once more Peter answered: "Lord, thou knowest that I love thee."

"Feed my lambs."

For the third time, Jesus repeated His question: "Simon, son of John, lovest thou me?"

Peter was deeply troubled by his Master's insistence. Had Jesus looked into his heart and found there no real love? Was he deceiving himself? But his conscience assured him of his love for his Lord. In a voice that shook with emotion, he replied: "Lord, thou knowest all things, thou knowest that I love thee."

"Feed my sheep."

Because Peter did love Jesus deeply, his great sin was forgiven him: "Many sins are forgiven (him), because (he) hath loved much"

(Luke 7:47). And not only did Jesus forgive him, but He also carried out His promise of making him head of the Church, the Supreme Pastor of all His members: "Feed my lambs. . . . Feed my sheep."

It was then that Simon, son of John, the poor fisherman from Bethsaida, the perjured Apostle, received the triple crown of Ruler, Teacher and Pastor. Invested with this power and humbly conscious of the dignity conferred on him, Peter, now become the cornerstone of the Church, was to stand up fearlessly in the face of the Sanhedrin's wrath; he was to brave the terrors of the deep, establish his see in the city of the Caesars, and on the ruins of the Roman Empire was to found another empire that would have no end. Thousands of victims would perish under the executioner's axe, be devoured by wild beasts and consumed in the flames, but their blood, the blood of martyrs, was to be the seed of Christians. Races and nations, princes and monarchs, were to rise up against the Anointed of the Lord and His Vicar, only to dash themselves fruitlessly against the immovable Rock. The centuries would pass, tyrants disappear, dynasties fall; empires would crumble into dust and the world would be shaken with violent convulsions, but the Church, founded by Christ and ruled by Peter, would continue its triumphant march. Like its Divine Founder, it would go about doing good, spreading light, consolation and hope, gathering to its maternal heart and sheltering under its mantle all men of good will.

Not only did Jesus make Peter the Supreme Head of the Church, but He also conferred on him another privilege, that of dying on the cross. Just as He, the High Priest, had suffered death on a cross, so would His Vicar. Solemnly He said to Peter: "Amen, amen, I say to thee, when thou wast young, thou didst gird thyself and walk where thou wouldst. But when thou art old thou wilt stretch forth thy hands, and another will gird thee, and lead thee where thou wouldst not."

In these mysterious words our Lord was making a veiled reference to the kind of death whereby Peter was to glorify God. The prophecy was fulfilled in the capital of the world, on the lowly hill of the Vatican, from which Peter's tomb now sheds its radiance over the whole earth.

Rising to His feet, Jesus began to take leave of His disciples. As He did so, He turned once more to Peter, and referring to what He had just told him, and perhaps also to the Apostle's former protestations of being ready to go with Him to death, said to him: "Follow me."

It was as if He said: "I have foretold that you will die as I did. Do not falter, do not shrink before trials. Follow me to the end." Supernaturally enlightened, Peter understood perfectly the meaning of his Master's prophetic words and realized the fate that awaited him. But he also wished to find out what would happen to John, who had followed Jesus and him as they drew apart from the group of disciples: "Lord, and what of this man?"

Although his question was inspired mainly by his love for John and his desire that the beloved disciple, too, should know his own fate, it must not have been entirely free of vain curiosity, for it earned him an answer that sounded like a rebuke: "If I wish him to remain until I come, what is it to thee? Do thou follow me."

Peter should not have concerned himself with John's lot. If Jesus willed that John was not to suffer martyrdom or any form of death, but was to remain alive until He returned, it was no concern of Peter's.

As is clear, our Lord made no statement about the fate reserved for John; yet the first Christians took His words to mean that the beloved disciple was not to die. John himself protested against this interpretation: "This saying therefore went abroad among the brethren, that that disciple was not to die. But Jesus had not said to him, 'He is not to die'; but rather, 'If I wish him to remain until I come, what is it to thee?'" (21:23).

APPARITION ON A MOUNTAIN IN GALILEE
(Matt. 28:16–28)

This episode is recorded by St. Matthew alone, and he does not tell us the name of the mountain in question. All we know is that "the eleven disciples went into Galilee, to the mountain where Jesus had directed them to go." Most likely the eleven Apostles were accompanied thither by some of the disciples.

All at once Christ appeared to them, and they fell on their knees in worship. But, as the evangelist tells us, some doubted—a very strange reaction considering the fact that they had already seen Him several times and had ascertained the reality of His Resurrection. It is quite possible, though, that their doubt was only a momentary uncertainty, not about the truth of the Resurrection, but about the identity of the person who had appeared so suddenly. Or perhaps it was not the Eleven who doubted, but some of the disciples who had come with them.[41] In any case, they regained confidence when Jesus spoke to them.[42] His words are of supreme importance: "All power in heaven and on earth has been given to me. Go, therefore, and make disciples of all nations, baptizing them in the name of the Father, and of the Son, and of the Holy Spirit, teaching them to observe all that I have commanded you; and behold, I am with you all days, even unto the consummation of the world."

What far-reaching powers, what a glorious mission, what a magnificent promise! To the Apostles and their successors belonged the prerogative of teaching, not merely to one race but to all peoples and nations, the principles of the Faith, the truths which they would have to embrace if they wished to gain eternal life. They were to administer baptism, the gate through which souls enter to become members of the kingdom of God on earth. They were entrusted with the power of governing the Church and with the mission of leading men along the path traced out by the Saviour. And to encourage them to fulfill valiantly this high office despite the storms which the world would certainly raise against them, Christ assured them of His continued presence, an unfailing guarantee of ultimate triumph.

The Last Apparition and Ascension Into Heaven
(Acts 1:1–11)

The forty days of Christ's glorified life on earth were drawing to a close. Now it was time for the Son, the Conqueror of death and hell, to go to receive from His Father the reward of His victory. Wishing to bid farewell to His beloved disciples, He invited them to a last reunion, a final intimate meal. As He reclined at table, He consoled them for His approaching departure, reminded them of some of His instructions, and charged them not to leave Jerusalem because

[41] Lepin, followed by Lagrange, proposes a translation of the phrase οἱ δὲ ἐδίστασαν (Matt. 28:17) which eliminates the difficulty—"those who had doubted." Thus it would be a reference to *past* doubts. The solution is indeed both very convenient and philologically possible; yet, with Fr. Buzy, we do not think it admissible.

[42] After examining at length all the other solutions, Fr. Severiano del Páramo gives this one in "Un problema de exégesis neotestamentaria," *Est. Bibl.,* 14 (1955), 296.

there the Father's promise was to be fulfilled in them. They would receive the gift of the Holy Spirit, the Comforter, of whom He had already told them. Then He added: "For John indeed baptized with water, but you shall be baptized with the Holy Spirit not many days hence."

How attentively and with what deep feelings of loving sorrow did the disciples and especially our Lady, who no doubt was there with the holy women, listen to these words which they knew were their beloved Master's final message! But in the midst of these tender, sorrowful emotions, there was sounded a strange, discordant note which shows once more how deeply rooted in the minds of some of the disciples was the idea of a temporal kingdom:

"Lord," they asked, "wilt thou at this time restore the kingdom to Israel?"

Jesus must have felt a pang of melancholy compassion for those who, even after His terrible Passion, still cherished dreams of national glory. But He did not judge the moment opportune for stressing the spiritual nature of His kingdom, as He had done so often already. Instead, He contented Himself with saying: "It is not for you to know the times or dates which the Father has fixed by his own authority; but you shall receive power when the Holy Spirit comes upon you, and you shall be witnesses for me in Jerusalem and in all Judea and Samaria and even to the very ends of the earth."

When He had said this, He and the Apostles and the rest of the company arose from the table, and, leaving the city, they went down towards the Cedron by the very same road which they had traversed forty days ago in such melancholy circumstances. Crossing the brook, they began to climb the slope of Mount Olivet, and as they walked the members of the group were torn between two emotions, joy at their Master's triumph and sorrow at His departure. When they reached the summit of the hill, Jesus looked round on them with tender eyes, raised His holy hands in blessing, and, as they watched in ecstatic awe, He was lifted up towards heaven. While they stood spellbound, their eyes fixed upon His receding figure, an "envious cloud" hid Him from their sight. But still they remained, gazing up to heaven. "And . . . behold, two men stood by them in white garments, and said to them, 'Men of Galilee, why do you stand looking up to heaven? This Jesus who has been taken up from you into heaven, will come in the same way as you have seen him going up to heaven.' "

Then, with hearts full of joy at their Master's triumph, they descended the hill and returned to Jerusalem.

It would be too much to expect the rationalistic critics to refrain from making violent attempts at casting doubt upon so glorious and supernatural an event as the Ascension. Their "explanations" of the miracle can be reduced to three main types: the Ascension was either a fable, a myth, or an interpolation.

Fable: The Ascension was a fraud, some rationalists maintain, because two of the evangelists (Luke and Mark) who had affirmed that Jesus had risen from the tomb and was still living, were unable to say where He was and were therefore driven to take refuge in the fable that He had disappeared from the face of the earth by ascending into heaven.

But the prologue of St. Luke's Gospel shows us that the evangelist was acutely conscious of his duties as an historian. He scrutinized documents, interrogated eyewitnesses, and inquired into tradition. In a word, he gathered every shred of information that could throw light on the course of the events which he was about to relate. Now it is inconceivable that an author so concerned with accuracy and gifted with such a keen sense of history would have even thought of debasing his work by including in it an obvious fable.

Myth: Other rationalist critics, realizing that the fable theory was completely unscientific and unacceptable, took another tack, which, however, led to the same result. According to these critics, when the Christian community found that Jesus had disappeared from among them, they concluded that He must have gone to God and they wove the legend of the Ascension about His departure from the earth.

No one denies that popular fancy can evolve legends which belong to the category of myths. But such myths are totally incompatible with the spiritual atmosphere in which the first generations of Christians lived. Now, Christ's trial and condemnation, His pain-filled Passion and His inglorious death on the gibbet of the cross were all well-known, and they are described in considerable detail by the four evangelists. Is it likely, then, that popular imagination would have woven a myth so glorious as the Ascension about a criminal who had been cursed by the people and condemned by the civil and religious authorities, and that not in some dim far-off era but in the full light of recent history? Such a procedure must be regarded as a moral impossibility.

Interpolation: The interpolation theory does not deserve the compliment of a refutation, for it is a last desperate expedient devoid of even the appearance of likelihood. The Ascension passage appears in all the codices and all the versions, and deleting it from the text would be tantamount to amputating a healthy limb. Only an obstinate resolve to remove by fair means or foul the importunate testimony of Christ's Ascension could make a critic go to such extremes.[43]

Christ, then, ascended into heaven, there to take His place at the right hand of the Father and to receive the praise that is His due: "And I beheld, and I heard a voice of many angels round about the throne, and the living creatures and the elders, and the number of them was thousands of thousands, saying with a loud voice, 'Worthy is the Lamb who was slain to receive power and divinity and wisdom and strength and honor and glory and blessing.' And every creature that is in heaven and on the earth and under the earth, and such as are on the sea, and all that are in them, I heard them all saying, 'To him who sits upon the throne, and to the Lamb, blessing and honor and glory and dominion, forever and ever' " (Apoc. 5:11–14).

> *To the King of the ages,*
> *who is immortal, invisible,*
> *the one only God,*
> *be honor and glory forever and ever.*
>   AMEN.
>   (1 Tim. 1:17)

---

[43] Cf. V. Larrañaga, *La Ascensión del Señor en el Nuevo Testamento* (Madrid, 1943), pp. 29 *ff.*

Maps

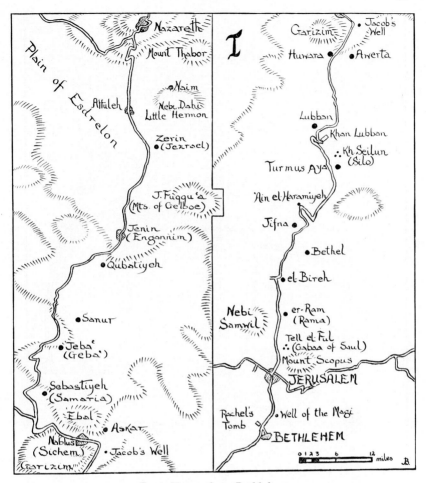

From Nazareth to Bethlehem.

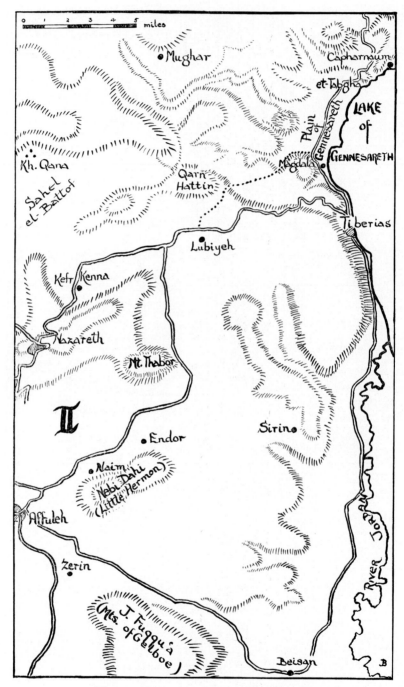

Western Shore of the Lake of Gennesareth.

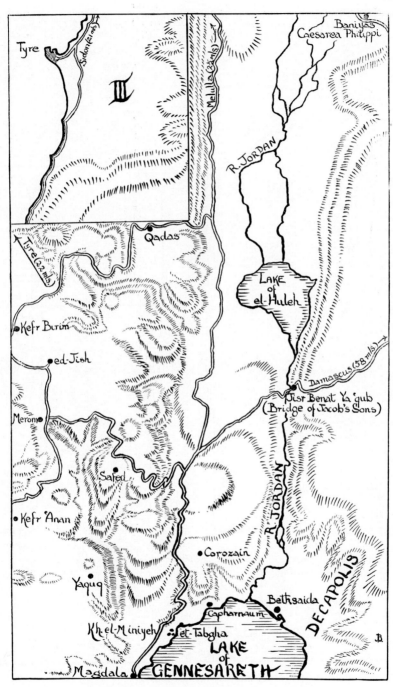

District north of the Lake of Gennesareth.

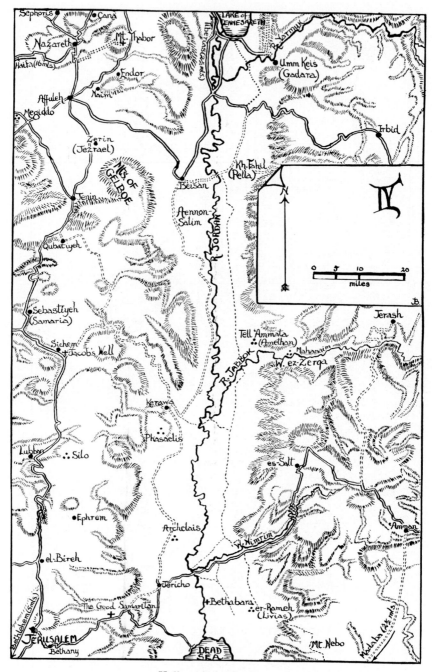

Valley of the Jordan.

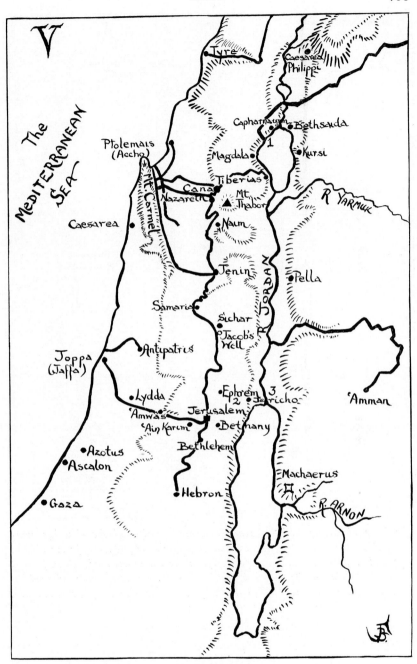

The Holy Land.

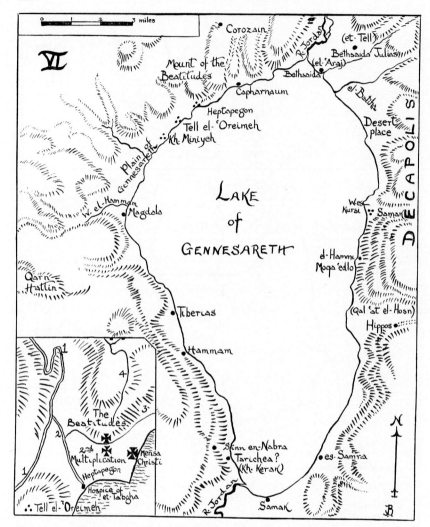

The Lake of Gennesareth. The crosses mark the sites of the churches com-
memorating the Beatitudes, the Second Multiplication (pp. 775 f.; see also p.
424) and the Mensa Christi, respectively. 1: the Damascus road, which follows
the ancient Via Maris; 2: road to the Hospice of el-Tabgha; 3: road to
Capharnaum; 4: path leading to the hospice on the Mount of the Beatitudes.

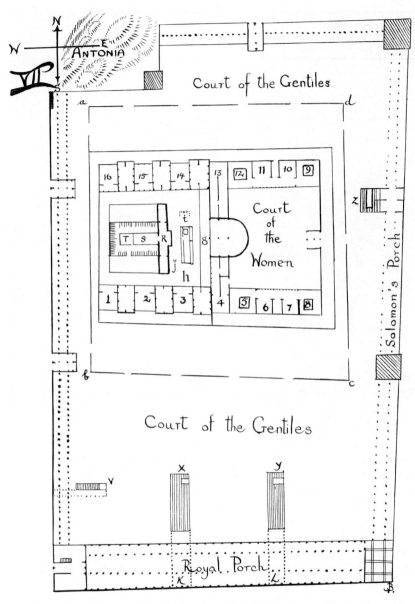

The Temple: g: Court of Israel; h: altar of holocausts; t: table for preparing victims; j: great bronze vessels; P: Court of the Priests; R, S, T: the Sanctuary (R: the Vestibule; S: the Holy Place; T: the Holy of Holies); a, b, c, d: wall separating the Court of the Gentiles from that of the Jews; V, X, Y, Z: staircases leading to the outer gates; 1–16: compartments set aside for the service of the Temple; K: double gates; L: triple gate.

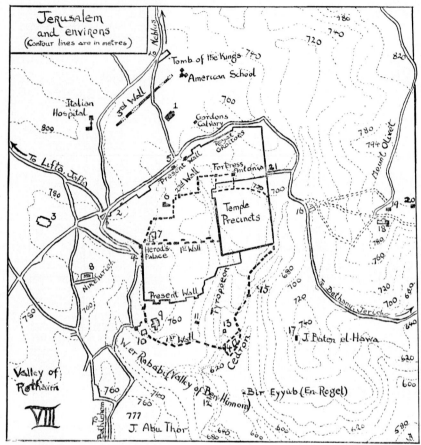

Jerusalem and Environs. 1: Basilica of St. Stephen; 2: Qasr Jalud; 3: Birket Mamilla; 4: Jaffa Gate; 5: Damascus Gate; 6: the Holy Sepulchre; 7: Pool of Ezechias (Hammam el-Batrak); 8: Pontifical Biblical Institute; 9: the Cenacle; 10: Gobat's School, and Protestant cemetery; 11: property of the Assumptionist Fathers; 12: Haceldama; 13: Pool of Siloe; 14: the King's Pool; 15: Fountain of the Virgin (Gihon); 16: Gethsemani; 17: property of the Benedictines; 18: Church of the Pater Noster (the Eleona); 19: site of the Ascension; 20: Russian Orthodox convent; 21: St. Stephen's Gate.

Index

el-Muchraqa (mountain), 6

Murillo, Fr.
  regarding Caiphas as high priest, 683
  regarding dove and baptism, 192

Mustard seed, parable of, 383

NABLUS (city), 7, 278 n., illus: 279

Nahr ez-Zerqa (river), 484

Nails, used in the Crucifixion, 728

Naim
  city, 350
  widow of, miracle of son, 350–351

Nakedness, of victims in stoning, 728–729

Nathanael (apostle), 774
  first meeting with Jesus, 217–221
  prophecy of Jesus to, 221

Native women of Cana, illus: 230

Nazareth, 77–78, 218
  hidden life at, 150–166, 344–399
  illus: 78, 79, 80, 97, 398
  Mary's return to, 108–111
  meaning of word, 149
  to Bethlehem (chart), 791

Neapolis (city), illus: 282

Nebi Dahi (mountain), 350

Nebi Samwil (mountain), 6

Nechao, and king of Juda, 227

Negeb (desert), 3, 4, 6, 11

Neighbor, love of, 485–487

Neo-Platonists, belief concerning logos, 95

Nephtali (tribe), 236

Neronias (city), 25

Net, parable of, 384

New Law
  and Christ, 178 n.–179 n.
  and John the Baptist, 178 n., 179–181
  and Mosaic Law, relationship, 339–346

New Testament, and logos, 96–97

Nicodemus, 28, 577
  burial of Christ, 741, 744–751 *passim*
  Jesus' conversation with, 256–268

Nicopolis (village), 765, 769

Nikefurieh (hill), 115

Noe, 542

OATHS, 342

Obedience of Jesus, 158–161

Official's son, cure of, 286–290

Old Law and New Law, contrasted, 322–323

Old Testament
  and logos, 96–97
  and the Beatitudes, 335

Onias (priest), 145 n.

Ophel (hill), 625, 663, 670

Ordination, 644

Origen, regarding 'Amwâs, 767–769

Ortas (village), 765

Our Father, the (prayer), 343, 498–501
  and prayers of the Jews, 501–502
  Jesus teaches the disciples, 495–502
  texts of, 497–498

Oven tombs, 743

PACORUS (king), 16

Pain, spiritual, of Christ, at Crucifixion, 736–737

Palace of high priest, parts of, 694–695

Palestine
  derivation of name, 3
  division in time of Christ, 6–8
  fertility of land, 8–11
  geography of, 3–13
  population at time of Christ, 12–13

Palestinian shepherd, illus: 126

Palm Sunday procession, illus: 567, 569

Paneion (Caesarea), restored, 24

Panis subcinericius, 160

Papias (Bp. of Hierapolis)
  on Gospel of St. Peter, 48
  on St. Mark's Gospel, 48–49

Parables, 371–385
  of mercy, 522–524
  of reprobation, 582–585

Paralytic, cure of, 291–296, 316–320

Passion of Christ
  foretold by Christ, 436–438, 553–554, 574–576
  preludes to, 562–600
  route of, 674–675

Passover(s), 243–268, 552, 629–637
  celebrated by Christ, 63–69

Patibulum, 726 n.

Paton, L. B., identification of pool of Siloe, 293

Paul, St.
  imprisoned, 6
  scourging of, 710

Peace, gift of, 651–654

Peacemakers, The, 338

Pearl of great price, parable of, 384

Pedagogium, 727 n.

Pella (city), refuge for Christians, 7, 8, 484, 719

Penal code, in Jesus' time, 690–691

Penance, teaching of John the Baptist, 183–185

Pentecost
  dispute concerning date of, 632–633
  feast of weeks, 244

A NOTE ON THE TYPE

IN WHICH THIS BOOK IS SET

This book is set in Baskerville, an Intertype face, created from the original types used by John Baskerville, the eighteenth-century type-founder and printer. This type has long been considered one of the finest book types ever developed. The letters are wide and open and have a businesslike approach. The finer hairlines give exquisite delicacy. The heavier strokes give color and strength. The relation of the two in combination gives a brilliant effect and makes for easy reading. The book was composed and printed by the York Composition Company, Inc., of York, Pa., and bound by Moore and Company of Baltimore. The typography and design are by Howard N. King.